ACLS History E-Book Project
Reprint Series

The ACLS History E-Book Project (www.historyebook.org) collaborates with constituent societies of the American Council of Learned Societies, publishers, librarians and historians to create an electronic collection of works of high quality in the field of history. This volume is produced from digital images created for the Project by the Scholarly Publishing Office and the Digital Library Production Service at the University of Michigan, Ann Arbor. The digital reformatting process results in an electronic version of the text that can be both accessed online and used to create new print copies. This book and hundreds of others are available online in the History E-Book Project through subscription.

Many of the works in the History E-Book Project are available in print and can be ordered either directly from their publishers or as part of this series. For information refer to the online Title Record page for each book. Inquiries regarding this series can be directed to info@hebook.org.

ACLS
HISTORY E-BOOK

http://www.historyebook.org

THE
POLITICS
of GRAND
STRATEGY

ritain and France Prepare for War, 1904-1914

Samuel R. Williamson, Jr.

". . . one of the most important studies of both British and French policies in the decade before the First World War."

Paul M. Kennedy

The Politics of Grand Strategy

Britain and France Prepare for War, 1904–1914

AFTER TEN YEARS.

The Politics of Grand Strategy

Britain and France Prepare for War, 1904–1914

Samuel R. Williamson, Jr.

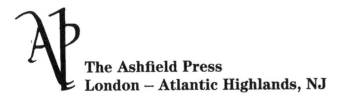

The Ashfield Press
London – Atlantic Highlands, NJ

First published in hardback 1969 by Harvard University Press

Paperback edition with new preface first published 1990 by
The Ashfield Press Ltd., 3 Henrietta Street, London WC2E 8LU
and 171 First Avenue, Atlantic Highlands, NJ 07716

© Samuel R. Williamson, Jr., 1969, 1990

Library of Congress Cataloging-in-Publication Data
Williamson, Samuel R.
    The politics of grand strategy: Britain and France prepare for
war, 1904–1914 / Samuel R. Williamson, Jr. — Pbk. ed.
    p. cm.
    Includes bibliographical references.
    ISBN 0–948660–13–9
    1. World War, 1914–1918—Causes. 2. Great Britain—Foreign
relations—France. 3. France—Foreign relations—Great Britain.
I. Title.
D511.W657   1990   89–27401
327.42044—dc20   CIP

British Cataloguing-in-Publication Data
A CIP record for this book is available from the British Library

Printed in the United States of America

For Frances and Ruthven

Preface to the Paperback Edition

Twenty years have passed since the publication of *The Politics of Grand Strategy*. During that time the opening of important archives and the ramifications of Fritz Fischer's redefinition of the debate over the origins of World War I have resulted in frequent contributions on the years covered by this study. Although much of the recent work focuses on eastern Europe and the Balkans, the role of Britain and France in the tragedy of 1914 continues to attract prominent scholars. The Anglo-French military conversations remain at the center of most historical examinations of entente diplomacy, despite increased attention to structural factors within the international system and to the relationship between *Aussen-* and *Innenpolitik*.

New archival material answers many important questions for which insufficient evidence was available in the mid-1960s. In Britain, the diaries and private papers of Maurice Hankey, Venetia Stanley, and others permit a clearer view of military and political considerations affecting the policy process in London. The opening of the papers of Raymond Poincaré in the Bibliotèque Nationale provides some help in assessing how Paris viewed the evolving military arrangements with Britain from 1912 to 1914. Other private paper collections have also appeared in France during the past twenty years, including those of Georges Louis, Pierre de Margerie, and Alexandre Ribot. Greater access to official records, including those of the intelligence agencies on both sides of the Channel, has clarified a number of bureaucratic issues that were necessarily sketchy to historians before 1969.

These collections constitute the basis for a broad range of published work on many aspects of the Anglo-French path to war in 1914. Especially important contributions have been made in three areas: 1) the broader context of strategic planning, including intelligence assessment, 2) the effects of the Anglo-French military relationship on politics and diplomacy on both sides of the English Channel, and 3) the role of the staff talks in the critical decisions of July and August 1914. Although these publications have identified key elements that were missing or incomplete in the historical record in the 1960s, they have not forced any significant changes in the argument or underlying premises first advanced by this book in 1969.

A number of those works place the continental commitment more firmly within the framework of British strategic thought. John Gooch, Keith Wilson, and David French have all illuminated broader aspects of war planning, while Nicholas d'Ombrain has focused on the bureaucratic machinery of strategic decisionmaking.[1] The effect of the continental strategy on British Army tactics has been dealt with effectively by Tim Travers, while John Coogan has assessed that strategy's impact on Britain's traditional maritime policy.[2] The prominent role of British Army officers in changing the nation's grand strategy also points out the importance of continued study of the social and intellectual background of both military and naval officers, along the lines of work by Brian Bond, Edward Spiers, and Byron Farwell.[3] A fuller understanding of the education, strategic training, and political biases of senior soldiers and sailors promises to improve understanding of the roots of British military involvement on the Continent. These works, however, have only deepened this author's commitment to the centrality of the staff talks and to the critical importance of Sir Henry Wilson in the transformation of British grand strategy.

A number of important contributions have also been made on the French military since 1969. Douglas Porch has elaborated the military context for French strategic policy with many materials unavailable in the 1960s. Christopher Andrew and A. S. Kanya-Forstner have suggestively interpreted the colonial context of that policy.[4] Equally important contributions on the domestic political constraints shaping French military policy have come from Gerd Krumeich and Inge Saatmann.[5] Finally, Jack Snyder, Joseph Arnold, and Michael Howard, among others, have elaborated the importance of offensive tactics in French strategic thought before the war.[6]

The relatively new field of the history of intelligence assessment has added substantially to our understanding of strategic decisionmaking before World War I. The recent opening of military and naval intelligence files in both countries has given scholars access to an element of the planning process that was almost totally closed in the 1960s. Christopher Andrew, Paul Kennedy, Jan Karl Tannenbaum, and Thomas Fergusson have pioneered the study of that murky area in Britain and France before 1914.[7] Work thus far, however, indicates that institutional intelligence assessment had little, if any, effect upon operational planning in the development of the Entente Cordiale.

Anglo-French politics and diplomacy constitute a second area in which major work has been done since 1969. The contributions of Zara Steiner and John Keiger in "The Making of the 20th Century" series discuss the emerging bureaucratic politics, global relationships, and colonial commitments.[8] Both also accept the general conclusions of this study regarding the importance of the military relationship in the development of each state's grand strategy. New archival material enabled John and Peter Coogan to trace the dissemination of knowledge on the staff talks through the British Cabinet.[9] The essays on the foreign policy of Sir Edward Grey, collected and edited by F. H. Hinsley, provide a variety of significant additions to the literature of British diplomacy.[10] Studies by Paul Kennedy, Raymond Poidevin, George Kennan, and Erwin Hölzle, among others, further clarify the international context within which the military entente evolved.[11] Specific crises, including that of July 1914, have been examined from a variety of perspectives.[12] A. J. A. Morris has contributed two important works on domestic pressure groups in Britain, while Jean-Jacques Becker has compiled a wealth of information of French public opinion.[13] Paul Gordon Lauren and Zara Steiner have focused on institutional pressures on diplomacy.[14] Important advances have also been made in the study of British opposition to the evolving commitment to France.[15]

The continuing wave of biographies of British and French politicians and diplomats has provided additional material for the historian. Recent studies of Grey, Asquith, Campbell-Bannerman, Lloyd George, Haldane, and Clemenceau have clarified political issues and filled in important gaps in our understanding of those individuals.[16] Middle-level diplomats like Hardinge and Crowe, and unofficial emissaries like Lord Esher have also started to attract scholarly attention.[17] Military biographers, always a flourishing group in Britain, have produced important works on Hankey, Fisher, and many others since the 1960s.[18]

Finally, the British decision to dispatch the BEF remains controversial twenty years after the publication of this work. Trevor Wilson, however, has confirmed the argument put forth here that British intervention represented not a moral obligation, but the reasoned strategic judgment of key members of the British Cabinet.[19] In London, foreign policy considerations triumphed over domestic politics to bring Britain to the timely aid of the Third Republic.[20]

No attempt has been made to cite all the relevant literature published since 1969 on the general topic of Anglo-French relations and the coming of World War I. The great extent of that literature indicates the continuing fascination of historians for the origins of the Great War. New evidence, new interpretations, and new areas of exploration have surfaced almost every year since the publication of the first edition of this book. Over the years I have rethought many of the questions posed by this study. My current research on the Austro-Hungarian empire's road to war in 1914 seeks to solve many of those same historical problems.

The Politics of Grand Strategy was researched and written as the United States became progressively involved in Vietnam. Fundamental issues raised in this study, including the proper balance in civil-military relations, the role of military contingency planning, and the dynamics of great-power alliances remain at the core of research in the history of international relations and strategic studies. The two decades have also continued to see serious questions raised about the willingness and ability of staff officers to pursue policies not directly approved by the civilian leadership of the state involved. The Anglo-French military conversations of 1904–1914 raised many of those same questions. The answers to those questions, then and more recently, merit the continual attention of concerned citizens and scholars.

In assessing the recent literature, my former graduate students at the University of North Carolina at Chapel Hill have been invaluable. I am especially grateful to Peter Coogan for his help in preparing this summary.

January 1989
Samuel R. Williamson, Jr.
The University of the South

Notes:

1. John Gooch, *The Plans of War: The General Staff and British Military Strategy, 1907–1916* (Oxford, 1974); Keith M. Wilson, "To the Western Front: British War Plans and the 'Military Entente' with France before the First World War," *British Journal of International Studies*, 3 (April 1977); John McDermott, "The Revolution in British Military Thinking from the Boer War to the Moroccan Crisis," *Canadian Journal of History*, 9 (August 1974); David French, *British Economic and Strategic Planning, 1905–1915* (London, 1982); and Nicholas d'Ombrain, *War Machinery and High Policy: Defence Administration in Peacetime Britain, 1902–1914* (Oxford, 1973). A suggestive overview is Michael Howard, *The Continental Commitment* (London, 1972).

2. Tim Travers, *The Killing Ground: The British Army, the Western Front and the Emergence of Modern Warfare, 1900–1918* (Winchester, Mass., 1987); and John W. Coogan, *The End of Neutrality: The United States, Britain, and Maritime Rights, 1899–1915* (Ithaca, N.Y., 1981).

3. Brian Bond, *The Victorian Army and the Staff College, 1854–1914* (London, 1972); Edward M. Spiers, *The Army and Society, 1815–1914* (London, 1980); and Byron Farwell, *Mr. Kipling's Army* (New York, 1981).

4. R. D. Porch, *The March to the Marne: The French Army, 1871–1914* (Cambridge, 1981); and Christopher Andrew and A. S. Kanya-Forstner, *The Climax of French Imperial Expansion, 1914–1924* (Stanford, 1981). William I. Shorrock, *French Imperialism in the Middle East* (London, 1976), is another important study of colonial influences on French diplomacy.

5. Gerd Krumeich, *Armaments and Politics in France on the Eve of the First World War: The Introduction of Three-Year Conscription, 1913–1914*, trans. Stephen Conn (Leamington Spa, 1984); and Inge Saatmann, *Parlament, Rüstrung und Armee in Frankreich, 1914–1918* (Düsseldorf, 1978).

6. Jack Snyder, *The Ideology of the Offensive: Military Decision Making and the Disaster of 1914* (Ithaca, N.Y., 1984); Joseph Arnold, "French Tactical Doctrine, 1870–1914," *Military Affairs*, 42 (April 1978); and Michael Howard, "Men Against Fire: The Doctrine of the Offensive in 1914," in *Makers of Modern Strategy: From Machiavelli to the Nuclear Age*, ed. Peter Paret (Princeton, 1986).

7. Christopher Andrew, *Her Majesty's Secret Service: The Making of the British Intelligence Community* (New York, 1986); Andrew, "France and the German Menace," in *Knowing One's Enemies: Intelligence Assessment before the Two World Wars*, ed. E. R. May (Princeton, 1986); Jan Karl Tannenbaum, "French Estimates of Germany's Operational War Plans," ibid.; Paul M. Kennedy, "Great Britain before 1914," ibid.; and Thomas Fergusson, *British Military Intelligence, 1870–1914: The Development of a Modern Intelligence Organization* (Frederick, Md., 1984).

8. Zara Steiner, *Britain and the Origins of the First World War* (New York, 1977); and John F. V. Keiger, *France and the Origins of the First World War* (London, 1983). Other important surveys include Richard Langhorne, *The Collapse of the Concert of Europe: International Politics, 1890–1914* (New York, 1980); F. R. Bridge and R. Bullen, *The Great Powers and the European States System, 1815–1914* (London, 1980); and James Joll, *The Origins of the First World War* (London, 1984).

9. John Coogan and Peter Coogan, "The British Cabinet and the Anglo-French Staff Talks, 1905–1914: Who Knew What and When Did He Know It?", *Journal of British Studies*, 24 (Jan. 1985).

10. F. H. Hinsley, ed., *British Foreign Policy under Sir Edward Grey* (Cambridge, 1977). The article by K. I. Hamilton, "Great Britain and France, 1911–14," is especially important.

11. Paul M. Kennedy, *The Rise of Anglo-German Antagonism, 1860–1914* (London, 1980); Raymond Poidevin, *Les origines de la première guerre mondiale* (Paris, 1975); George F. Kennan, *The Fateful Alliance: France, Russia, and the Coming of the First World War* (New York, 1984); and Erwin Hölzle, *Grossbritannien, Russland und Deutschland: Studien zur britischen Weltreichpolitik am Vorabend des Ersten Weltkrieges* (Mannheim, 1978).

12. To cite just a few of many examples: Geoffrey Barraclough, *From Agadir to Armageddon: Anatomy of a Crisis* (New York, 1982); J.-C. Allian, *Agadir 1911* (Paris, 1976); and Steven E. Miller, ed., *Military Strategy and the Origins of the First World War* (Princeton, 1985).

13. A. J. A. Morris, *Radicalism against War, 1906–1914* (London, 1972); Morris, *The Scaremongers: The Advocacy of War and Rearmament, 1896–1914* (London, 1984); Peter Rowland, *The Last Liberal Government: Unfinished Business, 1911–1914* (London, 1971); Jean-Jacques Becker, *1914: Comment les français sont entrés dans la guerre* (Paris, 1977); and G. W. Chapman, "The Decision for War: The Domestic Political Context of French Diplomacy, 1911–1914" (unpublished doctoral dissertation, Princeton University, 1971).

14. Zara Steiner, *The Foreign Office and Foreign Policy, 1898–1914* (Cambridge, 1969); and Paul Gordon Lauren, *Diplomats and Bureaucrats: The First Institutional Responses to Twentieth Century Diplomacy in France and Germany* (Stanford, 1976).

15. The best of these is K. M. Wilson, "The Opposition and the Crisis in the Liberal

Cabinet over Foreign Policy in November 1911," *International History Review*, 3 (1981).
16. Keith Robbins, *Sir Edward Grey* (London, 1971); Stephen Koss, *Asquith* (London, 1976); John Wilson, *C-B: A Life of Sir Henry Campbell-Bannerman* (London, 1973); Michael Fry, *Lloyd George and Foreign Policy* (Montreal, 1977); Peter Rowland, *Lloyd George: A Biography* (London, 1975); Bentley Gilbert, *David Lloyd George: A Political Life* (Columbus, 1987); Edward Spiers, *Haldane: An Army Reformer* (Edinburgh, 1973); and David Robin Watson, *Georges Clemenceau: A Political Biography* (London, 1974).
17. Briton Busch Cooper, *Hardinge of Penshurst: A Study in the Old Diplomacy* (South Bend, Ind., 1980); and Peter Fraser, *Lord Esher* (London, 1973).
18. Stephen W. Roskill, *Hankey: Man of Secrets*. Vol. I: *1877–1918* (London, 1970); John F. Naylor, *A Man and His Institution: Sir Maurice Hankey, the Cabinet Secretariat, and the Custody of Cabinet Secrecy* (Cambridge, 1984); R. F. Mackay, *Fisher of Kilverstone* (New York, 1973).
19. Trevor Wilson, "Britain's Moral Commitment to France in August 1914," *History*, 64 (1979). See also Wilson, *The Myriad Faces of War: Britain and the Great War* (New York, 1986); and Keith Wilson, "The British Cabinet's Decision for War, 2 August 1914," *British Journal of International Studies*, 1 (1975).
20. Michael Gordon, "Domestic Conflict and the Origins of the First World War: The British and German Cases," *Journal of Modern History*, 66 (1974); David French, "The Edwardian Crisis and the Origins of the First World War," *International History Review*, 4 (May 1982); Stephen J. Valone, "'There Must be Some Misunderstanding': Sir Edward Grey's Diplomacy of August 1, 1914," *Journal of British Studies*, 27 (1988).

Preface

In October 1910 General Henry Wilson expressed doubts about whether British regimental officers would be interested in "the topography of a funny little country like Belgium, although most of them may be buried there before they are much older." Within four years his prophecy began to come true. Before eight years were out, 37,326 British officers and 672,287 other ranks died in battle in Belgium and France. What follows is the story of why those soldiers went to the Continent in 1914.

The Anglo-French entente exercised a decisive influence upon European diplomacy in the last years before World War I. But, despite voluminous research on the origins of the war, the entente's political content and its strategic ramifications have not been studied in detail. Politics between allies or, more precisely in this case, politics between entente partners have traditionally not received as much attention as relations between the Triple Alliance and the Triple Entente, or between specific members of the opposing alliance systems. Yet the frictions and cooperation within each of the entente-alliance alignments played a crucial role in the evolution of international politics before 1914. Moreover, the military and naval arrangements that were derived from those systems shaped both the diplomatic and the strategic options of the respective member nations. The secret conversations between the French and British Staffs not only reinforced entente ties, they also encouraged a British strategic commitment to continental intervention which was ultimately realized in 1914. At the same time, every aspect of the entente relationship—diplomatic, military, and naval—was influenced by the demands of party politics, the machinations of aggressive bureaucracies, and the foibles of personal ambition. Domestic and foreign affairs were inseparable in the history of the entente.

Extensive new archival and manuscript material in Belgium, Britain, and France, as well as significant new historical studies on topics impinging on the Paris-London relationship, now permit an analysis of the politics of the Entente Cordiale. It is my hope that this study will add new perspectives to the continuing re-examination of the content and style of the "old diplomacy" as it existed before 1914.

It is a pleasure to thank the following foundations, publishers, and individuals for their help and cooperation. For financial support: the Danforth Foundation, the John Anson Kittredge Educational Fund (and Mr. Walter Muir Whitehill in particular), the Army Research Office, the American Philosophical Society, and Harvard University (for the Emerton Traveling Fellowship and other amenities). For library and archival assistance: the staffs of the Bibliothèque Nationale, the Bodleian Library of Oxford University (especially Mr. D. S. Porter), the British Museum, the Public Record Office (especially Mr. J. G. Wickham, Mr. L. G. Seed, and Mr. E. A. Timings, F.S.A.), Widener Library of Harvard University, and the United States Military Academy Library.

For the right to quote from archival and private papers I thank and acknowledge: the gracious permission of Her Majesty Queen Elizabeth II: the Royal Archives at Windsor; the permission of Her Majesty's Stationery Office for the use of Crown-copyright records in the Public Record Office: Admiralty, Foreign Office, and War Office Archives; General de Cossé Brissac: Archives du Ministère de la Guerre at the Château de Vincennes; Rear Admiral C. R. Fliche and M. Audouy: Archives du Ministère de la Marine, Paris; Georges Dethan, Conservateur: Archives du Ministère des Affaires Etrangères and the papers of Paul Cambon and Théophile Delcassé, Paris; P. H. Desneux: Archives des Affaires Etrangères et du Commerce Extérieur, Brussels; Mme. M.–R. Thielemans and the Archives Générales du Royaume: the Papers of Georges Helleputte, J. van den Heuvel, Paul Hymans, François Schollaert; the Trustees of the British Museum: the J. A. Spender Papers, the Balfour Papers; the third Earl of Balfour: miscellaneous Balfour letters; Mr. Nigel Arnold-Forster: the Arnold-Forster Papers; Mr. Mark Bonham

Carter: the Asquith Papers; the Earl Mountbatten of Burma: the Battenberg Papers; Marjorie, Lady Pentland: the Campbell-Bannerman Papers; Dr. K. W. Humphreys, Chief Librarian of Birmingham University Library, on behalf of the Chamberlain family: the Austen Chamberlain Papers; Mr. Martin Gilbert and Fladgate & Co.: the Churchill Papers; the late third Viscount Esher and the fourth Viscount Esher: the Esher Papers; Mr. Hector Munro, M.P.: the Spencer Ewart Diaries; the third Baron Fisher: the Fisher Papers; Sir William Goschen: the Goschen Papers; Sir Robin Edward Dysart Grey: the Grey Papers; the second Earl Haig and Mr. Robert Blake: the Haig Papers; Mrs. E. Campbell Fraser: the Haldane Papers; Helen, Lady Hardinge of Penhurst: the Hardinge Papers; Mr. A. W. H. Pearsall and the Trustees of the National Maritime Museum: the Kelly Papers; the eighth Marquess of Lansdowne: the Lansdowne Papers; Mr. A. J. P. Taylor and Beaverbrook Newspapers, Ltd.: the Lloyd George Papers; Sir Victor Mallet: the Mallet Papers; David McKenna: the McKenna Papers; the Warden and Fellows of New College, Oxford: the Milner Papers; the late Sir Harold Nicolson and Mr. Nigel Nicolson: the Nicolson Papers; General Lord Robertson of Oakridge and the Trustees of the Centre for Military Archives, University of London King's College: the Robertson Papers; Mr. L. P. Scott: the Scott Papers; the third Baron Mottistone: the Seely Papers; Lady Elizabeth Arthur: the Spring-Rice Papers; Lieutenant Commander P. K. Kemp (ret.): the Tweedmouth Papers; Major C. J. Wilson (ret.): the Wilson Diaries. Every effort has been made to locate holders of literary rights; where this has proved impossible, apologies are offered in advance.

For quotations from unpublished manuscripts and printed books I wish to thank: Professors Theodore Ropp and Bernard K. Dehmelt; Charles Scribner's Sons and the Hamlyn Publishing Group, Ltd.: Sir Winston Churchill's *The World Crisis*, vol. I; Ivor Nicholson & Watson and A. P. Watt & Son: *Journals and Letters of Reginald, Viscount Esher*, vols. II–III, edited by Maurice V. Brett and Oliver, Viscount Esher; Jonathan Cape Ltd.: *Fear God and Dread Nought: the Correspondence of Admiral of the Fleet Lord Fisher of Kilverstone*, vol. II, edited by Arthur J. Marder; Oxford University Press: Arthur J. Marder's *From the Dreadnought to Scapa Flow*, vol. I; Cassell and Company, Ltd., and Charles Scribner's Sons: Sir C. E. Callwell's *Field-Marshal Sir Henry Wilson: His Life and Diaries*, vol. I.

I am especially grateful to the late first Baron Hankey, who kindly granted me an interview, to Professors Pierre Renouvin and J.–B. Duroselle, who helped me locate archival materials in France, and to Sir Basil Liddell Hart, who read the manuscript and gave me other generous assistance. For research and secretarial assistance I must thank Teresa Berry, Helen Vinton, Wendy Norton, Jane Walker, and Alice Methfessel. The cartographer is Mr. Edward J. Krasnoborski. To Colonel G. A.

Lincoln, U. S. Military Academy, under whom I served for three years, I am particularly grateful; he understood the time required for this project and his encouragement was unceasing. I owe much to Professor John L. Snell, who first suggested the topic. To Professor Ernest R. May I am indebted for kindnesses too numerous to recount; his advice, his example, and his friendship have sustained me at every stage of the research and writing. To Joan, for whom Anglo-French relations has been a staple for seven years of marriage, I am grateful for many things, most of all for patience and confidence. To my parents, to whom this book is dedicated, I say simply thank you.

Lexington, Massachusetts   S. R. W.
November 1968

Contents

Abbreviations

Adm.	Admiralty Archives
Archives Guerre	Archives du Ministère de la Guerre
Archives Marine	Archives du Ministère de la Marine
Belg. Arch.	Belgian Foreign Ministry Archives
B.D.	*British Documents on the Origins of the War, 1898–1914*
Cab.	Cabinet and Committee of Imperial Defence Archives
C.I.D.	Committee of Imperial Defence
D.D.F.	*Documents diplomatiques français, 1871–1914*
D.M.O.	Director of Military Operations
D.N.I.	Director of Naval Intelligence
F.O.	Foreign Office Archives
G.P.	*Die grosse Politik der europäischen Kabinette, 1871–1914*
Int. Bez.	*Die internationalen Beziehungen im Zeitalter des Imperialismus*
K.D.	*Outbreak of the World War: German Documents Collected by Karl Kautsky (Kautsky Documents)*
M.A.E.	Archives du Ministère des Affaires Etrangères
RA	Royal Archives
W.O.	War Office Archives

The Politics of Grand Strategy

Britain and France Prepare for War, 1904–1914

1 | The Formation of the Entente Cordiale 1898–1904

April 8, 1904, was no ordinary day at Whitehall. In the corridors of the Foreign Office clerks hurried to complete last minute arrangements. Senior officials came and went from the spacious office of the Foreign Secretary overlooking St. James's Park and Horse Guards Parade. Pens were readied, chairs and tables arranged. At mid-morning the Marquess of Lansdowne, the Foreign Secretary, arrived. After checking the preparations, he seated himself behind his wide eighteenth-century desk and impatiently began to go through the dispatch boxes. Exactly at eleven o'clock the Foreign Office usher appeared at the door, announcing His Excellency, the ambassador of the Republic of France, M. Paul Cambon.

After the usual round of pleasantries the two men settled down to business. On a nearby table were the products of nine months of arduous negotiations—a series of colonial agreements. Upon these accords Lansdowne and Cambon, now surrounded by Foreign Office personnel, affixed their signatures. With this act old animosities were buried, past humiliations forgotten, new cooperation and support pledged. Anglo-French relations were entering a new phase. If the Entente Cordiale did not yet exist, at least the foundations for it were in place.

This pleasant scene of April 1904 contrasted sharply with earlier bitterness in Anglo-French diplomacy. Only six years before, in 1898, Fashoda had been an ugly word in both countries as war over the Upper Nile seemed imminent. Tempers had flared, tension had mounted as Horatio Herbert Kitchener confronted Captain Jean Baptiste Marchand's small party at Fashoda. British diplomatic pressure, deftly backed by naval power, finally forced the French government to renounce its attempt to control the headwaters of the Nile. From that nadir relations between London and Paris gradually improved. Indeed, the underlying forces behind this improvement were already at work in 1898.

Lord Salisbury's third and final government found the policy of "splendid isolation" increasingly less splendid as the nineteenth century drew to a close. At every turn the Franco-Russian alliance of 1894, the scramble for imperial gains, and the aggressiveness of German diplomacy harassed and confounded British policy-makers. Some within the Cabinet, exasperated by these developments, advocated a reorientation of British policy. In early 1898, when China appeared on the verge of partition, Joseph Chamberlain, the Colonial Secretary, took the initiative and broached the possibility of an alliance to the Germans. This overture received no encouragement from Berlin or from Lord Salisbury, and anxiety within the Cabinet about Britain's international posture continued. Nor did the victorious denouement of the Fashoda incident ease this concern. The start of the Boer War the following year served to emphasize anew the dangers of isolation. Finally, in late 1900, after the Boxer Rebellion in China, Chamberlain, Arthur Balfour, and Lansdowne persuaded the Prime Minister to make a slight departure from splendid isolation: in early October he reluctantly accepted an Anglo-German accord on the integrity of China.[1]

Several weeks later, on November 12, Lord Lansdowne assumed the aging Salisbury's duties as Foreign Secretary. Though Salisbury remained Prime Minister and retained a desk at the Foreign Office, his effective control over foreign affairs was significantly diminished. Equally important, Lansdowne's arrival ensured a more dynamic policy, one more to the tastes of the younger men in the Cabinet. A shrewd, prag-

1. On the development of British policy before 1904, see J. A. S. Grenville, *Lord Salisbury and Foreign Policy: The Close of the Nineteenth Century* (London, 1964); George W. Monger, *The End of Isolation: British Foreign Policy, 1900–1907* (London, 1963); Ian H. Nish, *The Anglo-Japanese Alliance: The Diplomacy of Two Island Empires, 1894–1907* (London, 1966); William L. Langer, *The Diplomacy of Imperialism*, 2nd rev. ed., 2 vols. in 1 (New York, 1951); Zara S. Steiner, "The Last Years of the Old Foreign Office, 1898–1905," *Historical Journal*, 6 (1963), 59–90; and Christopher Howard, *Splendid Isolation* (New York, 1967).

matic Whig aristocrat who did not shrink from responsibility, he came to his new post anxious to efface the memory of an unhappy tenure at the War Office. He brought no inflexible prejudices or unalterable conceptions about the conduct of foreign affairs. Rather, the fifty-five-year-old minister's sole concern upon taking office was the improvement of Britain's international position. To attain this goal Lansdowne was not fussy about the means, willing as he was to negotiate with any power whose help might bolster British interests: Germany, Russia, France, Japan, Italy, or the United States. A skillful negotiator, patient, doggedly stubborn once he had determined upon a course of action, he brought a new sureness and a new spirit to British diplomacy. Despite Salisbury's continued presence in the Cabinet, within a year Lansdowne had achieved a clear ascendancy over his Unionist colleagues in the formation of British foreign policy.[2]

The new Foreign Secretary's first task in late 1900 was the improvement of Britain's situation in the Far East. He initiated discussions for an Anglo-German alliance for that area only to find the German price —British membership in the Triple Alliance—too high. Undaunted, he then attempted to negotiate with the Russians but was rebuffed on two separate occasions during 1901. He persisted: having failed to reach an accord with the Germans or Russians over China, he reconsidered and decided to accept a Japanese offer for negotiations. The talks, which began in July 1901, were adroitly handled by Tadusu Hayashi, the Japanese ambassador; by December they had attained a momentum which even Salisbury could not overcome.[3] In these negotiations Lansdowne had the strong support of the Admiralty; Lord Selborne, the First Lord, and his advisers were especially anxious to release vessels from the Far Eastern station for duty nearer home.[4] Although others in the Cabinet were less enthusiastic about a Japanese connection, the Foreign Secretary gained final Cabinet approval for an alliance in mid-January 1902.

A few days later, on January 30, Lansdowne and Hayashi signed a five-year defensive alliance. The terms of the alliance were brief and unambiguous: both countries promised to maintain the integrity and status quo of China and Korea; if, in the achievement of these goals, either ally became involved in a defensive war with a single power, the other ally would remain neutral and seek to limit the conflict; only if two powers fought an ally was the other obligated to render assistance. The strate-

2. On Lansdowne as Foreign Secretary see G. P. Gooch, *Before the War: Studies in Diplomacy*, 2 vols. (London, 1936–1938), I, 1–86; and Lord Newton, *Lord Lansdowne: A Biography* (London, 1929).
3. Compare Grenville, *Lord Salisbury*, 344–369, 390–416; Nish, *Anglo-Japanese Alliance*, 124–184, 204–218, 229–232.
4. For example: memo by Selborne, Sept. 4, 1901, quoted in Zara S. Steiner, "Great Britain and the Creation of the Anglo-Japanese Alliance," *Journal of Modern History*, 31 (March 1959), 29–31. See also Arthur J. Marder, *The Anatomy of British Sea Power: A Study of British Naval Policy in the Pre-Dreadnought Era, 1880–1905* (New York, 1940), 427–434; Monger, *The End of Isolation*, 49–50, 57–58.

gic and naval aspects of the alliance were spelled out in a secret note. In this each country agreed to maintain in "so far as may be possible" a naval force which would be superior to that of any third nation in the area. In addition there were provisions for peacetime consultations between the respective military and naval authorities.[5] The first such consultations, it may be added, took place in the summer of 1902 in London, when the service representatives met to plan joint action against the Dual Alliance, to prepare signal codes, and to discuss the possibility of combined naval maneuvers.[6] When the Anglo-French staff talks began several years later, the War Office and the Admiralty were not entirely unfamiliar with the problems of joint strategic planning.

The conclusion of the Anglo-Japanese alliance opened a new era in British foreign policy. Despite recent contentions to the contrary, the alliance was a significant step away from the tradition of splendid isolation. By it Lansdowne committed Britain to a course of action which he hoped would discourage further Russian adventures in Manchuria; yet he also had to face the prospect of honoring this commitment if Russia did not desist. By any criteria this written, binding obligation to take action constituted a new departure for British diplomacy.[7] Furthermore, though the accord simplified Lansdowne's problems in Asia, it complicated them in Europe. The alliance increased the necessity for better Anglo-French relations lest the two countries be drawn into war because of their allies; at the same time, by eventually facilitating Japan's victory over Russia, the alliance enhanced France's need for British support.

After the humiliation of Fashoda, French foreign policy also entered a period of transition and flux. Théophile Delcassé, the Foreign Minister in successive governments from 1898 to 1905, labored assiduously to strengthen France's international position. Originally a successful journalist and diplomatic commentator for the republican journals *République française* and *Paris*, Delcassé entered the Chamber of Deputies in 1889. Thereafter his energy, knowledge, and ambition brought him handsome dividends: in 1893 he became Undersecretary of State for Colonies and in 1894 Minister of Colonies, a position he held until

5. The text of the accord is in G. P. Gooch and Harold W. Temperley, eds., *British Documents on the Origins of the War, 1898–1914,* 11 vols. (London, 1926–1938), II, no. 125.
6. Admiralty and War Office Archives, Public Record Office, London, Adm. 116/1231b, 1231c, W.O. 106/48; Marder, *Anatomy of British Sea Power,* 430–434; Nish, *Anglo-Japanese Alliance,* 251–253.
7. A. J. P. Taylor, *The Struggle for Mastery in Europe, 1848–1918* (Oxford, 1954), 400–401. See also Lillian M. Penson, "The New Course in British Foreign Policy, 1892–1902," *Transactions of the Royal Historical Society,* 4th ser., 25 (1943), 121–138; and the two perceptive articles by Christopher Howard, "Splendid Isolation," *History,* 47 (February 1962), 32–41, and "The Policy of Isolation," *Historical Journal,* 10 (1967), 77–88.

June 1895. Then in June 1898, just before the Fashoda confrontation, he became Foreign Minister. To this office Delcassé brought fixed prejudices and goals. Suspicious, sometimes contemptuous of Germany, he had been an early proponent of the Franco-Russian alliance; and, at other times in the 1890's, he had urged improvement of France's relations with Italy and Great Britain. But complementing, and sometimes competing with, his desire to ensure France's position in Europe was a fervent determination to make France *the* Mediterranean power—a concern that significantly shaped his policies toward Russia, Britain, Italy, and Germany, as well as Egypt and Morocco.[8] It was, moreover, the diminutive, bespectacled minister's activities in the Mediterranean that provided the decisive impetus for the improvement of Anglo-French relations.

But in 1898–1899, just following Fashoda, Delcassé's immediate priority was reinforcement of the Franco-Russian alliance. He wanted both to revitalize an arrangement that seemed verging on collapse and to reshape it to meet the contingency he feared most: the breakup of the Habsburg system. Delcassé dreaded the possibility that Germany might gain the Habsburg holdings along the Adriatic Sea and thus endanger his grandiose plans for the Mediterranean. To counter this prospect he persuaded the Russians in August 1899 to extend the duration of the alliance so that it became coterminus with the current European balance of power. Put differently, he cemented the alliance until the Habsburg spoils were divided to French satisfaction.[9] The French minister also sought to expand the military features of the partnership, partly to safeguard France from Germany but more immediately to strengthen his position vis-à-vis Britain.[10] Although St. Petersburg accepted this transformation and consolidation, the Tsar's government remained resolutely hypnotized by the lure of the Far East. Eventually this Russian preoccupation meant more trouble with London.

The French minister was perhaps more successful as he worked to improve relations with Italy. In this instance both Mediterranean and European considerations guided his policy. In 1900 the two governments negotiated a mutually beneficial secret accord over North Africa which recognized Italian rights in Tripoli and French in Morocco. Then two years later Delcassé secured an Italian promise to undertake no aggres-

8. Christopher Andrew, "German World Policy and the Reshaping of the Dual Alliance," *Journal of Contemporary History*, 1, no. 3 (1966), 137–151, and "France and the Making of the Entente Cordiale," *Historical Journal*, 10 (1967), 89–105. Along with Andrew's major study (*Théophile Delcassé and the Making of the Entente Cordiale* [New York, 1968]), the following are helpful: Charles W. Porter, *The Career of Théophile Delcassé* (Philadelphia, 1936); Albéric Neton, *Delcassé, 1852–1923* (Paris, 1952); and Gooch, *Before the War: Studies in Diplomacy*, I, 87–183.
9. Andrew, "Greman World Policy," 140–147; cf. Langer, *Diplomacy of Imperialism*, 597–599.
10. Pierre Renouvin, "L'orientation de l'alliance franco-russe en 1900–1901," *Revue d'histoire diplomatique*, 80 (July–September 1966), 193–204.

sive action against France should the latter become involved in a war.[11] This secret pledge, which effectively offset Italy's alliance obligations to Germany, was a major triumph for Delcassé. With it he not only secured France's southeastern frontier, he also drove a wedge into the Triple Alliance. In the future neither Berlin nor London could afford to ignore the growing cordiality of Franco-Italian relations.

Toward Germany and Britain Delcassé pursued a cautious, prudent policy in his first years at the Quai d'Orsay. The rightist agitation for closer ties with Germany, a call particularly insistent at the height of the Dreyfus affair, found no favor with the French minister.[12] For him the "lost provinces" of Alsace and Lorraine posed an insurmountable barrier to closer or friendly ties with Berlin. France would maintain correct relations with Germany and no more. Meanwhile he carefully watched Berlin's contacts with St. Petersburg and London, ever alert for the slightest shift in the alliance structure. He probed at first, then became increasingly circumspect with the British. In the early phases of the Boer War he hoped to exploit Britain's isolation to regain a foothold in Egypt; but this desire came to nothing—and after mid-1900 he scrupulously avoided antagonizing London for any reason. Instead he worked with his Anglophile ambassador, Paul Cambon, to ameliorate some of the bitterness in Anglo-French relations.[13]

Delcassé's diplomatic efforts were not, however, confined to the great powers. He also embarked upon an active colonial policy in Morocco. Aided by the geographical proximity of Algeria and by the continuing unrest in the Moorish kingdom, he worked to exploit the chaos in Morocco for the benefit and completion of France's North African empire. Strong rule came to an end in Morocco in 1900 with the death of the Grand Vizier, Ba-Ahmed. The weak and inexperienced Sultan, Abd-el-Aziz, was possessed of sporadic good intentions to reform his kingdom; but rebellions soon became common, disorder frequent, the opportunities and excuses for European intervention plentiful. In this environment Delcassé's policy of "peaceful penetration" made steady progress. Paris refused to define the Algerian-Moroccan border and thus retained a pretext for border incursions and encroachments. At the same time the French worked to increase their economic position in Morocco; and they prevailed upon the Sultan to accept a French military mission.[14]

11. Barrère to Delcassé, Jan. 10, 1901, Ministère des Affaires Etrangères, *Documents diplomatiques français, 1871–1914*, 2nd ser., 14 vols. (Paris, 1930–1955), I, no. 17; Barrère to Delcassé, July 10, 1902, *ibid.*, II, no. 329. Also see Eugene N. Anderson, *The First Moroccan Crisis, 1904–1906* (Chicago, 1930), 19–34.
12. Langer, *Diplomacy of Imperialism*, 566–570.
13. *Ibid.*, 662–672; Andrew, "France and the Making of the Entente Cordiale," 93–99; Keith Eubank, *Paul Cambon: Master Diplomatist* (Norman, Okla., 1960), 65–68.
14. The French policy was so active that Madrid, in April 1901, thought there must be an Anglo-French understanding on Morocco. Durand to Lansdowne (tele-

To protect these gains in Morocco Delcassé diligently tilled the diplomatic terrain. He removed possible Italian objections with the 1900 accord and in 1902 he opened negotiations with Spain for a settlement; nor did he at first, as would later be the case, neglect German interests as he contemplated compensation elsewhere in Africa in return for German cooperation in Morocco.[15] Delcassé was particularly careful about London's financial and strategic interests in Morocco, and during 1901 he repeatedly assured Lansdowne that France sought only to maintain the status quo in Morocco—an explanation the Foreign Secretary did not find entirely convincing.[16] In fact Lansdowne's continuing apprehension about French designs in Morocco explains in part his willingness to discuss colonial issues with Paris in 1902.

The signing of the Anglo-Japanese alliance presented a profound challenge to French foreign policy. In the first place it necessitated an apparent extension of the Dual Alliance to cover the Far East.[17] Then, because of Russia's ambitions in the Orient, the new alliance increased the possibility of an Anglo-French conflict. Finally, any friction between London and Paris, for whatever reason, might jeopardize Delcassé's colonial adventure in Morocco. To protect the Dual Alliance, to avoid trouble with Britain, and to gain a "free hand" in Morocco: these considerations dictated the improvement of Anglo-French relations, and the first significant steps came in early 1902.

During that spring Lansdowne and Paul Cambon saw each other with increasing frequency. They discussed a number of mutual problems: the Japanese alliance, the current boundary encroachments in Siam, French fishing rights in Newfoundland, even the possibility of a royal visit to Paris. But not until midsummer, after Balfour had replaced Salisbury as Prime Minister, did their conversations grow more specific. On July 23 Cambon noted that the Moroccan status quo, that is the integrity of Morocco, might prove impossible to maintain; he suggested that both countries should be "prepared for eventualities." France, the ambassador observed, could easily accept the future neutralization of Tangier.[18] Two weeks later he renewed this discussion, suggesting this time that they consider the "liquidation" contingencies in Morocco. On both occasions the Foreign Secretary refused to swallow Cambon's bait. He per-

---

gram, henceforward referred to as tel.), Apr. 23, 1901, B.D., II, no. 314. See also Pierre Guillen, L'Allemagne et le Maroc de 1870 à 1905 (Paris, 1967), 653–697.

15. Andrew, "France and the Making of the Entente Cordiale," 99.

16. P. Cambon to Delcassé, July 10, 1901, D.D.F., 2nd ser., I, no. 323; Lansdowne to Monson, Jan. 22, 1902. B.D., II, no. 320; Monger, The End of Isolation, 38–42; A. J. P. Taylor, "British Policy in Morocco, 1886–1902," English Historical Review, 66 (July 1951), 366–368.

17. "Texte de la déclaration franco-russe," Mar. 20, 1902, D.D.F., 2nd ser., II, no. 145; Monger, The End of Isolation, 70–71.

18. Lansdowne to Monson, July 23, 1902, B.D., II, no. 321; P. Cambon to Delcassé, July 23, 1902, Paul Cambon: correspondance, 1870–1914, ed. Henri Cambon, 3 vols. (Paris, 1940–1946), II, 72–75.

sistently avoided any sanction of an eventual partition and instead trumpeted the virtue of maintaining the Moroccan status quo. But Cambon made some progress with these overtures, for Lansdowne was attracted by the prospect of an agreement over Siam and he did promise to bring the Moroccan problem before the Cabinet in October.[19] Another point emerged from these discussions: Lansdowne's concern over German interests in Morocco, a concern which seemed warranted to the French ambassador. Cambon in fact urged Delcassé to consider discussing Morocco with Berlin, but the minister refused to make this move, fearing a renewal of German demands for acceptance of the Alsace-Lorraine frontier.[20]

When the Lansdowne-Cambon talks were resumed in October, the Foreign Secretary's opposition to discussing "liquidation" had stiffened considerably. For one thing the Sultan, having heard of the earlier discussions, had asked London to guarantee his government for seven years, a request which the British evaded but found embarrassing. Perhaps more important, the Admiralty and the War Office had submitted memoranda urging the retention of the status quo to protect Britain's strategic interests at the Straits of Gibraltar. The Admiralty demanded, at a minimum, the neutralization of Tangier and the denial to France of the Moroccan coast from Mazagan northward.[21] On October 15 Lansdowne bluntly told Cambon that he was unwilling to consider any future liquidation of the Sherifian kingdom: even if he had been, the projected French terms for a settlement were insufficient. British policy would support the integrity of Morocco and work toward that end. On this discordant note the topic of the Moorish kingdom was dropped.[22] Talks during the remainder of October and November centered upon Anglo-French differences in Siam.

But the Moroccan question refused to disappear. In early December a rebellion flared against the Sultan, endangering the lives of foreigners, and prompting strident demands for European protective action. This awkward development produced a shift of both French and British policy toward Morocco. Delcassé now altered his earlier position and accepted Lansdowne's views on the maintenance of the status quo. Such a policy, the French minister readily appreciated, offered the best means

19. Lansdowne to Monson, Aug. 6, 1902, B.D., II, no. 322; cf. P. Cambon to Delcassé, Aug. 9, 1902, D.D.F., 2nd ser., II, no. 369.
20. P. Cambon to Delcassé, Aug. 12, 1902, Delcassé Papers, Archives du Ministère des Affaires Etrangères, Paris, vol. III.
21. Monger, The End of Isolation, 79. Oddly, in view of their later intransigence about German gains in Morocco, the Admiralty and the War Office in late 1902 favored a three-way partition of Morocco between Germany, France, and Britain, ibid., 81.
22. Lansdowne to Monson, Oct. 15, 1902, B.D., II, no. 325; cf. P. Cambon to Delcassé, Oct. 23, 1902, D.D.F., 2nd ser., II, no. 456. Privately Paul Cambon was fearful that Wilhelm II would intrude into the Moroccan issue: Cambon to Delcassé, Oct. 23, 1902, Delcassé Papers, vol. III.

of momentarily thwarting foreign and especially German intervention. At the same time, from the British viewpoint, the preservation of the status quo conveniently kept Tangier out of French hands. More significantly, Lansdowne now feared that European intervention in Morocco could not be postponed or avoided much longer. To protect Britain's strategic interests Lansdowne on December 31 agreed with Cambon that if intervention proved necessary, it should be conducted by Spain, France, and Britain, the three most interested parties.[23] That is, the French won London's consent for a policy which in effect excluded Germany from Morocco. "At first it was only a tentative, provisional, decision," writes Monger, "forced on him [Lansdowne] by circumstances; only later could it be seen that it was the first move toward an entente." [24]

In early 1903 Delcassé and Lansdowne followed a cautious "wait and see" policy toward Morocco. They helped Sultan Abd-el-Aziz negotiate another loan; they quieted Spanish fears about an imminent partition; they permitted Sir Arthur Nicolson and Saint-René Taillandier to cooperate more frequently. Nearer home the Delcassé-Lansdowne determination to settle Moroccan affairs without Germany won King Edward VII's support. But, as an uneasy calm returned to the Moorish kingdom, no further action was necessary for the moment.[25]

Anglo-French relations, meanwhile, became increasingly friendly. Negotiations were opened for an arbitration treaty and in March the *Times* talked of an Anglo-French rapprochement.[26] This trend was greatly stimulated by the highly successful, and unexpectedly so, visit of King Edward to Paris in early May. At first the ebullient, bon vivant monarch encountered a certain coolness. Shouts of *Vive Marchand! Vive Fashoda! Vivent les Boers! Vive Jeanne d'Arc!* greeted him the first day. But on the second day Edward's friendly smile, his easy command of French, his obvious sincerity, and his acknowledged love of Paris (and its ladies) captivated the fickle Parisians. By the time of his departure open, warm enthusiasm for him was obvious. On the more official side the visit helped also. Edward indicated clearly to the French his own growing distrust of Germany and his desire for friendship between the two cross-Channel neighbors.[27] Two months later French President

23. Delcassé to P. Cambon, Dec. 30, 1902, *D.D.F.*, 2nd ser., II, no. 548; P. Cambon to Delcassé, Dec. 31, 1902, *ibid.*, no. 552; Lansdowne to Monson, Dec. 31, 1902, B.D., II, no. 330. See also Lansdowne to Balfour, Jan. 1, 1903, Balfour Papers, British Museum, Add. MSS, 49728; Balfour to Lansdowne, Jan. 2, 1903, *ibid.*
24. Monger, *The End of Isolation,* 112.
25. Saint-René Taillandier to Delcassé, Mar. 10, 1903, *D.D.F.*, 2nd ser., III, no. 131; P. Cambon to Delcassé, Jan. 29, 1903, *ibid.*, no. 49.
26. On the arbitration treaty see Sir Thomas Barclay, *Thirty Years: Anglo-French Reminiscences, 1876–1906* (Boston, 1914).
27. Andrew, "France and the Making of the Entente Cordiale," 103–105; Sir Philip Magnus, *King Edward the Seventh* (London, 1964), 308–314; Sir Frederick Ponsonby (Lord Sysonby), *Recollections of Three Reigns* (New York, 1952), 243–249.

Emile Loubet's visit to London further reinforced the new friendship. But Loubet's trip had an even more important by-product: it brought the French Foreign Minister to London. On July 7 Delcassé and Lansdowne met at the Foreign Office for a lengthy discussion of Anglo-French differences over Morocco, Newfoundland, Siam, Nigeria, and Egypt. Although this conversation settled nothing, it initiated the exchanges which eventually culminated in the April 1904 accords.

During subsequent negotiations three issues were particularly vexing: Egypt, the fishing rights at the Treaty Shore in Newfoundland, and Morocco.[28] At the start the French tried to exclude the Egyptian questions—the management of the Caisse de la Dette, the control of the Sudan, and British occupation—from the discussions. Stubbornly and skillfully Lansdowne resisted, finally making any British agreement about Morocco contingent upon a settlement on Egypt. In this he received valuable support, including a few pushes, from Lord Cromer, the British Consul General in Egypt.[29] At last Delcassé yielded, consenting to recognize formally what the Marchand-Kitchener confrontation had already demonstrated: British control of Egypt and the Sudan. The Newfoundland fishing issue, hardy perennial that it was, troubled the negotiations until the very end. In this case the British sought to curtail French fishing practices at the Treaty Shore; the French in turn demanded a territorial award for their alleged losses. After rejecting a number of British offers, Delcassé eventually accepted the Iles de Los, near Conakry on the west coast of Africa, and border adjustments along the Gambia River and in the area of Sokoto.[30]

The fate of Morocco, when compared with the haggling over fishing rights, was relatively easy to resolve. Both governments expressed hopes for the continuance of the Moorish kingdom but took certain precautions for the future. France, because of its adjoining territory, was recognized as having certain rights "to preserve order in that country, and to provide assistance for the purpose of all administrative, economic, financial and military reforms which it may require." [31] France also promised to pursue a policy of commercial equality and to negotiate an accord with Spain over Morocco. The latter provision reflected London's rightful concern lest the French try to slight Madrid on the Moroccan spoils.

But Delcassé's most important concession for a "free hand" in Morocco, aside from yielding in Egypt, was his careful respect for British strategic interests in the Mediterranean. Britain was clearly determined to have unchallenged passage through the narrow eight-mile Straits of

28. The negotiations are traced in Monger, *The End of Isolation*, 128–137, 144–148, 157–159; see also Anderson, *Moroccan Crisis*, 87–102.
29. For example: Cromer to Lansdowne, July 17, 1903, *B.D.*, II, no. 359.
30. P. Cambon to Delcassé, Jan. 14, 1904, *D.D.F.*, 2nd ser., IV, no. 178; Lansdowne to P. Cambon, Feb. 5, 1904, *B.D.*, II, no. 389.
31. A copy of the Anglo-French accords is in *B.D.*, II, no. 417.

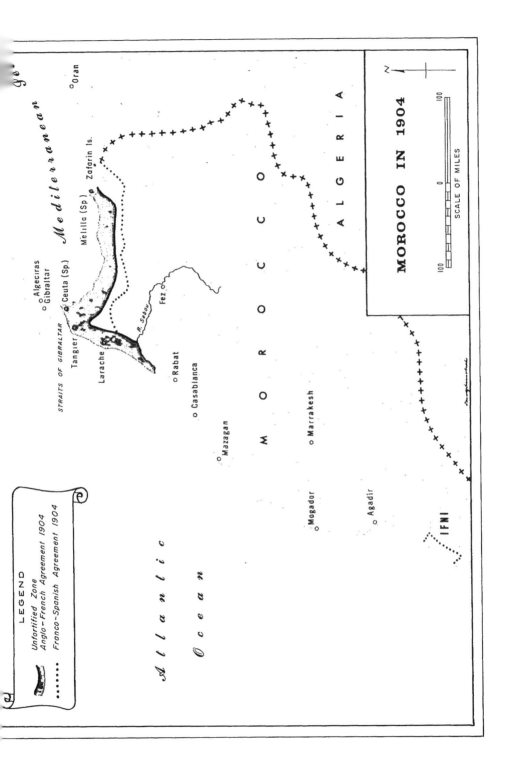

LEGEND

Unfortified Zone
Anglo-French Agreement 1904
Franco-Spanish Agreement 1904

MOROCCO IN 1904

SCALE OF MILES

Mediterranean

Atlantic

Ocean

STRAITS OF GIBRALTAR

R. Sebou

MOROCCO

ALGERIA

IFNI

°Oran
Zafarin Is.
Melilla (Sp.)
Ceuta (Sp.)
Algeciras
Gibraltar
Tangier
Larache
Fez
°Rabat
°Casablanca
°Mazagan
°Marrakesh
°Mogador
°Agadir

Gibraltar. In practice this meant keeping the coastline opposite the Big Rock either in weak Moorish or Spanish hands or under British control.[32] Delcassé, who had no intention of allowing Britain to control both sides of the Straits, offered to let Spain control the critical sector of the Moorish coast if a partition took place. But for a time even this safeguard seemed inadequate to the British services: in late July 1903, for example, the War Office restated its opposition to any settlement which allowed the Moors to lose control of the coastline. British gains in Egypt, the Army insisted, would not offset British losses in Morocco. In early August the Admiralty, somewhat less dogmatically, echoed this concern.[33] Finally, on December 14, the problem reached the Committee of Imperial Defence. There Lieutenant General Sir W. G. Nicholson, the Director of Military Intelligence, reiterated his unalterable opposition to any accord; but this time he received no support from his naval colleagues. Admiral Walter Kerr, the First Sea Lord, maintained that the Army's objections, which dealt chiefly with naval problems, were not "of sufficient importance to outweigh the advantages which this country would derive from the adoption of the Agreement as a whole." All the Admiralty required were Spanish pledges to retain the Zafarin Islands and to cede none of the Moorish littoral to France. This view the C.I.D. now accepted.[34]

With this strategic guidance in mind Lansdowne acted to acquire protection for Britain's naval interests. The final accord declared that "to secure free passage of the Straits of Gibraltar" the two governments would permit no fortifications (except the Spanish ones already there) between Melilla, near the Algerian border, and the right bank of the River Sebou on the Atlantic coast. In a secret clause the French also agreed that this same territory would go to Spain if Morocco were ever partitioned.

The agreements on Egypt and Morocco, unlike those on Newfoundland, Siam, the New Hebrides, and Madagascar, possessed two additional features: there were public clauses which promised mutual diplomatic support for rights in Morocco and Egypt, and there were secret clauses for the future disposition of those countries. The "support" clauses were the product of Cromer's determination to have French diplomatic backing in Egypt. But they had other, more significant long-term ramifications for London. By obligating Britain to support France's favored position in Morocco, the pledge increased the chances for An-

32. On this strategic concern, see P. Cambon to Delcassé, June 11, 1901, D.D.F., 2nd ser., I, no. 278.
33. Monger, The End of Isolation, 130–131; cf. memo by Prince Louis of Battenberg, then Director of Naval Intelligence, Aug. 7, 1903, Cabinet and Committee of Imperial Defence Archives, Public Record Office, London, Cab. 17/56.
34. Minutes of the 28th meeting of the C.I.D., Cab. 2/1. H. O. Arnold-Forster, the Secretary of State for War, also thought Nicholson did not fully appreciate the accord's benefits: diary entry, Nov. 20, 1903, Arnold-Forster Papers, British Museum, Add. MSS, 50335.

glo-German friction. In subsequent years this provision would become the most important aspect of the entire Anglo-French accord, for diplomatic support could only be meaningful if backed by military and naval force. When the Balfour government unhesitatingly accepted the responsibility to render diplomatic assistance, it demonstrated a naive unawareness of the European aspects of the Moroccan problem.[35]

The secret clauses were less significant. In the main they simply spelled out what the public terms clearly implied: London and Paris would have a virtual "free hand" in Morocco and Egypt if circumstances required it; Spain was guaranteed possession of the northern coast if the Moorish kingdom dissolved. Keeping the clauses secret was understandable. If published, they would have added further mockery to the lip service paid Moroccan integrity and unduly alarmed Madrid. Also, for London and Paris to have baldly revealed their intentions in Egypt and especially in Morocco would certainly have provoked a reaction from Berlin. In sanctioning the secret clauses the British Cabinet once more, as in the case of the Japanese alliance, indulged Lansdowne's penchant for secret diplomacy. Only later did the constitutional and the practical dangers of this procedure become apparent.[36]

The Russo-Japanese War was exactly two months old when Lansdowne and Cambon signed the completed accords on April 8. Throughout the negotiations the possibility of a clash in the Far East had acted as a stimulus, with London and Paris both anxious to reduce the possibility of becoming embroiled in a war because of their allies. But the Anglo-French accords did not arise, as has been suggested, chiefly from the pressures of Asia. In the first place the bargaining moved too slowly to warrant such an evaluation.[37] Despite numerous opportunities, the C.I.D. did not consider a possible accord until December 1903. At that time the British military advisers, quite oblivious to the talks with Paris, urged active intervention in a Russo-Japanese war.[38] Further, Delcassé, despite the tension in the Far East, did not fully reveal the nature of the Anglo-French talks to his own Cabinet colleagues until late February.[39] And when the French sought to hasten the talks, they made no ap-

35. The Cabinet papers indicate that neither the "support" nor the secret clauses were discussed by the Cabinet. Cab. 41/28, 29.
36. On the secret clauses see P. Cambon to Delcassé, Mar. 11, 1904, D.D.F., 2nd ser., IV, no. 342; Lansdowne to Monson, Mar. 11, 1904, B.D., II, no. 398; Harold Temperley, "British Secret Diplomacy from Canning to Grey," Cambridge Historical Journal, 6 (1938), 23–24. The secret clauses were finally published in November 1911.
37. E. W. Edwards, "The Japanese Alliance and the Anglo-French Agreement of 1904," History, 42 (February 1957), 19–27; Nish, Anglo-Japanese Alliance, 287. Significantly, Balfour's letters to Edward VII, recounting the main points discussed by the Cabinet, make no mention of Far Eastern tension until December 1903 (Cab. 41/28).
38. Monger, The End of Isolation, 151–152.
39. Lansdowne to Monson, Mar. 2, 1904, B.D., II, no. 394; Monson to Lans-

peal to Lansdowne on the basis of the Far Eastern situation. Instead Delcassé employed a more circuitous, though no less effective, method: he had Cromer informed in Cairo that his beloved scheme for Egyptian reform was in jeopardy.[40] Moreover, even after hostilities began, the talks nearly deadlocked over French fishing rights. As late as April 2, Lansdowne wrote the Prime Minister that he had informed the French "that if we cannot come to terms over Newfoundland the whole arrangement will have to go." [41] On the other hand, the entente accords did ease the predicament in the Far East created initially by the Anglo-Japanese alliance and accentuated by the war. Britain and France no longer had to stand, or at least appear to do so, in opposition because of their alliance partners.

From the start the Anglo-French accords, though essentially colonial in inspiration and results, possessed European significance. In large measure this stemmed from the problem of Morocco. In August 1902 Lansdowne had acknowledged that Germany might demand participation in any Moroccan settlement; yet four months later, in December, he shifted his position and accepted Delcassé's pleas that Germany be excluded from any Moroccan intervention. In the 1904 arrangement Lansdowne not only reaffirmed this exclusionist policy, he expanded it. Britain was now obligated to render diplomatic support to a French policy which deliberately bypassed Berlin on Morocco. Nor did Lansdowne do this blindly, for on March 23, 1904, he wrote Sir Frank Lascelles, the British ambassador in Berlin: "It will be interesting to see how Germany takes our transaction with regard to Morocco. She was always supposed to have des convoitises in that direction. It will be no less interesting to see what line she takes as to Egypt." [42] For his part Delcassé adhered to a course that ensured international complications. Although Russia was deeply involved in the Far East, the French Foreign Minister continued to disregard the fundamental connection between his European and his Mediterranean policies. He forgot that if the Kaiser challenged his exclusionist approach to Morocco, France and Britain would be confronted with a basically European, not colonial, problem.[43]

Further, London's pledge to support France over Morocco decisively shaped the future of Anglo-German relations. After the abortive talks in early 1901 about an alliance, relations between London and Berlin had progressively deteriorated. The alarming growth of the German Navy, bitter press exchanges, and the repercussions from the brief joint inter-

downe, Mar. 7, 1904, Foreign Office Archives, Public Record Office, London, F.O. 27/3665.

40. Cogordan to de La Boulinière (Cairo, tel.), Jan. 19, 1904, D.D.F., 2nd ser., IV, no. 198; Cromer to Lansdowne (tel.), Jan. 21, 1904, B.D., II, no. 387; P. Cambon to H. Cambon, Jan. 9, 1904, Cambon: correspondance, II, 107.

41. Lansdowne to Balfour, Apr. 2, 1904, Balfour Papers, Add. MSS, 49728.

42. Lansdowne to Lascelles, Mar. 23, 1904, Lansdowne Papers, Public Record Office, London, F.O. 800/129.

43. Porter, Delcassé, 190–194, 221–229; Andrew, Théophile Delcassé, 268–273.

vention in Venezuela fostered animosities and raised suspicions.[44] Moreover, the new intimacy and warmth of Anglo-French relations accelerated the growing coolness between Germany and Britain.[45] In 1902 several within the Cabinet still favored closer ties with Berlin; by 1904 the option was no longer acceptable nor even considered. Yet the Balfour government embraced with surprising readiness a policy which could only intensify Anglo-German differences. London had embarked upon a course which could only result in a further departure from "splendid isolation," indeed a policy which made a return to isolation impossible.

The strategic implications of the 1904 accord also reinforced its European and Anglo-German connotations. The Moroccan treaty stemmed from the necessities of British grand strategy. For at least a century the Admiralty had assumed that British ships would have unfettered movement through the Straits of Gibraltar—an assumption made possible by British possession of Gibraltar and an ineffectual Moorish kingdom on the opposite littoral. After 1900 one of these premises appeared threatened: France's policy of "peaceful penetration" into Morocco endangered British interests. If a strong naval power such as France occupied the coastline, Britain's naval position in the Mediterranean would be seriously jeopardized. London had either to prevent this development or to reach an accord with Paris which would have the same effect. With the Admiralty's support, Lansdowne chose the latter alternative and effectively secured the neutralization of the coastline.[46] From the start, however, both the Foreign Secretary and the Sea Lords regarded this safeguard as minimal; any attempt by any party to overturn or circumvent it would be cause for alarm.

The changing climate of Anglo-French relations was not immediately reflected in the military and naval planning of either country. Possible operations against the Franco-Russian alliance continued to absorb the energies of British planners; the requirements of *guerre de course* and an invasion of England still occupied the French staffs when they were not worrying about Germany. But in neither country did strategic considerations dominate the activities of the high commands. Rather, problems of organization, morale, materiel, and reform were everywhere the order of the day.[47]

The Royal Navy was no exception. Under the guidance of Lord Sel-

44. Monger, *The End of Isolation*, 42–45, 62–70, 82–84, 99ff; Marder, *Anatomy of British Sea Power*, 456–467; E. L. Woodward, *Great Britain and the German Navy* (Oxford, 1935), 63–86.
45. Cromer recognized this very early; Cromer to Lansdowne, Nov. 27, 1903, quoted in Newton, *Lord Lansdowne*, 285–286.
46. Marder, *Anatomy of British Sea Power*, 472–476, 574–575.
47. A comparative survey of these developments, as well as those in Russia and Germany, is found in Gerhard Ritter's *Staatskunst und Kriegshandwerk: Das Problem des "Militarismus" in Deutschland*, vol. II: *Die Hauptmächte Europas und das wilhelminische Reich, 1890–1914* (Munich, 1960).

borne, the First Lord (1900–1905), the British Navy sloughed off its Victorian torpor to become an effective, efficient fighting instrument. Better ships were constructed and tactics were improved, the fleet mobilization accelerated, and the Mediterranean station strengthened. In this work Selborne was ably assisted by Admiral Walter Kerr (the First Sea Lord until October 1904), by the vigorous and imaginative Admiral Sir John Fisher (Selborne's Mediterranean Commander and later his Second, then First Sea Lord), and by the consistent support of the Cabinet.[48] In 1889 Britain had adopted the two-power naval standard and at first met its requirements with a margin to spare. But the formation of the Franco-Russian alliance, the development of the Japanese and American navies, and the increases in the German fleet made this standard seem less relevant to Britain's imperial position. In practice the Admiralty came to gauge British naval strength against that of the Dual Alliance. By 1901, after the French embarked upon a new building program, this modified yardstick appeared in some danger, hence one of the attractions of the Japanese alliance.[49]

But the Franco-Russian alliance not only furnished the Admiralty with a construction standard, it also kept the British strategists busy. Because the Russian Black Sea Fleet was expected to join the French in the Mediterranean in case of war, that sea was always regarded as the principal theater of operations.[50] Fisher in 1900 argued that "you could no more change the Mediterranean from being the vital strategic centre than you can change Mount Vesuvius!"[51] If war came, the Admiralty planned for the Channel Fleet to join its Mediterranean counterpart and together proceed to attack the French fleet. While this operation was underway, a forward detachment would go beyond Malta to watch the Turkish straits and protect the Suez Canal. Not until late 1904 were these war plans substantially altered.[52] By then the growth of the German Navy, the decay of the French fleet, Russia's defeats in the Far East, the improvement in Anglo-Italian relations, and, not least, the signing of the Entente Cordiale dictated a shift in British strategic preparations from the Mediterranean to the North Sea.

48. The standard work is Marder, Anatomy of British Sea Power; also see his From the Dreadnought to Scapa Flow: The Royal Navy in the Fisher Era, 1904–1919, vol. I: The Road to War, 1904–1914 (London, 1961), 3–13.

49. The comparative naval strength of the powers can be judged, however roughly, by the available first- and second-line battleships. In 1901 Britain had 28 battleships, France 17, Germany 14, Russia 14, the United States 7, and Japan 5: Woodward, Great Britain and the German Navy, 449.

50. After 1892 the Admiralty had conceded that Russia could probably force the straits: Marder, Anatomy of British Sea Power, 152–161.

51. Fisher to Austen Chamberlain, Nov. 12, 1900, Austen Chamberlain Papers, Birmingham University Library, box 7; also see Fisher's lecture on the Mediterranean, quoted in Admiral Sir R. H. Bacon's The Life of Lord Fisher of Kilverstone, 2 vols. (Garden City, N.Y., 1929), I, 170–171.

52. The various Mediterranean war plans are in Marder, Anatomy of British Sea Power, 396–411, 495–496.

The German naval programs of 1898 and 1900 elicited no alarmed reaction from the Admiralty.[53] By 1902, however, this placidity was rapidly waning. One of the first officials to become nervous was H. O. Arnold-Forster, the Parliamentary and Financial Secretary at the Admiralty. Deeply impressed by what he had seen on a visit to Kiel and Wilhelmshaven, he drafted a Cabinet memorandum in September 1902 asserting that "Germany must be regarded as a possible enemy." To meet this danger he urged the construction of a naval base on Britain's east coast, an increase in the strength of the Home Fleet, and a revision of British war plans.[54] Another who shared Arnold-Forster's concern was Sir John Fisher, then Second Sea Lord. In that summer of 1902 Fisher stressed the German threat to a newspaper friend and asked him to agitate for an Anglo-French alliance.[55] And in October Lord Selborne told the Cabinet that he was "convinced that the great new German navy is being carefully built up from the point of view of a war with us." The naval estimates, the First Lord indicated, required at least an additional three million pounds to ensure complete maintenance of the two-power standard.[56]

During the next two years British alarm over the expanding German naval program steadily mounted, and numerous speeches, articles, and pamphlets warned of its challenge. Archibald Hurd, for example, cautioned his readers to "remember that Germany promises to be our most serious rival in sea-power." [57] And the *Daily Mail* (February 5, 1903) reminded its readers: "While great naval power in the hands of Britain cannot constitute a menace, in the hands of Germany it will be a grave peril to the world, the more so as the recent history of German policy is one of daring aggression, and as the want of space at home compels Germany to conquer the colonies of others or perish." [58] But the growing public concern was not immediately reflected in the Admiralty's war plans. Indeed, Arthur J. Marder has found no evidence that the German threat caused any modification of British plans before 1904. The first schemes aimed specifically at Germany were not drafted until July of that year, at which time Prince Louis of Battenberg, the Director of Na-

53. *Ibid.*, 288–301, 456–464; Woodward, *Great Britain and the German Navy*, 48–50.
54. Memo by Arnold-Forster, "Notes on a Visit to Kiel and Wilhelmshaven, August, 1902, and General Remarks on the German Navy and Naval Establishment," September 1902, Cab. 1/3/289.
55. Fisher to Arnold White, Aug. 6, 1902, Arthur J. Marder, ed., *Fear God and Dread Nought: The Correspondence of Admiral of the Fleet Lord Fisher of Kilverstone*, 3 vols. (London, 1952–1959), I, 259–262.
56. Memo by Selborne, "Naval Estimates, 1902–1903," Oct. 10, 1902, Cab. 37/63/142.
57. "The Kaiser's Fleet," *Nineteenth Century and After*, 52 (July 1902), 34–42.
58. Quoted in Marder, *Anatomy of British Sea Power*, 466. See also Woodward, *Great Britain and the German Navy*, 50–55; Oron J. Hale, *Publicity and Diplomacy with Special Reference to England and Germany, 1890–1914* (New York, 1940), 263–265.

val Intelligence, outlined several proposals for the employment of torpedo boats and destroyers, while also suggesting a way to block the
mouth of the Elbe River. These brief and rather farfetched plans constituted the Admiralty's planning for an Anglo-German war at the time
of Fisher's appointment as First Sea Lord in October 1904.[59]

Fisher, who often talked about a pre-emptive or "Copenhagen" attack against the German fleet (in imitation of the British seizure of the
Danish Navy in 1807), quickly gave British strategy an anti-German orientation. In late 1904 he ordered a sweeping redistribution of British sea
power with the major shift occurring in the Mediterranean. Four battleships were transferred from there to a new Channel Fleet (the former
Home Fleet), raising this fleet's strength to twelve battleships and ready-
ing it for immediate operations in the North Sea. The old Channel Fleet
became the Atlantic Fleet and retained its eight battleships. This new
Atlantic Fleet, now located at Gibraltar, was expected to serve in a
"swing" capacity, available to reinforce either the Channel or the Mediterranean Fleets as circumstances required.[60] It should be emphasized,
however, that these were fleet shifts and no more; precisely how these
ships would be employed still remained an open, and as yet unconsid-
ered, question. Still, with this wholesale realignment of British naval
power, Fisher entered 1905 convinced that the Royal Navy could defeat either a German or a French challenge.

British military policy-makers likewise reacted slowly to the changing
diplomatic situation. Nor should this have been altogether surprising,
for the British Army in these years remained shaken by its disastrous experience in the Boer War: because of that dismal performance it became the subject of intensive reappraisal, undergoing investigation by
three royal commissions in three years and experiencing two ill-advised
reform schemes.[61] The first royal commission, chaired by Lord Elgin, began its investigation in 1902. The voluminous evidence formed an impressive indictment of the Regular Army: poor preparations, inadequate
organizational structure, ineffective leadership, and outdated strategy
were included in the bill of particulars. The Elgin Report left little
doubt that the Regular Army and the War Office needed drastic reorganization; the old Cardwell system of linked battalions appeared
doomed.[62] The Norfolk Commission, which studied the auxiliary forces

59. Marder, Anatomy of British Sea Power, 479–482.
60. Ibid., 475, 491–492.
61. There is still no satisfactory study of the British Army for this period, but
the following are helpful: Albert V. Tucker, "The Issue of Army Reform in the
Unionist Government, 1903–5," Historical Journal, 9 (1966), 90–100; John K.
Dunlop, The Development of the British Army (London, 1938); Paul Kluke,
Heeresaufbau und Heerespolitik Englands vom Burenkrieg bis zum Weltkrieg (Munich, 1932); and J. E. Tyler, The British Army and the Continent, 1904–1914
(London, 1938).
62. For every battalion abroad, there was a corresponding replacement at home;
named for Edward Cardwell, the Secretary of State for War in Gladstone's first

in 1903, reached similar conclusions about their shortcomings. It found the Militia and the Volunteers inadequately trained and equipped for their home defense role.[63] Confronted with this catalogue of criticism, the Balfour government in late 1903 moved to implement some of the reforms suggested by the two commissions.

In October the Prime Minister appointed an extraordinary committee composed of Lord Esher, Sir John Fisher, and Sir George Clarke, with full authority to reorganize the War Office. The trio, working from November 1903 to February 1904, produced impressive results.[64] Their first recommendations, however, dealt not with the War Office, but with the Committee of Imperial Defence which Balfour had informally established in 1902 to improve the management of defense policy. They urged legal status for the C.I.D., the employment of a full-time secretary, and provisions for an adequate staff.[65] For the War Office per se the Esher Committee prescribed the abolition of the post of Commander in Chief, the formation of an Army Council, the development of a genuine General Staff, and the decentralization of Army administration. Although some of the committee's suggestions were still not achieved when the Conservative government fell in 1905, Balfour wasted no time on three items: Parliament gave legal status to the C.I.D., Sir George Clarke was selected as its first secretary,[66] and an Army Council was appointed.

Proceeding apace with the work of the commissions were the reform efforts of the successive War Ministers in the Balfour Cabinet, St. John Brodrick (1900–1903) and Arnold-Forster (1903–1905). Both men, by anticipating the reports of the commissions, created more confusion than enduring results in their attempts to reshape the Regular Army. Brodrick's proposals called for an army of six corps, with three corps (120,000 men) always ready for overseas duty. But this program, with its heavy manpower requirements and obvious expense, never had a chance.[67] And when Arnold-Forster arrived on the scene in September

Cabinet (1868–1874). On this see Albert V. Tucker, "Army and Society in England, 1870–1900: A Reassessment of the Cardwell Reforms," *Journal of British Studies*, 2 (May 1963), 110–141.

63. To the dismay of the Balfour ministry, the Norfolk Commission recommended compulsory training for home defense, advice which the Cabinet declined to accept.

64. On their work, see Maurice V. Brett, ed., *Journals and Letters of Reginald, Viscount Esher*, 2 vols. (London, 1934), II, 26–52; Marder, *Fear God and Dread Nought*, I, 288–305; Dunlop, *Development of British Army*, 167–168, 198–213.

65. On the C.I.D., see Lord Hankey, *The Supreme Command, 1914–1918*, 2 vols. (London, 1961), and Franklyn Arthur Johnson, *Defence by Committee: The British Committee of Imperial Defence, 1885–1959* (London, 1960).

66. Clarke, later Lord Sydenham, was a former governor of Victoria, Australia; he had served in the Army and had a wide reputation as a military writer. See his *My Working Life* (London, 1927).

67. Earl of Midleton (St. John Brodrick), *Records & Reactions, 1856–1939* (New York, 1939), 138–158; Dunlop, *Development of British Army*, 130–140, 156–162; Kluke, *Heeresaufbau und Heerespolitik*, 36–46.

1903, he abandoned the corps format for his own radical innovation: division of the Army into two separate categories, a long service army for overseas duty and a short service force for home defense. In addition he wanted a striking force of 20,000 regulars for emergencies. This unorthodox scheme encountered severe opposition from the Army, Parliament, the King, and the Prime Minister. When the Balfour regime ended in December 1905 the old Cardwellian system still held sway and Army reform remained unachieved.[68]

These contradictory reform programs were not the only cause of vacillation in British military policy. Contributing to the turmoil was the continuing debate within the government over the Army's role in British defense. During the 1890's the Army and the War Office had been guided by the Stanhope memorandum (1891), which defined the Army's duties as: home defense, supplying replacements for overseas garrisons, and preparing two corps for operations in colonial areas. The memo had explicitly remarked that "it will be distinctly understood that the probability of the employment of an Army Corps in the field in any European war is sufficiently improbable to make it the primary duty of the military authorities to organize our forces efficiently for the defense of this country." [69] After the Boer War Stanhope's guidelines with their stress on home defense were sharply questioned. By 1903 most in the Cabinet, including Balfour and Arnold-Forster, accepted the contention of the "blue water" school that the Navy could block any invasion threat.[70] The C.I.D. studies on invasion, begun first in 1903, also seemed to confirm this view, though Lord Roberts and others were not entirely convinced. In the opinion of the C.I.D. and Balfour the Army no longer existed for home defense, but rather for duty in India and South Africa, "conceivably (but only barely conceivably) for the defense of Canada," and for small raids against the colonial holdings of other powers. In particular the requirements of Indian defense against a possible Russian threat were now accepted as shaping both the size and the strategy of the Army.[71] The Army retained responsibility for home defense against raids, but possible overseas employment against the Dual Alliance now became its primary concern. In late 1904, well after the signing of the

68. Tucker treats the troubles experienced by Arnold-Forster in "The Issue of Reform," 91–99; also H. O. Arnold-Forster, The Army in 1906: A Policy and A Vindication (New York, 1906), and Mary Arnold-Forster, The Right Honourable Hugh Oakeley Arnold-Forster (London, 1910), 231–300.
69. Quoted in Dunlop, Development of British Army, 307.
70. Opposing the "blue water" school was the "bolt from the blue" group, which emphasized the dangers of a surprise attack and the need for an adequate army to defend Britain. The proponents of these positions were not, however, divided strictly along Army-Navy lines.
71. Balfour to Kitchener, Dec. 3, 1903, Balfour Papers, Add. MSS, 49726; also the memo by Balfour, "Our Present Minimum Military Requirements and Proposals for Fulfilling Them by a Reorganization of the Regular Army and Militia," Feb. 24, 1905, Cab. 17/13.

entente, amphibious operations against French colonies were still being perfected by the War Office.[72]

Although Stanhope's policy on home defense was seriously challenged after the Boer War, his injunction against continental involvement was not. Nevertheless, the mounting Anglo-German antagonism combined with the apparent need to redefine the Army's mission prompted some limited reconsideration of Britain's military relations with the Continent. An abortive move in this direction was made in January 1902. At that time Lieutenant Colonel William R. Robertson, then head of the foreign section of military intelligence, solicited Foreign Office guidance on Britain's treaty obligations to Belgium if Germany (or France) violated its neutrality. In his memorandum Robertson suggested that naval action would probably constitute Britain's primary response with military assistance "restricted to the number of troops adequate to afford ocular proof of our share in the war." But Lord Lansdowne, who saw Robertson's memo in March, refused to rule out entirely extensive land action: "I have always understood that our military system provided for the immediate dispatch of a small force beyond the limits of these islands and that we contemplated the possibility of sending out an Army Corps as soon as we had time to mobilize." Any enthusiasm generated at the War Office by this observation, however, was more than offset by Salisbury's stuffy attitude. The Prime Minister noted on Robertson's paper: "It does not seem to me that much profit will be derived from meditations of this kind. At least I am sure I can make no useful contribution. . . . Our treaty obligations will follow our national inclinations and will not precede them." [73]

Apparently the Prime Minister's rebuff was effective. Although Robertson remained concerned about Britain's role in preserving the balance of power, there were no other studies during 1902 about intervention on the Continent.[74] When preliminary planning for an Anglo-German war started in 1903, amphibious operations against German colonies or Heligoland were considered the Army's most likely task.[75] With this evaluation the *Army and Navy Gazette* (December 5, 1903) agreed, assert-

72. Memo, "British Naval and Military Policy in a War with France," dated winter, 1904–1905, quoted in Marder, *Anatomy of British Sea Power*, 550–568.

73. W.O. 106/44; also in Valerie Cromwell, "Communication: Great Britain's European Treaty Obligations in March 1902," *Historical Journal*, 6 (1963), 272–279; Robertson noted this memo in *From Private to Field-Marshal* (London, 1921), 132–133.

74. See, e.g., the memo by Robertson, Nov. 10, 1902, Robertson Papers, King's College Library, London, 1/2.

75. Memo by Robertson and E. A. Altham, "I. Military Resources of Germany and Probable Methods of their Employment in a War Between Germany and England; II. Memorandum on the Military Policy to be Adopted in a War with Germany," Feb. 10, 1903, revised Feb. 23, 1904, Cab. 3/1. In December 1903 Balfour wrote Selborne that "I do not want Antwerp to be occupied by a Great Power but I do not think such an event would be fatal to this country," Balfour Papers, Add. MSS, 49707.

ing "it would savour of madness to enter into any Continental struggle with such a handful, such a mere morsel to be swallowed whole by any one of the great military Powers." The fragmentary evidence indicates that the problem of continental involvement to help Belgium was merely speculated upon, not studied, before 1905.[76] The War Office, like the Admiralty, had expended little strategic thought on the demands of an Anglo-German war. In spite of the entente and the bitterness between London and Berlin, British war plans in late 1904 were primarily oriented against the Dual Alliance.

The French armed services were similarly characterized by change, adjustment, and reform in the years after Fashoda. Unfortunately, much of this effort produced unimpressive, indeed negative, results. For the French Army, as it coped with the aftermath of l'affaire Dreyfus, this period was particularly trying.[77] Final collapse of the uneasy truce between the aristocratic officer corps and the bourgeois politicians had come in the summer of 1899 when the reconvened Army court refused to quash Captain Dreyfus' conviction. Angered by this intransigence, Premier Waldeck-Rousseau had General de Galliffet, his Minister of War, impose sweeping changes upon the officer corps. Generals were relieved of their posts; three members of the Conseil Supérieur de la Guerre (henceforth called the War Board) were retired; promotions became the sole prerogative of the minister. President Loubet publicly pardoned the Jewish officer. Moreover, in 1900 when General de Galliffet balked at further measures against the officer corps, the Premier replaced him with General Louis André, one of the few genuinely republican generals. This appointment had instant repercussions: General Delanne, the Chief of Staff, and General Jamont, the designated wartime commander, resigned. As their replacements the government selected Generals Jean Marie Toussaint Pendezec and Henri Joseph Brugère, both more noted for their attachment to the Republic than for their military achievements.[78]

76. The Robertson-Altham memo of February 1904, noted above, speaks of a paper to follow on the problem of a German violation of Belgium. But a search of the W.O. and C.I.D. files has failed to produce such a study, nor do the 1905 studies refer to such a memo.

77. No standard work on the pre-1914 French Army exists, but the following deal with selected aspects of French military history: Eugène Carrias, La pensée militaire française (Paris, 1960); Richard D. Challener, The French Theory of the Nation in Arms, 1866–1939 (New York, 1955); Henry Contamine, La revanche, 1871–1914 (Paris, 1957); Raoul Girardet, La société militaire dans la France contemporaine (Paris, 1953); Paul-Marie de la Gorce, The French Army: A Military-Political History, trans. Kenneth Douglas (New York, 1963); David B. Ralston, The Army of the Republic: The Place of the Military in the Political Evolution of France, 1871–1914 (Cambridge, Mass., 1967).

78. General Louis André, Cinq ans de ministère (Paris, 1907), 26–45; diary entries for May 29–30, June 29, July 3–4, 1900, in Abel Combarieu, Sept ans à l'Elysée avec le Président Emile Loubet (Paris, 1932), 64–66, 73–76; Jacques Chaste-

Under André the Army experienced a prolonged purgatory. The minister came into office with the unenviable mandate to make the Army loyal to the Republic, and to achieve this goal he exploited a variety of police information about the loyalties of the officer corps. In addition his subordinates, possibly without his full knowledge, instituted a pernicious network of informers. Designed to ferret out suspected royalists, the system in practice became one in which Freemasons worked to exclude overzealous Catholic officers. At the same time André, despite the military implications, agreed to a reduction in compulsory service from three to two years (finally achieved in 1905). In this he satisfied ardent republicans who feared that three-year tours would make the Army too professional and thereby erode the idea of the nation in arms. Finally, in late 1904 a parliamentary uproar over the informers forced André's resignation. But by then his attempts, however necessary, to ensure the Army's loyalty to the regime had caused great havoc: embittered officers, shattered morale, and French security jeopardized.[79]

While the Army suffered from André's misguided zeal, Brugère and Pendezec labored to improve French strategy. Their first concern was the improvement of coordination and planning with their Russian counterparts. Staff visits became more frequent and thorough. In these meetings an overall strategic scheme for the Dual Alliance emerged, adequate for war both against Britain and against Germany. The 1900–1901 preparations against Britain provided for a French invasion force along the English Channel, the establishment of a defensive line in eastern France, and the strengthening of French coastal defenses to thwart reprisal raids. If war came the Russians were expected to apply pressure in Tashkent to threaten India. Certain steps, including French loans for railway construction in Tashkent, were taken to implement these plans.[80]

But the Dual Alliance preparations against Britain never received as much attention as did the plans for war with Germany. In this case, an immediate two-front struggle offered the alliance its only chance of success. The French were expected to withstand the initial blows of a major German offensive in the west until Russia's superior numbers could become effective in the east. In all of the staff conferences before 1914 the French officers constantly pleaded with the Russians to accelerate their mobilization and to expand the number of Russian troops available. By 1903 the French Staff had Russian assurances of some significant

net, *Histoire de la troisième république*, vol. III: *La république triomphante, 1898–1906* (Paris, 1955), 166–172, 211–212.

79. André, *Cinq ans*, 170–178, 297–334; Emile Combes, *Mon ministère: mémoires, 1902–1905* (Paris, 1956), 242–247; Louis Garros, *L'armée de grand-papa, de Gallifet à Gamelin, 1871–1939* (Paris, 1965), 129–147.

80. Memo by Brugère, "Compte rendu du Plan XV," 1902, Archives du Ministère de la Guerre (Archives Guerre), Château de Vincennes, Paris, "Plan XV," box 123; Renouvin, "L'orientation de l'alliance franco-russe," 193–204; memo by Pendezec, n.d. [1901], D.D.F., 2nd ser., I, no. 112.

help by the twelfth day and more substantial contingents ready by the eighteenth day. Later the French planners would discover that these were pious promises and no more. Nevertheless, under General Pendezec, the French Chief of Staff, the strategic planning of the Dual Alliance did improve; the requirements of a two-front war were considered; and both Paris and St. Petersburg were more confident of their ability to defeat the Germans.[81]

General Brugère, France's chief strategic planner and the man who would lead the French Army if war came, also worked on a second, closely related task: to ensure that France could withstand a German onslaught. To improve France's defensive posture the general drafted a new war plan, Plan XV, which the War Board approved in 1903. Like its predecessor, the new plan reflected the defensive-offensive views of General Marie Joseph de Miribel, three times Chief of Staff, and General Guillaume Bonnal, a professor at and later head of the Ecole Supérieure de Guerre. In this defensive-offensive strategy, writes Sir Basil Liddell Hart, "the Germans were to be encouraged to commit themselves to an invasion, and when entangled they would be struck by a counteroffensive." [82] In Plan XV Brugère expected to concentrate three French armies along the German frontier: one in the region near Epinal, another in the Toul-Nancy area, and a third near Verdun, facing Metz. The General thought these dispositions, coupled with the French reserve capability, would enable his forces first to blunt the German attack in Lorraine and then to launch an offensive of their own.[83] But Plan XV, like its successors, had a major weakness: despite reports of German rail construction around Aix-la-Chapelle, it made few significant provisions for defense along the Belgian frontier, the area which German planners already considered crucial for their attack plans.[84] Whatever its limitations, Plan XV along with the staff work of the Dual Alliance composed French strategic preparation after Fashoda.

The French Navy did not present an impressive appearance in 1904. A creditable rival of the Royal Navy in 1901, it was now a fourth-class

81. Memo by Pendezec, August 1903, D.D.F., 2nd ser., III, pp. 605–614; General Moulin to André, Apr. 23, 1904, ibid., V, no. 55; Alfred Vagts, Defense and Diplomacy: The Soldier and the Conduct of Foreign Relations (New York, 1956), 112–113.

82. "French Military Ideas before the First World War," in A Century of Conflict, 1850–1950: Essays for A. J. P. Taylor, ed. Martin Gilbert (London, 1966), 136.

83. "Etude sur les Plans I à XVII," n.d. [1919], Archives Guerre, "Histoire des Plans I à XVI [sic]," box 104; Ministère de la Guerre, Etat-Major de l'Armée: Service Historique, Les armées françaises dans la grande guerre, 68 vols. (Paris, 1923–1939), tome I, vol. I, pp. 7–10; General Arthur Boucher, Les lois éternelles de la guerre, 2 vols. (Paris, 1923–1925), II, 97–129; A. Marchand, Plans de concentration de 1871 à 1914 (Paris, 1926), 147–156.

84. See, e.g., Lt. Col. Gallet (military attaché in Brussels) to André, July 18, 1903, D.D.F., 2nd ser., III, no. 360; André to Delcassé, Oct. 15, 1903, ibid., IV, no. 11.

force. Chiefly responsible for this rapid decline was the durability of an outdated and discredited theory of naval warfare. In the 1880's Admiral Théophile Aube, in search of a raison d'être for a French fleet, had returned to the eighteenth-century concept of *guerre de course*. Steam-powered vessels and the success of the Confederate raiders convinced Aube that modernized *guerre de course* offered France the means to overcome the insular British. Fast cruisers and torpedo boats would destroy British commerce and shell English coastal towns while at the same time protecting the French coasts. Such operations, the Admiral had argued, would so disrupt British life that the Cabinet would be compelled to seek peace even though the battleship fleet remained intact. Aube's views won a wide and immediate audience—among politicians because torpedo boats were cheap, among French officers because a multitude of vessels offered them the possibility of command. Theodore Ropp has described the situation: "In every [continental] country, the torpedo boat, the cruiser, and the little ships were the hope of the younger men; in France, where conditions of advancement and favoritism were worst of all, the Young School had found its solution and its leader." [85] For nearly two decades, with some exceptions, the *jeune école* ruled supreme.

In the late 1890's the strength of the *jeune école* slowly waned, in part from the broadsides fired by Captain Alfred Thayer Mahan. Unsparingly critical of the stress on the destruction of commerce, the American officer insisted that only defeat of the enemy fleet would assure naval superiority; and for this battleships, not torpedo boats, were required.[86] Mahan's strictures, the surge elsewhere toward battleships, and the possibility of Russian naval help spurred a partial revival of offensive naval thought in France.[87] Admiral Alfred-Albert Gervais, the fleet commander in the Mediterranean at the end of the century, drafted offensive plans for defeating the British Navy;[88] moreover, the French government, especially during J. L. de Lanessan's tenure as Naval Minister (1899–1902), appeared willing to authorize the necessary naval vessels

85. Theodore Ropp's unpub. diss., "The Development of a Modern Navy: French Naval Policy, 1871–1904" (Harvard University, 1937), 265, 258–341; see also his article "Continental Doctrines of Sea Power," in *Makers of Modern Strategy: Military Thought from Machiavelli to Hitler*, ed. Edward M. Earle (Princeton, 1943); 446–450; also Vice Admiral Salaun, *La marine française* (Paris, 1934), 16–25. Henri Le Masson, "Douze ministres . . . ou dix ans d'hésitations de la marine française," *Revue maritime*, 233 (June 1966), 710–733.
86. On Mahan's views, see Donald M. Schurman, *The Education of a Navy: The Development of British Naval Thought, 1867–1914* (London, 1965), 60–82.
87. There were Franco-Russian naval talks in 1901 but no convention resulted: Renouvin, "L'orientation de l'alliance franco-russe," 201–203; Quai d'Orsay memo, Dec. 21, 1901, *D.D.F.*, 2nd ser., III, pp. 603–605.
88. Staff memo, "Memorandum envisageant les mesures à prendre en cas de guerre contre l'Angleterre," Apr. 2, 1898, Archives du Ministère de la Marine, Paris, BB4 2680; Ropp, "Development of a Modern Navy," 511–525; Marder, *Anatomy of British Sea Power*, 469.

for effective offensive operations. In 1900 the Parliament approved a new construction program calling for six battleships of the "Patrie" class (14,865 tons) and five armored cruisers. *Guerre de course* and defensive action no longer seemed to dominate French strategy.[89]

But appearances proved deceptive. In June 1902 Camille Pelletan, a doctrinaire radical and *jeune école* advocate, succeeded de Lanessan. From every standpoint his two and a half year administration represented a profound setback for the French Navy. In the government-owned dockyards his repeated concessions to labor unions occasioned numerous strikes and a virtual paralysis in naval construction. Mounting labor costs in turn prompted budget revisions at the expense, naturally enough, of the 1900 battleship program. By 1905 none of the "Patrie" class was finished, nor had any other battleships been voted since 1900. Not content with these savings, Pelletan cut costs in other ways: coal supplies were reduced, naval maneuvers curtailed, and a third of the Mediterranean squadron decommissioned during the winter.[90]

More important, the minister pressed the strategic views of the *jeune école* upon the admirals. Commerce raiding and defensive warfare were once more in favor, if not among the naval writers at least at rue Royale, where it mattered. Furthermore, technological improvements in the submarine, a weapon so obviously suitable for *guerre de course*, reinforced Pelletan's views and strength.[91] One of those who supported his stance on submarines was Vice Admiral François Fournier, a longtime adherent of the *jeune école*. In March 1904 Fournier argued strongly that submarines provided the only quick method for France to regain its naval power: with them, he insisted, the Entente Cordiale with Britain, which he regarded as an "instinctive tendency," would become an imperative for London. Once this occurred, France would have a durable guarantee of security. While the French Navy under Pelletan's guidance was constructing better submarines and torpedo boats, the British and German designers worked on larger battleships (and were thinking about the *Dreadnought* class).[92] The results were predictable. When Pelletan departed in January 1905, Admiral von Tirpitz' new fleet had substantially surpassed its French rival in number, tonnage, and firepower. France was now a fourth-class naval power.

Although the Anglo-French accords occasioned no immediate revision of grand strategy in either country, the arrangements did promote

---

89. Le Masson, "Douze ministres," 732–733; J. L. de Lanessan, *Le programme maritime de 1900–1906*, 2nd ed. (Paris, 1903).

90. On his administration the Oliver F. Guihéneuc Collection at Widener Library, Harvard University, a unique newspaper file devoted to the French Navy from the 1880's to 1916, is most helpful.

91. Ropp, "Development of a Modern Navy," 540–548; Marder, *Anatomy of British Sea Power*, 355–371.

92. Memo by Fournier, Mar. 1, 1904, Archives Marine, BB4 2681.

better political relations. In Britain the agreements received a warm and enthusiastic reception, from Conservatives because they clearly ensured British control of Egypt, from Liberals and radicals because they meant a reconciliation with republican France. Sir Edward Grey, the future Liberal Foreign Secretary, spoke for most when he told the Royal United Service Institution that it would be "necessary for us as a nation to depart from our old policy of splendid isolation. Splendid isolation, I think, is no longer the policy for us, and I am glad to see in one respect, at any rate, we have departed from it."[93] Only Lord Rosebery, the former Liberal Prime Minister, had misgivings about Britain becoming entangled with continental and especially French problems. Across the Channel the entente received a somewhat less enthusiastic welcome. Some charged Delcassé with having sold out French interests in Egypt for no appreciable or immediate gains in Morocco; others claimed the accord was another example of Delcassé's yielding to British pressure. But on the whole the settlement won French approval and ultimately that of the French Parliament.[94]

With the entente signed the two governments worked to avoid any friction that would compromise it. In June and July, for instance, they cooperated to hush up the Gordon incident, in which a retired British colonel described by the War Office as "an old fossil without any military aptitude" was mistakenly arrested by the French Army and charged with spying. Lansdowne feared that the colonel would take his story to the rapacious British press and thus damage Anglo-French relations. Paul Cambon warned Delcassé that the French were "so little accustomed to respect individual liberty that [they] could not understand the emotion that an affair of this kind could cause" in Britain. Gordon was, of course, released.[95] Meanwhile, the French Foreign Minister worked to expand the entente by improving Anglo-Russian relations; but the effort faltered after the Dogger Bank incident of October 1904, when the Russian Baltic Fleet fired on some English trawlers in the North Sea. Delcassé did, however, manage to avert serious complications for the new entente by persuading his Russian allies to accept arbitration of the episode.[96] He also reached an accord with Spain over Morocco and this further protected British interests at the Straits of Gibraltar. By the end

93. Grey's comments were delivered at the Royal United Service Institution on June 27, 1904; see Lt. Carlyon Bellairs, "The Standard of Strength for Imperial Defence," *Journal of the Royal United Service Institution*, 48 (September 1904), 1019–1020.
94. On the general reception see Anderson, *Moroccan Crisis*, 104–109; Oron J. Hale, *Germany and the Diplomatic Revolution: A Study in Diplomacy and the Press, 1904–1906* (Philadelphia, 1931), 77–79; see also the perceptive contemporary article by F. de Saint-Charles, "L'accord franco-anglais et l'Europe," *Revue d'histoire diplomatique*, 18 (1904), 454–475.
95. Minute by Sir T. H. Sanderson (Permanent Undersecretary), June 6, 1904, F.O. 27/3688; P. Cambon to Delcassé, June 6, 1904, Delcassé Papers, vol. III. (Unless noted, all translations are by the author.)
96. Monger, *The End of Isolation*, 167–175.

of 1904 this frequent Anglo-French cooperation was subtly converting the Entente Cordiale into something more than a colonial deal: it was becoming a useful partnership.

The improvement of Anglo-French relations had an impact on the already strained ties between London and Berlin. Calchas (J. L. Garvin), writing in *Fortnightly Review*, put it bluntly: ". . . the *entente cordiale* is fundamentally incompatible with an Anglo-German rapprochement in any shape or form."[97] The now bitter Anglo-German naval race simply reinforced this attitude. Fisher's redistribution of the fleet in late 1904 was regarded by the German press as an undisguised anti-German demonstration. The Kaiser came to feel that Britain was only waiting for the chance to attack. Nor were Wilhelm II's fears eased by the tirades of British journalists who talked wildly of a "Copenhagen" attack on the German fleet. The outburst in February 1905 of Arthur Lee, the Civil Lord of the Admiralty, who imprudently asserted that Britain might possibly take preventive naval action in certain circumstances, did nothing to ease German apprehension. Within the Cabinet Lansdowne had little success in his efforts to curb the rising anti-German sentiment. The days of cordiality in Anglo-German relations were long past.[98]

After April 1904, Franco-German ties were, as earlier, essentially formal and correct. In March Delcassé had informed Berlin of a pending settlement with Britain. But the French minister never gave the German government a copy of the accord, nor did he ever discuss it with Berlin.[99] And the Germans received no copy of the Franco-Spanish treaty on Morocco. As had been the case since 1901, Delcassé continued studiously to ignore Germany on the issue of Morocco. Count Bernhard von Bülow, the German Chancellor, bided his time. He supported Spain in the negotiations over Morocco but otherwise took no action during 1904 to offset the Anglo-French accords. The Chancellor still believed that a mere German hint "would cause France to apply to her for sanction of the French penetration of Morocco."[100] When this occurred the German government would be able to exact its price over Morocco.

But in December 1904 events in Morocco overturned the calculations of Bülow and Delcassé. Sultan Abd-el-Aziz, now comprehending the

97. 76 (Sept. 1, 1904), 402.
98. Lascelles to Lansdowne, Dec. 23, 1904, Lansdowne Papers, F.O. 800/129; Lascelles to Lansdowne, Dec. 28, Dec. 30, 1904, B.D., III, nos. 65a and b; Monger, *The End of Isolation*, 175–180; also Jonathan Steinberg, "The Copenhagen Complex," *Journal of Contemporary History*, 1, no. 3 (1966), 23–46.
99. For example, Delcassé to Bihourd (tel.), Oct. 12, 1904, D.D.F., 2nd ser., V, no. 371; Anderson, *Moroccan Crisis*, 125–127.
100. Bernard Karl Dehmelt, unpub. diss., "Prince Bülow's Moroccan Policy, 1902–1905" (University of Pennsylvania, 1963), 191. See also Norman Rich, *Friedrich von Holstein: Politics and Diplomacy in the Era of Bismarck and Wilhelm II*, 2 vols. (Cambridge, England, 1965), II, 680–685, 688–691; Guillen, *L'Allemagne et le Maroc*, 755–811.

danger posed to him by the provisions of the entente agreement, ordered all foreign military missions to leave Morocco. French pressure
forced a withdrawal of this order and permission for a French mission to
proceed to Fez. But the damage was done. The Sultan had revived the
issue of Morocco's integrity and again placed it upon the international
stage.[101] The overtures were ended; the first Moroccan crisis was about
to begin.

101. Saint-René Taillandier, *Les origines du Maroc français: récit d'une mission
1901–1906*, 3rd ed. (Paris, 1930), 213–224; Hale, *Germany and the Diplomatic
Revolution*, 81–93.

2 | The Entente Challenged: The First Moroccan Crisis, 1905

Throughout 1904 Théophile Delcassé pursued a relentless Moroccan policy. By steady and careful negotiation he gained British and Spanish assent for the "peaceful penetration" of the Sherifian kingdom; convinced that he had covered his most exposed fronts with the Spanish and British agreements, he now resolved to claim his reward. Nothing could alter this determination: not the Russian defeats in the Far East, nor the apparent restiveness in Berlin, nor the unimpressive condition of the French Army and Navy, nor his own insecure position in the new government of Maurice Rouvier, nor even the Sultan's sudden determination to resist French demands. Instead the start of 1905 witnessed an acceleration of French assaults on Morocco.

Delcassé's policy centered upon forcing the Sultan to accept a comprehensive scheme of reforms for the police, the banks, and the army, which would naturally be carried out with French technical, financial, and military assistance. In January 1905 Saint-René Taillandier traveled to Fez to present the program to Abd-el-Aziz. To the consternation of the French the Sultan, with unofficial encouragement from the German representatives in Morocco, resisted the reform proposals; and in mid-February he convened an assembly of notables, many of whom were anti-French, to discuss the entire question of reform. At this point the French envoy attempted to intimidate the Sultan by insisting that the reform program had the endorsement of all the interested European powers.[1] This imprudent act provided Berlin with a perfect pretext for intervention in Moroccan affairs. On March 14 Chancellor von Bülow assured the Reichstag that Germany's economic interests in Morocco would be upheld, and five days later it was announced that the Kaiser would stop at Tangier during his forthcoming cruise to the Mediterranean. This act, Bülow made clear to His Majesty, would "embarrass M. Delcassé, thwart his plans, and benefit our economic interests in Morocco." For a year Bülow had waited for Delcassé to approach Berlin on Morocco; now the Chancellor acted to make the French come to Canossa.[2]

On March 31 the Kaiser landed at Tangier. Mounted on a white horse and dressed in full military regalia, Wilhelm II was an impressive sight in the hot, dusty, crowded streets of Tangier. His statements during the brief stay were no less impressive, or explosive. He gave the Sultan's representative, Abd-el-Malek, assurances that Germany recognized the integrity of Morocco and would protect its economic rights there by supporting an independent Sultan.[3] This demarche not only openly challenged the French policy of peaceful penetration, it also called into question the support provisions of the 1904 Anglo-French accord.

The Tangier visit represented the first step in Germany's escalation of the Moroccan issue. During 1904 Bülow and Friedrich von Holstein had first considered, then rejected a stronger stand on Morocco, deciding to let events take their course. By early 1905, however, both men realized that Delcassé had no intention of rewarding Germany for acquiescence to a French take-over in North Africa. Holstein, the longtime political adviser at the Wilhelmstrasse, now pushed for and got Bülow's consent for a tougher policy. Germany would support the independence of the Sultan, defend the principle of the economic open door, and demand an international conference on Morocco. These political moves would, Holstein reasoned, make it "impossible for the French to cash their agreement with Britain, and France could be taught that an agreement with

1. Taillandier, Les origines du Maroc français, 225–247; Hale, Germany and the Diplomatic Revolution, 97–100.
2. Bülow to Wilhelm II, Mar. 20, 1905, Johannes Lepsius, Albrecht Mendelssohn Bartholdy, and Friedrich Thimme, eds., Die grosse Politik der europäischen Kabinett, 1871–1914, 40 vols. (Berlin, 1922–1927), XX, pt. 1, no. 6563; see also Rich, Holstein, II, 691–694.
3. De Chérisey to Delcassé (tel.), Apr. 2, 1905, D.D.F., 2nd ser., VI, no. 222; Michael Balfour, The Kaiser and His Times (Boston, 1964), 255–256.

Britain without the sanction of Germany was worthless." [4] By posing as the protector of Moroccan independence, Berlin could administer French colonial ambitions a sharp rebuff and also protect German economic interests. At the same time the French might be made to see the value of closer Franco-German relations. Bülow and Holstein did not intend, at least initially, to confront the entente as such with a direct challenge. But the mere achievement of their goals vis-à-vis France necessarily implied an attack upon the worth of the 1904 Anglo-French settlement. [5] Certainly the Kaiser realized the implicit ramifications of his Tangier caper. On April 1, the day after the visit, he told Prince Louis of Battenberg, then on duty in the Mediterranean: "As to France, we know the road to Paris, and we will get there again if needs be. They should remember no fleet can defend Paris." [6]

Repercussions from the Tangier episode upon Delcassé's policy and position were not long delayed. The Foreign Minister, convinced that the Germans wanted to overturn the entente, offered to negotiate bilaterally with Berlin. He made this offer first privately, then publicly on April 7 in the Chamber of Deputies, and later directly, on April 13, to Prince Radolin, the German ambassador. Further, Delcassé sent Maurice Paléologue, then a subdirector of political affairs at the Quai d'Orsay, to Berlin to initiate talks on Morocco. [7] Although the French overtures sorely tempted Bülow, Holstein remained firmly opposed to any bilateral talks. All Delcassé got for his efforts was official silence. On the other hand the German press clearly indicated what Berlin wanted: an international conference on Morocco. In addition, Delcassé's readiness to negotiate soon suggested another goal to the Kaiser's government: the possibility that the French minister might be ousted. [8]

Delcassé not only found the door closed in Berlin, he also discovered

4. Rich, *Holstein*, II, 693. See also Dehmelt, "Bülow's Moroccan Policy," 233–279; Bülow's distorted account, *Memoirs of Prince von Bülow*, trans. F. A. Voigt and G. Dunlop, 4 vols. (Boston, 1931–1932), II, 121–128; and Guillen, *L'Allemagne et le Maroc*, 813–880.

5. Rich's argument that Holstein did not seek war in 1905 is convincing, *Holstein*, II, 696–713; but cf. Gordon A. Craig, *From Bismarck to Adenauer: Aspects of German Statecraft* (Baltimore, 1958), 43–44 n. 37. On the alleged economic motives behind German and French policy, see Pierre Guillen, "L'implantation de Schneider au Maroc: les débuts de la compagnie marocaine, 1902–1906," *Revue d'histoire diplomatique*, 79 (April–June 1965), 113–168; cf. George W. F. Hallgarten, *Imperialismus vor 1914*, 2nd rev. ed., 2 vols. (Munich, 1963), I, 567–569, 599–638.

6. Note by Battenberg, Apr. 1, 1905, Lansdowne Papers, F.O. 800/130; see also Newton, *Lord Lansdowne*, 332–334.

7. Pierre Muret, "La politique personnelle de Rouvier et la chute de Delcassé, 31 mars–6 juin 1905," *Revue d'histoire de la guerre mondiale*, 17 (July and October 1939), 221–231; Maurice Paléologue, *Un grand tournant de la politique mondiale, 1904–1906* (Paris, 1934), 300–307; Porter, *Delcassé*, 229–237; Andrew, *Théophile Delcassé*, 275–278.

8. Rich, *Holstein*, II, 699–706; E. Malcolm Carroll, *Germany and the Great Powers, 1866–1914: A Study in Public Opinion and Foreign Policy* (New York, 1938), 514–520.

that support for his active Mediterranean policy was rapidly disappearing in France. Overnight he became the target of French press attacks. The nationalist press, which had never been enthusiastic about the entente, tartly observed that "for thirty-four years we have refrained from a war against Germany for the recovery of Alsace-Lorraine. Does M. Delcassé wish to go to war for Morocco?" De Lanessan, formerly Naval Minister and Cabinet colleague of Delcassé's, wrote in the radical Siècle that it was entirely appropriate for Germany to defend its interests in Morocco.[9] Perhaps more importantly, Delcassé's persistent failure to cultivate his colleagues in the French Parliament now began to hurt. The precariousness of his position, which both London and Berlin appreciated, was plainly revealed on April 19: in a savage, bitter debate at the Palais Bourbon, Delcassé was assailed for having ignored Germany's bona fide interests in Morocco. So devastating were the attacks that only Rouvier's timely intervention in the debate managed to prevent the government from falling. The Premier quelled the uproar by assuring the Chamber that Franco-German negotiations were in progress and that hereafter he would assume personal responsibility for French foreign policy.[10]

Rouvier's pronouncement did more than save his Cabinet. It ended Delcassé's unhampered freedom in the direction of French diplomacy. The Foreign Minister, immediately recognizing this, submitted his resignation the next day. Two days later (April 22), at the insistence of President Loubet, Paul Cambon, Edward VII, and Rouvier, he withdrew the resignation; but things were never quite the same. Delcassé remained adamantly opposed to any international conference, insisting that it would negate his plans for Morocco and perhaps divide the entente. Rouvier, for his part, refused to accept this line of reasoning. He had already pressured Delcassé to deal directly with Berlin and now, more convinced than ever of the need for peace, he embarked upon a tortuous series of secret conversations with the Germans in hopes of finding a solution, even at the expense of his erstwhile Cabinet colleague. Rouvier, moreover, was increasingly alarmed by the strong British support which Delcassé was receiving; he feared that British succor might either provoke a German attack upon France or be part of a British plan to trigger a Franco-German war. By late April 1905 the two top French policy-makers were sharply divided over the entente. The fate of that agreement appeared to many—especially in London—to depend upon Delcassé's retention of power.[11]

9. *Patrie*, Apr. 6, 1905, quoted in Hale, *Germany and the Diplomatic Revolution*, 109; *Siècle*, Apr. 1, 3, 1905.
10. France, *Journal officiel: débats parlementaires, Chambre des Députés, 1905*, I (Apr. 19, 1905), 1539–1550; Hale, *Germany and the Diplomatic Revolution*, 109–115.
11. Muret, "La politique personnelle de Rouvier," 306–318; Porter, *Delcassé*, 238–244.

Britain's initial reaction to the Tangier incident was somewhat confused. Lansdowne and Balfour at first were not disposed to take the visit very seriously. But the *Times* and most of the British press, in sharp contrast to their French counterparts, immediately treated the Kaiser's stop as a deliberate maneuver to wreck the growing Anglo-French friendship. On April 4 the *Times* called Wilhelm II an agent provocateur and urged France to stand firm. Two days later Printing House Square went further and asserted that "our character for staunchness and loyalty has been covertly impugned, and although the devices employed have been so transparent that they have deceived no one, it is well that our detractors should have an answer as to the meaning of which there can be no mistake." [12]

At the Foreign Office the emerging anti-German clique completely agreed with the *Times*. Eyre Crowe and Louis Mallet, then assistant clerks, saw the Moroccan crisis as a German attempt to cripple the entente; and as the tension increased, Lansdowne gradually came round to their outlook. On April 9 he wrote Lascelles in Berlin that Germany had "really no cause for complaint either of us or the French in regard to the Moroccan part of the Agreement." [13] Two days later the Foreign Secretary agreed to support Delcassé in opposing any international conference on Morocco. Two other factors helped to stiffen the British reaction to the German demarche: anxiety about the future of the entente if Delcassé disappeared from the Quai d'Orsay and fear that the Germans would gain a Moroccan seaport. Both apprehensions were reinforced by Rouvier's announcement on April 19 that he would negotiate, followed the next day by word of Delcassé's resignation. Suddenly the entente agreement and Britain's strategic position were in jeopardy. To protect these closely connected national interests now became the overriding concern of British diplomacy.

The first to grasp the political importance of the port issue was Louis Mallet. On April 20 he told J. S. Sandars, Balfour's private secretary, that Germany might ask for a port in the negotiations over Morocco. This would be done, Mallet felt, "to prove to the French the valuelessness of an understanding with England in which they will succeed if we do not back them up. How far are we prepared to go? I would not hesitate but would let the French know when they come to us that we would fight if necessary." [14] Two days later, after learning of Delcassé's prof-

12. *Times*, Apr. 6, 1905; see also *The History of THE TIMES*, vol. III: *The Twentieth Century Test, 1884–1912* (London, 1947), 410–416. George Monger's study on British foreign policy is particularly helpful in the delineation of Britain's response.
13. Lansdowne to Lascelles, Apr. 9, 1905, Lascelles Papers, Public Record Office, London, F.O. 800/12. As early as April 4 Mallet had written Cecil Spring-Rice (then First Secretary in St. Petersburg) that the episode at Tangier had fanned the "flames of the distrust and dislike of Germany" and brought London "closer to France," Spring-Rice Papers, London.
14. Mallet to Sandars, Apr. 20, 1905, Balfour Papers, Add. MSS, 49747. On April

fered resignation, Mallet expressed his fears about a German seaport to Lord Lansdowne. How would Britain react, the assistant clerk asked, if Germany, having ousted Delcassé, now pushed for a port. Mallet urged that the French be told that Britain would see them through the crisis. These considerations alerted Lansdowne. He told his subordinate to consult with the Admiralty. Fisher's reply, Mallet wrote later, was " 'of course the Germans will ask for Mogador and I shall tell Lord L. that if they do we must *at least* have Tangier—of course it is all rot and it would not matter to us whether the Germans got Mogador or not but I'm going to say so all the same.' " The clerk, who thought the First Sea Lord simply longed "to have a go at Germany," promised Fisher that he would help convince Lord Lansdowne.[15]

The Admiral immediately kept his part of the bargain. That same day he wrote Lansdowne that a Moroccan port in German hands would be detrimental to British interests. Only Tangier would be adequate compensation if this occurred.[16] Lansdowne immediately translated the First Sea Lord's admonition into action. From his estate at Bowood, near Bath, he wired Arthur Balfour on April 23: "Germany may press France for a port on the Moorish coast. Admiralty think this fatal. May I advise the French Govt. not to accede without giving us a full opportunity conferring with them as to the manner in which demand might be met?"[17] The Prime Minister, who came unexpectedly to Bowood that Sunday, agreed to the idea.[18] The next day Lord Lansdowne sent instructions to Sir Francis Bertie which repeated his original message to Balfour and added: "German attitude in this dispute seems to me most unreasonable having regard to M. Delcassé's attitude and we desire to give him all the support we can."[19] Monger rightly observes that this was a very strong telegram "which without actually committing Britain to the use of armed force certainly implied its possibility."[20]

In Paris Bertie sent an "urgent" note to Delcassé, saying he had "an important communication [on behalf of his] Government on the subject of Morocco." On April 25 the ambassador delivered an *aide-mémoire* which repeated Lansdowne's instructions. The appreciative Delcassé assured Bertie that there was no question of a port concession and prom-

18 Mallet had surmised in a letter to Spring-Rice that the Kaiser wanted a port: "The Emperor is cruising with a suite of 40 persons including 9 retired Admirals!" Spring-Rice Papers.

15. Mallet to Bertie, Apr. 24, 1905, quoted in Monger, *The End of Isolation*, 189.

16. Fisher to Lansdowne, Apr. 22, 1905, Marder, *Fear God and Dread Nought*, II, 55.

17. Lansdowne to Balfour (tel.), Apr. 23, 1905, Balfour Papers, Add. MSS, 49729.

18. Balfour later had second thoughts about the dangers of a Moroccan port in German hands, Balfour to Fisher, Apr. 26, 1905, Marder, *Fear God and Dread Nought*, II, 57; but Sir George Clarke of the C.I.D. strongly backed the Admiralty position, Clarke to Balfour, Apr. 29, May 4, 1905, Balfour Papers, Add. MSS, 49701.

19. Lansdowne to Bertie (tel.), Apr. 22, 1905, B.D., III, no. 90. The date in the Foreign Office files is Apr. 23, F.O. 27/3708.

20. *The End of Isolation*, 190–191.

ised to guard against any such demand. The best thing for Britain and France to do, he told Bertie, was to show that the entente was a "living force." [21]

King Edward's five-day visit to Paris in early May satisfied French requirements perfectly. Although the monarch counseled prudence to his hosts, the mere fact of his visit publicly appeared, as Paul Cambon put it, "to tie English interests to French." Despite Edward's preference for a quiet departure, Delcassé came to Gare du Nord to see the King off so as "to emphasize the Entente with England." [22] Lansdowne also helped. In late April he authorized G. A. Lowther, the British minister in Tangier, to go to Fez to assist Saint-René Taillandier. Then on May 3 the Foreign Secretary, while not committing himself to a course of action, reminded Cambon of British apprehension about a German port at Mogador. These official displays of British support for the entente had parallels in the British press: in the Nineteenth Century, for example, O. Eltzbacher called for closer Anglo-French ties—for an alliance to replace the vague agreement "which does not give a sufficient guarantee of mutual assistance and of national security either to Great Britain or to France." [23]

These demonstrations of British friendship strengthened but did not guarantee Delcassé's position. Berlin remained officially silent, while indicating in the press and through other channels that it would only be satisfied with an international conference. This the French Foreign Minister still opposed.[24] Then, in early May, the situation relaxed somewhat, chiefly because the Germans had to persuade the Sultan to call a conference before Berlin could resume diplomatic pressure.

At home Delcassé's position remained ambiguous and insecure. The press attacks upon his provocative foreign policy did not abate. And British support for him continued to disturb Maurice Rouvier, whose dread of a Franco-German clash was undiminished. The Foreign Minister, having learned of Rouvier's secret overtures to Berlin, tried repeatedly to convince him of the need to resist German demands and of the value of British help. But this businessman turned politician was skeptical, both of British motives and of the worth of British assistance.[25] None-

21. Bertie to Delcassé, Apr. 24, 1905, Delcassé Papers, vol. VIII; Bertie to Delcassé, Apr. 24, 1905, B.D., III, no. 91; Bertie to Lansdowne, Apr. 25, 1905, ibid., no. 93.

22. Bertie to Lansdowne, Apr. 25, May 5, 1905, Lansdowne Papers, F.O. 800/127. See also Sir Sidney Lee, King Edward VII, 2 vols. (London, 1925–1927), II, 342.

23. Lansdowne to Lowther (tel.), Apr. 21, 1905, F.O. 413/37; Lansdowne to Bertie, May 3, 1905, B.D., III, no. 86; P. Cambon to Delcassé, May 3, 1905, D.D.F., 2nd ser., VI, no. 390. Quotation from O. Eltzbacher, "The Balance of Power in Europe," Nineteenth Century and After, 57 (May 1905), 796.

24. Muret, "La politique personnelle de Rouvier," 316–321; Anderson, Moroccan Crisis, 211–220; Rich, Holstein, II, 704–706.

25. Muret, "La politique personnelle de Rouvier," 321–330; Paul Cambon to Henri Cambon, Apr. 29, May 4, 8, 13, 1905, Cambon: correspondance, II, 186–195; Combarieu, Sept ans à l'Elysée, 306–308.

theless, Delcassé placed more and more reliance upon British support, which he came to regard as the surest way to surmount both his domestic and his international problems. Strongly backed by Cambon and by Camille Barrère, the French ambassador to Italy, Delcassé tried to consolidate and extend British help as May progressed.[26]

A major step in this direction came when Cambon, at Delcassé's prompting, saw Lord Lansdowne on May 17 to review recent events, including British support on the port issue. The Foreign Secretary concluded that the "two Governments should continue to treat one another with the most absolute confidence, should keep one another fully informed of everything which came to their knowledge, and should, so far as possible, discuss in advance any contingencies by which they might in the course of events find themselves confronted." These comments, though probably intended by Lansdowne to restrain the French, were interpreted in an entirely different sense by Cambon. He saw them as a "most clear" and "most spontaneous" British offer to coordinate policy. He informed Delcassé that the British government was "completely ready to talk with the French government on measures to take if the situation became threatening." [27] In these differing assessments of the interview lay the germ of Cambon's belief that Lansdowne was offering a virtual alliance to France. This belief the ambassador retained and exploited all the way to 1914; and in 1905, it was his version of the talk that reached Paris.

There this latest sign of British friendship had a mixed reception. Delcassé regarded it as further proof of the wisdom of his policy; Rouvier saw it as another attempt to push France into trouble with Germany. On May 21 Delcassé, Cambon, Barrère, and Eugène Etienne, Minister of the Interior, met with President Loubet and Rouvier at the Elysée Palace to discuss the Moroccan situation. The entire question of British support was thoroughly aired. The Premier, still anxious for peace and afraid of German intentions, remained cautious about the alleged British offer. He instructed Cambon to reply evasively but not to reject Lansdowne's offer to discuss contingencies. In this way he hoped to retain British support without undermining his negotiations with Berlin.[28]

Throughout May each new development in France was closely scrutinized by the British policy-makers. Louis Mallet continued to insist that the entente needed strengthening, both as a protection to British interests and as a means of preventing a separate Franco-German accord on Morocco. Bertie, uneasy with Rouvier in power, urged a separate arrangement with Spain to safeguard Britain's interests in the western

26. P. Cambon to Delcassé, May 8, 1905, D.D.F., 2nd ser., VI, no. 416; P. Cambon to H. Cambon, May 13, 1905, Cambon: correspondance, II, 193–195.
27. Lansdowne to Bertie, May 17, 1905, B.D., III, no. 94; P. Cambon to Delcassé, May 18, 1905, D.D.F., 2nd ser., VI, no. 443; P. Cambon to Delcassé, May 18, 1905, Cambon: correspondance, II, 195–196.
28. Muret, "La politique personnelle de Rouvier," 332–334 n. 130.

Mediterranean.[29] Lord Lansdowne, however, now deeply embroiled in Far Eastern problems, grew steadily less apprehensive about the situation in Europe; he soon began to have second thoughts about his May 17 conversation with Paul Cambon—so much so that he tried to clarify its importance. An opportunity arose when the French ambassador wrote to thank him for the British offer to talk things over. On May 25 Lansdowne replied that he wanted to make it clear "that there should be full and confidential discussions between the two Gov[ernmen]ts, not so much in consequence of some acts of unprovoked aggression on the part of another Power, as in anticipation of any complications to be apprehended during the somewhat anxious period through which we are at present passing." [30] Read literally, this note carried two clear restrictions. First, there was no hint, no mention of military or naval assistance, despite the reference to "unprovoked aggression." Second, the "full and confidential discussions" referred to the immediate period of tension, not to future foreign policy issues. Any discussions were intended to cover no more than the crisis at hand, and at no point was there a suggestion of an alliance.[31]

But Lansdowne, despite his belated clarification, had in fact already added new dimensions to the entente relationship. In April he had promised Delcassé "all support" against a German attempt for a Moroccan port; further, he had offered to discuss ways to counter a German demand if it came. These assurances were followed by Lowther's dispatch to Fez, the royal visit to Paris, and the offer on May 17, even in Lansdowne's words, "to discuss in advance any contingencies." A promise of diplomatic support to France could reasonably be interpreted as a fulfillment of the 1904 accord; but a willingness to coordinate policy in advance suggested an intimacy more often associated with membership in an alliance. Impressed by this succession of British gestures, Cambon can hardly be blamed for believing an alliance possible.[32] For his part, Lansdowne certainly hoped that British steadfastness would save the entente from the German assault while also shoring up Delcassé's political position. At the same time Lansdowne's expressions of support can be viewed as a warning to Paris, as a reminder that Britain would not tolerate a Moroccan port in German hands. London in 1905, as in 1911,

29. Mallet to Short, May 6, 1905, Balfour Papers, Add. MSS, 49747; Bertie to Mallet, May 19, 1905, Bertie Papers, Public Record Office, London, F.O. 800/164.

30. Cambon's letter to Lansdowne is in P. Cambon to Delcassé, May 25, 1905, D.D.F., 2nd ser., VI, no. 455; Lansdowne's reply is in his dispatch to Bertie, May 31, 1905, B.D., III, no. 95.

31. The question of the alleged alliance offer is discussed fully in Monger, *The End of Isolation*, 197–198, 199 n. 2; Elie Halévy, *Imperialism and the Rise of Labour, 1895–1905*, trans. E. I. Watkin, 2nd rev. ed. (London, 1951), 425–428 notes.

32. One gesture did not materialize: Delcassé turned down Oxford's offer of an honorary doctorate of civil law (P. Cambon to Delcassé, May 3, 1905, Delcassé Papers, vol. III).

never completely trusted the French government (especially its Premiers) in its relations à deux with Germany.[33] In any event, Britain's support for France, despite Lansdowne's misgivings, was helping to transform the Entente Cordiale.

The Foreign Secretary's letter of May 25 sought to restrict British support to a specific crisis. But Cambon and Delcassé viewed it as meaning exactly the opposite—as a first step toward a defensive alliance. Lansdowne's previous backing, combined with the less than lucid prose of the May 25 note, may have drawn them to this conclusion; but, even more likely, both men wanted to see, and therefore saw, what they judged to be an implicit offer of alliance. Such an offer, the ambassador realized, carried certain domestic political risks for Delcassé, and he urged the Foreign Minister to be careful: "To accept the conversations," he wrote on May 29, "is to enter into the way of a general entente which would in reality constitute an alliance, and I am uninformed if the French Government would be disposed to accept such accords." When Delcassé, in spite of Rouvier's opposition to closer Anglo-French ties, ordered Cambon on May 30 to accept the alleged British offer, the ambassador balked. How could he answer Lord Lansdowne, Cambon asked on June 1, "if he proposed to have the Army and Navy Chiefs of Staff meet in view of threatened eventualities?" The veteran diplomat told Delcassé that they should thank Lansdowne again for the "alliance" bid, while avoiding acceptance of it.[34]

This prudent advice came too late to help the Foreign Minister. On May 28 the Russian fleet was defeated at Tsushima, and on the same day the Sultan rejected the French reforms and called for an international conference on Morocco: these developments quickly brought a resumption of German pressure for Delcassé's ouster. At first Rouvier rebuffed the German demands, then on June 3 agreed in the hope that Delcassé's departure would ease Franco-German tension and permit a reasonable settlement of the Moroccan dispute.[35] At a dramatic Cabinet meeting on June 6 Delcassé insisted that the Germans were only bluffing and stressed Britain's offer of a virtual alliance. If France failed to exploit this opportunity London, he warned, might seek closer relations with Berlin; the entente would be destroyed and France isolated against Germany. Rouvier, on the other hand, voiced doubts about British motives, about the value of British military and naval aid, and about the preparedness of the French Army; he also held, perhaps more cogently, that the country would never accept a war over Morocco. Furthermore,

33. Taylor, *The Struggle for Mastery in Europe*, 430–431.
34. P. Cambon to Delcassé, May 29, 1905, *D.D.F.*, 2nd ser., VI, no. 465; Delcassé to P. Cambon (tel.), May 30, 1905, *ibid.*, no. 470; P. Cambon to Delcassé, June 1, 1905, *ibid.*, no. 480. See also Paléologue, *Un grand tournant*, 341–342, 346–347.
35. Muret, "La politique personnelle de Rouvier," 336–350; Andrew, *Théophile Delcassé*, 296–297.

he promised that an honorable agreement could be reached with Germany. In the ensuing debate even President Loubet, a staunch backer of Delcassé on other occasions, sided with Rouvier. The former journalist submitted his resignation.[36]

Delcassé had scarcely cleared the papers from his office at the Quai d'Orsay when the German chargé d'affaires in Paris, Hans von Flotow, received information, late on June 6, that Delcassé had spoken of a British alliance offer at the Cabinet meeting.[37] When confronted on June 11 by German inquiries about this alleged offer, Sir Frank Lascelles (the British ambassador in Berlin) flatly denied to Bülow and Holstein that any such offer had ever been made. To stop further talk on the subject Lansdowne reiterated the denials on June 16 and again on June 28 to Count Paul von Wolff-Metternich, the German ambassador in London. But, afraid these denials might be misunderstood, Lansdowne on the same day warned that Germany should not "light-heartedly" go to war with France, for public opinion might force British support for France.[38] Berlin, with reluctance, accepted the British denials. Then, on July 12, Gaulois publicly declared that Delcassé had been pledged British assistance; once more Lascelles and Lansdowne repeated that no such proposal had ever been made. This continued furor provoked Lansdowne to complain privately that this time "Delcassé (or the reporter)" had gone too far. "I am," the Foreign Secretary lamented, "suffering heavily" for the French mistakes in Morocco.[39]

During the remainder of June Rouvier struggled to improve Franco-German relations. To his surprise—indeed, dismay—the German government did not relent on its demand for a conference to deal with reforms in the Moorish kingdom. At length Rouvier agreed to Berlin's call for an international gathering, but only after making careful stipulations about the agenda. In effect Bülow and Holstein got their conference, and the French the right to decide what would be discussed.[40]

Cambon, meanwhile, worked to repair the damage caused by Delcassé's abrupt fall. He had cabled the Premier on June 7 that it was "extremely important not to allow them to believe here that the retirement of M. Delcassé could bring about a rupture of our entente with England.

36. See the memo on the Cabinet meeting by Joseph Chaumié, Minister of Justice in the Rouvier Cabinet, June 6, 1905, D.D.F., 2nd ser., VI, pp. 601–607; Bertie to Lansdowne, June 10, 1905, B.D., III, no. 96; Combarieu, Sept ans à l'Elysée, 315–317. The Delcassé Papers add nothing significant on his fall.
37. Flotow to Bülow, June 7, 1905, G.P., XX, pt. 2, nos. 6853, 6854.
38. Lascelles to Lansdowne, June 12, 1905, B.D., III, nos. 97, 98; Bülow to Metternich, June 11, 1905, G.P., XX, pt. 2, no. 6857; Lansdowne to Lascelles, June 16, 1905, B.D., III, no. 99; Metternich to Bülow (tels.), June 16, 28, 1905, G.P., XX, pt. 2, nos. 6858, 6860; P. Cambon to Rouvier (tel.), June 16, 1905, D.D.F., 2nd ser., VII, no. 74.
39. Lansdowne to Lascelles, Aug. 5, 1905, Lascelles Papers, F.O. 800/12; see also Lascelles to Lansdowne, Aug. 3, 1905, Lansdowne Papers, F.O. 800/130.
40. Rich, Holstein, II, 707–713; Anderson, Moroccan Crisis, 234–256.

In this connection I have found some signs of apprehension among the King, the Prince of Wales and Lord Lansdowne."[41] Nor were the ambassador's fears excessive, for Balfour wrote Edward VII on June 8 that "Delcassé's dismissal or resignation" demonstrated that France could not be reckoned as an effective power. "She could no longer be trusted not to yield to threats at the crucial moment of negotiation. If, therefore, Germany is really desirous of obtaining a port on the coast of Morocco, and if such a proceeding be a menace to our interests, it must be to other means than French assistance that we must look for our protection."[42]

Cambon, given these attitudes in Britain, had no easy task. He pointedly assured British leaders that Rouvier was firmly attached to the entente and he made sure the Foreign Office knew each step of the Franco-German negotiations over Morocco. These efforts did help to ameliorate British concern over French dependability. On June 21 the Cabinet agreed to inform Cambon that Britain would generally follow the French lead on Morocco. This would, Balfour told the King, be "in strict conformity with the principles of the 'entente cordiale' and will probably conduce to an amicable arrangement of the whole matter, unless indeed the German Emperor means serious mischief."[43] In practice the policy first meant not blocking Rouvier's search for a solution, then accepting a conference on Morocco; all that London demanded was French opposition to any port concession to Germany. By July 12 the Foreign Secretary was able to assure Cambon that while Delcassé's fall had hurt the entente, the "British Government would support France by the means which France considered best" on Morocco. But he also expressed the hope that France could avoid further complications on the question.[44]

Within his own department Lord Lansdowne advocated the same qualities of prudence and caution about Anglo-French relations. The entente, he believed, needed time to adjust, to mend, to settle. Thus he turned aside suggestions that the agreement be expanded to cover more than Morocco. On July 10 he told Reginald Lister, the chargé d'affaires in Paris, that the French had never asked London "how far we should be prepared to go in supporting them against Germany." And he added: "We have been giving a good deal of thought to the question, but until it is asked I doubt whether we should be wise to volunteer a statement.

41. P. Cambon to Rouvier, June 7, 1905, D.D.F., 2nd ser., VII, no. 3.
42. Balfour to Edward VII, June 8, 1905, Cab. 41/30; Lee, *Edward VII*, II, 344. For similar sentiments, see Arnold-Forster's diary entry for June 7, 1905, Arnold-Forster Papers, Add. MSS, 50348; Newton, *Lord Lansdowne*, 341–342; also Mallet to Spring-Rice, June 6, 1905, Spring-Rice Papers.
43. Balfour to Edward VII, June 22, 1905, Cab. 41/30.
44. Lansdowne to Bertie, July 12, 1905, B.D., III, no. 152. See also Lansdowne to Bertie, June 27, 1905, F.O. 27/3704; P. Cambon to Rouvier, July 14, 1905, D.D.F., 2nd ser., VII, no. 224.

The moment would not, in my opinion, be a very opportune one for suggesting either to the Cabinet or to the country any extension of the understanding already arrived at. Recent events have, I am afraid, undoubtedly shaken people's confidence in the steadfastness of the French nation." [45]

Lansdowne's reluctance to extend the scope of the entente was shared in France but for different reasons. André Tardieu, the foreign editor of *Le Temps*, expressed it well on July 14: "As much as we are attached to the friendship of England, we equally believe that an alliance would risk bringing us into useless complications. . . . Why dream of imprudent extensions? Let us guard that which exists, instead of compromising it by ambitious developments." Afraid of being drawn into an Anglo-German naval fight in which France would needlessly suffer, Tardieu, like Rouvier, urged a policy of "sincerity, loyalty and independence." [46]

London and Paris thus refused to contemplate an alliance. Both governments, however, were fully determined not to let the entente falter before German pressure. A long and conveniently scheduled exchange of fleet visits afforded a perfect opportunity for fanfare and stress upon the entente. The British ships visited Brest during Bastille Week, the French vessels came to Portsmouth in early August. No expense was spared to make the occasions spectacular. Special trains, special entertainment, special receptions, including a huge banquet in London's Westminster Hall, highlighted the festivities. [47] In the press coverage of these events one observation stood out: the *Times* saw the naval exchanges as a poignant reminder that the entente might signify something more than a diplomatic agreement. The sight of British and French warships lying side by side at Brest was a "symbol that means much." [48]

These public manifestations of Anglo-French good will contrasted sharply with the mounting Franco-German bitterness. The French press, which had offered little sympathy to Delcassé on his ouster, now began to acknowledge the difficulties of negotiating with the Kaiser's government. The heavy-handed German attempt at Björkö to woo the Russian Tsar away from the French alliance simply reinforced French suspicions, and by mid-August even the nationalist press, hitherto unenthusiastic about the entente, had altered its tone. For the nationalists, Eugen

45. Lansdowne to Lister, July 10, 1905, Lansdowne Papers, F.O. 800/127; Lister to Lansdowne, June 30, July 10, 1905, *ibid*. See also Monger, *The End of Isolation*, 202–205.
46. *Le Temps*, July 22, 1905; Francis Charmes, "Chronique de la quinzaine," *Revue des deux mondes*, 5th ser., 28 (Aug. 1, 1905), 718–719.
47. The Admiralty first suggested these visits in January 1905; in mid-March Delcassé accepted the idea and then leaked it to the press to offset the Kaiser's stop at Tangier.
48. July 12, 1905. See also Hale, *Germany and the Diplomatic Revolution*, 170–174.

Weber writes, the entente became "an indispensable and indeed in-disputable part of the structure of French foreign policy." [49] No less affected by these developments was Maurice Rouvier. Dubious, wary, indeed alarmed about British friendship in April and May, the Premier now came to appreciate Britain's loyalty to France.[50] By summer's end there could be little doubt, public or private, that the Entente Cordiale had survived German attempts to upset or disrupt it.

Bülow and Holstein had raised the Moroccan issue in an attempt to drive a wedge between Britain and France. But by challenging the en-tente on Morocco the German government placed itself in a false posi-tion, for the Moroccan threat involved both Britain's support of the 1904 accord and Britain's strategic interest over the port question. That invincible pair, "honor and interest," brought the entente partners into a closer, if still vague, relationship in the way a simple continental issue would never have done.[51] Slowly but surely German pressure was trans-forming the colonial arrangement into an effective instrument for polit-ical cooperation. The German policy had other, equally significant effects, for it prompted London and Paris to review their respective war plans should more serious trouble arise over Morocco. One result of these studies was the mutual realization that a cross-Channel neighbor might be a useful companion in a war with Germany.

In April Admiral Fisher had strongly deprecated the possibility of a German port in Morocco. In fact, he had preferred that Britain do more than give diplomatic support to France. "This seems a golden oppor-tunity," he wrote Lansdowne on April 22, "for fighting the Germans in alliance with the French, so I earnestly hope you may be able to bring this about. . . . All I hope is that you will send a telegram to Paris that the English and French Fleets are *one*. We could have the German Fleet, the Kiel Canal, and Schleswig-Holstein within a fortnight." [52] The Foreign Secretary turned aside this bellicose proposition, labeling it a "characteristic effusion." Still, "it would be amusing," he noted on April 23, "to confront our colleagues with the seizure of the German Fleet, the Kiel Canal and Schleswig-Holstein as a fait accompli at our next meeting. We can't go as far as that, but I do think we might let the French Government. . . ." Lansdowne's private papers give no indication of what he meant to let the French government know.[53]

49. *The Nationalist Revival in France, 1905–1914* (Berkeley, 1959), 31–34; E. Malcolm Carroll, *French Public Opinion and Foreign Affairs, 1870–1914* (New York, 1931), 208–219.
50. See, e.g., Bertie to Lansdowne, July 27, 1905, F.O. 27/3706.
51. Anderson, *Moroccan Crisis*, 325.
52. Fisher to Lansdowne, Apr. 22, 1905, Marder, *Fear God and Dread Nought*, II, 55.
53. Lansdowne to Balfour, Apr. 23, 1905, Balfour Papers, Add. MSS, 49729. A notation on the letter states that the Prime Minister arrived at Bowood unexpectedly, thus preventing its completion.

In any case, there was no official mention of Fisher's desires to the French.

The First Sea Lord, as the crisis continued, resolved to have the entire question of war plans studied within the Admiralty. On June 24 he ordered Captain Charles L. Ottley, the Director of Naval Intelligence, to prepare a memorandum on the condition of the War Fleet in case it had to act suddenly to assist France. Two days later Ottley reported that the fleet was ready. He also pointed out that with France as an ally, Britain could, if necessary, withdraw ships from the Mediterranean; to take advantage of this possibility he recommended that the Admiralty "exchange views with the French naval authorities in order that there should be no misunderstanding or confusion in applying the overwhelming superiority which the Alliance could bring to bear." This recommendation was not acted upon during 1905.[54]

Ottley's memorandum on war plans was sent, as a matter of course, to Admiral Sir Arthur K. Wilson, Commander in Chief of the Channel Fleet and the man immediately responsible for the execution of British naval strategy. The Admiral's response reflected a shrewd appreciation of Britain's changing strategic position. He warned on June 27 that if Britain became involved in a Franco-German war, the role of the Navy would necessarily be diminished. In such a war military action, not naval, would be decisive. Even a naval blockade would be of little help to France in the demands of continental land warfare. What might be of assistance, suggested Wilson, would be amphibious operations along the German coastline, possible objectives to include the capture of fortifications at the mouth of the Elbe and operations within the Baltic. Simultaneous attacks of this type, he thought, draw significant numbers of German troops from the French frontier. With these comments Wilson aligned himself with Fisher on the need for and value of coastal operations against Germany.[55]

In early July Ottley drafted a scheme for amphibious operations. In this he made good use of the findings of the Plumer Committee, which had just studied the September 1904 amphibious maneuvers along the Essex coast. His completed report, "Preparation of Plans for Combined Naval and Military Operation in War," accurately reflected the changed conditions confronting British defense planners. The Moroccan trouble had for the first time raised the possibility of helping France rather than of fighting her, of meeting Germany with an ally rather than alone. All former planning for combined operations, Ottley pointed out, dealt with overseas attacks against German or French colonies. Now, however, with naval predominance assured because of a French ally, Britain

54. Memo by Ottley, "British Intervention in the Event of an Attack on France by Germany," June 26, 1905, quoted in Marder, *Anatomy of British Sea Power*, 502–503. There were no naval conversations until 1906.
55. Quoted in Marder, *Anatomy of British Sea Power*, 504–505.

might take certain tactical risks. Among such risks Ottley included attacks along the Schleswig-Holstein coast or elsewhere so "as to relieve the pressure upon France through the passes of the Vosges."[56]

But such dangerous operations required extensive prior preparation. To achieve the necessary interservice coordination, Ottley proposed that the Committee of Imperial Defense establish a permanent subcommittee on combined operations. The recommendation, strongly backed by Fisher and Balfour, won the approval of the C.I.D. on July 20: a subcommittee composed of service personnel and chaired by the Prime Minister was authorized to act as the center for the strategic coordination of British defense policy. Among its functions would be the study, review, and preparation of military operations against any power with whom war was considered possible. The subcommittee would also allocate the duties of each service in these attack schemes. Events soon proved that it was easier to define the responsibilities of the subcommittee than to make it operate effectively.[57]

The committee's failure to function, either in 1905 or later, stemmed chiefly from the divergent strategic conceptions held by the War Office and the Admiralty about the future role of the British Army. The case of a straight Anglo-German war posed no problem. Both services agreed that land operations against the military might of Germany would be foolish, dangerous, and ineffective. The seizure of German colonies, they admitted, constituted the only opportunity for the use of the Army; both also recognized that colonial operations would not bring Germany to defeat. But the Moroccan crisis provided the Army, as it did the Navy, with the prospect of a strong continental ally against Germany. This development enabled the General Staff to revise its strategic assumptions and ambitions. Suddenly colonial raids no longer seemed sufficient to the military; nor were they eager for amphibious raids against the heavily fortified German coasts. The 1905 crisis permitted the General Staff to consider a more ambitious role for the Army: the right to participate on the Continent in a Franco-German war. This desire ensured trouble with the Admiralty.

The Kaiser's stop at Tangier caught the Army in the process of revising its strategic outlook. In 1902 Colonel Robertson had, it will be remembered, sought guidance from the Salisbury government about Britain's obligation to uphold the neutrality of Belgium; and at that time the future Field Marshal thought naval action with some small military assistance would constitute Britain's probable response. But for his efforts at planning Robertson received no encouragement, rather a partial rebuke. When in 1903 he had reviewed the Army's role in an

56. Drafts of this report are in Cab. 17/5, 17/95; quoted in part in Marder, *Anatomy of British Sea Power*, 505–507.
57. Minutes of the 76th and 77th meetings of the C.I.D., Cab. 2/1; Clarke to Balfour, July 11, 1905, Balfour Papers, Add. MSS, 49701; Monger, *The End of Isolation*, 207–208.

Anglo-German war, operations against Heligoland and the German colonies were considered the most likely task for the military establishment. No attention was directed toward British involvement on the Continent. Then in 1904 Robertson's efforts at strategic planning received a major boost with the formation of the General Staff and its Directorate of Military Operations.[58] The Directorate assumed responsibility for both intelligence work and operational planning. Headed by Major General J. M. Grierson, who was assisted by Robertson and Colonel C. E. Callwell, the Directorate launched a series of studies on probable strategies in case of war with France, Russia, or Germany.[59] The most extensive and significant of these early exercises was the "strategic war game" carried out in April and May 1905, the first thorough British evaluation of the problems of continental warfare.

Grierson announced the war game to his staff in January 1905. In his introduction to this *Kriegsspiel* Grierson noted that Belgian military writers thought a Franco-German war would see the Germans attack through Belgium in an attempt both to exploit their military manpower and to avoid the French fortifications. Personally, the Director of Military Operations (D.M.O.) doubted that the Germans would gain much by such a flanking attack. It would take them at least twenty-one days to reach the Mons-Namur axis and "by this time the great battles in Lorraine will have been fought, and the larger the detachment sent through Belgium the less will be the chances of German success in these decisive struggles." In any event, the Belgians obviously expected British help. But such assistance carried certain risks for Britain: the large continental armies might swamp the small British contingent; moreover, "by locking up our mobile forces in Belgium we place our army as a hostage in the hands of our allies, and, at the same time take away from our maritime campaign the best part of its sting, energy and decision." [60] Grierson preferred, as Robertson had in 1902, to send just enough military help to show proof of Britain's commitment. Yet the D.M.O. appreciated that his planners must also consider what Britain would do if it did resolve to send a major force to the Continent.

In the war game France and Germany were assumed to have reached a stalemate along the Lorraine frontier, after which the Germans would decide to drive through Belgium to reach Chimay and Givet along the Franco-Belgian frontier. In the attack an estimated eight German corps and three cavalry divisions (473,050 men) would take part, a figure which corresponded closely to the actual German war plans then in effect. To counter this force the hundred thousand-man Belgian Army would need immediate British reinforcements. But such help, the war

58. Paul Guinn, *British Strategy and Politics, 1914 to 1918* (Oxford, 1965), 7; Robertson, *From Private to Field-Marshal*, 137–139.
59. See, e.g., "War with Germany and Russia Combined—France Neutral," by Lt. Col. H. D. Drake, Feb. 8, 1905, W.O. 106/48.
60. "Strategic War Game," 1905, W.O. 33/364.

game amply demonstrated, would be neither immediate nor sizable. Thirty thousand British troops could be sent in three weeks, a total of 50,000 in the first month. Landing at Antwerp, they would concentrate at Brussels for assaults upon the German lines of communications. Operations into Germany or in France were ruled out, in the latter case because they "would simply have prolonged the strategical front of the French Army, and might also have led to other political complications." The overall conclusion of this strategic exercise was that if the Belgians could hold out, an Anglo-Belgian force would be able to apply effective pressure on the German communications system after the tenth day of British mobilization. Beyond that nothing appeared certain.[61]

In many respects the game, played out at Camberley, the Staff College, perfectly summarized the complex issues that would confront British strategists and the Anglo-French talks in the years before 1914. Among the problems were the direction and size of the German offensive, Belgium's capability to defend itself, the mode and extent of British help, the location and employment of British forces if they were sent, the logistical requirements for moving British troops, the question of command coordination. Each of these topics would be the object of prolonged study during the next nine years. As the issues were settled, Britain's commitment to a continental strategy would grow.

The organization of the General Staff and Grierson's own preoccupation with an Anglo-German war had prompted the first serious, analytical study of the demands of continental war. The prolongation of the Moroccan crisis forced the British strategists to transfer their efforts into the realm of the practical. The man chiefly responsible for this was Sir George Clarke, Secretary of the C.I.D.

In early August, at the same time the Anglo-Japanese alliance was being renewed, Clarke called the Prime Minister's attention to the position of Belgium. The Secretary, who professed no illusions about the sanctity of international treaties, asserted that the signatory powers would "act solely in accordance with their interests at the moment." He thought the 1839 treaty would be useful only as casus belli should Britain find it necessary to help Belgium against an invader. The strength of the French frontier forts, Clarke noted, and the weak state of Belgian defenses meant that Germany had far more need in 1905 than in 1870 to contemplate operations through Belgium. Such a German move would force the British, traditionally concerned with the maintenance of the European balance of power and with the fate of the Low Countries, to consider direct aid to the Belgians.[62] But such assistance required planning and study. Clarke thus urged Balfour on August 17 to

61. *Ibid.*
62. Memo by Clarke, "Treaty Guarantees and Obligations of Guaranteeing Powers," Aug. 1, 1905, Cab. 4/1; see also Sanderson to Clarke, Aug. 10, 1905, Cab. 17/69.

let the General Staff "prepare a paper discussing (1) the military advantages (if any) which Germany or France might expect by a violation of Belgium territory and (2) the measure of resistance which Belgium if backed by us, would be able to offer to such a violation. Possibly also (3) the time we should require to put the two Army Corps, or the equivalent, into Antwerp." Balfour, after some delay, assented and the General Staff began its study.[63]

In late September the Directorate of Military Operations completed its report. Predictably, it exploited the results of the recent war game. The British Staff still thought the Germans would refrain from an initial attack through Belgium; instead, the first great battles would be in Alsace-Lorraine and then, should there be a deadlock, the Germans would sweep into Belgium and rapidly overcome the Belgian defenses along the Meuse. The paper noted that the recent war game had shown that "two army corps could be landed in Belgium by the twenty-third day after the order to mobilize had been given. The calculation was made on the assumption that the first twenty transports would be ready by the tenth day." It was possible, the paper concluded, that the Admiralty would be able to reduce the transport time required.[64] The memorandum was never discussed by the C.I.D.; nevertheless, it provides an excellent summary of the direction of British military thinking in mid-1905. Because of Belgium, the Army had begun not only to consider military operations upon the Continent, but also to study the requirements of such operations. In the opinion of the British historian J. E. Tyler, this was the "first rather tentative and unsubstantial appearance in history of the later famous B.E.F." [65]

In the possible movement of British troops to Belgium the Army expected ready cooperation from the Admiralty—a misapprehension, for already sharp differences were developing between the two services over the proper continental strategy for Britain. The dispute began innocently enough. In late August Colonel Callwell sent a paper to Captain George Ballard, an Assistant D.N.I., on "British Military Action in the Case of War with Germany." In keeping with his own published views on the subject, he asserted the value of amphibious operations. He thought a Baltic operation in the Schleswig-Holstein area might detain as many as 400,000 German regulars, reducing in turn their availability for the French frontier. Callwell asked Ballard to help work out the details for such an attack. The naval captain promptly wrote for more

---

63. Clarke to Balfour, Aug. 17, 1905, Balfour Papers, Add. MSS, 49702; Clarke to Sanderson, Aug. 16, 1905, Lansdowne Papers, F.O. 800/117; Sydenham, *My Working Life*, 185–186.
64. General Staff memo, "The Violation of the Neutrality of Belgium During a Franco-German War, Sept. 29, 1905," Cab. 4/1; also see "The Military Resources of France," Aug. 23, 1905, W.O. 33/363; Monger, *The End of Isolation*, 209–211, 229–230.
65. *British Army*, 20.

information from the Directorate; he wanted to complete the plans for a coastal raid by October 1.[66]

Ballard's hopes for speedy action suffered total frustration. Bureaucratic malaise set in at the War Office. First Callwell went on leave, then Captain Adrian Grant-Duff, who had actually drafted the August memorandum, demurred to Ballard's request for immediate details, saying "the arrangements on the coast in question are so efficient, and our numbers so small that it is very difficult to see in what way we can intervene to any really useful purpose." [67] Two days later, on September 9, Grant-Duff made his position more explicit in an office memo. Further study of the Baltic operation, he wrote, had led him to conclude that even if Britain had its entire army available for an amphibious attack, there was no military object worth the risk. He conjectured that the Admiralty's insistence upon this operation revealed its doubts about the sufficiency of combining British naval action with French land forces against Germany. What this really implied, he remarked, was that without "a powerful army to back our sea power we can exert little influence on the peace of Europe. If the Admiralty accept this conclusion we have taken the first step towards real reform." [68]

Meanwhile, Grant-Duff's evasive reply of September 7 surprised Ballard. He again wrote to the Directorate, only to discover this time that Grant-Duff was on leave. An impatient Ballard had to wait two more weeks, and in the meantime his demands for an "authoritative statement" received another setback within the Directorate. On September 26 Robertson expressed serious doubts about the entire exchange of letters and memoranda between relatively junior staff officers. Such correspondence might commit the Directorate to a position not acceptable to its head, General Grierson, or to the General Staff. Robertson ordered that in the future memoranda were to go to the Admiralty only if they had been officially requested by the Admiralty and cleared by the General Staff.[69]

Callwell, on returning from leave in early October, acted swiftly to settle the question of a Baltic operation. He wrote Ballard on October 3 and apologized for having "to a certain extent" misled him in the first paper. Still, "on these kind [sic] of matters second thoughts are often best, especially when first thoughts are the result of hasty considerations of the subject." Callwell also enclosed another paper on war with Germany, which he warned could "not be taken to be in any way authorita-

66. W.O. 106/46; Ballard to Grant-Duff, Sept. 2, 1905, ibid.; for some of Callwell's views on amphibious operations see his Military Operations and Maritime Preponderance (London, 1905).

67. Grant-Duff to Ballard, Sept. 7, 1905, W.O. 106/46.

68. Office memo by Grant-Duff, "British Military Action on the Baltic Coast in the event of war between Germany and Great Britain and France in alliance," Sept. 9, 1905, ibid.; see also the memo by Drake, Sept. 20, 1905, ibid.

69. Ballard to Grant-Duff, Sept. 9, 1905, ibid.; minute by Robertson, Sept. 26, 1905, ibid.

tive but I think the C.G.S. [Chief of the General Staff, General Sir Neville Lyttelton] and D.M.O. [Grierson] who are as you know away, would probably concur in it." [70] In this memo Callwell left no doubt that the Directorate had shifted its views on the employment of the British Army. A Baltic scheme, the Colonel now declared, was impractical and of doubtful military value. Instead the British Army should help the French field army. Callwell's justification for action on the Continent revealed the new tenor of British military thinking:

> An efficient army of 120,000 British Troops, might just have the effect of preventing any important German successes on the Franco-German frontier, and of leading up to the situation that Germany crushed at sea, also felt herself impotent on land. That would almost certainly bring about a speedy, and from the British and French points of view, satisfactory peace. [71]

The lure of military involvement on the Continent is not a sufficient explanation of this reversal of views within the Directorate of Military Operations, from acceptance of a Baltic expedition on the one hand to outright rejection on the other. A more fundamental reason was the Army's realization after several extensive studies that Baltic operations, while theoretically appealing, were virtually impossible to execute. All military and naval planning before 1914 contained elements of fantasy but the various amphibious schemes propounded by the Admiralty had an excessive share. The strategical and tactical flaws which the Army discerned in 1905 were never wholly eliminated from the later naval proposals.

Among the weak points was the obvious danger of moving troop transports through mined coastal waters or through the Baltic straits. If fear of mines and torpedo boats rendered close blockade too dangerous to be undertaken, the Army held that this same prudence should apply to the use of troop ships. The War Office also felt that the Admiralty underrated the German coastal defense system with its excellent rail network: even if a landing could be achieved, Army officers thought the *Landwehr* forces would still be able to destroy any British force, regardless of its size. And this meant that coastal raids would not tie down any significant fraction of regular German troops, so that coastal operations would neither threaten Berlin nor relieve the pressure on the Franco-German frontier. That such operations might provide the Navy with an advanced naval position, either an island or a coastal area, from which to operate destroyers was never adequately appreciated by the Army. Finally, the General Staff discerned contradictions in the Admiralty's plans for the use of the Army. To give effective help to France in the opening, and

70. Callwell to Ballard, Oct. 3, 1905, *ibid.*
71. Memo by Callwell, "British Military Action in case of War with Germany," Oct. 3, 1905, *ibid.*; partially reprinted in Marder, *Road to War*, 386.

in military opinion the decisive, stage of a war, operations along the German coasts would have to be launched at once. Thus timed, surprise diversionary attacks might upset the German mobilization and allow the French to achieve an early victory. Yet the Admiralty estimated that it would take from five to fourteen weeks to prepare the necessary transports and to gain full command of the sea. In the Army's opinion this delay effectively precluded any amphibious attacks, for by that time the German coastal defenses would be perfected and the main battles fought on the French frontier.[72]

These objections to amphibious raids ended Ballard's hopes for a quick agreement. But the Army's new position had other ramifications as well: it doomed the C.I.D. subcommittee on combined operations, and the recently authorized group apparently never met;[73] the divergence over strategy made War Office-Admiralty cooperation on naval transport matters sporadic and inconsistent; and, perhaps more significantly, Callwell's October memo indicated that if the problem of Belgium had initially prompted consideration of continental action, direct assistance to France was now also attracting the attention of British military planners. This clash of strategic views foreshadowed the War Office-Admiralty friction so characteristic of the remaining prewar years.

On October 10 Admiral Fisher, then vacationing at Levico in the Tirol, wrote Arthur Balfour a long, private memorandum. In it he asserted that it was never contemplated that Britain "could or would undertake single-handed a great military continental war, and that every project for offensive hostilities was to be subsidiary to the action of the Fleet, such as the occupation of isolated Colonial possessions of the enemy, or assistance of an ally by threatening descent on the hostile coast, or otherwise effecting a diversion on her behalf."[74] In addition the First Sea Lord praised the joint subcommittee as a valuable asset to the Prime Minister, especially as a means of "DRAWING THE ARMY OUT OF ITS QUAGMIRE 'OF ONE MAN WAITING ON AN-OTHER!' You will see how silently it will work a revolution in the War Office! They will be FORCED to be ready, forced to get on, forced to co-operate and finally forced to be efficient!"[75] Fisher's enthusiasm for the

72. For a summary of these criticisms, see the memo by Major J. D. Fasson, "Memorandum on the Feasibility of Landing a British Force of 100,000 Men on the coast of Germany . . . in active alliance with France in a War against Germany," Nov. 10, 1905, W.O. 106/46; also see Arthur J. Marder, From the Dreadnought to Scapa Flow: The Royal Navy in the Fisher Era, 1904–1919, vol. II: The War Years: To the Eve of Jutland, 1914–1916 (London, 1965), 176–198.

73. Hankey, Supreme Command, I, 62; Monger, The End of Isolation, 228 n. 7, 229–231.

74. Memo by Fisher, "The Elaboration of Combined Naval and Military Preparations for War . . . ," Oct. 1905, enclosed in Fisher to Sandars, Oct. 10, 1905, Balfour Papers, Add. MSS, 49711.

75. Fisher to Sandars, Oct. 10, 1905, ibid. Fisher to Clarke, Oct. 12, 1905, Marder, Fear God and Dread Nought, III, 29–30.

subcommittee as a curative for the Army's troubles both revealed his anxiety for the coastal operations and also betrayed his concern at the new trend in strategic thought within the General Staff. In such a committee Fisher might just manage to impose his strategic views upon his military counterparts. The Admiral's enthusiasm for close coordination, which in his terms meant subordination of the Army to the Navy, soon faded as the General Staff continued to study continental intervention. Fisher's refusal to cooperate not only heightened the interservice differences over strategy, it also allowed the Army's ideas to go unchallenged. Equally important, these strategic differences were apparent before the military conversations with France ever began.

If the Moroccan crisis found the British services in a state of some confusion and disagreement, their difficulties paled in comparison to the chaos that was the French Navy and Army. Although Gaston Thomson now headed the French Naval Ministry, he was unable to correct immediately the damage wrought by Pelletan's application of the outdated ideas of the *jeune école* to naval strategy and socialism to naval shipyards. The role of the French Navy in the crisis of 1905–1906, except for the symbolism of the fleet visit to Portsmouth, was negligible.

The French Army was also in a state of disrepair. Its morale, strained first by the Dreyfus affair and then by André's use of informers and the two-year service law, was virtually shattered. Maurice Berteaux's appearance as Minister of War in January 1905 just slightly improved the situation. Furthermore, there were serious divisions within the French high command over the strategy to be employed against Germany. In Britain sharp strategical cleavages existed between the two services; in France they existed within the Army. Friction within the high command stemmed in part from its very structure, a structure that remained intact until July 1911: on the one hand there was the Vice President of the War Board, who in peacetime drafted mobilization plans and in war acted as the Commander in Chief (Generalissimo) of all French field forces, and on the other there was the Chief of Staff, responsible for the day-to-day operation of the Army and for the execution of plans prepared by the Generalissimo. At best the differences between these spheres of responsibility were arbitrary. For the system to work the two men at the top had to complement, not compete with, each other. This was seldom the case, certainly not in 1904 and 1905 with General Brugère as Generalissimo and General Pendezec as Chief of Staff.[76]

Tension between the two men took a new turn in the late summer of 1904. In August the General Staff, under Pendezec's direction, took the

76. On the friction between Pendezec and Brugère, see Raymond Brugère to M. Paléologue, Oct. 14, 1932, in "Le plan Schlieffen et le 'Vengeur': deux lettres," *Revue des deux mondes*, 8th ser., 12 (Nov. 15, 1932), 427–428; on Brugère's vanity, Combarieu, *Sept ans à l'Elysée*, 103–104. See also Ralston, *The Army of the Republic*, 291–296.

unusual step of asking members of the War Board (composed of generals who in war would command the various armies) to comment upon new evidence gathered on German war plans, among which were the staff papers on the so-called *Vengeur* documents. The story behind French acquisition of these German documents in the winter of 1903–1904 remains confused and uncertain. In 1932 Maurice Paléologue, who had been one of Delcassé's assistants in 1904, asserted that a disillusioned German staff officer had betrayed the outlines of the Schlieffen Plan to French agents. Subsequent studies have cast grave doubts about Paléologue's accuracy both on the alleged betrayal and in his summary of the new information.[77] Certainly there was no question, as the French diplomat implied, of the Schlieffen Plan having been revealed, since the Plan did not go into effect until late 1905. But the French General Staff from whatever source did obtain information in early 1904 which conveyed a fairly accurate impression of Count von Schlieffen's current thinking. The Second Bureau (Intelligence) spent the entire spring trying to verify the details of the documents, discovering on a number of points that they did not have enough information to test the authenticity of the revelations.[78] Finally in August the General Staff drafted a memo embodying the new information and cautiously noting their uncertainties about it.

This staff paper, comparable in many ways to the British war game, credited Germany with twenty-eight army corps. Of these, sixteen were expected to be deployed in Alsace-Lorraine, nine to be concentrated in the area around Aix-la-Chapelle, and three to serve as a link between the Lorraine and Aix-la-Chapelle deployments. The Staff thought the northern German corps would launch a flanking move through southern Belgium, south of the Meuse and Sambre, aimed at Chimay-Mézières-Stenay; the German forces in Lorraine would, meanwhile, take the brunt of the French offensive. In this assessment French intelligence had in fact discerned the major features of the German plans then in force: Schlieffen did plan a limited enveloping move through southern Belgium while also advancing from Lorraine. The French were mistaken only in the number of German corps assigned to the swing through Belgium—seven, not nine. Unfortunately French intelligence did not repeat this

77. Paléologue, "Une prélude à l'invasion de la Belgique, 1904," *Revue des deux mondes*, 8th ser., 11 (Oct. 1, 1932), 481–524; Wolfgang Foerster, "Ist der deutsche Aufmarsch 1904 an die Franzosen verraten worden?," *Berliner Monatshefte*, 102 (November 1932), 1053–1067; Louis Garros, "Préludes aux invasions de la Belgique," *Revue historique de l'armée*, 5 (January–March 1949), 17–30; Contaime, *La revanche*, 95–97.

78. "Note au sujet des documents S. R. nos. 2474 et 2500 relatifs à la concentration allemande," Feb. 8, 1904, Archives Guerre, "Plan XV," box 123; "Etude de la possibilité d'une offensive allemande par la Belgique," Feb. 10, 1904, *ibid.*; "Note sur le document S. R. no. 2474, de 1904, relatif à la concentration allemande (étude faite au point de vue des transports)," Apr. 12, 1904, *ibid.*; untitled memo, May 10, 1904, *ibid.* Excerpts from the memo of Feb. 8, 1904, are in *D.D.F.*, 2nd ser., IV, p. 277 n. 1 and *ibid.*, V, pp. 366–369 notes.

mistake in its later studies. One point proved especially troublesome to the French officers: how to reconcile the obvious German intention to violate Belgian neutrality with a massive concentration of German forces in Lorraine. At almost the same time Count von Schlieffen was also studying this problem; he would eventually decide to eliminate the contradiction by strengthening the German right flank—a step French intelligence would never fully appreciate before 1914. To counter the German move through Belgium the French General Staff, anxious to leave Plan XV basically intact, proposed the creation of an Armée du Nord out of reserve divisions; this force could move into the Mézières-Sedan area after mobilization, hinder the German troops, and provide a useful screen while French forces conducted a major offensive in Lorraine.[79]

This new information on German plans and the Staff proposals to meet the new development were circulated to the War Board in August 1904. In their replies some of the members conceded that the Germans might try a flanking move. But, with one exception, none of the generals thought the new intelligence data warranted any overall changes in Plan XV. Most insisted that the new information dealt only with a variation of the main German plan of attack in Alsace-Lorraine, a variation made possible by Russia's involvement in the Far East. In any case, the generals thought the Staff's proposed use of reserve divisions would suffice to check a German flanking move through southern Belgium.[80] General Jacques Duchesne, however, sharply disagreed with his colleagues, protesting that neither Plan XV nor the General Staff proposals would be adequate to halt a German advance through Belgium. He called for a complete shift of French forces northward and for the abandonment of any blind offensive along a narrow front in Lorraine. Adoption of this course of action would, he asserted, enable the French to meet the Germans maneuver for maneuver in northern France, with the French Army eventually launching a counterattack in this direction. But the General Staff flatly rejected Duchesne's suggestions, contending that the General's ideas would cost France territory and reduce French forces in the one area (Lorraine) where France could mobilize more men than Germany. And the Staff doubted that France could launch offensive action in the north.[81] This critical evaluation of Duchesne's views was mild compared to General Brugère's scathing treatment of the entire proceeding.

79. "Note sur des renseignements récents relatif à la concentration des armées allemandes," Aug. 13, 1904, Archives Guerre, "Plan XV," box 123. The memo is partially reprinted in D.D.F., 2nd ser., V, no. 308. The German war plans for 1904–1905 are summarized in Gerhard Ritter, The Schlieffen Plan: Critique of a Myth, trans. Andrew and Eva Wilson (London, 1958), 41–43.
80. For the answers of the War Board, see Archives Guerre, "Plan XV," box 123; Garros summarizes them in "Préludes aux invasions de la Belgique," 26–28.
81. Duchesne's reply, Oct. 8, 1904, and the General Staff's comments are in Archives Guerre, "Plan XV," box 123.

The explosion came at the War Board meeting on February 18, 1905. Brugère began by denouncing the General Staff's action (and by extension Pendezec) in soliciting comments from subordinate commanders about alterations to his war plan. The Generalissimo demanded a stop to this practice and declared that Plan XV would be adequate for any emergency. Then he turned on Duchesne. He belittled the idea of major changes in Plan XV and said that Duchesne was too ignorant of the details of the plan to offer constructive suggestions. Nor did Brugère stop here: he completely dismissed the General Staff proposal to increase the cover forces along the French frontier as protection against a sudden German attack.[82] This last action so angered General Pendezec that he appealed directly to Premier Rouvier on February 20, warning of a German surprise attack along the French frontier and insisting that new intelligence information showed a need for revision of Plan XV to meet the new circumstances. But Pendezec's appeal brought no changes; and Brugère's obstinancy continued. The Generalissimo repeatedly refused Pendezec's requests in April and May for alterations in Plan XV that would strengthen the frontiers and guard against a German move through Belgium.[83]

This friction within the French high command gave Rouvier little cause for satisfaction as the Moroccan crisis unfolded, nor did the foreign reports ease his concern over the possibility of war. Intelligence confirmed rumors that the Germans had placed orders with Krupp (to be completed in 1906) for new, improved field artillery pieces; the acquisition of these 75-millimeter weapons would remove one of France's few advantages over the German Army. From St. Petersburg the news went from bad to worse. Russian defeats were followed by army mutinies and rebellion, and three years at least would be needed before the Russian Army would be ready to fight again.[84] Nor did the prospect of British military and naval aid, should it actually be forthcoming, stir Rouvier's enthusiasm: the British Navy, he had noted sarcastically in April, had no wheels—it could protect British interests, but not Paris.[85] And General Pendezec rated the Swiss army of more practical worth than that of the British.

But continuation of the 1905 crisis prompted a French reappraisal of the value of British assistance. Reports of an alleged offer of a British alliance, followed by the rousing success of the fleet visits, encouraged second thoughts. So also did Camille Barrère's report from Rome that

82. Minutes of the War Board, Feb. 18, 1905, Archives Guerre, "Procès-verbaux du Conseil Supérieur de la Guerre," box I.
83. Annex, D.D.F., 2nd ser., VI, pp. 604–607; Paléologue, Un grand tournant, 316–318, 358.
84. Delcassé to Berteaux, May 23, 1905, Archives du Ministère des Affaires Etrangères, Paris, "Allemagne," n.s. 29; note by Pendezec, May 26, 1905, enclosed in Berteaux to Delcassé, May 27, 1905, D.D.F., 2nd ser., VI, no. 457; General Louis Moulin to Berteaux, June 27, 1905, ibid., VII, no. 148.
85. Radolin to Bülow, Apr. 27, 1905, G.P., XX, pt. 2, no. 6635.

the British military attaché had insisted that the British were stronger than France believed: indeed, the attaché had boasted that Britain could immediately send 200,000 men to France and in ten days another 400,000.[86] In London Major Victor Jacques Marie Huguet, the French military attaché, was likewise reaching some new conclusions about the British Army. On his arrival in late 1904 Huguet had been scornful of what he and most continental soldiers of the time regarded as a mere colonial army, and a poor one at that. But his studies and observations forced a revision of his views on the British military establishment. In his 1905 reports he acknowledged that the British Army, alone of the European military systems, was utilizing the lessons of the Boer War. Although Huguet disliked Britain's failure to accept some kind of conscription, he reported that Arnold-Forster's reforms would increase the value of the Army. The striking success of the 1905 summer maneuvers won the attaché's special praise.[87]

In October Huguet went on leave to Boulogne. While he was at home a newspaper report bluntly reminded Europe that the Entente Cordiale could have more than diplomatic value: on October 7 Le Matin, the Paris daily, announced that Britain had offered France a defensive alliance prior to Delcassé's dismissal. Stephen Lauzanne, the editor and a close friend of Delcassé's, asserted that London had verbally promised to mobilize the British fleet, to seize the Kiel Canal, and to land a hundred thousand men in Schleswig-Holstein. Moreover, the British had offered to put the proposition in writing.[88]

The source of Lauzanne's accurate exposé of British naval strategy remains obscure. The Delcassé papers contain a record of a June conversation with Le Matin's editor, but there is no mention of any naval operation. During 1905 there were no Anglo-French naval conversations which might have revealed Fisher's pet project. Lord Sanderson, then Permanent Undersecretary at the Foreign Office, later remarked that there was much loose talk in naval circles in 1905, some of which might have found its way to Paris; this remains the most plausible explanation.[89] At the time Sanderson privately noted that the story in question was untrue; if it had come from the former French Foreign Minister, it confirmed the view "that Delcassé can on occasion tell the most whopping falsehoods." He also took pains to assure Metternich, the German ambassador, that the report was "pure invention," adding somewhat inaccurately that "the contingency of a *rupture* between France and Ger-

86. Barrère to Rouvier, July 9, 1905, M.A.E., "Grande Bretagne," n.s. 19.
87. Huguet, *Britain and the War: A French Indictment*, trans. H. Cotton Minchin (London, 1928), 3–4; Huguet's reports for 1905 are in Archives Guerre, "Attachés militaires: Angleterre," box 6.
88. Carroll, *French Public Opinion*, 218–219; Hale, *Germany and the Diplomatic Revolution*, 195–200.
89. Memo of Delcassé-Lauzanne conversation, June 23, 1905, Delcassé Papers, vol. V; Sanderson to Harold Temperley, Aug. 17, 1922, B.D., III, no. 105. Compare Andrew, *Théophile Delcassé*, 281–286.

many had never to my knowledge been discussed, or indeed mentioned on either side." [90]
This renewed talk of a British alliance aroused General Brugère, who contacted the vacationing Huguet and requested that he undertake a private study. In particular the Generalissimo wanted to know how many troops Britain could mobilize and the time needed to ferry them to the Continent. Huguet's answers were sent on November 18. In the event of war, the attaché estimated that Britain could mobilize three corps, totaling 118,000 men; of these 60,000 would be reservists. The I and II Corps, composed mainly of British regulars, would be ready within a few days, but the III Corps would be delayed by the integration of reserves into the units. There were other disadvantages: even if shipping were available, for example, embarkation, which would begin on the fifteenth day, could not be completed until the twenty-fifth or twenty-eighth day. This delay, Huguet emphasized, would place the British on the Continent after the first big battles. Further, the value of the British reservists, whom he termed "mercenaries," was suspect, and the Army's antiquated field artillery had not yet been replaced. On the basis of this information Huguet concluded that "a landing in Europe of an English army of 100 to 120,000 men in case of a Franco-German war, is not exaggerated; it is possible and even probable; but, for various reasons, it is doubtful that this aid could be truly effective or capable of seriously influencing the march of events." [91]
Although Huguet somewhat exaggerated the probable size of British military assistance, neither he nor his superiors now dared to ignore the possibility of such assistance. The approach of the long-awaited international conference on Morocco made this a matter of simple prudence. In Paris General Jean Brun, who had replaced Pendezec as Chief of Staff, initiated measures to evaluate possible British assistance. On November 9 he asked the Quai d'Orsay to prepare a program for eventual military and naval discussions with the British, even if that nation did not openly declare itself an ally of France.[92]
The interest of the French high command in the value and nature of British military aid paralleled the growing belief of the British General Staff that Britain's military role in the future would be on the Continent. But to intervene effectively on the Continent required detailed plans, schedules, and arrangements with numerous military, naval, and civilian

90. Sanderson to Lascelles, Oct. 10, 1905, Lascelles Papers, F.O. 800/12. Lansdowne noted in late October that he had only accepted with qualifications Paul Cambon's account of their May 17, 1905, talk; minute on Bertie to Lansdowne, Oct. 24, 1905, F.O. 27/3707.
91. Huguet to Etienne, Nov. 18, 1905, Archives Guerre, "Attachés militaires: Angleterre," box 6; reprinted with omissions (including the term "mercenaries") in D.D.F., 2nd ser., VIII, no. 137.
92. Paléologue, Un grand tournant, 411. In August 1905 Brun claimed he was having Huguet make a survey of the British Army, but there is no record of this in the archives (ibid., 395–396).

authorities, and to achieve this degree of preparation one needed information and assistance from the potential ally. Brun was apparently the first soldier to recognize this necessity for the exchange of information; the question now became one of implementation. The appearance of a new British government and apprehension over the possible collapse of the Algeciras conference provided the occasion for the first "conversations" between Anglo-French military and naval authorities.

3 | The Military Conversations Begin
1905–1906

Ten years of Conservative rule in Britain ended in December 1905 with the fall of the Balfour government. The departure of Balfour's Cabinet was neither widely lamented nor entirely unexpected: for weeks political circles had anticipated the formation of a Liberal government under Sir Henry Campbell-Bannerman. The prospective change of administrations caused some apprehension among those who favored a continuation of Conservative defense and foreign policies. Lord Esher, for example, sincerely feared that a new Cabinet might disband the Committee of Imperial Defence, a move which he successfully worked to prevent. Others were concerned lest a Liberal Cabinet swing away from France and toward Germany. Herbert Paul in the *Nineteenth Century* gave succinct expression to this fear: "England and France standing together are at this moment the best security for the peace of Europe, and French sympathies can only be retained if both parties in England show themselves equally anxious to retain it." [1]

1. Herbert Paul, "Liberals and Foreign Policy," *Nineteenth Century and After,* 58 (November 1905), 855; see also Esher to Balfour, Oct. 5, 1905, *Journals and Letters of Esher,* II, 114–115.

This foreboding about the possible course of Liberal foreign policy worried Sir Edward Grey, the man whom everyone regarded as the next Foreign Secretary. In mid-October he mentioned his apprehensions to J. A. Spender, a close friend and the editor of the *Westminster Gazette*. Britain, Grey mused, was "running a real risk of losing France and not gaining Germany; who would want us, if she [Germany] could detach France from us." The future minister added that he planned to combat this possibility by making a major policy address in the City, which he hoped Spender would emphasize in his paper.[2] In the speech on October 21 Grey outlined the main tenets of future Liberal foreign policy: first came the alliance with Japan and friendship with the United States; next was the maintenance of the Entente Cordiale with France; finally, Grey expressed hopes for more satisfactory relations with Russia and Germany. But improved ties with Berlin, the Liberal imperialist cautioned, could not come at the expense of Britain's good relations with France. Nine years later, in 1914, these views and this man would still shape the direction of British diplomacy.[3]

Grey's strong affirmation of the entente was pleasant news for the French, for a French success at the approaching Moroccan conference would depend on the steady support of the British government. Throughout the closing months of 1905 the French Embassy in London had paid close attention to the utterances of Liberal spokesmen. Generally Paul Cambon was delighted with what he heard, especially when Grey, on assuming office on December 11, reiterated his loyalty to the entente.[4] Yet, the veteran French diplomat had lingering doubts. There were too many variables in the equation to suit his logical, orderly, precise temperament. What influence, for instance, would the radical and peace-loving Campbell-Bannerman exert upon the formation of foreign policy? Then there were the problems of Grey's inexperience and the fact that the parliamentary elections in January would naturally absorb the attention of the new Liberal Cabinet. Prominent Liberals, moreover, were participating in a series of well-planned December meetings that proclaimed the virtues of Anglo-German friendship.[5] Each of these considerations made Cambon uneasy; each also made him anxious to test the temper of the new government. Perhaps the new Foreign Secretary

2. Grey to Spender, Oct. 19, 1905, Spender Papers, British Museum, Add. MSS, 46389.

3. The speech is quoted in George M. Trevelyan, *Grey of Fallodon* (Boston, 1937), 102–104. On Grey at the Foreign Office, also see Viscount Grey of Fallodon, *Twenty-five Years, 1892–1916*, 2 vols. (New York, 1925); Monger, *The End of Isolation*; Zara Steiner, "Grey, Hardinge and the Foreign Office, 1906–10," *Historical Journal*, 10 (1967), 415–439. For a highly critical view, see Hermann Lutz, *Lord Grey and the World War*, trans. E. W. Dickes (New York, 1928).

4. P. Cambon to Rouvier, Oct. 25, 1905, *D.D.F.*, 2nd ser., VIII, no. 79; P. Cambon to Rouvier, Dec. 14, 1905, M.A.E., "Grande Bretagne," n.s. 20.

5. P. Cambon to Rouvier, Dec. 5, 12, 1905, *D.D.F.*, 2nd ser., VIII, nos. 196, 219.

could be brought to reaffirm and even to extend the Lansdowne statements of April and May. The moment had come for the initiation of military and naval conversations.

How and why did the Anglo-French staff talks start? What did they reflect about British strategy? Why were they not immediately revealed to the British Cabinet? What role did Belgium play in the military conversations? What did these initial staff exchanges manage to settle? To these frequently asked questions the availability of new sources and new studies now permit some definite answers.[6] If the answers focus chiefly upon Great Britain, it is because the momentous decision was London's: whether voluntarily to bind Britain, if it fought, to the military fortunes of France.

The start of the conversations extended from December 15, 1905, to January 31, 1906. During this six-week period there were roughly three centers of activity: the French—diplomats, soldiers, and sailors; Grey, his fellow ministers, and his Foreign Office subordinates; and the C.I.D. with its Army, Navy, and civilian members. At times the activities of these groups were isolated, at times their paths were inextricably entwined and confused. Lieutenant Colonel Charles à Court Repington, the military correspondent of the *Times*, belonged to none of these groups yet curiously linked them all.[7] From the tangled bustle they created emerged first a period of "unofficial" military and naval talks, then the more familiar "official" conversations which continued until 1914.

The residents of Albert Gate, the French Embassy, made the first moves. In December 1905 Paul Cambon completed his seventh year as French ambassador to the Court of St. James. At sixty-two he looked and was the embodiment of all that is meant by the phrase "old diplomacy": his finely featured face, his piercing eyes, his strong jaw, his abundant gray hair and whiskers conferred upon him an aristocratic air. To these physical attributes were added a sure self-confidence, a sense of independence, and a calm, determined willingness to make the most of any situation. Distrustful of popular opinion and disdainful of the bureaucratic structure of the Quai d'Orsay, he preferred discreet negotiations for the adjustment of international differences. Together with his brother Jules, then stationed in Madrid and soon to go to Berlin, and Camille Barrère in Rome, Paul Cambon was part of a formi-

6. The following are most helpful: Sir George Aston, "The Entente Cordiale and the 'Military Conversations,' " *Quarterly Review*, 258 (April 1932), 363–383; J. D. Hargreaves, "The Origin of the Anglo-French Military Conversations in 1905," *History*, 36 (October 1951), 244–248; Monger, *The End of Isolation*, chap. ix; Ritter, *Staatskunst und Kriegshandwerk*, II, 78–97; Vagts, *Defense and Diplomacy*, 118–123.

7. See the essay on Repington in Jay Luvaas, *The Education of an Army: British Military Thought, 1815–1940* (Chicago, 1964), 291–330; *The History of THE TIMES*, III, 462–467.

dable trio that worked to ensure that France never again faced Germany alone.[8]

The approach of the Algeciras conference and alarming news from Germany convinced the ambassador in mid-December that a Franco-German clash might not be distant. Paris had learned from Alfonso XIII, the young Spanish monarch who had recently visited Berlin, that Germany was making extensive military preparations. This news upset the French on two counts: fear about German intentions toward France and worry that Alfonso might move into the German camp. To counter the latter uncertainty, Premier Rouvier ordered Cambon to seek King Edward's help in keeping Madrid in line.[9] Armed with Rouvier's instructions, the French ambassador decided the time had come to probe once more the position of the British government on the entente.

On December 20 Cambon saw Edward at Buckingham Palace. In the course of a lengthy audience the ambassador relayed the reports from Alfonso and the news about German military activity. The King, who was inclined to think the German preparations were a bluff, promised to watch Berlin and also to keep Alfonso in line. Successful on these points, Cambon turned to a larger subject: he tried, the ambassador later told Rouvier, "to sound the King on the assistance that we [France] could eventually expect from England." He began by reminding Edward of the German rumors about a British offer to send a hundred thousand men to the Continent. The monarch denied the rumors, but admitted that Britain could send the troops. At this point, however, Edward abruptly broke off the conversation, leaving a puzzled Cambon to speculate why:

> Did he wish to say that with a Liberal Cabinet we could not induce the British Government into military action, or did he wish to express the idea that in any case England must limit itself to naval action? I don't know. But it seemed to me that army assistance did not seem to the King to be envisaged at the moment. Going further, I recalled that Lord Lansdowne had remitted by Sir F. Bertie to M. Delcassé a memorandum proposing to talk in case the German Government made excessive pretensions over Morocco, that a little later he showed himself desirous of examining in advance with us all eventualities of a general order which could arise in the course of actual difficulties, that the fall of M. Delcassé and the change of the Government in England had not permitted the conversations to continue on this subject, and that I had no instructions to resume them, that I did not know if the new Government would be disposed to pursue the examination to which the Marquess of Lansdowne had invited us and that I asked if I could ask my Government for instructions in this sense.

8. On Paul Cambon see Eubank, *Paul Cambon*, and Henri Cambon, *Paul Cambon: ambassadeur de France, 1843–1924* (Paris, 1937).
9. Rouvier to P. Cambon, Dec. 18, 1905, *D.D.F.*, 2nd ser., VIII, no. 246.

"Do it," said His Majesty, "seek authorization to discuss everything with Sir E. Grey. It will be very useful." [10]

This conversation accurately portrays the indefinite status of the entente at the end of 1905. The two countries *were* closer because of the events of April and May; but Cambon clearly exaggerated the extent of Lansdowne's proposals and somewhat misrepresented why there had been no discussion, during six months, of "éventualités." The conversation with Edward also furnishes conclusive evidence that there were no military or naval conversations during the Lansdowne period. Had there been, Cambon would certainly have mentioned them, either in this frank discussion with Edward or in his subsequent reports.[11] On the other hand the interview hinted at a growing French awareness of the desirability of British military aid. Cambon was, after all, familiar with Huguet's earlier study on British military resources. Yet the French were quite uncertain about the prospects and the nature of actual British aid. Indeed, this very uncertainty prompted Cambon's overtures to Edward for new Anglo-French discussions. The King's strong encouragement to Cambon may have stemmed from a genuine concern over German military preparations; but more likely his endorsement came from a desire to commit the Liberal government to a stronger entente policy than it might normally have pursued.[12] At the same time the interview displayed Cambon's scrupulous regard for Rouvier's attitude; he wanted closer Anglo-French relations, but only if Paris approved. The ambassador, buoyed by his success with the King, journeyed down the Mall and across Horse Guards Parade to see Sir Edward Grey at the Foreign Office.

The Foreign Secretary had now been in office nine days. Tall, with stooped shoulders that concealed his height, Grey possessed a head which despite his beaked nose would have made a Roman senator proud. Blessed with an impeccable pedigree of Liberal forebears, the new minister was a north country gentleman thrust into a great office by a sense of duty to his country and obligation to his party. Force of character, elegance of expression, devotion to principle, and a certain liberal moral view of the world were the main features and assets of his diplomacy. Offsetting these, at least initially, were his lack of experience and his scanty acquaintance with European history and statesmen. A sensitive lover of nature, Grey was often intensely parochial and insular, capable of self-deception, and frequently inflexible in his views.[13] From

10. P. Cambon to Rouvier, Dec. 21, 1905, *ibid.*, no. 262; see also P. Cambon to George Louis (tel.), Dec. 20, 1905, *ibid.*, p. 359 n. 3.
11. Hargreaves, "The Origin of the Anglo-French Military Conversations in 1905," 245.
12. Taylor, *The Struggle for Mastery in Europe*, 435–436.
13. Bryon Dexter, "Lord Grey and the Problem of an Alliance," *Foreign Affairs*, 30 (January 1952), 298–309; Algernon Cecil, *British Foreign Secretaries, 1807–1916: Studies in Personality and Policy* (New York, 1927), 317–363.

the start he resolved that Britain would never have to face Germany alone. To achieve this he would keep the Entente Cordiale strong and be a careful exponent and practitioner of the balance of power (despite his later denials of this fact), while ensuring that nothing endangered Britain's naval supremacy. The challenges posed by the Moroccan crisis and the demands of the French provided Grey with a literal baptism of fire.

When Paul Cambon saw the Foreign Secretary on December 20, Morocco dominated their discussion. On this point Grey renewed his earlier promise that Sir Arthur Nicolson, the British ambassador to Spain, would give France steady support at Madrid and at the conference. He also emphasized that the entente "remained one of the essential factors of the foreign policy of the new Cabinet." These reassurances must have been a distinct relief to Cambon, who did not push things further; the conversation ended without any mention of Lord Lansdowne's earlier statements. But before leaving the Foreign Office, Cambon did stop to see Lord Sanderson, the Permanent Undersecretary. In their chat the ambassador asked "*incidentally* if he did not remember the offer which had been made by the former Secretary of State of Foreign Affairs . . . of discussing all the eventualities which could come out of the actual crisis. Sir Thomas answered that it seemed to him that the proposition of the Marquess of Lansdowne was aimed only at eventual German pretensions on Morocco." Reporting to Paris, Cambon conceded that Morocco was "in fact the object of the first memorandum remitted to M. Delcassé"; but Sanderson, he added, had apparently forgotten the later suggestions or "it is possible that he had not known them." In any case, the Undersecretary's alleged lapse of memory was more than balanced by Edward's warm support for closer ties.

The next day, December 21, Cambon wrote Rouvier for instructions in case "it would be desired to seek some guarantees from London." [14] On this occasion, unlike those in May and June, the French Premier was more receptive to the prospect of closer Anglo-French relations. He sanctioned Cambon's request for authorization (December 23) but asked that he avoid a firm, binding agreement. Still afraid of being trapped in an Anglo-German naval war, Rouvier preferred the benefits of an accord without its liabilities.[15] At this point, however, Cambon decided to defer any new moves until he could personally see Rouvier about still another development.

The ambassador had not been the only member of the French Embassy active on December 20. That morning Major Huguet met, apparently

---

14. P. Cambon to Rouvier (italics mine), Dec. 21, 1905, *D.D.F.*, 2nd ser., VIII, no. 262; cf. Grey to Bertie, Dec. 20, 1905, *B.D.*, III, no. 197; Grey to Nicolson, Dec. 21, 1905, *ibid.*, no. 200.
15. Rouvier to P. Cambon (tel.), Dec. 23, 1905, *D.D.F.*, 2nd ser., VIII, no. 265.

by chance, Major General Grierson on Rotten Row in Hyde Park. Their talk gradually turned to the Franco-German situation and the General expressed the belief that Great Britain would not stand aside if war came. Upon close questioning Grierson admitted that the General Staff had recently considered the problem of intervention in a continental war. And he indiscreetly confirmed Huguet's personal estimates that at least 100,000 British troops, and perhaps as many as 120,000, were avail-' able. This capability, the Director of Military Operations conceded, was somewhat weakened by the lack of new field artillery. Without giving any indication of how a British force might be employed, the General ridiculed the notion of a Schleswig-Holstein operation. On this note the men parted, agreeing to meet the next day.[16]

At their second meeting Grierson was both more loquacious and more indiscreet. He told Huguet that the Army's recent study on intervention had not only envisaged the use of three corps, but also two additional divisions from troops on colonial duty in the Mediterranean. It was hoped that the latter divisions might arrive at Marseilles by the eighteenth day. On the employment of British troops, Grierson felt that the British force would be most effective aiding the Belgians in Belgium. He planned to have the Aldershot corps in Brussels on the twelfth day, with all three corps at Brussels by the thirtieth day; with help from the Admiralty, Grierson thought the time might be reduced to twenty-one days. Although the General preferred, and would continue to prefer, an operation in Belgium, he said the troops could, if necessary, land at Calais. In this case the small British force would "unite with the French forces, of whom it would, for example, form the left wing." But Grierson warned Huguet that though the General Staff had considered the problem of cooperation with France, such considerations could not "prejudice the decision that the Government would take at a given moment." [17] How often the French were to hear this in the next eight years! Thus ended the only direct exchanges of information between British and French military personnel during the period of "unofficial" conversations. Cambon had made the opening diplomatic move to bring about closer relations with the new Liberal government. But Huguet had succeeded in having the first practical discussions about the military and naval aspects of such cooperation. Delighted with Huguet's achievement, Cambon, as noted above, decided to consult with Rouvier before mentioning closer ties to Sir Edward Grey.

16. This meeting can be dated from the French documents; see Huguet to Etienne, Dec. 20–21, 1905, *ibid.*, no. 256. Grierson in January 1906 misrepresented both the date and the number of meetings, claiming he had seen the attaché only once on the "16th or 18th December," Grierson to Sanderson, Jan. 11, 1906, *B.D.*, III, no. 211; Monger, *The End of Isolation*, 238–239.
17. Huguet to Etienne, Dec. 20–21, 1905, *D.D.F.*, 2nd ser., VIII, no. 256. See also D. S. MacDiarmid, *The Life of Lieut. General Sir James Moncrieff Grierson* (London, 1923), 215–216; Huguet, *Britain and the War*, 4–5.

Others, meanwhile, were also examining the problems of British participation in a possible Franco-German war. At 2 Whitehall Gardens, home of the C.I.D., Sir George Clarke had given the problem thoughtful study. What he saw did not please him. On December 15 he wrote Lord Esher (appointed by Balfour as a permanent member of the C.I.D.) and complained bitterly of the failure of both services to take what he considered elementary precautions for a possible breakdown of the Moroccan conference. Citing this lack of preparations and his fear of a German drive through Belgium, the Secretary sought with Esher's help to remedy a deplorable situation.[18]

On December 19 Clarke held the first of several informal conferences with Esher, Ottley, and General Sir John French, the commander at Aldershot. Strangely enough, Grierson, the man responsible for planning military operations, was absent. None of the quartet at this time favored a major commitment of British forces upon the Continent in a Franco-German war; rather, they preferred some kind of coastal operation. Such a preference meant, of course, ignoring the General Staff's attitude toward amphibious schemes at the very time Grierson was perfecting plans for intervention to help Belgium. Nor could Ottley have been ignorant of the Army's dislike of coastal assaults. He certainly knew of Callwell's letter in October and had seen the D.M.O. himself on December 15. All of this prompts the suspicion that Captain Ottley, with Fisher's approval if not instigation, still hoped to impose an amphibious operation on the Army through the auspices of the C.I.D.[19]

In their talks Clarke, Esher, French, and Ottley considered a variety of coastal operations. Their favorite was one which called for one hundred thousand French troops to join a like number of British forces for a landing on the German coast. They did concede, grudgingly, that the French might be reluctant to release men for such an operation. In spite of their strong preferences for amphibious operations, the group considered direct intervention upon the Continent. Here their attention centered upon Belgium: unlike Grierson, they doubted that the Belgians could hold the Meuse forts—and if the forts fell, then not only would the British troops arrive too late to help the Belgians, they might also be trapped in Belgium. The idea of aiding the Belgians by helping the French held no appeal; yet the four men concluded that the "assistance of all kinds that we could bring to the alliance is probably much greater than the French anticipate." [20]

But to facilitate this assistance required, as Clarke and his associates

18. Clarke to Esher, Dec. 15, 1905, Esher Papers, Watlington Park, Oxfordshire, "Clarke Letters," vol. V. Clemenceau on Dec. 13 told Esher that secret military and naval preparations were needed; Monger, *The End of Isolation*, 239–240.
19. Grierson's work on the mobilization plans, which began on Dec. 18, was apparently done independently of the Clarke group; MacDiarmid, *Grierson*, 215; cf. Monger, *The End of Isolation*, 241.
20. "Notes of Conferences Held at 2, Whitehall Gardens, December 19, 1905 . . . January 19, 1906," Cab. 18/24.

recognized, accurate information about the French and Belgian schemes of mobilization. The first to act on this problem was General French. On Christmas Day he wrote Esher, asking his help in arranging a meeting with Major Huguet. French thought the attaché's inquiry to him about British artillery could be made "an excuse for both of us to perhaps extract some information out of him." The General added, in a comment which shows his distance from Grierson, that he had "arrived at the conclusion that such 'separation' as would be brought about by the 'Baltic' plan would *not* be too dangerous." Four days later Sir George Clarke also resolved to establish closer ties with the French; he would use the British attaché in Paris "to sound the French General Staff on some points." [21] Before Clarke could act, an incident occurred which greatly simplified the initiation of direct contacts with Paris.

The *Times* on December 27 printed an article entitled "France and Germany," by its military correspondent. In it Repington strongly denounced the movements which promoted Anglo-German rapprochement, warning that Germany had belligerent intentions against Britain's entente partner. The article naturally caught the attention of Major Huguet, though he already knew of Repington's extensive sympathies for France and his bitter dislike of Germany. During the June crisis (and again in December) the correspondent had offered Huguet the use of the intelligence service of the *Times* if war should come.[22] With this December article as a point of departure, the Major now decided to exploit his contacts with the influential ex-officer and former British attaché to Belgium and Holland (1898–1902).

On December 28 Huguet met Repington for dinner, and afterward they talked for five hours. Their wide-ranging discussion touched upon the article, the state of British and French naval preparations, and the precautions recently taken by the French Army. Repington, who at this time did not share Huguet's fears about a German thrust through Belgium, cautioned the attaché that under no circumstances should France violate, or even be provoked into a violation of, Belgian neutrality. To do so would alienate a British public otherwise favorable to participation in an anti-German war. The conversation turned at length to the key question: actual British assistance in a Franco-German war. His colleagues at Albert Gate, Huguet remarked, were greatly disturbed by Grey apparent failure to affirm Lansdowne's statements about British support for France. Nor would the Major be satisfied with Repington's confident assertion that Grey completely shared Lansdowne's views.

21. French to Esher, Dec. 25, 1905, quoted in Gerald French, *Some War Diaries, Addresses, and Correspondence of Field-Marshal the Right Honble. The Earl of Ypres* (London, 1937), 110; Clarke to Esher, Dec. 29, 1905, Esher Papers, "Clarke Letters," vol. V.

22. Huguet to Berteaux, Sept. 2, 1905, Archives Guerre, "Attachés militaires: Angleterre," box 6; Huguet to Etienne, Dec. 30, 1905, *ibid.*; cf. *D.D.F.*, 2nd ser., VIII, no. 300. Repington claimed he made this offer with the knowledge of the editor of the *Times*, G. E. Buckle.

"Yes, we feel that," retorted Huguet, "but it may be a question of prompt action and immediate discussions." Certainly the journalist realized "how extremely important it was for his Government to possess formal assurances upon which they could count." [23] It is impossible to know exactly what motives prompted the French officer to broach the delicate question of Lansdowne's alleged assurances, or to know what he calculated to gain by doing so. Huguet had, nevertheless, selected the right man, for the energetic Repington spared no trouble in conveying the French views to various British officials.

The next day he sent a special delivery letter to Grey, then on vacation at Fallodon. In it Repington faithfully reported Huguet's concern over the immediate situation, particularly Grey's alleged failure to acknowledge Lansdowne's statements. The Foreign Secretary's reply was immediate and unequivocal: "I am very interested to hear your conversations with the French Military Attaché. I can only say that I have not receded from anything which Lord Lansdowne said to the French, and have no hesitation in affirming it." [24] The wording of this reply suggests that Grey was either unaware or uncertain or both about the extent of Lansdowne's promises. But the new minister had no desire to give the appearance of doing less than his Conservative predecessor had done. Thus he simply gave a blanket affirmation to the journalist's query. If Huguet hoped for more than a general expression of support from Grey, he was disappointed.

Others besides the Foreign Secretary quickly learned of Repington's talk with Huguet. On Saturday, December 30, the correspondent saw both Lord Esher and Admiral Fisher. The First Sea Lord assured Repington that Grey would be absolutely faithful to the entente. If there was any trouble, Fisher suggested that Rouvier mention the subject to Bertie. Then the Admiral added his own indiscretion to that of Grierson's by outlining for Repington the probable action of the British fleet should war come. Fisher was confident the Channel Squadron alone would crush the German Navy; all he wanted from the French, he insisted, was their help in forming a submarine-destroyer cordon across the Dover-Calais straits. The next day Repington forwarded these opinions to Huguet, adding that if the situation became threatening, Fisher would act on his own authority. Therefore, if the French Navy was not ready for immediate action when war came, the British would have finished the fighting before the French ever arrived on the scene. [25]

23. Repington to Grey, Dec. 29, 1905, Grey Papers, Public Record Office, London, F.O. 800/110; Huguet to Etienne, Dec. 30, 1905, D.D.F., 2nd ser., VIII, no. 300; Charles à Court Repington, The First World War, 1914–1918, 2 vols. (Boston, 1920), I, 2–3.
24. Grey to Repington, Dec. 30, 1905, Grey Papers, F.O. 800/110. See also Repington, The First World War, I, 4; Monger, The End of Isolation, 242–243.
25. Repington to Huguet, Dec. 31, 1905, Archives Guerre, "Plan XVII: Armée W," box 147b; Repington, The First World War, I, 4.

The French Naval Ministry, it should be added, learned more directly of Fisher's views. On January 2 the First Sea Lord had a conversation with Captain Mercier de Lostende, the French naval attaché, about the Moroccan conference and about British naval preparations. Their talk, the present documentation indicates, marks the only time in 1905 or 1906 that Anglo-French naval conversations occurred. The occasion was a simple, unofficial meeting in which Fisher repeated what he had told Repington about the fleet concentration and about the power of the Channel Squadron. The Admiral gave no hint that Britain wanted more help than French submarines in the Strait of Dover. There was no sug-gestion of exchanging signal books or of distributing duty assignments within the Channel, nor did Fisher offer any details about British war plans or express any wish for more talks. In short, Fisher spoke, de Los-tende listened. Not until late 1908 was Fisher again to admit that the French Navy might be able to help Britain, or to discuss cooperation with French naval officers.[26]

Repington's evangelism on behalf of the French had thus far had only limited results. Grey had responded in platitudinous tones about upholding the entente; Fisher had indicated he really did not need French help to defeat the Germans. The journalist found Sir George Clarke in an entirely different frame of mind, however, and Clarke's re-action altered everything. The Secretary of the C.I.D. wanted military information from the French General Staff; the French attaché wanted contacts with the British military authorities. With Repington's assist-ance as a middleman these desires were linked, so that it becomes vir-tually impossible to assign France or Britain final responsibility for hav-ing started the conversations. Despite Clarke's later modesty about his role in the conversations, he pursued and executed the first systematic exchange of military information with the French.[27] On New Year's Day, 1906, he wrote Esher:

> I enclose an interesting letter from Repington. As he is in contact with the Fr. Mily. Attaché, I have asked if he would sound him on some points as to which we want information. This will be much safer than using our Mily. Attaché in Paris. It is very necessary to do nothing that would alarm the Govt. and besides the W.[ar] O.[ffice] would balk. The tragic facts of the situation are that:
> 1. If the Germans proceeded to unprovoked aggression, the feeling in this country would demand our cooperation.
> 2. If the Germans violate Belgium we come in automatically. I am not sure that the French Govt. realizes either of these prop-ositions.

26. Leon Geoffray to Rouvier (tel.), Jan. 2, 1906, M.A.E., "Grande Bretagne," n.s. 20; de Lostende to Thomson, Jan. 2, 1906, D.D.F., 2nd ser., VIII, no. 308; Marder, Road to War, 116–117.

27. Compare the statement by Clarke (later Lord Sydenham) of July 19, 1927, B.D., III, no. 221.

And the next day Esher heard again from Clarke, "I think Repington may be about to get the information we want, and I do believe we can trust him absolutely. Except we three, however, it is best *no one should know anything.*" [28]

But the Secretary was not content just to improve the state of Anglo-French military preparations: he also thought naval cooperation and coordination with France might be required. The First Sea Lord, of course, did not share this opinion. Although the two headstrong men could agree initially on the value of amphibious raids, they soon quarreled on a host of other issues. As early as January 2, Clarke complained to Lord Esher that Fisher had no war plan save "smash the Germans" and that the only help the Admiral wanted from the French was the use of some submarines. "Submarines in the Straits of Dover will be *entirely useless,*" wrote the Secretary, "though possibly a danger to us and the French. I hope to see Ottley shortly and to find out what he has been doing since our little conference. We ought to have ready a complete plan of joint naval action to propose to the French if the need arises." [29] Clarke's attempt to use Lord Esher to push and prod the First Sea Lord, however, brought no immediate results. In the meantime the military conversations drew closer as Repington continued his gadfly role.

On January 3 the journalist lunched with General Grierson. Almost certainly the earlier Huguet-Repington discussions were mentioned. In the course of this meeting the D.M.O. stressed his adamant opposition to any form of coastal operation, a view which Repington shared. If Belgium were attacked, the General thought Britain could put two divisions at Namur on the thirteenth day and the entire Army into Antwerp within thirty-two days. [30] The discussion apparently reinforced Repington's determination to get some staff talks underway.

That same day he wrote Grey again, this time stressing the "extreme importance of an understanding with France concerning joint naval and military co-operation in case of need." He was confident the Foreign Secretary recognized that, "owing to the extreme rapidity with which modern war is conducted, the hour for hostilities is too late for the initiation of measures of defense, if these are to be successful." Then he outlined the dangers of a German attack upon Belgium and Holland—a hazard he thought warranted military talks with the Low Countries. He also revealed that he had talked with Huguet several days before about Anglo-French cooperation if war came. The attaché, he reported, "strongly advocated assistance to Belgium," and Repington thought this would be "(1) easiest for the present Government to assent to (2) most useful as a direct help to France in the decisive quarter and (3) most suitable to our naval and military organization. That Huguet should ad-

28. Clarke to Esher, Jan. 1, 1906, Esher Papers, "Clarke Letters," vol. VI; Clarke to Esher, Jan. 2, 1906, *ibid.*; Repington, *The First World War,* I, 4–5.
29. Clarke to Esher, Jan. 2, 1906, Esher Papers, "Clarke Letters," vol. VI.
30. Repington, *The First World War,* I, 5.

vance this course is pretty clear proof that France has no designs in this quarter." [31] There is no record of Grey's reaction to these proposals. But in any event he now knew firsthand the military value of advance preparations, of the crucial position of Belgium, and of Repington's contacts with Huguet.

The Times' correspondent meanwhile tirelessly continued his rounds. On January 5 he saw Huguet once more: most of their conversation centered upon the possibility of British action in Belgium. The Major noted that London had never given France any reason to believe that an attack on Belgium would necessarily bring British forces into the field. If this was indeed the case, then the French General Staff would be relieved. Huguet also raised the problem of what Britain would do if intervention in Belgium proved impossible. In his opinion the British troops could be attached to the French left flank, between Verdun and Mézières.[32] Repington spent the rest of the afternoon at 2 Whitehall Gardens with Esher and Clarke. Their meeting marked a turning point in the period of "unofficial conversations," for they decided to utilize their liaison with Huguet. Two precautions were taken: it was to be understood by the attaché that the British government could "continue the conversations or drop them as they pleased," and Repington would continue to act as the intermediary. Clarke then drafted a set of eleven questions dealing with French intentions toward Belgium, the problems of possible Anglo-French collaboration, and the probable nature of German war plans. Huguet personally carried the questionnaire to Paris, leaving on Sunday, January 7. In a very real sense the staff talks had begun.[33]

Clarke's work was not over. He reconvened his informal "preparedness" group the next day (January 6), with French, Esher, and Ottley present. They first considered General French's mobilization arrangements for the Aldershot command, then Ottley reported on the naval precautions in effect. Next the committee returned to the vexing question of what to do with the British Army. At length they abandoned—for many of the General Staff's reasons—the idea of a Baltic or coastal raid. What prompted this reversal of preferences is not clear. Grierson in a staff memo on January 4 had reiterated his support for operations in Belgium; in fact, if this proved impossible or unnecessary, the D.M.O. wanted "to reinforce the French army and so stem the tide of German invasion." He felt that such British help "to the French field force must come at once, owing to the fact that the moral effects of a first success would have an enormous influence on the course of such a war." [34] Although Grierson's ideas were available, there is no indication that any

31. Repington to Grey, Jan. 3, 1906, Grey Papers, F.O. 800/110.
32. Repington, The First World War, I, 5.
33. Ibid., 5–10; a shortened version of the questions is in D.D.F., 2nd ser., VIII, no. 389. These questions form the total of the written "unofficial" conversations; Clarke apparently never saw Huguet during this period.
34. Memo by Grierson, "Memorandum upon the Military Forces Required for Oversea Warfare," Jan. 4, 1906, W.O. 106/44.

of the quartet had seen them before the meeting; and the D.M.O., again unaccountably absent, still played no part in the chats.[35] For whatever reasons, the group now opted for some variety of continental land operations: "Any military co-operation on the part of the British army," they concluded, "if undertaken at the outset of the war, must take the form either of an expedition or direct participation in the defence of the French frontier." [36] The concomitant of this decision was the need for information about French plans, and on this point Clarke had already acted. Until Major Huguet returned from Paris with the French answers, the Whitehall Gardens group could make little additional progress.

The focus of activity in Anglo-French relations now shifted to the Foreign Office. There Sir Edward Grey was not "altogether comfortable" about possible developments at Algeciras.[37] He wrote Richard Haldane, the Secretary of State for War, on January 8 that a situation "might arise presently in which popular feeling might compel the Government to go to the help of France and you might suddenly be asked what you could do." Fisher was ready, commented the Foreign Secretary, "by which I take it he means that his ships are so placed that he can drive the German fleet off the sea and into shelter at any time. I don't want you to give any definite answer in a hurry but I think you should be preparing one." [38]

Grey also took precautions of his own. On January 9 he summoned Clarke to the Foreign Office for a report on defense arrangements. The C.I.D. Secretary assured Grey that "possibilities" were being considered, then used the occasion to mention the need for French views on co-operation; in addition he revealed his contacts with Huguet. Grey accepted the necessity for information from the French and agreed that it was "impossible to approach the French through official channels to ascertain what their views on co-operation are, as this would give the idea of an offensive and defensive alliance which does not exist." Pointing to the necessity for secrecy in these matters, Clarke confided that he "had said nothing to C.[ampbell]-B.[annerman] and he [Grey] seemed to think it was better not to do so at this stage. Of course if Grierson will play up loyally and intelligently there is no need in involving the P.M. just now." [39] Grey thus gave his approval, not only to Clarke's

35. Clarke was very fearful of leaks in the War Office; see, e.g., Clarke to Esher, Jan. 9, 1906, Esher Papers, "Clarke Letters," vol. VI; Monger, The End of Isolation, 245–246.
36. "Notes of Conferences Held at 2, Whitehall Gardens," Cab. 18/24. For another view of Clarke's thinking, see Clarke to Kitchener, Jan. 5, 1906, Kitchener Papers, Public Record Office, London, P.R.O. 30/57/34.
37. Grey to Lord Tweedmouth, Jan. 7, 1906, Campbell-Bannerman Papers, British Museum, Add. MSS, 41231.
38. Grey to Haldane, Jan. 8, 1906, quoted in Sir Frederick Maurice, Haldane: 1856–1928, 2 vols. (London, 1937–1939), I, 172–173.
39. Clarke to Esher, Jan. 9, 1906, Esher Papers, "Clarke Letters," vol. VI.

furtive contacts with the French, but also to concealing them from the leader of the Cabinet.

The Foreign Secretary made no mention of this conversation when he wrote that night to the Prime Minister, who was campaigning in Scotland. Grey reviewed the foreign scene for his chief and stated that with the French, "matters stand as Lord Lansdowne left them. I have promised support in accordance with Article IX, and have let it be known at Madrid and Rome that we shall give this. I have not said a word of anything more and the French have asked no inconvenient questions." But there were reports, wrote Grey, that indicated the Germans were preparing for war; he thought the "steps taken imply precautions, but not intentions" and doubted there would be war. But he told Campbell-Bannerman the War Office ought "to be ready to answer the question, what could they do if we had to take part against Germany if, for instance, the neutrality of Belgium was violated. Fisher, of course, is prepared to answer the question for the Admiralty at any moment, but that only means driving the German fleet to anchor in Kiel and stay there." Grey assured the Prime Minister that at present he had no difficulty "as to what to say or do, but I am apprehensive of what may happen at the Conference when I may have to ask for a decision at a critical moment." [40] This sober, confident assessment did not misrepresent the dangers of the situation. But it did conceal Grey's acquiescence to Clarke's contacts with the French. And within twenty-four hours the Foreign Secretary would find himself confronted with some "inconvenient questions" that would prove difficult to answer and to evade.

On January 10 Paul Cambon, just returned from Paris, went to see Grey, and their talk heralded the second and final stage of the "unofficial" conversations. The first phase had witnessed the brief, informal discussions by Grierson and Fisher with the French attachés, and Clarke's initiation of secret exchanges through an intermediary. The second stage saw the culmination of the "unofficial" talks and their shift to an "official" status.

At this meeting the French ambassador reminded Grey of the dangers of the Moroccan situation, and mentioned Lord Lansdowne's alleged offer to discuss "eventualities." Cambon declared: "It had not been considered necessary at the time to discuss the eventuality of war. But it now seemed desirable that this eventuality should also be considered." He indicated that Rouvier shared this view. It was not necessary, he conceded, "nor indeed expedient, that there should be any formal alliance, but it was of great importance that the French Gov(ernmen)t should know beforehand whether, in the event of aggression against France by Germany, Great Britain w(oul)d be prepared to render to France armed assistance." Grey's reaction was one of evasion: he cited the election con-

40. Grey to Campbell-Bannerman, Jan. 9, 1906, quoted in Grey, *Twenty-five Years*, I, 114–115.

fusion and asserted that the Cabinet could not discuss the matter before late January. Although he noted that "public opinion in England would be strongly moved in favour of France," Grey cautioned that he was in no position "to pledge the country to more than neutrality—a benevolent neutrality if such a thing existed." Rebuffed, Cambon said he would raise the topic again after the elections. In the meantime, the French envoy suggested that "unofficial communications between [the] Admiralty and War Office and the French Naval and Military Attachés should take place as to what action might advantageously be taken in case the two countries found themselves in alliance in such a war." Some communications, Cambon added, had already passed, and might be continued. "They did not pledge either Gov(ernmen)t." Since Grey "did not dissent from this view," he gave Cambon a partial victory.[41] Though unwilling to promise armed support, Grey did not block the exchange of military and naval information.

The record of this important conversation had a restricted circulation, going only to King Edward, Campbell-Bannerman, and Lord Ripon, the Lord Privy Seal, and apparently even to them only in an abbreviated version that made no mention of staff talks. Certainly this was the case with the version received by the Prime Minister; and because Ripon and the King made no reference to the conversations when they acknowledged the dispatches, it appears that they too were kept in the dark on this point.[42] Campbell-Bannerman's reaction on the larger issue of armed support for France was that Paris could not expect an answer until the elections were over. Ripon, for his part, opposed anything beyond diplomatic support.[43] The King's reaction will be considered in another context.

Lord Sanderson, who attended the Grey-Cambon talk on January 10, was upset by the ambassador's revelations of "unofficial conversations." Because Fisher had participated in the naval exchanges, these did not alarm him. But the military exchanges did: he thought Cambon's remarks "looked very much as if the conversations which we know Col. a'Court [sic] Repington has had with the French Military Attaché had been taken by the latter and by the Embassy as being authorized by our General Staff." [44] Sanderson, always lukewarm to closer ties with

41. Grey to Bertie, Jan. 10, 1906, B.D., III, no. 210a; P. Cambon to Rouvier, Jan. 11, 1906, D.D.F., 2nd ser., VIII, no. 385. Paris already knew, thanks to Mallet's indiscretion, that Grey had warned the German ambassador (Metternich) on Jan. 3 that public opinion might force British participation in a Franco-German war, Geoffray to Rouvier, Jan. 7, 1906, M.A.E., "Grande Bretagne," n.s. 20.

42. Compare the official record of the conversation with the shorter one (Grey to Campbell-Bannerman, Jan. 10, 1906, Campbell-Bannerman Papers, Add. MSS, 41218); see also Monger, The End of Isolation, 249–250, and Mallet to Bertie, Jan. 11, 1906, Bertie Papers, F.O. 800/164.

43. Lucien Wolf, Life of the First Marquess of Ripon, 2 vols. (London, 1921), II, 292–293; John A. Spender, The Life of the Right Hon. Sir Henry Campbell-Bannerman, 2 vols. (London, 1923), II, 249–251.

44. Minute by Sanderson, Jan. 11, 1906, B.D., III, no. 210b.

France, began to investigate. He asked Grierson whether he had had any direct or indirect contact with Major Huguet. Somewhat abashedly the D.M.O. admitted misrepresenting having seen the attaché in December, but he denied verbally and by letter that he had ever sought any information from the French attaché. At the same time Grierson took the offensive and pleaded

> that, if there is even a chance of our having to give armed assistance on land to France or to take the field on her side in Belgium in consequence of a violation of Belgian territory by the Germans, we should have as soon as possible informal communications between the military authorities of France and/or Belgium and the General Staff. There are a great many points which we must settle before we can make our plans for the despatch of a force to join either the French or the Belgian armies, and these we cannot settle without information which the staffs of these armies alone can give us. . . . To make our help effective we must come *at once* with every available man. First successes are everything, and if the French could gain those they would "get their tails up" and all would go well.[45]

Sanderson sent the results of his inquiries to Sir Edward Grey, then campaigning in Northumberland. The Foreign Secretary, who earlier had agreed with Clarke about the value of unofficial talks, now had second thoughts about such exchanges. Although still anxious for the military information, he decided, assisted perhaps by Sanderson's concern over departmental responsibility, that the War Office should have full control over such communications. In short, Grey wanted the talks put on a direct, official basis. Clarke's indirect overtures had the practical effect, therefore, of both facilitating and prompting the institution of official staff conversations. Grey took a major step in this direction on January 12.

Haldane came to Berwick that day for a political rally on Grey's behalf. After the speeches, the two close friends discussed the problem of communications with the French. Ironically, the minister responsible for army matters appears to have been unaware of Clarke's surreptitious activities; the rigors of the election campaign and Haldane's own concern about army reform account in part for his ignorance. But Clarke, fearing leaks at the War Office, had also deliberately kept the General Staff uninformed. Haldane's lack of information did not, however, prevent him from accepting Grey's views on the desirability of direct, authorized staff talks.[46] The next day, Saturday, January 13, Grey notified Sanderson: "I have now spoken to Mr. Haldane as regards the War Office and he is willing that the French Military Attaché should com-

45. Grierson to Sanderson, Jan. 11, 1906, *ibid.*, no. 211.
46. Grey, *Twenty-five Years*, I, 73; Lord Haldane, *Before the War* (London, 1920), 30–31, and *An Autobiography* (New York, 1929), 202–203.

municate with Gen[eral] Grierson. The communication must be solely provisional and non-committal." [47]

Two days later, on January 15, the conversations became official. Sanderson sent written Foreign Office approval for Grierson to begin talks "for the purpose of obtaining such information as you require as to the methods in which military assistance could in case of need be best afforded by us to France and vice-versa." It was to be "understood that the whole matter was being studied academically." [48] That same day Grey also saw Cambon. Once again the Foreign Secretary balked at any promises about armed assistance, nor could he promise Cabinet consideration of the matter for at least two weeks. But he balanced this news by reminding the ambassador of the naval and military conversations. Fisher, Grey promised, would take care of naval problems, and Haldane had authorized direct talks between Grierson and Huguet. Although these exchanges "did not commit either Government," they henceforth had government approval and patronage. [49] Valuable in themselves, the staff talks also helped Grey turn aside or postpone the more encompassing and more embarrassing French demand for a pledge of military help if war came. On January 16, the day the Algeciras conference opened, Grierson and Huguet had their first "official" meeting; at the same time the D.M.O. ordered Lieutenant Colonel N. W. Barnardiston, the attaché in Brussels, to open talks with the Belgians. [50]

Despite assertions in their memoirs, there is no evidence that Grey and Haldane obtained the Prime Minister's authorization to put the conversations on an official basis. Neither Grey's private nor official accounts of the January 15 talk with Cambon make any reference to Campbell-Bannerman's sanction of the discussions. The Foreign Secretary, moreover, gave his formal assent for such talks on January 13, the day before Campbell-Bannerman even acknowledged receiving the account of the first Grey-Cambon interview. Haldane later claimed that he had traveled to London to gain the Prime Minister's consent for the staff talks; yet at no time between January 13 and January 15 was Campbell-Bannerman in London—he did not return from Scotland until January 26. [51] Grey and Haldane in fact presented the Prime Minister with

47. Minute by Grey on the Cambon to Rouvier dispatch of Jan. 11, 1906, B.D., III, no. 212. On Jan. 14 Haldane ordered General Lyttelton, the Chief of the General Staff, to have Grierson ready for talks; Haldane to Grey, Jan. 17, 1906, Grey Papers, F.O. 800/102.

48. Sanderson to Grierson, Jan. 15, 1906, B.D., III, nos. 214, 217a.

49. Grey to Bertie, Jan. 15, 1906, ibid., no. 215; P. Cambon to Rouvier, Jan. 15, 1906, D.D.F., 2nd ser., VIII, no. 417; Grey to Tweedmouth, Jan. 16, 1906, B.D., III, p. 203. In a personal note to Bertie, Jan. 15, 1906, Grey downgraded the value of British help and called this action "sheer precaution"; ibid., no. 216.

50. MacDiarmid, Grierson, 216.

51. Grey to Bertie, Jan. 15, 1906, B.D., III, nos. 215, 216; Haldane, An Autobiography, 203. Haldane's daily letters to his mother make no mention of a meeting with the Prime Minister in London; Haldane Papers, National Library of Scotland, Edinburgh; see also Monger, The End of Isolation, 250–251.

a fait accompli on the staff talks; exactly when Campbell-Bannerman first learned of the talks is not clear, but it was almost certainly not until his return to London in late January. If the conversations do not appear to have had the Prime Minister's advance approval, he nevertheless made no specific objection to them, either in January 1906 or later. Further, at the time the talks got underway Grey and Haldane genuinely expected that the Cabinet would discuss the entire question of support for France; this might explain their handling of the issue in mid-January.[52]

Events leading to the authorization on January 15 of official staff talks were but one aspect of the developments taking place during the final phase of "unofficial" conversations. On January 11 Major Huguet returned from Paris with the French response to Clarke's questionnaire. In Paris, Generals Brun and Brugère and Ministers Etienne, Thomson, and Rouvier had studied the queries: their answers comprise the main source of information on French attitudes about military and naval cooperation before the talks got started. The French expressed hopes that one or two British divisions could arrive as early as the fifth or sixth day of mobilization, thereby giving a great boost to French morale. They wanted the British troops joined with the French armies and under French command, while conceding that all naval affairs would be directed by Britain. The French, who made clear their opposition to coastal operations, declined to say just how British troops would be used; nor did they give hints about their own military plans except to pledge no violation of Belgian neutrality. Their information on German war plans, which reflected Brugère's views, was that a German attack would come between Metz and Thionville sometime after the twelfth day. These answers, plus some intimations that Brugère planned a narrow frontal attack in Lorraine, constitute the major results of Clarke's unofficial contacts with the French.[53]

Almost certainly the French answers were discussed when Clarke reconvened his ad hoc group on January 12, at which time General Grierson joined the original quartet of Ottley, French, Esher, and Clarke. The requirements of continental military operations dominated their discussion. Captain Ottley reported that the movement of 50,000 troops across the Channel, starting on the fourth day, could be completed on the fifteenth day of mobilization. Grierson then explained that it was impracticable to try and prepare the III Army Corps for such an opera-

52. Grey to Campbell-Bannerman, Jan. 10, 1906, Campbell-Bannerman Papers, Add. MSS, 41218; minute by Grey, Jan. 18, 1906, on Bertie to Grey, Jan. 13, 1906, B.D., III, no. 213; Campbell-Bannerman to Grey, Jan. 21, 1906, Grey Papers, F.O. 800/100.
53. Repington, The First World War, I, 6–11; "Demandes formulées par le colonel Sir George Clarke," n.d., D.D.F., 2nd ser., VIII, no. 389; memo by Esher, "Memorandum on the Work of the Defence Committee in Anticipation of Possible Hostilities," Jan. 20, 1906, Esher Papers, "Private Papers, C.I.D., 1908–1909," vol. A.

tion. Thus it was concluded "that if it should be decided to employ troops in co-operation with the French, the force employed should be limited in the first instance to 2 Army Corps, 4 Cavalry Brigades, 2 Brigades of Mounted Infantry [roughly 100,000 men]." The force would be completely mobilized by the tenth day, though there was no indication when it would arrive in its entirety on the Continent. Consideration of where the British forces would be concentrated after their arrival was deferred. But, for naval reasons, Antwerp no longer figured as the landing point; instead the safer French Channel ports became the immediate destination of British troops. This shift in plans was an early indication that Belgium—once the raison d'être for any British operation on the Continent—was already losing ground to military considerations and to the possibility of operations in France.[54]

With the military preparations moving at a steady pace, Sir George Clarke renewed his inquiries about the state of naval preparations. On Saturday afternoon, January 13, the Secretary had a long, acrimonious meeting with Fisher. "It was all very unsatisfactory," complained Clarke. "Fisher is convinced that there will be no trouble, so is not greatly interested, though of course he admitted that we ought to exercise such prevision as is possible." For his part, the First Sea Lord assured Clarke that the Royal Navy was ready and would need only a little help from the French in the Dover straits. The Admiral brushed aside the suggestion of preparing code books in case French help became necessary. More importantly, he flatly refused to be a "party to military co-operation with the French on French territory." Nor would he promise to help in ferrying troops across the Channel, arguing that this might hinder other fleet operations. Then why, Clarke retorted, talk about moving troops into the Baltic, a far more complex operation? "He [Fisher]," commented the Secretary, "denied this and did not seem to think the difficulty too great; but I could see he had never studied the question at all." [55]

Clarke immediately informed Esher and Repington of this unprofitable conversation. The latter was deeply disturbed by Fisher's opposition to the employment of British troops on the Continent, feeling that if the British did not show "a disposition to share in the real struggle at the decisive point, good-bye to all ideas of a French alliance! It is not for me to say whether Sir John is right or wrong to refuse to give any general indication of the task he would like to assign to the French navy in case of war. They have agreed to accept Sir John's plan, but he had not one to offer." Repington lamented to Esher that "the French navy prac-

54. "Notes of Conferences Held at 2, Whitehall Gardens," Cab. 18/24. See also Ottley to Fisher, Jan. 13, 1906, B.D., III, p. 186n; Monger, The End of Isolation, 246–247.

55. Clarke to Esher, Jan. 13, 1906, Esher Papers, "Clarke Letters," vol. VI; also Repington, The First World War, I, 11–12.

tically shows its readiness to follow the Admiralty lead, and there is no lead given. I thought we had a St. Vincent at Whitehall, but apparently I was mistaken." Fisher's attitude on troop transport caused Repington even greater concern. "You see, it is useless for me to tell H.[uguet] that we shall begin to arrive on a certain day and be ready to entrain so many days later if Sir John is not prepared to cover the crossing. I understand that Ottley saw no difficulty in this." [56]

Clarke and Repington hoped that Viscount Esher would intervene with the First Sea Lord, but Esher's loyalties were with Fisher and the maneuver came to naught. The Admiral made his position quite clear to Esher on January 14. "What does Clarke's letter which you sent to me resolve itself into. There are no naval plans for war because he doesn't know them!" After all, Fisher added, "the French War Office haven't told the English War Office their plans. What fools if they did. To peril their military plans for the military drop in the ocean that our military support signifies. So also the English Admiralty intend to keep their own Counsel!" Four days later he made explicit his opposition to Clarke's activities: he forbade Ottley to attend any further conferences at Whitehall Gardens. A provoked Clarke could only comment: "The difficulties of getting anything to go right in this muddle-headed-country are enormous." [57]

Despite the rebuff, Clarke gathered his other colleagues on January 19 to make a final assessment of British preparations. This meeting, though held after the staff talks had become official, may be considered the last act of the period of unofficial conversations. Once the talks achieved official recognition, Grierson saw Huguet personally and the Directorate of Military Operations took control of Anglo-French military planning. Never again before 1914 did the C.I.D. play an active part in the entente conversations.[58] At this final session Grierson reported that further changes would enable them to have the Aldershot corps in France by the twelfth day. Making only brief mention of Belgium and none of where the troops might be concentrated, the minutes of the conference stated that: "It was understood that in the event of the British force being employed on the French frontier, its status would be that of an independent body under the general control of the French Commander-in-Chief." Otherwise there was little significant discussion. Their participants satisfied with the state of preparations, the conferences at White-

56. Repington to Esher, Jan. 14, 1906, Esher Papers, "Army, 1905–6," vol. III; also Esher to M. V. Brett, Jan. 14, 1906. *Journals and Letters of Esher*, II, 134–135.

57. Fisher to Esher, Jan. 14, 1906, Esher Papers, "Letters and Memoranda, 1898–1906," vol. I (also in Marder, *Fear God and Dread Nought*, III, 30–31, where it is incorrectly speculated as Feb. 18, 1906). See also Ottley to Clarke, Jan. 18, 1906, Esher Papers, "Clarke Letters," vol. VI; Clarke to Esher, Jan. 18, 21, 1906, *ibid*.

58. John Mackintosh, "The Role of the Committee of Imperial Defence before 1914," *English Historical Review*, 77 (July 1962), 490–503; Hankey, *Supreme Command*, I, 62. Clarke continued to have informal contacts with Huguet; Repington to Esher, Feb. 15, 1906, Esher Papers, "Army 1905–6," vol. III.

hall Gardens—no longer needed now that official conversations were underway—adjourned indefinitely.[59]

The part played by Sir George Clarke during the period of unofficial conversations remains difficult to evaluate. For the first and only time before 1914 a Secretary of the C.I.D. actively espoused and promoted a scheme of strategic thought. This excursion into strategy cannot be damned offhand as the work of an amateur, or as the meddling of an early version of the civilian strategists of the Cold War: for Clarke's military reputation was considerable and his appreciation of the changing strategic position of Britain was well in advance of most of his contemporaries. Because he was the first Secretary of the C.I.D. there were no precedents to guide him in a time of crisis; and he could perhaps reasonably assume that he should be checking upon the state of British defense preparations. With an election in progress and the Prime Minister out of London, his actions appear prudent and sensible.

Nevertheless, he did exceed the role envisaged for the C.I.D. and its Secretary: his contacts with the French were an incursion into the formation of foreign policy. Regardless of the disclaimers, his official position gave the talks a special significance. Also, his confident assurance to the French that a German violation of Belgium would automatically bring British assistance was a view not entirely shared either by the Foreign Office or by the services. Further, having taken these steps, Clarke deliberately failed to apprise the Prime Minister of his actions. And his distrust of the War Office led him to ignore the department chiefly concerned with military intervention. His impetuous nature also brought him into collision with Fisher: the results of this feud not only brought about Clarke's departure in 1907, they rendered nugatory the C.I.D. as a possible institution to bring about the coordination of British strategy. After this time, Fisher virtually boycotted the C.I.D. in protest of Clarke's intrusions into what the Admiral regarded as his special province. Yet he, too, must shoulder some of the blame for this feud; his unwillingness to accept criticism and his arrogant confidence in the superiority of materiel led him to neglect war plans and to cling to outdated strategic notions. When he finally realized that the Army wanted no part of a Baltic operation, Fisher simply withdrew from the fray and kept his own counsel. The stage was set for long, arduous, and often bitter debates within the British government over a national defense policy.

Clarke, while he was overreaching his prerogatives, was still far too clever a politician to keep Campbell-Bannerman entirely uninformed about the conferences at Whitehall Gardens. On January 27 he discussed them with the Prime Minister, who "was not at all inclined to be alarmed at what I told him we had done." In fact Campbell-Bannerman hoped to hold a C.I.D. meeting the next week.[60] Haldane and Grey

59. "Notes of Conferences Held at 2, Whitehall Gardens," Cab. 18/24.
60. Clarke to Esher, Jan. 27, 1906, Esher Papers, "Clarke Letters," vol. VI.

likewise brought their chief up-to-date on developments; he in turn made no attempt to stop the conversations, but instead reluctantly acquiesced, urging that extreme care be taken to keep them secret. He did not, as he later wrote Ripon, "like the stress laid upon joint preparations. It comes very close to an honourable undertaking; and it will be known on both sides of the Rhine." [61]

Although the conversations were now authorized and official, there remained the larger policy question for the British government: how to answer the French plea for a promise of armed support if war came? At the first Cabinet (January 31) following the election, the question was not mentioned; nor was it later discussed. Yet Grey used the Cabinet as a convenient excuse to avoid a written pledge of support when he saw Cambon on January 31. Citing the conversations as an example of their intimacy, the Foreign Secretary emphasized that there were already close relations between the two nations: thus a formal pledge was unnecessary and would only cause trouble with the Cabinet, many of whose members were radicals. Such a pledge, moreover, would amount to a defensive alliance and this could not be kept from Parliament. Grey then tried to define the conditions of Britain's support. He warned Cambon that London would not fight just to put France in Morocco; however, he admitted that if the Germans tried to disrupt the entente by an attack on France, then Britain would probably give assistance. In 1905 Lansdowne had worried first about a Moroccan port and only secondly about the entente, whereas Grey now minimized Morocco and stressed the entente: the Entente Cordiale was acquiring a significance of its own. The Foreign Secretary ended this conversation with the gracious assurance that the French could again raise the issue at any time.[62]

Lord Sanderson saw Cambon on February 1. The Permanent Undersecretary, who retired that very day, spelled out more completely the British position, stressing the Cabinet's traditional dislike for hypothetical discussions and advance commitments. Sanderson urged that the entente be left as it was—intimate political relations and staff conversations, but no defensive alliance. Cambon, Sanderson reported, appeared satisfied with this ambiguous but promising relationship.[63] At any rate, the ambassador did not revive the question of British armed support for France or even mention the conversations again until late 1906, when there was, as Campbell-Bannerman rightly forecast, a flurry of German press reports about an Anglo-French military convention.

61. Campbell-Bannerman to Ripon, Feb. 2, 1906, quoted in Spender, *Campbell-Bannerman*, I, 257.
62. Campbell-Bannerman's letter to the King after the Jan. 31 Cabinet contained one sentence on Morocco, Campbell-Bannerman Papers, Add. MSS, 52512; Grey to Bertie, Jan. 31, 1906, B.D., III, no. 219; P. Cambon to Rouvier, Jan. 31–Feb. 1, 1906, D.D.F., 2nd ser., IX, pt. 1, no. 106.
63. Memo by Sanderson, Feb. 2, 1906, B.D., III, no. 220b; Monger, *The End of Isolation*, 266–274.

During the protracted conference at Algeciras (January–April), Anglo-French relations continued close and cooperative. Although Grey was inclined to be conciliatory toward Berlin on occasion, he firmly supported French demands on the key question of who controlled the police in the Moroccan ports.[64] The entente's importance to his policy received unequivocal expression on February 20 when he told his Foreign Office staff: "If there is war between France and Germany it will be very difficult for us to keep out of it. The *Entente* and still more the constant and emphatic demonstrations of affection (official, naval, political, commercial, Municipal and in the Press), have created in France a belief that we should support her in war." He warned that "if this expectation is disappointed the French will never forgive us. There would also I think be a general feeling in every country that we have behaved meanly and left France in the lurch." [65] Above all, the Foreign Secretary did not want to be isolated against Germany. His support for France at Algeciras was therefore constant, though some disagreement arose in March when the French suspected London of wavering.

In early April the Algeciras conference ended. The fiction of Moroccan independence was preserved but France and Spain took control of the police in eight Moroccan ports. Berlin had only succeeded in reducing, not preventing French and Spanish encroachments in Morocco, and this at a very high political cost: German pressure had consolidated and reinforced the Entente Cordiale. Furthermore, while the conference was in progress, Anglo-French relations were acquiring a military and naval significance hitherto unconnected with them. The staff talks, perhaps originally intended to cover only the immediate danger of a war in 1906, were soon a permanent part of the entente. Unwilling to pledge British help to France in all conditions, Grey nonetheless encouraged the expectation of such help through his strong diplomatic policy and his tolerance of the staff talks.[66]

After January 15 the military conversations were on an official basis. Exchanges of military information between the Anglo-French staffs, and with the Belgians, began immediately. Yet the existence of these staff conversations was not revealed to the full British Cabinet in 1906. The most frequent explanations, or excuses, advanced for Grey's failure to inform the Cabinet may be briefly stated: (1) Grey was an inexperienced Cabinet minister in the midst of an election campaign and did not realize the full importance of the French demands; (2) the conversations were merely a logical extension of the terms of the 1904 accord and

64. On Anglo-French relations during the conference, see Anderson, *Moroccan Crisis*, 348–396; and Monger, *The End of Isolation*, 274–280. Grey was willing, and he had Admiralty approval, to yield on a Moroccan port; but French reaction to such reports was so violent that he had to disavow any intention of a concession.
65. Memo by Grey, Feb. 20, 1906, B.D., III, no. 299.
66. Sidney B. Fay, *The Origins of the World War*, 2nd rev. ed., 2 vols. in 1 (New York, 1930), I, 210.

thus involved no question of policy; (3) the conversations had begun in the Lansdowne period; (4) Campbell-Bannerman as Prime Minister, not Grey, had the final responsibility for bringing the talks before the Cabinet; (5) the death of Grey's wife on February 1 detained him so long at Fallodon that the issue was forgotten when he returned to London; and (6) the talks were purely departmental matters and thus permissible if the responsible ministers were informed.[67]

New evidence makes these explanations, already attacked on a number of grounds, quite suspect. On January 18 Lord Tweedmouth, the First Lord of the Admiralty, wrote Grey from Sandringham that King Edward approved of the desire to be ready for "eventualities," but was concerned about the "constitutional gravity" of such developments. However inexperienced Grey might have been, this warning from the King could have left no doubts about the significance of closer relations with France. And Edward's reaction certainly implied that he for one regarded the French demands as more than a logical extension of the 1904 agreements or as a mere departmental matter.[68] The other explanations suffer from evidence sent by Paul Cambon to Paris on February 1. Cambon wrote that he had been confidentially informed that at Windsor during the weekend of January 27–29 Edward, Campbell-Bannerman and Grey had agreed to conceal the talks from the Cabinet. They feared that the extension of the Anglo-French accords

> must give rise to a Cabinet discussion and that at present this consultation would have some inconveniences, for certain Ministers would be astonished at the opening of official talks between the military administrations of the two countries and of the studies which they have worked out in common. They [the King, the Prime Minister, and the Foreign Secretary] have thus thought that it was better to keep silent and to continue discreetly the preparations which would put the two governments in a position to plan and act rapidly in case of need.[69]

The source of this information remains a mystery. Nevertheless, the revelation provides, for the first time, a reasonable if not altogether commendable explanation of why the Cabinet was never informed. Anxious to avoid a radical challenge to his pro-French policy, Grey convinced Campbell-Bannerman of the prudence of this step: party unity would be preserved and the continuity of foreign policy assured. As George Monger notes, the Foreign Secretary, both in approving the staff talks

67. Trevelyan, Grey, 140, 152–160, notes most of these; see also Grey, Twenty-five Years, I, 72–86; Temperley, "British Secret Diplomacy from Canning to Grey," 25–32; Monger, The End of Isolation, 253–256.

68. Tweedmouth to Grey, Jan. 18, 1906, Grey Papers, F.O. 800/87; the King's comments referred specifically to the Grey-Cambon discussion of Jan. 10.

69. Cambon to Rouvier, Jan. 31–Feb. 1, 1906, D.D.F., 2nd ser., IX, pt. 1, no. 106. See also A. J. P. Taylor, "La Conférence d'Algésiras," Revue historique, 208 (October–December 1952), 240–241; Grey to Campbell-Bannerman, Jan. 19, 22, 1906, Campbell-Bannerman Papers, Add. MSS, 52514.

and then in concealing them, showed an indifference to the Cabinet that verged on unconstitutionality.[70]

Certain Cabinet ministers and the King, concerned that Britain be prepared for all emergencies, sanctioned and concealed the unprecedented staff discussions with France. Regardless of assurances that Britain was not committed by these talks, their existence opened a new era; nor did the French let the British forget this in the recurring international crises before 1914. A precedent was established in 1906 which equally served strong-willed generals like Henry Wilson and indecisive Prime Ministers like Asquith. The conversations brought Britain closer to participation in a continental war. Perhaps without realizing it, the small group of British ministers had moved toward the Army's view that Britain had a role to play on the Continent if Germany attacked France or Belgium. That Count von Schlieffen was coincidentally drafting a new German war plan which envisaged massive attacks on Belgium and France demonstrated that, for once at least, British military planners had rightfully discerned the future.

Two final and closely connected questions about the start of the conversations remain: What did these first official staff talks settle? What part did Belgium play in the arrangements? With the Navy these questions can be answered simply: nothing. Fisher's only contact with the French had come, as noted earlier, during the "unofficial" phase of the conversations when he requested French submarines and destroyers to help in the Dover-Calais area. Despite badgering by Clarke and Repington, the Admiral had remained confident of British self-sufficiency at sea and never saw de Lostende again during the crisis.[71]

The French military attaché was more successful. Huguet and Grierson met frequently from January 16 through the first of May.[72] On two occasions the General traveled to the Continent, once to inspect the ports of Boulogne and Calais, once to visit the areas around Lille, Valenciennes, Namur, and the Belgian Ardennes.[73] From these forays and extensive staff work the Anglo-French planners settled details on the size of the British force, the dates of its arrival, and the supply and transportation of the force in France. Grierson indicated, somewhat to Huguet's surprise, that only two corps (not three) would be available; this force would total approximately 100,000 men.[74] For naval reasons and

70. Monger, The End of Isolation, 255–256; on the larger question of Cabinet responsibility, see John Mackintosh, The British Cabinet (London, 1962), 316–324.
71. Clarke to Esher, Feb. 17 [?], 1906, Esher Papers, "Clarke Letters," vol. VI; Esher to Clarke, Feb. 18, 1906, Journals and Letters of Esher, II, 144–145; Esher to Fisher, Feb. 18, 1906, ibid., 145.
72. The British records on the 1906 Anglo-French conversations, including those used by the editors of the British Documents, were apparently destroyed during the Battle of Britain. The French files are intact and complete.
73. MacDiarmid, Grierson, 216–217; Huguet to Brun, Mar. 8, 1906, Archives Guerre, "Plan XVII: Armée W," box 147b.
74. "Note de l'Etat-major général anglais," Jan. 22, 1906, D.D.F., 2nd ser., IX,

reasons of convenience the British forces would, the Admiralty willing, land at Calais, Cherbourg, and Boulogne. The first British units would start debarking on the fourth day after mobilization, with the total force in France by the fifteenth day. From these ports the French rail system would move the troops forward; the French would supply food during the trip to the zone of concentration.[75]

The location of this zone was not, however, arranged precisely during these first Anglo-French staff talks—in fact, the evidence on this point is scanty and contradictory. Esher on January 20, before the official talks were in full progress, mentioned possible operations between Verdun and Mézières, which would have been on the French left under the provisions of Plan XV. But Paléologue on January 13 wrote that the French Chief of Staff, General Brun, wanted the British troops at Maubeuge on the twelfth day, from which he hoped they could check any German drive through Belgium. This location also corresponds with the French rail tables which mark Amiens as the final destination.[76] Yet by September 1906 Brun had altered his opinion. At the September maneuvers he told Grierson that the French wanted British troops at Vouziers on the Aisne River as a prolongation of the French left flank. When the British General protested, saying he preferred to operate in Belgium, Brun conceded that the British could "penetrate first on Belgian territory in case of necessity." Grierson accepted this notion without enthusiasm and apparently with reservations.[77] Shortly afterward Major General J. S. Ewart replaced Grierson as D.M.O.; at this time there was still no firm agreement within the entente on the utilization of the British Army.

The failure to settle on a precise zone of concentration in France for Armée W stemmed from a variety of factors. In Paris the French General Staff welcomed the prospect of British aid, but made no alterations in their plans because of it. The French appear to have vacillated between using the British Army as an extension of the French left wing and keeping it as a reserve force; their indecision may have been linked to Brugère's completion of his belated revisions of Plan XV. There was another, equally practical reason for the Anglo-French failure to define a zone of concentration: Haldane's army reforms and the switch from the corps to the division organizational format necessitated a complete

---

pt. 1, no. 34; Huguet attributed, incorrectly, the reduction in British forces to Admiral Fisher's and General French's desire to keep some troops for coastal operations; "Note du colonel Huguet," Jan. 26, 1906, *ibid.*, no. 68.

75. The landing tables of Jan. 30 and a revision of Apr. 11, 1906, are in Archives Guerre, "Plan XVII: Armée W," box 147b; also "Résumé des questions examinées par les Etats-majors français et anglais," May 10, 1906, D.D.F., 2nd ser., X, no. 48.

76. Paléologue, *Un grand tournant*, 424–425; "Note de l'E. M. F. du 5 mai 1906, en réponse à la note de l'E. M. W. du 8 mars 1906," Archives Guerre, "Plan XVII: Armée W," box 147b.

77. Memo by Paléologue, Sept. 18, 1906, D.D.F., 2nd ser., X, no. 208; Paléologue, *Un grand tournant*, 433–435.

revision of all the troop and transport arrangements agreed upon by
Grierson and Huguet between January and May. In early May the
French attaché unhappily reported that nothing could be done until
these revisions had been completed.[78]

But the Anglo-Belgian military conversations were probably the major reason for the entente's failure to define how the British Army would
be employed. The talks between Brussels and London reflected and
caused a certain ambivalence in British military planning during 1906—
nor should this have been unexpected. It was apprehension about Belgian neutrality which had first drawn the attention of British planners
back to the Continent. In 1905 the war game at Camberley and the September staff work were prompted by Belgium and not by the Entente
Cordiale. Moreover, when Grierson seriously got down to preparing for
British intervention on the Continent, his attention and his preferences
for action centered upon helping the Belgians in Belgium. The Directorate of Military Operations' conclusion in 1906 that the German
threat to Belgium would be immediate and not delayed gave added urgency to Anglo-Belgian preparations.

British military concern about Belgium had its diplomatic and political counterpart. Sir George Clarke in 1905 had stressed the importance
of Belgium to Balfour. Although Clarke's contention that a violation of
the neutral state would bring an automatic British response was not
unanimously accepted, his view remained in circulation.[79] Indeed, it
formed a part of Clarke's questionnaire to the French General Staff in
1906; and, more importantly, it served as a premise in Grey's thinking.
Just as Grey worried more about the entente than had his predecessor,
so also he emphasized Belgian neutrality: on February 1, 1906, for example, he told the Belgian minister, Count Charles de Lalaing, that
"your country has always been considered as sacred, as a kind of sanctuary." "Yes," responded the Belgian envoy, "a sanctuary of which England was the guardian priest. 'It is still our manner of seeing today,' Sir
Edward Grey replied." [80]

The Foreign Secretary's concern took practical form: he authorized
the Anglo-Belgian staff talks.[81] Beginning on January 18, they were conducted by Barnardiston, the British attaché, and Major General G. E. V.

78. Huguet to Brun, May 6, 1906, Archives Guerre, "Plan XVII: Armée W," box
147b. The code prefix "W" was given the British force at this time, but not, as
Barbara Tuchman suggests, in honor of Henry Wilson, who played no role in the
preparations until 1910 (*The Guns of August* [New York, 1962], 54).
79. Sanderson for one rejected the idea; Sanderson to Clarke, Aug. 10, 1905,
Cab. 17/69.
80. Lalaing to Favereau, Feb. 1, 1906, Belgian Foreign Ministry Archives, Brussels, "Correspondance politique: Légations," Great Britain, vol. VI. See also Jonathan E. Helmreich, "Belgian Concern over Neutrality and British Intentions, 1906–
1914," *Journal of Modern History*, 36 (December 1964), 416–419.
81. Perhaps through oversight or because there was a change of British ministers
to Brussels during this time, no mention of the conversations was made to the Belgian Foreign Ministry by either Sir C. Phipps or Sir A. Hardinge; see *B.D.*, III,
p. 203 n. 1.

Ducarne, Chief of the Belgian General Staff.[82] During the next three months their planning reached a level of great complexity and thoroughness. Ducarne eased persistent British fears that Brussels might consent to a German violation of Belgian Luxembourg, making evident his intention to see Belgium prepared to defend itself. Barnardiston likewise made clear Britain's intention to help Belgium after a German invasion —while always insisting that these prior preparations carried no absolute British commitment. Rail tables, provisions for maps and liaison officers, and supply arrangements were quickly settled. In these talks Grierson, through his attaché, emphasized his preference for British intervention in Belgium in spite of the initial landings in France. Such intervention would, in the D.M.O.'s opinion, not only have greater appeal to the British public, but would give the British Army more independence than if it were connected to the French left flank.[83]

On the important question of British troop concentration Grierson and Ducarne had little difficulty in agreeing. British operations, based on the assumption that Belgian forts could resist the initial German assaults, would seek to meet two developments: a German jab toward Antwerp or a flanking move through the Belgian Ardennes-Meuse region. If the Germans struck toward Antwerp, the British troops would move from the French ports to the Brussels-Aarshot-Louvain area, joining there the 120,000-man Belgian Army. Together they would try to block a German drive toward Antwerp. Should the Germans try the more probable flanking maneuver, Grierson planned for the British troops to detrain in the Dinant-Ciney-Namur triangle, then move to the Dinant-Namur line: these Belgian areas were Grierson's favorite choice for the British concentration.[84] In September 1906 he personally reiterated to Ducarne that he still preferred that Britain fight in Belgium.[85] It would thus appear that the Anglo-Belgian staff talks hold the key to the entente's

82. I have been able to locate only a fragment of the original records on the Anglo-Belgian military talks; the indications, however implausible, are that both sets of documents were destroyed by the ravages of war. Fortunately, the editors of the British Documents reprinted a nearly complete file from the British side. In 1914 German troops captured the records of the Belgian General Staff, and during World War I the German propaganda machine published the records to show that Belgium had compromised its neutrality before 1914: thus the Belgian records are also available, after a fashion. On the problems posed by the Anglo-Belgian talks, see Carl Hosse, Die englisch-belgischen Aufmarschpläne gegen Deutschland vor dem Weltkriege (Zurich, 1930), and A. de Ridder, "Encore les conventions anglo-belges," Revue belge des livres, documents & archives de la guerre, 1914–1918, 7 (April–June 1931), 218–238.
83. The records of the talks are in B.D., III, pp. 186–201; also see J. Wullus-Rudiger, La Belgique et l'équilibre européen, 2nd ed. (Paris, 1935), 310–317; F. Vandaele, "Les 'conversations' anglo-belges d'avant guerre," Revue belge des livres, documents & archives de la guerre, 1914–1918, 8 (January–April 1932), 59–72, 98–102.
84. Grierson to Barnardiston, Feb. 27, Mar. 20, 1906, B.D., III, no. 221; Tyler, British Army, 48–51. On the question of using Antwerp as a base of operations, see D. H. Thomas, "The Use of the Scheldt in British Plans for the Defence of Belgian Neutrality, 1831–1914," Revue belge de philologie et d'histoire, 41 (1963), 449–455.
85. Memo by Paléologue, Sept. 18, 1906, D.D.F., 2nd ser., X, no. 208.

failure in 1906 to coordinate more closely the deployment of British troops.

But however crucial Belgium was in initially attracting British military attention to the Continent, factors were already present which would ultimately force London to reconsider conducting operations in the Belgian kingdom. Anglo-Belgian political relations, regardless of Grey's protestations, were poor. King Leopold took great offense at British criticism of his rule in the Congo, and this issue would continue to exacerbate relations between London and Brussels.[86] Also, the Anglo-Belgian talks revealed practical military problems which could not be ignored: the British could not move enough troops to the Belgian Meuse in time; the crucial days for the German drive into Belgium would come after the tenth day of German mobilization, and at that time the available British troops would only total 35,000; not until the sixteenth day would the entire British force of nearly 100,000 men be available to help the Belgians, and this would be too late for effective assistance along the Meuse.[87] And the poor condition of the Belgian Army at the 1906 maneuvers prompted British misgivings, especially when it was compared with French troops.[88] Finally, there was always the possibility that the Belgians might back out of the preparations, refuse to defend themselves, and permit the Germans to cross their territory. The British planners before 1914 remained convinced that the Belgian Ardennes would be the probable scene of British operations if war came; but increasingly France, not Belgium, came to be viewed as the proper starting point for British action.

In the first months of 1906 Grey's foreign policy preserved and strengthened the entente. At the same time the military concomitants of a pro-continental policy received their first thorough examination: the problems of British intervention on the Continent were defined and the means to meet them authorized by a small segment of the British Cabinet. But by May 1906 staff talks were everywhere in abeyance. Barnardiston's transfer ended the Anglo-Belgian talks, which were never resumed. The British General Staff turned its attention to the demands of reform and a possible Anglo-Turkish war. Huguet could only wait impatiently for a chance to resume the talks, yet the absence of any European crisis at the end of 1906 carried the lull into 1907. At that point a series of C.I.D. investigations began which not only occupied the entire General Staff but also had long-term significance for the future of Anglo-French military and naval relations.

86. Helmreich, "Belgian Concern over Neutrality," 418–419; Mary E. Thomas, "Anglo-Belgian Military Relations and the Congo Question, 1911–1913," *Journal of Modern History*, 25 (June 1953), 157–165.
87. Barnardiston to Grierson, Mar. 30, 31, 1906, B.D., III, no. 221, pp. 197–199.
88. Grierson to Edward VII, Sept. 10, 1906, Royal Archives, Windsor Castle, RA W27/36; MacDiarmid, *Grierson*, 218–222.

4 | Preparing for War: British Defense Policy 1906–1910

The lull in the military conversations continued until Brigadier General Henry Wilson became Director of Military Operations in August 1910. During this interval (1906–1910) the War Office and the Admiralty reformed and perfected the instruments of British military and naval power; at the same time the services also revised and elaborated their war plans and strategies. The C.I.D. and the Liberal Cabinet worked to clarify and to define the overall aims and requirements of British defense policy. Each of these developments profoundly influenced the course of Anglo-French military relations.

The British Army was among the least attractive legacies bequeathed the Liberal government by its predecessor. Criticized and belittled after its Boer War performance, it had experienced three investigations and two major reforms within a three-year period: embittered officers, half-attained reforms, and an untried General Staff were the chief results. In the new government the unenviable task of reforming and reorganizing the Army went to Richard Burdon Haldane, a vain, rotund Scottish lawyer who brought a keenly analytical and flexible mind to the War Office. He had hoped and schemed to be Lord Chancellor in the new government, but Campbell-Bannerman had refused. Rather than be excluded altogether from the seat of power, the Liberal imperialist had asked for the dubious privilege of heading the War Office, a veritable graveyard for ambitious ministers. Haldane, unlike his two immediate predecessors, had no preconceived program for healing the Army's ills. Shortly after taking the seals of office he told the Army Council that he "was a young and blushing virgin just united to a bronze warrior and that it was not expected by the public that any result of the union should appear until at least nine months had passed." [1] On the other hand Haldane from the start accepted the "blue water" theory of British strategy, that is to say, he trusted the Navy to defend Britain from invasion and felt the Army's role lay overseas. "The first purpose," he told Parliament in July 1906, "for which we want any army is for oversea war. The Fleet defends our coast." This principle, which meant a complete break with the Stanhope memorandum and its emphasis upon defense, served as the fundamental premise of Haldane's efforts. In the next seven years he managed to create a military force which could later be described as "incomparably the best trained, best organized, and best equipped British Army which ever went forth to war." [2]

The creation of an expeditionary force absorbed much of Haldane's attention during 1906. His efforts came none too soon. Grierson's confident assertion that Britain could send 100,000 men to the Continent in fifteen days had turned out, under closer scrutiny, to be something of an exaggeration; 80,000 men within two months appeared a more accurate estimate.[3] To improve this unsatisfactory situation Haldane decided to create an overseas force of six divisions. In a lengthy speech to Parliament on July 12, 1906, he indicated that the new Expeditionary Force would consist of 158,000 men, organized into six infantry divisions and four cavalry brigades (later one cavalry division). Of this force more than a third would be soldiers on active duty, while Regular Reserves and the Militia (later replaced by the Special Reserves) supplied the remainder of the manpower. Henceforth regulars would serve seven years with the colors, five with the reserve; all service remained voluntary. To make this increased force of six divisions palatable to his fellow Liberals, Haldane promised financial savings and overall troop reductions of 20,000 men, mostly from colonial garrisons. His tactics were successful, for the Liberals, delighted with the reductions in estimates and soldiers,

1. Maurice, *Haldane*, I, 168–169.
2. Great Britain, *Parliamentary Debates: Commons*, 4th ser., 160 (July 12, 1906), 1080; Committee of Imperial Defence, *History of the Great War, based on Official Documents: Military Operations: J. E.* Edmonds, *France and Belgium, 1914*, I, 3rd ed. (London, 1933), 10.
3. Haldane, *Before the War*, 32.

were largely apathetic about the implications of the new Expeditionary Force. Except for Balfour's complaint that 100,000 men were enough to handle any foreseeable emergency, including action on the Continent, there was little parliamentary debate about the new force; and at no point, beyond vague talk of overseas duties, did Haldane furnish any indication of how the divisions would be used. Without substantial alteration, the proposals he outlined were put into effect in January 1907.[4]

Haldane met greater opposition in his attempts to reorganize the second-line or auxiliary forces. The Militia, the Yeomanry, and the Volunteers, designed to serve as a home defense force and as a possible vehicle for the emergency expansion of the Regular Army, were antiquated organizational forms perpetuated by local interests and the inertia of tradition. To overcome the opposition Haldane solicited, received, and exploited the support of Edward VII. This assistance and the relative passivity of Conservative leadership (who were willing to let someone improve the Army) enabled Haldane to carry out his program for the auxiliary forces. He suppressed the Militia as an organization, replacing it with the Special Reserves, who were liable for service overseas, supplied personnel for infantry units, and handled support and transport responsibilities in the Expeditionary Force—they were technically, in fact, first-line troops. Haldane planned for a total of 80,000 in this category. At the status of purely second-line forces the Volunteers, dating from mid-Victorian times, were replaced by the Territorial Force administered by County Associations (the War Office, however, retained full control over the training of the "Terriers"). Upon the mobilization of the Expeditionary Force, the territorials would be called for a six-month training period. After training they would relieve regulars in home defense work and, it was hoped, volunteer for service overseas. With this revitalized second-line force Haldane hoped to provide both for home defense and for the expansion of the Expeditionary Force in case of a major war. His original goal of 300,000 men was nearly reached by 1910, though there was a steady diminution after that.[5]

Briefly stated, these were the major Army reforms undertaken by Haldane. By September 1907 he had secured parliamentary approval for all of them, but actual implementation extended well into 1909. With few adjustments the reforms survived intact until the outbreak of war in 1914 when Lord Kitchener, who accepted the British Expeditionary Force (B.E.F.), overturned Haldane's provisions for second-line expansion forces. Of the components of the reform, the most important for Anglo-French relations was of course the new Expeditionary Force.

4. *Parliamentary Debates: Commons,* 4th ser., 160 (July 12, 1906), 1075–1119, 1161–1168; Dunlop, *Development of British Army,* 251–257; Kluke, *Heeresaufbau und Heerespolitik,* 77–96.
5. Dunlop, *Development of British Army,* 268–290; Elie Halévy, *The Rule of Democracy, 1905–1914,* trans. E. I. Watkin, 2nd rev. ed. (London, 1952), 174–186; Kluke, *Heeresaufbau und Heerespolitik,* 96–109.

What was the purpose of the B.E.F.? The answer given by the Liberal government in 1906 to this question was neither so clear-cut nor explicit as its members and its historians have claimed. In 1906 most at Whitehall, like Haldane, generally subscribed to the blue water view that the Army existed for overseas activity. Beyond this vague principle members of the government seldom agreed, and their differences of opinion are readily explicable: Britain in 1906 faced not one but two strategic situations which might prompt the dispatch of the Expeditionary Force, one in India, the other on the Continent. In the last years of the Balfour government Indian considerations and requirements had dominated defense discussions, but by 1906 India had to share the spotlight with the Continent. Now in the public at large many of those who sought sizable increases in the British Army also cited potential European requirements to support their demands. The Earl of Erroll in May 1906, for example, warned that Britain could not be indifferent to a German attack on Belgium. "I imagine that in consideration of the *entente cordiale* we should be bound in honour to take steps to prevent such a contingency if our friend and neighbour were threatened by a flank attack from this direction." A few months later Major H. Bannerman-Phillips stressed that Britain should be ready to put a "sufficiently large expeditionary force in position to support the Belgian Army on land— not as an act of aggression, but as a police duty, carried out in the interests of peace and in fulfillment of her guarantee." [6] And then there was Lord Roberts, who wanted a large British force raised by conscription and available to meet any contingency; the Field Marshal now gave the Continent equal billing with Indian and home defense needs.[7] Within the new government Haldane and the General Staff were also coming to regard a European war as the Army's most likely task. But others, such as Sir George Clarke, Lord Esher, and most in the Cabinet—as well as Balfour—argued that trouble along the northwest frontier of India was more probable. Because of the divided opinions, India and the Continent competed for attention, for resources, and for priorities in 1906: the result was a vigorous extended dialogue within the government, and especially the C.I.D., over the size and the raison d'être of the Expeditionary Force.

In early 1906, as the Moroccan crisis began to ease, India once more attracted the attention of the C.I.D. On March 1 Esher implored Campbell-Bannerman to authorize a Committee study of the requirements of India because those, he insisted, should govern the size of an expeditionary force. Esher got his way, and several days later the C.I.D. dis-

6. Earl of Erroll, "Parliament and the Army," *Nineteenth Century and After*, 59 (May 1906), 867; Maj. H. Bannerman-Phillips, "Great Britain as Guarantor of Belgium's Neutrality," *United Service Magazine*, 33 (August 1906), 531. See also E. N. Bennett, "Playing at Soldiers," *Nineteenth Century and After*, 61 (May 1907), 742–751.
7. The Earl Roberts, *A Nation in Arms* (London, 1907), 111, 142, 180, 198, 200.

cussed Indian defense requirements. On this occasion Grey and Haldane, pointing to Russia's recent defeats and the existence of the Anglo-French entente, demanded a reduction in the peacetime garrison in India. But the other C.I.D. members declined to rule upon Indian needs without the opinion of Lord Kitchener, head of British forces in India. The Prime Minister ordered John Morley, the Indian Secretary, to sound Kitchener on the military situation—a process which took some months.[8]

In the absence of a definitive statement on Indian needs, Haldane was left free to seek guidance elsewhere on the size of the Expeditionary Force: in effect this meant a consideration of the requirements of continental operations. Grierson's January memorandum, which advocated a British Army capable of placing 120,000 men in Belgium or France, the ideas of Colonel Gerald Ellison (Haldane's military assistant), and the new minister's own appreciation of the continental situation all influenced the planning of the future B.E.F.[9] Yet at no point during 1906 was there a thorough review, either in the War Office or elsewhere, of the requirements of continental warfare. And throughout that year the War Minister consistently refrained from citing European requirements as a justification for an increased overseas force. The closest he came to an overt admission about possible continental demands was in late July when he noted that the "change in the political circumstances of the day has made it possible, for the present, to divert exclusive attention from the North-West frontier of India, and to consider other possible contingencies." Otherwise, Haldane talked only generally of the force being used for "overseas war."[10]

Uncertain of Indian requirements and afraid to talk of European needs because the radicals in the Cabinet might be alarmed, Haldane in 1906 had to turn elsewhere for public justification for his Expeditionary Force. He fell back on the nearly sacrosanct Cardwellian principle of linked battalions: one at home for each overseas. Instituted first in 1872, this concept had guided British military policy until Arnold-Forster's attempt to form distinct overseas and home service armies. In returning to Cardwell's scheme Haldane won the support of many traditionalists, including Campbell-Bannerman, a fact that became apparent on July 6 when the C.I.D. tackled the problem of army reform. Belatedly the Prime Minister recognized that Haldane had elaborated a plan for an expeditionary force without having first received an authoritative state-

8. "Military Requirements of the Empire—Note by Lord Esher," Feb. 28, 1906, Cab. 17/94; Esher to Campbell-Bannerman, Mar. 1, 1906, *Journals and Letters of Esher*, II, 146–149; minutes of the 85th meeting of the C.I.D., Cab. 2/2/1.
9. Memo by Grierson, "Memorandum upon the Military Forces Required for Oversea Warfare," Jan. 4, 1906, W.O. 106/44; "Military Organisation: Note by Sir G. S. Clarke," Jan. 31, 1906, Cab. 17/13; Haldane, *Before the War*, 31–33; memo by Robertson, "The True Standard of Our Military Needs," 1906, Robertson Papers, 1/2.
10. Great Britain, War Office, *Memorandum by the Secretary of State for War on Army Reorganization*, July 30, 1906 (Cd. 2993).

ment of imperial needs. Defending his actions, Haldane told the C.I.D. he had used Cardwell's principle to make the "most efficient dispositions of the minimum establishment which must be maintained at home in view of the existing peace distribution of foreign garrisons." The invocation of Cardwell's dictum satisfied the Committee; without further discussion they approved Haldane's proposals "as a principle on which to organize the regular forces." [11] Later, in December 1906, a C.I.D. subcommittee on army reform gave blanket approval to the details of the new Expeditionary Force. Their report was in turn accepted by the Cabinet Committee on the Army in January 1907.[12] That same month Haldane issued formal orders to implement the formation of the new overseas force.

From the welter of undetermined but admittedly large Indian requirements, preferences for continental action, and adherence to the Cardwellian principle there emerged the six-division Expeditionary Force. At no time had either the needs of India or the Continent been systematically appraised. Indeed, Haldane told the Cabinet in December 1906, after the scheme was completed, that it was impossible "to calculate . . . according to an abstract standard for the requirements of the Empire. What the requirements for the defence of the Empire are depends, to a large extent, at all events on policy." [13] Several months later he publicly admitted that "the size of this Expeditionary Force is not decided by, nor is it pretended that it is at all commensurate with the strategical needs of the Empire." Haldane, using the Cardwellian principle as a guide, and possibly a crutch, had organized a force which simply made the best use of available British troops.[14]

In January 1907 Esher belatedly tried again to secure an adequate survey of Indian requirements. He dogged Campbell-Bannerman until the Prime Minister in mid-January 1907 appointed a subcommittee to study the needs of an Indian campaign. After six lengthy meetings it was concluded that "the military organisation of Great Britain should be such as to enable 100,000 men to be dispatched to India during the

11. Minutes of the 90th meeting of the C.I.D., Cab. 2/2/1; also see the Cabinet letter, Campbell-Bannerman to Edward VII, July 3–4, 1906, Campbell-Bannerman Papers, Add. MSS, 52512. The Prime Minister had been Financial Secretary under Cardwell at the War Office.

12. "Report of the Sub-Committee . . . [on] the Scheme of Military Organization," Dec. 14, 1906, Cab. 17/13; minutes of the 94th meeting of the C.I.D., Dec. 20, 1906, Cab. 2/2/1. When Asquith informed the Prime Minister of the Cabinet committee's approval, he expressed the hope "that the term 'Expeditionary Force'—which is by suggestion, at least, a misnomer—will drop out of the scheme," Asquith to Campbell-Bannerman, Jan. 9, 1907, Campbell-Bannerman Papers, Add. MSS, 41210.

13. Memo by Haldane, "Note on Army Reorganization," Dec. 18, 1906, Cab. 37/85/102.

14. Haldane, "The Military System of the Future in the British Empire," Journal of the Royal United Service Institution, 51 (October 1907), 1185. St. John Brodrick from the start caught Haldane's reliance on the Cardwell system, "Mr. Haldane's Proposals," Nineteenth Century and After, 60 (September 1906), 356–366.

first year of war." Lord Hankey, who tended to overstress the role of the C.I.D., erroneously claims that this decision was the "original basis upon which Haldane's scheme was worked out." [15] In actuality, by the time the C.I.D. had ascertained this figure, the main part of Haldane's work was complete and in the process of execution.

The subcommittee's studies were not, however, without value. The figure of 100,000 men furnished Haldane with an effective argument with which to defend the size of the Expeditionary Force: the Indian requirements, when combined with the 40,000 men on other colonial assignments, roughly equaled the size of the B.E.F. Later those who challenged the strength of the Regular Army were blithely and incorrectly informed that its size had been determined by the C.I.D.; the Army claimed it had merely met the responsibilities imposed upon it. The subcommittee's work and the problem of India also helped the War Office in other ways. Because the Indian demands involved large numbers of men, supplies, and transportation facilities, they forced the Army to solve problems which could also occur in a continental operation. As Lord Esher remarked, "to be prepared for that eventuality [India] is to be prepared for all others." [16] On one point India was especially useful, providing the Army with an excuse to demand Admiralty cooperation on transportation arrangements. Although the arrangements studiously avoided any reference to European ports, they remained, thanks partly to Admiralty intransigence, useful guidelines for the Directorate of Military Operations in computing troop movements to the Continent.

By late 1907 the demands of India no longer attracted substantial attention from British defense planners. Diplomatic developments had encouraged this process. Anglo-Russian relations had steadily improved under Grey's watchful guidance: from the start he had wanted Russian help in restoring, or perhaps overturning, the balance of power against Germany; he feared the Kaiser's periodic flirtations with the Tsar; he suspected German intrigues in Persia and elsewhere in the Near East. Satisfactory relations with St. Petersburg would alleviate or remove these dangers. Prolonged Anglo-Russian negotiations conducted by Sir Arthur Nicolson, who was at this point the British ambassador to Russia, led to an August 1907 treaty that reduced tension along the northwest frontier of India while outlining a potential division of spoils in Persia. The pressure on India was further eased by Russia's new concern over the troublesome Balkans.[17]

15. "Report and Minutes of Evidence of a Sub-Committee . . . to Consider the Military Requirements of the Empire as Affected by the Defence of India," May 1, 1907, Cab. 16/2; Hankey, *Supreme Command*, I, 61.
16. Esher to Edward VII, Jan. 21, 1907, *Journals and Letters of Esher*, II, 217–218.
17. Monger, *The End of Isolation*, 281–295; Beryl J. Williams, "The Strategic Background to the Anglo-Russian Entente of August 1907," *Historical Journal*, 9 (1966), 360–373.

The improvement in Anglo-Russian relations was not duplicated in Anglo-German affairs. Throughout 1906 and 1907 there were mutual exchanges of visits by German and British mayors, newsmen, and monarchs. King Edward in fact veered round to a more amicable relationship with his nephew, Wilhelm II. But each step, indeed each hint, toward better relations with Berlin sparked recriminations from Paris and from the anti-German clique in the Foreign Office, now strengthened by Eyre Crowe's promotion to Senior Clerk. Sir Edward Grey listened to and accepted the protests of the French and of his subordinates.[18] Rather than risk an improvement in Anglo-German relations, he found himself driven closer to France. He assured his Foreign Office colleagues that he would do all in his power "to maintain" the entente; and he informed Paul Cambon in early November 1906 that "if a subject like the Algeciras Conference was to arise again, France might depend upon it that our support would be just as strong and our attitude as firm as it had been before."[19] By 1907 preservation of the Entente Cordiale had become the cardinal feature of Grey's diplomacy.

But the anti-German direction of Grey's policy took other forms as well. The British and the French concluded separate understandings with Spain to preserve the status quo in the Mediterranean and along the Atlantic coasts—arrangements aimed at preventing German pressure upon the weaker Spain for a port concession. Unable to prevent the conclusion of a status quo accord in the Baltic between Denmark, Russia, Germany, and Sweden, London pressured Berlin to accept France in a similar North Sea arrangement.[20] The thrust of Grey's policy was shown in more mundane ways as well: in mid-1907, for example, he forbade, for fear of antagonizing the French, a visit to Germany by the Coldstream Guards' band.[21] Finally, the naval race intensified Anglo-German ill will as Admiral von Tirpitz began a new building program in the *Dreadnought* class. This led to new animosity and tension between Berlin and London, heightened by the Kaiser's imprudent letter to Lord Tweedmouth about naval expenditures in March 1908.

These international developments pushed the question of Britain's military relations with the Continent again into the foreground. The relationship had not, of course, been entirely neglected by the General Staff during the period of army reorganization. In late 1906 and early 1907 the Directorate of Military Operations had prepared a series of studies on possible military operations in Belgium and the Netherlands

18. See, e.g., Mallet to Lord Knollys, June 6, 1906, RA W49/46; "Memorandum by Mr. Eyre Crowe . . . on the Present State of British Relations with France and Germany," Jan. 1, 1907, B.D., III, pp. 397–433.

19. Minutes by Grey on Bertie to Grey, Oct. 27, 1906, F.O. 371/74; the dispatch without minutes is in B.D., III, no. 441; Grey to Bertie, Nov. 8, 1906, ibid., no. 442.

20. Monger, *The End of Isolation*, 296–331; see also Folke C. Lindberg, *Scandinavia in Great Power Politics, 1905–1908* (Stockholm, 1958).

21. Grey to Knollys, Oct. 6, 1907, Haldane Papers, 2907; Monger, *The End of Isolation*, 328–329.

that served to emphasize the problems, already revealed by the Anglo-Belgian staff talks, that would handicap British operations in Belgium. British assistance, to be of any value, would require 100,000 soldiers in Louvain or Namur by the tenth day of mobilization, and this the planners thought impossible. A few months later in April 1907, the General Staff concluded that the Belgian Army was unreliable and "might only too soon become demoralized and panic stricken." The Staff proposed that "close co-operation with the actual French Army might perhaps be a more effectual way of ridding Belgium of her invaders." And in any case the Staff recognized that "the same set of railway lines from Calais, Boulogne, and Havre, would lead British forces debarking at these ports equally to the French left or the Belgian right [and] would perhaps enable us to defer a decision upon this point until the very last moment." [22]

The demands of continental intervention received further attention when the C.I.D. began its hearings on the danger of invasion in November 1907. Pressure from Lord Roberts and from Repington of the *Times* was responsible for the hearings; they hoped to so discredit Haldane's home defense scheme that the government would be forced to adopt conscription. The popular climate helped this attempt. Thanks to the alarmist speeches of Lord Roberts and his cohorts in the National Service League, clamor rose about the dangers of invasion and the need for some form of compulsory service.[23] A spate of popular, fictionalized accounts about a future Anglo-German war kept the issue alive. William le Queux's *Invasion of 1910* (to which Roberts wrote the preface) appeared in March 1906—translated into twenty-seven languages and serialized in the *Daily Mail*, it sold over a million copies. Le Queux graphically described the invasion and a subsequent succession of German victories. I. F. Clarke has noted how he rubbed in the disaster: "repulsive Prussian troopers shoot down helpless women; terrified Londoners dig their graves under the eyes of the German firing squads; brutal proclamations commanded the requisitioning of everything from private possessions to country houses." [24] The moral of this and similar tales was clear: Britain was exposed to a "German bolt from the blue" and required a larger army for home defense. With such arguments Repington and Roberts persuaded Balfour and finally Campbell-Bannerman that the situation warranted a new examination of the invasion issue.[25] The Prime Minister appointed a special C.I.D. subcommittee which met sixteen times from November 27, 1907, to July 28, 1908.

22. Memo by Grant-Duff, "War with Germany in Defence of Belgian Neutrality," Jan. 4, 1907, W.O. 106/46; General Staff memo, "Our Position as regards the Low Countries," Apr. 8, 1907, Cab. 18/24; "The Military Resources of Belgium," December 1906, W.O. 33/417.
23. Theodore Ropp, "Conscription in Great Britain, 1900–1914: A Failure in Civil-Military Communications?," *Military Affairs*, 20 (1956), 71–76.
24. I. F. Clarke, *Voices Prophesying War, 1763–1984* (London, 1966), 144–152.
25. Balfour to Campbell-Bannerman, June 20, 1907, Cab. 1/7/740.

The hearings examined both the naval and military aspects of home defense. On the naval side the hypotheses advanced by Repington and Roberts for a successful German invasion were dismissed by Admiral Fisher as "sheer impossibility"; he assured all who would listen that the Royal Navy could defend the British Isles from any harm.[26] But the First Sea Lord was finally driven to admit that the Germans had sufficient naval tonnage to initiate a surprise raid or attack and, despite his objections, this admission led the subcommittee to decide that the Army should be prepared to repel at least two simultaneous raids of 12,000 men each. Such military preparations would compel the enemy to use at least 70,000 men in any invasion attempt. A force of this size, they reasoned, could never elude Fisher's fleets.[27] On the military side the subcommittee's review indicated that, while the Army was improving, few of Haldane's reforms were entirely completed. General Lyttelton, Chief of the General Staff, and General Ewart, the D.M.O., indicated that only four of the new divisions could be ready within fifteen days. Because the B.E.F. still needed auxiliary personnel and transport equipment, only two divisions could be sent to the Continent within a fortnight. In the category of second-line troops the formation of the Territorial Force had only just begun; administrative confusion characterized all aspects of this attempt to replace the Volunteers.[28] In each area the War Office promised, and produced, great improvements within the next year. But in the sensitive sphere of home defense the subcommittee took a more cautious stance: upon the departure of 100,000 men for India "there will be left in this country during the first six months a sufficient number of regulars and other troops to deal with a force of 70,000." [29] In practice this would mean that two of the six B.E.F. divisions would stay at home.

The General Staff reacted strongly to this potential reduction in the Expeditionary Force. On June 2, 1908, it reminded the subcommittee that leaving two divisions at home "renders possible alliance between ourselves and one of the continental Powers of less value to the latter than would be the case if we could at once set free the whole of our Regular military strength for service abroad." Britain, the Staff argued, needed an adequate army to fulfill its treaty obligations and to maintain the "traditional policy of upholding the balance of power in Europe.

26. Fisher to Esher, Dec. 13, 1907, Marder, *Fear God and Dread Nought*, II, 154; Fisher to Clarke, Sept. 12, 1907, *ibid.*, 131–133. Fisher was not especially cooperative with the subcommittee; see, e.g., Esher to Fisher, Aug. 29, 1907, *Journals and Letters of Esher*, II, 247–248.
27. Minutes of 5th and 11th meetings of the subcommittee, Feb. 4, Apr. 2, 1908, Cab. 16/3A.
28. Minutes of 9th and 11th meetings of the subcommittee, Mar. 12, Apr. 2, 1908, *ibid.*
29. "Invasion: Report of a Sub-Committee . . . to Reconsider the Question of Oversea Attack," Oct. 22, 1908, *ibid.*

According as the strength and efficiency of our military forces increase or decrease, so does the value of our friendship to any continental nation." [30] By arguing Britain's possible military value to a continental nation the Army had boldly and officially served notice that continental operations, not India nor home defense, held priority in its planning and expectations. The ambiguity which had characterized Britain's military preparations now began to disappear.

Haldane found himself, at this same time, stating these same points as he defended the size of the Expeditionary Force against attacks from fellow Cabinet ministers. In late May 1908 Winston Churchill and David Lloyd George, perhaps encouraged by Fisher, began a vigorous assault upon the Army.[31] Churchill's target for reductions was the B.E.F., which he labeled a "dangerous and provocative" force. Demanding that Haldane abandon the Cardwellian system, he suggested that groupings of battalions might serve the draft needs of the colonies and India. This, the Board of Trade Minister felt, would enable the Expeditionary Force to be reduced to 100,000 men; any consequent financial savings would be available for naval needs. Churchill's attack upon the hitherto unchallenged Cardwellian principle forced Haldane to reveal more clearly the War Office views on the purpose of the B.E.F. He informed the Cabinet that Churchill ignored "the possibility of our being called upon to operate on the Continent of Europe." He observed that "Great Britain in the past has almost invariably taken steps to assist and reinforce her continental allies when a strong and aggressive power has attempted to upset the balance of Power in Europe. She has also certain treaty obligations which might compel her to intervene on the Continent." [32] Churchill was unimpressed by this argument. His reply, though ultimately to no avail, was devastatingly to the point:

> No proportion exists between British land forces and great contingencies. The troops maintained in the U. Kingdom are not, never have been, and probably will never be, equal to dealing with any peril of first-class magnitude. They bear no relation to the military needs which would arise in the course of a struggle with Russia upon the Indian frontier, or with Germany upon the Continent. Arguments are therefore, in my opinion, irrelevant which are based upon the assumption that there exists at present between the British Army and these tremendous possibilities some nice adjustment which a

30. Memo by the General Staff, June 2, 1908, Cab. 1/7/740.
31. Fisher to Esher, May 5, 1908, Marder, *Fear God and Dread Nought*, II, 175–176; cf. Peter de Mendelssohn, *The Age of Churchill: Heritage and Adventure, 1874–1911* (London, 1961), 402–404. For Churchill's early views on the Army, see Randolph S. Churchill, *Winston S. Churchill*, vol. II: *1901–1914: Young Statesman* (Boston, 1967), 16–20.
32. Memo by Churchill, "Memorandum for Cabinet Committee on Estimates," June 18, 1908, Cab. 1/7/664; memo by Haldane, "Reply to Mr. Churchill's Memorandum . . . ," June 26, 1908, Esher Papers, "C.I.D., 1908–9," vol. A.

dozen battalions of infantry or a million or two in money would fatally derange.[33]

The young minister had in fact touched upon the grand weakness of Haldane's Expeditionary Force, a numerical weakness which became all too apparent by the end of August 1914. Caught between the radical demands for army reductions and the conscription demands of Lord Roberts, Haldane had simply employed in a more effective form the regular forces which he found upon his arrival in office. From the start, therefore, the size of the Expeditionary Force was more a product of circumstance than of a frank assessment of possible needs: it was, in short, a political expedient which bore little correspondence to actual British needs or obligations. Despite the validity of his argument, however, Churchill was unable to prevail against this expedient. In July 1908, helped by Asquith and King Edward and by widespread suspicion of Churchill's motives, Haldane survived the radical attacks.[34]

The War Minister's justification of the B.E.F. in continental terms mirrored the main lines of General Staff thinking during the summer of 1908. In June and July Major Grant-Duff undertook a thorough review of British military policy in the event of an Anglo-German war, considering every possible area for British military action: Denmark, Holland, the Schleswig-Holstein coast, Belgium, and France. Operations in all of these areas save France, he concluded, would be dangerous and probably unproductive. He thought the only course open to Britain if Germany violated Belgium would be "to prolong the left of the French Army." This help would, he emphasized, have a great moral impact upon the French. But Grant-Duff had reservations about fighting in France if Germany for some reason ignored Belgium altogether. In this case he thought it was "just questionable whether the British Expeditionary Force mobilized and equipped with sea transport, ready to go anywhere at any moment, might not be a greater source of anxiety to the Germans than if it were actually employed in the field from the outset."[35] This idea, which echoed the Admiralty proposals of 1905 for the amphibious use of the British Army, disturbed Grant-Duff's superior, Colonel Count Gleichen, head of the operations section of the Directorate of Military Operations. Gleichen, a supporter of continental involvement, disliked the uncertainty about the future use of the British Army. He wanted, he told Grant-Duff, to get help from General Ewart on the principles arrived at by the C.I.D. about the Army's future role.[36]

33. Memo by Churchill, "A Note Upon British Military Needs," June 27, 1908, Cab. 37/94/89; also see his "A Note Arising Out of the Conversation at the Cabinet Committee on Estimates on the 29th June 1908," Cab. 37/94/93.
34. Esher to Knollys, June 26, 1908, *Journals and Letters of Esher*, II, 324–325.
35. Memo by Grant-Duff, "Military Policy in a War with Germany," July 2, 1908, W.O. 106/46; memo by Grant-Duff, "The Netherlands, Germany, and the United Kingdom," July 1, 1908, *ibid*.
36. Gleichen's minutes are on Grant-Duff's memo of July 2, 1908.

Gleichen's desire for guidance was soon fulfilled: in late October 1908 another special subcommittee of the C.I.D. was authorized to examine Britain's military relations with the Continent. These hearings confirmed that the primary role of the British Army now lay in Europe, not in India; that Europe, not the Empire, was now the recognized focus of British military and naval activity.[37]

The French were attentive observers of every stage of Haldane's army reforms. Lieutenant Colonel Huguet reported voluminously and usually enthusiastically about the changes taking place. In January 1907 he remarked that Britain was at last realizing that it needed an army and navy "to guarantee the security of its territory, to assure the defense of its colonies, to permit it to intervene on the Continent, and to make there, in case of necessity, its influence felt." [38] Although an ardent supporter of conscription, Huguet came to doubt the wisdom of Lord Roberts' persistent attacks upon the Territorial Force and his repeated talk of the dangers of a German invasion. The attaché correctly feared that this criticism would not only weaken the Territorial Force, it might also cause the B.E.F. to remain at home if a European emergency arose.

But Huguet's generous praise of British military efforts was not always echoed in Paris. In particular, the doughty French Premier, Georges Clemenceau, heaped scorn upon the British Army. He never allowed an opportunity to pass without pressing British officials for a stronger army, without stressing the value of entente cooperation, and without deprecating the worth of the British Navy.[39] His quick, impetuous tongue caused trouble on more than one occasion. In November 1906 his spur-of-the-moment comments in the French Senate appeared to substantiate German rumors of an Anglo-French military convention. The British Foreign Office spent some anxious days fearful that British politicians would take up their cudgels about such an accord; in fact, Grey was prepared "to avoid a public denial" if he were asked the question, but no questions came and the issue faded.[40] Then in April 1907 Clemenceau ruffled Anglo-French relations more seriously with impru-

37. At no point between 1906 and 1908 were the military conversations cited as a justification for the Expeditionary Force or as determining the role of the British Army. But the conversations, which continued on a sporadic basis as will be seen, certainly reinforced the General Staff's predilection for action on the Continent.
38. Huguet to General Georges Picquart, Jan. 7, 1907, Archives Guerre, "Attachés militaires: Angleterre," box 6; also see the frequent articles in *Revue militaire des armées étrangères*, published by the French General Staff.
39. Huguet to Picquart, July 20, 1909, D.D.F., 2nd ser., XII, no. 255. Clemenceau on various occasions complained to King Edward, Campbell-Bannerman, Grey, Goschen, Haldane, and Bertie; see, e.g., the memo by Grey of his talk with the Premier, Apr. 28, 1908, quoted in Grey, *Twenty-five Years*, II, 302–307.
40. Minute by Grey, Nov. 24(?), 1906, B.D., III, no. 444; Bertie to Grey, Nov. 21, 1906. *ibid.*, no. 443; P. Cambon to G. Louis, Nov. 23, 1906, D.D.F., 2nd ser., X, no. 305; P. Cambon to Stephen Pichon, Nov. 24, 1906, *ibid.*, no. 307; Moltke to Bülow, Nov. 24, 1906, G.P., XX, pt. 2, no. 7232 and note.

dent demands during the Parisian visit of the prickly, sensitive Sir Henry Campbell-Bannerman. Clemenceau's call for a larger British Army caused the visiting Prime Minister to retort that "he did not think English public opinion would allow of British troops being employed on the Continent of Europe." A dismayed Clemenceau immediately sought a clarification from Sir Francis Bertie, asking if Campbell-Bannerman was aware of the military conversations. Grey and Bertie hastened to rectify things with assurances that the Prime Minister knew of the conversations. They also denied that he had said the British would not, under any circumstances, send troops to the Continent. In the last analysis, noted Grey, British public opinion would decide on the issue of intervention; but should Britain fight, the French could be assured it would be with all their resources, naval and military.[41] These explanations eased the situation, and the rest of 1907 passed uneventfully for the entente.

The state visit of President Fallières to London in May 1908 saw the resumption of Clemenceau's efforts to strengthen the entente. He had Tardieu in Le Temps raise the issue of an Anglo-French alliance. Citing the dangers which accrued to France because of the entente and the Anglo-German naval race, the journalist called for a stronger British Army and for a military convention. His line of reasoning was typical of the French attitude toward the naval race: they were anxious to see it continue because it drained the German treasury—at the same time they exploited the race to justify further claims for British military support. Tardieu's call for closer Anglo-French ties was generally approved by other French journals.[42] But in Britain there was only a scattering of support for closer relations; even the Times, whose anti-Germanism by now was Pavlovian, failed to see the need to give the entente "a wider scope and a more formal character. Any efforts to do either could but tend, we are confident, to defeat their own object and would expose the whole policy of the entente to misconstructions which it is not in the interests of either England or France to have placed upon it."[43] The French press clamor prompted no new Anglo-French political talks. The Foreign Office regarded Tardieu's demands for a larger army as inopportune and unwise. Sir Charles Hardinge, the Permanent Undersecretary, surmised that "at the best our army can never have more than a moral effect on the Continent since we could never send an expedition

41. Bertie to Grey, Apr. 11, 17, 1907, B.D., VI, nos. 9, 11, 13; Grey to Bertie, Apr. 13, 19, 1907, ibid., nos. 10, 14; Campbell-Bannerman to Grey, Apr. 12, 1907, Grey Papers, F.O. 800/100; P. Cambon to Pichon, April 20, 1907, D.D.F., 2nd ser., X, no. 472; R. B. Jones, "Anglo-French Negotiations, 1907: A Memorandum by Sir Alfred Milner," Bulletin of the Institute for Historical Research, 31 (1958), 224–227.
42. Le Temps, May 26, 28, 30, 1908; Lister to Grey, May 28, 1908, B.D., VI, no. 95.
43. May 28, 1908; cf. J. Ellis Barker, "The Triple Entente and the Triple Alliance," Nineteenth Century and After, 64 (July 1908), 1–17; Geoffray to Pichon, June 3, 1908, D.D.F., 2nd ser., XI, no. 372.

of more than 150,000 men while Continental armies are counted by millions." And Grey felt that "the real counterforce to the German army must be the French and Russian armies, while we maintain naval supremacy." [44] Nor did the French demands help Haldane, who was busy defending the size of the Expeditionary Force within the Asquith government.

But Clemenceau was relentless. At Marienbad that summer he again mentioned to Edward the need for a stronger British Army, and when he found the King receptive to the idea he was convinced that finally his pleas were succeeding. He was mistaken. The August overture sorely irritated Asquith, who had succeeded Campbell-Bannerman in April. The new Prime Minister told Grey that while the French Premier railed against the ignorance of British public men, his own was great if he thought the British were "going to keep here a standing army of half or three quarters of a million men, ready to meet the Germans in Belgium if and when they are minded to adopt that route for the invasion of France." And he complained that Clemenceau "completely ignores the existence—from a military point of view—of his Russian ally." [45] This statement indicates that Asquith viewed the continental problem as a Belgian one; it also suggests that he felt six divisions were a sufficient British military force. In addition there was the implication that in a major war Britain's most useful assistance to France would be naval.

Asquith's reaction epitomizes the confusion of purpose so characteristic of British strategic thinking in mid-1908. In the past two years the Liberal government had strengthened and expanded its political relationship with France; simultaneously it had authorized the formation of an Expeditionary Force and maintained Britain's naval supremacy over Germany. Still, there had been no attempt to correlate the requirements of the entente policy with British military planning. The General Staff, and the French, thought in terms of British action on the Continent. But the soldiers drafted their plans without guidance from their political masters and without any confidence that the schemes would ultimately be realized. The Royal Navy, on the other hand, believed that it would have the paramount function in any Anglo-German war. Until 1908 the Liberal Cabinet, preoccupied with domestic legislation and with rebuilding the Army, had simply let the problem of strategic coordination drift. Nowhere was this more apparent than in the development of British naval war plans.

In the autumn of 1906 Admiral Fisher ordered the second installment

44. Minutes by Hardinge and Grey on Lister to Grey, May 28, 1908, F.O. 371/455. There were commercial talks later in 1908 and also some discussion about French treaty rights in Muscat.
45. Asquith to Grey, Sept. 7, 1908, Grey Papers, F.O. 800/100; see also Lee, *Edward VII*, II, 628–630; Clemenceau to Pichon, Aug. 29, 1908, D.D.F., 2nd ser., XI, no. 434.

in his program of fleet redistribution. Aimed at a more effective concentration of British naval power in home waters, the reorganization created a Home Fleet on reserve status from ships taken from the Mediterranean, the Atlantic, and the Channel Fleets. This new arrangement, unlike the first redistribution in late 1904, met a hostile reception. Ex-Navy men and popular naval writers, already at odds with Fisher over the introduction of the *Dreadnought* class of all-big-gun ship, blasted this arrangement as poor strategy on the ground that it weakened the stronger fleets for the benefit of a reserve one of dubious quality. Officials at the Foreign and Colonial Offices also bitterly assailed the new distribution, as did Sir George Clarke at the C.I.D. (a factor in his removal and appointment as a colonial governor in mid-1907).[46]

With characteristic vigor the First Sea Lord waged an energetic counterattack. To silence his critics outside the government he utilized the services of four loyal and distinguished naval writers, Julian Corbett, Archibald Hurd, James R. Thursfield, and Arnold White, who readily penned a series of sturdy defenses on Fisher's behalf.[47] Meanwhile Fisher resisted the Foreign Office complaints, chiefly those of Sir Charles Hardinge, that the redistribution meant a neglect of Britain's world interests: he insisted that protection of the British Isles against the growing German Navy offered the best protection of imperial interests. Moreover, the Admiralty asserted that harmonious relations with France facilitated these moves: "This being the case, our only potential foe now being Germany, the common-sense conclusion is that the outlying fleets no longer require to be maintained at the strength which was admittedly necessary a year or two ago when France and Russia were our most probable opponents." [48] When these explanations failed to end Hardinge's criticisms, Admiral Fisher reminded Campbell-Bannerman of the financial savings gained by the new redistribution; thereafter the Prime Minister sustained the First Sea Lord against the barbs of other departments.

The new fleet concentration necessitated a revision of naval war plans. In late 1906, in the absence of a naval staff, Fisher ordered Ottley, the D.N.I., to join Captain Slade of the new Naval War College and Captain Ballard, a former Director of Naval Operations, in drafting a set of naval war plans; Hankey (then a Captain in the Marines) acted as sec-

46. Marder, *Road to War*, 71–75; Fisher to Edward VII, Oct. 22, 1906, Marder, *Fear God and Dread Nought*, II, 102–105; Clarke to Ponsonby (Campbell-Bannerman's private secretary), Nov. 20, 1906, Campbell-Bannerman Papers, Add. MSS. 41213; on the Foreign Office complaints, see F.O. 371/364.

47. See, e.g., Corbett's "Recent Attacks on the Admiralty," *Nineteenth Century and After*, 61 (February 1907), 195–208; cf. Admiral Cyprian A. G. Bridge, "Amateur Estimates of Naval Policy," *Nineteenth Century and After*, 60 (December 1906), 883–888.

48. Memo by Ottley, Dec. 13, 1906, Tweedmouth Papers, Naval Library, Ministry of Defence, London, box 2; the same point is made in A. Hurd, "The British Fleet and the Balance of Power," *Nineteenth Century and After*, 61 (March 1907), 377–394; Monger, *The End of Isolation*, 309–313.

retary to the group. Their plans and Admiral A. K. Wilson's observations upon them comprised the Admiralty's approach to naval strategy before 1911. That Fisher would actually have used these plans is doubtful. Still, they were the only war plans completely worked out during his tenure as First Sea Lord and he later cited them in defending his strategic preparations.[49]

The central feature of the plans was four highly detailed schemes for operations against Germany. The overriding purpose of each was to force the German Navy out into the North Sea where a decisive naval battle could be fought. The planners reckoned that sooner or later the destruction of German commerce on the high seas, the blockade of German ports, and the enforced idleness of the German merchant fleet would ensure the appearance of the German battle fleet. The effectiveness of this economic pressure, as Hankey later admitted, was sharply overestimated, while the resources of Germany were grossly underestimated. To supplement this purely naval pressure there were two plans that provided for amphibious operations. Among the projected schemes were closure of the Elbe, the bombardment of German coastal fortifications, and seizure of the isle of Borkum in the mouth of the Ems by three thousand Marines. Borkum, the planners hoped, could serve as an advanced destroyer base. These initial amphibious operations did not envisage army assistance: Ottley and his colleagues, convinced that the Marines could be embarked with less public speculation and that they were better trained, assigned the Army the minor role of occupation forces once Borkum was taken. There was no mention of British military operations upon the Continent.[50] A year later the Admiralty revamped and enlarged the proposals of Fisher's strategy committee. "War Plans—Germany, W. 1, W. 2" set forth in even greater detail plans for operations against Borkum and the isle of Sylt and for the bombardment of Heligoland.[51]

In both the 1907 and the 1908 plans there were contingency provisions for French naval aid. In the initial plans the British fleet was expected to withdraw from the Mediterranean if France came into the fray. The French in this case would be entrusted with protecting common entente interests. In the October 1908 scheme, "War Plan—England and France v. Germany, W. 3," the provisions for French assistance were more explicit: Britain would exert its naval power in the North Sea

49. Fisher to Grey, Jan. 23, 1908, Marder, *Fear God and Dread Nought*, II, 155–157; Fisher to McKenna, May 26, 1908, *ibid.*, 177–179.
50. A complete set of the plans with A. K. Wilson's comments is in Adm. 116/1043b; the plans alone are in *The Papers of Admiral Sir John Fisher*, ed. Lt. Comdr. P. K. Kemp, II (London, 1964), 316–468. Julian Corbett wrote the introduction to the plans, Slade the general review of the international situation, based on his "War with Germany," Sept. 1, 1906 (Adm. 116/1036b), while Hankey and Ballard worked out the details; Hankey, *Supreme Command*, I, 39–40; also, interview with Lord Hankey, Aug. 16, 1962.
51. "War Plans . . . ," June 1908, Adm. 116/1043b, I.

and upper Channel while the French conducted blockade work both in the Shetland-Norway area and in the lower Channel, from Ushant to Lands End. French forces in the Mediterranean were "to remain where they are, in order to prevent the intervention of Italy and Austria on Germany's behalf, and release the British Mediterranean Fleet, which will be recalled to England." [52] The Admiralty plans made quite clear, therefore, the potential naval benefits of the Anglo-French entente.

These war plans received some circulation within the naval high command. Sir Arthur Wilson—"old 'Ard 'Art," as he was known to the blue-jackets—gave them general approval. Like the planners, he disliked the idea of a close blockade, wanted to capture Borkum, and desired a closure of the Elbe; but his attention was focused, as it had been in his 1905 comments on strategy, on the possibility of combined military and naval operations. Wilson still felt that the Army's participation in an Anglo-German war would be limited to the threats of coastal attacks. Even with a French ally he believed the "only way in which we could give serious assistance to France would be by a floating army, making raids on different parts of the German coasts and so diverting troops from the main theatre of war. . . . To make such a diversion effective the raids must be carried out with a certain recklessness of life and yet not pushed so far as to risk being cut off entirely." [53] One such operation, he noted, was the capture of the Cuxhaven fortress at the mouth of the Elbe, which could be achieved by sending obsolete ships up the river to fire on the fort while troops attacked from the rear. This dubious idea remained one of the Admiral's pet schemes, even into World War I.

If Wilson accepted the proposals as useful and helpful, Admiral Lord Charles Beresford, who had succeeded him as commander of the Channel Fleet, viewed them as unsound and inadequate. Yet Beresford, for all his fuss and agitation, failed to produce more than vague alternatives.[54] A more perceptive, discerning appreciation of the inadequacies of Fisher's plans came from the then Captain Herbert Richmond. In May 1909 the future Admiral and naval historian wrote that the

Admiralty plans are to my mind the vaguest amateur stuff I have ever seen. I cannot conceive how they were discussed or what ideas governed the framers of them. Weak dissipation of force all along the line is the most marked characteristic. No governing idea at all except that the enemy's Fleet is to be brought to action—which is stated as being the principal object. . . . Fisher, supreme in his contempt for history and distrustful of all other men, will neither

52. *Ibid.*
53. "Remarks on War Plans by Admiral of the Fleet Sir A. K. Wilson, V.C., G.C.B., G.C.V.O.," May 1907, *ibid.*; see also the Admiralty memo "Forcing the Defences at Cuxhaven," Oct. 5, 1908, *ibid.*
54. Beresford's undated, untitled critique is in Adm. 116/1037, along with other Beresford correspondence on war plans; see also Marder, *Road to War*, 88–104, 186–203.

seek nor accept counsel. He generalises about war, saying it is to be made terrible, the enemy is to be hit hard & often, and many other aphorisms. These are not difficult to frame. But a logical & scientific theory of war is a different matter.[55]

Richmond's indictment was especially relevant to one problem—the Admiralty's apparent vacillation about the Army's role in an Anglo-German war. The 1907 war plans, as has been seen, envisaged only a minor role for the Army. But the 1908 schemes talked of creating a diversion that would force Germany to divide its forces and "thus relieve pressure on the Franco-German frontier. To do this the British and the French Fleets must be used to destroy or neutralize that of Germany while expeditionary forces of British troops operate against the German coasts and distract attention from the land campaign." Yet this same plan, "War Plan . . . W. 3," asserted that one of the most pressing requirements was the dispatch of the Army to France "in order that it shall exert its greatest influence, moral as well as physical. The actual operation of transferring the troops and their impedimenta from the English to the French coast is one of no difficulty." [56] Contradictions between points of view in a single war plan are not unusual; sometimes the unresolved ambiguities are deliberate. Nevertheless, this plan suggests that the Admiralty strategists had given little systematic attention to the Army's consistent hostility since 1905 to amphibious operations and had not thought very carefully about the demands of a cross-Channel move. In any event, Admiral Fisher had not let his views be altered one iota by the Army's new concern for the Continent. In August 1907, when arguing against an invasion hearing, Fisher held that "a force of 70,000 British troops, complete in all arms, is a weapon essentially necessary to give effect to the activity of the Fleet, 'a projectile to be fired by the Navy,' as Sir E. Grey said." He thought such a force, assembled in the North Sea, "would constitute such a menace to Germany as would probably occupy a very considerable portion of the German army in providing for the unknown point of landing of this British raiding force." [57] A few weeks later he told Edward VII that British "intervention in [a] Continental struggle by regular land warfare is impracticable, and combined naval and military expeditions must be directed by us against the outlying possessions of the enemy." [58] Fisher's views had obviously not shifted since January 1906 when he refused to ferry troops to France.

By the middle of 1908 the strategic preparations of the Royal Navy

55. Quoted in Arthur J. Marder, *Portrait of an Admiral: The Life and Papers of Sir Herbert Richmond* (Cambridge, Mass., 1952), 48–49.
56. Adm. 116/1043b, I.
57. Memo by Fisher, Aug. 22, 1907, Cab. 1/7/740.
58. Fisher to Edward VII, Oct. 4, 1907, Marder, *Fear God and Dread Nought*, II, 139–141. Also see Col. G. Aston, "Combined Strategy for Fleets and Armies: Or 'Amphibious Strategy,' " *Journal of the Royal United Service Institution*, 51 (August 1907), 984–1004.

for war were nearly complete. Fleet redistributions had concentrated British naval power in or near the North Sea. War plans were drafted that would exploit Britain's naval superiority. Auxiliary plans for the use of amphibious operations were ready. In all of these preparations one theme was dominant: the Royal Navy, as in days of old, would bear the brunt of Britain's efforts against the forces of the German Kaiser. Traditional British reliance upon sea power remained the safest, surest guide for the future. But this strategic doctrine and its assumptions were already under attack. The General Staff, not unmindful that Waterloo and not Trafalgar had finally toppled Napoleon, was veering away from its preoccupation with India and the colonies. After 1905 each service had made its own studies, developed its own plans, and drafted its own orders without regard to any overall concept of British strategy and without much regard for interservice cooperation. The General Staff recognized this lack of political guidance and generally welcomed the C.I.D.'s help. But Fisher continued to regard the C.I.D. as an intruder, an attitude that ensured trouble when the C.I.D. attempted to coordinate military and naval policy. This attempt was not long in coming.

In October 1908 Asquith, at the insistence of Ottley (Secretary of the C.I.D. after August 1907), appointed a subcommittee to study the military needs of the Empire as influenced by the Continent. Specifically the subcommittee was to furnish the War Office with some indication "as to the general policy of His Majesty's Government with regard to the employment of a British military force on the Continent of Europe, as would enable the General Staff to concentrate their attention only on such plans as they might be called upon to put into operation." [59] On the committee, which met on December 3 and 17, 1908, and on March 23, 1909, were Asquith, Haldane, McKenna, Hardinge, Ewart, Nicholson, Slade, Bethell, French, Crewe, Esher, and Fisher.

The subcommittee viewed the continental issue in its broadest terms. Belgium, which had initially triggered British military concern about the Continent, continued to lose importance. An early Foreign Office memorandum, for example, suggested that the Cabinet decision to send help to France would "be more easily arrived at if German aggression had entailed a violation of the neutrality of Belgium, which Great Britain has guaranteed to maintain." [60] But most of the committee, while sharing the Foreign Office's pragmatic realism, concluded that assistance to France could not be left to turn upon the "mere point of Belgian neutrality." Thus they decided to investigate every possible location and method of exerting influence upon the Continent.

59. "Subcommittee Report on the Military Needs of the Empire," July 24, 1909, Cab. 16/5; the complete records of the investigation are in that file.
60. Foreign Office note, Nov. 11, 1908, *ibid.*; also see the memo by Crowe, "Memorandum respecting Belgian Neutrality and Great Britain's Obligation to Defend it," Nov. 15, 1908, B.D., VIII, no. 311.

The Admiralty, Lord Esher, and the General Staff offered a variety of proposals for achieving British goals in Europe. The naval suggestions were familiar and predictable: Fisher and his subordinates argued that economic pressure against Germany would be sufficient—the vast German overseas trade and the alleged German dependence upon imports of raw materials and foodstuffs automatically ensured that maritime pressure would bring Germany to its knees. The soldiers, preferring not to challenge Admiralty statistics, simply commented that France would be beaten by the German armies before economic pressure could become effective.[61] Nor did the Army think more highly of an Admiralty plan for operations in Denmark. In this case Fisher's lieutenants advocated a French military expedition into the Baltic, with the Royal Navy furnishing naval support to their French comrades in arms.[62]

In the first stages of the committee's work Fisher was reluctant (for Fisher) to comment upon coastal operations. He told Esher on March 15, 1909, that he did not want to discuss such expeditions and "never will, as our military organization is so damnably leaky! but it so happens for two solid hours this morning I have been studying one of them of inestimable value only involving 5,000 men and some guns, and horses about 500—a mere fleabite! but a collection of these fleabites would make Wilhelm scratch himself with fury!" [63] In the end Fisher was unable to maintain his self-imposed silence. At one of the subcommittee meetings (probably March 23) the War Office plans so irritated him that he unleashed a vicious, bitter attack upon Haldane and the Army. Turning to the realm of strategy, he proclaimed that "there was a stretch of ten miles of hard sand on the Pomeranian coast which is only ninety miles from Berlin. Were the British army to seize and entrench that strip, a million Germans would find occupation; but to dispatch British troops to the front in a Continental war would be an act of suicidal idiocy." [64] In spite of this outburst, the tide was running against the Admiral's views on military strategy.

This soon became evident when Lord Esher, Fisher's close and devoted supporter, tried to bridge the gap between Admiralty and General Staff thinking. A gifted, articulate backstage manipulator, Viscount Esher served on the C.I.D. as its only nongovernment member. Although his anomalous position on the C.I.D. attracted parliamentary criticism, his genius for organization and his friendship with Edward made him

61. Admiralty memo, "The Economic Effect of War on German Trade," Cab. 16/5; General Nicholson made this observation at the March 23, 1909, meeting.

62. Admiralty memo, "Naval Operations in Denmark," Feb. 4, 1909, Cab. 16/5; minutes of 3rd meeting of the subcommittee, March 23, 1909, ibid.

63. Fisher to Esher, March 15, 1909, Marder, Fear God and Dread Nought, II, 232–233.

64. Fisher's outburst has usually been dated as December 1908, but his letter to Esher and the minutes of the subcommittee would indicate the March 23 meeting as the occasion; Bacon, Life of Fisher, II, 182–183; Marder. Road to War, 387–388; minutes of 1st meeting of the subcommittee, Dec. 3, 1908, Cab. 16/5.

useful to any government in power.[65] On good terms with both Fisher and Haldane, Esher on occasion tried to mediate Army-Navy differences. Such was the case in 1908. But another factor influenced Esher's decision to enter the strategic arena: in early November 1908 he learned, to his dislike, that the French wanted any British troops sent to the Continent placed under a French commander. And Huguet had candidly admitted to him that France wanted British help not just for morale reasons, but because the British divisions would reduce the two hundred thousand-man disparity between German and French first-line troops.[66] Contrary to Huguet's impression, Esher was not overjoyed at the prospect of extensive British involvement in France; and he expressed this dislike in a paper prepared for the subcommittee in which he suggested that British participation on the Continent be limited to twelve thousand mounted troops under an independent commander. Elsewhere, the Navy would bear the brunt of the struggle. These proposals were a clever attempt by Esher to touch all bases—French wishes for help, Admiralty demands for the dominant role, the Army's desire for action.[67] But the General Staff and Esher's old friend General French flatly rejected this proposal as inadequate, and Esher's role as peacemaker came to naught.[68]

The subcommittee eventually concluded, to Fisher's dismay, "that a military *entente* between Great Britain and France can only be of value so long as it rests upon an understanding that, in the event of war in which both are involved alike on land and sea, the whole of the available naval and military strength of the two countries will be brought to bear at the decisive point." [69] In the discussions the General Staff indicated what it regarded as the decisive point. Skeptical of the Belgian Army and the durability of the Meuse forts, the generals opposed an operation in Belgium; the fact that Germany might not violate Belgian neutrality reinforced this view. Coastal descents were naturally held to be useless, which led the Army to urge the deployment of four infantry divisions and a cavalry division as a "reinforcement to the French left." Landing at French ports, this force would be ready for action

65. On the parliamentary criticism see, e.g., Esher to Knollys, March 19, 1907, *Journals and Letters of Esher*, II, 225–227.
66. Diary, Nov. 9, 1908, *ibid.*, 357–358; Huguet to Picquart, Nov. 9, 1908, *D.D.F.*, 2nd ser., XI, no. 558; see also Esher's diary for another meeting with Huguet, Jan. 14, 1909, *Journals and Letters of Esher*, II, 365–366.
67. "Sub-Committee . . . The Assistance to be given by Great Britain to France if she is attacked by Germany. Note by Lord Esher," Dec. 14, 1908, Cab. 16/5. Esher elaborated these ideas in a private memo for Edward VII, Jan. 3, 1909, Esher Papers, "Imperial Defence."
68. Minutes of 2nd meeting of the subcommittee, Dec. 17, 1908, Cab. 16/5; note by French, Jan. 5, 1909, *ibid.*
69. "Sub-Committee Report on the Military Needs of the Empire," July 24, 1909, Cab. 16/5.

by the twentieth day, probably in a reserve function near Reims or Amiens.[70]

The prospect of helping the French in France brought the military conversations before the C.I.D. for the first time since January 1906. Hardinge in the March 23, 1909, meeting stated that France had no assurance of British military help; "the only grounds upon which the French could base any hopes of military assistance were the semi-official conversations which had taken place between the French Military Attaché and our General Staff." And in this case the French had been informed that "the force that we could send would be a comparatively small one. The French considered that the moral effect of the co-operation of English soldiers would be very great." [71] The Undersecretary's mention of the staff talks provoked no discussion or comment from the group, not even from Asquith, whose own knowledge of the talks was sketchy. Not until August 1911 were the military conversations again mentioned at a C.I.D. meeting.

The subcommittee's final report reflected the pro-continental policy implied by the staff talks. It indicated that "the expediency of sending a military force abroad, or of relying on naval means only, is a matter which can only be determined when the occasion arises by the Government of the day." Recognition of this fact was a significant gain for the Army. In the future if a crisis developed the Army was assured that at the very least its strategic views would get a hearing. More important, the subcommittee also recommended that the General Staff work out plans for intervention. Although the group wanted plans for the defense of Antwerp, they agreed with the Staff's preference for intervention "in which the British force shall be concentrated in rear of the left of the French army, primarily as a reserve." [72] Creation of the western front had come a step closer.

The subcommittee's report, which the C.I.D. adopted, conferred respectability on the strategy of intervention. The Army had won an important victory in the ill-defined realm of civil-military policy formulation. Three years after its formation the Expeditionary Force was now recognized as having a possible European function; equally important, naval views on the employment of the Force were clearly disavowed. Armed with this C.I.D. endorsement, the military bureaucracy proceeded to elaborate and polish its plans for operations in France. The Admiralty emerged from the hearings with its plans for economic warfare also approved. But Fisher was too shrewd not to realize the implications of the subcommittee's report. His subsequent behavior paralleled

70. General Staff memo, Nov. 27, 1908, *ibid.*; memo by French, Jan. 5, 1909, *ibid.*; memo by Ewart, Mar. 5, 1909, Grey Papers, F.O. 800/102.
71. Minutes of 3rd meeting of the subcommittee, Mar. 23, 1909, Cab. 16/5.
72. "Sub-Committee Report on the Military Needs of the Empire," July 24, 1909, *ibid.*

his performance of January 1906; he and the Admiralty remained uncooperative. Thus, though Reginald McKenna and Fisher had promised in the subcommittee to ferry troops to the Continent, the Admiralty made no effort to implement this promise with the appropriate transport tables.[73] When Henry Wilson became D.M.O. in August 1910, there was still no agreement on the naval movement of the Expeditionary Force to the Continent.

In 1909 the C.I.D. provided a forum for the presentation of current military and naval strategies; it did not provide coordination of those strategies. In the absence of enforced coordination or cooperation, the services continued to develop their plans along narrow departmental lines. The C.I.D.'s failure as a coordinating institution mainly reflected Asquith's personal inclination to postpone troublesome problems until the last possible moment. And since the Prime Minister headed the C.I.D. it was his responsibility to reconcile differing concepts.[74] But Asquith's task was not rendered any easier by the Admiralty: indeed the problem of coordination became worse after A. K. Wilson succeeded Fisher as First Sea Lord in January 1910.[75] Not until the second Moroccan crisis did a reluctant Prime Minister finally act on the issue of interservice cooperation. Until that point British defense policy, in spite of the existence and efforts of the C.I.D., remained diffuse, uncoordinated, contradictory.

The Anglo-French staff talks continued on an infrequent basis during the period of army reform and strategic debate in Britain. Their infrequency, plus Huguet's own dislike of General Ewart, the D.M.O., later caused the attaché to belittle the achievements of the military conversations between late 1906 and 1910.[76] But Huguet failed to acknowledge how much of Ewart's time and energies were absorbed in the creation, organization, and training of the new Expeditionary Force. The now available diaries of General Ewart make it quite clear that reforming the Army's structure was no small task. They also reveal his concern over the secretive nature of the Anglo-French preparations. In late April 1907, after four months of work and worry about scheme "W.F.," he wrote: "I often wonder where it will ultimately land our Foreign Office—and me." A few months later, after seeing Huguet, he noted that their relationship was amicable; but he felt that "these military conversations with France are not very satisfactory. Only two or three members of the Cabinet know about them. I wish we had a regular alliance. It may come as a result of German hostility." In succeeding years the General

73. McKenna made the promise at the Dec. 3, 1908, meeting.
74. Mackintosh, "The Role of the Committee of Imperial Defence before 1914," 490–503; Johnson, *Defence by Committee*, 95–101.
75. Memo by Ewart, Dec. 13, 1909, W.O. 106/45; Esher to Balfour, Dec. 31, 1909, *Journals and Letters of Esher*, II, 431–432.
76. Huguet, *Britain and the War*, 7–10.

became more convinced that an alliance was desirable: "If our politicians were only patriots, an Anglo-French-Russian Alliance would be the best answer to German aggressiveness." Near the end of his term as D.M.O. Ewart perceived and supported the large manpower demands which a continental intervention would necessitate. "The only true defence is offence . . . Lord Roberts and his henchmen are out of date. The ideal of the future is imperial coordination by land and sea, the whole power of the Empire being concentrated at the decisive point." [77] In the final analysis Ewart's unglamorous work on the Expeditionary Force made it easier, despite the numerous problems still unresolved, for Henry Wilson to devote his attention to strategy, mobilization, and the military conversations. And if the British were paying less attention to the staff talks in these years, the French were not pressing especially hard.

Moreover, whatever Huguet's later complaints, there was substantial Anglo-French agreement by January 1908 about the size of the British forces destined for France, their arrival dates, and their rail movements from the French ports. In August 1907, with the explicit permission of the Foreign Office and with a written disclaimer of British obligation, the General Staff furnished Huguet with a revised set of troop tables. Four infantry divisions and a cavalry division (110,000 men) would be in France by the end of the eighteenth day, and this would ensure the involvement of the Expeditionary Force in the war's opening battles. The details of the arrival were quite complete: at Calais 1,701 officers, 47,675 soldiers, and 4,202 horses would land during the eighteen-day period.[78]

But though there was substantial agreement on these logistical problems, there was still correspondingly little accord on where the British troops would be concentrated. In the C.I.D. discussions General French had indicated that he *expected* the Army to have a reserve function around Reims or Amiens. But in August 1909 Esher, who saw French often and whose son Maurice was French's aide, remarked that "Laon is the place where, if the General [French] ever fights the Germans, I presume he will assemble his forces." [79] On the other hand, the French General Staff, without ever communicating its views to London, had apparently decided by 1908 upon a zone of concentration for the B.E.F. Two rail studies reveal plans for moving the British from the Channel ports to the triangle formed by Cambrai, St. Quentin, and Arras, not

77. Diary, Apr. 20, July 31, 1907, June 7, 1908, July 12, 1909, Ewart Papers, Williamwood, Kirtlebridge, Dumfriesshire, Scotland.
78. "Note du Chef de l'Etat-major général britannique," July 26, 1907, D.D.F., 2nd ser., XI, no. 95; subsequent revised tables were furnished in 1908, 1909, 1910. See also "Note résumant les principals dispositions prévue le cas d'une coopération militaire F.W.," Jan. 8, 1908, Archives Guerre, "Plan XVII: Armée W," box 147b.
79. Esher to M. V. Brett, Aug. 25, 1909, *Journals and Letters of Esher*, II, 401; also see memo by Ewart, July 1909, W.O. 106/46.

distant from the Belgian frontier.[80] From this location the British, perhaps contrary to their own expectations, would have had an active, not reserve, function in meeting any German drive through southern Belgium. Of course, since the French Staff doubted the Germans would come that far west into Belgium, this deployment might have been considered by Paris as a reserve role. In any case, the Huguet-Ewart talks never settled how the Expeditionary Force would be utilized.

The problem of British troop concentration impinges upon the larger question of what influence, if any, the prospect of British aid had upon French military strategy. To answer this, one must consider the status of French strategic planning on the eve of the second Moroccan crisis.

80. Note by the Third Bureau (Operations), French General Staff, Dec. 9, 1907, Archives Guerre, "Plan XVII: Armée W," box 147b.

5 | French Strategy in Transition, 1905–1911

The leadership of the French Army in early 1911 remained divided between the Chief of Staff and the Generalissimo. The latter continued to have responsibility for developing French war plans and for submitting them to the War Board for approval. In July 1910 the new Generalissimo, General Victor Constant Michel, had started this complicated process of instituting a new war plan: after reviewing Plan XVI, drafted in 1907–1908, he had decided that its provisions against a German drive through Belgium were entirely, indeed dangerously, inadequate. In February 1911 he submitted his main proposals for a new plan to General Brun, then Minister of War.

Michel's basic strategic assumption was that if war came, Germany would cross neutral Belgium not only below the Meuse and the Sambre, but also deep into the "heart" of the kingdom. The General supported this assertion by pointing to the Anglo-German naval rivalry, to German ambitions for Antwerp, and to the massive rail network in Westphalia. He also emphasized the practical consideration that only Belgium offered enough room for the German Staff to maneuver its vast man-power. Although Michel expected British help in blocking the German offensive through Belgium, he believed that France's ultimate salvation depended upon the proper utilization of its own military resources.

France's first task, the General argued, was to overcome its numerical inferiority vis-à-vis the German Army. Correctly anticipating that the Germans would make full use of reserve troops, he advocated that France do likewise. Upon mobilization he wanted a reserve regiment to join each regular regiment; the resulting demibrigade would be commanded by a regular colonel. Michel estimated that this arrangement could add as many as 70,000 men to each French corps. As a result France would possess the equivalent of forty corps, just two short of the German total.[1] But there were two drawbacks to this proposal: Michel's belief that reserve troops could fulfill a fighting function was not widely shared—most French military men were openly scornful of the value of reservists. Nor did his associates like the prospective delay in French mobilization that the incorporation of reserves into demibrigades would cause—in their opinion a delay of two or three days was intolerable, for it ensured that France would have to adopt a defensive strategy. Michel disagreed. He could use the argument that General Félix Saussier had first advanced in 1899: a German flanking move, because of the distances and logistical problems involved, would require more time to execute than a straight German attack through Lorraine. This delay in the German attack would, Michel believed, offset any slowness in French mobilization.[2]

But the most radical feature of Michel's proposed plan was its disposition of French troops. He wanted to concentrate 680,000 men (eleven corps) along the Franco-Belgian frontier from Lille to Mézières, to which he would add any British contingents. Not only would these enormous concentrations be in a position to thwart a German swing maneuver, they could also be used to launch a French counteroffensive once the Germans had violated Belgian neutrality. Michel, like Count von Schlieffen, thus contemplated *offensive* operations in the one area available for the successful manipulation of large armies. The inevitable corollary of this intention to counterattack through Belgium was the

1. Memo by Michel, "Concentration et plan d'opérations," Feb. 10, 1911, *Les armées françaises*, tome I, vol. I: *Annexes*, no. 3; also see Michel's memo of June 15, 1911, included in "Séance du Conseil Supérieur de la Guerre du 19 juillet 1911," *ibid.*, no. 4. On May 2, 1910, the War Board had discussed the dangers of a German move through Belgium and the use of forts to check it, Archives Guerre, "Procès-verbaux du Conseil Supérieur de la Guerre," box J.
2. On the professional attitude toward reserve troops, see Challener, *The French Theory of the Nation in Arms*, 75–87; Joseph Monteilhet, *Les institutions militaires de la France (1814–1932): de la paix armée à la paix désarmée*, 2nd rev. ed. (Paris, 1932), 251–265; "Séance du Conseil Supérieur de la Guerre du 19 juillet 1911," *Les armées françaises*, tome I, vol. I: *Annexes*, no. 3; Joseph J. C. Joffre, *The Memoirs of Marshal Joffre*, trans. T. Bentley Mott, 2 vols. (London, 1932), I, 8–10.

abandonment of the traditional French concentration of forces along the Alsace-Lorraine frontier. Michel wanted to reduce by at least seven corps the forces assigned by Plan XVI to this area. Even then he planned to have 300,000 men available for deployment on the front from Luxembourg to the Swiss border, and he expected to bolster this defensive front with four additional corps, including the XIX Corps from North Africa. Marshal Joffre's later stricture that Michel exposed Paris to a German breakthrough must be regarded as simply a plaintive plea of self-defense for Joffre's own heavy concentration of troops along the Lorraine sector.[3]

Events later demonstrated the wisdom of Michel's radical war plan; his contemporaries were not so kind. To understand their rejection of Michel's proposals and his subsequent dismissal in July 1911, as well as the failure of the entente staff talks to influence French planning, it is necessary to examine both the nature of French military thought and the war plan (XVI) then in effect.

The war plans drafted by Generals Brugère (1903), de Lacroix (1909), and Michel reflected the influence of the counteroffensive or defensive-offensive school of French strategy. This doctrine, which owed much of its content to General Bonnal of the Ecole Supérieure de Guerre, had gained wide acceptance in the 1890's. It appealed to those who longed to see France adopt something more aggressive than a defensive stance behind the long chain of frontier forts from Belfort to Verdun. But the proponents of the strategy tempered their desire for the offensive with a realistic appreciation of France's military situation. They were especially cognizant of the numerical inferiority of French armies and the strategic advantages conferred upon Germany by the possession of Lorraine. Thus Bonnal and those influenced by him stressed the need for adequate defensive safeguards. Advance troops and cover forces would first locate and engage the enemy, while the rear armies would concentrate and prepare to attack. Once the advance guard discerned the extent and direction of the enemy attack, the counterattack could be launched without fear of being outmaneuvered. Counterforce, applied at the decisive point, would result in a French "offensive" victory. This strategy afforded a degree of flexibility and adaptability unknown either to the purely defensive or to the purely offensive schools of military thinking: it enabled the commander to meet a known force with force in an offensive movement which, it was hoped, could overcome the impetus of the enemy attack. Although the strategy implied that there would be no preconceived plan of counterattack, most of its exponents expected the German attack, and the French reply, to occur

3. "Concentration et plan d'opérations," Feb. 10, 1911, *Les armées françaises,* tome I, vol. I: *Annexes,* no. 3; Joffre, *Memoirs,* I, 17–18. Also see *Les armées françaises,* tome I, vol. I, 13–15.

in Lorraine.[4] Brugère's Plan XV and its variants clearly demonstrated this.

Plan XV originally envisaged a massive concentration of troops along the Lorraine frontier. In 1905 Brugère had persistently refused to modify these arrangements, despite intelligence reports indicating a probable German attack through the Belgian Ardennes. Finally in early 1906 he agreed to shift some of his troops northward, establishing a new Fifth Army (two corps) south and west of Verdun at Bar-le-Duc—over fifty miles from the Belgian-Luxembourg frontiers. Brugère refused to make any further provisions to meet a German flank attack. He still felt, as he had earlier, that a German drive through Belgium would weaken the Germans in Lorraine, and this would in turn facilitate a French offensive in that sector.[5] Had the new Schlieffen Plan been tested in 1906, the German armies would have reached Paris on schedule.

General Alexis Hagron, Brugère's successor, made further adjustments to Plan XV in early 1907. More French forces were moved northward so that Verdun was now fully shielded. But the bulk of French military power still remained heavily centered upon the Lorraine frontier. Neither Brugère nor Hagron satisfied the prime requirement of the counter-offensive strategy: adequate defensive arrangements. Failure to appreciate or accept the implications of intelligence reports accounted in part for this; but like their successors, Brugère and Hagron also gave excessive emphasis to their expected offensive operations in Lorraine. Moreover, they remained confident that the speed of French mobilization along the Lorraine front would ensure a decisive French victory there, balancing any German successes elsewhere.

These two Generalissimos paid little, if any, attention to the benefits conferred by the Entente Cordiale. There were, for example, no precise provisions for utilizing the British troops mentioned in the staff conversations. While the French in 1906 and 1907 probably expected the British to fulfill a reserve function on their left flank, nothing had actually been settled. More predictably, both Generals failed to exploit another possible benefit of the new entente: the reduction of French troops assigned to protect coastal areas against the threat of British invasion. Over two hundred thousand men (regulars, reserves, and territorials) were allocated to this work. And both men also retained the "mobilisation réduite" ("M. R.") which permitted a partial mobilization in an Anglo-French war in which Germany stayed neutral. It provided for the maintenance of coastal forces and potential invasion troops at Calais

4. Carrias, La pensée militaire française, 278–285, 295; Jay Luvaas, "European Military Thought and Doctrine, 1870–1914," in The Theory and Practice of War: Essays Presented to Captain B. H. Liddell Hart, ed. Michael Howard (London, 1965), 77–81.

5. For Brugère's early views on a flanking move, see "Compte rendu du Plan XV," 1902, Archives Guerre, "Plan XV," box 123; for outlines of Plan XV and its variants, see Les armées françaises, tome I, vol. I, 9–10; "Etude sur les Plans I à XVII," Archives Guerre, "Historie des Plans I à XVI," box 104. See also Andrew, Théophile Delcassé, 252–253.

without hampering operations against Germany. Not until July 1908, four years after the conclusion of the Anglo-French accord, did the French high command finally abandon "M. R." [6] Its abandonment was one result of the new war plan then being drafted by General de Lacroix.

In mid-1907 Hagron resigned abruptly in protest over the condition of the French Army, and General Henri de Lacroix succeeded him. A former military governor of Lyon, the new Generalissimo brought a sense of urgency, determination, and perception to the development of French strategy. In less than two years he drafted and installed Plan XVI. Despite Michel's recommendations and the later revisions by Joffre, Plan XVI remained the French war plan until early 1914. This longevity and the persistence of misconceptions about Plan XVI make its development and provisions of special interest.

In August 1907 de Lacroix sent Georges Picquart, the Minister of War in Clemenceau's government, two brief studies emphasizing the need for a new war plan. In these he observed that for thirty years the majority of French forces had been concentrated on the Alsace-Lorraine frontiers, below the Paris-Metz line. These dispositions, the General held, took scant account of new developments in German strategic thinking; Plan XV with its extension of the French left flank north of Verdun was but a step in the right direction. France had to be prepared for a possible German attack through Belgium. There were practical reasons as well for drafting a new war plan: the vastly improved French rail system would permit new flexibility and quicker offensive action; the loss of manpower from the two-year service law had to be compensated.[7]

The new Generalissimo also insisted to Picquart and to the War Board on February 15, 1908, that the changing international scene both prompted and permitted the formation of a new plan. British friendship and goodwill, for instance, would permit substantial reductions in the coastal defense forces, allowing them to be reassigned to the northeastern front. In addition de Lacroix discarded Plan "M. R." in order to ease the problems of the Fourth Bureau, which handled transportation.[8] On the other hand, he told the War Board that direct British assistance was only "problematical," and in his final plan he assigned no role to British forces.[9] The railway studies undertaken in 1906 simply indicate that the French Staff expected the British to concentrate be-

6. "Compte rendu du Plan XV," 1902, Archives Guerre, "Plan XV," box 123; "Note au sujet de la mobilisation réduite dans le Plan XVI," July 7, 1908, Archives Guerre, "Plan XVI," box 133.
7. "Note sur suject de l'établissement des bases d'un nouveau Plan," Aug. 2, 1907, ibid.; de Lacroix to Picquart, Aug. 12, 1907, ibid.
8. Les armées françaises, tome I, vol. I, 10; "Défense des côtes," December 1907, Archives Guerre, "Plan XVI," box 128; "Bases du Plan—Note de Présentation," February 1908, ibid.
9. De Lacroix used this term in the War Board, Feb. 15, 1908, Archives Guerre, "Procès-verbaux du Conseil Supérieur de la Guerre," box J; a partial account of the meeting is in Les armées françaises, tome I, vol. I: Annexes, no. 2.

tween Amiens and the Belgian frontier. Aside from these rather marginal aspects, the entente and the prospect of British help had only limited impact upon the drafting of Plan XVI. At the same time, France's improved relations with Italy encouraged de Lacroix to shift the XIV and XV Alpine Corps northward. Further, the prospect of Italy's probable neutrality spurred hopes that the XIX Corps could be moved from North Africa to the metropolitan area in case of war.[10] The French General Staff, like its British counterpart, was soon to discover that the French Navy could be difficult about the movement of troops in the initial days of war.[11]

The manifold problems of France's Russian ally nearly balanced the gains attained by good relations with Rome and London. The Russian Army, still suffering from the chaos and disorganization caused by the Russo-Japanese war, was not expected to be ready for even minor offensive action before 1910. After 1906 the members of the French Embassy in St. Petersburg expended most of their energies pleading with the Russians to revamp their mobilization plans, to construct strategic railways, and, above all, to promise offensive action against Germany.[12] General Brun, the Chief of Staff, traveled twice to Russia in search of a commitment for some kind of offensive action. On these occasions (1907 and 1908) the Russians diligently avoided any promises, even of diversionary action along the German-Polish frontier. In fact, each time the French pressed for offensive action the Russians evaded or gave the vaguest promises, while displaying their customary cupidity with regard to French loans for railway construction. By 1909 all that had been secured by the French were Russian promises to accelerate mobilization. Thus, in spite of the longtime military convention with Russia, French military planners could not count with certainty on Russian help if war came. Above all, Paris could not be confident of Russian offensive action which might compel the Germans to reduce their forces in the west.[13]

Defense against a German attack was of course de Lacroix's primary

10. Whether the General Staff knew of the 1902 secret treaty with Italy, in which the latter virtually pledged neutrality, is unclear. In January 1906 Paléologue discussed the effect of better Franco-Italian relations with General Brun; Paléologue, *Un grand tournant*, 426–427. But Joffre claimed the Staff did not learn of the treaty until June 10, 1909; Joffre, *Memoirs*, I, 37; cf. Lt. Col. Jullian (military attaché in Rome) to Picquart, Oct. 26, 1908, *D.D.F.*, 2nd ser., XI, no. 508.

11. See, e.g., the memo by the Fourth Section (Transportation), May 3, 1910, Archives Guerre, "Plan XVI," box 134.

12. See, e.g., General Moulin to Picquart, Nov. 25, 1906, *D.D.F.*, 2nd ser., X, no. 310; "Note du Ministre de la Guerre," July 21, 1908, *ibid.*, XI, no. 412; Moulin to Picquart, Sept. 2, 1908, *ibid.*, no. 442; Lt. Col. Pierre Matton to Picquart, Mar. 6, 1909, *ibid.*, XII, no. 88.

13. The records of these staff talks are in Bompard (French ambassador to Russia) to Pichon, Aug. 5, 1907, *ibid.*, XI, no. 116; and "Procès-verbal de l'entretien, du 24/11 septembre 1908 entre les Chefs d'Etat-major généraux des armées russe et française," *ibid.*, no. 455.

responsibility. Unlike some of his associates, the Generalissimo took seriously the intelligence estimates that Germany planned a move through part of Belgium. Familiar with the works of Bernhardi and with Prussian military habits, he believed a German flanking action accorded with both German traditions and intentions.[14] Moreover, as Lieutenant P. de Lanet had demonstrated in *Spectateur militaire* in late 1906 and early 1907, there were purely technical considerations which dictated a German drive into the neutralized state. The French forts, the need for room to maneuver the German corps, the German rail system around Aix-la-Chapelle, the exposed position of Paris: all of these were reasons for a German flanking attack via Belgium.[15] De Lacroix, who did not share the young officer's belief that the Germans might cross the Meuse, nevertheless worried about defending against a German assault from the north.

But his ability to organize such a defense was complicated by the attitude of the Belgians themselves. The somewhat meager reports of Lieutenant Colonel E. A. R. Siben, the French military attaché in Brussels, emphasized that Belgium would mobilize and defend its neutrality in a Franco-German war.[16] Yet at the same time the ruling Catholic party adamantly refused to increase Belgian field forces and also sanctioned new fortifications around Antwerp. Consequently some French planners believed that if war came, the Belgians would simply retire to Antwerp and only emerge to join the obvious victor. Nor was Paris happy in 1907 when the Belgian Parliament finally ratified an agreement (signed in 1903) authorizing the construction of two German-financed railways between Stavelot-Malmédy and Aix-la-Chapelle-Louvain.[17] And Leopold's bitterness at British press attacks upon his Congo policy did not help entente relations with Brussels. From these conflicting developments de Lacroix obviously could possess little certainty about Belgium's role if war came.

In a Franco-German war the General expected, as did Joffre later, that the Germans would not commit their full resources in a turning maneuver above the Meuse-Sambre. Instead he thought the Germans would launch a swing maneuver of two armies through the Belgian Ardennes, in the direction of Verdun-Sedan. He believed, again as Joffre

14. Minutes of the War Board, Feb. 15, 1908, Archives Guerre, "Procès-verbaux du Conseil Supérieur de la Guerre," box J. "Note lue par le général de Lacroix . . . 15 février 1908," *Les armées françaises*, tome I, vol. I: *Annexes*, no. 2.

15. P. de Lanet, "La neutralité de la Belgique en 1906," *Spectateur militaire*, 65 (Nov. 15, 1906), 307–318; 66 (Jan. 15, 1907), 136–149.

16. See, e.g., Siben to Picquart, May 2, 1907, *D.D.F.*, 2nd ser., X, no. 486; also see two works by Albert Duchesne, "L'Armée et la politique militaire belges de 1871 à 1920 jugées par les attachés militaires de France à Bruxelles," *Revue belge de philologie et d'histoire*, 39 (1961), 1102–1109, and *Les archives de la Guerre et de la Marine à Paris et l'histoire de Belgique* (Brussels, 1962), 69–74.

17. See, e.g., Crozier to Pichon, Mar. 3, 1907, M.A.E., "Belgique," n.s. 20; Picquart to Pichon, May 8, 1907, *D.D.F.*, 2nd ser., X, no. 493.

did, that the major German offensive would come on the Lorraine frontier. In reality, the Schlieffen-Moltke arrangements called for three armies to cross into and through Belgium, sweeping as far as Lille; two armies to cross through Luxembourg and turn on Verdun; and two others, helped by the forts at Metz and Thionville, to protect Strasbourg and Lorraine.[18]

This glaring misestimate about German intentions remains difficult to explain or accept. Although French military intelligence was compromised by the Dreyfus affair, it had by 1904, as seen earlier, accurately discerned the probable thrust of German war plans. But its reports thereafter were never so perceptive or prescient. Brugère's stubborn refusal to respond to the warnings of French intelligence may have dampened the Bureau's inclination to dispute prevailing preconceptions. Later, the enthusiasm of the *offensive* school tended to minimize the importance of intelligence to French planners. Before 1914 French intelligence and many French officers recognized that Germany would violate Belgian neutrality, but they refused to believe that the Germans would cross the Meuse or Sambre. France paid a high price for this miscalculation.

Within this framework of inadequate intelligence estimates, changing international relations, and limited manpower reserves, de Lacroix drafted Plan XVI. Like its predecessors, the new plan reflected the views of the defensive-offensive school of French strategy. Practical considerations required de Lacroix's retention of this strategy: because overall French mobilization was two days slower than the Germans, he had no choice but to adopt a *défense stratégie* in the opening phase of the war. He assured his colleagues on the War Board that this did not, however, mean a passive defense, for "if the enemy engages us, we [France] have the will to make a decisive riposte." The details of this strategy he spelled out to the War Board on February 15, 1908. The major defensive innovations were more troops in the area around Vouziers and the concentration of a new Sixth Army at Châlons on the Marne. The Sixth Army, which he alternately described as the "secret army" or the "army of maneuver," could be deployed at any point along the Belgium-Luxembourg frontier, where, it was hoped, a German sweep toward Verdun could be stopped. Although de Lacroix preferred to move still more troops northward, he informed the War Board that prudence, and tradition, demanded that at least ten corps (in four armies) be left along the Verdun-Epinal line.[19]

18. Minutes of the War Board, Feb. 15, 1908, Archives Guerre, "Procès-verbaux du Conseil Supérieur de la Guerre," box J; "Note lue par le général de Lacroix . . . 15 février 1908," *Les armées françaises*, tome I, vol. I: *Annexes*, no. 2; de Lacroix to Picquart, Oct. 21, 1907, Archives Guerre, "Plan XVI," box 133; Ritter, *The Schlieffen Plan*, 134–148.
19. "Note lue par le général de Lacroix . . . du 15 février 1908," *Les armées françaises*, tome I, vol. I: *Annexes*, no. 2; minutes of the War Board, Feb. 15, 1908,

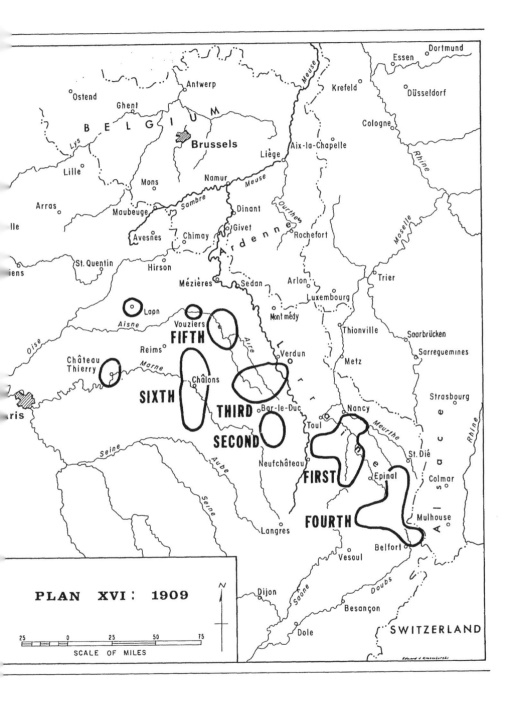

PLAN XVI: 1909

SCALE OF MILES

25   0   25   50   75

These defensive dispositions were also the key to the new plan's offensive capability, for de Lacroix planned a double counteroffensive: one the traditional attack in Lorraine, launched as soon as the main lines of the German assault were discerned; the other an entirely different type of counterattack conducted by the "army of maneuver," which, just skirting the Belgian border, would attack across southern Luxembourg into the area north of Thionville.[20] De Lacroix hoped this offensive would smash or divide the German thrust as it came through the Ardennes toward Sedan-Verdun; he also thought it would avert complications which a planned premeditated counterattack through Belgium might incur. He knew that any offensive move into Belgium risked alienating not only the Belgians but also the British—and, while the French generals had little esteem for Belgian and British forces, none wanted to create additional enemies or to lose. possible support. On the other hand, the Generalissimo was convinced the Germans would violate Luxembourg. He declared flatly to the War Board that "it is presumed that we can pass into Luxembourg, since the Germans already control the railways and would certainly use them in time of war." Should the Germans also violate Belgium, operations in that sector would then be reconsidered.[21]

Not all of the General's colleagues were happy with this new offensive scheme. General Charles Ferdinand Millet urged the War Board to keep the main offensive operation in Lorraine, for this was the surest way to reconquer the "lost provinces." The Generalissimo, who assured Millet that the offensive in Lorraine would not be neglected, insisted that an attack on the left would lead "to a most rapid decision." He further defended the new plan as conferring greater flexibility upon the Commander in Chief. "Besides the plan, based upon the strategic defensive at first, is conceived as permitting a vigorous offensive attack. If the front must yield some territory it will find itself solidly supported; the army of maneuver will intervene at this moment in order to take the offensive by the left, or even if need, by the center or right if the circumstances dictate this to the commander in chief." [22] At length the Generalissimo convinced his fellow generals. In late 1908 the logistical tables for the new scheme were completed; in March 1909 Plan XVI became operational.

The prospect of British military assistance and the military conversations failed to exert any measurable influence on the formation of Plan XVI. But the British were not entirely forgotten. Each year a number of

Archives Guerre, "Procès-verbaux du Conseil Supérieur de la Guerre," box J. An outline of the plan can also be found in Marchand, Plans de concentration, 169–181.
    20. Compare Joffre, Memoirs, I, 16–17.
    21. Minutes of the War Board, Feb. 15, 1908, Archives Guerre, "Procès-verbaux du Conseil Supérieur de la Guerre," box J.
    22. Ibid.

high-ranking French officers visited the British maneuvers, and their impressions about the Expeditionary Force underwent a progressive change. In 1908 General Michel reported to the War Board that only three British divisions of dubious quality were ready; and that year there was sharp, almost unkind criticism in *Correspondant* about the amount of potential British help available.[23] The French officers who visited Britain in 1909 came away with better impressions—General Léon Durand, for example, informed the Chief of Staff in October that the *"British field army constitutes a real force,* having the serious military qualities of order, discipline, endurance, training, and resistance." [24] After 1908, furthermore, there was a steady expansion in French interest about the British Army. By 1910 General Langlois, writing in *Revue des deux mondes,* could assure his compatriots that the Expeditionary Force was "capable of taking vigorous action in a European conflict." [25]

But there was no agreement during de Lacroix's tenure on how this British force would be deployed. Nor did the Generalissimo offer London any indications about French war plans. In 1906 Huguet had unofficially informed Repington that the French would be concentrated along a narrow forty-kilometer front in Lorraine; the troops would be in the Napoleonic lozenge, the reserves echeloned in the rear.[26] Then in 1908 the attaché told Lord Esher that the French plan was defensively oriented, designed "to hold lightly the frontier—nearly 300 miles—with their reserves in rear, ready to deliver a strong counter-attack." Esher gathered that the French thought "the Germans can only advance through the 'gap' [Toul-Epinal] or by violating the neutrality of Luxembourg and Belgium. They proposed to wait on the defensive." [27] As late as August 23, 1911, Henry Wilson was forced to admit to the C.I.D. that he had no *precise* information about French strategic intentions. Not until two weeks later did Huguet confide some of the details to the chief British planner.[28] Before that point London had had little or no official indication about French plans; this in turn paralleled the general absence of British influence before 1911 upon the formation of French war plans. Ironically, this lack of British influence contrasted sharply

23. *Ibid.;* "La vérité sur la puissance militaire et maritime de l'Angleterre," *Correspondant,* 233 (Nov. 10, 1908), 418–448.

24. Durand to Brun, Oct. 29, 1909, Archives Guerre, "Attachés militaires: Angleterre," box 26; also see memo bv General Jules du Pontarice de Heussey, Oct. 11, 1909, Archives Guerre, "Plan XVII: Armée W," box 147b.

25. General Langlois, "L'armée anglais," *Revue des deux mondes,* 5th ser., 55 (Feb. 15, 1910), 872. After 1908 *Spectateur militaire* and *Revue militaire des armées étrangères* carried numerous articles on the British Army.

26. Repington, *The First World War,* I, 11; also see the memo by Esher, "Memorandum of the Work of the Defence Committee in Anticipation of Possible Hostilities," Jan. 20, 1906, Esher Papers, "Private Papers, C.I.D., 1908–1909."

27. Diary, Nov. 9, 1908, *Journals and Letters of Esher,* II, 358.

28. Minutes of the 114th meeting of the C.I.D., Cab. 2/2/2; diary, Sept. 9, 1911, Sir C. E. Callwell, *Field-Marshal Sir Henry Wilson: His Life and Times,* 2 vols. (London, 1927), I, 103.

with the sweeping effects which probable intervention on the Continent was having upon Britain's military strategy.

While de Lacroix and Michel converted the theoretical ideas of the counteroffensive into war plans, another strategic concept was steadily gaining favor within the French Army. The growth of the "offensive" school—*offensive à outrance*—can be quickly recapitulated. The doctrine's antecedents were the works of Ardant du Picq and Captain Gilbert and the alleged lessons of the Napoleonic Wars and the Wars of German Unification. From these sources the school extracted the idea that will or resolution or morale, not materiel factors, determined the outcome of battles. If an army resolved that it would not be beaten, that army became in fact unbeatable. On a more practical level the true expression of the will to victory came only when an army executed offensive actions, for the offensive was the key to victory: without offensive operations no great battle would occur and thus no victory was possible. The defensive, the theorists contended, was valuable only if it conserved forces for deployment elsewhere on the offensive. They scorned the counteroffensive strategy as weak and timorous, unsuitable for and unworthy of French character. France, they stressed, should launch an offensive attack as soon as hostilities commenced. Such an attack would achieve decisive results before the Germans could make any significant gains, regardless of their strategy.[29]

The most noted exponent of this concept of French strategy was General Ferdinand Foch, then head of the Ecole Supérieure de Guerre. From his lectures at the Ecole, where he had taught in the 1890's, there had emerged two major works on strategy: *Des principes de la guerre* and *De la conduite de la guerre*.[30] Both studies demonstrated Foch's heavy reliance upon, and misunderstanding of, Clausewitz. In both he stressed the importance of the will to victory and the value of the offensive. To these strategic attitudes he added four somewhat redundant principles: economy of force, freedom of maneuver, security of forces, and the free disposition of forces. Although Foch occasionally recognized that the strategic defensive had merits, his works betrayed an uncompromising faith in the offensive.[31]

If Foch, building upon du Picq and Clausewitz, laid the foundations of the French offensive school, it was the military journals that ensured circulation of these ideas. In 1902 Commandant Lamey was writing in

29. On the offensive school see Carrias, *La pensée militaire française*, 285–302; Stephen Possony and Etienne Mantoux, "Du Picq and Foch: The French School," in Earle, *Makers of Modern Strategy*, 206–233; Boucher, *Les lois éternelles de la guerre*, II, 132–153; Bernard Brodie, *Strategy in a Missile Age* (Princeton, 1959), 40–59; Tuchman, *The Guns of August*, 28–37.
30. Paris, 1903; Paris, 1904.
31. B. H. Liddell Hart, *Foch: The Man of Orleans* (Boston, 1932), 23–30, 63–66.

the *Journal des sciences militaires* that "the offensive alone can obtain decisive results." [32] Thereafter articles on the offensive and the need for strong, disciplined morale filled the pages of the professional magazines. One writer tersely summed up the interconnection between morale and the offensive by holding that "the efficacy of fire power in time of war reposes above all on the morale of the soldier." [33] And another emphasized that "moral force is a quality of mind which permits the soldier to surmount the depressing impression produced by the dangers, the privations, the fatigue, and the spectacle of all the horror which war engenders." [34] Morale, discipline, the will to victory would together produce a victorious offensive. In conducting this offensive the soldiers were reminded that "the fear of losses is immoral." [35] The battles of World War I bore grim testimony to the persistency of this belief.

But neither the military publicists nor Foch would have achieved their goal of offensive warfare without the assistance of Lieutenant Colonel François Loyzeau de Grandmaison. Chief of the operations section of the French General Staff, this officer was an ardent disciple and interpreter of Foch. He was also an active propagandist for the theory of offensive war. In *Dressage de l'infantrie* he insisted that the morale factor dominated all others in warfare: to obtain victory one must have esprit offensive, "in order to be the conqueror one must make the enemy afraid; when one is afraid, he is beaten. The only way to make the enemy afraid is to attack resolutely without worrying about who is the strongest." [36] Within the French high command proper the argumentative, dogmatic de Grandmaison inveighed against the weaknesses of the counteroffensive. By lumping the counterattack school with that of the purely defensive, he successfully managed to discredit both. His most effective attack came in early 1911 at two conferences held in the newly established Centre des Hautes Etudes in which he extolled the virtues of offensive action. General Michel, who was present, responded so poorly to de Grandmaison's arguments that he lost considerable personal prestige and hastened the demise of the counteroffensive school.[37]

The advocates of the offensive overlooked, or disregarded, what in retrospect appear to be a number of strategical and tactical realities. Their insistence upon the value of élan and resolution led them to ignore the materiel factors of warfare. They underrated the need for heavy artillery

32. A. Lamey, "Etude sur le service en campagne et la deuxième partie des règlements de manoeuvres de l'infantrie," *Journal des sciences militaires*, 15 (August 1902), 271.
33. General Daudignac, "Les réalités du combat," *Spectateur militaire*, 70 (Jan. 1, 1908), 16.
34. "Le moral . . . ," *Spectateur militaire*, 58 (Jan. 1, 1905), 23.
35. Commandant Jette, "La hantise des pertes et l'esprit d'offensive," *Revue militaire générale*, 5 (February 1911), 217.
36. Third ed. (Paris, 1908), 68, 89.
37. Joffre, *Memoirs*, I, 9; François Loyzeau de Grandmaison, *Deux conferences* (Paris, 1912); Boucher, *Les lois éternelles de la guerre*, II, 134–138.

and increased fire power, while failing to appreciate the defensive potential of the machine gun. Commanders and troops alike, Liddell Hart later observed, discovered in 1914 that "bullets—the hardest of facts—can overcome the will of the commander by shattering the bodies of his men." [38] Equally important, the stress on the offensive led to an almost flippant disregard for German strategy. The long tradition of French intellectual arrogance found expression within the French Army. Vast amounts of time were spent deprecating the output of German military writers; far too little time was spent in analyzing what the published works of Schlieffen and others revealed about probable German strategy. A former French officer, Eugène Carrias, has recently confessed that "this constant affirming of our superior intellectual comprehension, in spite of numerous translations of German works on military art and history which revealed the German methods and which no French writer understood, was proof of a weakness more important than any one in France realized." [39] Reinforcing this disregard for German strategy was the offensive school's belief that a victorious French attack in northern Lorraine would sever any German turning move from its base of operations. Some offensive theorists, even less cogently, reasoned that a German flanking move would help France because it would weaken German forces in Lorraine. Finally, there was another important by-product of this stress upon the offensive: reserve troops were further discredited. Successful offensive operations, the theorists contended, required disciplined professional soldiers, and reserve troops were to be avoided. Thus the offensive school strongly supported efforts in 1913 to increase military service to three years, thereby increasing the number of active troops.[40] Skepticism about reserves also prompted the French Staff to presume, incorrectly, that their German counterparts shared their contempt for reserve troops. Not until 1914 would the dangers of neglecting materiel factors, German strategic writings, and the reserves cast doubt upon the wisdom of the *offensive à outrance*. In the meantime the offensive school reigned supreme.

In July 1911 the offensive adherents won their most crucial victory: the ouster of Michel as Generalissimo. In this triumph they were assisted by a wave of parliamentary attacks upon the structure of the French high command. In the Senate on June 19 Count de Tréveneuc and retired General Langlois, editor of the prestigious *Revue militaire générale*, demanded the abolition of the post of Generalissimo: at the

38. Foch, 30; General Gaston Duffour, *Joffre et la guerre de mouvement, 1914* (Paris, 1937), 115–120.
39. *La pensée militaire française*, 289; see, e.g., Pellé (French military attaché in Berlin) to Berteaux, Mar. 28, 1911, D.D.F., 2nd ser., XIII, no. 204, in which Pellé speaks of the German military bluff.
40. Challener, *The French Theory of the Nation in Arms*, 81–89; Joffre; *Memoirs*, II, 592–595; John C. Cairns, "International Politics and the Military Mind: The Case of the French Republic, 1911–1914," *Journal of Modern History, 25* (September 1953), 273–285.

very least they wanted the French Army to have the same commander in peace and war, rather than a system whereby the Generalissimo supplanted the Chief of Staff upon the outbreak of war. Four days later these views were reiterated in the Chamber of Deputies by André Hesse, Admiral Amédée Bienaimé, and General Jean Pedoya. General François Goiran, who was the third Minister of War in four months, ineptly defended the old command structure and flatly rejected the suggestion that one man run the French Army. But the deputies thought otherwise, overturning the Monis government on this question on June 23.[41] Eight days later, with the appearance of a German gunboat at Agadir, the second Moroccan crisis began.

In the new Cabinet formed by Joseph Caillaux on June 27, Adolphe Messimy was Minister of War. A former career officer turned politician, Messimy shared many of the attitudes and predilections of the offensive school; moreover, he regarded the overthrow of Goiran as a parliamentary mandate for reforms in the French high command. These considerations and the Moroccan situation ensured trouble for Michel—and it came quickly. Messimy met Michel for the first time on July 2 and was thoroughly unimpressed. He judged the Generalissimo to be a weak officer, crushed by the burdens of his office. Further, from the start he rejected Michel's scheme to utilize reserve troops. When he asked other generals for their opinions of Michel, the answers seemed to confirm his initial evaluation. The minister then asked for Michel's resignation, but the Generalissimo refused, demanding instead that the War Board pronounce upon the use of reserves.

The Board met on July 19 at the Ministry of War on rue Saint Dominique. Michel outlined his plans for the reserves and field artillery; both were resoundingly defeated. Because the use of the reserves was crucial to Michel's strategic dispositions along the Franco-Belgian frontier, he never presented his radical new war plan for consideration.[42] That his colleagues would have looked favorably upon a shift of French forces to the Belgian frontier and away from Lorraine seems unlikely. Joffre, who later discovered Michel's plan in his office safe, belittled it by quoting Napoleon: " 'How can anyone think of returning to such foolishness?' "[43] For the moment, Plan XVI of 1909 remained in effect.

Under fire from all sides, including unprecedented press attacks, Michel finally resigned on July 21. A week later the *Journal officiel* an-

41. France, *Journal officiel: débats parlementaires*, Sénat, 1911, I (June 19, 1911, 1st session), 797–800; *Journal officiel: débats parlementaires, Chambre des Députés, 1911*, II (June 23, 1911), 2513–2521. See also Ralston, *The Army of the Republic*, 326–332.
42. Adolphe-Marie Messimy, *Mes souvenirs* (Paris, 1937), 74–76; minutes of the War Board, Archives Guerre, "Procès-verbaux du Conseil Supérieur de la Guerre," box J; *Les armées françaises*, tome I, vol. I, 14–15; "Séance du Conseil Supérieur de la Guerre du 19 juillet," *ibid.*, tome I, vol. I: *Annexes*, no. 4.
43. Joffre, *Memoirs*, I, 17.

nounced the appointment of Joffre as Chief of the General Staff; the post of Generalissimo was abolished. France no longer possessed a divided high command. Messimy and Joffre now turned their attention to an infinitely more complex and dangerous assignment: the possibility of German aggression over the Agadir incident. This danger prompted a complete review of Plan XVI and a renewal of interest in the possibility of British military assistance.

6 | The Entente Under Stress, 1908–1911

The Moroccan crisis of 1911 exerted a profound impact upon Anglo-French relations. The jolt of the Agadir incident prompted both governments to reconsider every facet of the entente relationship—diplomatic, military, naval. The two powers, influenced and guided by these evaluations, withstood the German challenge. At the same time the military and naval conversations emerged from the crisis with new substance and importance. This chapter and the three that follow examine these developments, starting with the political and diplomatic context in which the staff talks had been occurring.

Anglo-French relations, from August 1908 when Clemenceau badgered Edward VII about the British Army until the Agadir incident, can be quickly reviewed. Three issues dominated the exchanges between the two entente partners: London's reaction to Moroccan affairs in 1908–1909 and to the Entente Cordiale in general; the recurrent question of Anglo-German naval negotiations; and, finally, French efforts in early 1911, before Agadir, to extend and reinforce the entente system.

In late September 1908 the Casablanca incident, provoked when an impetuous German consul sought to conceal deserters from the Foreign Legion, disturbed the relative calm of Franco-German affairs. At first negotiations to resolve the episode made steady progress; then in early November Berlin and Paris reached an impasse over German demands for a French apology. The international situation, already tense because of Vienna's annexation of Bosnia-Herzegovina, grew dangerous, and Morocco once again threatened to become the catalyst of international politics. This sudden and unwelcome development alarmed London; at the Foreign Office senior officials hurried to define the limits of British support for France. Yet the French, curiously, never pressured London for a firm affirmation of loyalty. And Grey, who preferred a prudent, cautious approach, restricted British support to endorsement of the French arbitration proposals—beyond this he refused to go without Cabinet instructions. Before he could seek such instructions, the crisis abruptly ended with a German retreat.[1]

But Grey had not confused prudence with weakness. On November 5 he had alerted the Admiralty to the dangers of the Casablanca discord and requested that it be ready "to make preparations in case Germany sent France an ultimatum and the Cabinet decided that we must assist France." [2] Had the issue of support for France ever reached the Cabinet, the outcome appears predictable. Esher, who actively participated in the military preparations, indicates that by November 12 Grey, Haldane, and Asquith, without any French pressure, had resolved to aid France. "Haldane told Asquith that if we failed France, he would not give ten years' purchase for the British Empire. This," thought Esher, "was very straight and courageous. Grey never wavered or doubted." [3] Mounting anti-German antagonism, stimulated by the Kaiser's injudicious comments about Britain in the *Daily Telegraph* interview of late October, clearly redounded to France's benefit.

Not until Franco-German tensions had eased was there any mention of military or naval conversations. Then, on November 24, Cambon pressed Grey for the initiation of naval conversations to complement the military talks. The Foreign Secretary, who had thought such talks were already in progress, readily agreed to discuss the question with Reginald McKenna, the First Lord of the Admiralty.[4] But Grey never returned to

1. Minutes on Bertie to Grey, Nov. 4, 1908, *B.D.*, VII, no. 129.
2. Grey to McKenna, Nov. 5, 1908, *ibid.*, no. 132; Fisher later wrote that Grey thought them on the "very brink of war," Fisher to Knollys, Dec. 22, 1908, Marder, *Fear God and Dread Nought*, II, 204–205.
3. Diary, Nov. 12, 1908, *Journals and Letters of Esher*, II, 359–360; also see the entries for Nov. 5, 9, 1908, *ibid.*, 355–358; P. Cambon to Pichon, Nov. 25, 1908, *D.D.F.*, 2nd ser., XI, no. 566.
4. Grey to Bertie, Nov. 24, 1908, *B.D.*, VI, no. 106.

this subject with Cambon during 1908; indeed, not until 1912 did the two men again discuss either variation of the staff conversations. In any event, in late 1908 France could have had no doubts about the loyalty and reliability of its entente partner. Paris, as London soon discovered, did not always reciprocate this trust.

In mid-January 1909 the Foreign Office learned of the impending conclusion of a Franco-German agreement on Morocco. Surprise, then apprehension prevailed at Whitehall. Fears were dispelled only when London learned that no British economic interests were in jeopardy. Assured on this point, Hardinge decided the settlement was "a complete vindication of the Anglo-French 'entente.' The Germans have thrown up the sponge." [5] Grey, who conceded there was some political advantage "that France and Germany should agree not to quarrel about Morocco," was less confident about German sincerity.[6] He tempered his felicitations to Cambon with the blunt reminder that the "political weather . . . was very uncertain, and I thought it desirable to keep the *Entente* between France and England as fresh and vigorous in the sunshine, as it had been during the storms of the Algeciras Conference and on other occasions. At the same time there was no reason why we should not enjoy the sun while it shone." [7]

But almost immediately there was a cloudy period. In March 1909 the sputtering antagonism between St. Petersburg and Vienna over the Balkans threatened to flare into war. Grey and the Liberal government promised Russia diplomatic support but would go no further. This British hesitancy caused some concern among French policy-makers; Paul Cambon, sounding Hardinge on what Britain would do if war came, got an equivocal answer: the most the Permanent Undersecretary would acknowledge was that "already several newspapers envisaged the necessity of British intervention." Cambon nonetheless concluded that in the final analysis "English opinion would not permit the government to remain immobile." [8] When Russia backed down before the German ultimatum in late March, Cambon's assessment was not put to the test. The slowly evolving Anglo-French-Russian Triple Entente, though somewhat shaken, had survived.

With the easing of Balkan tensions, Anglo-French relations entered a

5. Hardinge to Grey, Feb. 6, 1909, *B.D.*, VII, p. 140 n.; cf. P. Cambon to Pichon, Feb. 12, 1909, M.A.E., "Grande Bretagne," n.s. 10: see also E. W. Edwards, "The Franco-German Agreement on Morocco, 1909," *English Historical Review*, 78 (July 1963), 483–513.
6. Grey's minute on Bertie to Grey, Feb. 6, 1909, *B.D.*, VII, no. 149.
7. Grey to Bertie, Feb. 16, 1909, *ibid.*, no. 158. Paul Cambon personally disliked the Quai d'Orsay's attempt to improve Franco-German relations, and he wanted to retort by concluding a new Anglo-French commercial accord; Hardinge to Bertie, Feb. 4, 1909, Hardinge Papers, Cambridge University Library, vol. 17.
8. P. Cambon to Pichon, Mar. 20, 1909, Pichon Papers, Bibliothèque de l'Institut de France, Paris, 4396; also see M. B. Cooper, "British Policy in the Balkans, 1908–9," *Historical Journal*, 7 (1964), 274–279.

period of prolonged serenity. During this interlude their entente faced no major challenges, domestic or external. In the summer of 1909 Clemenceau renewed his appeals to King Edward about the British Army; he fared no better than before. Later that year, in December, Robert Blatchford, a well-known British publicist, published a series of lurid, alarmist articles on the German danger in the *Daily Mail*. For Britain's salvation he urged conscription and military aid to France. Though these comments stirred considerable discussion, they failed to alter the direction or tenor of British policy.[9]

In 1910 only minor issues ruffled relations between London and Paris. The first came in February when Grey learned of Aristide Briand's arguments for new French naval increases. Claiming that France had moral obligations to Britain because of alleged naval conversations, Clemenceau's successor told the French Cabinet that France must be ready to fulfill its share of the agreements. Grey, though unhappy at any mention of entente obligations, declined to protest Briand's contentions. He preferred instead to adhere to Walpole's maxim, "let sleeping dogs lie," on the delicate question of obligations.[10]

Grey's caution was reinforced when Asquith, on March 21, was asked by William Byles in the House of Commons "whether any treaty or naval or military convention of which this House is yet uninformed exists between this country and France, by which the French Navy is to maintain absolutely free and secured against all danger the English commerce which passes down the Mediterranean to use the Suez Canal and by which there is assured to French and English flags, in case of conflict, the absolute mastery of the Mediterranean." The Prime Minister, using a reply drafted at the Foreign Office, assured the Commons that "no treaty or convention of the nature specified by my hon. friend exists between this country and France." [11] In a legal sense this response was impeccable; there was no formal or informal naval convention. But there were military conversations, a development clearly contrary to the spirit of the question and to the position of the radical wing of Asquith's party. Although Asquith had successfully evaded the full implications of the parliamentary query, the government recognized anew that the staff conversations must be extremely guarded and discreet. When Stephen Pichon, the French Foreign Minister, visited London in May 1910 for the funeral of Edward VII, there was no mention either of the military conversations or of expanding the entente relationship.[12]

9. These articles are summarized in Hale, *Publicity and Diplomacy*, 373–377.
10. Bertie to Grey, Feb. 10, 17, 1910, B.D., VI, nos. 331, 333; Grey to Bertie, Feb. 12, 19, 1910, *ibid.*, nos. 332, 334.
11. *Parliamentary Debates: Commons*, 5th ser., 15 (Mar. 21, 1910), 769. There was a curious forerunner to this parliamentary question: on Nov. 11, 1908, a private citizen, F. H. Mayhew, wrote the Foreign Office about a possible military convention with France. The Foreign Office, of course, refused to discuss the issue; F.O. 371/456.
12. Colonial and other related topics were discussed; memo of Grey-Pichon talk, May 19, 1910, M.A.E., "Grande Bretagne," n.s. 21.

Although the entente remained secure during 1910, Paris nevertheless became uneasy when the secret Anglo-German naval talks were resumed. The French always viewed these negotiations as an accurate barometer of the international climate. Despite Grey's frequent assurances after 1908 that French interests would be safeguarded in the naval negotiations, Paris remained dubious.[13] The French in fact need not have worried, for Grey remained solidly attached to the entente as the cornerstone of British foreign policy. In May 1910, for example, he emphasized that no Anglo-German formula could prevent "the same sort of support as I gave to France at the time of the Algeciras Conference and afterwards until she settled her difficulty with Germany."[14]

The French also had positive grounds for desiring the naval race to continue. Soldiers and diplomats alike recognized that Anglo-German ill will strengthened France's position: France became valuable to Britain.[15] Moreover, the continuing naval race drained money from the German Army budget; the French never appreciated that the same race deprived the British Army of money. In any case, successive French governments followed the sporadic naval talks closely, hopeful that Anglo-German differences were irreconcilable. These hopes were somewhat shaken in late 1910 and early 1911 by proposals to exchange naval information; for the first time some type of Anglo-German agreement appeared likely. Grey once more, in February 1911, sought to erase French concern by promising to include France in any political formula growing out of a naval accord.[16] Three months later, to Paris' relief, the naval talks stalled once again.

What particularly disturbed the French about the new naval talks was their timing. They closely followed the unexpected Potsdam conversations on November 4–5 between the Tsar and the Kaiser. Rumors of an impending Russo-German accord for the Near East, when combined with new Anglo-German naval negotiations, suggested to some French policy-makers that the Triple Entente was in trouble. Although there were assurances from St. Petersburg about the durability of the Dual Alliance, Paris remained doubtful.[17] And Pichon's own position was not made any easier by press and parliamentary discussions which

13. These negotiations are traced in Marder, *Road to War*, 171–177, 221–233, and Woodward, *Great Britain and the German Navy*, 253–307. On French concern and British assurances, see, e.g., P. Cambon to Pichon, Jan. 6, 1910, *D.D.F.*, 2nd ser., XII, no. 394, and Bertie to Grey, Nov. 20, 1909. *B.D.*, VI, no. 206.
14. Grey to Sir Edward Goschen, May 5, 1910, *B.D.*, VI, no. 361.
15. Huguet to Picquart, Mar. 18, 1909, Archives Guerre, "Attachés militaires: Angleterre," box 9.
16. P. Cambon to Pichon, Jan. 12, Feb. 3, 1911, *D.D.F.*, 2nd ser., XIII, nos. 116, 136; Grey to Bertie, Feb. 3, 1911, *B.D.*, VI, no. 429. In early March the Cabinet considered the French role in a naval accord; Asquith to George V, Mar. 9, 1911, Asquith Papers, Bodleian Library, Oxford University, box 6.
17. Pichon to Louis (tel.), Dec. 30, 1910, *D.D.F.*, 2nd ser., XIII, no. 107; P. Cambon to Pichon, Jan. 12, 1911, *ibid.*, no. 116; Bertie to Grey, Feb. 4, 1911, *B.D.*, X, pt. 1, no. 672.

criticized the alliance, the Entente Cordiale, and the general direction of French foreign policy.[18]

In early February Pichon's troubles were compounded when the debate shifted to the French Senate. There, in an attack upon French foreign policy, Senator Gustave de Lamarzelle on February 2 criticized not only the Potsdam talks, but also the lack of any recent Anglo-French military conversations. This indiscreet exposé forced Pichon to retort "that never had the *entente cordiale* been more complete and more intimate than today." In fact, "never had the diplomatic situation of France been more assured than today." But in replying to his critics the Foreign Minister carefully avoided any discussion of the military conversations,[19] and his evasion, instead of denial, of the de Lamarzelle charges confirmed for many (including the German Embassy) that such talks had occurred.[20]

A by-product of this criticism of French foreign policy was the demand that France review her ties with Britain. André Tardieu, as in 1908, belittled the relative sterility of the entente as such and argued that it had to become more effective to be of any value to France.[21] Others, such as the political commentator Francis Charmes, writing in *Revue des deux mondes*, asserted that the time had come for France and Britain to initiate military conversations; perhaps, he remarked, there had already been such talks. In any case what crime would the countries commit in discussing "certain eventualities"? One logical area for discussion, he wrote, was the Dutch proposal to fortify Flushing—a step which would prevent the use of the Schelde in wartime by the Belgians and, equally important, by the British. Charmes concluded his appeal for closer Anglo-French relations with a classic description of the entente as it evolved before the war: "As there is no positive alliance, there would be no question of absolute obligation; they would keep their liberty, but they do not want to be caught unprepared and obliged to mediate and coordinate in the moment when they must also act." [22]

The widespread public concern about the nature of the entente was paralleled within the French government. Briand had already suggested to Bertie in mid-January that the Triple Entente should become more vigorous and "more communicative" and thereby prevent a repetition of

18. These attacks are summarized in Francis Charmes, "Chronique de la quinzaine," *Revue des deux mondes*, 6th ser., 1 (Jan. 15, 1911), 472–480; Commandant de Thomasson, "La malaise de la triple entente," *Questions diplomatiques et coloniales*, 31 (Feb. 1, 1911), 129–138. Also see the debates in the Chamber of Deputies, Jan. 12–13, 1911, *Journal officiel: débats parlementaires, Chambre des Députés, 1911*, I, 11–23, 29–42.

19. *Journal officiel: débats parlementaires, Sénat, 1911*, I (Feb. 2, 1911), 106–113; *Le Temps*, Feb. 1, 4, 1911.

20. Schoen to Bethmann, Feb. 8, 1911, *G.P.*, XXIX, no. 10520, pp. 66–68 notes; Metternich to Bethmann, Feb. 7, 1911, *ibid.*, no. 10521.

21. *Le Temps*, Feb. 4, 1911.

22. Charmes, "Chronique de la quinzaine," *Revue des deux mondes*, 6th ser., 1 (Feb. 15, 1911), 947–953.

Potsdam.[23] A month later, on February 13, French policy-makers including Briand, President Fallières, Pichon, General Brun, and Georges Louis, the ambassador to Russia, reviewed the military terms of the Dual Alliance. During the discussion Pichon revealed his intention to use a Russian inquiry about the staff talks as an excuse "to resume the conversations remaining in suspense with England." [24] Also, the Quai d'Orsay regarded the new Austrian naval program as a further reason for "new military conversations with England." [25] Potsdam directly, the resumption of Anglo-German naval talks less directly, had prompted the French to re-examine the health of the entente. Their prescription for its continued long life was a new dose of military conversations.

The Foreign Office followed carefully French discussions about the value of the entente. Eyre Crowe, a Senior Clerk at the Foreign Office and a bitter foe of Germany, agreed with French criticisms. "For purposes of ultimate emergencies it [the entente] may be found to have no substance at all," he wrote on February 2, 1911, "for an entente is nothing more than a frame of mind, a view of general policy which is shared by the government of two countries, but which may be or become so vague as to lose all content." [26] Sir Arthur Nicolson, the new Permanent Undersecretary, shared Crowe's attitude. A determined exponent of Britain's place in the European balance of power, Nicolson had already asserted on January 23 that the balance required British willingness to furnish its "friends or allies, in case of necessity, some assistance of a more material and efficient kind than we are at present in a position to offer them." Many people, he wrote in late February, "do not understand that, were the Triple Entente to be broken up, we should be isolated and compelled to do the bidding of the Power which assumed the hegemony in Europe. Moreover in the present circumstances we are certainly not strong enough to stand alone." [27]

Although the permanent officials personally desired to help the French, they recognized the political pressures on the Asquith government against open military ties with France. Awkward parliamentary questions in March about "obligations to France to send troops, in certain eventualities, to assist the operations of the French Army" reminded them of the danger of attempting any new move toward France.[28] On

---

23. Bertie to Grey, Jan. 18, 1911, Grey Papers, F.O. 800/52.
24. "Procès-verbal d'une conférence tenue chez M. le Président de la République," Feb. 13, 1911, D.D.F., 2nd ser., XIII, no. 152; on the Russian overture, see Isvolski to Sazonov, Feb. 3/16, 1911, René Marchand, ed., Un livre noir: diplomatie d'avant-guerre d'après les documents des Archives russes: novembre, 1910–juillet, 1914, 2 vols. (Paris, 1922–1923), I, 37–38.
25. Minute on Barrère to Pichon, Feb. 10, 1911, D.D.F., 2nd ser., XIII, no. 150.
26. Minute by Crowe on Bertie to Grey, Jan. 31, 1911, F.O. 371/1117.
27. Nicolson to Cartwright, Jan. 23, 1911, Nicolson Papers, Foreign Office Library, London, vol. I/1911; Nicolson to Goschen, Feb. 28, 1911, ibid.
28. Parliamentary Debates: Commons, 5th ser., 23 (Mar. 30, 1911), 1490; for various drafts of Grey's response, see F.O. 371/1116.

the other hand, Grey, who assured the House of Commons that there was no such obligation to France, later admitted that he "purposely worded the answer so as not to convey that the engagement of 1904 might not under certain circumstances be construed to have larger consequences than its strict letter." [29] The Foreign Secretary, like his subordinates, wanted the best of all worlds. Once more he found deliberate ambiguity a useful technique to confuse and evade.

In February Briand's government had resolved to seek closer relations with London, but there was no attempt to implement this decision until April. At that time Jean Cruppi, who had succeeded Pichon as Foreign Minister, quickly discovered Grey's personal and political inclination to leave the entente alone. Friction first occurred on April 5 when Cruppi proposed a Senate declaration which stated that Britain and France "would remain friends and united in the presence of every eventuality, and they could entrust to their respective Governments, the care of giving a precise form to their entente when the moment came." Afraid this sentence would lead to "inconvenient questions" about "an offensive and defensive alliance," Grey, aided effectively by Bertie, secured the deletion of the remarks.[30] This action, which followed closely upon Grey's public denial of any military commitment to France, thoroughly rattled the new French Foreign Minister, who, on April 8, asked Bertie if the British Cabinet had changed its attitude toward France.[31]

At the same time the Foreign Office received a long dispatch from Colonel W. E. Fairholme, the British military attaché in Paris. In summarizing an extensive conversation with General Foch, then Commandant of the Ecole Supérieure de Guerre, the attaché related Foch's demands for closer Anglo-French military cooperation and preparation. British military help, Foch had asserted, would both increase French morale and offset superior German numbers; but France could not set aside the necessary rolling stock to move British troops "unless indeed it had received a previous assurance that it could count with certainty on the arrival of the British contingent." Upon such an agreement, Foch predicted, "may depend the result of the war and consequently, the fate of Europe." [32] Grey, who assessed Foch's remarks as a French call for a military convention, limited the circulation of the attaché's dispatch to Asquith, Haldane, and Lord Morley. The latter's inclusion meant that Grey, in contrast to his actions in January 1906, no longer entirely ignored the more radical wing of the Cabinet.

Foch's proposals had scarcely been received in London when Sir Fran-

29. Grey to Bertie, Apr. 10, 1911, B.D., VII, no. 206.
30. Bertie to Grey (tel.), Apr. 5, 1911, ibid., no. 200; Grey to Bertie, Apr. 6, 1911, ibid., no. 201; Bertie to Grey, Apr. 6, 1911, Grey Papers, F.O. 800/52; Grey to Bertie, Apr. 8, 1911, ibid.
31. Bertie to Grey, Apr. 9, 1911, B.D., VII, no. 205.
32. Fairholme's report was included in Bertie to Grey, Apr. 9, 1911, ibid., VI, no. 460.

cis Bertie reported still another French overture for closer relations. On April 12 Cruppi, still peeved by Grey's attitude, reminded the British ambassador of "the inflammable state of the political atmosphere in and out of Europe." Given this situation, the French Foreign Minister thought that it "behooved the French and British Governments to carry matters further as regards possible co-operation in certain eventualities than had hitherto been done." "He did not mean," Bertie added, "a formal Convention but an understanding which would not bind the two Governments to act but which would define what the joint action should be in case they had to co-operate." [33] These remarks left few doubts that the French were probing for a possible expansion of the entente relationship.

Eyre Crowe, by now apprehensive about the renewal of German ambitions in Morocco, thought Cruppi's suggestion deserved "the most careful consideration." [34] Grey was equally impressed, but for rather different reasons. On April 16 he wrote Asquith:

> Please look at Bertie's desp: No 168 Secret of April 13. I have marked it for you, Morley, and Haldane and I would suggest that as soon as Haldane returns it you and Morley sh[oul]d have a talk with him.
> Early in 1906 the French said to us "will you help us if there is a war with Germany?"
> We said "we can't promise—our hands must be free."
> The French then urged that the Mily. Authy. should be allowed to exchange views—ours to say what they could do—the French to say how they would like it done, if we did side with France. Otherwise, as the French urged, even if we decided to support France on the outbreak of war we shouldn't be able to do it effectively. We agreed to this. Up to this point C.B., R.B.H. and I were cognizant of what took place—the rest of you were scattered in the Election.
> The military experts then convened. What they settled I never knew—the position being that the Govt. was quite free, but that the military people knew what to do if the word was given.
> Unless French war plans have changed; there should be no need for anything further, but it is clear we are going to be asked something. [35]

Grey's letter raises several important points. After three years in office the Prime Minister was finally being informed by his Foreign Secretary of the full extent of Anglo-French relations. Grey's failure to brief Asquith earlier was, given the tone of his letter, almost certainly an oversight on his part and no more. Moreover, this was not Asquith's first

33. Bertie to Grey, Apr. 13, 1911, *ibid.*, VII, no. 207.
34. Minute by Crowe, *ibid.*
35. Grey to Asquith, Apr. 16, 1911, Grey Papers, F.O. 800/100; reprinted with changes in Grey, *Twenty-five Years*, I, 91–92.

opportunity to become knowledgeable about the staff talks: at the 1909 C.I.D. hearings on the Continent, which he had chaired, Sir Charles Hardinge had mentioned the staff conversations. In any case, the Prime Minister now knew part of the story of how the talks began. More significant was Grey's failure to mention the 1907 staff exchanges, which had taken place with explicit Foreign Office approval, and his unawareness of Henry Wilson's full-scale resumption of the military conversations in late 1910. The Foreign Secretary's ignorance of these developments, plus his confession that "what they settled I never knew," suggests that Grey's conduct and control of British foreign policy left something to be desired. On the one hand, he consistently refused to extend the political nature of the entente; on the other, he consistently refused to appreciate that the staff talks negated much of his prudent approach to Anglo-French relations. Having failed to inform the Cabinet in 1906 about the conversations, he committed the equally grave error of failing to control the talks once underway.

The reactions of Grey's Cabinet associates—Asquith, Haldane, and Morley—to the prospect of French demands remain unknown. And, despite the deteriorating situation in Morocco, the expected French demarche for more extensive ties never materialized. Paul Cambon never broached the issue with the Foreign Secretary. Instead Cruppi preferred to intimate to Bertie the need for closer relations without formally demanding them. On May 14 Bertie noted privately that what Paris wanted was "something more visible to Germany and useful to France than the existing *Entente.* . . . The French Government have found it very useful in restraining Spain, but they do not feel sure how far they could rely on it if Germany became threatening or bluffed." Such an arrangement would also be valuable to Britain, for it might prevent France from yielding on a matter vital to British interests. Yet Bertie held no illusions about the political feasibility of a more tangible accord with France. To mitigate this obstacle, indeed to avoid it, he suggested that "everything military and naval ought to be arranged unofficially to meet the contingency of British and French forces *having* to act together. Otherwise in these days of quick locomotion we might arrive a day too late for the fray and find our essential interests already compromised. Perhaps," he concluded, "these arrangements *have* been made." [36]

Bertie's assessment of the British political scene proved accurate, for Grey, who discussed this letter with Asquith, made no move to meet the French desires. As Nicolson aptly observed on May 17: "You [Bertie] can quite understand that there is considerable hesitation here to binding ourselves to any definite course of action in view of possible eventualities." For his part the Permanent Undersecretary had personal

36. Bertie to Nicolson, May 14, 1911, B.D., VII, no. 269.

reservations about the effectiveness of Bertie's suggested alternative—the establishment of unofficial military and naval talks. Although there had been a "certain amount of desultory talk" with the French, Nicolson doubted that "a concerted plan of action will ever be settled." [37] Nicolson, like his superiors, had misjudged the character, ability, and ambitions of Henry Wilson.

After the middle of May the French ended their sporadic and indirect efforts to put some starch into the entente. Yet at this very time the Moroccan situation was becoming more and more dangerous. This paradox introduces a puzzling aspect into any consideration of the entente in early 1911: with evident trouble ahead in Morocco, why did Paris fail to pursue the question of closer Anglo-French relations? Pichon's departure from the Quai d'Orsay in early March, after five years as Foreign Minister, certainly upset French policy. His successor in the Monis government, Cruppi, knew little of foreign policy. These two facts surely explain part of the vacillation in French diplomacy. In addition, the rapid flux of Moroccan developments monopolized French attention. Nor had Paris received any encouragement to seek an expanded relationship with Britain: rather, Sir Edward Grey had denied the existence of a military convention, then altered Cruppi's speech, and consistently ig-nored French hints to review the entente. The French may have decided to avoid an open British rebuff.

There remains another possible explanation. By May 1911 the military conversations, which had languished between 1908 and 1910, were again underway. Thanks to the efforts of Brigadier General Henry Wilson, the new Director of Military Operations, the staff talks had not only been renewed but substantially expanded. The Monis government, aware of the revived military conversations and familiar with Britain's diplomatic and strategic interests in Morocco, may well have concluded that it was adequately prepared to meet any crisis over Morocco.

The background of the second Moroccan crisis can be quickly sketched. From the start the 1909 Franco-German accord on Morocco had proved abortive: the two governments could never agree upon a division of the economic spoils. Their disputes were further complicated by the steady deterioration of the Sultan's authority. By the end of 1910 Morocco was in a state of anarchy. Then, in February 1911, the Zaer tribesmen in the Gharb region revolted, threatening Fez and its European inhabitants—or so the French claimed. The revolt supplied the French with a perfect pretext to expand their control beyond the terms assigned at Algeciras.[38]

37. Nicolson to Bertie, May 17, 1911, *ibid.*, no. 275.
38. Ima C. Barlow, *The Agadir Crisis* (Chapel Hill, N.C., 1940), 75–168; also André Tardieu, *Le mystère d'Agadir* (Paris, 1912), 363–420.

The idea of a French expedition to relieve Fez received scant encouragement from Berlin or Madrid or London. On April 9 Jules Cambon, the French ambassador to Berlin, warned that if France were to violate the Act of Algeciras Germany would demand a Moroccan port. Despite this and a subsequent warning, the Monis government on April 23 authorized preparations for a relief expedition. Five days later Alfred von Kiderlen-Wächter, the German Secretary of State for Foreign Affairs, pointedly reminded Cambon that a prolonged French stay at Fez would nullify the Act of Algeciras.[39] When the expedition drew nearer Fez in early May, the Germans, strangely enough, grew taciturn, making no significant observations on Moroccan developments. Kiderlen even left Berlin for a six-week cure at Bad Kissingen. This interlude caused the suspicious Arthur Nicolson to fear the worst: "I expect," he wrote, "that Germany calculates that in that time France will have plunged herself up to her neck in Moorish affairs and that the moment will have arrived for Germany to step in and demand her price."[40] Nicolson was right: the trap was set, the French plunged ahead.

France's unilateral action in Morocco alarmed its Iberian neighbor. Madrid, encouraged by Berlin, concluded that the French were embarking upon the partition of Morocco envisaged in their secret 1904 accord. Justly afraid of French ambitions, the Spanish resolved to gain their share of the Moroccan loot. For several weeks British pressure delayed Spanish action, but could not prevent it.[41] On June 8 Spanish troops landed at Larache and Alcazar; the partition of Morocco had begun.

The British government, obligated by its 1904 accord to give France diplomatic support on Moroccan affairs, scrutinized each phase of developments in the Moorish kingdom. In April London, like Berlin, had urged caution and restraint upon Paris—advice that was ignored in spite of French recognition of the value of British friendship. In fact, to ensure complete British support on Morocco the French reverted to the proven technique of 1905: Paul Cambon on April 28 mentioned the possibility of a German port in Morocco.[42] It is doubtful that the argument influenced British policy on this occasion; nevertheless, in early May the British appeared to be loyal "friends." London pledged support to France on Morocco and Nicolson stated that Britain did not "intend to waver in the slightest in the attitude which we adopted at Algeciras

39. J. Cambon to Cruppi, Apr. 9, 1911, D.D.F., 2nd ser., XIII, nos. 221, 222; J. Cambon to P. Cambon, Apr. 17, 21, 1911, ibid., nos. 234, 246; J. Cambon to Cruppi (tel.), Apr. 28, 1911, ibid., no. 267. Joseph Caillaux, Finance Minister in the Monis government, later claimed that the Quai d'Orsay had concealed Cambon's warnings from the French Cabinet, Agadir: ma politique extérieure (Paris, 1919), 92–96.
40. Nicolson to Bertie, May 11, 1911, B.D., VII, no. 263.
41. On British pressure see, e.g., Grey to Sir Maurice de Bunsen, May 2, 1911, ibid., no. 242; de Bunsen to Grey, May 3, 1911, ibid., no. 246.
42. Memo by Nicolson, Apr. 28, 1911, ibid., no. 230; P. Cambon to J. Cambon, Apr. 30, 1911, Cambon: correspondance, II, 318.

in 1906." [43] And Grey, at the time of the Kaiser's visit to London in mid-May, stoutly defended French action at Fez, allegedly asserting that "England in any case and under all circumstances would fulfill its obligations to France." [44] Paul Cambon, though pleased by these signs, remained personally convinced that Britain would offer no more than diplomatic support on Morocco.[45]

The ambassador's suspicions were justified. Behind the facade of support for France the Foreign Secretary possessed profound reservations about French policy. On May 25 Grey bluntly told Paul Cambon that the French, on reaching Fez safely, should restore order and depart at once. A week later, with the French still at Fez, he wrote Bertie: "We are already skating on very thin ice . . . and every week that the French remain at Fez the ice will get thinner." By June 9 Grey was resigned to the predicament, reluctantly concluding that the French were "too deeply in to get out and they will have to go through with a partition of Morocco, in which there will be some difficult and rough water to navigate, and some price to be paid. But if the disagreeable day can be put off so much the better." [46]

Jules Cambon shared Grey's apprehension over the situation and wanted, if at all possible, to avoid any German participation in a division of Morocco. To achieve this goal he was willing to arrange a comprehensive Franco-German colonial settlement; in pursuit of this policy he visited the vacationing Kiderlen at Bad Kissingen on June 21 and 22. During their discussions the ambassador stated firmly that France could not allow Germany in Morocco, but simultaneously he held out the possibility of other colonial compensation for Germany. Kiderlen, apparently amenable, told him: "Bring us something from Paris." [47] A hopeful, optimistic Cambon departed for the French capital. His efforts and his hopes were in vain; he never had enough time to explore a colonial arrangement with the new Caillaux government. On July 1 the German gunboat *Panther* appeared at Agadir for the ostensible purpose of protecting German economic interests in the area, in reality to pressure Paris. Grey's "disagreeable day" had arrived.

The *coup d'Agadir* transformed the Moroccan question into an international crisis. The reaction of the Entente Cordiale to this belligerent

43. Nicolson to Sir George Buchanan, May 10, 1911, Nicolson Papers, vol. II/1911.
44. Count Alexander Benckendorff to A. Neratov, May 10/23, 1911, B. de Siebert, ed., *Graf Benckendorffs Diplomatischer Schriftwechsel*, 4 vols. (Berlin, 1928), II, no. 403; see also Metternich to Bethmann, May 22, 1911, G.P., XXIX, no. 10561; P. Cambon to Cruppi (tel.), May 19, 1911, D.D.F., 2nd ser., XIII, no. 308.
45. P. Cambon to J. Cambon, May 23, 1911, *Cambon: correspondance*, II, 320, 323.
46. Grey to Bertie, May 25, June 1, 9, 1911, B.D., VII, nos. 288, 307, 314.
47. On these talks see J. Cambon to Cruppi, June 22, 1911, D.D.F., 2nd ser., XIII, no. 364.

German gesture must now be considered: as with the first Moroccan affair an abundance of evidence, especially the Asquith, Grey, and Nicolson Papers, permits a more extensive evaluation of British than French policy—but, once more, it was the British response which was decisive because it sharply influenced the limits of French intransigence toward Berlin.

In the first weeks after Agadir the lines of British and French policy were never entirely clear. The confusion stemmed partly from clashes within the policy-making machinery of both countries: in France, for example, there was undisguised hostility among those who created policy. On one side were the younger diplomats who controlled the Quai d'Orsay, such as Maurice Herbette, the Chef de Cabinet, Edmond Bapst, Directeur des Affaires Politiques, and Alexander Conty, the Directeur-Adjoint des Affaires Politiques. Impetuous, proud, and willing to risk trouble with Germany, these "Young Turks" gained importance in 1911 because of the rapid turnover and inexperience of the foreign ministers. Cruppi succeeded Pichon in early March and was in turn succeeded by Justin de Selves in late June; neither man had any experience in the making of foreign policy. Opposing the Quai d'Orsay group were the older ambassadors, the Cambon brothers, Camille Barrère in Rome, and Georges Louis in St. Petersburg. Although the ambassadors wanted France to gain Morocco, they realized not only the dangers of German opposition but also the need for caution, conciliation, and compensation. They therefore resisted both the provocative proposals of the "Quai clique" and its attempt to manipulate de Selves, Caillaux's Foreign Minister. In late July the ambassadors were joined by Caillaux himself, who had grown suspicious of both de Selves and the Quai group. The Premier's intervention ensured the triumph of a prudent, reasonable approach to Moroccan affairs; that this approach would prevail in the first days after Agadir was less certain.[48]

Within the machinery of British foreign policy there also existed distinct, if not always conflicting, approaches. Sir Arthur Nicolson had replaced Hardinge in mid-1910 as Permanent Undersecretary. The appointment of the former ambassador to St. Petersburg strengthened the ranks of the anti-German faction at the Foreign Office now spearheaded by Eyre Crowe. A frail, pallid individual, Nicolson possessed most of the attitudes and prejudices of the opposition Unionists; indeed, his contacts with Unionist leaders would be frequent and occasionally suspect. Deeply attached to the maintenance of the Anglo-Russian understanding

48. On this friction see, e.g., P. Cambon to H. Cambon, May 31, 1911, *ibid.*, XIII, no. 329; P. Cambon to Cruppi, June 29, 1911, *ibid.*, no. 370. Also see Caillaux, *Agadir*, 109–113, 155–156, 159–161, 174–176, and his *Mes mémoires*, 3 vols. (Paris, 1942–1947), II, 147–153. That all was not well at the Quai d'Orsay became public in November 1911; Bapst was relieved as Political Director and Herbette faced a departmental investigation; *Le Temps*, Nov. 12–13, 1911; *Times*, Nov. 14–15, 17, 1911.

he had negotiated, Nicolson disliked and opposed any step toward Berlin that might endanger his handiwork. He soon became the most consistent, and persistent, advocate within the government for closer ties with France and Russia.[49] During the Agadir crisis the Nicolson-Crowe combination was joined by Sir Francis Bertie, the longtime British ambassador in Paris. Agadir simply reinforced their convictions and prejudices toward Germany. Their narrow, somewhat inflexible, appraisal of the international scene was rejected by Lord Loreburn (the Lord Chancellor), Lord Morley, and the radical wing of the British Cabinet. At first during July the latter group would, surprisingly, manage to impose its policy upon the government. Britain would offer diplomatic support to France but nothing more.

The man caught between these divergent approaches was Sir Edward Grey. Patient, wary, and persistently evasive, the Foreign Secretary tried to bridge the gulf between the Cabinet and the Foreign Office.[50] But his duties far exceeded this domestic task; he also faced the complex and connected problems of keeping the entente intact and frustrating German ambitions while not encouraging the French to go to war. His role was pivotal in Anglo-French relations, and from the start he urged a policy of conciliation and concession upon France.

The *Panther's* arrival at Agadir completely surprised the three-day-old Caillaux government. De Selves, inexperienced and hotheaded, immediately wanted to retort in kind: he proposed the dispatch of a French ship to Moroccan waters. This bellicose notion found no favor with either Caillaux or his Minister of Marine, Théophile Delcassé. Disregarding their opposition, de Selves proceeded to order Paul Cambon to sound Grey about sending a ship to Mogador, a port not far from Agadir.[51]

The Foreign Secretary, out of London for the weekend, postponed action on the French request until he could see Asquith on Monday morning, July 3. That afternoon Cambon visited Grey at the Foreign Office. Throughout the interview the ambassador urged that the entente partners send ships to Morocco; finally Grey agreed, but deferred a positive commitment until the Cabinet could meet the next day.[52] Cambon returned to Albert Gate convinced the British would send a ship, and widespread British press support for France strengthened his confidence —the *Times*, for instance, had promised that very morning that Britain would "not be disloyal or unfaithful" to the spirit of the entente. And

49. Nicolson's career is treated in Harold Nicolson, *Sir Arthur Nicolson, Bart., First Lord Carnock: A Study in the Old Diplomacy* (London, 1930); also see Frans Gosses, *The Management of British Foreign Policy Before the First World War, Especially During the Period 1880–1914*, trans. E. C. Van Der Gaaf (Leiden, 1948).
50. Taylor, *The Struggle for Mastery in Europe*, 469.
51. De Selves to P. Cambon (tel.), July 1, 1911, D.D.F., 2nd ser., XIV, no. 1; also editorial note, *ibid.*, p. 2.
52. Grey to Bertie, July 3, 1911, B.D., VII, no. 351; P. Cambon to Caillaux (tel.), July 3, 1911, M.A.E., "Allemagne," n.s. 34.

the *Westminster Gazette* (July 3), which was generally regarded as having close connections with the Foreign Office, stressed France's "special political interests, which no other nation possesses in Morocco," and her "genuine causes for anxiety which are different in kind from the diplomatic solicitude of other Powers for future spheres of action." But the ambassador soon found that his hopes had been excessive; his disappointment stemmed directly from the Cabinet's intervention in the policy process.

In contrast to the first Moroccan crisis, the second saw the active participation of the British Cabinet in the formation and direction of foreign policy. In fact the main lines of British policy for the entire crisis emerged from the Cabinet meeting of July 4, at which it was resolved to remain faithful to the 1904 obligations to France, to oppose German demands for negotiations *à trois* over Morocco, and to propose instead negotiations *à quatre* (Britain, Spain, France, and Germany) to settle the issue. On instructions from the Cabinet, Grey that day notified the German ambassador, Count Metternich, of these decisions. But while the Cabinet agreed to fulfill Britain's treaty commitments to France, it firmly refused to send any ship to Morocco. Grey was ordered to remind the French "that they must recognize that largely by their own action, a return to the status quo ante has become difficult, if not impossible, and that it may therefore become necessary to give a more definite recognition than before to German interests in Morocco." Not content with suggesting a partition of Morocco, the Cabinet also spelled out British conditions for such an eventuality: "(1) no German port on the Mediterranean shore (2) no new *fortified* port anywhere in the Moroccan coast (3) the open door for British trade." [53] Although they professed loyalty to the entente the British, so long as their Moroccan interests were safeguarded, had no qualms should the French lose part of their share of the 1904 arrangement.

Paul Cambon learned of these decisions shortly after the Cabinet had adjourned. Grey attempted to cushion the ambassador's disappointment on the ship issue by stressing British "treaty obligations" and British opposition to any negotiations on Morocco which excluded London. Then, almost in passing, he observed that Paris should consider compensation to Germany, possibly even in Morocco. Cambon, still angry about the ship decision, missed the meaning of this remark; his dispatch attached no special significance to it. [54]

If the logic behind Grey's suggestion was lost on Cambon, it was not on Joseph Caillaux: the Premier immediately cabled the ambassador (July 5) that there could be no compensation for Germany in Morocco.

53. Asquith to George V, July 4, 1911, Asquith Papers, box 6; cf. Grey to Count de Salis, July 4, 1911, *B.D.*, VII, no. 356; Metternich to Wilhelm II (tel.), July 4, 1911, *G.P.*, XXIX, no. 10592.
54. P. Cambon to Caillaux (tel.), July 4, 1911, *D.D.F.*, 2nd ser., XIV, no. 19; Grey to Bertie, July 4, 1911, *B.D.*, VII, no. 355.

Thus alerted, Cambon asked Grey the next day to indicate what the Cabinet meant by compensation. To his astonishment the Foreign Secretary revealed that Britain, in spite of its previous strategic views, could now accept an unfortified German port in Morocco. Cambon's Gallic temper flared. France, he declared, would never accept a German foothold in Morocco. Bitterly denouncing the entente's failure to send ships, he warned that Germany could easily fortify any harbor. Faced with this outburst, Grey hastened to assure the ambassador that Britain would not force an unacceptable policy upon France. This assurance only slightly mollified Cambon's unhappiness with Britain's new flexibility on Morocco.[55]

British willingness to yield a port in Morocco deserves further comment. It seems, first of all, to have marked a radical departure from all previous British strategic policy. Both in the negotiations for the entente and then during the first Moroccan crisis, London had been especially sensitive about who possessed Moroccan ports. The port issue had indeed prompted the much misunderstood exchanges between Lansdowne and Delcassé in April and May 1905. Yet, during the Algeciras conference in early 1906 Admiral Fisher had agreed if necessary to accept a German port in Morocco; when rumors of this view reached the French, Grey denied any change in the British position.[56] The French consequently were misled and unaware of the true Admiralty position on Morocco. Thus in 1911 the British attitude toward a port, though new neither to Grey nor to the Admiralty, completely flabbergasted the French. Moreover, the new British attitude deprived Paris of an effective technique for rallying the entente: the appeal to British strategic interests.[57] Although they refused to abandon completely their favorite tocsin, the French thereafter began to shift their appeals to a higher plane, to the preservation of the entente relationship on its own merits and as a matter of honor. In this approach they were helped by the blunderings of Kiderlen, by British fears of Germany, and by a British sense of obligation to France growing out of the 1904 agreement.

This friction between the entente partners in early July was known only to the officials involved. To the public and to Germany—and somewhat to the Kaiser's amazement—the British appeared the dependable "friends" of France. If some radical press organs thought France had possibly provoked German action, the entire British press condemned Germany's bellicose behavior.[58] And France received more public support when Asquith spoke in the House of Commons on July 6, the same

55. P. Cambon to Caillaux (tel.), July 6–7, 1911, D.D.F., 2nd ser., XIV, no. 36; Grey to Bertie, July 6, 1911, B.D., VII, no. 363.
56. Tweedmouth to Campbell-Bannerman, Feb. 2, 1906, Campbell-Bannerman Papers, Add. MSS, 41231; Tweedmouth to Grey, Feb. 25, 1906, Grey Papers, F.O. 800/87; Grey to Tweedmouth, Feb. 28, 1906, ibid.
57. Bertie to Grey, July 6, 1911, B.D., VII, no. 361.
58. Hale, Publicity and Diplomacy, 384–385.

day Cambon was learning the precise limits of the actual support. The German action, declared the Prime Minister, had created a new situation in Morocco, one which involved British interests; he reminded the Commons that Britain, because of the 1904 accord, had special obligations to France. In short, on the public level the entente appeared to react to the new crisis as a well-defined unit. British backing seemed assured.[59]

In Paris, in the meantime, certain lines of policy were likewise beginning to emerge. If these lines were less clearly defined, they were also more susceptible to change—changes caused not only by German demands but also by the pressures of France's friends and allies. On two key points French officials were agreed: no territorial concessions to Germany in Morocco and a strong preference for bilateral negotiations with Berlin.[60] Beyond these points French policy hinged upon the crucial question: what did Germany want from France? Unofficial reports from Berlin in early July suggested that Kiderlen wanted to bargain in the Congo-Cameroon area, and this impression was soon reinforced. On July 8 Baron von Schoen, the German ambassador to France, assured de Selves that Germany had no territorial ambitions in Morocco, only in the French Congo. And the next day Kiderlen emphasized to Jules Cambon that the French Congo offered an area for possible compensation; four days later he repeated the idea. This apparent German willingness to reach a quick agreement over the Congo raised French hopes.[61]

The hopes proved illusory. On July 15 Berlin revealed the extent of its territorial demands: the cession of virtually the entire French Congo. The temerity and scope of the German demand immediately unsettled the international climate. Paris regarded the suggestion as a deliberate attempt to wreck negotiations; Jules Cambon concluded that the Germans still wanted an Atlantic port, either at Agadir or Libreville. By July 18 the Franco-German negotiations were on the verge of collapsing. A situation which had so recently appeared capable of solution was now dangerously near an explosion.[62]

While Paris and Berlin probed each other on the Congo, British officials continued to debate how far to support France in its drive for Morocco. At first the radical views within the Cabinet continued to prevail: Britain would afford diplomatic backing to France yet could accept Germany in Morocco. On July 10 Grey not only reiterated this position

59. Parliamentary Debates: Commons, 5th ser., 27 (July 6, 1911), 1341.
60. See, e.g., Caillaux to P. Cambon (tel.), July 5, 1911, D.D.F., 2nd ser., XIV, no. 22; Caillaux to J. Cambon (tel.), July 4, 1911, ibid., no. 21.
61. Berckheim (Councillor of the Berlin Embassy) to Caillaux (tel.), July 3, 1911, ibid., no. 16; J. Cambon to de Selves, July 10, 1911, ibid., nos. 51, 54; J. Cambon to de Selves (tel.), July 13, 1911, ibid., no. 65.
62. J. Cambon to de Selves (tel.), July 16, 1911, ibid., no. 71; J. Cambon to P. Cambon, July 16, 1911, ibid., no. 73.

to Cambon, he also refused to consider sending entente ships as a countermove. France, the Foreign Secretary bluntly declared, had one of two choices: adhere to the Act of Algeciras or give Germany adequate compensation, in or out of Morocco.[63]

The Cabinet's stance on Morocco disturbed Grey's colleagues at the Foreign Office. Encouraged and abetted by Bertie, they pressured the Foreign Secretary to alter the tenor of British policy. Bertie, moreover, attempted to change it on his own initiative, flatly promising de Selves on July 11 that Britain would never allow a German port on the Atlantic coast of Morocco.[64] This blatant contradiction of Grey's earlier statement, which Bertie "claimed" not to have received, put the ambassador in an awkward position. Strongly defending his actions, Bertie wrote Nicolson on July 12: "If the French get to think that we are ready to give way to Germany we shall help to throw them into the Teuton embrace." He was also "equally confident that the German Government if we join with the French in refusing to agree to the establishment of a German port, call it what you may, on the Atlantic Coast of Morocco, may bluster, but there will be nothing else." [65] Crowe agreed entirely with Bertie's assessment. Caustically noting the variety of opinions received in the past from the Admiralty, the Senior Clerk demanded that the Naval Lords draft a written policy statement on the question of a German port in Morocco; quite clearly he expected that this requirement would change naval opinion. Grey assented to the request.[66]

The opposition from Bertie and Crowe forced the Foreign Secretary to defend his position. On July 13 Grey wrote the ambassador that Admiral A. K. Wilson, the First Sea Lord, and Reginald McKenna, the First Lord of the Admiralty, would be "perfectly satisfied with an arrangement that included an undertaking not to fortify any port in Morocco. We should then have a Treaty right as well as the Sea Power (which we now have) to prevent it." Having made his point, Grey observed that a partition of Morocco would create a "great fuss," possibly forcing Britain to demand concessions elsewhere. In any event, since France objected to having Germany in Morocco, he thought it "unnecessary to discuss question of bringing it into the negotiations." [67] Bertie remained unconvinced and suspicious. On July 16 he predicted that if the Germans discovered London had "no unalterable objection to their having a commercial port, and in these days there are no limits to indiscretions, they may squeeze the French." "Selves," he wrote, "was very

63. P. Cambon to de Selves (tel.), July 10, 1911, *ibid.*, no. 48; Grey to Bertie, July 10, 1911, B.D., VII, no. 368; J. Cambon to de Selves (tel.), July 10, 1911, M.A.E., "Allemagne," n.s. 35.
64. Bertie to Grey (tel.), July 11, 1911, B.D., VII, no. 369; Bertie to Grey, July 12, 1911, *ibid.*, no. 372.
65. Bertie to Nicolson, July 12, 1911, *ibid.*, no. 376.
66. Minute by Crowe on Bertie, July 12, 1911, *ibid.*, no. 372.
67. Grey to Bertie, July 12, 13 (tel.), 1911, *ibid.*, nos. 375, 377; also Grey to Asquith, July 13, 1911, Grey Papers, F.O. 800/100.

much taken aback by the change of attitude which Cambon found or thought he noticed in H(is) M(ajesty's) Government as regards a German port on the Atlantic Coast of Morocco." [68] The news of Kiderlen's demands in central Africa seemed to confirm Bertie's fears; he too regarded the proposal as a mere pretext for a Moroccan port.

The Foreign Secretary's continuing refusal to exceed the instructions of the Cabinet alarmed Crowe and Nicolson. The excessive German demands in the Congo now conveniently buttressed their bureaucratic campaign on France's behalf. No longer would the two plead the port question with the Foreign Secretary; instead they began to urge Grey to contemplate the future of Europe—that is, they exploited his fear of a Britain isolated against Germany. "Germany," wrote Crowe on July 18, "is playing for the highest stakes. If her demands are acceded to either on the Congo or in Morocco . . . it will mean definitely the subjugation of France. . . . This is a trial of strength, if anything. Concession means not loss of interests or loss of prestige. It means defeat, with all of its inevitable consequences." He insisted that "the defeat of France is a matter vital to this country." Therefore it was of little use to discuss "the particular conditions which might or might not be put up with, before deciding the larger and dominant question whether England is prepared to fight by the side of France if necessary. This is the question to be wisely considered and firmly decided. On this decision everything else depends." Arthur Nicolson concurred. He thought the government had "to decide whether they will remain true to their engagements to France and maintain the present groupings of Powers, so essential to the preservation of peace, or whether they will leave Germany to settle matters with France." "The only hope of keeping the peace," the Undersecretary declared, "is for us to range ourselves alongside of France, as we did in 1905 and 1906, and show a united front to German demands, the character of which it is superfluous to specify." [69]

These arguments impressed the Foreign Secretary, who even acknowledged to his subordinates that the entente was in danger. Yet, there remained the practical problem of how to protect this valuable but ambiguous accord. Grey's alternatives, given the radical predominance in the Cabinet, were limited. The political environment appeared to rule out any unequivocal stand with France, or against Germany. Indeed, even less ambitious action also seemed circumscribed. This the Foreign Secretary discovered on July 19 when he sought the Cabinet's permission to propose an international conference should the Franco-German negotiations deadlock. The invitations to the meeting should plainly stipulate, Grey argued, that if Germany refused to attend, Britain would then act to protect its own interests. This threatening proposal encoun-

68. Bertie to Nicolson, July 16, 1911, B.D., VII, no. 386.
69. Minutes by Crowe and Nicolson on Bertie to Grey (tel.), July 18, 1911, ibid., no. 392.

tered vigorous resistance from the radicals in the Cabinet, especially from Lord Loreburn, who was opposed, Asquith informed the King, "on the ground that our direct interest in the matter was insignificant, and that, as a result of such a communication, we might soon find ourselves drifting into war." Loreburn carried the Cabinet; there would be no threat attached to any conference proposal. Britain would simply suggest a conference where it would "work in concert with French diplomacy." The radicals further insisted that France be notified that Germany's admission to Morocco "under proper conditions . . . would not be regarded by us as fatal to British interests, and could not be treated by us as a *casus belli*." [70]

Once more the Cabinet had firmly decreed the outlines of British policy. But this time Grey, by now convinced of Germany's threat to the Entente Cordiale, paid less heed to his colleagues' advice. At the conclusion of this Cabinet, he privately sounded Asquith about the desirability of warning Metternich that a collapse of bilateral negotiations would bring active British intervention in the Moroccan problem. Britain might, opined Grey, even send a ship to Morocco. "I fear lest irreparable harm may have been done by continued silence and inaction." [71] These demands marked a turning point in Grey's approach to the Moroccan crisis. His policy of restraint upon France was henceforth joined by one of rigid sternness toward Germany.

On July 20 Sir Francis Bertie presented the French Foreign Minister with a note embodying the Cabinet decisions of the preceeding day: if the negotiations deadlocked, Britain would propose an international conference. Then came the bombshell. At such a conference the British government would be "unable to treat as an unconditional *casus belli* any such admission of Germany to Morocco, though they could not, except in concert with France and on conditions satisfactory to her suggest or deal with it." London, moreover, expected consultation "about any step envolving [sic] serious consequences" for the British government, including presumably a partition of Morocco.[72] It was this memorandum of July 20, not the Mansion House speech, which warned Paris against a Moroccan settlement at British expense.[73] More importantly, the British memorandum unmistakably defined the limits of Britain's support for France.

Grey elaborated upon these limits in a private letter to Bertie on July 20: "We cannot go to war in order to set aside the Algeciras Act and put France in virtual possession of Morocco . . . if we go to war it must

70. Asquith to George V, July 19, 1911, Asquith Papers, box 6.
71. Grey to Asquith, July 19, 1911, B.D., VII, no. 399.
72. Grey to Bertie (tel.), July 19, 1911, ibid., no. 397; Bertie to Grey, July 20, 1911, ibid., no. 403. On July 24, 1911, Nicolson confessed to Goschen that "I was able however to modify our communication very considerably, and since its dispatch I think matters have got in a far better groove"; Nicolson Papers, vol. II/1911.
73. Compare Taylor, The Struggle for Mastery in Europe, 471.

be in defense of British interests." Grey, like the Cabinet, wanted no war over Morocco. Of the acceptable solutions to the crisis, he preferred an arrangement in the French Congo. Barring that possibility, he opted for a Spanish-French-German partition of Morocco, with some reward to Britain. As a last resort there might be a return to the *status quo ante*, which would at best be a "cumbrous troublesome and temporary expedient." Bertie, who had already experienced the anger of Caillaux and de Selves over the official memorandum, prudently decided not to "frighten" them with Grey's personal thoughts on the flexibility of British policy. "They might feel that they were about to be deserted by us for the benefit of Germany." [74]

The ambassador had correctly gauged French feelings. The official French reply to the British memorandum curtly denied that the negotiations had broken down and pointedly emphasized British treaty obligations. Under no circumstances would France yield territory, "however small," in Morocco.[75] On July 21 both de Selves and Caillaux reiterated each of these points with Bertie; Caillaux, whose suspicions about British dependability had been increased by the demarche, complained bitterly that he was unable to comprehend British policy. He attacked the notion of a German port in Morocco and warned that German troops in the Moorish kingdom would "make it impossible for France to transfer to Europe for use against Germany the Algerian troops. This impossibility," he contended, "would be an injury to British as well as to French interests." The Premier appealed not only to Britain's strategic interests but also to British honor. "If France was to be deserted (lachée) by England and left to face Germany alone in the controversy it would be a serious blow to the Entente between France and England, a great shock to French public opinion and the consequences might be very serious." [76]

Reports from Berlin reinforced French concern about the unity and effectiveness of the entente. On July 20 Kiderlen, infuriated by French press leaks about Germany's Congo demands, informed Jules Cambon that, should the talks fail, Germany would "press to the end" for an application of the Algeciras accord. Cambon retorted that France would go as far as Germany would. The language and tone of this interview were disturbing.[77] The possibility of war made British support more necessary than ever. Had Caillaux and de Selves known the full scope

74. Grey to Bertie, July 20, 1911, *B.D.*, VII, no. 405; Bertie to Grey, July 21, 1911, *ibid.*, no. 407. Grey had written that Bertie could use as much of the secret note as he thought "discreet" in "helping the French to clear their minds"; Grey to Bertie, July 20, 1911, Bertie Papers, F.O. 800/165.
75. Bertie to Grey (tel.), July 20, 1911, *B.D.*, VII, no. 401; "Note pour l'ambassade de Grande-Bretagne," July 20, 1911, *D.D.F.*, 2nd ser., XIV, no. 88.
76. Bertie to Grey, July 21, 1911, *B.D.*, VII, no. 408; Caillaux thought the memo indicated an Anglo-German deal over the Moroccan ports, Caillaux, *Mes mémoires*, II, 130–139.
77. J. Cambon to de Selves (tel.), July 21, 1911, *D.D.F.*, 2nd ser., XIV, no. 90.

of developments in London on July 21, they would have rested easier. At the Foreign Office Sir Edward Grey was now ready for a policy of firmness toward Berlin. Armed with Nicolson's argument that a disgruntled France would. hurt Britain's naval interests in the Mediterranean, Grey managed to gain Cabinet approval on July 21 for a "hard line" toward Germany.[78] He was authorized to remind Berlin of its failure to respond to the British statement on Morocco made seventeen days earlier. He was also to inform Metternich that "it must be clearly understood that we should recognise no settlement in Morocco in which we had not a voice." Neither Grey nor the Cabinet feared Germany in Morocco, only a Germany which ignored British interests in Morocco. Later that morning Grey conveyed the Cabinet warning to the German ambassador.[79] Within hours an incident that was as surprising as it was dangerous made their conversation superfluous.

At a Mansion House dinner that evening, Chancellor of the Exchequer David Lloyd George delivered a routine after-dinner speech to an audience whose main attention in recent days had been on the struggle over the power of the House of Lords. At the conclusion of his remarks he made some less than impromptu observations about British foreign policy. Commenting upon Britain's role as a world power, the Welsh radical pledged that Britain would never renounce this role simply to keep the peace. Nor would it look with favor upon negotiations which touched upon British interests but which did not include Britain. This "would be a humiliation intolerable for a great country like ours to endure. (Cheers.) . . . National honour is no party question. (Cheers.)" [80] With this strong, though vague, assertion of British interests in Morocco, the British government was now *publicly* pledged to support its entente partner, come what might. The policy of firmness toward Germany was thus reiterated; but at the same time the policy of restraint upon France appeared overturned.

The origins, the motives, and even the exact meaning of Lloyd George's peroration remain obscure. That the maneuver was deliberate —checked and approved at least by Asquith and Grey—is certain.[81] Further, as Oron Hale has pointed out, there was apparent coordination with certain newspapers to ensure both full coverage of the speech and that the remarks would be harshly applied to Germany.[82] Beyond this the evidence is tentative, scant, and often contradictory on two key

78. Minute by Nicolson, July 21, 1911, *B.D.*, VII, no. 409.
79. Asquith to George V, July 21, 1911, Asquith Papers, box 6; Grey to Goschen, July 21, 1911, *B.D.*, VII, no. 411; Metternich to Bethmann, July 21, 1911, *G.P.*, XXIX, no. 10617.
80. *Times*, July 22, 1911.
81. On the origins of the speech see David Lloyd George, *War Memoirs*, 6 vols. (Boston, 1933–1937), I, 39–43; Grey, *Twenty-five Years*, I, 215–217, 232; Winston S. Churchill, *The World Crisis, 1911–1918*, 4 vols. (New York, 1923–1929), I, 42–46; Lord Riddell, *More Pages From My Diary* (London, 1934), 20–21.
82. *Publicity and Diplomacy*, 387–391.

points: why did Lloyd George suddenly intrude into the formation of foreign policy, and what role did Grey play in the episode? News of the German demands upon France may have genuinely stirred Lloyd George from his fixation on domestic politics. Or possibly the speech was a personal attempt to divert public attention from the constitutional crisis or to exploit the growing anti-German sentiment for private political gain. But who gave the Chancellor the notion of speaking on the Moroccan issue at Mansion House? It was perhaps Churchill or one of the senior Foreign Office officials who was responsible. On July 24 Nicolson remarked that the "speech of Lloyd George . . . was no sudden inspiration but a carefully thought out one"; he was confident the French would now be "quite tranquillized as to our attitude." [83]

Grey's role is equally unclear. Since late May he had consistently evaded any pretence of an unconditional guarantee to help the French; but the Mansion House speech seemed an abandonment of that position. Yet, as the French soon discovered, Grey's basic policy continued to be one of caution and evasion. Why? Because Lloyd George's speech, though indeed a warning to Germany, was more importantly a political move by Asquith and Grey to curtail radical control of Britain's policy toward the Moroccan question. Grey had by July 19 become greatly exercised at radical incursions into his traditional preserve.[84] And in the next two days the Crowe-Nicolson-Bertie theme that the entente was in danger found increasing favor with the Foreign Secretary. Without necessarily overturning the "restraint-firmness" formula, he and the Prime Minister sought to reduce radical influence by both the content of the pronouncement and the participation of the pronouncer. They achieved their goals: the Mansion House remarks effectively muted the Cabinet's direction of foreign policy, alarmed the Germans, and assured the French.

The speech drastically altered Anglo-German relations. There was now no room or reason for a German misunderstanding of the British position. If the Wilhelmstrasse wanted to keep Britain out of the negotiations, then it must renounce any territorial ambitions in Morocco. On July 24 the Germans took this step; Metternich assured Grey that Germany had no territorial designs on the Sherifian kingdom. But despite the German disclaimer, Anglo-German tensions mounted. The very next day, July 25, Metternich strongly protested the Mansion House remarks, ominously declaring that a collapse in the negotiations must bring a return to the *status quo ante* in Morocco, "whether that were agreeable to France or not"; moreover, he opposed any suggestion of an

83. Nicolson to Sir Fairfax Cartwright (British ambassador to Vienna), July 24, 1911, B.D., VII, no. 418; Nicolson to Goschen, July 24, 1911, Nicolson Papers, vol. II/1911; see also Churchill, *Young Statesman*, 504–505.
84. Grey to Asquith, July 19, 1911, B.D., VII, no. 399.

international conference on Morocco.[85] The acrimonious interview so disturbed the Foreign Secretary that he told Churchill and Lloyd George that he had " 'just received a communication from the German Ambassador so stiff that the Fleet might be attacked at any moment. I have sent for McKenna to warn him!' " [86]

This frantic moment marked the peak of Anglo-German hostility during the second Moroccan crisis. Tensions eased somewhat on July 27 when the Germans renewed their assurances about Morocco and the British promised acceptance of any settlement arranged outside Morocco. In the House of Commons that same day Asquith firmly restated British interests in Morocco, but in calm and nonbelligerent tones.[87] These developments, combined with some progress in the Paris-Berlin talks, helped to mollify Anglo-German relations in early August. Although there were minor flurries in August and September, neither Berlin nor London again allowed their feelings to intrude too deeply upon the underlying issue at hand—Franco-German relations.

Lloyd George's assertions troubled Anglo-German relations; they also thoroughly confounded his radical associates within and without the government. During the early weeks of the crisis the *Manchester Guardian*, mouthpiece for the radical wing of the Liberals, had maintained "that neither their obligations to France nor their strategic position on the Atlantic coast of Morocco were sufficient cause to justify going to extremes." [88] Apparently unaware of the Cabinet's willingness to accept a German presence in Morocco, C. P. Scott, editor of the *Guardian*, had severe reservations about British policy which were simply reaffirmed by the Mansion House speech. Scott, in London, protested to Asquith, Grey, and Lloyd George (July 22 and July 25) about a policy on Morocco that could "lead to war." His pleas were not eminently successful. Grey made it clear he would leave the government if he could not give France "such support as would prevent her from falling under the virtual control of Germany and estrangement from us." Scott could only respond that Britain should not be more French than the French.[89]

Scott's radical friends within the Cabinet were equally unhappy over Lloyd George's excursion into foreign affairs. Until this point the radicals had successfully blocked Grey's proposals to send a ship, had delayed efforts to warn Germany, and had ruled out Morocco as a casus belli. In short, the Cabinet had substantially shaped British foreign policy, in decided contrast to the Unionist-Liberal performance in the first

85. Grey to Goschen, July 24, 25, 1911, *ibid.*, nos. 417, 419; Metternich to Kiderlen (tel.), July 25, 1911, G.P., XXIX, no. 10626.
86. Churchill, *The World Crisis*, I, 44–45.
87. Grey to Goschen, July 27, 1911, B.D., VII, no. 430; Metternich to Kiderlen (tel.), July 27, 1911, G.P., XXIX, nos. 10633, 10634.
88. On the *Guardian*'s attitude, see Hale, *Publicity and Diplomacy*, 391.
89. J. L. Hammond, *C. P. Scott of the Manchester Guardian* (London, 1934), 161, 153–163.

Morocco imbroglio. Yet Lloyd George, whose help the radicals needed if they wanted to retain their influence, had now forsaken them—without even mentioning his proposed remarks to the Cabinet. His desertion especially angered Lord Loreburn and Lord Morley (the Lord Privy Seal), the two most prominent radicals besides the future Prime Minister himself. On Thursday, July 27, before Asquith spoke in the Commons, Loreburn and Morley approached the Prime Minister and the Foreign Secretary, asking that they make clear that Britain had "no wish to interfere between France and Germany and to undo the effect of Lloyd George's speech." Morley, who sympathized with German resentment of the speech, observed that the Mansion House discourse reminded him "uncomfortably of Gramont's on July 6, 1870: received with tremendous applause, followed by bottomless mischief." He hoped that Asquith would "efface—so far as may be—the natural and inevitable effects of the deliverance which I cannot help but regard as really unfortunate." [90]

Loreburn and Morley were disappointed. The Prime Minister virtually restated, in somewhat clearer terms and moderate tones, Lloyd George's demand that any negotiations over Morocco include Britain. "That would be our right as a signatory of the Treaty of Algeciras; it might be our obligation under the terms of our Agreement of 1904 with France; it might be our duty in defence of British interests directly affected by further developments." And Asquith added, for the benefit of the radicals, "I would venture, in the general interest, to make a strong appeal to the House, not on the present occasion to enter into further details or open up controversial ground." [91]

While the radicals were clearly unhappy about British policy after July 21 and their lack of control over it, they never waged a full-scale fight on the issue within the Cabinet. On July 31 Grey gained, "after considerable discussion," unlimited authorization to call a conference if the Franco-German talks collapsed. Otherwise the radicals failed to press for an exhaustive Cabinet debate, either upon Lloyd George's remarks or upon British policy.[92] The continuing crisis over the House of Lords, as well as a wave of strikes, may well have pre-empted their attention; or perhaps they had decided to wait for a more propitious moment to challenge Grey's policy.[93]

In late August, however, Loreburn renewed his attack on Grey's performance during the crisis. Having possibly heard rumors of the staff

90. Loreburn to Grey, July 27, 1911, Grey Papers, F.O. 800/99; Morley to Asquith, July 27, 1911, Asquith Papers, box 13.
91. *Parliamentary Debates: Commons*, 5th ser., 28 (July 27, 1911), 1827–1828.
92. See Asquith to George V, July 25, Aug. 1, 1911, Asquith Papers, box 6. In contrast to Grey's handling of other major issues, on this occasion the Cabinet received copies of most of the important dispatches, though not of course the numerous private letters between the Foreign Office and Paris. The dispatches circulated to the Cabinet are in Cab. 37/107.
93. The latter explanation was advanced by the *Times*, Nov. 21, 1911.

talks, he wrote Grey that "I greatly fear that France expects our military and naval support." He warned that "I believe you could not give it if you wished, in this which is a purely French quarrel. I believe you could not carry it in the present House of Commons except by a majority very largely composed of Conservatives and with a very large number of [the] Ministerial side against you and this would mean that the present government could not carry on." In these circumstances France should not expect material aid from Britain; "they ought to be told we cannot go beyond diplomatic support in this quarrel." Loreburn's strictures were again ineffectual. Grey, who claimed that only the Cabinet could authorize such a statement, refused to vary his policy.[94]

The Mansion House episode gave added impetus to the already smoldering radical dislike of Grey's management of British policy. In the first weeks after the *Panther's* arrival at Agadir, the radicals in the Cabinet had effectively shaped the limits of British support for France. Their intervention in the policy process first provoked the hostility and the opposition of the permanent officials at the Foreign Office, then that of Grey as well. Nor of course did the radicals' willingness to accept the Germans in Morocco appeal to Paris. With the Chancellor of the Exchequer's speech all of this suddenly changed. The definite erosion of radical control over policy in late July provoked abiding resentments within the Cabinet that, in November 1911, reached new heights with the radicals' discovery of the military conversations.

It would, however, be a mistake to assume that radicals alone were displeased with British policy. There were other dissidents as well, among them Lord Stamfordham, one of the King's private secretaries and an unbending conservative. On July 23 he wrote Nicolson, expressing distrust "of French alliances and . . . belief of a natural affinity of England to Germany. If Germany chooses to establish herself at Agadir what business have we to object. If France was not in such a blue funk of Germany we should not be mixed up in this question at all." His views were also ignored, for Lloyd George's decisive utterance had, as Oron Hale writes, openly committed the government "to the foreign office view that the issue was no longer a deal in African real estate, but the foundations of their foreign policy in Europe. At all costs the understanding with France must be preserved."[95]

The Mansion House oratory affected and influenced Anglo-French relations no less than it did Anglo-German tension and the role of the British Cabinet. The French press, unaware of the resentment caused by the British memorandum of July 20, welcomed the words of the

94. Loreburn to Grey, Aug. 25, 1911, Grey Papers, F.O. 800/99; Grey to Loreburn, Aug. 30, 1911, *ibid.*
95. Stamfordham to Nicolson, July 23, 1911, Nicolson Papers, vol. III/1911; Hale, *Publicity and Diplomacy*, 392.

Chancellor of the Exchequer, seeing his remarks not only as proof of the unity of British policy, but as an impressive reaffirmation of the value and vigor of the entente. And *Le Temps* on July 22 observed: "Is there any need to remark that the well-known opinions of M. Lloyd George, his liberalism, his pacifistic tendencies, his sentiments toward Germany underline the importance of his declaration." He had warned Berlin of the dangers of a "policy of bluff." [96]

The makers of French policy—Caillaux, de Selves, and the Quai d'Orsay officials—were naturally encouraged by this new statement of British intentions. Since it followed by twenty-four hours the signing of a joint staff accord on the military conversations, the French officials hoped these two displays of goodwill, not the qualifying memorandum, represented London's true policy.[97] Yet there remained the question: how far did British support actually extend? With Lloyd George's declaration Paris faced afresh the problem of deciding where the entente really stood. The French soon discovered there would be no definite or conclusive answer to this question, for the Mansion House remarks were no "blank check" for Paris.

On July 25 Paul Cambon began the sounding operations. His first results were pleasing. Grey, though still hoping diplomatic support would suffice, agreed with Cambon that the situation might arise when it would be necessary "prévoir toutes les éventualités," a comment that nearly duplicated Lansdowne's remarks of 1905. Two days later came Asquith's parliamentary statement on Britain's obligations to France. London now appeared determined, prepared, and united in its intention to support the entente.[98]

But the limits of this support soon became evident. On July 27 and 28 Cambon and Grey discussed three of the central issues in the crisis: would London press for a conference in spite of known German opposition, what would London do if German troops landed at Agadir, and would Britain "collaborate militarily" to prevent a German landing. On each point Grey disappointed the French. He absolutely refused to commit Britain to do more than summon a conference; any further commitments, he insisted, would compromise events—and to send a ship to Morocco was to take a step toward war.[99] "We could not contemplate such a step without being able to take into full consideration all the circumstances which might exist at the time." Put more bluntly, the Foreign Secretary preferred to wait and see. He closed his conversation with Cambon with the gratuitous observation that for a "protectorate" in

96. See also Carroll, *French Public Opinion*, 243–244.
97. Caillaux, *Agadir*, 138; the joint staff accord is discussed in Chapter 7.
98. P. Cambon to de Selves (tel.), July 25, 1911, *D.D.F.*, 2nd ser., XIV, no. 102; Grey to L. D. Carnegie, July 25, 1911, *B.D.*, VII, no. 421.
99. De Selves to P. Cambon (tel.), July 27, 1911, *D.D.F.*, 2nd ser., XIV, no. 110; P. Cambon to de Selves (tel.), July 27, 28, 1911, *ibid.*, nos. 113, 118; P. Cambon to J. Cambon, July 30, 1911, *ibid.*, no. 129.

Morocco, France should be willing to grant compensation to Germany.[100] British policy would, in short, continue to be one of firmness and restraint, regardless of the more bellicose public statements.

The British responses to Cambon's overtures arrived in Paris at a crucial moment; for in Berlin, also on July 28, the talks between Jules Cambon and Kiderlen had stalled on the issue of concessions. Grey's evasive refusals, coming at this point, helped to revive French misgivings about British dependability. Among those especially distrustful of London was Joseph Caillaux. While aware of the sympathy of the Foreign Office functionaries for France, the Premier never underestimated the power of the radicals within the British Cabinet. Lloyd George's saber rattling eased his apprehension for a moment, but Grey's pronouncements merely renewed his doubts. He complained afterward that "the English Government . . . constantly supported the solution, which from the first day had envisaged: the concession of compensation to Germany; beyond that, it reserved action, refusing to say what would be its attitude, if, for one reason or another, an agreement could not be established between France and Germany." [101]

Although Caillaux favored compensation for Germany, he was determined to avoid any partition of Morocco. Indeed, his attachment to this goal led him to resort to a highly dangerous bluff on July 31—he had the Army and Navy prepare mobilization orders, calculating that the German government had enough spies about "to learn these secret orders which may open their eyes to the fact that France cannot be pushed further." [102] But this willingness to indulge in a bluff was not typical of the usually sensible Caillaux: he had already made secret contacts with the German Embassy and with Jules Cambon in hopes of achieving a peaceful settlement.[103]

Several factors strengthened the Premier's predilection for peace. One was a realistic appraisal of the defects of the French Army; his reorganization of the high command eloquently reflected these shortcomings and his awareness of them. Moreover, General Joffre, when asked, informed Caillaux that France did not possess that seventy-percent chance of success recommended by Napoleon as the guideline for war or negotiations. Nor did Caillaux have much confidence in Russian dependability or military effectiveness.[104] Finally, Britain's hesitancy to

100. Grey to Bertie, July 28, 1911, B.D., VII, no. 433.
101. Caillaux, Agadir, 138–141, and Mes mémoires, II, 137–139; see also Rudolph Binion, Defeated Leaders: The Political Fate of Caillaux, Jouvenel, and Tardieu (New York, 1960), 36–48.
102. Bertie to Grey, July 31, 1911, B.D., VII, no. 447.
103. On Caillaux's "private" diplomacy, see his Agadir, 161–171; "Notes de M. Fondère: conversations Lancken et Caillaux," July 25, 1911, D.D.F., 2nd ser., XIV, no. 105; "Notes de M. Jules Cambon," March [?] 1912, ibid., pp. 752–760. On Aug. 21, 1911, Bertie informed Grey of rumors about communications between Caillaux and the German Embassy; Grey Papers, F.O. 800/52.
104. Caillaux, Agadir, 141–146; Joffre, Memoirs, I, 14–15.

act, evén after Mansion House, shaped the Premier's decisions, and he never found it easy to be enthusiastic about the merits of help from the small British Army. In this connection there occurred the only exchanges on the diplomatic level about the military conversations.

On July 24 Jules Cambon had implored Paris to establish military collaboration with London. De Selves quickly assured him that this question, which "was posed several years before . . . is becoming a reality." But the nature of the "reality" troubled Caillaux, and in early August he told Bertie that the British Army, though excellent, would be too small for the European war that he felt was eventually bound to come. Would there be any chance, he asked the ambassador, of getting Japan to send troops to Europe. Bertie, who offered no opinion, labeled the entire conversation "wild talk." Neither the question of British military assistance nor the staff talks reappeared at the diplomatic level during the remainder of the crisis.[105]

The French policy-makers, meanwhile, continued to ponder and explore the larger question of Britain's ultimate intentions if the Franco-German talks collapsed. Each time the negotiations with Berlin faltered the French resumed their probing operations. On August 13, for example, de Selves asked Paul Cambon to try once more to discover what Britain would do if German troops debarked at Agadir. At first Grey deferred an answer, then responded by reminding the ambassador of the connection between actions in Moroccan waters and trouble on France's eastern frontiers. Instead of a provocative move, the Foreign Secretary recommended an international conference as the first step should the talks break off. But, "in the actual situation," Grey saw no necessity to take action and thought the entente could "await events." The Foreign Secretary had again avoided any definite promise of action, either if the Germans refused a conference or if they landed at Agadir. In an attempt to mitigate the effects of this second British rebuff, Cambon deliberately stressed to Paris that Grey had spoken "of England as if she was the ally of France on the same bases as Russia, and he did not seem to doubt for an instant that his Government would shirk her *obligation* to sustain us." [106] The ambassador's optimism and confidence could not diminish Caillaux's distrust of London. At this point the Premier employed still another approach: on August 20 he told Bertie that France planned to send ships to Mogador and Saffi if German troops debarked. If this happened, he hoped that the British would join in the operation. Grey reacted immediately. In no uncertain terms he warned against sending

105. De Selves to J. Cambon, July 26, 1911, *D.D.F.*, 2nd ser., XIV, no. 108; Bertie to Grey, Aug. 3, 1911, *B.D.*, VII, no. 455.
106. P. Cambon to de Selves, Aug. 16, 1911, *D.D.F.*, 2nd ser., XIV, no. 184; Jules Cambon was quite bitter over Grey's evasion, J. Cambon to de Selves, Aug. 20, 1911, *ibid.*, no. 198. On Aug. 17 the British Cabinet renewed its opposition to sending any ship to Moroccan waters; Asquith to George V, Aug. 17, 1911, Asquith Papers, box 6.

ships without first consulting London; should a break occur, Germany must appear the responsible party. Yet, for the third time, Grey declined to indicate what Britain would do in such circumstances.[107]

Throughout August and early September the British consistently avoided any policy commitment beyond the convening of an international conference. Churchill's drastic proposal to convert the Triple Entente into an alliance if the talks failed never got beyond the Foreign Office.[108] Grey's reluctance to go further reflected his own continued preference for a prudent, sober policy of firmness toward Germany, restraint upon France. The Foreign Secretary had disliked the radical attempts, especially those of Loreburn, to dictate policy during July; on the other hand, his own handling of the crisis would continue, even after the Mansion House speech, to be close to what the radicals desired. Grey had accepted the Foreign Office contention that the entente was in jeopardy because of German machinations, and he had approved Lloyd George's public commitment to France and against Germany. But he also shared the radical fears that France might be encouraged to war, thus his private and more important dealings with the French saw him adamant and inflexible against any precipitate French action. The Foreign Secretary had in fact successfully fused the Foreign Office and radical views, in the process strengthening his own position within the policy machinery. Paris possessed, therefore, Asquith's and Lloyd George's assurances of support; Paris read repeated press stories of British loyalty to its treaty obligations; Paris enjoyed British help in Berlin. The French had all the appearances of British support, but somewhat less of the substance or reality of support.

Nor could the French be entirely certain about their Russian allies. In mid-August the Caillaux government learned of the imminent conclusion of Russo-German negotiations over the Middle East. This news was followed by other unpleasant signs. On August 18 Alexander Isvolski, now the Russian ambassador in Paris, abruptly observed that war over a few miles of African territory would be unfortunate; shortly thereafter he proposed that Emperor Franz Josef of Austria be invited to mediate the Franco-German dispute. From St. Petersburg Ambassador Georges Louis reported widespread sentiment for peace.[109] And the Russian Chief of Staff, General Jakov Zhilinskii cautioned General

107. Bertie to Grey (tel.), Aug. 20, 1911, B.D., VII, no. 485; Grey to Bertie (tel.), Aug. 21, 23, 1911, ibid., nos. 487, 511; P. Cambon to de Selves (tel.), Aug. 23, 1911, D.D.F., 2nd ser., XIV, no. 205.
108. Churchill to Grey, Aug. 30, 1911, quoted in Churchill, The World Crisis, I, 63–64.
109. Isvolski to Neratov (tel.), Aug. 5/18, 1911, Otto Hoetzsch (ed.), Die internationalen Beziehungen im Zeitalter des Imperialismus, 3rd ser. (4 vols. to date; Berlin; 1939–), I, pt. 1, no. 341; Isvolski to Neratov, Aug. 7/20 (tel.), Aug. 8/21, 1911, ibid., nos. 348, 350; de Selves to Louis (tels.), Aug. 21, Sept. 1. 1911, D.D.F., 2nd ser., XIV, nos. 200, 234; Louis to de Selves (tel.), Aug. 22, 1911, ibid., no. 201.

Auguste Dubail, then in Russia for the annual military talks, on the need to avoid war.[110] The Dual Alliance was shaky. Confronted with Grey's evasions and uncertain about Russia, the French wisely decided to come to terms with Germany.

In early August Kiderlen and Jules Cambon were unable to agree on a common basis for negotiation. Later in the month the exhausted Kiderlen left Berlin for a brief rest and Jules Cambon returned to the French capital. At this point Premier Caillaux, alarmed and worried by the slowness of the negotiations, decided to take a more active and open role in the formation of French policy. At a series of high-level meetings on August 22, 23, and 25, the French defined for the first time, amazingly enough, exactly what they wanted in Morocco on the one hand and what they would concede on the other. The overriding guideline for their policy became: the more Germany yields in Morocco, the more compensation it receives in the Congo. Paris further resolved that the future of Morocco would have to be settled before the talks turned to compensation; no longer would the negotiations attempt to solve both questions at once. Armed with these instructions, Jules Cambon returned to Berlin, and on September 4 he and the German Foreign Minister resumed their talks; at last they began to make genuine progress.[111]

The French decision to adopt a businesslike attitude about the Moroccan crisis came none too soon, for Grey and the British leaders were, like the Russians, increasingly appalled at the possibility of war over compensations in the French Congo. Also, Grey knew, thanks to Jules Cambon's indirect appeal for British pressure on Paris, that the "peace faction" in the French government needed reinforcing. In early September he therefore emphasized that "the extent to which British support is forthcoming, if trouble is ahead, must depend upon its being clear that France has had no reasonable and honourable way of avoiding it." [112] He told Paul Cambon on September 5 that France must make some concessions because of British public opinion. The French ambassador readily understood this implicit warning, informing Paris that "militarily, England is ready; we know the Government desires to help us; but to pass from desire to action, it must be pushed by national opinion, and it is very anxious about our attitude, for a mistake on our part would suffice to delay the movement of opinion which it needs to

110. Louis to de Selves (tel.), Sept. 1, 1911, D.D.F., 2nd ser., XIV, no. 235.
111. "Notes de M. Jules Cambon," March [?] 1912, ibid., pp. 755–760; Caillaux, Agadir, 176–189; Messimy, Mes souvenirs, 60–62. See also Pierre Renouvin and J.-B. Duroselle, Introduction à l'histoire des relations internationales (Paris, 1964), 429–433.
112. Grey to Bertie, Sept. 4, 1911, B.D., VII, no. 531. On Cambon's appeal through Goschen, see Goschen to Grey (tel.), Sept. 4, 1911, Grey Papers, F.O. 800/62; Grey to Goschen (tel.), Sept. 5, 1911, ibid.

act." [113] Britain, Cambon added, "would not send a boat, a man to Morocco if we break the talks, you can be sure"; indeed France might destroy the entente if it broke off the negotiations. [114] The French ambassador had realistically discerned the extent of British support.

The need for such limits seemed confirmed when reports began to reach London of the bellicose spirit sweeping France. Colonel Fairholme, the military attaché, reported that in the French Army "the balance of evidence is in favour of a war at the present moment." [115] Although Arthur Nicolson thought it would be hard "to find a more favorable opportunity [for war] either for France or ourselves," Grey, then vacationing, was less sanguine. Afraid of a repeat of 1870, he wrote the Undersecretary on September 13 that he did "not like the indication . . . that the French Army are so ready that they might prefer war now. Nevertheless," he confessed, "I am glad they are ready." [116]

Grey's apprehensions about French militancy and French diplomacy were not realized. Although the Quai d'Orsay clique steadfastly resisted any significant compensation to Germany (to the point of repeatedly leaking stories to the press), Kiderlen and Cambon made steady progress throughout September, helped in part by a financial panic in Berlin and in part by the Italian attack upon Tripoli on September 28. [117] These events encouraged both governments to conclude their Moroccan differences; on October 11 they accepted a draft arrangement, and three weeks later (October 28) they agreed on the compensations. Finally, on November 4, Kiderlen and Cambon signed the formal accords: France gained a protectorate status in Morocco; Germany received extensive, and worthless, territory in the French Congo.

In the last stages of the Franco-German negotiations the question of Moroccan ports recurred, but this time in the context of Anglo-French relations. In late September Ambassador Bertie asked if London planned to secure a French guarantee about the nonfortification of all Moroccan ports, not just those covered by the 1904 treaty. Bertie, citing Morocco's strategic value to Britain, noted that "as the Naval Advisers of His Majesty's Government would see great objection to the establishment of a German fortified naval base on the Atlantic coast of Morocco, and the friends of to-day may be the enemies of to-morrow I conclude that

113. P. Cambon to de Selves, Sept. 6, 1911, D.D.F., 2nd ser., XIV, no. 272; cf. P. Cambon to de Selves (tel.), Sept. 5, 1911, ibid., no. 263.
114. P. Cambon to de Selves, Sept. 6, 1911, ibid., no. 274.
115. Fairholme's report is in Bertie to Grey, Sept. 8, 1911, B.D., VII, no. 644. On French sentiment, see Carroll, French Public Opinion, 246–247.
116. Nicolson to Hardinge, Sept. 14, 1911, Nicolson Papers, vol. IV/1911; Grey to Nicolson, Sept. 13, 1911, ibid.
117. On the press leaks see, e.g., Berckheim to des Touches, Sept. 21, 1911, quoted in Caillaux, Mes mémoires, III, 301–302. Caillaux later claimed that he triggered the financial panic, Agadir, 193–199.

they would also see objection to a French fortified naval base on that coast." Grey consulted the services on the matter; both recommended that Britain get a guarantee to cover the coastline below the Sebou River. The Foreign Secretary, however, finally decided to attach no conditions to British acceptance of the Moroccan settlement. Rather, he promised to seek such a guarantee when the tensions had cooled; but this promise was not fulfilled.[118]

The status of the entente in October and November influenced Grey's postponement of the sensitive port issue. As pressure from Berlin had diminished, the cross-Channel partners had drifted apart. Discord over Spanish rights in Morocco was partly responsible: Caillaux's persistent attempts during October to balance concessions in the French Congo with a reduction of Spanish rights in Morocco got no encouragement from London. The British, anxious for strategic reasons to have the Sherifian empire in the hands of two powers, badgered Paris to be more amenable to Madrid. Grey feared the French actions would "drag the *entente* in the mud, and would have the most disastrous effect on public opinion." [119] On November 8 he angrily wrote Bertie: "We can have nothing to do with a line that is mean and dishonourable. We have got to keep France straight in this matter, or to part company with her. I wish of all things to avoid the latter alternative, but we can only do so by carrying the former. This we shall carry." [120]

Anglo-French friction was intensified by Caillaux's repeated aspersions about the value of the British Army and of the entente. Ambassador Bertie, who strongly defended the entente, asked the Premier "whether he really meant that, in his opinion, it would be advantageous to France that it [the entente] should not exist, as in such case I would so report to you [Grey]. He replied he did not mean that, but he thought that it was being made to work to the disadvantage of French interests." [121] These remarks, which imperiled the basic foundations of British policy, antagonized even that ardent Francophile Arthur Nicolson, who on November 7 retorted testily and not without exaggeration that it was "one of the strangest admissions I ever heard from a French statesman and it shows a curious want of perception, for had we not stood so manfully by France during the recent crisis, I doubt if she would have been able to obtain all that she has acquired." Hopefully, Caillaux's statement was "merely . . . an ebullition of temper, and I am quite sure that on this point he will be unable to carry either the French President or members of the French Cabinet with him." For "it would never do," the

118. Bertie to Grey, Sept. 28, 1911, B.D., VII, no. 567; Admiralty to Foreign Office, Nov. 3, 1911, *ibid.*, no. 620; Grey to Bertie, Nov. 14, 1911, *ibid.*, no. 683.
119. Grey to Carnegie, Oct. 30, 1911, Cab. 37/108/138.
120. Grey to Bertie, Nov. 8, 1911, B.D., VII, no. 631.
121. Quoted in "Extract from Annual Report for France for the Year 1911," *ibid.*, no. 337; on President Fallières's displeasure with Britain, see diary, Nov. 17, 1911, Georges Louis, *Les carnets de Georges Louis*, 2 vols. (Paris, 1926), I, 214.

Undersecretary later wrote Ambassador Buchanan in Russia, "that others should think that any cause of friction between us and France was likely to occur." [122]

Another factor complicated the Anglo-French relationship. In early November the Quai d'Orsay leaked the secret terms of the Franco-Spanish treaty of 1904; Le Temps then published what purported to be the secret clauses of the entente accord. Since the radicals were already attacking Grey about alleged secret commitments to France, the French disclosures sorely embarrassed and irritated the Foreign Office. Grey, to head off further domestic repercussions, decided to publish the treaties in full. Before doing so he sought and obtained Lord Lansdowne's permission; in granting the permission the former Foreign Secretary added, interestingly, "we shall at any rate hear no more of the confident statements, which are still being made, to the effect that we had bound ourselves by these articles to afford one another material assistance of a definite kind in certain eventualities." [123]

This series of petty but annoying quarrels with Paris ended in late November. The French gave way on Spanish rights in Morocco, Caillaux controlled his tongue, and attention shifted to the various parliamentary discussions about the Moroccan episode. Furthermore, Grey's extensive review of British foreign policy in the House of Commons on November 27 helped the entente.

In this speech Grey hoped to achieve a number of objectives: to defend his foreign policy, to disarm his radical critics, and to reassure Britain's friends, while still holding an olive branch toward Berlin. After reviewing the Moroccan crisis, replete with denials of any military commitments to France, he sharply denounced those critics who advocated a return to the policy of "splendid isolation. . . . As a matter of fact," he asserted, "that policy, which would be disastrous, is not a policy. It is the negation of policy." Neither the European power structure nor the dangers of the naval race would permit Great Britain to stand aside. Nor, he continued, would such a policy gain the friendship of Germany. He lectured his radical colleagues that "one does not make new friendships worth having by deserting old ones. New friendships by all means let us make, but not at the expense of the ones we have. . . . We intend to retain them unimpaired." And he added: "But I trust that the fact that we have with France during the last seven months gone hand-in-hand through a great deal of rough diplomatic weather, without for a moment losing touch with each other, will have its influence in perpetuating in France and here confidence in our mutual good faith and

122. Nicolson to Goschen, Nov. 7, 1911, Nicolson Papers, vol. V/1911; Nicolson to Buchanan, Nov. 21, 1911, ibid., vol. VI/1911. See also Nicolson to Stamfordham, Nov. 29, 1911, ibid., and "Memorandum by Sir E. Crowe respecting Franco-German Negotiations," Jan. 14, 1912, B.D., VII, pp. 821–826.
123. Minutes by Crowe, Langley, Nicolson, and Grey on Bertie to Grey, Nov. 11, 1911, B.D., VII, no. 675; Lansdowne to Grey, Nov. 22, 1911, ibid., no. 706.

goodwill, our intention to keep in touch." [124] Grey left no doubt that Britain's good relations with France remained the cardinal principle of his foreign policy.

This resounding pledge of allegiance to the Entente Cordiale pleased the French press, if not all members of the French government. Caillaux remained bitter over Britain's failure to adhere to his anti-Spanish schemes. But Justin de Selves praised Anglo-French relations and generally shared the view expressed in the *Journal des débats* that the entente, "far from being barren or perilous . . . is, with the Russian Alliance, the best safeguard of our national interests and of peace reposing upon the balance of power." [125] The Entente Cordiale, which had once more survived German pressure from without, had also weathered stresses from within.

The termination of the second Moroccan dispute settled more than a Franco-German question: it also saw France collect its share of the 1904 Anglo-French accord. The act of collection ended Britain's formal obligation to render France diplomatic support; yet it scarcely affected the viability of the entente, for what had begun initially as a colonial accord had long since grown into a far more extensive relationship. The blusterings of German diplomacy, the demands of the naval race, and France's prolonged hostility to Germany had given the entente partners a community of interests that extended far beyond Morocco. After 1911 growing Franco-German antagonism and British naval requirements in the Mediterranean merely fortified the trends of close cooperation already established, not only in the political sphere, but also in the military and naval.

124. *Parliamentary Debates: Commons*, 5th ser., 32 (Nov. 27, 1911), 60–61, 64–65; also in B.D., VII, no. 721.

125. Quoted in the *Times*, Nov. 29, 1911; Bertie to Grey, Dec. 3, 1911, B.D., VII, no. 731.

7 | Agadir Confirms Britain's Continental Strategy

The Agadir challenge provoked more than a diplomatic reaction from the Entente Cordiale. The possibility of war over Morocco gave new impetus and urgency to the military conversations. In Britain the "false alarm" reopened the strategical debate over the utilization of the British Army and provided an invaluable test of the war preparations of both services. Moreover, the military precautions of the summer caused some within the Cabinet to question the implications of the entente.

Amid the turmoil within the British defense establishment in 1911 there was one constant: Brigadier General Henry Wilson. Appointed Director of Military Operations in August 1910, the future Field Marshal soon became a major figure in Anglo-French relations. Lanky, horse-faced, arrogant, at forty-six he already had a reputation for insubordination, intrigue, and strongly held opinions. Contemptuous of politicians, especially Liberal ones, the Anglo-Irish officer constantly consorted with Lord Roberts for conscription and with the Ulstermen against Home Rule. Despite this questionable military behavior and his loose, caustic tongue, Wilson managed to keep his position as D.M.O. His retention stemmed mainly from his acknowledged competence as a staff officer: his energy, ability, and sense of professionalism contrasted sharply and favorably with the normal pattern of dilettantism so characteristic of the British officer before 1914. Wilson thought about the problems of continental warfare, spending much of his spare time cycling along the Franco-German-Belgian frontiers; by contrast most of his contemporaries, and rivals, devoted themselves to the minutiae of army life, and to polo matches.[1]

The General brought three other assets to his new post: well-placed contacts in the French Army, a sure sense of how the next European war would unfold, and strong convictions about the future role of the British Army. In 1909, while still at Camberley as head of the Staff College, he had solicited the friendship of Ferdinand Foch, his counterpart as head of the Ecole Supérieure de Guerre. After their first rather awkward meeting in December 1909, Wilson and Foch met often to discuss strategy.[2] This friendship and similar contacts, plus an ample command of French, enhanced Wilson's effectiveness as the officer responsible for staff talks. These French ties, furthermore, reinforced the General's longstanding belief in the inevitability of a Franco-German war—at some point the Germans would be tempted, he thought, to use their superior military machine to crush the Dual Alliance. Confident that Russia would not worry the German General Staff unduly, he expected a massive German assault in the west followed by the subsequent defeat of France. Germany would then dominate Europe, a development he regarded as distinctly hostile to Britain's political interests, to its economic prosperity, and to its maritime supremacy.[3]

The gloomy prospect of German hegemony in Europe made Wilson an early and ardent champion of British military intervention on the Continent. At Camberley he formulated a number of staff exercises on the problems of British intervention. As D.M.O. he preached intervention "day and night," Admiral Fisher complained at one point in 1911.[4] But the General was not only convinced of the necessity for British intervention, he was certain that Britain would intervene. This belief

1. General French in 1904 thought Wilson should have his "wings clipped"; Fisher in 1910 complained of "indiscipline amongst the subordinate Generals who seem to prosper by being insubordinate"; French to Esher, Sept. 8, 1904, French, *Some War Diaries*, 102; Fisher to Mrs. R. K. McKenna, mid-December 1910, Marder, *Fear God and Dread Nought*, II, 344. On Wilson's career, see Callwell, *Wilson*, and Basil Collier, *Brasshat: A Biography of Field Marshal Sir Henry Wilson* (London, 1961).
2. See, e.g., diary, Oct. 13, 1910, in Callwell, *Wilson*, I, 88.
3. On this see Wilson's memo to Nicholson, Aug. 11, 1911, W.O. 106/47, and his memo "The Military Aspects of the Continental Problem," Aug. 15, 1911, Cab. 4/3/2.
4. Fisher to Spender, Feb. 27, 1911, Marder, *Fear God and Dread Nought*, II, 359; interview with Lord Hankey, Aug. 16, 1962.

stemmed from his undeviating assumption that Germany would cross Belgium in its drive westward and thus allow Britain to intervene as a guarantor of Belgian neutrality.

In November 1910 Wilson thought (not inaccurately) that the German attack through Belgium would *cross* the Meuse River with perhaps forty divisions and swing northward as far as Brussels.[5] Later, however, he modified this prognosis following a Directorate of Military Operations study on the problem and after April 1911 always insisted that the Germans would *stay below* the Meuse to avoid antagonizing the Belgians, crossing Belgium on a line from Liège to Verdun.[6] This revised (erroneous) estimate of German plans did not of course disturb the possibility of British military intervention. The new predictions, moreover, had a practical aspect which Wilson could not have overlooked: they made the case for intervention more appealing.

Previous justifications for British intervention had centered upon the boost it would give French morale and the reduction, though slight, it would make in the numerical disparity. But Wilson, thanks to his revised estimate of German plans, could argue that British assistance might make the difference between a French victory and a French defeat. If the Germans remained below the Meuse to avoid offending the Belgians, the German staff would have only seventeen available roads on which to move troops. Since each route could accommodate at most three divisions, a German attack would be limited to fifty-one divisions. Consequently, the entente with its forty or more French and six British divisions could meet the Germans on roughly equal terms: a combined Anglo-French force might administer a decisive check to a German flanking move. But the outcome depended upon the presence of British troops, otherwise the French would be defeated. Britain became responsible for the fate of France.[7]

This explanation of the value of British assistance furnished Wilson with an effective argument in his campaign for intervention. Yet it did so at the expense of his appreciation of German strategy. Because his revised evaluations of German intentions fortified the rationale for intervention, he became less and less inclined to re-examine the problem of a German attack through Belgium. The natural disinclination of the strategic planner to rethink his assumptions also held true for Wilson.

5. Huguet to General Brun, Nov. 4, 1910, Archives Guerre, "Plan XVII: Armée W," box 147b; Pellé to Berteaux, Mar. 7, 1911, D.D.F., 2nd ser., XIII, no. 180.

6. The Directorate study, done by Colonel Count Gleichen and C. B. Money, concluded that the first clash would come on the fourteenth day at Stenay and Montmédy; Lord Edward Gleichen, *A Guardsman's Memoirs: A Book of Recollections* (Edinburgh, 1932), 340–341. Wilson's diary indicates he received the report on Mar. 9, 1911, Wilson Diaries; Wilson to Nicholson, March 15, 1911, W.O. 106/49. Also see Wilson's memo, "The Military Aspects of the Continental Problem," Aug. 15, 1911, Cab. 4/3/2.

7. Wilson's most effective use of this argument came at the Aug. 23, 1911, meeting of the C.I.D., Cab. 2/2/2.

As a result he would delude himself, and others, about the real dangers which would confront the British Expeditionary Force on the Continent. In any case, his official position enabled him to do more than talk about the merits of intervention—the D.M.O. could work within the War Office and through the military conversations to prepare the B.E.F. for continental warfare. His efforts came none too soon.

Upon arriving at the War Office in 1910 Wilson quickly discovered that all was not well with the Expeditionary Force. Despite four turbulent years of Army reform, glaring deficiencies still remained in the Army's mobilization preparations. By late October the new D.M.O. was expressing dissatisfaction "with the state of affairs in every respect. No rail arrangements for concentration and movements of either the Expeditionary Force or Territorials. No proper arrangements for horse supply, no arrangements for safeguarding our arsenal at Woolwich. A lot of time spent writing beautiful but useless minutes. I'll break all this," he promised himself, "somehow." [8] But at first he made little progress. He found General Sir W. G. Nicholson, Chief of the Imperial General Staff, more interested in "drafting inter-departmental minutes" than in "our preparations for war. . . . I don't think the idea, or expression, of *war* crosses his mind or lips once a month." [9] The "scandalous state of affairs" persisted.

In early January 1911 Wilson was still uncertain how long it would take to mobilize four divisions. Completely exasperated with his superiors, the General at this point launched a vigorous personal campaign to revamp the Army's mobilization arrangements. Four divisions ready for action in a war's opening battles became his immediate goal: to achieve it he badgered fellow officers, complained incessantly to the Secretary of State for War, and usurped responsibility from his colleagues. With the help of Haldane and Grey (who in addition to his Foreign Office duties served as a railway director), he tackled the problem of moving troops from their mobilization areas to the ports of embarkation. In March he reached a tentative accord with the chairman of the London and South-Western Railway to have the Expeditionary Force embarked at Southampton by the ninth day of mobilization. Locating an adequate supply of horses proved more difficult. Handicapped by a decline in the equine population and by the phlegmatic Quartermaster General H. S. G. Miles, Wilson at the time of the Agadir crisis still lacked enough horses to meet all the mobilization requirements.[10]

The D.M.O.'s most vexing transportation problem, however, involved

8. Diary, Oct. 25, 1910, in Callwell, *Wilson*, I, 89. Where the dates in Callwell are imprecise, they have been checked against the original diaries.
9. Nov. 2, Dec. 17, 1910, Wilson Diaries.
10. Wilson to Nicholson, Jan. 12, 1911, W.O. 106/49; Jan. 23, Mar. 13, 17, 1911, Wilson Diaries; Callwell, *Wilson*, I, 91–92, 97–98.

the shipment of the Expeditionary Force to France. To solve this issue he needed the cooperation and assistance of the Navy. In December 1908, Reginald McKenna, First Lord of the Admiralty, had agreed at the C.I.D. hearings to move the Army across the Channel: the promise remained just that, as the Admiralty made no effort to honor McKenna's pledge. In February 1910, over a year after the hearings and well before Wilson's appointment, the War Office implored the C.I.D. to establish departmental coordination because "the preparation of certain schemes of military operations . . . have now reached a stage beyond which they cannot be developed without naval collaboration. . . . [I]t seems essential that a plan of embarkation should be thoroughly worked out." [11] The plea went unheeded, and in October 1910 Wilson renewed it—this time to General Nicholson; in his appeal the D.M.O. suggested reviving the stillborn permanent subcommittee on combined operations which Balfour had instituted in July 1905.[12] But Nicholson disliked this suggestion and recommended instead that Wilson establish a modus vivendi with his naval counterpart Rear Admiral Alexander Bethell, the Director of Naval Intelligence. In December Wilson and Bethell discussed embarkation arrangements. Then in February 1911 Lieutenant Colonel F. W. Kerr sent retired Admiral Robert Groome, head of the Naval Transport Department, a set of revised mobilization tables. No reply was received from the Admiralty, and another new set of tables was personally handed to Bethell on May 8; but by the end of June the Admiralty still had not responded. Later the naval authorities would excuse this inaction on the somewhat dubious grounds that the tables had never been officially transmitted to the Sea Lords. Although Wilson and Bethell had a brief discussion in early July on which French ports the B.E.F. would use, no firm arrangements on troop transport had been settled by late August 1911. And at that time Admiral Sir A. K. Wilson, the First Sea Lord, completely repudiated Groome's contacts with the War Office. Not until Winston Churchill assumed responsibility at the Admiralty would the naval transport arrangements become a reality, and even then there would be delays.[13]

Although Henry Wilson's immediate objective was the preparation of four divisions for action in Europe, he also began investigating methods of increasing the scale of British aid to France. In late 1910, for example, he asked Douglas Haig, then Chief of Staff to the Commander in Chief of the Indian Army, to explore the difficulties of utilizing British regulars stationed in India. Initially Haig felt that the Indian response would be limited to releasing Egyptian garrisons for continental

11. General Staff memo, "Questions Requiring Inter-Departmental Consideration," Feb. 22, 1910, Cab. 38/16/3.
12. "Draft of letter asking for assembly of Permanent Sub-Committee of Imperial Defence," October 1910, W.O. 106/47.
13. Wilson to Bethell, June 30, 1911, W.O. 106/50; memos by Wilson, July 7, 8, Sept. 22, 1911, *ibid.*; memo by Nicholson, Sept. 25, 1911, *ibid.*

duty.[14] Later however, in 1911, he completed plans for Indian troops to fight in Europe proper. Ordered by Lord Hardinge, the Indian Viceroy, to destroy these plans because they contradicted the official policy of the Indian Army, Haig discreetly disobeyed—in 1914 the scheme proved quite valuable.[15]

Despite the lure of assistance from the colonies, Wilson harbored no illusions about its immediate availability. Any dependable increase in the Expeditionary Force, pending the unlikely institution of conscription, must come from the military establishment at home. The D.M.O. soon recognized that the easiest way to increase the Force was to overturn the C.I.D.'s 1909 ruling on continental operations. At that time the Committee had restricted any British participation on the Continent to a cavalry and four infantry divisions, with two divisions remaining at home to protect against invasion. Wilson's plan to overcome this restriction was simple: he would obtain Haldane's and Nicholson's consent to complete the mobilization arrangements for the entire B.E.F., then present the Committee with a fait accompli. This he proceeded to do. By late March 1911 he could write that "we settled that the whole of the infantry of the 6 divisions would embark on the 4th day, cavalry 7th day, artillery 9th day. We will work out this in detail and see what will have to be done." [16]

In late May Wilson gave Nicholson the new mobilization dates necessary to move all six divisions to France, and the latter immediately ordered Ewart, the Adjutant General, to incorporate these dates and requirements into the mobilization orders. For the next seven months a committee of the General Staff—stimulated of course by Agadir—revised the schedules and arrangements required for a mobilization of the entire B.E.F.[17] While the August stress revealed that total mobilization was impossible, by mid-1913 the Army seemed capable of realizing this goal, thanks to Wilson's persistence.

The General's efforts to expand the Expeditionary Force and to accelerate its mobilization necessarily required an updating of the arrangements previously settled with the French General Staff. Wilson from the start had injected a new spirit into the military conversations. In contrast to Ewart, who remained cautious and circumspect in his contacts with the French, the new D.M.O. believed Anglo-French relations to be "vital for both countries." His sympathy for the French and his desire

14. The date of Wilson's request is uncertain; see Haig to General Hamilton Gordon, Jan. 2, 1911, Haig Papers, National Library of Scotland, Edinburgh, box 89; note on Wilson's memo, "The Military Aspects of the Continental Problem," Aug. 5, 1911, Cab. 4/3/2.
15. Alfred Duff Cooper, *Haig*, 2 vols. (London, 1935–1936), I, 118–119; John Terraine, *Ordeal of Victory* (Philadelphia, 1963), 48–49; Callwell, *Wilson*, I, 106.
16. Diary, Mar. 21, 1911, in Callwell, *Wilson*, I, 92; see also "Memo by Major Gorton on the progress of the Scheme for the despatch of the Expeditionary Force during the half-year ending June 30th 1911," W.O. 106/49.
17. On the work of the General Staff committee, see W.O. 32/534/79/2856.

for intervention naturally buttressed the importance he attached to the conversations. Further, he promised Huguet that the staff talks guaranteed the certainty of British assistance. This attitude would, of course, more than offset the scrupulous lip service Wilson paid to the proposition that the conversations were noncommittal.[18]

Wilson had few kind words for the results of the previous Anglo-French talks. He thought they were "disgraceful" and "a pure academic paper arrangement of no earthly value to anyone."[19] But his initial reaction was to leave intact the arrangements agreed upon by Grierson, Ewart, and Huguet. Not until March 1911, with work on expansion of the B.E.F. well under way, would he give serious attention to overhauling the staff accords.

On March 23 Wilson informed Huguet that all six divisions would be in France by the fourteenth day; this would make the British Army available for action around the seventeenth day. But, he pointed out, achieving this earlier arrival of British troops, four days ahead of the old schedule, would necessitate three immediate alterations in the previous arrangements. First, Rouen and Le Havre must be used as ports instead of Cherbourg. Second, the French must accept his radical proposal for surmounting the temporary shortage of horses that would occur on British mobilization. In his new scheme all infantry units would arrive in France before their cavalry components and in advance of the cavalry division, and all convoy and artillery detachments dependent upon horses would follow the infantry units, not accompany them. Although these changes speeded the arrival of the Expeditionary Force, they also effectively disrupted unit integrity, temporarily deprived the infantry of its support elements, and created additional problems in reunifying the units after their arrival in France; moreover, the proposals entailed a complete revision of all movement tables. Finally, the earlier arrival of British troops, coupled with their increase in numbers, would place new demands upon the French rail system, and new arrangements would have to be made to avoid conflicting with French mobilization.[20] In these initial adjustments of the staff arrangements Wilson made no mention, significantly, of a British zone of concentration. The only hint on this comes from the French rail tables, which still designated the Arras-St. Quentin-Cambrai area of northwestern France: apparently the studies never reached London.[21] But at least Wilson had renewed the staff talks and begun the revision of the intervention arrangements.

18. Huguet to General Brun, Nov. 4, 1910, Archives Guerre, "Plan XVII: Armée W," box 147b. The French records and Wilson's diaries permit a detailed reconstruction of the staff talks during Wilson's tenure.
19. Jan. 9, 1911, Wilson Diaries.
20. Huguet to Berteaux, Mar. 24, 1911, Archives Guerre, "Plan XVII: Armée W," box 147b.
21. "Note sur les modifications proposées à la organisation des Transports W," May 13, 1911, ibid.

Throughout the spring of 1911 the two staffs leisurely worked on the organizational and logistical problems created by the accelerated arrival of the B.E.F. The *Panther's* appearance off the Moroccan coast suddenly changed all this, and Huguet and Wilson met three times within a week to review the progress of the mobilization arrangements. Not everything was satisfactory. When the attaché indicated strong French opposition to the arrival of the infantry without its equine complement, the General on July 7 became adamant, insisting there was no other method of moving all six divisions to France. Nor was Huguet especially happy to learn that the Admiralty disliked the still applicable Ewart-Huguet accord calling for troop landings at Calais and Boulogne. Admiral Bethell would contemplate troop movements to Boulogne, but not to Calais because of its proximity to the North Sea.[22] These early July meetings with Huguet graphically illustrated Wilson's key problem during the summer crisis: how to bridge the gap between the half-completed provisions of a new scheme and the drawbacks of an old one still in effect. In an attempt to ease the dilemma he decided to deal directly with his French counterparts, and on July 20 he traveled to Paris. That the trip had Haldane's approval is not certain, that it did not have the Cabinet's sanction is certain.[23] This trip and its resulting memorandum brought a major amplification in the nature of the military conversations.

Wilson arrived in Paris at a bad moment for the French Staff. The day before, General Michel had been outvoted in the War Board on his proposal to use reserve troops; the pending changes in the French high command meant that Wilson's negotiations were conducted in a partial vacuum. General Auguste Dubail, Chief of the French Staff under the old organization, and Adolphe Messimy, the War Minister, represented the French; Joffre, the future head of the Army, played no part in the talks. On the afternoon of July 20 Wilson and Huguet met with Messimy, Dubail, General Regnault, and Lieutenant Colonels Hallouin, Crepy, and Vignol "to determine the conditions of eventual participation of an English army in French operations in the North East, in a war against Germany." After observing that his presence could not be construed as committing his government, Wilson softened this point, as Messimy noted, by remarking that the "good work of the general staff, prepared in cooperation and in advance, could singularly influence the definitive decision." After a long, rambling two-hour discussion Wilson and Dubail signed a memorandum summarizing the status of the entente's military arrangements. The Expeditionary Force would be composed of six divisions of infantry and a division of cavalry, totaling one

22. Huguet to Dubail, July 7, 13, 1911, *ibid.*; July 10, 1911, Wilson Diaries.
23. In his diary Wilson noted that a last-minute meeting with Haldane and Nicholson delayed his departure for Paris; presumably therefore Haldane knew of the trip; diary, July 19, 1911, in Callwell, *Wilson*, I, 96.

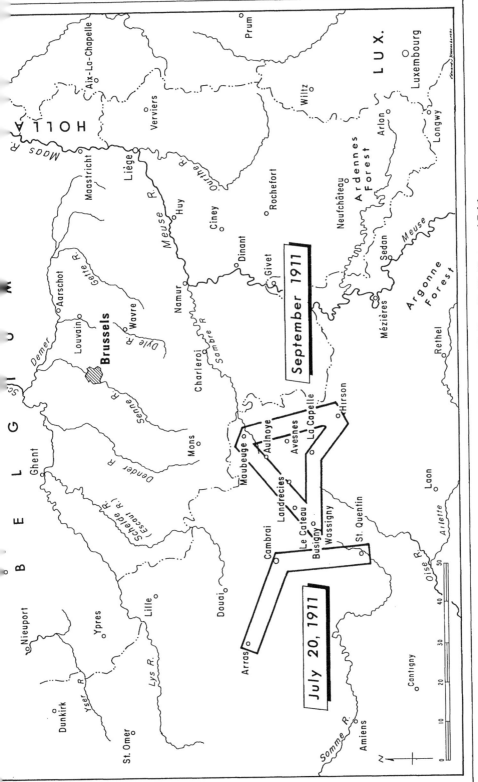

CONCENTRATION OF THE B.E.F. : 1911

hundred fifty thousand men. In accordance with Wilson's unorthodox preferences, the infantry units would arrive first, landing at Rouen and Le Havre on the fourth day. Rail movements of these troops would start on the fifth day. All combatants were expected to be in the staging area by the thirteenth day.[24]

The most important aspect of the Wilson-Dubail accord was the assignment of a zone of concentration to the British force. Despite five years of intermittent Anglo-French talks the problem had never been adequately examined. In 1906 Grierson had clearly preferred action in Belgium. Afterward, the technical problems inherent in a Belgian operation had convinced the British Staff that the Expeditionary Force would be better deployed in France, probably in a reserve capacity along the Franco-Belgian frontier. The French Staff had never communicated the 1907 rail studies mentioning Arras-Cambrai-St. Quentin as a zone, and how much Wilson knew of these studies is unclear, though Huguet in November 1910 reported that the General regarded Amiens as the first destination of the B.E.F.[25] But in early 1911, as will be seen, Wilson was once more attracted by the potential that an operation in Belgium would confer. In any event, the memorandum of July 20 was the first formal acknowledgment of a staging area: it was the familiar St. Quentin-Cambrai-Arras neighborhood. Unless the German forces crossed the Meuse, which neither Wilson nor the French thought likely, the British troops would be in primarily a defensive, reserve location.

Although the Wilson-Dubail accord defined a zone of concentration, the memorandum was fundamentally a logistical settlement of routine details rather than a plan of entente strategy. The ultimate deployment of the Expeditionary Force and the vexing problem of command were left unanswered. The agreement suggests, moreover, that neither party was entirely candid in the discussions. Wilson certainly appreciated that six divisions would not be ready for mobilization and that the plans for maritime transport left much to be desired. The French were equally silent about the problems caused by Michel's abrupt ouster, nor did they volunteer any information about Plan XVI. On the latter point Wilson himself certainly erred in not being more aggressive or demanding.[26] His elaborate justification for British intervention rested upon the assumption that France would be able to counter the main thrust of a German attack through Belgian Luxembourg. Yet he made no effort to determine if this was actually the case; in fact he only learned of the

24. "Memorandum of Meeting held on July 20, 1911, between General Dubail and General Wilson," Aug. 21, 1911, B.D., VII, no. 640; Messimy, Mes souvenirs, 267–268; diary, July 20–21, 1911, in Callwell, Wilson, I, 96.
25. Huguet to General Brun, Nov. 4, 1910, Archives Guerre, "Plan XVII: Armée W," box 147b.
26. On July 7, 1911, Wilson had assured Huguet that the Admiralty would give its "most absolute and effective help," Huguet to Dubail, July 7, 1911, ibid.; see also Tyler, British Army, 122.

proposed deployment of French forces in early September. Nevertheless, the July 20 memorandum infused new meaning into the Anglo-French military relationship—even with their Russian allies the French had never attained this level of coordination.[27] In many respects the signed statement resembled a de facto military convention. More importantly, despite its "noncommittal" clause, the agreement encouraged the French to expect British help, as would the Grey-Cambon letters of 1912, and this expectation in turn influenced the formation of French strategy.

After a further meeting with Messimy on July 21, Wilson returned to London. Having clarified his relations with the French, the General spent most of the rest of the summer improving the B.E.F., sending his intelligence agents abroad, and arguing the merits of intervention; and he managed, after checking first with Arthur Nicolson, to spend the first week of August at Cowes on vacation. During these summer weeks he saw Huguet occasionally, but there were no regular exchanges of information about the likelihood of war.[28] It was only in late August, and then from Fairholme's dispatches, that the D.M.O. learned anything definite about Joffre's views on French strategy.

The new Chief of the French General Staff, the attaché had written, thought war unlikely and had therefore embarked upon wholesale changes in the French war plan. Joffre was particularly worried about a German violation of neighboring Belgium. If it occurred, Colonel Fairholme "gathered" that Joffre planned "to hold them in check on that flank, and to attack vigorously on Alsace and Lorraine." In this connection the French commander placed the "very greatest importance to the co-operation of a British expeditionary force, which concentrating somewhere between Douai and Cambrai, and falling on the right flank of the German advance, might produce great, and even decisive, results." "In the main," Wilson penciled in his diary, "Joffre seems to agree with me." Then in early September Fairholme reported that in spite of Joffre's earlier calmness, "the balance of evidence is in favour of war at the present moment."[29]

Alarmed by this and other intelligence reports, Wilson sought out Colonel Huguet for another long and important discussion on September 9. He began by reminding the French attaché that if war came, Germany must appear the responsible party: if France seemed responsible, British opinion would be divided and "English intervention would find itself

27. See, e.g., the record of the 1911 Franco-Russian talks, Aug. 31, 1911, enclosed in Matton to Millerand, Feb. 23, 1912. Ministère des Affaires Etrangères, *Documents diplomatiques français, 1871–1914*, 3rd ser., 11 vols. (Paris, 1929–1936), II, no. 90.
28. The French archives contain only a "Note du Brigadier Général H. H. Wilson . . . sur le memorandum de la conférence du 20 juillet 1911," Archives Guerre, "Plan XVII: Armée W," box 147b.
29. Fairholme to Bertie, Aug. 24, 1911, B.D., VII, no. 641; diary, Aug. 29, 1911, in Callwell, *Wilson*, I, 102; Fairholme to Bertie, Sept. 7, 1911, B.D., VII, no. 644; see also the minute sheet on this report, F.O. 371/1119.

greatly retarded." The initial decision for intervention, he warned, would be the most difficult; once made, Britain would harness its entire resources to gain victory. Huguet took this admonition in stride and soon turned to Joffre's new plans for the Anglo-French forces. "He told me where the French G.[eneral] S.[taff] want us to go, and what their plans are. That is the first time I have been told." Exactly how much the General learned from Huguet about French plans is unclear, apparently not very much. But Wilson at least now knew of Joffre's preference that the British zone of concentration be in the Maubeuge-Hirson area, somewhat nearer the Belgian frontier.[30] This location would ensure British participation in a war's first battles regardless of whether the Germans attacked above or below the Meuse.

At this point the Wilson-Huguet conversation took an unexpected turn, focusing on a problem long familiar to the entente planners: how would Belgium react to a German violation of its neutrality? In 1906 General Ducarne had assured Barnardiston that Belgium would defend its territory against any infringement, however small. But after 1906 the Belgians appeared to shift their position somewhat; soon the British, French, and German Staffs were concluding that Belgium might just tolerate a German passage through Belgian Luxembourg rather than risk converting the entire country once more into the "cockpit of Europe." The reinforcement of the Antwerp fortifications, with its defensive connotations, strengthened this view. Moreover, as the entente partners drew closer together the Belgians themselves became more distant and suspicious of Anglo-French motives. The distrust was accentuated in early 1911 by the Flushing issue; the Anglo-French uproar over the Dutch proposal to fortify Flushing on the Schelde (and thus possibly block British help to Antwerp) struck many Belgians as unwarranted meddling in Belgian affairs. In turn the Belgian apathy on Flushing served to convince the entente that the Belgians would try to avoid trouble if war came.[31] Henry Wilson shared this view, telling the famous C.I.D. meeting of August 23, 1911, that the Belgians "would avoid committing themselves as long as possible in order to try and make certain of being on the winning side." [32]

Wilson's doubt about Belgium's political reliability was one thing, his military realism another. He had, of course, no use for the idle chatter of the popular journals with their talk of a military expedition to Antwerp. On the other hand, he possessed strong ideas about the strategical advantages that might accrue from an Anglo-Belgian operation in Belgium. Although not opposed to British operations in France with the

30. Huguet to Messimy, Sept. 10, 1911, Archives Guerre, "Plan XVII: Armée W," box 147b; diary, Sept. 9, 1911, in Callwell, *Wilson*, I, 103.

31. Helmreich, "Belgian Concern over Neutrality," 419–422; Thomas, "The Use of the Scheldt in British Plans," 456–465.

32. Minutes of the 114th meeting of C.I.D., Cab. 2/2/2; this phrase was omitted from the version published in the *British Documents* (VIII, no. 314).

French, he repeatedly gave attention to British action in the neutralized state and to improving Anglo-Belgian relations. In early 1911 he traveled to Brussels to see Lieutenant Colonel Tom Bridges, the British attaché, and to have dinner with General H. A. Jungbluth, Chief of the Belgian General Staff. The visit, which frightened the sensitive Brussels government, brought no tangible improvement in Anglo-Belgian ties.[33] A few months later, Wilson was reiterating what a difference dependable Belgian assistance might make in the course of a war; this time he urged General Nicholson to press the Foreign Office on the matter. Again his efforts brought no results.[34]

During the Agadir crisis Wilson returned to the idea of Belgian participation in a war, which he discussed at great length with Churchill and then with Colonel Huguet in their September 9 review of entente preparations.[35] In the latter talk the D.M.O. outlined a program of "persuasion" and "intimidation" for the entente partners to apply to Belgium: first, London and Paris could publicly renew their guarantee pledge, thereby easing Belgian fears about what might happen to Belgium after a war; then they could force a Belgian pledge of action if the Germans crossed south of the Meuse; finally, they could push for an improvement in the Belgian defense system. At the same time Wilson raised with Huguet the possibility of Anglo-Belgian offensive action along a line from Liège to Givet and Mézières. Such action, he observed, in "a region without resources and where the troops could not live without their convoys could have the most disastrous consequences" for the Germans. Huguet, who remained cool to the idea of an Anglo-Belgian operation, conveyed Wilson's thoughts to Paris.[36]

Once again the General earned only mixed results from his agitation about Belgium. There was no joint entente pressure upon Brussels, though the British did approach Julien Davignon, the Belgian Foreign Minister, on September 25 about a rumored agreement permitting German passage below the Meuse. Davignon categorically denied the existence of any such pact.[37] His firm denial and King Albert's belated ef-

33. Jan. 27, 1911, Wilson Diaries; also see his Jan. 14, 1910, talk with Foch about "combined action in Belgium," ibid. On the Brussels attitude toward Wilson's trip, see Helmreich, "Belgian Concern over Neutrality," 419.
34. Wilson to Nicholson, Apr. 24, 1911, W.O. 106/47; Aug. 30–31, Sept. 4, 1911, Wilson Diaries.
35. Diary, Sept. 4–5, 1911, in Callwell, Wilson, I, 102–103; Lloyd George to Churchill, Aug. 27, 1911, quoted in Frank Owen, Tempestuous Journey: Lloyd George, His Life and Times (New York, 1955), 212; Churchill to Grey, Aug. 30, 1911, quoted in his The World Crisis, I, 63–64; and Churchill to Lloyd George, Aug. 31, 1911, quoted in Churchill, Young Statesman, 512–513. Also see Churchill to Lloyd George, Sept. 4, 1911, Lloyd George Papers, Beaverbrook Library, London, C/3/15/8.
36. Huguet to Messimy, Sept. 10, 1911, Archives Guerre, "Plan XVII: Armée W," box 147b.
37. Ronald Macleay to Nicolson, Sept. 29, 1911, B.D., VIII, no. 318; Count de Manneville to de Selves, Sept. 30, 1911, D.D.F., 2nd ser., XIV, no. 382.

forts to strengthen the Meuse forts inspired entente hopes that Belgium might resist a German attack.[38]

But Wilson was not satisfied. After an October cycling tour along the Franco-Belgian frontier, he returned to Brussels to discuss the situation with the British Embassy. Following this visit he ruefully observed: "I think we ought to be able to snaffle those Belgians." On returning to London he immediately began to pressure Arthur Nicolson on the importance of "getting into closer touch with Belgium." [39] And he re-examined the military worth of an Anglo-Belgian operation, concluding that such action against a German flanking move would prove more effective than any possible juncture of British forces with the French left. Action on the Maubeuge-Brussels axis might occupy ten to fifteen German divisions. Yet, the appeal to Arthur Nicolson and the studies on Anglo-Belgian cooperation received little encouragement in late 1911. The Foreign Office deferred overtures to Brussels, possibly because of the Cabinet flap over the Anglo-French staff talks, and the French displayed no enthusiasm for Anglo-Belgian operations either in 1911 or later. In fact, in late October Huguet gave his government explicit assurances that the impetus for the British staff work on such operations had come from General French, not from Wilson—the latter, the attaché insisted, remained loyal to joint action with France.[40] During the rest of 1911 the Anglo-French talks, regardless of Wilson's views on Belgium, centered upon the details of British help to France in France.

The last days of September witnessed another burst of Anglo-French military activity. On September 21 Wilson furnished the French Staff with revised mobilization tables, defining precisely the number of British troops to be mobilized, their dates of mobilization, their ports of embarkation and debarkation, the number of horses to accompany them, and the amount of rear area support necessary to maintain them. For example, of the 150,000 British troops, 32,500 would debark at Rouen in the first fourteen days. Except for the 3,600 men assigned to port duty in Rouen, the remainder, along with their 16,795 horses, would be transported to the zone of concentration by the twelfth day.[41] This detailed planning mitigated, if not negated, the noncommittal phrases affixed to the staff talks.

A week later, on September 28, Wilson traveled to Paris to meet with the French Staff and be briefed on their estimates of German intentions and on the revisions of Plan XVI. On the first point French strategists

---

38. Memo by Bridges, Sept. 19, 1911, F.O. 371/1050; Bridges to G. Watson, Sept. 22, 1911, B.D., VIII, no. 317; Bridges to Villiers, Oct. 19, 1911, ibid., no. 319; Victor Duruy to Messimy, Sept. 7, 1911, D.D.F., 2nd ser., XIV, no. 279.
39. Oct. 24, 27, 1911, Wilson Diaries; see also Macleay to Nicolson, Oct. 28, 1911, Nicolson Papers, vol. V/1911.
40. Memos by Wilson, Nov. 11, 21, 1911, W.O. 106/47; Huguet to Messimy, Oct. 18, 1911, Archives Guerre, "Plan XVII: Armée W," box 147b.
41. Huguet to Dubail, Sept. 21, 1911, ibid.

insisted that Wilson had overestimated the number of German troops. They did not believe the Germans would use any reserve divisions in a Belgian operation, and they anticipated only seventy to seventy-five German divisions in the west, while Wilson had placed the figure at eighty-four. Without any attempt to clear up this important discrepancy, the British General accepted the erroneous evaluations. On the second point (French plans), the Staff showed Wilson "the concentration areas of their northern armies. Intensely interesting. Then they showed me papers and maps . . . showing in detail the area of concentration for our Expeditionary Force. In fact, by 12.30 I was in possession of the whole of their plan of campaign for their northern armies, and also for ours. I never spent a more interesting morning." [42] During this session Joffre confirmed that the British divisions would now be located near Maubeuge and La Capelle: the change in locale and concentration Wilson also accepted without hesitancy. In addition he and the French agreed that all British elements would be in their zones by the sixteenth day of French mobilization. These September 1911 arrangements would, it turned out, remain in effect until March 1913, being replaced then by another revision of British mobilization tables.

An equally important part of Wilson's trip was the establishment of friendly relations with the new French high command. Joffre, a "fine, manly, imperturbable soldier with much character and determination," made a favorable impression on him. On the evening of September 29 the D.M.O. dined with his old friends Huguet and Foch and with General de Curières de Castelnau, Joffre's principal strategic adviser. "After dinner we four retired to a private room and with maps we had an exhaustive talk on the whole problem, which was most satisfactory. Castelnau and Foch know their business thoroughly, and it is a real pleasure to discuss matters with them." And Wilson concluded, in a rare moment of satisfaction, "Altogether, I am greatly pleased with the result of my visit." [43]

The steady progress during October in the diplomatic negotiations over Morocco brought a slackening in the military conversations. Most of the essential work had been achieved.[44] Although arrangements for the maritime transport of the B.E.F. remained incomplete, Wilson now confidently believed that the Anglo-French preparations could withstand a practical test. With the relaxation of tensions the General, accompanied by a War Office subordinate, left for a holiday in Belgium and France. Cycling along the Lorraine frontier, near the Metz battlefield, they stopped at the village of Mars la Tour. While there, Wilson

42. Sept. 29, 1911, Wilson Diaries; diary, Sept. 29, 1911, in Callwell, *Wilson*, I, 104–105.
43. Callwell, *Wilson*, I, 105.
44. For a convenient summary of what had been settled by October 1911 see Huguet to Messimy, Oct. 18, 1911, Archives Guerre, "Plan XVII: Armée W," box 147b; also see Chapter 13.

wrote afterward, "we paid my usual visit to the statue of 'France,' looking as beautiful as ever, so I laid at her feet a small bit of map I have been carrying, showing the areas of concentration of the British forces on her territory." [45] This sentimental, symbolic act represented the true nature of Anglo-French military relations in late 1911. So long as Henry Wilson remained Director of Military Operations, he would use all of his considerable energies and persuasive powers to promote the cause of British military intervention on the Continent.

Henry Wilson and the War Office always treated the Moroccan imbroglio as potentially explosive; their Admiralty colleagues were more casual. Nonchalance pervaded the entire naval attitude toward the Agadir crisis. Admiral A. K. Wilson, then First Sea Lord, simply refused to believe that war might come, and the excitement of mid-July found him in Scotland for some shooting.[46] Concern about Britain's naval preparations, or rather the lack of any, came first from the C.I.D. On July 20, Rear Admiral Charles Ottley, the Committee Secretary, reminded Arthur Nicolson of the dangers of a German "bolt from the blue." When the Admiral repeated the warning to Eyre Crowe, Nicolson alerted Grey on July 24 about the possibility of a German sneak attack. Since Kiderlen had earlier requested that the German and British fleets avoid each other during their summer cruises, the ever suspicious Permanent Undersecretary thought it "just possible that he [Kiderlen] had in mind that our vessels should not see what the others were doing." Grey, however, took no positive action until the next day, July 25, when Metternich vehemently protested Lloyd George's speech at Mansion House. Then, according to Churchill, the Foreign Secretary warned McKenna that " 'the fleet might be attacked at any moment.' " [47] At last warning orders were issued.

These belated precautions came none too soon, for while the German High Seas Fleet cruised as a single unit in the North Sea, the British Home Fleet was widely scattered. At one point, in fact, the Admiralty lost contact with the German fleet. This development prompted Henry Wilson to write: "The whole thing is like a pantomime—or the Admiralty!" [48] On July 30 an anxious Winston Churchill inquired of Grey: "Our margins of naval strength are so big, if only we are ready: but are we ready? Are you absolutely *sure* we are ready?" [49] The young Home Secretary was soon convinced, especially after Admiral Wilson's performance at the C.I.D. three weeks later, that all was not ready with the Royal Navy. In September he told Henry Wilson that he was "very dis-

45. Diary, Oct. 16, 1911, in Callwell, *Wilson*, I, 105.
46. Hankey to Esher, Aug. 9, 1911, quoted in Marder, *Road to War*, 243; Hankey, *Supreme Command*, I, 83–84.
47. Ottley to Nicolson, July 20, 1911, Nicolson Papers, vol. III/1911; Nicolson to Grey, July 24, 1911, B.D., VII, no. 636; Churchill, *The World Crisis*, I, 44–45.
48. Diary, July 27, 1911, in Callwell, *Wilson*, I, 97–98.
49. Churchill to Grey, July 30, 1911, Grey Papers, F.O. 800/97.

satisfied with McKenna and Wilson and the whole place, and very angry that everybody should be away." [50]

Churchill's apprehensions about Admiralty preparedness received further corroboration in the middle of September. Despite the international tension, A. K. Wilson continued to scoff at concern over a surprise attack, saying "there was no known case and that Germany was precluded by the Hague Convention from doing anything of that sort." [51] This view, given the Japanese attack on Russia in 1904, struck Sir Arthur Nicolson as wholly absurd. He sought and received Grey's permission (September 17) to warn the Admiralty about the possibility of a "bolt from the blue," only to discover that the First Sea Lord was again away on leave. But this time Nicolson did manage to get at least some action from the Admiralty. The Second Sea Lord, Admiral George Egerton, immediately ordered fleet commanders to take precautionary measures and to move their vessels toward either Scapa Flow or Dover-Harwich. [52] Four days later, with the Moroccan negotiations going more smoothly, the naval precautions were eased with the permission of the Foreign Office. [53]

While the Admiralty continued business as usual during the Moroccan crisis, Henry Wilson at the War Office found the tension a heaven-sent opportunity to press for further improvements in the preparation of the Expeditionary Force. Much remained to be done. On July 8 the D.M.O., determined this time to make General Nicholson "face the problem," complained that the Force was short of both officers and horses and that British rifles and machine guns were poor. Wilson stressed, moreover, that he could not state exactly how long it would take the B.E.F. to mobilize. It was a "disgraceful" situation. [54] When General Charles Heath, the Director of Transport, and General Miles, the Quartermaster General, informed Nicholson that only four divisions were ready for action, an angered Wilson observed that "the scandal grows." In mid-August he drafted still another memo for the Chief of the Imperial General Staff, reiterating his unhappiness with the condition of the Expeditionary Force and again pointing out that he did not know when British divisions would take the field. [55]

Wilson's appeals for action had limited success. There were daily con-

50. Sept. 14, 1911, Wilson Diaries. See also Churchill to Asquith, Sept. 13, 1911; Churchill to Lloyd George, Sept. 14, 1911, quoted in Churchill, Young Statesman, 513–516.

51. Nicolson to Grey, Sept. 16, 1911, Grey Papers, F.O. 800/93; on Sept. 16 the Admiralty informed the Home Fleet commander that "desirable precautions should not be too obvious," Adm. 1/8256.

52. Nicolson to Grey, Sept. 16, 18, 1911, Grey Papers, F.O. 800/93; Grey to Nicolson, Sept. 17, 1911, B.D., VII, no. 647; Egerton to A. K. Wilson (tel.), Sept. 18, 1911, Adm. 1/8256.

53. The Army precautions were eased on Sept. 26, 1911.

54. Wilson to Nicholson, July 6, 1911, W.O. 106/49; July 4, 6, 8, 1911, Wilson Diaries.

55. Diary, July 27, 1911, in Callwell, Wilson, I, 97–98; Wilson to Nicholson, Aug. 16, 1911, W.O. 106/49.

ferences on mobilization arrangements, and the Staff worked hard to revise the logistical tables. General Ewart thought the war scare was "a real blessing from a War Office point of view as we are getting our house in order and for once the Finance branch are afraid to obstruct anything." [56] But the leadership from General Nicholson left something to be desired, at least in Wilson's opinion. At one point he disgustedly declared that in thirteen months Nicholson had not asked a single question about the B.E.F. or "given me the slightest assistance." While the danger of war lurked never far away, General Nicholson was deeply engrossed in a report on pack saddles. In fact, the Chief "talked absolute rubbish, disclosing an even greater ignorance of the problem than I had credited him with," wrote the D.M.O. "He did not even know where the Sambre was!" [57] Nevertheless, despite Nicholson's less than assertive leadership, the B.E.F. did experience a substantial improvement as a result of the steps taken during the crisis. If all six of Wilson's divisions were not ready for mobilization in late July, they were at least much nearer that goal by early October.

Wilson did not confine his energies to the Anglo-French staff talks and to the preparation of the B.E.F.: he also promoted the policy of military intervention on the Continent through personal contacts, War Office memoranda, and the C.I.D. On August 9, for example, he lunched with Grey, Eyre Crowe, and Lord Haldane. Their discussion naturally centered upon the danger of war over the Moroccan issue. When the Foreign Secretary asserted that Russia held the key to peace or war, the General flatly declared that Russia's position would in no way influence German war plans. Instead Russia's weakness meant that Great Britain "*must* join the French . . . *must* mobilize the same day as the French . . . *must* send all six divisions." These objectives, he observed, "were agreed to, but with no great heartiness." He left the group dissatisfied with Haldane's and Grey's grasp of the situation. In particular he regarded Grey as "an ignorant, vain, and weak man, quite unfit to be the Foreign Minister of any country larger than Portugal. A man who knows nothing of policy and strategy going hand in hand." [58]

A few days later Wilson's intervention evangelism took another form: the drafting of two closely reasoned papers designed to prove "conclusively that we *must* join France." These papers, which Nicholson requested and circulated under his name, dealt with both the necessity for British intervention and the value of such assistance. The protection of Britain's political interests in Europe was Wilson's major theme. If Britain remained aside or neutral in a war, France would suffer defeat and "Germany would attain to that dominant position which it has already

56. Diary, Sept. 1, 1911, Ewart Papers.
57. Sept. 6, 1911, Wilson Diaries.
58. Aug. 9, 1911, Wilson Diaries; diary, Aug. 9, 1911, in Callwell, *Wilson*, I, 98–99.

been stated it is an axiom of this country not to tolerate." [59] Should Britain participate, the complexion of the situation would change entirely. First of all, the entente powers would control the sea, a decided advantage if the war was prolonged. But to obtain this prolongation the Germans must be denied an early victory over the French, and to achieve this the French needed British help. The D.M.O., basing his argument on the available roads and on the assumption that the Germans would stay below the Meuse, declared that British aid would decisively influence the chances for an early victory over the Germans. "The early intervention of our six divisions would be more effective than the tardy presence of double their numbers." [60]

Wilson's appreciation of and solution for the continental situation sustained an immediate and prophetic challenge from a surprising source, the literate pen of the young Home Secretary. Impetuous, imaginative, ambitious, Churchill thought, talked, lived, and wrote politics. Even Lloyd George, something of a political animal himself, found it amusing that Churchill talked politics in the vestry of St. Margaret's Chapel only moments before his marriage to Miss Clementine Hozier. [61] But the young minister, though immersed in politics, also had a keen interest in grand strategy. Once critical, even contemptuous of the need for an Expeditionary Force, he found his "high-metalled spirit" exhilarated by the heady excitement of the Agadir crisis. [62] As a result, he experienced a veritable metamorphosis (much more so than did Lloyd George) in his attitude toward Germany and the alleged German threat. But this new understanding of the German menace did not mean that he accepted either Henry Wilson's estimate of the European scene or his idea of full-scale British intervention.

In a memorandum of August 13 Churchill assumed an extensive German violation of Belgium. Working from this premise, he boldly predicted that France would, because of its numerical weakness, be forced to take the defensive. "The balance of probability is that by the twentieth day the French armies will have been driven from the line of the Meuse and will be falling back on Paris and the south. All plans based upon the opposite assumption ask too much of fortune." Despite their expected gains, Churchill doubted that the Germans could achieve a complete victory. By the fortieth day, moreover, with the German lines fully extended, with the German economy under strain, and with Russian help becoming more meaningful, he thought the long-term advantages would shift to France. Given these probable developments, Brit-

59. Wilson to Nicholson, Aug. 11, 1911, W.O. 106/47.
60. General Staff memo, "The Military Aspects of the Continental Problem," Aug. 15, 1911, Cab. 4/3/2.
61. Riddell, More Pages From My Diary, 1.
62. Grey, Twenty-five Years, I, 229–230; for another view of Churchill during the crisis, see Trumbull Higgins, Winston Churchill and the Dardanelles: A Dialogue in Ends and Means (New York, 1963), 26–29.

ain's decisions became those of deciding when to intervene and with what force.[63]

Although the Home Secretary did not "exclude the plan of using four or six British divisions in these great initial operations," he preferred to limit British participation until the fortieth day. By that time he expected additional colonial troops to swell the available British force to two hundred ninety thousand men. An army of that size, "almost entirely composed of professional soldiers, would be assembled around (say) Tours by the fortieth day, in the rear of the French left (instead of being frittered into action in piecemeal), and would then become a very important factor in events." This army could begin assembling on the outbreak of war. Four divisions of the B.E.F. would immediately depart for France, the remaining two upon the establishment of a naval blockade. But until the fortieth day and the arrival of additional colonial help, the Expeditionary Force would remain in a reserve function.[64]

Henry Wilson, thinking Lord Kitchener and Sir John French were behind Churchill's proposals, wasted no time in attacking what he considered "a ridiculous and fantastic paper." His retort hammered at three points: he denied that the Germans would necessarily force the French into a defensive withdrawal off the Meuse; then he belittled the hope that colonial troops would be available within forty days; and he maintained that "the risks of a decision on the French-Belgian frontier are not so serious as are anticipated." Any postponement or delay in British intervention would increase, furthermore, the very danger Churchill envisaged. With active British help it could be "shown that the victory of Germany is by no means a foregone conclusion." [65] While Wilson did not entirely convince the minister with this reply, he nonetheless won his respect. Throughout the remainder of the Moroccan crisis the General remained in close, indeed intimate, contact with the future First Lord of the Admiralty—so much so that Nicholson mildly reprimanded Wilson about sending memos to Churchill.

If immediate British military intervention on the Continent prompted concern among Kitchener, French, and Churchill, this prospect met outright, unyielding opposition from Admiral A. K. Wilson and Reginald McKenna. In their opposition the naval high command enjoyed the moral support of Lord Fisher, then on holiday in Lucerne. On August 20 the former First Sea Lord wrote McKenna:

> Don't give me away to Spender or to "Napoleon B. [Haldane] by any chance word," but REST ASSURED that if the Government

63. Memo by Churchill, Aug. 13, 1911, quoted in Churchill, *The World Crisis*, I, 58–62. It is possible that Churchill saw the drafts of Wilson's papers of Aug. 11–12, 1911, but Wilson's diaries make no mention of it.
64. *Ibid.*
65. Diary, Aug. 15, 1911, in Callwell, *Wilson*, I, 99; Wilson to Nicholson, Aug. 15, 1911, W.O. 106/47.

land a single British soldier in France (*or even entertain any plans for it!*), there will be an upheaval in England that will cast them out of office. Sir John French once came to me about it as a tool of Sir William Nicholson, but I told him to go to Hell! The whole single object is compulsory service and an increase of the Army Estimates and military influence; I much fear the Prime Minister may be "nobbled" by Napoleon B.[66]

Admiral Wilson, meanwhile, acted to ensure that Asquith was not "nobbled" by the idea of continental intervention. In a specific rejoinder to Henry Wilson's memos, the First Sea Lord declared that as a naval power Britain's first responsibility was the destruction of the enemy fleet. Therefore, "naval opinion on any proposed action by the Army must be determined mainly by the extent to which it helps or hinders that object." And he renewed his 1905 warning: once committed to the Continent, the Army would drain off all other military and naval resources. If intervention would turn the tide for France, the Admiral remarked, then the Navy might consider it worthwhile, "but even the advocates of the scheme do not pretend that this is the case." Instead of continental involvement, he suggested that the C.I.D. reconsider its 1909 position on combined coastal raids. A single British division, kept at sea as a decoy, would divert the entire German coastal defense force. Yet even Admiral Wilson conceded in advance that his scheme had some shortcomings, saying at one point that "if no actual success is gained, the mere fact of keeping the field army in motion must tend to exhaust their [German] resources." [67] The First Sea Lord's rigid opposition to intervention left no doubt about the strategic differences between the two services; a "showdown" over British strategy, which could not long be postponed, came two days later.

On August 23 the C.I.D. held a remarkable, unprecedented all-day session to review British strategy. This meeting followed close on the heels of a series of important and bitter domestic developments—Agadir had been but one of an array of problems confronting British policymakers during the long summer. The constitutional crisis over the proper role for the House of Lords had finally been resolved in favor of the Commons in early August; but the settlement was almost immediately obscured by a wave of strikes, including one on the railways, which swept the country. For a time there was a genuine question of whether troops on strike duty would be able to mobilize if war came. But by August 23 the railway strike was over; Parliament had recessed; the Cabinet was about to disperse; even the oppressive heat had begun to abate. Now, before leaving London for their own holidays, the responsible

66. Fisher to McKenna, Aug. 20, 1911, Marder, *Fear God and Dread Nought*, II, 380.
67. "The Military Aspects of the Continental Problem—Admiralty Remarks," Aug. 21, 1911, Cab. 4/3/2; see also Aug. 21, 1911, Wilson Diaries.

ministers plus Churchill and Lloyd George gathered to discuss the possibility of a European war and the alternate strategic choices open to Britain. Participants in the meeting were Asquith, Lloyd George, Grey, Haldane, McKenna, Churchill, A. K. Wilson, Henry Wilson, John French, Nicholson, Bethell, Ottley, and Hankey. Notably absent were Lord Morley and Lord Esher, the former on vacation in Scotland, the latter recovering from an operation. Harcourt, Crewe, and Loreburn were uninvited; Kitchener rejected an invitation because "he was sure the Germans would beat the French" and he wanted "no part in any decision." [68] These absences were to be the source of considerable trouble, for Asquith, for the military conversations, and, ultimately in 1914, for British strategy.

The C.I.D. meeting had hardly begun when Reginald McKenna fired the first salvo: the Admiralty could furnish neither men nor ships to move troops across the Channel at the start of a war. When General Nicholson replied that the Admiralty Transport Division had already worked out the details, the First Lord claimed that Admiral Groome had not realized that Army and Navy mobilizations would be simultaneous. A. K. Wilson then intervened to say that he thought the entire expeditionary scheme had been discussed and dropped. In the ensuing exchanges Asquith made clear his unhappiness with the Admiralty's position. Instructing McKenna to investigate the misunderstanding over the transport question, the Prime Minister pointedly stated that "it should be understood that the question of time was all important. The simultaneous mobilisation of our army and that of the French, and the immediate concentration of our army in the theatre of war were essential features of the plan." The first round went to the Army.[69]

At this point Henry Wilson began his masterful, well-planned exposition upon the European military situation and British war plans. In his presentation Wilson insisted, as he had in the memos, that the approximate equality of Franco-German troops in the Maubeuge-Verdun sector would enable six British divisions to exert a decisive impact on the course of events. But, interrupted Churchill and French, what if the Germans crossed above the Meuse and swept through the Maubeuge-Lille gap? Brushing aside this possibility, the D.M.O. maintained that Germany dared not alienate a Belgium that otherwise would accept a German violation below the Meuse. Such a German sweep, moreover, would be dangerous and "would require so many men . . . that in present circumstances no advantage and a good deal of risk would accrue to the Germans by taking this course." In any case, should this danger materialize, the French could quickly throw ten divisions into the gap and

68. Diary, Sept. 6, 1911, Oliver, Viscount Esher, ed., *Journals and Letters of Reginald, Viscount Esher*, vol. III: *1910–1915* (London, 1938), 58.
69. The account of this meeting is based entirely on the minutes of the 114th meeting of the C.I.D., Cab. 2/2/2. Also see Churchill, *The World Crisis*, I, 53–56; Hankey, *Supreme Command*, I, 78–82; Marder, *Road to War*, 388–393.

the "Belgian army, though small, could not be ignored, and its strategical position upon the German flank was strong."

Churchill then shifted his angle of attack. What would happen to the British troops at Maubeuge, he asked, if the French were beaten along the Meuse. Wilson, who confessed he knew nothing of French plans for such a contingency, thought the Expeditionary Force would remain attached to the French left. The Home Secretary refused to accept this possibility, urging instead that the British divisions should cling to the coastline: he had in fact anticipated the problem of Dunkirk by twenty-nine years. Unable to reach agreement on this issue, Churchill suggested discussing the matter with the French. At this point Grey intervened to oppose such a step and then deliberately shifted the conversation. The young minister's question remained unanswered; Wilson continued his exposé.

British troops, he told the group, would move over the French railways to their zone of concentration near Maubeuge; concentrated by the fourteenth day, they would be available for the first fighting, which Wilson expected around the seventeenth day.[70] The mention of combat prompted McKenna, a navalist and a radical (in that order), to ask whether "the probable effect of our intervention with six divisions [was] so great that without it the French would not resist German aggression, while with it they would." Grey, always litmus-paper-sensitive to radical fears about Anglo-French relations, interrupted to say that Britain must "postulate that the French intended to fight. The main point was whether our intervention would make the difference between defeat and victory." The Prime Minister concurred. The point, he told the Committee, "which the Cabinet would have to decide was what we were going to do if we resolved to commit ourselves to support the French against a German attack." On this note the morning session adjourned.

In the afternoon the Admiralty had its innings. A. K. Wilson got things off to a promising start by pledging naval cooperation in the movement of the Expeditionary Force; but the olive branch soon wilted as the Admiral proceeded to denounce any dispatch of the B.E.F. to the Continent. Such an operation, he claimed, would start an invasion panic and force the Navy into a defensive role, while also depriving the Admiralty of troops required for amphibious operations along the German coast. Among the contemplated coastal raids were the capture of Wangeroog and Schillighörn at the mouth of the Jade and Weser and a troop landing at Büsum. The acquisition of these positions was imperative, the First Sea Lord pronounced, since they would serve as advanced bases for the destroyers engaged in close blockade duty. This re-

70. Wilson's mention of Maubeuge was at variance with the July 20 memorandum designating St. Quentin-Cambrai as the zone. In citing Maubeuge, Wilson anticipated Joffre's later decision on the matter, though exactly why he did so remains obscure.

turn to the doctrine of coastal raids, so long stressed by Fisher and discredited by the earlier C.I.D. studies, angered the irascible, salty-tongued General Nicholson, who declared that a century ago some of these operations might have had some value, "when land communications were indifferent, but now, when they were excellent, they were doomed to failure. . . . None of these places, so far as he could understand, had any essential importance for the naval operations."

Arthur Wilson simply ignored the thrust of Nicholson's objections and pushed on. He next outlined possible operations in the Baltic and against the island of Heligoland; the latter, he added, might require a division from the Army. At this Nicholson exploded. He asked "if the Admiralty would continue to press that view even if the General Staff expressed their considered opinion that military operations in which it was proposed to employ this division were madness." Grey was moved by this outburst to agree with the General, commenting that so "far as he could judge, the combined operations outlined were not essential to naval success, and the struggle on land would be the decisive one." But the First Sea Lord remained adamant about the need for such an operation, continuing to insist on the importance of the German islands as advanced bases. The most he would concede was that the Schillighörn expedition might not be necessary. Because this talk about close blockading contradicted Admiral Wilson's own published views about its dangers and because he offered no precise details to support the schemes, most on the Committee concluded that he had no war plans worthy of the name. Even Hankey, a staunch Fisherite and a supporter of Wilson, thought his ideas sounded as if they had been "cooked up" during the lunch break.[71]

Perhaps deciding that the best defense was a good offense, the First Sea Lord and the First Lord of the Admiralty renewed their attack upon the proposed plan of continental intervention. Already Wilson had claimed that language differences and logistical problems would render impossible any effective British assistance. Now McKenna reiterated the contention that the sudden departure of the B.E.F. "would result in great pressure being brought to bear upon the Government to tie the Fleet to the defence of our coast. The moral effect upon the English people would be so serious as to be disastrous." This invocation of home defense requirements brought the Prime Minister back into the discussion. Hoping to assuage the First Lord's apprehension, he reminded the group that the 1908 Subcommittee on Invasion had ruled that two divisions would stay in Britain at the start of any emergency; these, he was confident, would be sufficient to repel any German raids.

Asquith's attempt to reconcile the two positions simply made things worse, for Generals French and Archibald Murray (Director of the Territorial Force), supported by Lloyd George, asserted that the territorials

71. Hankey, *Supreme Command,* I, 81.

could repulse both German raids and invasion threats without the help of the regulars. When the First Lord and First Sea Lord refused to be convinced, Churchill asked the telling question: how, if the Admiralty established its close blockade, could any German ships escape in the first place? He observed that until that day the Navy had always claimed that any and all invasions and raids were impossible; now the Admiralty had suddenly reversed itself. McKenna admitted the point. The real job of the Committee, concluded Churchill, was to settle the "most effective method of employing our military forces in the event contemplated. Some risks had to be taken in war."

This apposite remark led Asquith to inquire what was the smallest British force that could intervene effectively on the Continent. Henry Wilson answered that while the General Staff preferred to send all six divisions, five would have a great moral effect. Nicholson went further, claiming that four divisions would be preferable to none. The Prime Minister, who leaned toward the latter figure, accepted these opinions without making any decision. Shortly afterward the meeting broke up, with McKenna still objecting to the removal of the entire B.E.F. and Arthur Wilson still demanding an Army division for amphibious operations. Quite clearly neither the Admiralty nor the War Office had convinced each other about the utilization of the British Army and the priorities of British strategy.

Several immediate observations must be made about this secret session of the C.I.D. First, the military conversations as such were not discussed in any detail, nor did Henry Wilson reveal the existence of the signed memorandum on British help to France; on the other hand, Wilson's presentation left no doubts about his intimacy with the French Staff. Second, the August review of British strategy was a unique, not a regular, occurrence for the C.I.D. The Committee had touched upon strategic matters in the past and would do so in the future, but this occasion was its only excursion before 1914 into the realm of grand strategy and overall strategic coordination. Nor would the C.I.D. ever again stop and fully reconsider Henry Wilson's arguments for intervention, or even the implications of intervention.[72] In 1912 the Committee would discuss Belgian neutrality and briefly mention British intervention; in 1913 a subcommittee would evaluate anew the problem of invasion but only touch upon the problem of Britain's overall strategy in a European war. The reasons for the Committee's circumspection, as will be seen, stemmed in part from the political repercussions of this meeting, in part from the absence of an international crisis before 1914 that would force a procrastinating Asquith and Cabinet to come to terms with the problem. Finally, one reason for the Committee's failure certainly sprang from the horrendous impression made by the Admiralty on August 23:

72. Mackintosh, "The Role of the Committee of Imperial Defence before 1914," 501–503.

contrasted with Henry Wilson's confident, lucid, and logical presentation, Admiral Wilson's views appeared vague, ill-advised, and dangerous. The resulting alarm over conditions at the Admiralty tended to obscure the inadequacies and shortcomings of the Army's strategic thought.
A. K. Wilson's poor performance had other equally significant aspects. Fisher and he had repeatedly stressed the need to keep their war
plans secret; in retrospect their talk of secrecy appears more a means of
masking unpreparedness than of protecting preparations. Admiral Wilson's bluster about taking Heligoland, for example, indicated to Admiral Ottley that the First Sea Lord had completely disregarded the
work of the Ballard-Hankey committee of 1907 which had ruled as unfeasible any assault upon that heavily fortified island. Ottley believed
that revival of the plan in 1911 could be directly attributed to the lack
of a naval war staff at the Admiralty.[73] The acrimonious exchanges between Arthur Wilson and Sir William Nicholson emphasized, moreover, that despite the C.I.D. the two services still evolved their strategies
in separate compartments; and for this the Admiralty was chiefly to
blame. In late 1909 Esher had complained that "the Admiralty is very
obstructive. . . . We come to decisions, and they are treated as the
amiable aberrations of a few well meaning but rather harmless amateur
strategists." [74] Although the C.I.D. had decided in 1909 that a British
Army might be employed upon the Continent, the Admiralty had hampered and frustrated all War Office attempts to settle the details of
troop movement. This lack of cooperation, which even Henry Wilson
tried to conceal, jeopardized the chances of effective British intervention.[75]

But the C.I.D. and Asquith shared responsibility for the lack of coordination and cooperation. From its start in 1903, the Committee cautiously walked around the delicate problem of interservice relations. The
1905 subcommittee on combined operations was stillborn; Fisher and
his successor were allowed to pursue their own desires. No efforts were
made to verify whether the services respected or even took notice of
C.I.D. rulings. As far as the Admiralty was concerned, the 1909 hearings
on the Continent were a "make-work" exercise. Whether Asquith could
have molded the Committee into an effective coordinating forum is another matter: faced with the constitutional struggle created by the People's Budget, he had other, more immediate and pressing problems.
Moreover, though he was capable of great ruthlessness to friend and foe
alike, Asquith had perfected the art of indecision and evasion as a positive political asset. The self-made Prime Minister, a product of Yorkshire,

73. Ottley to Churchill, Nov. 2, 1911, Cab. 17/8; memo by Ottley, Nov. 1, 1911,
ibid.
74. Esher to M. V. Brett, Dec. 29, 1909, *Journals and Letters of Esher*, II, 430.
75. Ottley to Nicolson, Apr. 4, 1911, Nicolson Papers, vol. II/1911; Hankey,
Supreme Command, I, 77–78, 82–84.

Oxford, and the bar, preferred to muddle through, to postpone decisions until the last possible minute. Defense problems, which he often never understood, were not immune from this treatment—nonetheless, the Prime Minister bore ultimate responsibility for British defense arrangements. In the C.I.D. he had a convenient instrument to implement and enforce coordination. Because of his repeated inaction, Asquith made possible the painful session of August 1911.

Historians, observers, and participants have generally agreed that the C.I.D. meeting of August 23 placed an imprimatur upon continental involvement. Hankey, who on August 24 thought that "no decision was arrived at," speaks for most when he later wrote that "from that time onward there was never any doubt what would be the Grand Strategy in the event of our being drawn into a continental war in support of France. Unquestionably the Expeditionary Force, or the greater part of it, would have been sent to France as it actually was in 1914." [76] Such judgments should not, however, conceal the fact that when the meeting ended, Henry Wilson had gained only a partial victory with the Prime Minister. Although convinced of the need for intervention, Asquith was still unhappy about the prospect. He wrote Haldane on August 31: "Sir A. Wilson's 'plan' can only be described as puerile, and I have dismissed it at once as wholly impracticable. The impression left on me, after consideration of the whole discussion, is . . . that, *in principle, the General Staff scheme is the only alternative* [italics added] but . . . that it should be limited in the first instance to the dispatch of 4 divisions. Grey agrees with me, and so (I think) does Winston." Ten days later Asquith wrote the War Minister that "the arguments as put in the W.O. letter are, of course, conclusive as against Sir A. W.'s scheme. I hope, however, that we may not have again to consider the contingency." [77]

Asquith's evident distaste for intervention steadily increased. At Balmoral Castle as guests of the King, he and Lord Esher on October 4 discussed British defense problems. "Then we talked," recorded Esher, "about the General Staff scheme of landing an army in France. The Prime Minister is opposed to this plan. He will not hear of the dispatch of more than four Divisions. He has told Haldane so." On the same day the viscount wrote his son that Asquith's views "would astonish dear old Pussy [Haldane] and the General Staff. If they, as they do, think that

76. Hankey to Fisher, Aug. 24, 1911, quoted in Marder, *Road to War*, 393; Hankey, *Supreme Command*, I, 82.
77. Asquith to Haldane, Aug. 31, 1911, Haldane Papers, 5909; Asquith to Haldane, Sept. 9, 1911, *ibid.* Lord Stamfordham also disliked the idea of sending troops to France; he feared German raids and thought the Army might have "to do Police work at home, deal with strikes, possibly revolution!" (Stamfordham to Nicolson, Sept. 19, 1911, Nicolson Papers, vol. IV/1911).

their strategic plan would be feasible, they are highly mistaken." [78] By late October Asquith's opposition had reached the point where he could assure McKenna that there was "no danger so long as he was P.M., as he was opposed to the scheme" of early intervention.[79] Considered from this vantage point, the strategical debate of August was unresolved. But Asquith's apparent hostility to intervention was offset by his actions elsewhere. Demands for new leadership at the Admiralty and a Cabinet crisis over the military conversations were also direct consequences of the C.I.D. meeting: the Prime Minister's reactions to them influenced the direction of British strategy, for they had the practical effect of nullifying his qualms about continental involvement.

The August meeting had hardly ended when Haldane presented his chief with a veritable ultimatum: unless the Admiralty installed a naval war staff and cooperated with the Army, he would resign. Furthermore, Haldane himself wanted to carry out the reorganization.[80] While Asquith pondered these demands the Secretary of State for War was experiencing other incidents which reinforced his determination to change things at the Admiralty. On August 29 the Navy requested that the Army "keep available a force of 6000 infantry, a field company of Royal Engineers, three batteries of artillery, a cyclist company (for scouting), a small telegraph company, and a few airmen" for combined operations in the North Sea. The Navy appeared incapable of recognizing, despite Nicholson's outburst in the C.I.D., that the Army wanted no part of such operations. The War Office on September 9 responded tersely that "operations of the nature and scale proposed could only end in disaster." [81] And Haldane was further irritated by the Admiralty's continued apathy on the transport issue.[82] In late September Haldane, joined now by Churchill, intensified pressure upon the Prime Minister for a change in naval leadership. Visiting Asquith at Archerfield, near Edinburgh, the two ministers focused their demands upon the issue of a naval war staff for the Admiralty. After several lengthy discussions they managed to convince the Prime Minister of the wisdom of a change.[83] But, to Hal-

78. Diary, Oct. 4, 1911, *Journals and Letters of Esher*, III, 61; Esher to M. V. Brett, Oct. 4, 1911, *ibid.*, 60.
79. Undated notes of the McKenna-Asquith conversation, Oct. 20, 1911, quoted in Marder, *Road to War*, 250. The manuscript record of the conversation is in the McKenna Papers, Churchill College Library, Cambridge, McKn 4/2.
80. Haldane to Asquith, Aug. [?] 1911, quoted in Maurice, *Haldane*, I, 283–284; J. A. Spender and Cyril Asquith, *Life of Herbert Henry Asquith, Lord Oxford and Asquith*, 2 vols. (London, 1932), I, 346.
81. Admiralty memo, Aug. 29, 1911, quoted in Marder, *Road to War*, 393; General Staff memo, Sept. 8, 1911, *ibid.*, 393–394.
82. Haldane to Asquith, Sept. 25 [28?], 1911, Asquith Papers, box 13; McKenna to Asquith, Sept. 19, 1911, *ibid.*; memo by Nicholson, Sept. 25, 1911, W.O. 106/50.
83. Haldane to Grey, Oct. 2, 1911, quoted in Maurice, *Haldane*, I, 284–286; Churchill, *The World Crisis*, I, 66.

dane's surprise and consternation, Churchill received the post; he and McKenna simply exchanged positions within the Cabinet.

Of Churchill's appointment Arthur Marder writes: "It should be stressed that Asquith reached this decision without choosing between the naval strategy of sea-war with a mobile army poised for landings on the enemy coast, and the 'continental' strategy of the Army, with the Navy's main role that of transporting a continental army and keeping its lines of communications open." [84] This appraisal misses the larger issue. Churchill and Haldane admittedly concentrated their attack upon the staff question; but Churchill's support for some form of continental intervention was already well known, revealed both in his papers of August 13 and 30 and by his performance in the C.I.D. Given Churchill's outlook, the transfer of Cabinet posts also meant a decision between strategies. This consequence, moreover, was not missed by Reginald McKenna.

On October 20 McKenna went to Archerfield to discuss with the Prime Minister the coming changes at the Admiralty. Ignoring entirely the naval staff issue—the alleged raison d'être for all the commotion—their rather unpleasant meeting centered upon continental strategy and the military conversations. McKenna resumed his efforts to hamstring intervention, demanding for the Navy the right to oppose any movement of troops to the Continent. He also wanted assurances "that in no case should our troops be employed in the first instance and the French should never be encouraged by such a promise. If the communications between the General Staffs were continued I would have to resign." Asquith, though defending the conversations as necessary, assured McKenna that he too opposed Henry Wilson's proposals. But the First Lord remained skeptical. He feared that Asquith "might be rushed into it by a situation being developed by the W.O. and Admiralty." Resenting this aspersion upon his control of the government, the Prime Minister cautioned McKenna that he was not a "figurehead pushed along against his will and without his knowledge by some energetic colleagues." Their discussion ended with Asquith stating that "he did not believe in war and that if he had thought that war were probable he would not have made the change." [85]

McKenna clearly grasped the most obvious impact of the Cabinet switch. He recognized, if Asquith did not, that the change in naval leadership would settle by extension the strategic question as well.[86] So long as he remained First Lord and Arthur Wilson First Sea Lord, the Navy

84. Road to War, 248.

85. Undated notes of the McKenna-Asquith conversation, Oct. 20, 1911, quoted in Marder, Road to War, 250–251.

86. Hankey and Fisher also regarded Churchill's appointment as a victory for the Army; Hankey to McKenna, Oct. 24, 1911, quoted in Stephen McKenna, Reginald McKenna, 1863–1943: A Memoir (London, 1948), 117; Fisher to Spender, Oct. 31, 1911, Marder, Fear God and Dread Nought, II, 409–410.

would oppose continental intervention. Churchill's appearance would almost certainly reduce or eliminate naval opposition to this military strategy. To avert this prospect, McKenna had sought to gain in advance for the Naval Lords a guarantee of veto power over Army operations. He had failed. All he got for his efforts was the Prime Minister's assurance that he too disliked Henry Wilson's war plan: this, McKenna soon realized, meant little.

On October 25 Churchill assumed command at the Admiralty, and his arrival justified many of his predecessors' worst fears. His friendship with the magnanimous Haldane immediately brought a new spirit of cooperation into War Office-Admiralty relations. Encouraged and guided by Haldane, the new First Lord proceeded to oust A. K. Wilson and to establish a naval staff to draft and review war plans.[87] Even more importantly, coastal operations were shelved as he accepted the military viewpoint on the role of the Army. Only later, in the spring of 1914, would he seek to resurrect the amphibious schemes. A grateful Henry Wilson wrote on November 21 that Churchill "will play in with us all he can, and I feel sure will do a great deal of good in the Admiralty." [88]

The dimensions of the change at the Admiralty were amply illustrated by an incident that occurred in mid-January 1912. On January 17 General Wilson spent the evening with Sir Francis Bridgeman, the new First Sea Lord, and Rear Admiral Sir Ernest Troubridge, the Chief of the new Naval Staff. "We had a long and intimate talk about things," Wilson later wrote, "and I am greatly pleased with their outlook and their most kindly feeling to me personally. They agree with all my proposals. I showed them my maps of the French and German concentration on the frontier and explained the situation. The most satisfactory evening I have spent for years." [89] Interservice cooperation had at last been achieved—on Army terms. The continental strategy was triumphant.

Another development, meanwhile, consolidated the victory for continental involvement. It, like the changes at the Admiralty, had begun in late August. Word of the extraordinary C.I.D. meeting with its mention of the staff talks soon reached those ministers who were uninvited, all of whom were radicals. Already angered by their loss of influence following Lloyd George's peroration at Mansion House, the Cabinet radicals—especially Morley, Loreburn, and Harcourt—were now infuriated, both over their exclusion from the meeting and over the news of the military conversations. John Morley's anger over the proceedings caused

87. On improved War Office-Admiralty relations, see, e.g., Haldane to Mary Haldane, Nov. 30, 1911, Haldane Papers, 5986. On the naval staff issue, see Marder, Road to War, 256–258, 265–266; Churchill, The World Crisis, I, 78–85, 90–92.
88. Diary, Nov. 21, 1911, in Callwell, Wilson, I, 107.
89. Diary, Jan. 17, 1912, ibid., 109–110.

Asquith to wonder who had told him of the meeting. Morley, Asquith remarked, "is quite the most impossible colleague that ever entered a Cabinet." [90]

Though peeved at Lord Morley, the Prime Minister himself possessed nagging doubts about the conversations and their implications. He reminded Grey in early September that "conversations such as that between Gen. Joffre and Col. Fairholme seem to me rather dangerous; especially the part which refers to possible British assistance. The French ought not to be encouraged, in present circumstances, to make their plans on any assumptions of this kind." But Asquith's desire for caution received no encouragement from the Foreign Secretary, who replied: "It would create consternation if we forbade our military experts to converse with the French. No doubt these conversations and our speeches have given an expectation of support. I do not see how that can be helped." [91] It might be hoped, observed Grey, that the Berlin-Paris negotiations were near a settlement, in which case this problem would be removed. The conversations continued; and so did Asquith's concern.

The plainspoken Lord Esher did little to allay the Prime Minister's anxiety about the conversations. In their early October discussion at Balmoral the viscount, always a useful *advocatus diaboli*, stressed the intimate connection between the staff talks and British defense policy. "I reminded him [Asquith] that the mere fact of the War Office plan having been worked out in detail with the French General Staff (which is the case) had certainly committed us to fight, whether the Cabinet likes it or not, and that the combined plan of the two General Staffs holds the field. It is certainly an extraordinary thing that our officers should have been permitted to arrange all the details, trains, landing, concentration, etc., when the Cabinet have never been consulted." Esher also pressed the Prime Minister on what he thought the chances were of having the B.E.F. in France within seven days, "in view of the fact that the Cabinet (the majority of them) have never heard of the plan." Asquith thought it "impossible!" [92] Despite the Prime Minister's agreement on these points, Esher personally doubted much would happen. "Although the P.M. showed that he had thought a good deal of these problems, he is lazy and hesitates to act upon his views. He despises the French Government and says that the brothers Cambon rule France in her foreign relations." [93] Events proved that Esher had correctly forecast not only the Cabinet's reaction but Asquith's as well.

90. Asquith to Haldane, Sept. 9, 1911, Haldane Papers, 5909. On Loreburn's reaction, see above, Chapter 6, pp. 156–157: also see Hammond. C. P Scott. 143–144; J. A. Spender, *Life, Journalism and Politics*, 2 vols. (London, 1927), I, 241–242: Haldane to Spender, Aug. 27, 1911, Spender Papers, Add. MSS, 46390.
91. Asquith to Grey, Sept. 5, 1911, quoted in Grey, *Twenty-five Years*, I, 92; Grey to Asquith, Sept. 8, 1911, *ibid.*, 93.
92. Diary, Oct. 4, 1911, *Journals and Letters of Esher*, III, 61–62.
93. This sentence was omitted in the published diaries; see Esher Papers, "Journal 1909–1914."

The approach of a new session of Parliament on October 24 found the political circuits in London buzzing with talk about the summer crisis. Some claimed the Liberals had used the danger of a war to end the rail strike in August, others spoke of promises to send troops to France within ten or fourteen days. Rumors about deficiencies at the Admiralty and about the military preparations became general.[94] Each new report antagonized, angered, aggravated the sensitive feelings of the radical ministers. Sir Almeric Fitzroy, Secretary of the Privy Council, observed on October 20 that there was a "distinct rift in the Cabinet on the amount of support to be given to France, Lord Morley, the Lord Chancellor, Harcourt, and John Burns having not seen eye to eye with their colleagues."[95]

The removal of McKenna from the Admiralty accentuated the rift in that it gratuitously supplied the radical bloc with another formidable ally. In their tête-à-tête of October 20 McKenna belabored Asquith about the ramifications of the conversations. Moreover, he had won the Prime Minister's consent to utilize C.I.D. information "to strengthen [his] position . . . with regard to communications between the General Staffs."[96] As a navalist he regarded the staff talks as the prerequisite for continental action; as a Liberal he suspected them of dangerously encouraging France to follow a bellicose foreign policy. Thus an end to the conversations would check the policy of intervention, preserve the Navy's strategy, and restrain the French. He failed, however, to achieve any of these aims, for Asquith refused to halt the staff talks.

In early November the Cabinet crisis over the staff talks reached its climax. At the Cabinet on November 1, as Asquith later informed George V, "Lord Morley raised the question of the inexpediency of communications being held or allowed between the General Staff of the War Office and the General Staff of foreign states, such as France, in regard to possible military cooperations without the previous knowledge or directions of the Cabinet." This charge forced the Liberal imperialists, Haldane, Grey, and Asquith, to defend both the conversations and their failure to inform the Cabinet of them. The three invoked a variety of justifications. First, they stressed that the talks had begun in 1906 under the auspices and approval of Sir Henry Campbell-Bannerman. Since his radicalism had been above reproach, the late Prime Minister's acquiescence in the conversations robbed the radicals of a telling argument. Then Asquith went to great trouble to assure the Cabinet that the conversations had in no way committed the government to a policy of intervention. He agreed with the radicals that it was "quite outside

94. See, e.g., Austen Chamberlain to Joseph Chamberlain, Oct. 12, 23, 26, 1911, quoted in Austen Chamberlain, *Politics from Inside: An Epistolary Chronicle, 1906–1914* (London, 1936), 360–361, 363, 367–368.

95. Sir Almeric Fitzroy, *Memoirs*, 2 vols. (London, n.d.). II, 466.

96. Memo of McKenna-Asquith conversation, Oct. 20, 1911, McKenna Papers, McKn 4/2.

the function of the military or naval officers to prejudge such questions." And both the Prime Minister and Sir Edward Grey insisted that the French government recognized Britain's lack of commitment. Asquith could also hold that the talks increased, not limited, the Cabinet's freedom of action since they made possible the act of intervention should the Cabinet so decide. What the Prime Minister did not acknowledge, and probably did not realize, was that the talks committed Britain, in case of intervention, to a particular military strategy of such magnitude as to constitute a policy decision. In that sense, regardless of Asquith's disclaimers, the conversations were indeed shaping policy, albeit only potential policy. In any case, the arguments failed to convince the radicals. After "considerable discussion" in which "no conclusion was come to," the Cabinet adjourned the matter until its next session.[97] While the opposition Unionists were fighting over who would succeed Balfour as party leader, Asquith was struggling to keep the Cabinet intact over foreign policy.

At its meeting on November 15 the Cabinet again took up Morley's complaint. Once more there was "a prolonged and animated discussion." In the debate Grey strenuously defended the conversations, insisting that neither diplomatic nor military engagements compromised Britain's "freedom of decision of action in the event of a war between France and Germany."[98] To illustrate that the French completely understood that Britain was not bound to intervene, the Foreign Secretary read an excerpt from a Cambon dispatch of September in which the French ambassador had warned Caillaux " 'that it would be exceedingly difficult for any British Government to take any action which was not supported by British public opinion.' " Observing that British opinion " 'was impetuous and did not reason very deeply,' " Cambon warned that France must avoid any appearance of being the aggressor in a war with Germany. Should France start something, " 'the result would be that France would not be able to count on British support.' "[99] But Cambon's assessment of the role of British opinion and the entente, however accurate, did not appease the radicals.

The fact is that the radicals remained unhappy about the military conversations. They feared that such talks "might give rise to expectations, and that they should not, if they related to the possibility of concerted action, be entered into or carried on without the sanction of the Cabinet." At length Asquith managed to bridge the differences by advancing two propositions which won unanimous approval: "(1) That no communications should take place between the General Staff here and

97. Asquith to George V, Nov. 2, 1911, Asquith Papers, box 6; Spender and Asquith, *Life of Asquith*, I, 349; cf. Lloyd George, *War Memoirs*, I, 45–48. Roy Jenkins, *Asquith* (London, 1964), 244–245.
98. Asquith to George V, Nov. 15, 1911, Asquith Papers, box 6.
99. From a minute by Nicolson, Nov. 2, 1911 (B.D., VII, no. 617). Grey noted on Nov. 16 that he had read Nicolson's entire paper to the Cabinet.

the Staffs of other countries which can, directly or indirectly, commit this country to military or naval intervention. (2) That such communications, if they relate to concerted action by land or sea, should not be entered into without the previous approval of the Cabinet." Significantly, Grey penciled on the Cabinet letter that he found the last paragraph "a little tight." [100]

These propositions eased the differences within the Cabinet, staving off further debate about the staff talks until mid-1912 and the start of the official naval conversations. More important, Asquith's formula did not halt the staff conversations. Future exchanges were restricted, but conversations already in progress were neither prevented nor stopped. Nor did the stipulation that the talks were noncommittal represent a significant new restriction, since Henry Wilson had always acknowledged this notion, while nullifying it with his unofficial assurances to the French. The vagueness of the propositions, moreover, reduced their value. The conversations involved "concerted action"; so were all day-to-day Anglo-French staff talks to be reported to the Cabinet, or only those which initiated new programs? The radicals almost certainly wanted information on both categories; they obtained it only on the latter. In 1912 Churchill would seek Cabinet approval for new naval talks, but thereafter the Cabinet would know nothing of the content of the naval conversations. Henry Wilson would of course make no attempt to keep the Cabinet informed of his regular discussions with the French. But perhaps most important, the continuance of the staff talks ensured the primacy of the strategy of continental intervention. By his formula, as with the shift of Churchill to the Admiralty, Asquith had supported the War Office's strategic preferences. Well might Haldane remark after the Cabinet meeting: "I emerge unhampered in any material point." [101]

While the Cabinet debated the staff talks, one individual fully appreciated that he was the intended target of the radical attacks: Brigadier General Henry Wilson knew that he was being accused of having "forced the pace during the crisis" and that the "peace party" in the Cabinet was calling for his head. Wilson, who was willing to resign to appease the "dirty, ignorant curs," got strong support from Sir William Nicholson and Lord Haldane. The latter, in fact, told Asquith he would resign rather than accept a change of policy which the D.M.O.'s ouster would imply. The upshot, Wilson soon concluded, would be to stop his "going to Paris . . . but not much else." [102]

100. Asquith to George V, Nov. 15, 1911, Asquith Papers, box 6.
101. Quoted in Mackintosh, The British Cabinet, 320 n. 28.
102. Nov. 16–18, 1911, Wilson Diaries; Callwell, Wilson, I, 106–107. Haldane had Nicholson draft a memo tracing the conversations from 1906: this Nov. 6, 1911, memo placed special stress on the noncommittal aspects of the talks and the earlier Foreign Office approval of them; it was apparently not circulated to the entire Cabinet. See B.D., VII, no. 639.

Asquith's compromise formula saved Henry Wilson and averted a possible Cabinet breakup. It did not end the dissatisfaction of the radicals outside the government, whose position was given strong backing by E. D. Morel in the November issue of the *Nineteenth Century*. Morel asserted that it was time to "examine sundry matters of vital national import and ask . . . in all soberness where this *entente* with France is leading us." The French had perverted the 1904 accord, making it "a shield under cover of which French ambitions can move." There was a real danger that the "nation had lost all control over its foreign policy." Throughout the Moroccan affair, Morel charged, the British had been more French than the French. He warned that the surest way to destroy the entente's power for good would be "to allow it to be converted by a faction in England and a faction in France into an instrument of aggression." [103] On the more practical level Arthur Ponsonby headed a group, centered at the New Reform Club, which demanded that the Commons be given more control over British foreign policy. In a letter to the *Times* on November 17, Ponsonby asserted that if the people "had any voice in the decision, matters of injured official pride, small points of diplomatic dispute, or wrangles over the position of distant territory would not be causes for which the people would consent to fight." Four days later the *Times* revealed that in July the radicals had nearly challenged Grey's policy. What they now wanted, reported the newspaper, was to know "the exact nature of obligations undertaken by this country at the time of the Anglo-French Agreement of 1904." [104]

The radical assault reached new heights in mid-November following an alarmist speech by Captain W. V. Faber, a Conservative M.P. Claiming that the Army had arranged with the French to send six British divisions, Faber announced that all had been frustrated by the Navy's failure to work out the details. These revelations, which Henry Wilson regarded as "disgraceful," were intended by Faber to damn the Admiralty.[105] Instead they exposed the Asquith government and especially the Foreign Secretary to sharper radical attacks. A "Grey Must Go" campaign began. Haldane on November 22 complained that "these are troublesome times. Foreign Affairs have given us so much anxiety. I had

103. Morel, "The National Interest in the Franco-German Dispute," *Nineteenth Century and After*, 70 (November 1911), 834–847; see also Catherine Ann Cline, "E. D. Morel and the Crusade against the Foreign Office," *Journal of Modern History*, 39 (June 1967), 126–131.
104. On the radical pressure see, Hammond, C. P. Scott, 163–164; Thomas P. Conwell-Evans, *Foreign Policy from a Back Bench, 1904–1918: A Study Based on the Papers of Lord Noel-Buxton* (London, 1932), 57–60; Hale, *Publicity and Diplomacy*, 415–417; A. J. P. Taylor, *The Trouble Makers: Dissent over Foreign Policy, 1792–1939* (Bloomington, Ind., 1958), 118–122.
105. Faber gave the speech at Andover on Nov. 9; it was reprinted in the *Daily Telegraph* on Nov. 20, 1911, and extracts are found in G.P., XXIX, pp. 261–263 notes; and Nov. 20, 1911, Wilson Diaries. Col. A. W. A. Pollock had said some of the same things in "Some Strategical Questions," *Nineteenth Century and After*, 70 (October 1911), 796–804.

Sir E. Grey in here late last night. We went through the speech which he proposes to make on Monday. He has done splendidly. There are many annoying things over which one has simply to keep silence." Two days later a worried Esher spoke of a "serious crisis. Fifteen members of the Cabinet against five. The Entente is decidedly imperilled. The Cabinet is so far intact. Edward Grey is to speak on Monday and Europe is awaiting his speech with some anxiety." [106]

Indeed, all Europe, especially the French and German governments, did await the Foreign Secretary's pronouncements. Paris and Berlin had watched closely as the radical pressure mounted upon the Liberal government. Both capitals now knew that the rumors of British military preparations were true, for Haldane on October 24 had deliberately informed Major R. Ostertag, the German military attaché, that Britain had taken certain military and naval precautions during the recent tension. This action, the War Minister had explained, was not prompted by any written obligation to France, nor did one exist; but, he warned, if Germany declared war on France, Britain would intervene. The warning led Kaiser Wilhelm II to write on the dispatch: "We must now reckon upon it." Haldane's frankness reinforced, of course, German interest in the radical pressure against Grey's policy. While Ambassador Metternich held few illusions about the chances of a radical success, he and Berlin were anxious to see what effect, if any, the attacks would have upon British policy.[107] The French were equally interested in the radical agitation, but for the opposite reasons. Georges Daeschner, the French chargé, also doubted that the radicals would be successful, but he disliked the trend: he feared the uproar would bring new demands for the improvement of Anglo-German relations. Further, Grey would be forced to explain that "there existed between France and England no engagement foreseeing a casus belli and that the British Government remains entirely free to take part in a war or to remain neutral." While factually exact, this denial would cause some surprise, and "un certaine déception," particularly if the Foreign Secretary denied there had been any military preparations.[108] The French fears were soon realized.

On November 27 Grey and Asquith went before the Commons to explain Liberal policy during the Agadir crisis. Both men sought to reconcile entente loyalties with reassurances to the radicals about the direction of British foreign policy. Grey spoke first, with seeming candor —unless one knew the whole story.

---

106. Haldane to Mary Haldane, Nov. 22, 1911, Haldane Papers, 5986; diary, Nov. 24, 1911, *Journals and Letters of Esher*, III, 74.
107. Report by Ostertag, Oct. 24, 1911, G.P., XXIX, no. 10652; Metternich to Bethmann, Nov. 1, 1911, *ibid.*, no. 10653.
108. Daeschner to de Selves, Nov. 16, 1911, M.A.E., "Grande Bretagne," n.s. 10; Daeschner to de Selves, Nov. 20, 24, 1911, D.D.F., 3rd ser., I, nos. 160, 210.

First of all let me try to put an end to some of the suspicions with regard to secrecy—suspicions with which it seems to me some people are torturing themselves, and certainly worrying others. We have laid before the House the secret Articles of the Agreement with France of 1904. There are no other secret engagements. . . . I saw a comment made the other day, when these Articles were published, that if a Government would keep little things secret, *a fortiori*, they would keep big things secret. This is absolutely untrue. There may be reasons why a Government should make secret arrangements of that kind if they are not things of first-rate importance, if they are subsidiary to matters of great importance. But that is the very reason why the British Government should not make secret engagements which commit Parliament to obligations of war. It would be foolish to do it. No British Government could embark upon a war without public opinion behind it, and such engagements as there are which really commit Parliament to anything of that kind are contained in treaties or agreements which have been laid before the House. For ourselves we have not made a single secret article of any kind since we came into office.[109]

Grey's speech could be squared with the facts, but just barely. His elegant sophistry deliberately distorted the intimacy of Anglo-French relations, while gliding past the military conversations. Were the staff talks not "of first-rate importance"? Were they subsidiary to matters of "great importance"? Had not his own Cabinet colleagues been kept in the dark about these matters? No doubt Grey felt that public opinion would be decisive, that without it the fruit: of the conversations would not be realized and that with it the talks would be legitimized. Yet his unequivocal statement perpetrated a distinctly false impression, indeed a deception, about the exact nature and extent of entente relations. Asquith simply added to this impression when he told the Parliament that

The House has heard from my right hon. Friend the Foreign Secretary, and I believe has heard with universal satisfaction, that the world is now in possession of the whole of our Treaty obligations on this subject. *There is no secret arrangement of any sort of kind which has not been disclosed*, and fully disclosed, to the public, and we ask, from that point of view, that our conduct should be judged by the measure of our Treaty obligations which Members of the House are able to ascertain precisely for themselves.[110]

The Asquith-Grey pronouncements checked but did not eliminate the radical unrest. The "Grey Must Go" drive continued into December, when there were renewed demands for a House of Commons committee

109. *Parliamentary Debates: Commons*, 5th ser., 32 (Nov. 27, 1911), 57–58.
110. Italics added; *ibid.*, 106–107.

on foreign affairs. On December 6 the Prime Minister again had to assure the House that no secret engagements bound Britain to give another power military or naval assistance.[111]

By the end of 1911 Asquith and Grey had survived the most dangerous of the radical challenges to their foreign policy. Within the Cabinet the Prime Minister had appeased his dissident colleagues by imposing a facade of restrictions upon the conversations, while assuring Grey, Haldane, and Churchill that the exchanges would not be terminated. Though personally unenthusiastic about continental operations, Asquith was politically unable or perhaps temperamentally unwilling to halt the military conversations. Or, he may have decided, as Grey had insisted earlier, that the cessation of the talks would disrupt the entente. In any case, the conversations continued.

Asquith and the Cabinet had committed themselves, if not to France, at least to a strategy of continental intervention. And the conversations were essential to intervention. What had begun as a temporary expedient in 1906 was now an established element of British policy. The direction of British strategy, perhaps unwittingly, had been determined.

111. *Ibid.* (Dec. 6, 1911), 1400.

8 | Joffre Reshapes French Strategy, 1911–1913

Joseph Jacques Césaire Joffre assumed command of the French Army on July 28, 1911. At fifty-nine, Messimy's third choice for the new post of Chief of the General Staff possessed an undistinguished military record. The son of a Pyrenean barrelmaker, General Joffre had fought in the Franco-Prussian war while a student at the Ecole Polytechnique; subsequently, much of his army service had been in the French colonies. In 1904 he returned to France to become the Director of Engineers, a task he performed with credit. Then, after serving as a divisional and corps commander, he became Director of Support Services for metropolitan France in 1910. A trained and competent engineer, Joffre understood well the organizational and logistical requirements of the French Army. The same could not be said for his appreciation of grand strategy: indeed, he had had no training or experience in this area, having not attended the Ecole Supérieure de Guerre or even commanded an army-size unit in the annual war games. Rather, he brought to his new post the proper political and religious credentials and a certain peasant capacity for making the right intuitive decision. These qualities had advanced him to the apex of the French military hierarchy; they would not be enough to ensure his success as France's chief strategic planner.[1]

Joffre shared most of the strong convictions and prejudices of the offensive school of military theorists. Confident that "the offensive alone made it possible to break the will of the adversary," he agreed with de Grandmaison and Foch that the counteroffensive was outdated, useless, and unworthy of the French Army. No longer would the French wait for the first blow and attack only when certain of the enemy's location. Although Joffre's later actions suggest that he never quite understood the limits of the "all-out offensive," his firm, zealous commitment to the doctrine influenced every facet of his strategic evaluations. Moreover, he could impose his views upon the Army, since the elimination of the divided high command removed any organizational barriers to the establishment of an "offensive" orthodoxy. Unlike his predecessors, Joffre bore responsibility for the preparation both of war plans and of the Army to implement them.[2] Assisting him in this work was General de Curières de Castelnau, a staff officer well acquainted with the details of Plan XVI and equally anxious for offensive action.[3]

In their planning the two generals faced a pair of especially vexing questions: what deference to pay to Britain's attitude toward Belgian neutrality, and what value to place upon British military assistance. Their answers may usefully be examined within the context of Joffre's reshaping of French strategy.

Changes in the French high command had come at a perilous moment. The Moroccan crisis, fanned by Lloyd George and excessive German demands in the Congo, looked ominously like the occasion for war, a prospect Joffre regarded with no great confidence. The recent shake-up of the Army's leadership, combined with the inadequacies of Plan XVI, suggested discretion rather than a rush for valor. The chances for victory were less than the seventy percent established by Napoleon: to improve these odds became the General's overriding concern.

His first step was to review intelligence estimates on Germany's probable strategy in case of war. Detailed information about the German rail network near Aix-la-Chapelle and Moltke's alleged annotations on a recently acquired 1906 *Kriegsspiel* reaffirmed Joffre's fear that Germany might strike through Belgium. But these intelligence estimates, not nearly so precise as their 1904 counterparts, furnished the General with

1. On Joffre's early career, see Pierre Varillon, *Joffre* (Paris, 1956), chaps. i–ii; General René Alexandre, *Avec Joffre d'Agadir à Verdun: souvenirs, 1911–1916* (Paris, 1932), 7–12; Alistair Horne, *The Price of Glory: Verdun, 1916* (London, 1962), 19–24.
2. Joffre, *Memoirs*, I, 30, 26–35; Alexandre, *Avec Joffre*, 13–23. See also Ralston, *The Army of the Republic*, 331–343.
3. Joffre preferred Foch, but Messimy blocked the appointment.

little guidance about the probable extent of a German sweep into Belgium.[4] Would such a drive be the major German attack in the west, or simply a secondary thrust to divert attention from the Alsace-Lorraine frontiers? How many German corps would be employed? Would reserve units be utilized? Would the Germans cross the Meuse into central Belgium? French intelligence, though confident the Germans would not use reserve troops or traverse the Meuse, offered only the vaguest answers to these questions. The paucity of intelligence placed Joffre in a difficult dilemma—he had to defend against a German flanking move, the extent of which remained unknown, yet not jeopardize his ability to wage offensive war. From both standpoints he disliked Plan XVI: it had insufficient provisions against a German attack through Belgium; it was, despite de Lacroix's provisions for a prompt counterattack, too defensive for Joffre's tastes. On the other hand, Michel's proposed new plan for a defensive stance along the entire Belgian frontier struck Joffre as equally unsuitable. Of his situation in August 1911 he later wrote: "I thus found myself faced . . . with an approved plan which manifestly did not correspond to the hypothesis of the most likely manoeuvre on the part of the enemy, and . . . with a tentative plan which exaggerated the importance of this hypothesis and thereby incurred the most dangerous risks." [5]

Joffre decided upon a hurried revision of Plan XVI. Variation Number 1 (completed in September) was his attempt to bolster the defenses along the Belgian frontier and at the same time prepare for offensive action elsewhere. The Fifth Army was shifted northward from Vouziers on the Aisne to Mézières, just six miles from the Belgian Ardennes. Supporting this force would be three cavalry corps, the XIX Corps from North Africa, and the B.E.F. concentrated round Hirson and Maubeuge. In sum, nearly three hundred fifty thousand men, or a fifth of the total military strength of the entente, would be deployed along the Franco-Belgian frontier. This composite force, Joffre was confident, could resist and repel any German move across southern Belgium. The changes prompted by Variation Number 1 along the Alsace-Lorraine borders were equally significant: de Lacroix's "army of maneuver" now became simply another frontier army centered on Verdun. The other four armies retained their old alignments, though they were moved closer to the frontier. From these positions Joffre planned to launch an immediate offensive. The major attack would be directed between Metz and Strasbourg, with the French troops around Verdun taking offensive action against any German moves from Metz and Thionville.[6]

4. Joffre, *Memoirs*, I, 18–19, 45–47; untitled French Staff memo on a German violation of Belgium, December 1909, Archives Guerre, "Plan XVII," box 137; diary, Sept. 29, 1911, in Callwell, *Wilson*, I, 104; *Les armées françaises*, tome I, vol. I, 15–16.
5. Joffre, *Memoirs*, I, 18.
6. Memo by Joffre, "Note du sujet du plan," Aug. 29, 1911, Archives Guerre, "Plan XVI," box 130; "Plan XVI: ordre de bataille," Sept. [?] 1911, *ibid.*, box

But Joffre was not content just to revise Plan XVI. He also strove to increase the effectiveness of possible military assistance from France's allies and friends. Before 1911 the Russians had, despite continual French pressure, refused to promise more than unspecified offensive action by the twentieth day of mobilization. In late 1910 even this minimum expectation was shaken when St. Petersburg withdrew several units from Russian Poland and the Tsar met with the Kaiser at Potsdam. Although General Sukhomlinov, the Russian Minister of War, assured Paris that Russia remained ready for military action, the French were apprehensive.[7] In an attempt to clarify things Joffre decided to send General Dubail to St. Petersburg for new staff talks in late August. During his visit Dubail repeatedly stressed France's desperate need for effective Russian aid. All the evidence, he told the Russians, pointed to a massive German assault in the west coming through Lorraine, Luxembourg, and Belgium. "With the aid of the English Army on its left wing," France planned to counter the German challenge with an immediate and vigorous offensive. But for this action to succeed the Russians had to strike simultaneously in the east. While insisting that the Russians needed four more years to recover from their Manchurian fiasco, General Zhilinskii, the Russian Chief of Staff, eventually agreed to undertake some offensive action by the sixteenth day in the hope of tying down at least five or six German corps otherwise employable on the western front. The vast expenditures and loans to the mercenary Russians seemed at last to have brought, and bought, results.[8]

With the British, or, more accurately, with Henry Wilson, the new French high command enjoyed increasingly intimate relations. Joffre paid far more attention to British assistance than had his predecessors. His revisions of Plan XVI contained detailed, elaborate provisions for the concentration of British troops. He was clearly confident of British help and ready to exploit it along the Belgian frontier. Again unlike his predecessors, Joffre was also more open and candid with the British officers. His discussions with Wilson, for example, about French intelligence reports and French plans for the employment of entente forces contrasted sharply with previous French reticence on such matters.[9]

Still, the new Anglo-French intimacy did not mean that there was

132; "Ordre aux 3e et 4e bureaux de l'état-major de l'armée," Les armées françaises, tome I, vol. I: Annexes, no. 5; Joffre, Memoirs, I, 22–23.

7. "Procès-verbal de l'entretien entre les Chefs d'Etat-major généraux des armées française et russe," Sept. 20–21, 1910, D.D.F., 2nd ser., XII, no. 573; Pichon to Brun, Dec. 7, 1910, M.A.E., "Russie," n.s. 40; Brun to Pichon, Dec. 14, 1910, D.D.F., 2nd ser., XIII, no. 83; Louis to Pichon, Dec. 23, 1910, ibid., nos. 101, 102; Matton to Brun, Feb. 17, 1911, ibid., no. 157.

8. "Procès-verbal de l'entretien du 18/31 août 1911, entre les Chefs de l'Etat-major des armées française et russe," D.D.F., 2nd ser., XIV, no. 232; Joffre, Memoirs, I, 23; Dubail to Messimy, September 1911, quoted in Caillaux, Mes mémoires, II, 143–144.

9. Memo by Joffre, "Note du sujet du plan," Aug. 29, 1911, Archives Guerre, "Plan XVI," box 130; diary, Sept. 29, 1911, in Callwell, Wilson, I, 104–105.

genuine joint strategic planning. There was joint consultation and some joint discussion, but Britain's military weakness and the lack of a positive British commitment made London the junior partner in the planning process. And this relationship was reinforced by Henry Wilson's own conception of the problem. Rabidly Francophile, the D.M.O. deferred far too frequently to French leadership, accepting almost without question French estimates on German intentions and French plans for the location of the B.E.F. Moreover, he failed to press for French candor about the overall nature of French strategy. Anxious to ensure British participation in a continental war, he was less concerned about the course such a war might take. But he never abandoned or compromised London's right to determine the employment of the Expeditionary Force once it had arrived in France. On this point there was, indeed, surprisingly little consultation among the entente partners—a fact which partly explains the confusion pervading British efforts in August 1914.

By late September 1911 Joffre's most immediate military problems appeared under control. A revision of Plan XVI was in effect, early Russian offensive action seemed assured, and British assistance appeared more certain than ever. As the Moroccan tension abated, the General began to consider the requirements for an entirely new war plan. The first prerequisite, he quickly decided, was an accurate statement of France's diplomatic commitments and understandings. It particularly rankled military planners to think that for seven years they had been ignorant of the 1902 secret convention with Italy; as a consequence two valuable French corps had been wastefully deployed along the Alps. Nor had the War Ministry ever received an official diplomatic appraisal of Anglo-French relations. In the General's opinion poor coordination between the Quai d'Orsay and rue St. Dominique needlessly complicated and hampered French strategic planning. Adolphe Messimy readily agreed with Joffre's desire for political guidance, but found Caillaux unwilling to discuss the matter in late September.[10]

Messimy, however, refused to take no for an answer and continued to press Joffre's case for political guidance in the formation of a new war plan. Finally, on October 11, Messimy and Joffre were allowed to plead for improved interdepartmental cooperation at a meeting of the Conseil Supérieur de la Défense Nationale, the lackluster French equivalent of the Committee of Imperial Defence. Citing the Italian example and emphasizing the urgent need for information about Belgium's probable attitude in a conflict, the War Minister requested that the Council "study all the questions" that might require or influence military operations. This sensible proposal was opposed by Foreign Minister Justin de Selves, who vehemently insisted that the Army should first disclose the military considerations, then the Quai d'Orsay would "make known the

10. Joffre, Memoirs, I, 37–38.

diplomatic possibilities; it will say whether it is or is not in agreement with the War Department."

Joffre strongly disagreed. The question of Belgium was, he declared, not simply a military one. Rather it was "above all in the province of diplomacy. If we violate Belgian neutrality first, we will become provocateurs. England will not join us. Italy will be able to declare against us. We will consequently be stopped," he emphasized, "by political considerations. If only military considerations count, we would have, on the contrary, the greatest interest in taking the offensive through Belgium." But de Selves remained unconvinced. He explained that during the Agadir crisis, when war seemed imminent, he and the General had agreed not to violate Belgium ahead of the Germans. Such departmental coordination was adequate; there was no need for any preliminary statement on the diplomatic situation. When Joffre and Messimy refused to abandon their demand for political assistance, the Foreign Minister grudgingly consented to informal conferences between representatives of the War Ministry and the Quai d'Orsay.[11]

On October 15 Joffre availed himself of the Foreign Minister's reluctant generosity: he sent the Quai d'Orsay a memorandum outlining a series of military problems with political overtones. Would the military convention with Russia, for example, "have the force of a Treaty"? Was there "complete agreement regarding the interdiction against our troops being the first to violate Belgian territory"? Given the predominance of German influence in Luxembourg, was that tiny country's neutrality also sacrosanct? And he raised the question of the entente relationship. He wanted to "know whether the relations established between the general staffs are the consequence of a treaty or of a written or verbal agreement between the two Governments, or whether they are the result of a tacit consent between them. Can it be expected that in all probability Great Britain will support us in a war with Germany?"[12]

The Foreign Ministry, moving with unusual vigor, supplied the guidelines in five days. Taking Russian help for granted, the Quai d'Orsay paid special attention to the problem of Belgium: France, it warned, could not violate the terms of the 1839 guarantee treaty on Belgian neutrality. But it softened this admonition by observing that Germany seemed "certain" to enter Belgium, and once that occurred France could take whatever measures were militarily desirable. Further, the diplomats placed no obstacles to preventive military action in Luxembourg, "since Great Britain had not the same interest in the matter of Luxembourg's neutrality as she had in Belgium's." On the question of British help the Quai d'Orsay refrained from advice; there was no attempt to

11. "Procès-verbal de la séance du Conseil Supérieur de la Défense Nationale du 11 octobre 1911," D.D.F., 2nd ser., XIV, no. 424.
12. This memo is summarized as quoted here in Joffre, Memoirs, I, 39–42; neither the French diplomatic nor military files contain a copy.

gauge the probability of British participation.[13] Yet, as the position on Luxembourg indicated, French officials, both military and civilian, recognized that the prospect of British intervention was inescapably linked to the neutrality of Belgium. This became quite evident in early 1912.

On January 12, General Joffre again brought the Belgian issue before the Council of National Defense. Declaring that a German move through the Belgian Ardennes was certain, he requested permission to launch offensive action through Belgium at the first news of a German attack, and the Council approved. In the debate over this request Delcassé, now the Naval Minister, pressed for an even stronger policy. Claiming that Belgian neutrality had originally been a British device against the French, he argued that the cordiality of entente relations might induce London to abandon its scruples about the 1839 accord. France would then be able to launch immediate offensive action through Belgium. Both Caillaux and de Selves hotly contested this notion, insisting that the British would never alter their position. France, lamented the Foreign Minister, had to accept the limitations at hand.[14]

Joffre continued to consider the merits of an immediate offensive through Belgium, however. He was possibly encouraged in this by bits and pieces of information reaching him about an apparent change of attitude among the Belgians. For years the French attachés in Brussels had sent skeptical, sometimes scathing reports about the ruling Catholic party's determination to defend Belgian neutrality and about the value of Belgian military preparations. Now the situation seemed to be shifting. King Albert after Agadir had implemented certain military precautions, and there were new signs of Belgian apprehension about Germany. Brussels appeared more realistic about its unenviable location between two overarmed neighbors.[15] Furthermore, in late January the French attaché reported that General Jungbluth, the Belgian Chief of Staff, had expressed the idea that neutrality was a "hindrance." There was the possibility that Belgium under the new King would pursue a more active foreign policy. Captain Victor Duruy, though doubting that the Belgians would choose a French alliance over a German one, reported that the situation had possibilities for France. Similar comments and impressions reached Joffre from Henry Wilson: in a conversation with Foch the D.M.O. repeated that General Jungbluth was pro-English and "very much in sympathy with us [France]." [16] These varied indications about a possible shift in Belgian sentiments may well have

13. *Ibid.*, 42–43.
14. "Note de présentation," Jan. 9, 1912, Archives Marine, ES 23; Caillaux, *Mes mémoires*, I, 213–214; Joffre, *Memoirs*, I, 47–48.
15. Albert Duchesne, "L'armée et la politique militaires belges de 1871 à 1920 jugées par les attachés militaires de France à Bruxelles," *Revue belge de philologie et d'histoire*, 39 (1961), 1092–1126.
16. Duruy to Alexandre Millerand, Jan. 25, 1912, D.D.F., 3rd ser., I, no. 522; "Conversation du général Foch avec le général Wilson . . . 4–5 février [1912]," Archives Guerre, "Attachés militaires: Angleterre," box 11.

convinced Joffre that an offensive through Belgium might not only be feasible, but also politically acceptable—even to the British. At any rate, the fall of the Caillaux government in late January provided the General with still another opportunity to broach the possibility of an immediate attack through the Belgian Ardennes.

On February 21 Raymond Poincaré, the new Premier, summoned an informal group to the Quai d'Orsay for a review of France's defense posture. Those present included Admiral Marie Jacques Charles Aubert, the new Chief of the Naval Staff; Paléologue, the new Director of Political Affairs; Millerand, the new War Minister; Delcassé, held over as Naval Minister; and Joffre. At the meeting Joffre once more advocated a French offensive across lower Belgium. Assuming that Britain would agree and that France "could come to an understanding with the Belgian Government beforehand," the General outlined the military rationale for such an operation. If war came, the French Army planned to launch immediate offensive action against Germany. The question was where—Lorraine, Alsace, or the Belgian Ardennes? Rough terrain and the fortress system ruled against an attack through the "lost provinces," leaving the Belgium-Luxembourg corridor the most attractive alternative for a French offensive. An assault in this area would not only counter any German flanking move, but would also gain swift passage to German territory. In addition, observed Joffre, such a maneuver "would make it possible for the British Army to participate more efficaciously in our operations, and the assistance of this army would bring us a marked superiority as compared with our adversaries." [17] But to be successful the French attack through Belgium had to be immediate. It could not depend upon whether the Germans actually violated Belgium, for if the Germans did not do so, the French forces would be hopelessly out of position. France must either plan to disregard Belgian neutrality or be content to accept an offensive on less favorable terms in Lorraine.

Joffre's appeal for action through Belgium again gained the support of Delcassé, this time joined by Millerand. But Poincaré refused to consider the possibility. He maintained that it would be difficult, if not impossible, to reach a prior agreement with the Belgians: diplomatic reports indicated that German influence within the Belgian government remained strong. Poincaré's principal opposition, however, stemmed not from the probable Belgian attitude but rather from the probable British reaction. Whatever the status of the entente, he feared that an offensive through Belgium would run the risk of alienating the unpredictable Anglo-Saxons.[18] Moreover, the Anglo-German talks then under way reinforced Poincaré's caution. He knew that in the negotiations

17. Joffre, Memoirs, I, 50–51.
18. Raymond Poincaré, Au service de la France: neuf années de souvenirs, 10 vols. (Paris, 1925–1933), I, 224–225; Antony Klobukowski to Poincaré, Feb. 12, 1912, M.A.E., "Belgique," n.s. 20.

Britain was demanding freedom to help France against any unprovoked German attack; yet this narrow definition of Britain's "obligation" to France encouraged few hopes that London would sanction a French offensive across Belgium. Nor could the French Premier ignore the ramifications of losing British military and naval help, so carefully arranged by the staff talks, through an injudicious attack northward. Poincaré thus ruled against any French offensive via Belgium. The most he would concede was permission to attack should there be the "positive menace" of German action. As Joffre later remarked: what was meant by a "positive menace"? [19] Confronted with Poincaré's adamant position about the neighboring kingdom, the General transferred his hopes for offensive action back to the area first envisaged in August 1911, that is, to Lorraine.

Poincaré, while rejecting Joffre's strategic desires, decided to probe the British position on Belgium. The Congo and the Anglo-German negotiations provided him with convenient excuses. On two separate occasions he had Paul Cambon emphasize to Arthur Nicolson the benefits which would accrue from British recognition of Belgium's 1908 annexation of the Congo: such action would end Anglo-Belgian bitterness, make the entente more attractive to Brussels, and reduce the German ability to cause trouble. Each time Cambon's pleas fell upon deaf ears; Nicolson would promise no immediate change in British policy.[20]

Poincaré's other approach to the Belgian issue involved the Anglo-German negotiations. In mid-March Paul Cambon casually mentioned to Nicolson that the mounting evidence of a German buildup near Aix-la-Chapelle "could only be explained by the intention of violating Belgian neutrality." If German scouts were on the verge of crossing into Belgium, "must we," Cambon asked him, "await the occupation of Belgium by the German army in order to advance on our side?" Nicolson replied simply, "c'est bien grave." [21] Later, when the Anglo-German negotiations for a possible neutrality formula failed to collapse, the French revived the hypothesis of possible action in Belgium. Cambon told Grey on March 29 that if "Germany concentrated troops upon Aix-la-Chapelle with the obvious intention of entering Belgium, France might be compelled to take the initiative." The implications could not have been clearer: the French might have to violate Belgian neutrality and thus a "neutrality formula" might deprive them of British assistance. But the Foreign Secretary, as usual, carefully avoided any comment upon Cambon's observation.[22] Much the same thing happened five days later when

---

19. Joffre, *Memoirs*, I, 51–53. London regularly informed Paris about the Anglo-German negotiations; see, e.g., P. Cambon to Poincaré (tel.), Feb. 13, 1912, D.D.F., 3rd ser., II, no. 30.

20. Poincaré to P. Cambon, Mar. 23, 1912, D.D.F., 3rd ser., II, no. 252; P. Cambon to Poincaré, Mar. 29 (tel.), May 2, 1912, ibid., nos. 271, 406.

21. P. Cambon to Paléologue, Mar. 21, 1912, ibid., no. 240.

22. Poincaré to P. Cambon, Mar. 28, 1912, ibid., no. 269; Grey to Bertie, Mar. 29, 1912, B.D., VI, no. 559.

the chargé cautioned Nicolson that a neutrality agreement with Berlin would be difficult to interpret. Such an accord, for example, might prevent "the entry of French troops into Belgian territory which the English and French staffs considered as necessary in certain cases." The Undersecretary again refused to be drawn, insisting instead that the chances for an Anglo-German agreement were slight.[23] Despite his trial balloons, Poincaré had learned precious little about the British attitude toward Belgium.

The Foreign Office's studied reticence on Belgian neutrality concealed a renewed British interest in the problem. At this very time both the Foreign Office and the C.I.D. were carefully examining Britain's probable relationship to Holland and Belgium in time of war. Eyre Crowe, in another of his thoughtful, lengthy memos, insisted in early March that Germany would almost certainly violate Belgium "on the very outbreak of war" and that Belgium would resist. He thought that Britain was "entitled, if so minded—not to say, bound—to come to the assistance of Belgium." Yet, if war came, Britain should do nothing that might alienate the Belgians; Britain, he cautioned, should be careful not to "place itself hopelessly in the wrong in the eyes of the world at the moment of entering on a life-and-death struggle."[24]

The Senior Clerk's sensitivity to Belgian feelings was not entirely shared by members of the C.I.D. In late April the Committee considered what action Britain should take if Belgium failed to resist German aggression. Haldane contended that Britain would under international law be justified in taking any action it so desired; Arthur Nicolson argued that Britain could take "steps to enforce . . . neutrality, even were she [Belgium] unwilling that we should do so." Churchill, on the other hand, thought "it would be a great pity if we had to rescue Belgium against her will." To avoid this unseemly development there was talk of discussing the matter with Brussels. Sir John French thought that "the Belgians were disposed to favour [Britain] . . . and that proposals would not be unwelcome." And he added that "it would certainly make an immense difference to a British army employed on the Continent which attitude the Belgians were to adopt."[25] When the C.I.D. adjourned on April 25, several aspects of British policy were quite clear. First, if Germany attacked Belgium, Britain would uphold its strategic interests with or without Belgian permission. Second, to avert friction with Brussels, attempts would be made to establish better Anglo-Belgian relations. Finally, there was not the slightest hint or suggestion of any form of preventive action by Britain or the entente prior to a German violation of Belgian sovereignty. Had Paris decided to press London in

23. A. de Fleuriau to Poincaré, Apr. 4, 1912, D.D.F., 3rd ser., II, no. 300.
24. Minute by Sir Eyre Crowe, Mar. 10, 1912, B.D., VIII, no. 321.
25. Minutes of the 116th meeting of the C.I.D. (Apr. 25, 1912), Cab. 2/2/3; see also "The Attitude of Great Britain towards Belgium in the event of a violation of Belgian Territory by Germany in Time of War," Apr. 9, 1912, Cab. 4/4/1.

less elliptical, ambiguous terms about a French offensive through Belgium, it would have received a decided rebuff.

While the C.I.D. was debating the need for closer ties with Brussels, Henry Wilson was hard at work on the same problem. In early March he had spent three days touring eastern Belgium—Stavelot, Liège, and Ciney. The excursion strengthened both his conviction that the Germans would try a flanking move and his belief in the value of Belgian assistance. In early April, on his own initiative, the D.M.O. attempted to revive the long-suspended Anglo-Belgian staff talks. On April 5 he crossed to Ostend to brief Lieutenant Colonel Tom Bridges about a demarche: the attaché was "to tell the Belgians that Britain could put 150,000 men 'at the decisive point and time' : . . but that the Belgians must play their part by further strengthening Liège and Namur and by calling for help as soon as their country was invaded." [26] If there was any mention of Anglo-French arrangements, Bridges was to plead ignorance.[27]

On April 23 Bridges attempted to carry out Wilson's mandate; the results were disastrous. Contrary to the D.M.O.'s expectations, General Jungbluth displayed not the slightest interest in Bridges' revelations about British capabilities. More importantly, Jungbluth took immediate umbrage at the attaché's imprudent assertion that Britain would intervene regardless of Belgian desires if Germany moved first. Bridges then compounded his faux pas by repeating the idea of unilateral intervention to General Michel, the War Minister. An angered, indeed enraged Michel declared that the Belgians could protect themselves and would fire upon any would-be British saviors.[28] His language was so violent in fact that Sir Francis Villiers sought out Davignon, the Foreign Minister, and assured him that Bridges' comments had no official sanction.[29] The damage, however, was done. Henry Wilson's ill-advised attempt to improve Anglo-Belgian ties had backfired.

The anger that greeted Bridges' remarks reflected a new stiffening of Belgium's attitude toward the entente powers. This toughness had begun in September 1911, coincidental with the Belgian military measures which had so impressed London and Paris. Thoroughly frightened by the Agadir crisis, Belgium's political and military leadership had undertaken a major re-evaluation of Belgian policy. Three questions in particular worried Brussels: how to devise a military strategy that would

26. Collier, *Brasshat: Biography of Henry Wilson*, 128.
27. Apr. 7, 1912, Wilson Diaries; cf. Lt. General Sir Tom Bridges, *Alarms & Excursions* (London, 1938), 62–63.
28. Note by Léon van der Elst (Secretary General of Belgian Foreign Ministry), Apr. 24, 1912, Great Britain, Foreign Office, *Collected Diplomatic Documents Relating to the Outbreak of the European War* (London, 1915), 360–361. See also Wullus-Rudiger, *La Belgique et l'équilibre*, 78–79, 321–322; Luigi Albertini, *The Origins of the War of 1914*, trans. and ed. Isabella M. Massey, 3 vols. (London, 1952–1957), III, 430–432.
29. Helmreich, "Belgian Concern over Neutrality," 424.

limit the destruction of Belgium, how to ensure that a guarantor nation did not force Belgium into a war against its will, and how to ensure that a protecting power, once invited, would leave. Slowly, over a period of months and after much debate, the answers emerged. Militarily the Belgian General Staff planned to oppose any violation of Belgium; at the same time they hoped to confine all the fighting to a small area, possibly to the province of Belgian Luxembourg. Simply stated, Belgium would resist, yet seek to avoid losing either its integrity or its neutrality.[30]

Among the possible guarantors of Belgian neutrality Great Britain got the most attention. The British military and naval preparations in 1911, the growing solidarity of the entente, and Britain's expressed interest in Antwerp and the Schelde convinced Brussels that London might rush, quite uninvited, to help Belgium;[31] this would virtually guarantee that all of Belgium would be exposed to the dangers of war. As a hindrance to any premature British action, the Belgian leadership secretly hoped the Dutch would fortify Flushing. Still, the Belgians could not altogether ignore the possibility that they might need external assistance. Anxious to avoid becoming the pawn of either a victorious Germany or France, Brussels decided to draft in advance a convention for any future protectors to sign; this, it was hoped, would guarantee the preservation of Belgian independence. From Belgian planning there emerged one unmistakable result: renewed determination to protect Belgium's neutral status, both politically and militarily. It was this prideful determination which Colonel Bridges' demarche aroused and alarmed. His mention of possible pre-emptive action simply reinforced Belgian fears about British intentions. By mid-1912 the chances for improved entente cooperation with Belgium were at an end, and during the remainder of that year the gulf grew wider.

In September and again in October General Michel, the Belgian War Minister, brutally rejected British suggestions that Germany contemplated a violation of Belgian neutrality. He made it quite clear, wrote Captain Howard Kelly, the naval attaché, "that in his opinion the dangers of a breach of Belgian neutrality lay more from England than anywhere else." Citing the British preparations in 1911, the General complained that Belgium now had to expect a British attack either at Antwerp or in conjunction with the French left. In the future the Belgians would have to defend against attacks from not one but three sides.[32] A few weeks later Michel expressed doubts to Colonel Bridges that Britain would act if the French violated Belgium, which meant that Great Brit-

30. *Ibid.*, 421–425; memo by Arendt, "En cas de guerre," November 1911, Belg. Arch., "Indépendance neutralité," X.
31. See, e.g., "Note au Baron de Gaiffer du 6 août 1912 sur la situation qui serait faite à la Belgique en cas de guerre," Belg. Arch., "Indépendance neutralité," XI.
32. Kelly to Villiers, Sept. 12, 1912, B.D., VIII, no. 324, note by van der Elst, Oct. 7, 1912, Belg. Arch., "Indépendance neutralité," XI.

ain was "a potential enemy, and as such, had to be watched and could no longer be regarded as the Power to which Belgium could confidently appeal for help." This dogmatism led Grey to comment curtly: "If Germany does not violate the neutrality of Belgium no one else will do so." [33] Michel's display of antagonism toward the entente, coupled with sharp attacks upon France in much of the Belgian press, stirred latent Anglo-French fears about Belgium's genuine willingness to defend its neutrality. This in turn increased apprehension about what Belgium might do if the entente were to resolve, unannounced and uninvited, to check a German attack.[34]

These unpleasant indications particularly worried Sir Edward Grey. So long as a weak and helpless Belgium resisted a German attack, Britain would unquestionably intervene on the Continent. But a German-Belgian détente would jeopardize all of this. Grey would find it difficult to win public support for British intervention if the Belgians permitted an invasion of their own country; moreover, the British would be deprived of Belgian military help, which Henry Wilson reckoned at "12 to 16 divisions." And even more dangerous to the chances for British intervention, given the new mood in Brussels, would be an impetuous French violation of the neutralized state. Such an attack would completely undermine one of the ostensible and most appealing justifications for Britain's continental strategy—the preservation of Belgian independence.

At the same time Grey faced a practical problem of how to communicate these fears to the ever-sensitive French government. On this point, however, he received unexpected help from Henry Wilson, who was equally disturbed by the trend of opinion in Brussels, so disturbed in fact that he wanted to reach an agreement with Paris on the treatment of a possibly hostile Belgium. These mutual concerns led the Foreign Secretary to authorize another Wilson trip to France.[35] The General could discuss his own problem and also caution the French Staff about an imprudent attack northward. Exactly eight months after Poincaré had first sounded London on preventive offensive action through Belgium, Henry Wilson brought the answer.

On November 26 Wilson bluntly warned General de Castelnau that if "France violates Belgian neutrality first, the Belgian Army will march with the Germans, and the English Government, perhaps put in the position of respecting neutrality, could find itself in a very embarrassing

33. Bridges to Villiers, Oct. 8, 1912, B.D., VIII, no. 326; minute by Grey, ibid. Grey specifically assured the Belgians on this point in 1913; see Grey to Churchill, Apr. 11, 1913, B.D., X, pt. 2, no. 472.
34. Memo by Davignon, Nov. 21, 1912, Belg. Arch., "Indépendance neutralité," XI. Minutes of the 120th meeting of the C.I.D. (Dec. 6, 1912), Cab. 2/3/1; also see Nicolson to Villiers, Dec. 30, 1912, quoted in Nicolson, First Lord Carnock, 398–399.
35. Diary, Oct. 22, 1912, in Callwell, Wilson, I, 118; Nov. 18–19, 26, 1912, Wilson Diaries; Ritter, The Schlieffen Plan, 88; Villiers to Grey, Nov. 22, 1912, F.O. 371/1300.

situation. Thus," he admonished, "the French Army has no interest in being the first to violate Belgian neutrality." The question of a hostile Belgium was an entirely different matter. "Would not the Belgians," the British General asked, "then become the objective of the English army?" No, responded de Castelnau, "les Allemands" would remain the object of the Anglo-French forces.[36] This view the D.M.O. accepted.

Joffre later wrote that Wilson's unequivocal pronouncement about Belgium was "of the very highest importance for it obliged me definitely to renounce all idea of a manoeuvre a priori through Belgium." [37] This assessment vastly exaggerates the importance of Wilson's trip. In actuality his comments simply supplied the coup de grace to any lingering plans Joffre might have had for an attack through Belgium—an early autumn staff study by Colonel Georges Demange had already turned down, on both military and political grounds, any such operation as a part of the new war plan.[38] But the fatal blow to Joffre's proposals had come much earlier, from the opposition of French politicians. Anxious to retain British friendship, with its military and naval potential, not to mention its economic resources, first Caillaux and then Poincaré blocked the demands for action in Belgium. In this sense the entente played an important, negative role in the formulation of French strategy. London's attitude constrained the French to settle for an offensive in Lorraine; ultimately this deployment would compound the errors and failures of French intelligence. A French attack through Belgium would have had little chance of success, but the concentration of forces for such an offensive might have placed France in a much stronger position to resist the eventual German onslaught. If Joffre bears the final responsibility for succumbing to the madness of the offensive à outrance, the elusive prospect of British help, or, more precisely, the ambiguous entente, shares the responsibility for creating the framework in which Plan XVII was elaborated.[39]

During 1912 Joffre and his staff labored over a new war plan. Simultaneously the popular and professional press was also analyzing the problems of French grand strategy. Most French commentators, like the French Staff, expected not only a German offensive along the Lorraine frontier, but also a flanking maneuver through Luxembourg-Belgium;

36. De Castelnau to Millerand, Nov. 27, 1912, Archives Guerre, "Plan XVII: Armée W," box 147b; Millerand to Poincaré, Dec. 12, 1912, D.D.F., 3rd ser., V, no. 53.

37. Joffre, Memoirs, I, 54; also see entry for Feb. 10, 1913, Maurice Paléologue, Au Quai d'Orsay à la veille de la tourmente: journal, 1913-1914 (Paris, 1947), 30-32.

38. Memo by Demange, "Note relative au dispositif de réunion et au plan d'opérations des armées du N.E.," n.d. [autumn 1912], Archives Guerre, "Plan XVII," box 137.

39. For a caustic French view on the British constraints, see Garros, L'armée de grand-papa, 186.

but this thrust through Belgium would, they believed, stay below the Meuse.[40] For example, Lieutenant Colonel A. Grouard, who predicted German attacks in the south aimed at Chaumont-Troyes and in the north at Verdun-Mézières, doubted that any German sweep would cross the Meuse. Only an occasional prophet warned that if the Germans came through Belgium they would do so in strength: General Gabriel Herment, writing in the *Journal des sciences militaires*, insisted that the Germans would overrun the Belgian forts along the Meuse and move to block British intervention by seizing the Channel ports. And General de Lacroix, the former Generalissimo, stressed the dangers implicit in a German attack through Belgium.[41] Nevertheless, public comment about German strategy generally stiffened Joffre's view that a German drive would stay in the Ardennes.

There was somewhat less agreement about how France should counter German strategy. The new "offensive" orthodoxy within the high command was shared by many of the military essayists.[42] Still, there were some like Captain Sorb who tempered their enthusiasm for offensive action with a perception of the dangers involved. He, for instance, wanted the French commander to take the initiative in seeking a decisive battle; yet, he also thought that circumstances (or defensive-offensive considerations) should dictate the direction of the French attack. He personally envisaged two arenas for offensive action, one in the Longuyon-Thionville area, the other in the Lunéville-Sarrebourg vicinity.[43]

A few other military analysts were even less enchanted by the idea of unconditional offensive action. General Bonnal, reviewing de Grandmaison's published lectures, ridiculed the Colonel's ideas as mere rhetoric and warned that sometimes a commander must assume the defensive. Emile Mayer, onetime officer turned military critic, repeatedly emphasized the defensive advantages conferred by the new artillery and firepower. But perhaps the most incisive challenge to the offensive mania came from Colonel Grouard, a man whose criticisms of Napoleonic strategy had already labeled him as a heretic among French military writers. In *France et Allemagne: la guerre éventuelle* Grouard refuted assurances that only offensive action offered a safe, sure, feasible panacea for France's military situation. He called instead for a return to a

40. See, e.g., Captain Sorb [Charles Cormier], *La doctrine de défense nationale* (Paris, 1912), 38–81; and Col. Arthur Boucher, *La France victorieuse* (Paris, 1911), 50–56.
41. Lt. Col. A. Grouard, *France et Allemagne: la guerre éventuelle*, 4th ed. (Paris, 1913), 83–110; General Herment, "Considérations sur la défense de la frontière du nord," *Journal des sciences militaires*, 5 (Oct. 15, 1912), 384–388; General de Lacroix, "Quelques mots au sujet de la neutralité de la Belgique," *Revue militaire générale*, 6 (September 1912), 273–276.
42. See, e.g., Captain Altmayer, "Je veux," *Revue militaire générale*, 6 (October 1912), 417–446.
43. Sorb, *La doctrine de défense nationale*, 82–101; cf. "De 1870 à 1912: à propos de la doctrine de défense nationale du Captain Sorb," *Journal des sciences militaires*, 2 (Apr. 1, 1912), 278–300.

defensive strategy with France waiting to counterattack. Such a counterattack could be launched through the Ardennes and thus disrupt if not stop a German flanking move. In sharp contrast to the offensive orthodoxy, he insisted that France at least avoid a decisive battle until Russian and British help was available.[44] Eventually Grouard's prognosis of France's military predicament proved accurate; in the short run his criticisms, like most external criticism of military policy, prompted no changes and perhaps even strengthened the hold of the offensive school —for Joffre's new war plan was the virtual incarnation of the *offensive à outrance*.

On April 18, 1913, after nearly twenty-one months of study, General Joffre presented the War Board with an outline of his new offensive plan (XVII). Manpower requirements, the probable nature of German strategy, and the proposed French response to that strategy formed the crux of his presentation. When the three-year service law was in operation, the General expected to have 710,000 men available in forty-six divisions. Every effort would be made to place the maximum number of troops in the northeast "in order to gain a decisive result"; but, in keeping with the tenets of the offensive theorists, twenty-five reserve divisions were assigned to secondary functions.[45] By contrast, Joffre estimated that Berlin would have 880,000 men available by the end of 1913, most of whom would be deployed on the western front. He regarded a German advance from Alsace and Lorraine as a foregone conclusion, with a German drive across Belgium toward Mézières as highly probable. But Joffre doubted that such a drive would traverse the Meuse, or that it would even be a part of the initial German assault. Nevertheless, if the Germans crashed through the Ardennes, he was confident that the French forces, aided by the B.E.F., could check them.[46] And like his predecessors, he believed that the French advances in Lorraine would more than offset German gains elsewhere.[47]

This grossly inaccurate estimate of German intentions reflected the Second Bureau's continuing ineptness. Even when the final concentration orders for Plan XVII were issued in early 1914, it was stated as

44. General Bonnal, "Considérations sur la tactique actuelle," *Journal des sciences militaires*, 5 (Oct. 15, 1912), 380–381. On Mayer and Grouard see Liddell Hart, "French Military Ideas before the First World War," 142–148; and Grouard, *France et Allemagne*, 69–73, 140–142, 198–201.

45. *Les armées françaises*, tome I, vol. I, 18–29; minutes of the War Board, Apr. 18, 1913, Archives Guerre, "Procès-verbaux du Conseil Supérieur de la Guerre," box J; "Plan XVII: avant propos," *ibid.*; Joffre, *Memoirs*, I, 66–98.

46. "Etude du plan d'opérations contre l'Allemagne, considérations d'ensemble," Apr. 18, 1913, Archives Guerre, "Plan XVII," box 137; diary, Apr. 19, 1913, Paléologue, *Journal, 1913–1914*, 104–105.

47. See the testimony of Joffre and General Alexandre Percin before the Briey Commission, May 23, July 4, 1919, France, Assemblée Nationale, Chambre des Deputés, session de 1919, *Procès-verbaux de la Commission d'Enquête sur le rôle et la situation de la métallurgie en France: défense du Bassin de Briey*, 2 vols. (Paris, 1919), I, 126–128, II, 158–159.

"probable that a great part of the German forces will be concentrated on the common frontier." Nancy, Verdun, and Saint-Dié were regarded, in that order, as the probable objectives of a sudden German attack. And in May 1914 French intelligence still insisted that any German move through Belgium would stay below the Sambre and Meuse as it headed for Montmédy and Hirson.[48] In actuality the Schlieffen-Moltke Plan would send two German armies across the Meuse, swinging as wide as Brussels and Lille. Also, the Germans would employ, contrary to expectations, reserve divisions on an equal footing with regular units. It was this calculation about reserve troops, a miscalculation perhaps fortified by an alleged German staff memo on the subject, which was possibly the crucial intelligence error.[49] If the Germans were to utilize only regular divisions, then their ability to launch a major sweep through Belgium seemed reasonably out of the question; yet French intelligence did receive information in late 1913 which suggested that the Germans might employ reserve divisions and, moreover, there were new reports in 1913 of German rail construction around Luxembourg and Cologne.[50] None of this information, however, produced any significant revision of Joffre's strategic plans.

On French strategy, the General's comments to the War Board were terse and to the point. He gave his subordinate commanders only the vaguest hints about the French offensive. Unlike de Lacroix with Plan XVI in 1908, Joffre was not forced to explain or to defend his intentions. There were several reasons for his reticence: in the first place his fellow generals did not demand more information, in itself a reflection of his increasing domination of the high command, nor were there any cantankerous old men like General Duchesne on the War Board to pose the penetrating or embarrassing question. Joffre's associates, Michel excepted, shared his faith in the offensive and élan; and implicit in these noble virtues was a certain disdain for plans that were too detailed, and therefore too confining to the spirit of the French soldier. Finally, Joffre could not reveal his attack scheme for the simple reason that he had

48. "Directives pour la concentration," Feb. 7, 1914, Les armées françaises, tome I, vol. I: Annexes, no. 8, p. 21; "Plan de renseignements," Mar. 28, 1914, ibid., no. 10, p. 44; "Analyse du plan de mobilisation pour l'armée allemande (édition 9 octobre 1913)," May 1914, Archives Guerre, "Plan XVII," box 149.
49. In early 1913 the French obtained a staff memo, ostensibly written by Col. Ludendorff, which inferred that reserve troops would not be utilized initially; Pichon to P. Cambon, Apr. 5, 1913, D.D.F., 3rd ser., VI, no. 210. However, in early 1914 the Journal des sciences militaires published an alleged German document, supposedly left in a train compartment, which outlined German war plans: in its reserve divisions were scheduled for employment but the German attack would remain south and east of the Belgian Meuse ("La concentration allemande," 16th ser., 7 [Feb. 15, 1914], 337–371).
50. L. Koeltz, La guerre de 1914–1918: les opérations militaires (Paris, 1966), 60–62; for reports of rail construction, see M.A.E., "Allemagne," n.s. 95. When the French military archives are reopened during 1969, scholars should be able to evaluate more thoroughly the failures of French intelligence before 1914.

not yet decided definitely where to attack. Lorraine remained the most obvious area for action, but Joffre occasionally resurrected the idea of a Belgian maneuver.[51] Not until early 1914 would he irrevocably opt for Lorraine. In the meantime the War Board had his assurances that the offensive would bring France victory, and bring it quickly.

In the course of his presentation Joffre offered the War Board a candid, and realistic, assessment of the value of British help. British cooperation, he declared, remained uncertain because London "wanted to make no engagement in writing." [52] Nor was there any guarantee that if Britain did intervene all six divisions would immediately depart for France. Indeed, even Henry Wilson was worried about the chances of the entire B.E.F. being available.[53] These uncertainties prompted Joffre to tell the War Board: "We will thus act prudently in not depending upon English forces in our operational projects." [54] On the other hand, the General made clear his expectation of British naval assistance, asserting that "the interest of English commerce was too evident for Great Britain to hesitate to fight on our side." [55] In sum, Joffre interpreted the military conversations for what they were: arrangements that facilitated British intervention but did not guarantee it. Yet this prudence should not obscure the point, already noted, that the lure of British help had forced him to renounce a possible Belgian operation. Certainly this limitation influenced France's grand strategy far more than the inclusion or noninclusion of the B.E.F. in Plan XVII.

In his strategic exposition Joffre said little about an essential prerequisite for a successful French offensive: Russian help. There was, on this count, no apparent cause for worry. Franco-Russian relations had never been more cordial or intimate. Poincaré's strong views on foreign policy and his trip to Russia in mid-1912 had eased Russian apprehensions about the Third Republic; and the rousingly successful visit of the Tsar's cousin (and future Commander in Chief of the Russian Army), Grand Duke Nicholas, to the French maneuvers in September 1912 had also helped. It was on this occasion that Nicholas' impetuous, Montenegrin-born wife, Anastasia, had asked for a small piece of Lorraine soil to carry back to Russia and talked wildly of the reunification of the "lost provinces" to France.[56] These public displays of goodwill were supported by the continuation of French-financed rail construction in

51. See Garros, "Préludes aux invasions de la Belgique," 36–37.

52. Les armées françaises, tome I, vol. I, 19; but see Captain Louis Le Merre's staff study (May 1912) which concluded that Britain would intervene on the Continent unless the Germans launched a surprise naval attack; Archives Guerre, "Attachés militaires: Angleterre," box 11.

53. Artus Henri de La Panouse (French attaché in London) to Millerand, Dec. 11, 1912, Archives Guerre, "Plan XVII: Armée W," box 147b; diary, Mar. 12, 1913, in Paléologue, Journal, 1913–1914, 75–76.

54. Les armées françaises, tome I, vol. I, 19.

55. Ibid.; cf. minutes of the War Board, Apr. 18, 1913, Archives Guerre, "Procès-verbaux du Conseil Supérieur de la Guerre," box K.

56. Louis Garros, "En marge de l'alliance franco-russe, 1902–1914," Revue historique de l'armée, 6 (January–March 1950), 29–30.

Russia and by steady improvements in the Russian Army. More importantly, General Zhilinskii pledged in the 1912 and 1913 staff talks that
eight hundred thousand soldiers would be deployed along the German
front, with some action beginning after the fifteenth day. The Russian
planners considered action in three different locations: toward Konigsberg, toward Allenstein in East Prussia, or across the Vistula past Thorn
toward Berlin (the latter, which the French repeatedly encouraged,
would have severed East Prussia from the Reich).[57] In 1914 the Russians actually did take the first two options, launching a double attack
toward Konigsberg and Allenstein.

A comparison of the Franco-Russian military arrangements with those
of the entente reveals several instructive differences. Staff consultations
between Paris and London after 1910 were virtually uninterrupted; those
between St. Petersburg and Paris remained on an annual basis. The in-
formality and frequency of the Anglo-French exchanges disabused each
party of some illusions about the other; the Franco-Russian talks were
always high-level and formal, with appearances replacing realistic thinking. Furthermore, in spite of the ambiguity of the entente, the French
displayed a trust in the British that was not repeated toward the Russians: Henry Wilson was not privy to every facet of French planning,
but he knew far more than the Russians did. For their part the Russians
were equally secretive with the French about their intentions, though
the problems of a two-front war naturally caused some strategic ambivalence in St. Petersburg. By the same token, geography necessitated
closer Anglo-French planning if the two countries hoped to cooperate
effectively in a common theater of war. Another factor could not help
but reinforce entente cooperation: when the British and French Staffs
agreed upon something, action followed. Such was not often the case
when the French and Russian experts settled upon a plan. Not surprisingly, as John Cairns has pointed out, "the French army seemed to
count almost more surely on the nation that refused an alliance than on
the nation treaty-bound." [58]

Joffre's presentation of the new plan in April 1913 provided the first
and last opportunity for any significant modification in the call for offensive action. The War Board neither then nor later seriously considered the merits of the proposal. In early May Etienne, the War Minister, accepted the new scheme without change; immediately the staff bureaucracy began work on the logistical and strategical details. Ten
months later, in February 1914, the Army commanders finally received
their respective plans of mobilization and concentration. In May, two
years and ten months after Joffre had assumed command, Plan XVII became operational.

The new plan covered every phase of French preparations: concentra-

57. *Ibid.*, 32–42; Joffre, *Memoirs*, I, 57–61; Poincaré, *Au service de la France*, I,
110–111. The records of the staff talks are in *D.D.F.*, 3rd ser., III, no. 200; *ibid.*,
VIII, no. 79.
58. Cairns, "International Politics and the Military Mind," 278.

tion assignments, border protection, transportation movements, and intelligence instructions. Everywhere the impress of the offensive school was clear. The orders succinctly stated: "Whatever the circumstances, it is the Commander in Chief's intention to advance with all forces united to attack the German Armies." [59] Unlike its German counterpart, Plan XVII did not, however, establish a precise schedule for offensive operations. In fact, the general orders permitted Joffre a remarkable degree of elasticity in taking the offensive. There were provisions for double offensives north and south of the Metz-Thionville complex; in addition, should the Germans violate Belgium, Joffre retained sufficient flexibility to shift the northern offensive attack to the northeast, through Luxembourg and the Belgian Ardennes. Regardless of their ultimate location, these offensive assaults were expected to bring about the decisive battle so dear to the offensive theorists. Once that battle was won, victory would quickly follow elsewhere.

To achieve this victory Joffre divided French forces into five armies. Three would be located along the Alsace-Lorraine frontier from Verdun to Epinal. Another army, the Fifth, would be assigned to the Franco-Belgian border from Montmédy to Sedan to Mézières, roughly the same assignment it had had since 1911. Despite a consensus about the risks of a German operation south of the Meuse (and Joffre's later protests notwithstanding), Plan XVII brought no notable improvement of France's immediate frontier defenses in the north. But Joffre did achieve new flexibility by reviving de Lacroix's idea of an "army of maneuver" which could be employed as the circumstances dictated or the commander chose.[60] This Fourth Army at St. Dizier, composed of three infantry corps and a cavalry division, could either join in the assault upon Thionville or shift northward to help the Fifth Army if the Germans came through the Ardennes. A semi-reserve force, it constituted Joffre's one concession to the counteroffensive school of French strategy, his one concession to the realities of his strategic dilemma. Significantly, none of the orders for Plan XVII made any mention either of a British zone of concentration or of the possibility of British help.[61]

There is no need for still another analysis or critique of Plan XVII, for earlier critics have reconnoitered the available terrain.[62] Several

59. Copies of these orders are in Les armées françaises, tome I, vol. I: Annexes, no. 8.
60. Joffre did not apply this label, but the comparison is obvious.
61. On July 4, 1919, Joffre claimed that the secrecy of the conversations prevented any mention of British assistance in the orders; Procès-verbaux . . . défense du Bassin de Briey, II, 140.
62. Among them see General Selliers du Moranville, Du haut de la tour de Babel (Paris, 1925), 97–109; Sir Basil Liddell Hart, Reputations (London, 1928), 22–29; and General Charles Lanrezac, Le plan de campagne français et le premier mois de la guerre (2 août–3 septembre 1914) (Paris, 1921), 15–48. For critical defenses of Joffre, see Duffour, Joffre et la guerre de mouvement, 96–105; Varillon, Joffre, 101–108.

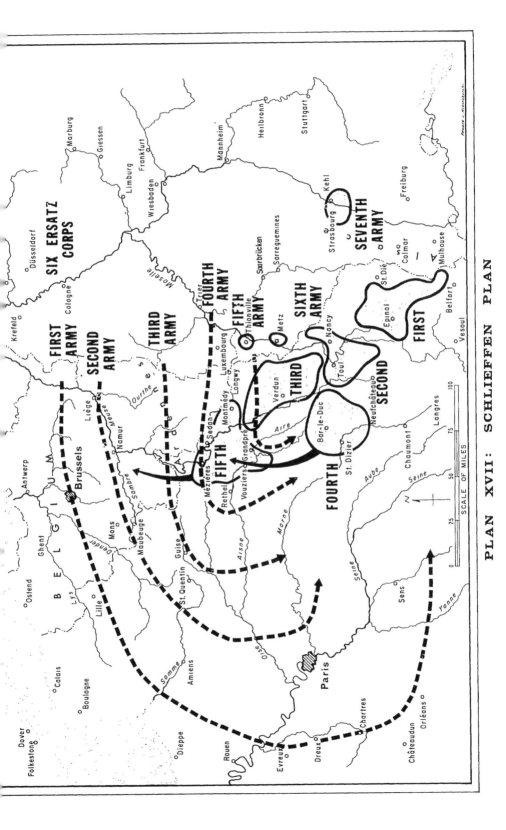

PLAN XVII: SCHLIEFFEN PLAN

points merit special emphasis, however. In the first place Plan XVII represented a fundamentally unsound compromise between the realities of France's military situation and the desires of its military leaders. French manpower resources were simply inadequate to meet both the requirements of security and the exigencies of offensive operations. In his determination to seize the offensive, Joffre neglected an equally important principle of warfare: security. Although uncertain about the extent of a German move through Belgium, he nonetheless concentrated his forces in Lorraine. Further, he completely exposed his left flank from Mézières to the sea with only the B.E.F., whose arrival he held as doubtful, available to protect part of this hundred ten-mile sector. In August 1914 four British divisions would face the might of two German armies. Admittedly British sensitivity over Belgian neutrality prevented French offensive action in the one area where it might have stalled the German drive. Yet London's attitude did not force the General to plan an attack against the heavily fortified area of Lorraine, nor to neglect the elementary requirements of security. Nor did it cause him to relegate twenty-five reserve divisions to secondary functions. For these decisions the allure of the "offensive" school remained the culprit.

In the second place, at no time did the British exercise a positive role in the formation of French strategy. Joffre and de Castelnau consulted and informed Wilson on certain issues, but in the main kept their own counsel. London's lack of influence upon French planning was in turn matched by the modest role conceived for "Armée W" by the French Staff. Located in the triangle Le Cateau-Hirson-Maubeuge, the British divisions would adjoin the French left flank and be available for defensive action. Although the B.E.F. might participate in a counteroffensive toward Dinant or Neufchâteau, none of Joffre's schemes envisaged active British assistance. In spite of Wilson's exhortations, Paris did not view British help as the so-called "decisive" factor in the opening stages of a war. But if dubious about the extent and reliability of British assistance, the French—soldiers and politicians alike—hesitated to forfeit this help by violating Belgian neutrality. The French regarded British intervention as a form of insurance, useful at a war's outbreak, imperative if the war was prolonged. The main problem was to get London involved on the Continent. Once Britain intervened, it would be committed to the cause of France, come what may.

In 1909 Henry Wilson asked Foch: " 'What would you say was the smallest British military force that would be of any practical assistance to you in the event of a contest such as we have been considering?' " " 'One single private soldier,' responded Foch on the instant, 'and we would take good care that he was killed.' " [63] French opinion never changed.

63. Callwell, Wilson, I, 78–79.

9 | The Naval Conversations Begin, 1911–1912

At the height of the Agadir crisis Théophile Delcassé, now Caillaux's Naval Minister, decided to review French naval plans. To his consternation he discovered there were no naval arrangements with London, no staff talks comparable to the military ones. Appalled, the chief architect of the entente immediately notified Justin de Selves, and on August 14 the Foreign Minister cabled Paul Cambon to initiate naval conversations without delay. Naval talks were *already* underway, the ambassador fired back, and had been since the Clemenceau ministry.[1] This might be true, de Selves retorted the next day, but Paris certainly knew nothing of any exchanges between the Admiralty and the French naval attaché. "It is necessary," he caustically observed, "that the latter quickly edify our Naval Staff on these results."[2] Stung by the rebuke, Cambon investi-

1. De Selves to P. Cambon (tel.), Aug. 14, 1911, *D.D.F.*, 2nd ser., no. 171; P. Cambon to de Selves, Aug. 14, 1911, *ibid.*, no. 175. Cambon later asked the Quai d'Orsay to delete his assertion about the naval talks, a request which Bapst obviously ignored.
2. De Selves to P. Cambon (tel.), Aug. 15, 1911, *ibid.*, no. 176.

gated and discovered that his confident assertion was groundless: there had been no extensive naval talks such as he had imagined.

Before the ambassador could remedy this deficiency, the naval attaché, Captain René Pumperneel, died suddenly on August 19. To avoid any further delays because of this unfortunate development, Delcassé sent Captain Mercier de Lostende (Pumperneel's predecessor) to London, ostensibly to attend the late attaché's funeral, in fact to see Admiral Sir A. K. Wilson about entente naval coordination. With the de Lostende-Wilson discussion effective naval conversations may be said to have begun. Although the subsequent exchanges in 1911 were limited and few, they opened the way for the intensive conversations which followed the collapse of the Haldane mission in early 1912.

Before the staff talks are considered, however, the sea power and strategic thinking of the entente navies deserve some attention. This is especially true for the French, whose prewar naval policy has largely been ignored by historians. In the years between the Moroccan crises the French Navy experienced a veritable revolution. France remained the fourth-ranking naval power, but the disastrous legacy bequeathed by the *jeune école* and by the Pelletan regime was slowly overcome. In this resurgence the theory of offensive naval warfare exerted a significant impact: the spell of the *jeune école* with its stress on defensive action was finally broken.

Offensive naval action had first won some currency in France in the late 1890's. Mahan's writings, emphasizing destruction of the enemy fleet, had blasted the propositions that *guerre de course* and defensive maneuvers could bring victory over a maritime rival. And his contentions about the political value of sea power had received fresh substantiation with the American victories of 1898. The high-water mark had come in 1900 when the Parliament had accepted J. L. de Lanessan's program for six battleships; but these gains were quickly erased during Pelletan's three years at rue Royale. Yet, throughout that dismal travail two developments were undermining the assumptions of the *jeune école:* the expanding, indeed superior, might of the German Navy and the formation of the Anglo-French entente. Torpedo boats and armored cruisers, the materiel of the defensive school, could no longer effectively defend French coasts and colonies from a German attack; at the same time, friendly relations with Britain eliminated the one potential enemy against whom *guerre de course* might have been effective. The need for a dynamic, positive approach to naval warfare seemed more and more self-evident to a number of French navalists.[3]

Among the foremost proponents of offensive naval strategy was the then young Lieutenant René Daveluy. In two volumes first published in 1902 and 1905, the future Admiral eloquently argued the value of of-

3. See Chapter 1, pp. 25–26.

fensive action at sea. In the second book, *Etude sur la stratégie navale*, he scoffed at the idea of commerce warfare and called instead for a "single fleet" to carry the fight to the enemy. To be on the defensive was to be beaten without doing anything: "The character of the offensive is to impose the attack instead of receiving it; it is supported in history by the fact that nearly all the victories have been gained on the enemy's coasts."[4] These views received wide circulation through their appearance in *Marine Rundschau*; and they were impressively endorsed in the next few years by Gabriel Darrieus, a former professor at the Ecole de Marine, and by de Lanessan, the former Naval Minister. Darrieus, echoing de Grandmaison, asserted that "a fleet is an offensive instrument, and the best method that any one has ever found of defending himself is to attack."[5] Nevertheless, while these naval writers preached the offensive, they also recognized that the French Navy was woefully unprepared to conduct this type of operation: in particular, it lacked battleships. Concomitant, therefore, with their emphasis upon offensive action was equal stress upon the development of adequate materiel to implement this policy.

Pelletan's exit from the Naval Ministry in January 1905 reopened opportunities for the offensive strategists. Gaston Thomson, Rouvier's Naval Minister, shared their conviction that the French fleet must be rebuilt for offensive action.[6] One of his first acts was to revamp the construction program, pushing for immediate completion of the six "Patrie"-class battleships voted in 1900 but delayed by Pelletan. And in 1907 he managed, despite Pelletan's criticism, to gain parliamentary approval for six more battleships as part of an eventual fleet of thirty-eight. But Thomson's political victories were partly balanced by his troubles with the conservative Conseil Supérieur de la Marine. In abeyance during Pelletan's tenure, the now resurrected Navy Board was composed of a group of venerable officers who formulated construction programs and naval strategy. Some of its members were noted neither for intellect nor for energy: one of them, in fact, only came to work in the afternoons, never in the mornings—except on payday.[7] Not especially zealous about anything, including the offensive strategy, some members like Fournier had well-defined views in favor of *guerre de course*.[8] In construction matters the Board refused to imitate Fisher and construct an all-big-gun battleship. Instead, after considerable delay, they decided in 1907 to con-

4. René Daveluy, *Etude sur la stratégie navale* (Paris, 1905), 58; see also his *Etude sur le combat navale* (Paris, 1902), and "Marine et marins d'hier, souvenirs de carrière de l'Amiral Daveluy, XXX: au Ministère de la Marine," *Revue maritime*, 218 (February 1965), 240–242.

5. Gabriel Darrieus, *La guerre sur mer: stratégie et tactique: la doctrine* (Paris: 1907), 203; J. L. de Lanessan, *Le bilan de notre marine* (Paris, 1909).

6. *Le Temps*, Aug. 3, 1905; *Le Matin*, May 29, 1906.

7. Daveluy, "Marine et marins d'hier," 242.

8. Paul Brière, *Un grand français: le vice-amiral François Ernest Fournier* (Mayenne, 1931), 164–167.

struct the "Dantons" (17,700 tons), though they were slower, less well armed, and had a smaller displacement than either the *Dreadnought* or its projected British and German successors (18,200 tons and more).[9] The ill effects of the Board's timidity and hesitation were further accentuated by the prolonged delays prevalent in the construction phase of any French naval program: French shipyards were usually twenty-five percent slower than those in Germany and Britain, thus the new "Dantons," already second-rate when ordered, were even more inadequate by the time of their delivery.[10]

Thomson, hampered by vacillating naval advisers, inefficient dockyards, and political vendettas, meant well but was unable to improve France's relative naval position. By 1908 this failure exposed him to mounting parliamentary and press criticism. Leading the attacks was the former Foreign Minister, turned naval expert, M. Delcassé. As chairman of the 1907–1908 investigation of the *Iéna* disaster (one hundred seventeen sailors killed), Delcassé became convinced that the French Navy remained unfit for its expected role in grand strategy. When the Chamber of Deputies debated the *Iéna* report in October 1908, his slashing attack upon the ineptitude of the naval administration so angered Thomson that he resigned on the spot.[11] His successor was Alfred Picard, a distinguished French engineer with little experience in maritime affairs.

A mere change of faces in the Clemenceau ministry was not enough to appease Delcassé. Continuing to complain about the Navy, he finally forced Clemenceau in late March 1909 to sanction a full-scale parliamentary investigation of the service. Predictably, the commission's report, completed three months later, contained a scathing indictment of French naval policy. Its main conclusion was simple and unambiguous: the Navy was in pathetic condition. It lacked adequate battleships, armament, and ammunition. French dry docks were not long enough to accommodate the already authorized "Dantons." French naval construction was slow, shoddy, expensive, and corrupt. Moreover, the naval high command was hopelessly and archaically organized. Nothing less than a complete reorganization of administrative procedures and structure would suffice to improve the quality of the Navy.[12] In July the Chamber of Deputies debated the commission's report during six separate sessions. The debate reached a frenzied climax on July 20, when Delcassé summarized the deplorable conditions within the Navy and fastened the blame squarely upon the Clemenceau ministry. In a desperate effort to save his government, the "Tiger" launched a vitriolic personal

9. See the minutes of the Navy Board for 1906–1907, Archives Marine, BB8 2428, 2429.
10. De Lanessan, *Le bilan de notre marine*, 292.
11. *Journal officiel: débats parlementaires, Chambre des Députés*, 1908, I (Oct. 16–17, 19, 1908), 1749–1793. On Delcassé's role, see Philippe Masson, "Delcassé, Ministre de la Marine," unpub. diss. (Paris, 1951), 3–14; Porter, *Delcassé*, 274–308.
12. The report is in France, *Annales de la Chambre des Députés: documents parlementaires*, LXXVII (1909), Annexe no. 2554, pp. 777–818.

attack on the former Foreign Minister, whom he accused of having taken France "to the doors of war" in 1905; he then demanded "if it was acceptable that the man who led us to Algeciras should implicate some ministers and accuse them of incapacity in the preparation of national defense!"[13] This time the veteran politician misjudged the temper of the Chamber; his slur upon Delcassé's patriotism enraged the deputies. The three-year-old ministry fell on a vote of confidence, 212 to 176.

In the first of Aristide Briand's eleven governments the naval portfolio did not go, as expected, to Delcassé. Instead Vice Admiral Boué de Lapeyrère, the energetic naval prefect at Brest, replaced Picard at rue Royale. Under de Lapeyrère's guidance the French Navy began to experience something of a "renaissance,"[14] which, like most renaissances, owed part of its triumph to the previous labor of others. For Picard, despite his sixty-four years and the criticism of Charles Bos in La vie maritime, had in fact stirred the Navy Board to action. The Board had begun to study an organic law for naval construction, to fix a ratio of cruisers to battleships, and to consider reorganization of the French dockyards. Moreover, Picard was hard at work on a sizable naval program for 1910 when he lost office.[15] De Lapeyrère built well upon these foundations.

An ardent advocate of offensive naval strategy, the Admiral readily agreed with his former colleagues on the Navy Board about the need for more battleships; the question was how many. The Board wanted forty-five; the officer turned minister maintained that twenty-eight was an adequate and more attainable figure. He justified this number on two grounds: the entente with Britain and financial limitations. The government, he explained, counted upon British naval help against Germany, so that the Austrian and Italian fleets were the standards against which French strength should be measured. A program of twenty-eight battleships would give France a one-ship margin in 1927. This figure, he assured his fellow admirals, was recognized by the government as the minimum fleet for France. Unhappy with this reasoning, some of the admirals were livid when de Lapeyrère invoked the financial argument. Vice Admiral Léonce Caillard vigorously protested that he could not comprehend why "the Minister of Finance had such a preponderant voice in determining national defense!"[16] Caillard's familiar complaint, repeated by countless services before and after 1909, was ultimately to

13. *Journal officiel: débats parlementaires, Chambre des Députés*, 1909, I (July 20, 1909), 2229–2243; also see G. Blanchon, "Le bilan de la marine," *Revue des deux mondes*, 5th ser., 52 (July 1, 1909), 137–171.
14. Marder uses this term in *Road to War*, 304.
15. See "Note pour le Conseil Supérieur de la Marine," Feb. 26, 1909, Archives Marine, "C.S.M., 1909(1)"; staff memo, "Composition de la flotte," Feb. 26, 1909, Archives Marine, BB8 1814.
16. Henri Le Masson, "Politique navale et construction de navires de ligne en France en 1914, I," *Revue maritime*, 202 (August–September 1963), 994–995; minutes of the Navy Board for May 17, 29, 1909, Feb. 2, 1910, Archives Marine, "C.S.M., 1909–1910"; Masson, "Delcassé, Ministre de la Marine," 50–60.

no avail: the Board accepted twenty-eight battleships as an adequate program.

Boué de Lapeyrère soon discovered that determining a naval program was easy compared to gaining parliamentary approval for it. While the deputies and senators might advocate, debate, and even demand a strong Navy, they were always reluctant to pay the price. This attitude, coupled with the Admiral's own political inexperience, handicapped his efforts to revive the Navy. Although he obtained authorization in April 1910 for the first genuine French dreadnoughts, the *Jean Bart* and the *Courbet*, Parliament never acted upon an organic naval law which would have committed France to a long-term building program; naval construction remained a year-to-year proposition. Nevertheless, de Lapeyrère had presented the politicians with a naval program which, for the first time since 1900, bore some relationship to France's naval requirements. His successor, more familiar with the mores of the political world and assisted by the aftereffects of Agadir, would achieve the results denied the Admiral.

Delcassé became Naval Minister in the Monis government on March 2, 1911. Now able to control what he had hitherto only been able to criticize, the diminutive deputy from Ariège immediately set out to improve the materiel of the French Navy. In March 1912 he persuaded the Parliament to adopt an organic naval law closely patterned on the one first submitted by de Lapeyrère three years before, providing for a French fleet of twenty-eight battleships by 1920.[17] In the debates over the program, Delcassé frankly acknowledged that it was only designed to make France supreme in the Mediterranean, not to match or to compete with the Germans in the North Sea. Further, he warned that the new program was the absolute minimum, even for the Mediterranean.[18] Indeed some deputies charged that his proposals were already below the minimum, arguing that by 1915 the combined Austro-Italian fleets would have a 10-7 edge in dreadnoughts, though not in battleships as such. And, in July 1912, de Lanessan submitted a supplementary naval program calling for a total of thirty-six battleships by 1920, but the most critics got was an acceleration in the rate of construction during 1913 that slightly improved French prospects in the Mediterranean.[19] Whatever its shortcomings, the Naval Law of 1912 was still a step in the right direction: in time France might conceivably possess a respectable offensive naval force.

While the theorists preached offensive action and successive ministers struggled to improve the Navy's materiel, French admirals faced the stra-

17. Masson, "Delcassé, Ministre de la Marine," 64–74.
18. *Journal officiel: débats parlementaires, Chambre des Députés, 1912,* I (Feb. 13, 1912), 304–340; *Le Temps,* February 1912, *passim.* Also see Gabriel Darrieus, "The Naval Problem," *Journal of the Royal United Service Institution,* 56 (July 1912), 929–956; this paper was presented on Jan. 13, 1912, at the Institut Maritime.
19. Le Masson, "Politique navale et construction," 996–998.

tegic necessity of employing the available French forces. In particular they were confronted with two interlocking issues: whether to concentrate their forces in the Mediterranean or in the Atlantic, or to divide them between those areas; and how to evaluate the probable role of the British Navy. These questions first received serious attention from the naval high command during the Algeciras conference. In mid-February 1906 Rear Admiral Aubert, then attached to the Naval Ministry, wrote a staff paper urging that all of France's battleships be concentrated in the Mediterranean: located there, they could mobilize more quickly and with less commotion than if in the Atlantic. Once mobilized, the twelve battleships would be ready for action against Italy or for dispatch northward to meet the German fleet.[20] Six weeks later, on March 31, 1906, the Navy Board met to consider Aubert's ideas and to conduct a general review of French naval strategy. The outcome of the meeting effectively shaped French naval strategy for the remaining years before the Great War.

The Board's session began with a review of German capabilities by Admiral Fournier, the designated fleet commander in case of war. The fundamental problem, he pointed out, was how best to concentrate France's inferior naval strength against a German Navy with an advantage of at least six battleships. Personally in favor of concentrating at Brest, Fournier thought it dangerous to expose France's northern coasts to a German attack and to expect French cruisers to hold out until battleships could arrive from the Mediterranean. Admiral Joseph Besson passionately agreed with Fournier, at one point exclaiming that "if we do not oppose the concentration at Toulon, we betray our country." On the other hand Admirals Camille Gigon and Jules Melchoir staunchly opposed a northern deployment. The former argued, without much perspicacity, that the Navy had to stay in the Mediterranean to move the XIX Corps from North Africa to France. Slightly more cogently, Melchoir declared that the real danger to French interests would come from an Italian move against Corsica and Tunisia; moreover, he saw no reason to concentrate France's entire strength either in the Mediterranean or in the Atlantic, especially since the Entente Cordiale assured unfettered movement for French ships through the Straits of Gibraltar. Admiral Marie Edgard de Maigret, who was presiding, then asked for a vote on whether the Navy Board should, in a war just against Germany, concentrate French forces in the north. The vote was unanimously in the affirmative. De Maigret then asked his colleagues whether they could accept a primary concentration in the Mediterranean if political considerations demanded it. The vote this time was 10–2 in the affirmative.[21]

At this point Gaston Thomson belatedly entered the meeting. After a

20. Memo by Aubert, "Note sur la répartition des forces navales," Feb. 13, 1906, Archives Marine, "C.S.M., 1906."
21. Minutes of the Navy Board, Mar. 31, 1906, *ibid.*

quick briefing, he launched into a justification for concentrating French naval forces in the Mediterranean, pointing to the dangers of an Italian mobilization, emphasizing the possible benefits of British assistance, and warning against any action that might compromise the Algeciras conference. Also, he urged the Board to look beyond the immediate dangers of a war, which he thought unlikely, and to consider instead the overall future situation. And he attempted to ease apprehensions about a Mediterranean concentration by promising frequent fleet exercises in the Atlantic and improved coastal defenses. Soon the admirals found other justifications or excuses, such as better port facilities and the better weather in the south, to support the minister's position. At length the Navy Board formally approved (10–2) the concentration of France's first-line forces in the Mediterranean and its second line in the north.[22]

The major factor behind this momentous decision remains, despite plentiful documentation, somewhat obscure. Friendship with Britain, for instance, was not ignored by the Board, but the entente was not the decisive or even the prompting factor behind the concentration in the Mediterranean. At this time there had been no naval conversations of any significance. Nor does French concern about Italian naval power explain the shift, for the admirals simply were not that alarmed about the Italians. That either the movement of the XIX Corps to metropolitan France or the defense of Algeria was a crucial factor seems unlikely. Furthermore, it appears doubtful that the move was a response to any realistic assessment of France's naval position vis-à-vis Germany. If it had been, Fournier's arguments for concentrating in the north could hardly have been refuted. The admirals' repeated allusions to political considerations and Thomson's own vigorous intervention suggest that, in the final analysis, the transfer was perhaps the result of pressure from the Midi politicians for a larger share of the naval budget. In any case, by early 1907 the withdrawal of the six battleships from the Northern Squadron was complete, leaving only six armored cruisers in the Atlantic. In the Mediterranean the French now possessed two squadrons: an active one composed of six battleships and a reserve one composed of the older battleships transferred from the Atlantic. Since the vessels formerly in the Northern Squadron were placed in a reserve status, the new distribution brought no spectacular improvement in French naval power in the Mediterranean. But a pattern was begun. France would henceforth center its naval might in the Mediterranean; as they were completed, new battleships would be added to those already there. Tacitly, if not explicitly, the French admirals now depended upon the British to handle the German fleet.

This tacit dependence upon Britain prompted some French navalists

22. *Ibid.;* also see the staff memo, "Avantages et inconvénients de la concentration des forces navales suivant qu'elles seraient dans la Nord ou dans la Méditerranée," June 22, 1906, Archives Marine, BB4 2707.

to speculate about the role of the entente. Spencer Dickson, the British vice-consul at Brest, for example, reported that French naval officers there thought the "changes in distribution are the result of an understanding with Britain, or, as it has been sometimes called, of the 'treaty of Portsmouth.' " [23] Even Boué de Lapeyrère, then serving as prefect at Brest, believed the French concentration in the Mediterranean was the result of a secret Anglo-French accord,[24] though in reality no such arrangements yet existed. The French war plans for 1908 made no provisions for British help. In a war against Germany alone or against the Triple Alliance, the French planned to concentrate in the Mediterranean and then to take the offensive—the location to be determined by the behavior of Rome and Vienna.[25] Not until late 1908 did French planners finally begin to grapple with the explicit problem of possible British help. Their initial reaction, fortified by Admiral Fisher's comments in December of that year, was that British assistance would not significantly alter either the logic of the 1906 dispositions or the nature of French plans. France would still handle the Mediterranean, while the British operated in the Channel and the North Sea.[26] Entente naval planning had not advanced beyond these broad considerations when de Lapeyrère took command in early 1909.

One of the Admiral's first actions upon arrival at the Naval Ministry was to nibble away at the 1906 decision to concentrate in the Mediterranean. In·August he returned the older battleships to Brest as the new Second Squadron, while shifting the six cruisers back to the Mediterranean. To most contemporary observers these shifts meant that Boué de Lapeyrère planned to re-establish France's naval position in the north. Was this in fact the case? Certainly the shifts were not the result of any accord with London; indeed Georges Louis (then at the Quai d'Orsay) recorded that de Lapeyrère sought to assure Admiral Fisher that the change was temporary.[27] And it is doubtful, despite Bos's repeated assertions in La vie maritime,[28] that the redistribution was designed either to furnish French admirals with more ships to command or to appease de Lapeyrère's friends in Brest. In this instance the Admiral's public statements probably contain the real explanation for the apparent change in naval policy. In February 1910 he assured the deputies that no funda-

23. Memo by Dickson, Mar. 5, 1907, F.O. 371/250. Archibald Hurd had suggested this earlier; see his "The Government and the Navy," *Nineteenth Century and After*, 60 (November 1906), 740.
24. Dickson to Foreign Office, Nov. 23, 1908, F.O. 371/453.
25. Aubert to Thomson, May 11, 1908, Archives Marine, BB4 2680; war orders, May 11, 1908, Oct. 6, 1908, Archives Marine, ED 37.
26. Memos by Aubert, "Note pour le Ministre sujet de la coopération des marines française et anglaise, en cas de guerre avec l'Allemagne," Nov. 15, 1908, Archives Marine, ED 37; and "Note au sujet de la conduite à tenir en cas de guerre avec la Triple Alliance, l'Angleterre étant notre alliée," Jan. 16, 1909, Archives Marine, BB4 2681.
27. Diary, Aug. 12, 1909, *Les carnets de Georges Louis*, I, 42–43.
28. Aug. 25, Sept. 10, Nov. 10, 1909, Mar. 25, 1910.

mental alteration in French naval strategy was contemplated; the Mediterranean remained France's foremost concern and the Second Squadron could always be brought back if necessary. Two practical considerations, he explained, dictated the "temporary" changes. First, he wanted to join the cruisers with the battleships they were designed to protect; second, the inadequate dry dock facilities at Toulon forced him to send the old battleships to Brest and Cherbourg if they were ever to be repaired. Only in this way could he get both squadrons into fighting condition—an impossibility as long as both had depended upon Toulon. Once the facilities at Bizerte could handle the repairs, French naval power, he promised, would again be completely centered in the Mediterranean. Moreover, de Lapeyrère predicated and justified his new building program solely in terms of the advantages it would confer in the Mediterranean. In short, even with him the Mediterranean remained the focal point of French naval strategy.[29]

One important ramification of the "temporary" fleet shift was a bitter public debate over the proper location of French naval power. J. L. de Lanessan, the former Naval Minister and a deputy from Rochefort, waged an active and persistent campaign for a northern concentration. In the Dépêche de Brest (September 9, 1910), for instance, he warned of the danger of German attacks in the north and pleaded for a fleet in the Atlantic. Since British ships would always be available in the Mediterranean, it was unnecessary, he insisted, for France to concentrate all of its naval might there also.[30] André Tardieu, writing in Le Temps, took furious exception to de Lanessan's analysis. Arguing that the onetime minister entirely ignored the expansion of the Austrian and Italian fleets, Tardieu emphasized that Britain's effectiveness in the Mediterranean was limited to the eastern basin: thus the French Navy, even if completely concentrated in that sea, would be pressed to prevent a junction of the Austrian and Italian fleets. Nor did the Navy have any real role in the north—the British would block any German threat long before it ever reached Calais. Tardieu maintained that France should trust to Britain in the North Sea, while the entente partners shared responsibility in the Mediterranean. These views were strongly endorsed by Charles Bos, who added that "the English Ambassador had expressed the surprise of his government at seeing a situation disturbed which had been agreed upon between France and Great Britain."[31] Though not borne out by the records, this allegation by Bos accurately emphasized what the Mediterranean concentration logically meant: French need for British help. Bos, however, exaggerated the foresight of the French government by think-

29. On parliamentary criticism and de Lapeyrère's defense. see Journal officiel: débats parlementaires, Chambre des Députés, 1910, I (Feb. 23–24, 1910), 1045–1046, 1064–1065, 1074–1080.
30. Le yacht also backed a concentration in the Atlantic; see, e.g., Aug. 28, 1909, Jan. 22, Apr. 9, 1910.
31. Le Temps, Sept. 11, 1910; La vie maritime, Sept. 25, 1910.

ing that this help was already arranged. While Tardieu and de Lanessan continued to argue well into 1911, the advent of Delcassé as Naval Minister appeared to reaffirm the primacy of the Mediterranean in French naval strategy.

Delcassé as early as 1909 had held that the Mediterranean was the Navy's principal concern. He thought protection of the lines of communication with North Africa was essential, and believed that if France could control the Mediterranean, its sea power would prove attractive to its allies and friends.[32] Once in office Delcassé did not publicly deviate from these earlier views. Although he did not immediately recall the squadron of aging battleships from Brest and Cherbourg, he indicated that the new "Dantons" and all French dreadnoughts would be assigned to the Mediterranean. And his defense of the Naval Law of 1912 centered entirely upon the advantages it would confer upon France in the Mediterranean.[33]

Officially, however, Delcassé's war orders for the fleet reflected surprising flexibility about the Mediterranean. In contrast to Thomson's 1908 orders, those of July 1911 designated Brest as the main operational port in any war fought singlehandedly against Germany or the Triple Alliance. Not until victory had been won in the north would the fleet return to face the Italians. Only if Great Britain fought alongside France would French forces stay in the south with the Channel entrusted to British care.[34] On the other hand, Delcassé almost certainly never expected to fight Germany alone. And on a practical, day-to-day basis, France's effective naval power continued to be located in the western basin of the Mediterranean. While dockyard limitations had prompted Boué de Lapeyrère to depart slightly from this emphasis, the completion of the "Dantons" in 1911 and their concentration in the Mediterranean more than offset the earlier return of the vintage 1890 battleships to Brest and Cherbourg. When seen in this perspective, the final transfer in 1912 of the aged battleship squadron to the Mediterranean was much less innovative than Poincaré dared admit in his negotiations with London that year.

Across the Channel, the years between Tangier and Agadir encompassed the zenith of the Fisher era. In Britain the requirements and technicalities of materiel reigned supreme, symbolized by the development of the *Dreadnought*. The construction of that all-big-gun ship—displacing 17,900 tons, turbine-powered, capable of twenty-one knots, and armed with ten twelve-inch guns—was a triumph of British engineering. It also

32. *Journal officiel: débats parlementaires, Chambre des Députés,* 1909, I (Mar. 25, 1909), 841; Porter, *Delcassé,* 280.
33. *L'excelsoir,* May 15, 1911; *La vie maritime,* June 25, 1911; *Journal officiel: débats parlementaires, Chambre des Députés,* session extraordinaire, III (Dec. 11, 1911), 3832.
34. War orders, July 29, 1911, Archives Marine, BB4 2681.

represented a personal triumph for Sir John Fisher, the First Sea Lord. No other military or naval figure in pre-1914 Europe so dominated his service as did the Admiral from 1904 to 1910. Inexhaustibly energetic, despite his age (he was sixty-three in 1904), and inescapably impulsive, both with his tongue and in his judgments, Fisher could be cunning, clever, and occasionally vindictive in the infighting that characterized British defense politics. During his reign the Scripture-quoting Admiral prodded, pushed, cajoled, and harangued the Royal Navy and the political establishment in his efforts to prepare Britain for war. In the main he achieved his goals, though not without significant costs to himself and to the morale of the Navy.

Fisher's major achievements were in preparing the materiel of the Navy for action and in persuading the Liberal government to pay for that materiel. He relentlessly scrapped vessels that had no fighting value; he instituted a nucleus-crew system for reserve ships which kept them manned with forty percent of their normal crews and thus ready for instant mobilization. The scrapping policy, which the Foreign Office disliked because it curbed "showing the flag," saved money, while the nucleus-crew arrangement raised the war proficiency of the overall naval establishment. Economy and efficiency were, as Marder notes, the hallmarks of Fisher's naval administration. In turn, the financial savings from these reforms enabled the Admiral to launch the dreadnought program without any major increase (there were in fact some reductions) in British naval estimates until the final year of his command (1909–1910). Moreover, the initial edge given by the *Dreadnought*'s completion in December 1906 and by Germany's failure to respond immediately allowed Fisher to slow the pace of naval construction, to the delight of the Liberal government. Some Conservatives and naval critics, however, deplored the pause in shipbuilding and the introduction of the *Dreadnought*, the latter because it nullified Britain's overwhelming superiority in conventional battleships. In 1906 and 1907 Fisher could easily demonstrate for the skeptics that Britain's naval superiority far exceeded the requirements of the two-power standard.[35]

Then in 1908 and 1909 the strains of the Anglo-German naval race began to show. Early in 1908 the Kaiser's government revamped its naval goals, aiming now for a grand total of fifty-eight battleships instead of thirty-eight. And, later in the year, Admiralty intelligence received a variety of reports suggesting that Berlin had secretly accelerated its construction of dreadnoughts. There were, as one expects from military establishments, dire predictions about the future of Britain's naval superiority. Some estimates predicted the Germans would have seventeen dreadnoughts by 1912, other sources calculated twenty-one. By comparison, Britain would have but eighteen: the two-power standard would be swept away, and possibly Britain with it. For months the gov-

35. This account draws chiefly upon Marder, *Road to War*, chaps. ii–viii.

ernment was racked by a major crisis over naval construction. Fisher and the Board of Admiralty demanded six new dreadnoughts for 1910, instead of the usual four. The radicals, led by Lloyd George and Winston Churchill, refused to be convinced of the German danger. Finally, after acrimonious, sometimes savage exchanges within the Cabinet and after repeated leaks by Fisher to the Conservative press, the Asquith government in early 1909 capitulated to Fisher's demands and then some.[36] As Winston Churchill put it later: "In the end a curious and characteristic solution was reached. The Admiralty had demanded six ships; the economists offered four; and we finally compromised on eight."[37] Britain's naval supremacy was assured, at least until the next scare; Fisher was again triumphant.

The First Sea Lord strikingly improved the materiel and training of the Royal Navy. As a strategic thinker his record was less impressive. His nasty feud with Admiral Lord Charles Beresford, while fanned by personal animosity, derived in part from the latter's aspersions about the Admiralty's war plans. When Beresford refused to remain quiet on this and other matters, he was unceremoniously removed from command of the Channel Fleet a year ahead of schedule. Ultimately the pompous, shallow Beresford had a certain revenge, as his demands forced Asquith to authorize a private C.I.D. investigation of naval plans. This challenge to the Board of Admiralty was thoroughly resented by Fisher. Though fully acquitted of the charge of having no war plans, the First Sea Lord was chastised by the Committee for his failure to institute a naval staff, and the reproof eventually brought about his retirement at the end of 1909. Admiral Sir A. K. Wilson, a trusted collaborator and friend, succeeded him in January 1910.[38] Subsequently Wilson's own failure to create a naval war staff would, as seen earlier, bring about his ouster by Churchill in November 1911.

Fisher's chief contribution to British strategy derived from his ruthless and farsighted redistribution of Britain's naval flotilla. In late 1904, when he took command, British preparations for a war against Germany were at best ad hoc and rudimentary. To remedy the situation he systematically began to concentrate British men-of-war in home waters. For Fisher, to be prepared for war meant being prepared to fight the most likely enemy. By early 1907 the preponderant might of the British Navy was located in and around the North Sea. In 1909 he further reorganized the Home Fleet so that it possessed sixteen fully commissioned battleships with eight in reserve. The Atlantic Fleet with six battleships was relocated at Dover, ready for action in either the North Sea or the At-

36. *Ibid.*; also see Woodward, *Great Britain and the German Navy*, 203–239. The Cabinet letters from Asquith to George V are most instructive on the development of the crisis.
37. Churchill, *The World Crisis*, I, 33.
38. Marder, *Road to War*, 88–104, 186–207.

lantic. When united, the Home and Atlantic Fleets were vastly superior to the German High Seas Fleet.[39]

This steady concentration of naval power in home waters was achieved only through drastic reductions in the strength of other stations. In these reductions the Mediterranean was not spared. The 1907 reorganization reduced Britain's battleships in that sea from eight to six, and this figure remained unchanged until 1912. Gradually these vessels would be outclassed as the French, Italians, and Austrians completed larger battleships and began dreadnoughts. The changing status and importance of the Mediterranean in British naval strategy was also reflected in the war plans drafted by the Ballard-Hankey group in early 1907. Each of that committee's schemes provided for French help; if this assistance materialized, the Admiralty intended to withdraw the remaining battleships from the Mediterranean and let the French protect British interests.[40] Moreover, in December 1908 Fisher told the French that he planned to abandon the Mediterranean in case of war, a view A. K. Wilson echoed at the time of Agadir.[41] The Admiralty, like its French counterpart with regard to the Atlantic, had resolved therefore long before 1912 to forego any sizable allocation of naval power in the Mediterranean. Nothing could be allowed to interfere with the preparations against Germany.

Fisher's main strategic problem was how to bring the German fleet to a decisive action. To achieve this the Admiralty considered and devised a variety of schemes that might pry or entice German ships from their safe havens: the use of blockades, the seizure of offshore islands such as Borkum, amphibious operations along the German coasts, the destruction and strangulation of German commerce on the high seas. Implicit in most of these plans was the efficacy of economic pressure upon an opponent, the belief that economic deprivation would have what Thomas Schelling calls a compellent effect upon the enemy. In this case the German Navy would be forced to risk an encounter with a superior British fleet.[42] Because British plans rested so heavily upon economic warfare, the Admiralty's attitude toward the Hague Conference and particularly the London Conference is difficult to unravel.

In both cases the Board of Admiralty cooperated willingly with the Foreign Office in discussions about an international prize court, blockade rules, neutral rights, and the definition of contraband. Further, despite restrictions placed by the Declaration of London on the conduct of economic warfare, the Admiralty raised no open or significant protests.

39. *Ibid.*, 40–43, 71–76.
40. These plans are examined in detail in Chapter 4, pp. 104–107.
41. Minutes of the 114th meeting of the C.I.D. (Aug. 23, 1911), Cab. 2/2/2. The 1907 accords with France and Spain, which sought to preserve the status quo in the Mediterranean, may also be considered as evidence of London's concern about its receding power in that area; Monger, *The End of Isolation*, 318–322.
42. Marder, *Road to War*, 367–395; Hankey, *Supreme Command*, I, 87–93; Thomas Schelling, *Arms and Influence* (New Haven, Conn., 1966), 69–91.

There was no challenge from the Navy, for example, about the three categories of contraband promulgated at the London Conference. What constituted absolute contraband was clear and unambiguous. But conditional contraband and free goods were defined, as the critics pointed out, so loosely as to render an effective blockade quite difficult.[43] Explanations for the Admiralty's curious ambivalence are at best tenuous and somewhat unconvincing, but several points should be noted. First, the fundamental work at the Hague and London meetings was handled by an interdepartmental committee of Admiralty and Foreign Office personnel. On both occasions officers enjoying Fisher's full confidence were the naval delegates: Ottley attended the two conferences and Rear Admiral E. J. Slade the one in London. The First Sea Lord, who thought "you can no more tame war than you can tame hell!" may simply have trusted his faithful subordinates to use their own judgments—in the case of the London Conference (1908–1909), which coincided with the crises over naval construction and Bosnia, Fisher obviously could devote little attention to the intricacies of international law. Second, there was significant pressure from the Foreign Office and the Liberal government to reach agreements on the maritime aspects of economic warfare. Third at no point did the Declaration of London ever reach the C.I.D.; if it had, naval objections would probably have appeared.

Finally, there are Machiavellian aspects that cannot be altogether discounted. The Naval Lords were genuinely concerned about Britain's ability to maintain the naval domination required for successful economic warfare. Because this supremacy might be in doubt, especially in the opening stages of a war, restrictions upon *guerre de course* could ensure useful protection for British commerce. So long as the naval issue remained undecided, the Declaration of London and the Prize Court offered convenient means to soothe neutral susceptibilities; then, when Britain could enforce a total blockade, the Declaration and other impediments could be disregarded at will. In the meantime, the admirals would have appeased their Liberal masters.[44]

Not all within the British defense establishment remained quiescent about the Declaration of London. A young Marine Captain, Maurice Hankey, then Ottley's assistant at the C.I.D., doggedly campaigned against the Declaration. In February 1911 he drafted a long, pungent memorandum entitled "The Declaration of London from the point of view of war with Germany," in which he outspokenly condemned the government both for its failure to bring the Declaration to the C.I.D.

43. Among the many criticisms of the Declaration, see T. Gibson Bowles, "The Declaration of London," *Nineteenth Century and After*, 65 (May 1909), 744–754 (an extract is in *B.D.*, VIII, no. 307); and Admiral Sir E. R. Fremantle, "The Declaration of London," *United Service Magazine*, 43 (April 1911), 1–12.
44. Hankey, *Supreme Command*, I, 99–101; minutes by Ottley, Feb. 17, 1911, F.O. 371/1278; Admiral Sir R. N. Custance, "The Naval Case for Ratifying the Declaration of London," *Nineteenth Century and After*, 71 (March 1912), 440.

and for its complete disregard of that document's impact upon British war plans. Britain, he insisted, would find itself unable to apply effective economic pressure against Germany. Doubtful that Britain's maritime supremacy was actually endangered, he particularly disliked the advantages given neutral nations by the Declaration. Any limitations upon the exercise of British sea power were, in his opinion, intolerable and unacceptable.[45]

Hankey's paper met a hostile reception. His superior, Admiral Ottley, a key participant in both conferences, strongly disputed his subordinate's conclusions, contending that the safeguards obtained for British commerce clearly outweighed any limitations imposed upon the conduct of economic warfare. Any restrictions would in any case only be temporary, that is, until the British Navy had destroyed the enemy fleet. Then the Declaration could be ignored with impunity. Though he disagreed with Hankey, Ottley did send the Captain's memo to the Foreign Office. C. J. B. Hurst, the department's legal expert and himself a delegate to the London Conference, belittled Hankey's assertion that economic coercion would decisively influence a war with Germany. He also expressed doubts about the Royal Navy's ability to control the sea lanes. "To my mind," Hurst concluded, "Captain Hankey advocates that the very solid advantages of the Declaration of London should be thrown away in the pursuit of a will of 'the wisp.' " Hankey did not let this civilian rebuff go unchallenged. He retorted a week later that economic pressure constituted Britain's only offensive weapon in a straight Anglo-German war. Were, he asked, "the solid and immediate advantages of the Declaration of London . . . so great as to outweigh the terrible handicap which it will place in the exercise of our sole weapon of offense. . . . To some it would seem preferable to act on the motto— Salus Civitatis, Suprema Lex." [46] Hankey's rejoinder proved no more successful than his original memorandum. During 1911 the government repeatedly pressed for ratification of the Declaration. At length, on December 7, Grey won its approval from the House of Commons, only to see the House of Lords emphatically reject it five days later. That opposition was never overcome.[47]

The Declaration of London only threatened the Admiralty's plans for economic warfare. The Army, on the other hand, had already effectively demolished the Admiralty's schemes for amphibious operations. After 1905 the War Office never seriously contemplated raids along the Ger-

45. Feb. 17, 1911, F.O. 371/1278; also see Hankey, Supreme Command, I, 94–101.

46. Minutes by Ottley, Feb. 17, 1911, F.O. 371/1278; minutes by Hurst, Feb. 27, 1911, ibid.; memo by Hankey, Mar. 8, 1911, ibid.

47. On Dec. 23, 1911, Grey told Churchill that while the Prize Court and the Declaration of London were "positively advantageous to this country," he wanted the Admiralty to review them before their reintroduction into Parliament; Grey Papers, F.O. 800/87.

man coasts. Each time the problem was studied, the results were the same: coastal raids would not be commensurate with the costs and risks involved. In spite of the insistent, glowing support of Sir John Fisher and Sir Arthur Wilson, the C.I.D. in 1909 and again in 1911 sided with the Army in rejecting amphibious attacks as unfeasible.[48] Yet these setbacks did not entirely purge the Admiralty of its fixation with coastal raids, and in June 1914 coastal raids were again reconsidered by the Navy.

Whatever its shortcomings, British naval strategy in the era of Fisher and Wilson reflected a shrewd appreciation of the value of the Entente Cordiale.[49] This was evident in Fisher's decision to concentrate British naval might in the North Sea, in the reductions of naval strength in the Mediterranean, and in the provisions for French help in the Admiralty's war plans. Yet this awareness and appreciation prompted neither of the First Sea Lords to go farther and actively coordinate his naval policy with the French. This failure stemmed in part from the extreme reluctance of these two men to discuss their war plans with anyone, much less foreigners. They probably believed that so long as the French generally knew what London expected, this was adequate coordination; moreover, their supreme confidence in the Royal Navy's ability to destroy the German fleet was conducive to casual treatment of possible French help. Before long, the steady expansion of the Triple Alliance navies, coupled with the revival of French sea power, would prompt the Admiralty to modify this aloof attitude; but in the meantime there were only isolated exchanges with the French naval attachés.

The naval conversations before 1911 can be quickly traced. In July 1905 Captain Ottley, the Director of Naval Intelligence, urged the coordination of naval plans with France. Nothing came of this suggestion. Fisher did not see the French naval attaché until the following January and then only for a very brief discussion, during which he assured de Lostende that the British Navy was ready for any eventuality—all he wanted from the French were submarines in the Dover-Calais straits. Despite the pleas of Sir George Clarke and Repington, the Admiral refused to be more explicit with Paris. This solitary exchange with de Lostende constituted the naval conversations of the first Moroccan crisis.[50]

The question of further talks did not arise again until the Casablanca incident of 1908. In an interview with Grey on November 24, Paul Cam-

48. See above, Chapters 4 and 7; see also Alfred Vagts, *Landing Operations: Strategy, Psychology, Tactics, Politics, From Antiquity to 1945* (Harrisburg, Pa.; 1946), 509–516; Vice Admiral K. G. P. Dewar, *The Navy From Within* (London, 1939), 144–145.
49. The 1913–1914 war plans will be considered in Chapter 13.
50. Memo by Ottley, June 26, 1905, quoted in Marder, *Anatomy of British Sea Power*, 502–503; de Lostende to Thomson, Jan. 2, 1906, D.D.F., 2nd ser., VIII, no. 308.

bon mentioned reports that London wanted "an informal discussion as to the form which Naval co-operation should take if war broke out, just as there had been a discussion about Military co-operation in 1905." Genuinely surprised by the ambassador's remarks, the Foreign Secretary replied that he thought such talks had already taken place. This was not the case, Cambon explained, though "it was well understood" that the British would be in charge of naval operations. Paris, he observed, needed guidance about possible British demands in case of war. Concurring in this observation, Grey promised to discuss the question with McKenna.[51]

Cambon's probe was successful. In early December de Lostende conferred with McKenna and Fisher at the Admiralty, receiving a succinct briefing on British war plans. Fisher informed him that while Britain could handle the North Sea unassisted, French torpedo boats and submarines were needed to patrol the Dover-Calais area. Otherwise, however, he thought France could concentrate all of its naval forces, including the six armored cruisers at Brest, in the Mediterranean; he revealed that Britain, in turn, would entrust the entire Mediterranean to French care, including the defense of Suez and Malta. Armed with these Olympian pronouncements, the attaché departed immediately for Paris. There, on December 18, he briefed Clemenceau, Pichon, Picard, and Admiral Aubert, Chief of the Naval Staff, on Fisher's proposals. After a brief discussion the quartet decided to accept the division of responsibility in principle, while requesting more time to study the situation in the Mediterranean.[52] Some weeks later, the date is unclear, de Lostende informed the First Sea Lord that Paris thought its naval strength was inadequate to protect the entire Mediterranean: at most the French Navy could only control the western basin. Presumably London accepted this evaluation of French naval strength.[53] In any event, there were no further naval discussions between the entente partners before Agadir.

The influence of the 1908 discussions upon French naval strategy appears minimal. The initial French decision to concentrate in the Mediterranean had come in 1906 without any consultation or coordination with London. Now, two years later, Fisher's belated allocation of responsibilities merely ratified an existing situation, rather than prompting a new one—his dicta simply buttressed the earlier French commitment to the Mediterranean. Yet, while the talks did not significantly influence the actual deployment of French forces, they nevertheless indi-

---

51. Grey to Bertie, Nov. 24, 1908, B.D., VI, no. 106. This dispatch, sent only to the King and Asquith, attributed the alleged desire for naval talks to Repington "or some unauthorized person."

52. Memo by Picard, Dec. 17 [18], 1908, Archives Marine, ES 10; cf. Marder, Road to War, 118. In July 1912 the French gave the Admiralty a brief record of the 1908 and 1911 talks; of the 1908 talks there is a marginal note that "on the wish of the British authorities, in order to maintain absolute secrecy, nothing was committed to writing on the subject"; Adm. 116/3109. The Admiralty copy also bears an undated and erroneous annotation stating that Fisher was not present at the meeting in 1908.

53. Memo by de Lostende, Aug. 29, 1911, Archives Marine, ES 10.

cated how London viewed the overall naval situation. And the French, once cognizant of the British position, took pains thereafter to justify any alteration in their fleet arrangements. In 1909, for instance, de Lapeyrère early and pointedly promised the British naval attaché that the shift of the old battleships to Brest was temporary, occasioned only by Toulon's incapacity and not by any fundamental change in French strategy.[54]

The 1908 talks had another and less predictable effect. In February 1910 Briand defended Boué de Lapeyrère's new naval program in the Cabinet by asserting that France must meet the duties assigned by the "British Authorities." He "could not accept the position," the Premier told his colleagues, "of its being said with any show of accuracy that France could not fulfil her moral obligations and was of no reliable aid at sea to England." Briand carried his point within the Cabinet but, possibly because of Grey's complaints to Bertie, he refrained from utilizing the argument with the Chamber of Deputies.[55] After this episode the topic of Anglo-French naval relations did not reappear in any context until the *Panther*'s arrival off the Moroccan coast.

After Agadir the French made the first move for more intimate naval ties. With Paul Cambon's permission, René Pumperneel discussed with Admiral A. K. Wilson (July 12) the need for a naval code for the entente. The First Sea Lord, "who immediately declared himself a partisan of the project," insisted on the importance of *"absolute secrecy."*[56] Although there are no records of subsequent Pumperneel-Wilson talks, it was this episode which convinced Cambon that regular naval conversations were in progress. The attaché's unexpected death in mid-August not only complicated the work on a naval code, it also hampered Delcassé's efforts to obtain more extensive naval coordination.

Until a new attaché could reach London, the French Naval Minister had to rely upon ad hoc expedients to maintain contact with Wilson. The first opportunity came when de Lostende was sent to London to attend Pumperneel's funeral. On August 24 the former attaché met with the First Sea Lord and briefed him about the 1908 discussions with Sir John Fisher. With little hesitation Wilson accepted the thrust of the earlier talks; quickly the two men arrived at a "convention en trois points." The British would direct all naval activity and each country would possess a clearly defined zone of operations; the French would patrol the western Mediterranean, the British the eastern basin. The only change from the 1908 proposals was in the third point: Wilson

54. Diary, Aug. 12, 1909, *Les carnets de Georges Louis*, I, 42–43.
55. Bertie to Grey, Feb. 10, 1910, *B.D.*, VI, no. 331; Grey to Bertie, Feb. 12, 1910, *ibid.*, no. 332. Grey privately disputed Briand's view of how to strengthen the moral obligation, telling Bertie (Feb. 19, 1910) that "what really strengthens the moral obligations between us is that France should keep up an Army and we a Navy at the highest possible pitch of strength"; *ibid.*, no. 334.
56. Pumperneel to Auvert (Chief of the Naval Staff), July 12, 1911, Archives Marine, ES 10.

preferred that British vessels watch the Dover-Calais straits, while the French guarded the lower Channel. These issues settled, de Lostende returned to Paris.[57]

Delcassé next sent Lieutenant Charles Gignon, a wireless expert, to London. In early September Gignon spent three frantic days working on a secret code and, on Delcassé's personal orders, securing a revision of the August 24 "convention." It was now decided that France would assume responsibility for the entire Mediterranean, the British keeping only enough cruisers there to protect commerce. Gignon also explored with the First Sea Lord and with Paul Cambon the possibility of a written naval agreement. Both men thought a written accord out of the question: Wilson disliked the idea because it would "put politicians into things," Cambon because the numerous German spies might discover such an agreement.[58] Gignon returned to Paris on September 7; after this burst of activity there were no further naval conversations until December. The lengthy intermission stemmed in part from Wilson's departure on leave in mid-September, in part from the turmoil within the Admiralty in October and November, and in part from the absence of a French naval attaché.

During this interval an incident occurred which accurately illustrated the respective roles of the British and French attachés in the staff talks. In late autumn Delcassé casually mentioned the naval conversations to Captain Kelly, the British naval attaché. Flabbergasted by this information, the attaché manfully pretended to know all the details of the talks. "I finally withdrew," Kelly later recalled. "I was seething with indignation. I took the afternoon train to London with the intention of resigning my appointment." The next morning he told Admiral Wilson that if he did not possess the confidence of the Admiralty he should be replaced. The First Sea Lord, who convinced him that this was not the case, suggested that he see the newly appointed Chief of the Naval Staff about the conversations. The attaché, appeased by Wilson's attitude, returned to his post.[59] In spite of his belated discovery of the naval talks (three months had elapsed), Captain Kelly remained ahead of his military counterpart: Colonel Fairholme was only informed of the military conversations in March 1911, some five years after they had begun.[60]

Even though both British attachés were now informed of the staff talks, the French ones remained the focal point of all transactions. With the exception of Colonel Barnardiston's role in Brussels in 1906 (the

57. Memo by de Lostende, Aug. 29, 1911, ibid.
58. Memo by Gignon, Sept. 11, 1911, ibid.
59. Captain Howard Kelly, "Journal as Naval Attaché: Feb. 16, 1911, to Mar. 16, 1914," National Maritime Museum, Greenwich, KEL/3, p. 23.
60. On Mar. 22, 1911, Henry Wilson noted that he had "told Fairholme much of our secret work," Wilson Diaries; also Huguet to Berteaux, Mar. 29, 1911, Archives Guerre, "Plan XVII: Armée W," box 147b. On this kind of activity also see Alfred Vagts, The Military Attaché (Princeton, 1967), chap. xvii.

Belgians had no attachés at that time in London), the British attachés throughout these years never played an active part in the conversations. The explanation for this is simple and self-evident: British attachés normally had their reports sent through the Foreign Office—by using the French attachés as the channel for communication, the Foreign Office was excluded, the chances for leaks and objections reduced, and the civilian ministers effectively bypassed.

Shortly after Kelly stumbled upon the existence of the naval conversations they were briefly resumed. On December 11 Captain Comte le Gouz de Saint-Seine, the new French attaché, paid his first visit to Admiral Sir Francis Bridgeman, Wilson's successor as First Sea Lord. In the course of their chat the Admiral warmly praised the distribution of French forces and expressed a desire to study a division of the Channel into distinct zones for action "against a common enemy." The attaché immediately relayed Bridgeman's proposal to Paris and five days later in a private letter reiterated the importance of resuming the staff talks. He stressed that Paris should exploit this chance "to study not only the coordination of the efforts of the flotillas, but also a plan of cooperation." The two navies could, for example, finally settle upon a code, upon recognition signals, and upon arrangements for ships seeking refuge from enemy attack. He closed his private letter with an impatient plea for instructions on how to proceed with the Admiralty.[61]

These instructions were considerably delayed in coming, for the attaché's urgent appeal ran afoul of the intricacies of the French naval bureaucracy. Admiral Paul Auvert, an Anglophobe of the old school and not at all enthusiastic about closer Anglo-French ties, simply sat on de Saint-Seine's request. When he had received no reply by early January, the attaché with Cambon's permission took the unusual step of circumventing the chain of command and of approaching Delcassé directly on the matter. Thus informed of the Chief of Staff's procrastination, Delcassé severely castigated the Admiral (in front of de Saint-Seine) and told him to leave political matters in the future to the politicians. He then proposed that the British be invited to outline their ideas on the defense of the Channel, while the French Staff did the same.[62] Yet, in spite of Delcassé's intervention, the naval talks gained no momentum. In March de Saint-Seine was again complaining of the French failure to seize Bridgeman's offer. Indeed, there were no significant naval exchanges until July 1912 when the talks were finally renewed on a regular basis.[63]

61. De Saint-Seine to Delcassé, Dec. 11, 1911, D.D.F., 3rd ser., I, no. 336; de Saint-Seine to Captain Mornet [?], Dec. 16, 1911, Archives Marine, ES 10.
62. Memo by de Saint-Seine; Jan. 20, 1937, *ibid.*, memo by Auvert. January 1912, *ibid.* In January 1912 a French memo, apparently never sent to London, proposed that the French watch the lower Channel and keep some ships near Calais and Dunkirk; "Collaboration des marines anglaises et françaises contre la marine allemande," *ibid.*
63. De Saint-Seine to Captain Mornet [?], Mar. 21, 1912, *ibid.*; also see the unpub. ms. by Lt. de Vaisseau Marie Bernard Touvet, "Guerre de 1914–18: la 2me

The reasons for this second lengthy interruption can only be conjectured, especially since Delcassé quickly accepted and pursued a Russian proposal in February for naval talks. The fall of the Caillaux government, the efforts to pass the Naval Law, and Auvert's replacement by Aubert in early February naturally caused some confusion in the Naval Ministry, which may have delayed the talks. Or perhaps the French were unsure about the quality of the Royal Navy; the repeated and widespread talk in London about the Admiralty's dismal performance in 1911 did not exactly inspire confidence. Yet, by late March, de Saint-Seine's reports could leave little doubt that the Admiralty under Churchill was fully prepared for all emergencies.[64] On their side the British, concerned with their own budgetary, building, and distribution problems, had little time to devote to serious staff talks. Moreover, these issues had to be settled before anything meaningful could be done on a joint basis. Finally, the entente governments may have preferred to wait until they knew the exact details and ramifications of the forthcoming German naval law, confident that the "convention" of the previous year would be adequate in the meantime. In any case, the conversations were not resumed until midsummer.

Although the naval talks of 1911 were infrequent and inexhaustive, they did apportion the broad strategic responsibilities of the two navies: British ships would guard the North Sea and upper Channel, French vessels the Mediterranean and lower Channel. But these arrangements suffered from two major weaknesses. There was nothing in writing, no naval equivalent to the Wilson-Dubail accord of July 20, 1911. More important, while the Cabinet knew of the past naval exchanges, it had not, under the terms of Asquith's restrictions, given its approval to any resumption of talks.

All this was soon to change, thanks to the demands of the Anglo-German naval race. The failure of the Haldane mission to ease naval competition forced the Cabinet to reconsider Britain's naval situation. In this review the naval conversations received close Cabinet scrutiny and, finally, approval. The French, alarmed by the Berlin-London negotiations, renewed their interest in closer entente naval relations. Because the Anglo-German negotiations in early 1912 acted as a catalyst to the staff talks, they have a special place in the history of the Anglo-French entente.

---

escadre légère," pp. 14–17 (part of a series prepared for the French Naval Staff by the Service Historique de la Marine in the early 1930's; a complete set is in Archives Marine).

64. On criticism of the Admiralty see, e.g., Admiral Sir E. R. Fremantle, "The Moroccan Crisis and Churchill's Clean Sweep," *United Service Magazine*, 41 (January 1912), 341–356; Lt. Alfred C. Dewar, "Naval Strategy and the Crisis of 1911," *ibid.* (March 1912), 583–589; Aubert to de Saint-Seine, Mar. 12, 1912, Archives Marine, BB7 100; de Saint-Seine to Aubert, Mar. 26, 1912, *ibid.*

10 | The Haldane Mission, 1912

The Agadir crisis and its aftermath alienated British radicals from the foreign policy of Sir Edward Grey. Inside the Cabinet, Morley, Loreburn, Harcourt, and eventually McKenna were driven to protest that the entente was not an alliance and that staff talks were irregular and dangerous. In the ensuing Cabinet crisis of late 1911 Asquith gave his radical colleagues assurances that the conversations would thereafter be closely controlled. Outside the government, the disclosures about British military preparations and the secret clauses of the 1904 entente, buttressed by reports of Russian intervention in Persia, triggered comparable radical assaults upon Liberal foreign policy. Although the Asquith-Grey pronouncements of late November eased some of the pressures upon the Liberal government, general public somnolence and indifference did not return. Complaints, accusations, denunciations, and severe press criticism of Grey's policy continued. As 1912 began, both the conduct and the substance of British diplomacy were under steady attack.

The so-called "New Radicalism" in particular distrusted the Foreign Office as an institution and as an elite. These radicals, including E. D. Morel and Arthur Ponsonby, charged the "British diplomatic machine" with having deliberately escalated the recent Franco-German quarrel over Morocco into an Anglo-German squabble. They feared that Grey's surreptitious advisers might force Britain to war over "a slice of Equatorial African forest, sparsely populated by primitive races and by a handful of fever-stricken white officials and rubber exploiters." Nor did the dissidents like the Foreign Office's penchant for secret diplomacy and for infrequent public explanations of British foreign policy. The critics demanded more, and continuous, information about the formation of policy, calling for the creation of a parliamentary commission on foreign affairs. And the radicals condemned Grey's attitude of "accept-my-policy-or-I-resign" as unbecoming a "modern democratic commonwealth." [1]

The radicals, joined occasionally by some Conservative supporters of Persian integrity, demanded a re-examination of the fundamental assumptions of British foreign policy. They assailed Grey's toleration of Russian efforts to thwart reform in Persia; they disliked Britain's complacent smugness; and they demanded an improvement in Anglo-German relations. Britain's obsession with naval power and the close ties with France, they asserted, naturally disturbed Berlin. Urging immediate naval negotiations with Germany, they also wanted a renewal of discussions about colonial matters and a cessation of talk about sending British troops to the Continent. In January the Manchester Liberal Federation called upon the Foreign Secretary to explain to the French that Britain was "under no obligation either of treaty or of honour to support French diplomacy in any future controversy, by the weight of the armed forces of this country, or by any such diplomatic action as might imply such assistance in the last resort." Britain should be free "to take such action as it may think that the circumstances of the occasion demand when any difficulty arises." [2] And Lord Rosebery told a Glasgow audience on January 13 that "no Glasgow merchant would do what we do in foreign affairs—that is, to engage in vast and unknown liabilities and affix his signature to them without knowing their nature and extent." [3] In short, the "trouble makers," to use A. J. P. Taylor's apt

1. E. D. Morel, "The True Story of the Moroccan Negotiations," *Nineteenth Century and After*, 71 (February 1912), 248; see also "Our Foreign Policy and its Reform," *Contemporary Review*, 10 (April 1912), 466–474; S. J. Low, "The Foreign Office Autocracy," *Fortnightly Review*, 91 (January 1912), 1–10; Conwell-Evans, *Foreign Policy from a Back Bench*, 68–77; Hale, *Publicity and Diplomacy*, 415–419; Taylor, *The Trouble Makers*, 118–127; John Murray, "Grey and His Critics," *Power, Public Opinion and Diplomacy*, ed. Lillian P. Wallace and William C. Askew (Durham, N.C., 1959), 140–171.
2. Jan. 12, 1912, quoted in Hammond, *C. P. Scott*, 164–165.
3. Quoted in the *Manchester Guardian*, Jan. 14, 1912; also see Sir F. C. Lascelles, "Thoughts on the Anglo-German Problem," *Contemporary Review*, 101 (January 1912), 1–9.

label, and their transient allies wanted nothing less than the abandonment, or at least the erosion, of the Triple Entente as the cornerstone of British diplomacy.

Grey was not without defenders, most of whom were in the Opposition party. The Conservative *Spectator*, for example, accused (January 27) the radicals of flagrant inconsistency, seeking "to court a European war in causes so sacred as the maintenance of anarchy in Persia and the restoration of Chinese power in Mongolia" on the one hand, demanding disarmament and a small army on the other. They wanted a foreign policy which combined "the maximum of interference and the minimum of friendship." The sudden radical alarm, the *Spectator* continued, came from "the discovery that in the successive crises of last year the liberal government meant business. So long as the *Triple Entente* could be represented as merely a piece of meaningless courtesy it might be tolerated. When it proved to be founded on common interests and their protection by common action it became at once matter for anathema." The Foreign Secretary, the journal noted, was to be congratulated on his moderation and restraint, on his preference for "the friendship of our allies and the maintenance of peace in Europe to the cheap praises of the organs which now declare that, in order to be free of Sir Edward Grey, they would put up with a Unionist Government." The Unionist M.P. Captain C. S. Goldman, writing in the *Nineteenth Century*, called for one more attempt at an Anglo-German naval agreement and, failing that, consideration of an open alliance with France and Russia. D. C. Lathbury insisted a month later in the same magazine on the continuation of the Triple Entente as the only sure way of preserving the peace.[4]

This public debate about the direction and tone of British diplomacy was soon paralleled by renewed debate within the Asquith Cabinet. Angered and at the same time frustrated by the events of late 1911, the radical ministers were a disgruntled group. McKenna was now solidly "anti-alliance," and Lord Loreburn found increasing support in January for his strictures of Grey's "extravagant championship of France"; moreover, the Lord Chancellor planned to revive the entire issue of staff talks, holding that "if we are to continue the present policy we'll need to send not 150,000 men but at least ½ million to be any good." If the Cabinet rejected his views, he planned to resign.[5] The radicals' capacity for troublemaking was also enhanced by the likely prospect that a supplementary German naval law (*Novelle*) was in the offing. Any German increase would almost certainly prompt another Cabinet crisis over naval estimates.

4. Also see the *Spectator*, Feb. 10, 17, 1912; C. S. Goldman, "Eleven Years of Foreign Policy," *Nineteenth Century and After*, 71 (February 1912), 217–232; D. C. Lathbury, "English Radicals and Foreign Politics," *ibid.* (March 1912), 589–598.

5. Memos, Dec. 2, 1911, Jan. 7, 22, 1912, C. P. Scott Papers, British Museum, Add. MSS, 50901.

Edward Grey possessed few illusions about the fragility of his détente with his radical colleagues. Politically he recognized that the radicals had to be either placated or short-circuited. Nor was he personally unsympathetic to some of their complaints; for in early 1912 he resumed the position he had adopted just after Agadir, that is, refusal to adhere to a totally inflexible posture on British policy.[6] The Foreign Secretary genuinely desired improved relations with Germany, but not at the expense of the entente; he wanted a reduction in the naval race, but with Britain's superiority preserved; he hoped for peace and the blessings of peace, but not peace and accommodation at any price. In early 1912 Grey was prepared to pursue these somewhat mutually exclusive aims. His willingness to negotiate took practical form just at the turn of the year: he sanctioned the resumption of the long-suspended Anglo-German talks on the exchange of naval information and indicated a readiness to discuss colonial issues with Berlin.[7]

Grey politically and personally favored an improvement in Anglo-German relations. His inclinations were not shared by his principal advisers, Sir Arthur Nicolson and Sir Eyre Crowe. The Senior Clerk's opposition took its usual form: a long and somewhat vitriolic memorandum. In it Crowe accused Caillaux of conspiring with the Germans over Morocco and asserted that Berlin had deliberately exploited Caillaux in an attempt to wean France from the entente. Britain, Crowe argued with more emotion than analysis, should not now over-react to the French Premier's presumed treachery. London should not turn to Germany simply out of spite for France. Instead, Britain should adopt for the moment an attitude of dignified reserve. Nicolson's resistance to a détente with Berlin was less open, more subtle, and equally implacable: charging that the international financiers were out to disrupt the Triple Entente, he advocated that no changes be made in British policy.[8]

This, then, was the situation at the beginning of 1912. Radicals were demanding improved Anglo-German relations. Radical ministers remained embittered about the staff talks. Grey and Winston Churchill at the Admiralty were anxious to avert another round of naval increases.[9] On the other hand, some within the "permanent government," that is, the professional advisers at the Foreign Office and elsewhere, were not disposed to facilitate or to encourage a settlement with Berlin. It was in this confusing, overheated atmosphere that the Haldane mission originated.

6. Grey, Twenty-five Years, I, 240–243; Taylor, The Trouble Makers, 127.
7. Grey to Goschen, Dec. 20, 1911, Jan. 2, 17, 1912, B.D., VI, nos. 480, 482, 487; Grey to Goschen, Dec. 29, 1911, Grey Papers, F.O. 800/62.
8. Memo by Crowe, Jan. 14, 1912, B.D., VII, pp. 821–826; Nicolson to Hardinge, Feb. 1, 1912, Nicolson Papers, vol. I/1912.
9. On Churchill's attitude, see his memo, Dec. 8, 1911, Adm. 116/940b, and The World Crisis, I, 95–96.

Preliminary maneuvers for the resumption of Anglo-German naval negotiations started in early January. Albert Ballin, managing director of the Hamburg-American Line, privately and on his own initiative broached the subject with Sir Ernest Cassel, a German-born internationál financier and naturalized British citizen. Cassel, who enjoyed entrée into the court circles of both countries, was a friend and financial adviser to Winston Churchill.[10] Initial soundings soon revealed a mutual desire by the civilian leadership for negotiations; Chancellor Bethmann Hollweg no less than Grey wanted to check spiraling naval expenditures. From the start, however, Grey, Churchill, and Lloyd George demanded German acceptance of a memo recognizing British naval supremacy and pledging no further German naval increases. In return for these concessions London offered to consider Germany's colonial ambitions and the possibility of "reciprocal assurances" against future aggressive designs or combinations. The Kaiser and Bethmann accepted these conditions, contingent upon British recognition of the Novelle as an integral part of the existing German naval program.[11]

On January 30 Cassel brought this German response to London, along with a sketch of the proposed new naval law. Upon close examination the Admiralty discovered that the Novelle called for three additional dreadnoughts in six years, a new third squadron, and substantial personnel increases. The implications for British naval policy were unmistakable. There would have to be immediate increases in naval construction and naval personnel; furthermore, British battleships would have to be withdrawn from the Mediterranean, which in turn would cause dependence upon France. And all of this would cost money: Churchill's first estimate was £3,000,000.[12]

On Friday, February 2, the entire Cabinet was informed about the new information from Berlin. The unhappy prospect of another naval crisis strengthened the sentiment for new naval negotiations. The radical desire for improved Anglo-German relations coalesced with the Admiralty's dislike of possible things to come. As a result, the Cabinet selected Lord Haldane to go to Berlin. He was to "feel the way in the direction of a more definite understanding," pointing out to the German government "the bad effect which would be produced on public opinion in both countries by a fresh development of naval rivalry, and would at the same time—if the question of naval competition can be got out of the way—indicate . . . readiness to deal in a cordial and gen-

10. Lamar Cecil, Albert Ballin: Business and Politics in Imperial Germany, 1888–1918 (Princeton, 1967), 181–183; Churchill, Young Statesman, 541–543.

11. The most recent accounts of these preliminaries and the subsequent mission are Marder, Road to War, 272–287, and Cecil, Ballin, 180–197; see also Walther Hubatsch, Die Ara Tirpitz: Studien zur deutschen Marinepolitik, 1890–1918 (Göttingen, 1955), 95–112.

12. Churchill to Grey, Jan. 31, 1912, quoted in Churchill, The World Crisis, I, 96–98; Marder, Road to War, 276.

erous spirit with German aspirations and interests." After Bethmann had reiterated his interest in negotiations, the Cabinet on February 6 gave final approval to Haldane's departure.[13] The next day this erstwhile barrister secretly left for Berlin, only to be recognized on the Channel steamer by a newspaper reporter. Instantly rumors spread about new Anglo-German negotiations.

Upon arrival in Berlin Lord Haldane had a series of frank, blunt discussions with the Kaiser, Bethmann, and Admiral von Tirpitz. Topics ranged from possible colonial exchanges to the limitation of naval increases. On the latter issue the minister found his task made more difficult by one of his colleagues at home: on February 9, with Haldane in Berlin, Churchill assured a cheering audience in Glasgow that Britain was determined to maintain its naval superiority and added, rather gratuitously, that the German Navy was a "luxury." These provocative comments not only angered the radical ministers, they placed Bethmann in a difficult position vis-à-vis Tirpitz. The Chancellor refused to drop the Novelle. The most he could offer was a slowdown in naval construction and this on the condition that Britain accept a formula which promised benevolent neutrality in a continental war. Such a bargain, Haldane made clear, was out of the question; he suggested instead that Britain simply promise not to join in any unprovoked attack upon Germany. Although Bethmann was unimpressed with the proposal, he agreed nonetheless to continue the talks. In addition he handed the British War Minister a confidential copy of the proposed German naval law. On February 11 Haldane, having finished his reconnaissance mission, returned to London.[14]

The Admiralty staff immediately began a minute evaluation of the Novelle brought back by Haldane. When the experts had finished, Churchill informed the Cabinet on February 14 that the German measure was far worse than the earlier information had suggested. The additional dreadnoughts, personnel, and squadron were threats in themselves; but the biggest danger, he pointed out, came from the thirty-three percent increase in German battleships in full commission, from eighteen to twenty-five. To counter this Britain would, with twenty-two battleships in full commission at home and at Gibraltar, have to rearrange its fleets—the remaining six battleships in the Mediterranean would have to be withdrawn. Moreover, in the next five years the German expansion would cost Britain approximately £14,295,000. This enormous amount alone, Asquith told the King on February 21, negated the chances for a viable political agreement with Germany. Yet, the Cabinet, still hoping for a modification of the Novelle, instructed Grey

13. Asquith to George V, Feb. 3, 7, 1912, Asquith Papers, box 6.
14. Haldane's account (drafted Feb. 10, 1912) is the single best source for what transpired in Berlin; B.D., VI, no. 506. Compare memo by Bethmann, Feb. 12, 1912, G.P., XXXI, no. 11362. On the Glasgow speech, see Churchill, Young Statesman, 544–546.

and Haldane to continue informal conversation's with Ambassador Metternich.[15] The talks were unproductive, and by the end of February the discussions were stalled.

The renewal of Anglo-German negotiations disturbed the ever-sensitive French. At the outset Grey had taken elaborate precautions to reassure Paris of his loyalty to the entente, promising that Paul Cambon would be apprised of any significant developments.[16] The press furor over Haldane's trip, however, made these private assurances seem rather inadequate. No one felt this more acutely than the proud, sensitive, often haughty Lorrainer now become French Premier, Raymond Poincaré. Determined to keep the entente intact (and if possible to expand it), this prosperous-looking lawyer speculated on how to offset the mounting public comment about Haldane's trip. At length he hit upon the idea of seeking Grey's approval for a press release saying one of two things: either that the French were privy to Haldane's journey, or that Henry Wilson had just visited the French Ministry of War. Paul Cambon, aghast at the latter suggestion, cabled Paris on February 9 that the Times had made it evident that the French had known in advance of Haldane's trip. "There is no need in my opinion," he concluded, "of speaking of the visit of General Wilson." Accepting his ambassador's assessment, Poincaré dropped, for the moment, the idea of a public statement.[17]

Other developments also softened Poincaré's anxieties about the entente. On February 9 Haldane paid a special visit to the French Embassy in Berlin, after which he and Jules Cambon drafted a dispatch saying that the Anglo-German talks aimed only for a détente, not for an entente. A few days later Grey further assuaged French fears by recounting to Cambon how strongly Haldane had defended Britain's military and naval preparations during 1911. The Germans, the Foreign Secretary emphasized, were warned that the measures would have allowed Britain "to go to the assistance of France if Germany had made an aggressive or unprovoked attack upon her: and Lord Haldane had explained that we could not tie our hands with regard to such an event. The difficulty was to find a formula that would express our attitude." Nicolson, at the same time, privately assured the ambassador that there was no chance of an Anglo-German accord.[18]

These repeated pledges about the entente soothed the nerves of the French policy-makers. But the secret assurances did not of course silence

15. Memo by Churchill, Feb. 14, 1912, Asquith Papers, box 106; Asquith to George V, Feb. 15, 21, 1912, ibid., box 6.
16. Grey to Bertie, Feb. 3, 1912, Cab. 37/109/12; P. Cambon to Poincaré (tel.), Feb. 7, 1912, D.D.F., 3rd ser., I, no. 628; Grey to Bertie, Feb. 7, 1912, B.D., VI, no. 498. The Russians were also informed of the negotiations with Berlin.
17. Poincaré to P. Cambon (tel.), Feb. 9, 1912, D.D.F., 3rd ser., II, no. 9; P. Cambon to Poincaré (tel.), Feb. 9, 1912, ibid., no. 15.
18. Grey to Bertie, Feb. 13, 1912, B.D., VI, no. 514; P. Cambon to Poincaré (tel.), Feb. 13, 1912, D.D.F., 3rd ser., II, no. 30.

French press comments about Anglo-German relations. Gabriel Hano-
taux, a former Foreign Minister, and other conservative writers waged a
vicious campaign against the entente. For them the Haldane episode
was simply another example of the treachery of "perfidious Albion." The
British intended to desert France and to abandon to Germany their
rights to the Portuguese colonies; the entente was bankrupt; France
must trust its fortunes to Russian help.[19] Disturbed by these attacks,
Poincaré prepared a rebuttal praising the entente's value to France and
sent it, as customary, to London for clearance. Grey, though appreciative
of Poincaré's domestic political needs, objected to one phrase which
implied joint cooperation in the maintenance of the European equilibrium. After considering a more innocuous phrase, he abandoned
Poincaré's statement altogether and drafted an entirely new one that
would ease French fears without saying too much. With uncharacteristic
humility, the French Premier accepted the substitute. On March 15,
using Grey's guarded rhetoric, Poincaré told the Chamber of Deputies
that France "had the assurance that if England desired to maintain
friendly relations with all the powers, there was nothing and there would
be nothing in its talks with another government which would weaken
the nature or hurt the cordial relations, the mutual understanding, and
confidence which are established between France and England (loud
applause)." [20]

The progress, meanwhile, of Anglo-German talks in early March could
give the French little cause for alarm. Berlin adamantly refused to
make any alteration in the *Novelle* without a neutrality pledge from the
British. Even the proverbially optimistic Haldane was convinced by
March 8 that Tirpitz and the German admirals had torpedoed Bethmann's attempt to negotiate.[21]

Then four days later, quite unexpectedly, Metternich sought out Haldane and announced that the naval law would be considerably amended
if Britain would accept a suitable political formula. Grey, still sensitive
to the need for a détente with Germany, readily embraced Metternich's
overture. On March 13 he drafted a formula which stated:

> England will make no unprovoked attack upon Germany and pur-
> sue no aggressive policy towards her.

19. On this see P. Cambon to J. Cambon, Feb. 27, 1912, *Cambon: correspondance*, III, 14–15, and Commandant de Thomasson, "Les causes et les conditions
d'un rapprochement anglo-allemand," *Questions diplomatiques et coloniales*, 33
(Mar. 1, 1912), 257–266.
20. Poincaré to P. Cambon (tel.), Feb. 26, 1912, *D.D.F.*, 3rd ser., II, no. 105;
P. Cambon to Poincaré (tel.), Feb. 28, 1912, *ibid.*, no. 119; see also Gooch, *Before the War: Studies in Diplomacy*, II, 153–155.
21. Memo communicated by Metternich, Mar. 6, 1912, *B.D.*, VI, no. 529; Grey
to Goschen, Mar. 6, 1912, *ibid.*, no. 530; memo by Churchill, "Admiralty Memorandum on New German Naval Law," Mar. 9, 1912, Cab. 37/110/43; Haldane to
E. Haldane, Mar. 8, 1912, Haldane Papers, 6011.

Aggression upon Germany is not the subject and forms no part of any Treaty understanding or combination to which England is now a party nor will she become a party to anything that has such an object.[22]

After clearing this formula with the Cabinet, the Foreign Secretary handed it to the German ambassador the next day. The following day (March 15) Cambon received a copy.

London's revived hopes for an agreement were short-lived. Ambassador Metternich, after having briefly glanced at Grey's proposal on March 14, deemed it unacceptable because there was no mention of British neutrality if Germany were attacked. The next day the ambassador upped his objections, insisting that it would take a promise of unconditional neutrality to bring any reduction in the German naval program. Against this demand Grey stood firm. Britain, he reminded Metternich, must keep its hands free with regard to France; it could not allow the Third Republic to be crushed. And he added, for good measure, that all "the military conversations or preparations of which he [Metternich] might have heard had meant simply that, improbable as such a contingency might be, we had considered what we should do if it arose and we decided to take action."[23] Thus a promise of unconditional neutrality was impossible: the ententes with France and Russia simply could not be jeopardized for a limited and perhaps transitory naval accord. All Grey would concede was an additional phrase expressing a desire for peace and promising that Britain would not "join" in any unprovoked attack upon Germany. On March 19 Metternich announced the Kaiser's rejection of the revised formula; Wilhelm II demanded an absolute neutrality clause as the sine qua non of any naval agreement, and this stipulation Grey again refused.[24]

In the meantime the diminishing chances for naval limitations received another jarring blow. The First Lord presented the 1912 naval estimates to the House of Commons on March 18. In his peroration Churchill warned that "circumstances" might necessitate new increases in shipbuilding; to avoid any misunderstanding, in the future the Admiralty would maintain a sixty percent margin over the dreadnoughts authorized by the 1908 German Naval Law, and any increases above that law would be met on a two-to-one basis.[25] This unambiguous dec-

22. Grey to Goschen, Mar. 14, 1912, B.D., VI, no. 537; Asquith to George V, Mar. 14, 1912, Asquith Papers, box 6.
23. Grey to Goschen, Mar. 15, 1912, B.D., VI, no. 539; Metternich to Grey, Mar. 14, 1912, ibid., no. 538; Bethmann to Wilhelm II, Mar. 15, 1912, G.P., XXXI, no. 11401.
24. Grey to Goschen, Mar. 16, 19, 1912, B.D., VI, nos. 544, 545; Cassel to Haldane, Mar. 17, 1912, Haldane Papers, 5909. Haldane now thought "nothing but an alliance" would prevent the Novelle; Haldane to E. Haldane, Mar. 18, 1912, ibid., 6011.
25. Parliamentary Debates: Commons, 5th ser., 35 (Mar. 18, 1912), 1549–1574; Churchill, The World Crisis, I, 110–111.

laration about future British naval strength, followed by Berlin's rejection of the March 14 formula and the subsequent publication of the *Novelle*, marked the end of any real possibility for an Anglo-German naval accord.

Nevertheless, the negotiations sputtered on for another month, rekindling French and Foreign Office apprehensions about the Entente Cordiale. On March 22 Sir Edward Grey notified Paul Cambon that the naval talks were suspended. Greatly relieved, the ambassador felt that "thus have vanished the hopes or the fears that little informed minds have placed upon the visit of Lord Haldane to Berlin." Everything would rapidly return to normal.[26]

Cambon's British counterpart in Paris was considerably less sanguine about the situation. On March 27 Sir Francis Bertie made a special trip to the Quai d'Orsay. Announcing that he came not as the ambassador but rather as a friend, he warned Poincaré that the Anglo-German talks were perhaps not finished: in fact, Berlin was still pressing for a neutrality agreement and Grey was being " 'very weak.' " He, Bertie complained, could not understand the Foreign Secretary's intentions. Any agreement that even mentioned neutrality would endanger the entente; with such a formula how would Britain react if Germany provoked France into committing the initial aggression? " 'If you,' " implored the ambassador, " 'speak to London with a little firmness, they will hesitate to commit the fault which I dread.' "[27] With this unusual maneuver Bertie embarked upon a personal campaign to frustrate the policy of his own government. Such a venture, it will be remembered, was nothing new for the ambassador, who, during the Agadir crisis, had on several occasions failed to inform—or rather had misinformed—the French government about Grey's views on a Moroccan port.[28] But this time Bertie carried his machinations a step further, boldly inviting the French Premier to subvert the policy of the Liberal government.

Poincaré quickly acted on Bertie's proposition. The next day he instructed Cambon to see Sir Edward Grey "without delay" and to stress French opposition to *any* formula which pledged British neutrality in a Franco-German struggle. Cambon was to emphasize France's loyalty to the entente and to observe that while "*no written convention bound the reciprocal goodwills of the two governments*, we [France] had consented to our General Staff entering into secret conversations with the English General Staff, and thus informing them of the most important

26. P. Cambon to Poincaré (tel.), Mar. 22, 1912, *D.D.F.*, 3rd ser., II, no. 244; Nicolson to Grey, Mar. 22, 1912, Nicolson Papers, vol. II/1912; Grey to Bertie, Mar. 22, 1912, *B.D.*, VI, no. 550.

27. Memo by Poincaré, Mar. 27, 1912, *D.D.F.*, 3rd ser., II, no. 266; Poincaré, *Au service de la France*, I, 170–172; cf. Bertie to Nicolson, Mar. 28, 1912, *B.D.*, VI, no. 556. Also see Gooch, *Before the War: Studies in Diplomacy*, II, 155–162.

28. In February 1912 Bertie had also intervened with George V against the naval talks; see memo by Bertie, Feb. 17, 1912, Bertie Papers, F.O. 800/187.

arrangements of our strategic plans." All France asked was that Britain not restrict its freedom of action by a neutrality formula.[29] For Poincaré's purposes at least, the military conversations, originally a product of strategic planning and German pressure, were now the fabric that bound the entente together. Military secrets, not necessarily political interests, were the new common denominator of Anglo-French relations.

Poincaré's instructions came none too soon. For Grey on March 29 informed Paul Cambon that the Cabinet had resolved to make one last attempt for an agreement with Berlin. Since the *Novelle* had not yet been acted upon, some ministers still thought that a political-naval accord might be reached. The Germans were therefore being asked to "indicate what it is they want which is not covered by the terms of that formula [of March 14]." Scarcely able to control his temper, Cambon testily asked what Berlin meant by neutrality. What, for instance, would Britain do if "Germany concentrated troops upon Aix-la-Chapelle with the obvious intention of entering Belgium" and France was "compelled to take the initiative." Germany would then appear the victim and Britain would have to stand aside. Grey, anxious to smooth ruffled feelings, promised that the formula would not tie British hands. And he expressed doubts that the Cabinet would in any case expand the original formula. Somewhat reassured, Cambon made no mention, despite Poincaré's suggestion, of the military conversations.[30]

Bertie and his like-minded friends at the Foreign Office, meanwhile, worked to supplement French pressure. The ambassador wrote both Grey and Nicolson, sharply castigating Liberal efforts to reach a neutrality agreement with Berlin. "We ought," he argued, "to have our hands entirely free so that if war come [sic] about we can there and then decide whether it is to our interests to take part in it, and when, and not be hampered by previous neutrality promises. Our aid to France might be too late unless forthcoming at the outbreak of the war, and her ill-fate would be ours later on." Anglo-German negotiations, he stressed, fostered French apprehensions about the strength of pro-German sentiment in "certain circles in England." Furthermore, any accord with Germany would cause trouble between France and Britain, and "would be observed by Germany only in so far and so long as it might suit her interests and convenience." Such an arrangement would therefore be "detrimental to the interests of France and dangerous to the peace of Europe." [31]

29. Poincaré to P. Cambon, Mar. 28, 1912, D.D.F., 3rd ser., II, no. 269 (italics in original).
30. Grey to Bertie, Mar. 29, 1912, B.D., VI, nos. 558 (tel.), 559; P. Cambon to Poincaré (tel.), Mar. 29, 1912, D.D.F., 3rd ser., II, no. 271; Poincaré to P. Cambon (tel.), Mar. 30, 1912, *ibid.*, no. 276. See also Asquith to George V, Mar. 30, 1912, Asquith Papers, box 6.
31. Bertie to Nicolson, Apr. 1, 1912, B.D., VI, no. 563 (Grey, Asquith, and the King saw this letter); Bertie to Grey, Apr. 3, 1912, *ibid.*, no. 564.

These sentiments were shared entirely by Sir Arthur Nicolson. His notes for Grey repeatedly emphasized French uneasiness and alarm about Anglo-German relations. Unless the French were "unequivocally" assured "that we retain our complete liberty of action in any possible eventualities," the Undersecretary feared that French "confidence . . . may wane even to the extent of seriously impairing our relations—and such a result would at once react on our relations with Russia. The ultimate consequences are not pleasant to contemplate." It was time, declared Nicolson, to end the search for formulas, "which are at best dangerous and embarrassing documents, and the signature of which would apparently, in present circumstances, affect our relations with France. . . . So long as Germany cannot rely on our abstention or neutrality, so long will she not be disposed to disturb the peace." [32] Nicolson's arsenal of objections also contained a persuasive strategic argument: a formula would not only hurt the Triple Entente, it would necessarily force Britain "to reconsider entirely the distribution of our naval forces, as we should not, as it apparently is the intention at present, practically leave the care of the Mediterranean to the French Navy." [33] To Nicolson the moral seemed clear and unambiguous: an unfriendly Germany would be less dangerous than an unfriendly France and Russia. Or put another way, any attempted rapprochement with Berlin, however limited, risked placing Great Britain in a state of dangerous isolation.

Grey, unmoved by these arguments, listened politely to the advice of his subordinates and then ignored it. For one thing, he rightly suspected Bertie of indiscretions and possibly connivance with the French. On March 29 he observed in a dispatch to Paris that Bertie and Paul Cambon had apparently discussed the neutrality formula. To conceal his intervention with Poincaré, Bertie responded with an elaborate, and false, explanation of how Cambon had procured his information.[34] More importantly, Grey disagreed with the premises of his subordinates' advice. He rejected their contention that a formula would necessarily hamper Britain's freedom of action. Although he promised that the Cabinet would never accept the word "neutrality" in an agreement, he consistently defended the March 14 formula, insisting that it would impose no restrictions on Britain. And at one point he retorted that it was "not reasonable that tension should be permanently greater between England and Germany than between Germany and France or Germany and Rus-

32. Nicolson to Grey, Apr. 4, 6, 1912, ibid., nos. 566, 567. Crowe was equally hostile to a continuation of the talks; see his minutes on Bertie to Grey, Apr. 3, 1912, ibid., no. 564.
33. Nicolson to Goschen, Apr. 15, 1912, ibid., no. 575. Nicolson also sent Grey a French dispatch from P. Cambon, then on vacation, describing the apprehensions of Fallières and Poincaré about British policy.
34. Grey to Bertie, Mar. 29, 1912, ibid., no. 559; Bertie to Grey, Apr. 3, 1912, ibid., no. 564.

sia." [35] Even in early April, after Asquith was ready to end the talks, Grey was still prepared to seek an agreement on the exchange of naval information.[36]

The Foreign Secretary's apparent willingness for some kind of agreement alarmed Bertie. Undeterred by Grey's earlier reprimand, he continued his campaign to influence British policy through the indirect approach. Once again he solicited French assistance and once again Poincaré agreed.[37] On April 12 the Premier ordered Paul Cambon, who was just returning to London, to express strong objections to any formula or political declaration. Fully alive to the importance of symbols in international politics, Poincaré wanted the ambassador to declare that "a paper of this kind, however weak it might be, will be interpreted in France as a voluntary abandonment of the entire policy followed since 1904." The entente, he observed, was not consecrated by any formal act. Rather it depended "on opinion and on the conversations of our General Staffs. Anything which would upset public sentiment will thus destroy it. England has the same interest as we of maintaining it and she knows with what loyalty we adhere to it." [38] As it turned out these instructions proved unnecessary, for on the same day Arthur Nicolson had notified de Fleuriau, the French chargé, of Bethmann's latest rejection of the British formula.[39] The *Novelle* would be presented unchanged to the Reichstag. The radicals' hope of changing the tone and the direction of British foreign policy was frustrated anew.

Reverberations from the Anglo-German talks had, however, only just begun. The Haldane mission and the subsequent exchanges had been painful reminders to Paris of the delicate nature of the entente relationship. The absence of any written mutual obligations, now that Morocco was settled, particularly disturbed French policy-makers. Concerned lest another round of naval negotiations actually disrupt the entente, Poincaré and Cambon spent much of 1912 searching for a more tangible and less ambiguous relationship with London.

Their first move came within days of the breakdown in the naval parleys. On April 15 Cambon outlined for Sir Arthur Nicolson the continuing apprehension of Raymond Poincaré about what Britain would do in case of war with Germany. The Premier, the ambassador commented, had not found the recent British assurances "sufficiently clear and precise"; or, put more simply, France wanted closer relations with

35. Minute by Grey on Bertie to Grey, Apr. 3, 1912, *ibid.*, no. 564; Grey to Nicolson, Apr. 5, 1912, Nicolson Papers, vol. III/1912.
36. Grey to Bertie (tel.), Apr. 9, 1912, B.D., VI, no. 569; Asquith to Grey, Apr. 10, 1912, *ibid.*, no. 571; Grey to Churchill, Apr. 12, 1912, Grey Papers, F.O. 800/87.
37. "Note de M. Poincaré à M. Paléologue," Apr. 10, 1912, D.D.F., 3rd ser., II, no. 319; Bertie to Grey (tel.), Apr. 10, 1912, B.D., VI, no. 570.
38. Poincaré to P. Cambon, Apr. 11, 1912, D.D.F., 3rd ser., II, no. 329.
39. De Fleuriau to Poincaré (tel.), Apr. 12, 1912, *ibid.*, no. 332.

Britain. To buttress this plea, Cambon reverted to that old and familiar canard: the alleged offer of a British alliance by Lord Lansdowne in 1905. In resurrecting the episode he clearly hoped to shame, or at least to push, the Liberal government into imitating its Conservative predecessor.

Nicolson handled Cambon's appeal brilliantly. First, he made clear his own personal preferences for closer ties with France. Then, having established his own position, he expressed serious doubts about the likelihood of the Liberal government accepting a more intimate relationship. Some within the Cabinet still desired an accommodation with the Germans, and this notion remained popular among the financiers and pacifists. In these circumstances, cautioned Nicolson, any French proposal that looked more or less like an alliance would encounter wide opposition in the government and in the public. "It would be far wiser," he confided, "to leave matters as they were—and not to strain an understanding which was at present generally popular, and did not by itself afford the slightest reason to any other country to resent or demur to it." [40] Nicolson's polite but firm refusal, which Cambon accepted "very well," won plaudits from the politicians. "I entirely approve the language used by Sir A. Nicolson," the Prime Minister minuted on April 18. Grey, on vacation at Fallodon, wrote Nicolson three days later that "you could have taken no other line with Cambon except what you did take." And the Foreign Secretary added that, on returning to London, he would "have to say the same; I shall however impress upon him that although we cannot bind ourselves under all circumstances to go to war with France against Germany, we shall also certainly not bind ourselves to Germany not to assist France." [41]

The opening gambit of the French campaign to reinforce the entente had been gently turned aside. Poincaré and Cambon, while not entirely surprised, were nonetheless disappointed.[42] They would have to be satisfied with the sentimental symbolism represented by the unveiling of statues of Victoria and Edward at Nice and Cannes in mid-April. But the French position was in fact much stronger than either the Premier or the ambassador realized, and the unsuspected strength came, ironically, from that long neglected aspect of Anglo-French relations: naval matters. Intensification of the Anglo-German naval race forced the Admiralty to reconsider its strategic dispositions. Churchill had signaled the results in March when he announced that the Malta-based Mediter-

40. Memo by Nicolson, Apr. 15, 1912, B.D., VI, no. 576; P. Cambon to Poincaré, Apr. 18, 1912, D.D.F., 3rd ser., II, no. 363. Nicolson, who wanted his memo to go no further than the Prime Minister, later admitted that it went "against my grain" to tell Cambon to wait; Nicolson to Goschen, Apr. 23, 1912, Nicolson Papers, vol. III/1912.
41. Asquith minute on Nicolson to Morley, Apr. 16, 1912, B.D., VI, no. 577; Grey to Nicolson, Apr. 21, 1912, ibid., no. 580.
42. Poincaré to P. Cambon, Apr. 30, 1912, D.D.F., 3rd ser., II, no. 396.

ranean fleet would soon be withdrawn to Gibraltar. The division of naval responsibilities envisaged in the Wilson-de Lostende "convention" of August 1911 would now become a reality, and France would have responsibility for entente and therefore British interests in the Mediterranean.

The naval issue, which in early 1912 had threatened the Entente Cordiale because of the Anglo-German negotiations, now presented Paris with an opportunity to tighten its bonds with London. Anglo-French naval relations, hitherto casual and infrequent, offered Paris the lever which its political and military policy had been unable to obtain for seven years. What Morocco had once been to the entente the Mediterranean now became.

11 | The Mediterranean and the Entente, 1912

On January 31, 1912, Winston Churchill warned Sir Edward Grey that a further expansion of German sea power would force him to bring "home the Mediterranean battleships." If this proved necessary, Britain would then have to rely "on France in the Mediterranean, and certainly no exchange of system [the entente] would be possible, even if desired by you." [1] This grim evaluation acquired even greater urgency when Haldane returned from Berlin with a copy of the *Novelle*. Tirpitz' proposed increases in the German fleet, especially in the number of ships in full commission, necessitated immediate and drastic changes in the dispositions of the Royal Navy. Without seeking guidance from the other responsible departments or from the C.I.D., Churchill and his new naval staff began to consider the adjustments necessitated by this disquieting intelligence.

1. Churchill to Grey, Jan. 31, 1912, quoted in Churchill, *The World Crisis*, I, 98; on the Admiralty and the Mediterranean in 1912, see Marder, *Road to War*, 287–308.

On February 2 the Chief of the War Staff, Admiral Troubridge, drafted arguments for and against the withdrawal of the six remaining battleships from the Mediterranean, emphasizing that such a move would reduce British influence upon Rome, prompt complaints from commercial interests, possibly provoke trouble in Egypt, and, above all, be hailed as a success for German policy. But to provide for only the simplest defensive protection against Austrian and Italian vessels would require, he noted, at least twelve British dreadnoughts by 1915. More importantly, Britain *had* to be superior in the North Sea because "the international situation as between Great Britain and Germany and her allies is to all intents and purposes a state of war without present violence." There was no mention in the Admiral's outline of what impact French assistance in the Mediterranean would have upon British dispositions.[2] Nonetheless, reliance upon France remained implicit in any withdrawal and for some of Churchill's confidants it seemed a "good thing." "What on earth is the use of our risking our existence for France," Lord Fisher asked (March 5), "if we get no return. Let the French take care of the Mediterranean, and a hot time they'll have of it with submarines poking about in that lake! We are well out of it."[3] In apparent agreement with this attitude, Churchill in early February ordered the War Staff to draft plans for a partial withdrawal from the Mediterranean.

The results of the Admiralty's unilateral efforts were revealed to the House of Commons on March 18 in Churchill's presentation of the 1912–1913 naval estimates, in the course of which he announced a sweeping reorganization and redistribution of British naval forces. The steady expansion of German naval power left the Admiralty with no choice but to concentrate still more warships in home waters. Britain's main line of defense would now become the First Fleet, composed of four squadrons of eight battleships each and a flagship in full commission. This fleet would be supported by four reserve squadrons of older vessels, divided into the Second and Third Fleets and available within days to reinforce the First Fleet. Three of the squadrons for the new First Fleet would come from the former Home and Atlantic Fleets and would operate from British ports. The fourth, Churchill indicated, would "be formed from the battleships now stationed in the Mediterranean, which will step into the place of the Atlantic Fleet and be based on Gibraltar instead of on Malta." From Gibraltar the squadron would

2. Memo by Troubridge, Feb. 2, 1912, Adm. 116/3099; memo by Churchill, Feb. 1, 1912, *ibid.* Also see Churchill's memo of Feb. 15, 1912, *ibid.*, and his Cabinet paper, "The Mediterranean Fleet," Mar. 15, 1912, Cab. 37/105/27.
3. Fisher to Churchill, Mar. 5, 1912, Marder, *Fear God and Dread Nought*, II, 437; on the Churchill-Fisher relationship during early 1912, see Churchill, *Young Statesman*, 564–569. In November 1911 Prince Louis of Battenberg had suggested that the six battleships could be withdrawn; see Battenberg to Churchill, Nov. 20, 1911, quoted in Admiral Mark Kerr, *Prince Louis of Battenberg: Admiral of the Fleet* (London, 1934), 233–234.

be available for immediate deployment with the First Fleet or for operations in the Mediterranean; but its movements, the First Lord conceded, would be regulated "by the main situation," meaning of course a naval war against Germany. In blunt terms, Britain no longer possessed adequate naval superiority to meet the German threat and simultaneously station a battleship squadron in the Mediterranean: in the future, British interests in that sea would be safeguarded by a cruiser squadron located at Malta.[4]

Surprisingly, Churchill's plan to withdraw the battleships from the Mediterranean sparked no immediate public uproar in either Britain or France. During the naval debates several speakers challenged the wisdom of the Mediterranean shifts, but the First Lord casually brushed aside their doubts with a blanket assurance that British interests would be safeguarded. Within the Asquith government proper there were no prompt demands for a review of British naval strategy. The prolongation of Anglo-German naval negotiations monopolized the attention of many within the Cabinet; there was, simply, little time left for the harassed policy-makers to reflect about broader strategic questions. Moreover, so long as the possibility of a naval agreement remained, the new fleet arrangements might prove unnecessary. The British press, meanwhile, was preoccupied with the new Home Rule bill and then with the *Titanic* tragedy. Even Colonel Repington, the sharp-eyed military correspondent of the *Times*, devoted only passing attention to the proposed fleet redistribution.[5]

Nor did the French readily grasp the full implications of Churchill's announcement. Paul Cambon, always sensitive to the slightest shift or imagined shift in British policy, foresaw no renunciation of Britain's political interests in the Mediterranean.[6] In Paris the ebullient Premier remained far too distraught by the continuation of Anglo-German naval talks to examine closely the ramifications of the Admiralty's new strategy. In the French press the steady Italian gains in the Italo-Turkish war, along with the *Titanic* story, filled editorial and news columns.

The collapse of Anglo-German negotiations in mid-April meant, among other things, that the Asquith government could no longer postpone a thorough evaluation of Britain's overall strategic situation. During the next three months British policy-makers argued constantly about the deployment of British sea power and the possible need for French help in the Mediterranean. After mid-May their work was complicated by Poincaré's realization that Britain's naval weakness in the Mediter-

4. *Parliamentary Debates: Commons*, 5th ser., 35 (Mar. 18, 1912), 1564. On Mar. 29, the Admiralty issued a circular letter on reorganization of its commands with May 1, 1912, the effective date; Marder, *Road to War*, 287–288.

5. See, e.g., the *Times*, Apr. 10, 1912. For a hostile view, somewhat later, see Admiral Sir E. R. Fremantle, "The Navy Estimates," *United Service Magazine*, 45 (May 1912), 109–124.

6. Cambon to Poincaré, Mar. 20, 1912, D.D.F., 3rd ser., II, no. 232.

ranean not only strengthened the French case for naval conversations, but also provided a perfect means to tighten the entente.

Churchill provided the initial impetus for a review of Britain's Mediterranean policy. In late April he persuaded Asquith to schedule a preliminary meeting of the Committee of Imperial Defence at Malta during their forthcoming inspection tour of the Mediterranean. Aided by Lord Kitchener, who could come from Cairo, Churchill believed they could have a useful discussion of "local matters." And, given the Prime Minister's proclivity for procrastination, there were "great advantages," Churchill noted to Hankey, in getting his "attention concentrated on the whole subject during a time when he will have full leisure from other things." [7] The First Lord's overture was successful; on April 29, just two days before the fleet shifts went into effect, Asquith instructed the C.I.D. "to consider the effects of the new naval dispositions on the strategic situation in the Mediterranean and elsewhere." The Committee was to examine the defense of Malta and Egypt, the protection of the Mediterranean trade routes, and "the degree of reliance to be placed on the co-operation of the French fleet." [8] This sweeping mandate to review the naval dispositions brought the Mediterranean issues into sharper focus.

The C.I.D.'s involvement in the policy process quickly placed Churchill and the Sea Lords (almost certainly to their surprise) on the defensive. They now found themselves forced to explain their earlier decisions. Churchill's principal defense was that the new arrangement provided the only logical solution to the German danger. The Mediterranean question had "been settled long ago by the brute force of facts. We cannot possibly hold the Mediterranean or guarantee any of our interests there until we have obtained a decision in the North Sea." British war plans for the last five years had envisaged the abandonment of the Mediterranean "as the first step consequent on a war with Germany & all we are doing is to make peace dispositions wh approximate to war necessities. It wd be vy foolish," he told Haldane on May 6, "to lose England in safeguarding Egypt." With Haldane the First Lord could employ another argument as well: "Considering you propose to send the whole Br Army abroad, you ought to help me to keep the whole Br Navy at home." [9]

As a second line of defense, Churchill and his advisers denied that the shifts would jeopardize Britain's political interests in the Mediterranean. They insisted that the battleship squadron at Gibraltar and the new cruiser squadron at Malta, along with assorted destroyers and submarines, would provide more than adequate protection. Yet, candor forced the Sea Lords

7. Churchill to Hankey, Apr. 25, 1912, Adm. 116/3099.
8. Asquith's instructions are in Hankey to Grey, Apr. 30, 1912, B.D., X, pt. 2, no. 381.
9. Churchill to Haldane, May 6, 1912, Haldane Papers, 5909; also quoted in Churchill, *Young Statesman*, 570.

and Churchill to admit their preference for the construction of a new battleship squadron for the Mediterranean. An Admiralty memo spelled it out quite clearly: "Ten more British dreadnoughts laid down in 1912–13 (or four, together with the purchase of the six battleships building or projected in British yards for foreign powers) would make the British position secure in both home waters and the Mediterranean from 1915 onwards without extraneous help." [10] The Navy's attitude toward appropriations for more dreadnoughts, Churchill wryly observed to Haldane, would be "that of a cat to a nice fresh dish of cream." But neither the First Lord nor his Staff harbored any illusions about receiving the additional three or four million pounds necessary to maintain a two-power standard in the Mediterranean and a sixty percent margin against Germany.

There remained the option of dependence upon France as a way to supplement British power in the Mediterranean. This prospect, however, was disliked by Churchill's naval advisers who distrusted France as a "country of unstable politics, with no particular sympathy towards British interests except in so far as they represent French interests as well." [11] And though he regarded French help as an unavoidable necessity Churchill, also, had no great enthusiasm for the situation. "If she [France] is our friend," he wrote Lord Haldane, "we shall not suffer. If she is not, we shall suffer. But if we win the big battle in the decisive theatre, we can put everything else straight afterwards. . . . Whatever the French do, my counsel is the same, & is first of all the laws of war—overpowering strength at the decisive point." [12] Uncomfortable about depending on France and realistic about the chances of further naval appropriations, the Admiralty in early May strongly reaffirmed the correctness of its initial decisions. In the future Britain would have to rely upon the battleship squadron at Gibraltar and the cruisers at Malta for the protection of its interests; the March dispositions would remain unchanged.

Across Whitehall the War Office was astir. The C.I.D. inquiry and the meeting at Malta galvanized the normally placid routine within that pillared Victorian atrocity. A thoroughly "fussed" Haldane disliked Churchill's precipitate decision to withdraw the battleships: he thought it changed the "fundamental basis" of existing plans and prevented taking any troop reinforcements from the Mediterranean. All of this would, he believed, considerably affect "the plan of operations of the Expeditionary Force." [13] Haldane's military advisers were equally dis-

---

10. "War Staff Memorandum on the Mediterranean Situation," April 1912, quoted in Marder, Road to War, 291.
11. Ibid.
12. Churchill to Haldane, May 6, 1912, quoted in Churchill, Young Statesman, 570. Nonetheless, in April the Admiralty did draft some notes on possible Anglo-French cooperation; they were seen by Churchill on Apr. 23, 1912; Adm. 116/3109.
13. "Memorandum by the Secretary of State for War [Haldane] on the Effect of the Loss of Sea Power in the Mediterranean on British Military Strategy," May 9, 1912, Adm. 116/3110; later reprinted as a General Staff memo, July 1, 1912.

turbed by the defensive problems created by the naval evacuation. Staff studies, which assumed that the Gibraltar squadron was unavailable and that the French fleet was occupied with troop movements, gloomily concluded that Cyprus, Malta, and Suez could fall within weeks to the Austrians, Italians, and Turks respectively.[14]

In full agreement about the dangers of the Admiralty scheme, Haldane and his principal assistants were at the same time in sharp disagreement about a solution to the Mediterranean problem. The Secretary of State for War, like the navalists, favored more battleships regardless of the cost. On the other hand Sir John French, now Chief of the Imperial General Staff, and Henry Wilson pressed for an open alliance with France. Haldane, resisting the entreaties of his subordinates, maintained that an alliance would drive Turkey into Germany's arms and also mean conscription. And he expressed doubts that Asquith and Grey would in any case accept an alliance—a comment which left Henry Wilson "cold." "They are," the D.M.O. added, "useless as they are ignorant." [15] Although Haldane gradually modified his personal position, the General Staff nevertheless had to consider how to reinforce the Mediterranean garrisons. Plans were drafted in late June for troop increases, the manpower to come from South Africa. As it eventually turned out, though, adjustments in the naval program and the situation in South Africa kept the Mediterranean garrisons from being strengthened.[16]

Ambitious generals at the War Office were not the only advocates of an alliance with France. At the Foreign Office Arthur Nicolson and Eyre Crowe also insisted that an alliance offered the best protection for British interests beyond Gibraltar. At a Buckingham Palace dinner on May 3, for example, Nicolson complained bitterly to Austen Chamberlain about Liberal foreign policy, declaring that it was unsafe to abandon the Mediterranean without a French alliance.[17] Nor did he confine his advocacy of an alliance to his numerous Conservative and military acquaintances; he openly argued it with the Foreign Secretary as well. If the Admiralty persisted in its Mediterranean schemes, Britain, Nicolson told Grey on May 6, had only three alternatives: to increase the naval budget, to make an alliance with Germany, or to come to an understanding with France. The first option he ruled out on the grounds of expense, the second as an unacceptable confession of British weakness. This left only "an understanding with France whereby she would undertake, in the early period of a war and until we could detach vessels from home waters,

14. See, e.g., C.I.D. memo, 92–C, "Papers Prepared by the General Staff—1. The Attack on Malta by Italy. 2. The Defense of Malta Against Deliberate Invasion," Cab. 4/4/33; see also Marder, Road to War, 291–292.

15. May 10, 1912, Wilson Diaries; also see diary, May 3, 7–8, 1912, in Callwell, Wilson, I, 112–113.

16. On the question of reinforcing the garrisons, see de La Panouse to Millerand, May 29, June 24, 1912, D.D.F., 3rd ser., III, nos. 50, 137.

17. Austen Chamberlain to Joseph Chamberlain, May 4, 1912, Chamberlain, Politics from Inside, 485–486; May 4, 1912, Wilson Diaries.

to safeguard our interests in the Mediterranean." Although France would probably ask "for some reciprocal engagement," the Undersecretary still felt that this approach offered Britain the "cheapest, simplest and safest solution" to its Mediterranean dilemma.[18]

Eyre Crowe reiterated these conclusions in a memo prepared for the belated C.I.D. inquiry in which he carefully scrutinized the new naval dispositions within the larger context of British policy in the Mediterranean. The political repercussions of a naval withdrawal were, he declared, enormous: Italy would once more become a faithful member of the Triple Alliance, Spain would drift into the German camp, British influence at Constantinople would deteriorate, Egypt would stand exposed. But he concluded that these unwelcome consequences "could to a certain extent be averted if the place of the British Mediterranean squadron were effectively taken by a powerful French fleet." [19] Both of Grey's principal advisers viewed the naval dispositions as catastrophic; both would accept foreign assistance in the protection of British interests.

The Foreign Secretary opposed the demands for a "defensive alliance." While unhappy about the bleak situation in the Mediterranean, he thought that any move toward a French alliance would break up the Cabinet. What he preferred, mindful of radical sensitivity, was to continue the policy of the "free hand" in European affairs; but he recognized, in the words of the Westminster Gazette, that "the condition of keeping the free hand is that we maintain our Navy at the necessary ratio of strength. Without that we inevitably become dependent on our neighbors and at the mercy of their combinations and alliances." [20] In short Grey, like Haldane, saw an increase in the naval estimates as the best solution to Britain's strategic problems. But he concurred entirely with Nicolson and Crowe about the need for a thorough reconsideration of the Mediterranean dispositions within the total framework of British foreign policy. It was thus with relief that the Foreign Office learned of the Cabinet's cancellation (May 10) of the scheduled C.I.D. meeting at Malta. There would still be informal conferences between Churchill, Asquith, and Kitchener, but all final decisions would be made in London.[21] The new naval arrangements could still be overturned, or at least modified.

As the Asquith government began to examine the fleet reorganization another factor came to be increasingly involved in their evaluations: the

18. Nicolson to Grey, May 6, 1912, B.D., X, pt. 2, no. 385. In a private letter to Bertie that day, Nicolson speculated that the French might ask for help on their eastern frontier; ibid., no. 384.
19. "Memorandum on the effect of a British Evacuation of the Mediterranean on Questions of Foreign Policy," May 8, 1912, B.D., X, pt. 2, no. 386.
20. May 16, 1912. See also May 15, 17, 1912, Wilson Diaries; diary, May 8, 1912, in Callwell, Wilson, I, 113.
21. Morley, Haldane, and Grey were the leaders in blocking a "preliminary" meeting of the C.I.D. at Malta; diary, May 13, 1912, in Fitzroy, Memoirs, II, 485–486. Asquith to George V, May 11, 1912, Asquith Papers, box 6.

entente relationship with France. Two issues were at stake: continuing French uneasiness about Anglo-German relations and French pressure for naval conversations. When Prime Minister Asquith informed the House of Commons (April 30) that Britain and Germany would continue friendly discussions, French fears were immediately rekindled. Indeed, Grey on May 3 had to reassure Cambon that the naval negotiations were over and that any future discussions would only touch upon colonial issues.[22] Even this assurance was only momentarily successful. In mid-May, Haldane's declaration in the House of Lords that Britain was free of a continental alliance, followed by news of the appointment to London of the veteran German diplomat Adolf Marschall von Bieberstein, aroused Poincaré's suspicions anew. Irritated by the persistent French sensitivity about Anglo-German relations, Grey had Bertie deliver a letter to the French Premier on June 5 denying once more that any negotiations were under way for a political formula and pledging British loyalty to France.[23] Cambon did not revive the issue.

Equally important for the entente were French efforts to resume the naval conversations. On May 4, despite Nicolson's recent injunction to move cautiously, the French ambassador revived—implicitly if not explicitly—the question of a closer entente relationship. Notifying Nicolson of the impending conclusion of a Franco-Russian naval accord, Cambon announced that his naval attaché wanted "to renew conversations" with the Admiralty. To buttress this demarche the ambassador recalled the de Lostende talks with the Admiralty in 1911 and placed special emphasis upon the earlier British decision to entrust the Mediterranean to French care. What Paris desired was that the British Navy "look after the Channel and the northern coast of France" while France, with a renovated fleet, undertook "the 'care of the whole of the Mediterranean.' " And Cambon also pointed out the possibility that France and Russia might solicit British participation in their new naval agreement. Saying he knew nothing whatsoever about any naval conversations, Nicolson deferred a definite answer on these points until he could see Sir Edward Grey.[24] With this overture, Cambon brought the naval conversations, hitherto infrequent, informal, and highly secret, before the Foreign Office and the Cabinet.

This conversation with the French ambassador disturbed Nicolson. Jealous of Foreign Office prerogatives in the formation of foreign policy, the Undersecretary disliked the idea of unauthorized naval talks. He thought confusion would result if the other departments "intervene in what are important foreign questions." In this case the staff talks demanded, at the very least, Grey's approval, if not that of the Cabinet.

22. Grey to Bertie, May 3, 1912, B.D., VI, no. 582; P. Cambon to Poincaré (tel.), May 3, 1912, D.D.F., 3rd ser., II, no. 411.
23. Grey to Bertie, May 31, 1912, B.D., VI, no. 589; "Communication de l'Ambassade britannique," D.D.F., 3rd ser., III, no. 71.
24. Nicolson to Grey, May 4, 1912, B.D., X, pt. 2, no. 383; also see Nicolson to Bertie, May 6, 1912, ibid., no. 384.

On the substance of Cambon's essay, Nicolson expected that Britain would soon have to decide about its policy toward France and Russia; London was going to be asked "to take a more active part than hitherto in mutual assistance." [25]

The ministerial reaction to the French request was characteristic: Asquith agreed with Nicolson that Cabinet sanction was needed for naval talks; Churchill, who also knew of the probe, warned that he would have to seek this sanction after their Malta trip because further naval talks were imperative; Grey, anxious to defend himself against the aspersions cast on his control of foreign policy, assured Nicolson that the Cabinet did know of the earlier naval exchanges. He did not, however, make clear exactly how or when the Cabinet had received this knowledge. On one point the three ministers were in total agreement: there would be, regardless of Cambon's pressure, no new naval talks until after the Malta meeting.[26] The French ambassador's maneuver for immediate talks had been forestalled.

Grey, faithful to the limitations imposed the previous autumn, duly notified the Cabinet on May 16 of the French probes for "possible naval cooperation between the two countries in the event of war." This information generated profound misgivings among the radical ministers. It became apparent, Asquith wrote George V, "that the whole Mediterranean situation must be resurveyed from the point of view both of policy & strategy," and such a study would begin when the Prime Minister and First Lord returned from the Mediterranean.[27] The French demand for naval talks had finally alerted the entire Cabinet to the long-range ramifications of Churchill's fleet reorganization. The Mediterranean problem would now face the scrutiny of both the C.I.D. and the Cabinet; the First Lord of the Admiralty still had to justify his fait accompli of March to his colleagues.

Before these strategic reappraisals could occur, the British and French press pounced on the Mediterranean issue. It all began on May 20 when the *Morning Post*, in commenting on Asquith's trip to Malta, called not only for more ships in the Mediterranean but also for an alliance with France. In succeeding days other Conservative journals, including the *Observer*, the *Daily Graphic*, and the *Spectator*, urged the conversion of the entente into an alliance. But outside the Conservative press these pleas found little support. Led by Scott's *Manchester Guardian*, the radical papers denounced an alliance as leading to conscription and as " 'an absurdly disproportionate remedy' for the situation." [28] If the choice was between an alliance, with its implied large army, and spending more for the Mediterranean fleet, the Liberal *Westminster Gazette* preferred the latter since it would leave Britain the master of its own policy. And

25. Nicolson to Grey, May 4, 1912, *ibid.*, no. 383.
26. Minutes by Grey, Asquith, and Churchill on Nicolson's report, *ibid.*
27. Asquith to George V, May 17, 1912, Asquith Papers, box 6.
28. Quoted in Marder, *Road to War*, 289–290; see also de Fleuriau to Poincaré, May 30, 1912, D.D.F., 3rd ser., III, no. 56.

the influential, anti-German *Times* concluded that agitation for an alliance was inopportune, unnecessary, and harmful; moreover, the *Thunderer* defended Churchill's fleet dispositions, insisting that they meant no evacuation of the Mediterranean—indeed, it asserted that the dreadnought squadron at Gibraltar would restore British strength in that sea to its 1904–1905 level.[29]

The Paris press added its own dimensions to the British debate over the Mediterranean. On May 22 *Le Temps* equated the British withdrawal with a treaty of alliance because it left France responsible for protecting entente interests in the Mediterranean. Given these circumstances, the journal insisted that the Poincaré government reconsider "the naval and international situation of the entente cordiale." *Figaro* went even further, maintaining that the fleet transfers constituted a virtual alliance for which Britain should promise France some quid pro quo, preferably military help on France's eastern frontier.[30] Other writers were more realistic about French chances for British concessions: Commandant de Thomasson told readers of *Questions diplomatiques et coloniales* that it was quite unlikely that a Liberal government would accept such a firm engagement, even though it would surely improve the chances for peace.[31] Press reports about closer Anglo-French relations eventually prompted official comment in France. On June 14 Poincaré, after acknowledging the demands for an alliance, informed the Chamber of Deputies that the "two friendly governments" were not in fact discussing the issue; nor was there any need to do so, he explained, for "the entente cordiale, in the absence of parchment, has the guarantee of an immense majority of favorable opinion in both countries." The entente gave each government freedom of action, while facilitating "the settlement of common problems and the search for mutual solutions in the problems of general policy."[32] This resounding endorsement of the entente temporarily muted French discussion about an alliance. In the relative calm that ensued, Raymond Poincaré sought the equivalent of an alliance through more devious means.

From the Malta conference in late May until the introduction of the supplementary naval estimates on July 22, the Liberal government devoted unprecedented attention to the resolution of Britain's problems in

29. *Westminster Gazette*, May 30, 1912; *Times*, May 27, 30, 1912.

30. Quoted without date in George Grahame (First Secretary of the Paris embassy) to William Tyrrell, May 27, 1912, Grey Papers, F.O. 800/53. Grahame personally thought Britain owed the French nothing for letting them be the "cocks of the walk" in the Mediterranean.

31. 33 (June 1, 1912), 641–645; also see Francis Charmes, "Chronique de la quinzaine," *Revue des deux mondes*, 6th ser., 9 (June 1, 1912), 717–720.

32. *Journal officiel: débats parlementaires, Chambre des Députés*, 1912, I (June 14, 1912), 1482. On Poincaré's pronouncement, also see Bertie to Grey, June 15, 1912, Bertie Papers, F.O. 800/165; Isvolski to Sazonov, May 24/June 6, 1912, George Abel Schreiner, ed., *Entente Diplomacy and the World*, trans. B. de Siebert (New York, 1921), no. 730.

the Mediterranean. The hostile sentiments of early May resembled mere skirmishes when compared to the heavy salvos now encountered by the Admiralty proposals. Politicians and the permanent government were in complete agreement about the urgent necessity to counter German naval expansion; but there were sharp, not to say violent, disagreements between and among the ministers and their advisers on how to defend Britain's interests in the Mediterranean. In the ensuing discussion four possible options emerged: an open alliance with France, a naval understanding with France, the construction of more ships for the Mediterranean, or general retention of the initial Admiralty plan for a cruiser squadron at Malta. Each alternative had drawbacks: expanded political responsibilities, larger naval budgets, or an apparent sacrifice of British interests and freedom of maneuver. More important, each option or combination of options represented fundamental choices in policy that would be difficult to reverse. British naval and defense planning had reached a turning point.

On May 22 Asquith, Churchill, and a small retinue of relatives and advisers boarded the Admiralty yacht *Enchantress* at Genoa. They then sailed for Elba, Paestum, and Syracuse on what Henry Wilson described as a "holiday at Govt. expense." The more official part of their cruise started on May 29 with their arrival at the island of Malta. Receptions, dances, and gunnery exercises were interspersed with consultations between the Prime Minister, the First Lord, and Lord Kitchener. The latter two, Violet Asquith noted in her diary, "seemed to get on *very* well together this time—which relieved me, as their relationship has always been a prickly one and Lord K. can't like the prospect of the Mediterranean ships going north." [33]

During three days of talks Kitchener, occasionally assisted by Asquith, applied steady, unrelenting pressure on Churchill. Finally the First Lord agreed to modify the naval dispositions: two, and possibly three, battle cruisers of the "Indomitable" class (17,200 tons) *and* a cruiser squadron of four "Devonshires" (10,850 tons) would be stationed at Malta. The battleship squadron at Gibraltar would retain its Mediterranean label and eventually contain eight dreadnoughts. Furthermore, Kitchener won pledges from Asquith and Churchill for a "definite agreement" with France. Britain would defend the French northern coasts, while an Anglo-French force guarded the Mediterranean. Significantly, however, the word "alliance" was carefully avoided. Basically the Malta compromise represented an attempt to fuse the fundamental Admiralty program of withdrawal with a naval agreement with France. As such, the concessions to Kitchener set an important pattern. [34]

33. April 29, 1912, Wilson Diaries; Violet Bonham Carter, *Winston Churchill: An Intimate Portrait* (New York, 1965), 217.
34. There was no mention of larger garrisons in the Mediterranean; Kitchener to Grey, June 2, 1912, *B.D.*, X, pt. 2, no. 392. The desirability of closer relations with

While Asquith and Churchill cruised in the Mediterranean, concern within the Establishment over Britain's naval position began to mount. Lord Esher, the occasionally meddlesome civilian member of the C.I.D., and Arthur Balfour, the recently deposed leader of the Conservative party, were especially disturbed. The viscount thought those who wanted every ship in the North Sea "mad." In his opinion the Mediterranean remained "the centre of naval strategic gravity in Europe." Convinced that only an adequate battle fleet in the Mediterranean would protect Britain's interests, he inveighed against the "illusion" of French help, both within the C.I.D. and with Cabinet ministers. He also actively preached, with some success, these views to George V.[35] Balfour, likewise unhappy with the strategic situation, proposed a radically different solution: he wanted an alliance. Public sentiment, he noted in a memo to Grey, would never allow Britain to stand aside if France were attacked; besides, a clearer definition of mutual obligations would not only help the general staffs with their preparations, it would also remove the entente from the dangers of diplomatic intrigue.[36] To devise and win support for a Mediterranean policy at once acceptable to these influential critics, to their radical colleagues, and to their advisers was the immediate problem confronting Churchill and Asquith on their return from sunnier climes.

The First Lord wasted little time in staking out his position. On June 15 he sent the Cabinet a paper justifying the removal of the old battleships and at the same time reassuring his fellow ministers that the Malta compromise would protect British interests. The withdrawal, he argued, was necessary on two grounds: he needed the personnel for more modern vessels in home waters, and the old battleships would be no match for the new Austrian and Italian dreadnoughts. He insisted, however, that Britain's position in the Mediterranean would be adequately protected by the cruiser squadron, the two battle cruisers, and the Mediterranean battleships now located at Gibraltar; and in addition there was the prospect of French assistance in that sea. In any war an Anglo-French combination could completely control the Mediterranean and protect entente interests "without impairing British margins in the North Sea." Churchill believed that "a definite naval arrangement should be made with France without delay." To make this suggestion palatable to the radicals, he stressed that the agreement would only come into force in

France had already been discussed by Churchill and his naval secretary, Rear Admiral David Beatty; see Churchill's draft memo, May 29, 1912, Adm. 116/3110 and Rear Admiral W. S. Chalmers, *The Life and Letters of David, Earl Beatty* (London, 1951), 112–113.

35. Esher to J. A. Spender, June 5, 1912, *Journals and Letters of Esher*, III, 93; diary, June 6, 12, 1912, *ibid.*, 94–95; memo by Esher for George V, June 17, 1912, RA G234.

36. Balfour to Grey, June 12, 1912, Grey Papers, F.O. 800/105; the memo is summarized in Blanche E. C. Dugdale, *Arthur James Balfour*, 2 vols. (New York, 1937), II, 71–73.

case of war: "It would not decide the question of whether they should be allies or not." It would, he assured them, simply allow the naval staffs to define their respective responsibilities in advance.[37]

Churchill's brief for the Malta compromise indicated no willingness to shift more cruisers to the Mediterranean or to build a new battleship squadron for service there. The compromise would, he soon discovered, satisfy neither the advocates of a larger navy nor those opposed to dependence upon France. This first became evident four days later, on June 19, at a stormy Cabinet session. In discussing increases in the naval estimates, Reginald McKenna (the former First Lord) voiced such strong disagreement with Churchill's entire program that he received Cabinet approval to draft an alternate scheme for consideration.[38]

During the next week the past and present occupants of the First Lordship exchanged literary daggers. Churchill, as usual, had the first and the last word. On June 22 he plaintively described how the *Novelle* reduced Britain's battleship margin over Germany to eight vessels (thirty-three to twenty-five). Eight of the British battleships were at Gibraltar, three and a half days away, and some ships were always in dry dock; the Germans, therefore, could launch a surprise attack on nearly equal terms. Consequently, there were simply no battleships left for dispatch to the Mediterranean. On the other hand, with a distinct change of tone he now conceded that the Mediterranean problem was urgent. He preferred a massive building program, costing £20,000,000, but even that would not help before 1916. In the interval the most feasible alternative, he repeated, was to make "an arrangement with France and leave enough ships in the Mediterranean to give her undoubted superiority." [39]

McKenna disagreed on every point (June 24). His program for the North Sea hinged on more effective use of reserve vessels and a willingness to risk some inequality before mobilization, which would in turn free several battleships for Mediterranean duty. Further, he assailed the idea of an "alliance" with France and charged that it was the "essential feature" of the Admiralty scheme. An increase in ships and personnel would, he told his colleagues, be preferable to being "driven by our weakness into dependence on an alliance with any European power."

Churchill responded the next day with a slashing and somewhat ill-tempered indictment of McKenna's ideas, asserting that they would give Britain only the barest equality in the North Sea even after mobilization and that a divided fleet guaranteed naval disaster. Yet nowhere did he note, much less discuss, McKenna's principal objection to the new naval

37. Memo by Churchill, "Naval Situation in the Mediterranean," June 15, 1912, Cab. 37/111/76; an extract, dated June 5, 1912, is quoted in Churchill, *Young Statesman*, 572–574.

38. Asquith to George V, June 20, 1912, Asquith Papers, box 6.

39. Memo by Churchill, "The Naval Situation, II," June 22, 1912, Cab. 37/111/78; see also "War Staff Memorandum on the Mediterranean Situation," June 21, 1912, Adm. 116/3109.

dispositions: dependence upon France. He may have hoped that his ruthless demolition of McKenna's proposals would demonstrate the paucity of the alternatives available to the Cabinet. Or he may have decided, given the radical grumblings within the Cabinet, that the less said about French assistance the better. In any event, the policy struggle temporarily shifted away from the memo-war and back to the Cabinet proper.[40]

On Thursday, June 27, the Cabinet spent a further fruitless session grappling with the naval problem. Churchill utterly failed to convince his colleagues of the validity of his Mediterranean policy: the prospect of dependence upon French naval power remained an anathema to the radicals. At length the Cabinet decided to postpone further consideration until after the C.I.D. had formally reviewed the problem on July 4.[41]

In the days before the July 4 meeting, an unlikely and unstructured "coalition" of radicals, Unionists, and imperialists emerged to oppose Churchill's Mediterranean schemes. The radicals, disliking the prospect of dependence upon France, and the Unionist-imperialists, distrustful both of the French and of any erosion of British power, were united in their demands for a thorough review of British naval policy. In the House of Commons Unionist members demanded complete information about the new Mediterranean dispositions and doubted—correctly—that the C.I.D. had originally been consulted about the redistribution.[42] In the House of Lords on July 2 a series of Unionist spokesmen—Lansdowne, Selborne, a former First Lord, and Brassey, editor of the prestigious *Naval Annual*—denounced the "evacuation" of the Mediterranean and Britain's apparent reliance upon France. Selborne declared that Britain should not have "to depend exclusively, or practically exclusively, on the loyalty and efficiency and courage of some ally for protection of all our interests in the Mediterranean." For these critics, the construction of a new battleship squadron in the Mediterranean was the only solution consistent with British interests and traditions. Lord Crewe, the Lord Privy Seal, and spokesman for the government on this occasion, flatly rejected the accusation that the Liberals planned to abandon the Mediterranean Sea. But he offered no hints of how the Cabinet proposed to meet the problems there, saying only that the choice between more ships, dependence upon friends, or going it alone was particularly difficult. That was not the kind of rejoinder or assurance that eased Unionist apprehensions.[43]

The *Times* also lent its prestige to the agitation. Shifting from its earlier endorsement of Churchill's proposals, by late June it opined that

40. Memo by McKenna, June 24, 1912, Cab. 37/111/79; memo by Churchill, "The Naval Situation, III," June 25, 1912, Cab. 37/111/80.
41. Asquith to George V, June 28, 1912, Asquith Papers, box 6.
42. *Parliamentary Debates: Commons*, 5th ser., 40 (June 25, 1912), 208–209; ibid. (June 26, 1912), 294.
43. *Parliamentary Debates: Lords*, 5th ser., 12 (July 2, 1912), 305.

his ideas had caused "serious uneasiness in the public mind." British strength now had to be "above all suspicion" in the Mediterranean. In early July, after the Lords' debate on the issue, the Thunderer pontificated that what the country wanted was "to have naval strength enough to keep its security in its own hands, in the Mediterranean as elsewhere, and not one ship or blue jacket less." [44]

Elsewhere that indefatigable imperialist Lord Esher worked to thwart an "abandonment" of the Mediterranean. He belabored Churchill directly on July 1, urging the First Lord to seek more men and more ships from a nation anxious to respond. And, more indirectly, he sought Balfour's assistance against Churchill's plans, insisting that either Britain would be supreme at sea or "she is relegated to the class of secondary Powers. These are not arguable propositions. They are fundamental and commonplace axioms of world policy." Yet Esher possessed few illusions about converting the "strong people" in the Cabinet to his way of thinking. "It means an alliance with France," he gloomily predicted to his son, "under the cover of 'conversations,' and conscription to cover Pussy (Haldane)'s traces at the War Office. Adieu to the sea command of Great Britain until after the next war. Perhaps then, for ever. Rome," he moaned unhappily, "had to call in the foreigner to help her when the time of her decadence approached. I shall, like Candide, cultivate my garden." [45]

The Unionist-Esher views also had their advocate within the permanent government. Sir Arthur Nicolson, who had initially favored closer relations with France to meet Britain's strategic needs, now advocated more ships. He implored Sir Edward Grey to reject the Malta "compromise" as unsatisfactory and inadequate. And, in a step that was quite out of character for a senior bureaucrat, he requested permission to miss the forthcoming C.I.D. session if he would be called upon to announce that the Foreign Office had accepted the Malta proposals. [46]

On the other side of the political spectrum, radical opponents of the Mediterranean withdrawal also rallied. Lord Morley, for example, now found his own mind "quite made up. No alliance, with or without a mask." And McKenna, in a Cabinet paper on July 3, renewed his frontal assaults upon "the policy of dependence on France." The questions of naval distribution and of more ships were unimportant, he contended, when compared to entering into "an alliance with its obligation to fight

44. June 29, July 3, 1912.
45. Esher to Churchill, July 1, 1912, *Journals and Letters of Esher*, III, 98–99; Esher to Balfour, July 1, 1912, *ibid.*, 95–98; Esher to Maurice Brett, July 2, 1912, *ibid.*, 99–100. On this occasion Esher's old comrade in arms, Lord Fisher, was on the opposite side and the latter actively lobbied in support of Churchill's program; Nicolson to Grey, June 21, 1912, Grey Papers, F.O. 800/94.
46. Nicolson to Grey, June 30, 1912, *ibid.* Nicolson to Goschen, June 24, 1912, Nicolson Papers, vol. V/1912. Nicolson's intimate, Henry Wilson, was now unhappily resigned to the naval reorganization; diary, June 26, 1912, in Callwell, *Wilson*, I, 113.

in a war not of our own making." "What terms would France ultimately demand from us as a condition of protecting us in the Mediterranean?" [47] As at Archerfield in October 1911, the Home Secretary sought to limit the scope of the entente and thus keep Britain out of France's continental quarrels. At that time he had hoped to prevent British involvement by stopping the military conversations, now he wanted to achieve this same goal by constructing more ships. This time, ironically, he would get his way about the ships—yet see reliance upon France increase nonetheless.

On July 4 McKenna carried his fight to the Committee of Imperial Defence. Unlike the momentous session of August 23, 1911, this meeting was well attended by both radicals and Liberal imperialists, including Asquith, Lloyd George, Grey, Haldane (who had replaced Loreburn as Lord Chancellor in June), Churchill, Sydney Buxton, Lewis Harcourt, John Seely (who had succeeded Haldane as War Minister), McKenna and Crewe. Their military and civilian advisers included Bridgeman, Battenberg, Troubridge, A. K. Wilson, Fisher, Henry Wilson, French, Nicolson, and Esher.

The rambling, six-hour session was dominated by Churchill and McKenna; they were, Fisher later wrote, "tearing each other's eyes out the whole time." [48] At the outset they clashed over what constituted adequate margins of naval strength in the North Sea and the Mediterranean. Despite McKenna's objections, Churchill steadfastly held to his sixty percent advantage over Germany as an imperative. To retain this edge and at the same time maintain a ten percent margin over Austria would require, he declared, the construction of six new dreadnoughts, a step he regarded as unlikely; but if the British and French cooperated, then the mere addition of two battle cruisers would ensure complete entente preponderance over any Austro-Italian combination. When McKenna called this idea "an alliance," Churchill retorted that the Admiralty had never assumed an alliance with France in making the new fleet distributions. Only two principles, insisted the First Lord, had guided their decisions: "(1) that we must maintain a continuous and certain superiority of force over the Germans in the North Sea, and (2) that all other objects however precious, must, if necessary, be sacrificed to secure this end."

Throughout the debate over fleet distribution McKenna demanded the retention of at least a one-power standard in the Mediterranean for the protection of trade. But the most Churchill would concede, without the assurance of a new squadron, was a "force sufficient to maintain our prestige and to support our diplomacy." At length Sir Edward Grey

47. Morley to McKenna, July 3, 1912, quoted in McKenna, *Reginald McKenna: A Memoir*, 147; memo by McKenna, July 3, 1912, Cab. 37/111/86.
48. Fisher to Cecil V. Fisher, July 5, 1912, Marder, *Fear God and Dread Nought*, II, 470–471.

acted to bridge the gap between the two positions, declaring that British policy needed a fleet that would be "free to operate in the Mediterranean as required. It would be better based on Malta, but that was not essential: freedom of movement was, and its freedom of movement should be emphasized on every occasion." The Foreign Secretary's intervention proved decisive and the Committee's conclusion, accepted over Churchill's protests, reflected a partial victory for McKenna. It stated that in the future "there must always be provided a reasonable margin of superior strength ready and available in Home waters. This is the first requirement. Subject to this we ought to maintain, available for Mediterranean purposes and based on a Mediterranean port, a battle fleet equal to a one-Power Mediterranean standard, excluding France." [49]

Esher, flushed with a sense of victory, left the meeting confident that the British could hold up their "heads once more in the Mediterranean and beyond." Diplomatic considerations, made more vivid by the continuing Italo-Turkish war, were, he wrote George V later that day, chiefly responsible for the success of Churchill's critics. Now, observed the viscount, "the whole matter: cost—amount of margin—etc.—is relegated to the Cabinet and the Admiralty to work out." Because McKenna, Lloyd George, and Harcourt had been so "staunch," he doubted that there would be any "backsliding" when the issue reached the Cabinet. "Anyhow," he rejoiced, "the Mediterranean is to have a Fleet of *Battle ships!*" [50] "Whatever the cost may be it is cheaper than a conscript army and any entangling alliance." [51]

The Unionist-Esher-McKenna "coalition" had won a significant victory of principle. But their triumph should not be exaggerated. The North Sea still retained first priority upon British naval strength and until new battleships could be constructed, the one-power standard in the Mediterranean would remain more a statement of intention than a firm realization of fact. The fragile nature of the C.I.D. détente on the problem readily became apparent when the Cabinet sought to convert principle into reality.

Four times in eleven days the Cabinet debated the naval question. The climax came on July 15–16 when the First Lord outlined his new plans for achieving a future one-power standard in the Mediterranean and for protecting British interests in the interim. By 1915 he wanted a squadron of eight dreadnoughts or battle cruisers there. To relieve the financial burden imposed by such a program, Churchill was hopeful that Canadian Prime Minister Sir Robert Borden, to whom he had explained

49. This narrative is based on the minutes of the 117th meeting, Cab. 2/2/3; also see the accounts in the *Journals and Letters of Esher*, III, 100, and Callwell, *Wilson*, I, 115.

50. Diary, July 5, 1912, *Journals and Letters of Esher*, III, 100; Esher to George V, July 4, 1912, quoted in Marder, *Road to War*, 294.

51. Esher to Fisher, July 9, 1912, *Journals and Letters of Esher*, III, 101; see also Esher to Balfour, July 23, 1912, *ibid.*, 102–104.

these ideas in the C.I.D. on July 11, could secure approval for the construction of three dreadnoughts.[52] Because of the prospect of Canadian assistance, Churchill and the Cabinet were able to postpone an immediate struggle over a large supplement to the announced naval estimates.

But a wrangle over Churchill's proposals for interim protection of the Mediterranean was impossible to avert. The First Lord maintained that four battle cruisers and a cruiser squadron would be adequate; his old antagonist Reginald McKenna strongly disagreed. At the session on July 15 the Home Secretary and former First Lord centered his criticism on three points. First, any straight Anglo-German war would force the Navy to withdraw the four battle cruisers from the Mediterranean. Second, Churchill's proposed force would be unable to hold its own against an Austrian fleet of three "Radetzkys" and two or more dreadnoughts. Third, he denied that the battleship squadron at Gibraltar, whatever its nomenclature, would or could perform any reliable function in the Mediterranean. What Britain needed, argued McKenna, was an unadulterated battleship squadron at Malta, able at all times to defend itself against any conceivable Austrian fleet. Yet, he could offer his colleagues no realistic advice on how to achieve this worthy goal. McKenna, as in October 1911, had scored valid points against the management of British defense policy without offering a viable alternative, a fact recognized by the Cabinet when it met again the next day. Churchill opened this sitting with a patient, point-by-point refutation of McKenna's objections. Promising that the battle cruisers would only be withdrawn in case of "some unlikely and unforeseeable emergency," he flatly assured the Cabinet that until 1915 and the completion of the dreadnoughts, the cruiser squadron and four battle cruisers would "be more than a match in the Mediterranean for any force that Austria could oppose to it." After heated debate Churchill carried his point; Asquith duly informed the King that "the Cabinet unanimously approved the proposal of the Admiralty." [53] There remained, however, one further question for the Cabinet to resolve.

From the start increased reliance upon French naval power was implicit in Churchill's Mediterranean strategy. This prospect he and the Admiralty accepted as a necessary imperative; this dependence Henry Wilson and Sir Arthur Nicolson welcomed generally with anticipation; this entanglement the radicals and some imperialists like Esher abhorred. Four months of pulling and tugging, coupled with the C.I.D.'s enunciation of a one-power standard, modified but did not remove Britain's need for French assistance. While the Royal Navy might be en-

52. Minutes of the 118th meeting of the C.I.D., July 11, 1912, Cab. 2/2/3; Marder, *Road to War*, 295–298.
53. The only records of these Cabinets are Asquith's single letter to George V, dated July 16, 1912 (and covering the sessions on both July 15 and 16), and a memo by Asquith, July 15, 1912, which summarized McKenna's views, Asquith Papers, box 6; also see Marder, *Road to War*, 294–295.

tirely capable of handling the Austrian fleet, it could not prudently ignore the possibility of engaging a combined Austro-Italian fleet (expected to include ten dreadnoughts by January 1915). In such an eventuality French help would be indispensable; not to arrange for this contingency would be the height of folly. However much the radicals might dislike it, their earlier reluctance to grant larger naval estimates had to some extent conditioned a strategic situation that could only be satisfied by closer naval relations with France. This unpleasant realization the Cabinet acknowledged in its July 16 meeting when it authorized the continuation of military and naval conversations with the familiar stipulation "that such communications were not to be taken as prejudicing the freedom of decision of either government as to whether they should or should not cooperate in the event of war." [54] For the radicals and Esher there remained only the consolation that by 1915 Britain might be able to dispense with any appearance of dependence upon France. In the meantime, the true victor of the Cabinet struggle over the Mediterranean was neither the Admiralty nor the radicals, but the entente.

The public learned of the Cabinet's position on naval policy in piecemeal fashion. Sir Edward Grey in the course of a Foreign Office debate on July 10 defended the concentration in the North Sea, while promising that Britain would "have some respectable force in the Mediterranean which is available for use at any time." [55] Churchill then provided the details of the government's decisions on July 22 when he introduced a supplementary naval measure for a million pounds. It was a masterful, clever, supremely political performance by the young First Lord: virtually ignoring the clamor about the Mediterranean, he emphasized in sweeping, bold phrases the threat posed by the new German naval law. Twenty-nine German battleships were now available for a sudden attack; against this force Britain could oppose but thirty-three battleships including the squadron at Gibraltar. All that prevented Britain from being outclassed was the Royal Navy's complete dominance of the pre-dreadnought category. To counter this danger Churchill announced that during the next five years dreadnought construction would be increased from seventeen to twenty-one units. The budgetary increases for the new program would not, however, come until the 1913 estimates, and he hinted broadly of possible Canadian help on the construction problem. Only after this sober review of Britain's plight vis-à-vis Germany did the First Lord turn, and then only briefly, to the Mediterranean. Four battle cruisers of the "Invincible" class and four new armored cruisers would go to Malta. This force, he promised the

54. Asquith to George V, July 16, 1912, Asquith Papers, box 6.
55. Parliamentary Debates: Commons, 5th ser., 40 (July 10, 1912), 1994.

Commons, together with the French fleet, would more than equal any possible enemy combination.[56]

The revised Admiralty policy enjoyed a mixed reception in Parliament and in the press. Although Arthur Balfour thought the new construction program cut "it rather fine," he generally supported Churchill's exposition. Other Unionists were not so kind; Lord Beresford, Arthur Lee, and Andrew Bonar Law assailed the Liberals for failing to launch a crash construction program and complained of makeshift arrangements in the Mediterranean.[57] And the Opposition press, joined by the *Times*, expressed grave reservations about robbing the North Sea to protect the Mediterranean; they too demanded an accelerated construction program. The Liberals both in Parliament and in the press reluctantly accepted the new program, though they were thoroughly dismayed at the steady increases in naval expenditures. The radical *Manchester Guardian* not only disliked the prospect of another round in the naval race, it objected even more strongly to Churchill's mention of France, labeling it the "most alarming single passage" in the speech. The *Guardian*'s apprehensions were, as it turned out, not entirely unjustified.[58]

By the end of July the naval debate subsided. The Admiralty's original policy, drafted without much reference to the other departments or to the deteriorating political situation in the Mediterranean, had been substantially modified. Steady pressure within and without the government had progressively forced Churchill, first at Malta and then in the C.I.D., to amend the initial dispositions. Instead of a single cruiser squadron, four battle cruisers and four modern armored cruisers, and ultimately some dreadnoughts, were now promised for the Mediterranean. This force could handle the Austrian fleet and adequately support British diplomacy. On the other hand, if Britain faced the Triple Alliance, the Royal Navy would have to abandon the Mediterranean until it could achieve victory in the North Sea. Since this prospect was unthinkable, the case for naval conversations with France seemed self-evident, even to the radicals. With the explicit approval of the Cabinet, still another dimension was added to the ambiguous but increasingly essential entente.

56. *Ibid.*, 41 (July 22, 1912), 838–864.
57. *Ibid.*, 864–946; *ibid.* (July 24, 1912), 1197–1308; *ibid.* (July 25, 1912), 1384–1498.
58. *Times*, July 23–24, 1912; *Westminster Gazette*, July 23, 1912; the *Guardian* quote is from Marder, *Road to War*, 299.

12 | The Political Consolidation of the Entente 1912

The failure of the Haldane mission and Tirpitz' *Novelle* forced the Admiralty to revise its Mediterranean dispositions. Despite the anguish of the radicals and of Lord Esher, British naval power in the Mediterranean was significantly reduced. Coming at a time when the Italians were already upsetting the traditional power configuration in the eastern Mediterranean, this change in British strategy necessarily prompted a reconsideration of French naval policy; in addition it furnished French policy-makers with a convenient pretext to resume their pressure for a closer technical and, if possible, political relationship with London. Furthermore, alterations in the French naval dispositions increased Paris' need for staff talks, so that by mid-July 1912 both sides were ready for the initiation of authorized naval conversations.

Publicly, Théophile Delcassé always emphasized the importance of the Mediterranean to French naval strategy. The newly completed "Dantons" were stationed there, and he justified his new building program in terms of that sea. Yet the *instructions de guerre* of July 1911 called for a concentration at Brest in case of war with the Triple Alliance; further, the six aging battleships which Boué de Lapeyrère had "temporarily" sent to the Atlantic in 1909 remained in northern waters. No one was more appalled by these inconsistencies and by the apparent division of French naval power than Vice Admiral Aubert, the new Chief of the French Naval Staff (February 1912). In 1906 Aubert had prepared, while serving as a staff officer in the Naval Ministry, the memoranda which convinced the Navy Board to concentrate France's effective sea power in the Mediterranean.[1] In succeeding years he had never wavered in his convictions about the importance of the Mediterranean.

In May 1912 Aubert launched a campaign to revise the current war orders and to reinstitute the 1906 decision locating all French battleships, however venerable, in the Mediterranean. French interests in the Mediterranean, communications with North Africa, and the possibility of luring German ships southward dictated, the Admiral stressed to Delcassé, a French plan to fight in that sea. To do otherwise would offer Italy and Austria-Hungary too great a temptation for mischief. Further, because the Germans might trap the battleships at Brest and because a dispersal of strength could lead to a "fatal" situation, Aubert insisted that the Third Squadron be recalled from the Atlantic. In all of this, he added significantly, "there is no question . . . of the possibility of an English alliance which [would] constitute a strong argument in favor of sending the Third Squadron into the Mediterranean."[2] By early July he had won Delcassé's assent for the transfer of the Third Squadron to the Mediterranean. Though resolved independently of the British (and of the Franco-Russian naval talks then in progress), the shift in French sea power re-emphasized France's dependence upon Britain for protection of its northern coasts. The coordination of entente naval activity in the English Channel became more imperative than ever.

At least one Frenchman did not, however, believe that the French Naval Staff understood the value of entente naval coordination. In May Paul Cambon had complained privately to Delcassé that his Naval Staff attached no great importance to staff talks. Although Delcassé had personally chastised Admiral Auvert (Aubert's predecessor) for delaying such talks, the ambassador thought that the naval high command still displayed no haste to get them under way. To stir things up Cambon proposed sending de Saint-Seine to Paris for new instructions.[3] Nor did the ambassador stop there: in late June he urged Poincaré to consider the initiation of naval conversations to include, possibly, the Spanish.[4]

1. See Chapter 9, pp. 232–234.
2. Memo by Aubert, May 7, 1912, Archives Marine, ED 37; see also undated, but early 1912, notes by Delcassé, Delcassé Papers, box 10.
3. P. Cambon to Delcassé, May 18, 1912, Delcassé Papers, vol. III.
4. Grey to Bertie, June 21, 1912, B.D., X, pt. 2, no. 395; also see Marder, *Road to War*, 299–308.

At length Cambon's appeals were successful. On July 10 de Saint-Seine had his first "staff" talk with Admiral Bridgeman since the preceding December. It did not settle much. The British wanted to delay further talks for another week, until the Cabinet had concluded its discussions. The attaché, for his part, confided that Delcassé planned to shift the old battleships from Brest to Toulon. Both the Admiral and the French Captain readily agreed that this change would necessitate a revision of their Channel arrangements of the previous September.[5]

Full-fledged, authorized naval talks began a week later, on July 17, when Churchill and Bridgeman briefed the French attaché on Britain's new Mediterranean arrangements. While confident that four battle cruisers and a cruiser squadron would "suffice until 1914 to protect British interests in the Mediterranean," Churchill expressed the hope that France would adopt a two-power standard in that sea. France, de Saint-Seine promised, was determined to maintain its position in the Mediterranean; this explained the recent decision to move the six battleships southward. On the issue of naval conversations per se, Churchill bluntly warned that such talks bound neither country nor became effective unless approved by the British Cabinet. Moreover, he insisted that such stipulations had to preface any technical agreement in order to prevent later misunderstandings. The rather one-sided interview ended with the First Lord promising de Saint-Seine a British draft on naval cooperation within a few days.[6] The Churchill-de Saint-Seine meeting pinpointed the two issues that would occupy the naval staffs for the next four months: technical arrangements on the one hand, the drafting of a suitable preamble or preface stating the nonobligatory nature of the staff talks on the other. It was, of course, the latter issue which posed the greatest problem as the entente partners struggled to redefine their relationship during the second half of 1912.

In the search for a suitable means to satisfy both members of the entente Sir Francis Bertie played a key role. As early as May the British ambassador had proposed that London meet the French demands for closer ties by an exchange of notes promising that the two governments would consult in time of danger. On July 17 he repeated the suggestion to Sir Edward Grey as a way of meeting the French demands for a quid pro quo for defending British interests in the Mediterranean. Grey, who feared such an exchange of notes "would be something like an alliance," agreed to put Bertie's idea before the Cabinet. But Grey's politi-

5. De Saint-Seine to Delcassé, July 10, 1912, D.D.F., 3rd ser., III, no. 189.
6. De Saint-Seine to Delcassé, July 18, 1912, ibid., no. 207; "Memorandum by Mr. Winston Churchill," July 17, 1912, B.D., X, pt. 2, no. 399. The Admiralty records indicate that the French attaché on July 17 also furnished the British with a record of the 1911 talks; see Adm. 116/3109. On July 2, 1912, Captain Kelly, the British naval attaché in Paris, wrote a lengthy memo urging an Anglo-French naval alliance. The report went to Ballard at Naval Intelligence where it was sidetracked; it did not reach Churchill until October, when the question of an alliance was thoroughly discredited; Adm. 116/8666; F.O. 371/1367.

cal associates refused to alter their original guidelines for the naval talks; the most the Foreign Secretary could offer Bertie (July 23) was the assurance that he [Grey] "would not remain in the Cabinet if there was any question of abandoning the policy of the Entente with France." The ambassador, for his part, remained convinced that Paris would not long be content with "nothing more promising than a warning that the arrangements between the experts were entirely without prejudice." [7] His proposal for an exchange of notes had, for the moment, been considered and cast aside.

In the meantime the French government was learning more precisely what the British meant by authorized naval conversations. On July 22 Grey emphasized to Paul Cambon that the naval talks were noncommittal, that in no case could the "experts" commit governments to a course of action. That could only be done "by what passed directly between Governments themselves." This observation the ambassador agreed with completely because it meant that "if we were asked whether there was a Military or Naval arrangement between the two Governments we could say there was none." But when Grey went on to remark that of course there was "no formal 'Entente,'" Cambon retorted that there was "a moral 'Entente' which might however be transformed into a formal 'Entente' if the two governments desired, when an occasion arose." Again the Liberal imperialist countered that the governments remained "perfectly free," and on this note of disagreement the two parted.[8]

The next day Admiral Troubridge presented the French attaché with the British proposals for naval cooperation. In the Channel there would be a simple division of the Strait of Dover, the French taking the eastern half, the British the western; there was no mention of the lower Channel. In the Mediterranean, Malta would be the dividing point, the British operating in the eastern half and the French in the western. Beyond these vague and general propositions—typical of much of British naval planning before 1914—the Admiralty offered no suggestions for the execution of the mutual responsibilities. There was, however, no lack of political specifics in the draft, for Churchill had inserted a lengthy preamble stating that the "agreement" was not binding and that the dispositions of the two fleets "have been made independently because they are the best wh(ich) the separate interest of each country suggests, having regard to all the circumstances and probabilities; and they do not arise from any naval agreement or convention." [9] Accepting the entire memorandum without comment the attaché, duly allowing for the Parisian August, promised a French reply in mid-September.

7. Bertie to Nicolson, May 9, 1912, B.D., X, pt. 2, no. 388; memo by Bertie, July 25, 1912, Bertie Papers, F.O. 800/165.
8. Grey to Carnegie, July 22, 1912, B.D., X, pt. 2, no. 400.
9. Ibid., p. 602; cf. Delcassé to Poincaré, Sept. 17, 1912, D.D.F., 3rd ser., III, no. 420.

This Admiralty memo provoked the French reaction Bertie had predicted: Paul Cambon immediately complained that the British wanted "9/10ths of the naval force of France" to go to the Mediterranean, yet would give Paris no "guarantee" that Britain would protect France's exposed northern coasts. The French would certainly require "some assurances that British naval aid would be forthcoming for the Channel and Atlantic coasts." [10] Cambon's apparent misconception about what had prompted the French fleet shift and his poorly veiled demand for a binding engagement irritated the British. Grey held that the French could not demand such an assurance: "if they do raise it we shall have to consider how it can be met without altering the first article of the Draft Naval Agreement." Churchill, who verified anew what he had actually told de Saint-Seine, charged Cambon with completely distorting the meaning of the suggested preamble. The fleet dispositions were independent decisions, the First Lord argued, and the staff talks only involved "the co-operation of forces thus independently disposed." [11]

Churchill's views were flatly contradicted by Paul Cambon on July 26. His interview with Grey that day starkly revealed the dangers inherent in unsupervised staff discussions between military experts: for the ambassador insisted that as early as 1907 Admiral Fisher and the French naval command had divided responsibilities for the Mediterranean. "Eventually the French," Grey recorded, "had said that they would look after the whole of the Mediterranean, and Sir John Fisher had said that we would look after the North Sea and Channel. It was in consequence of these conversations that France had concentrated her fleet in the Mediterranean." [12] Unable to exploit the 1912 fleet shifts, Cambon had cleverly harked back to an earlier epoch. That he misrepresented the evolution of French naval strategy is evident, as France's initial decision to concentrate in the Mediterranean had come in 1906 solely as the product of the Conseil Supérieur de la Marine—the unofficial talks of 1908, not 1907, had simply reaffirmed earlier French assumptions about British help along the northern coasts. Moreover, if Cambon's analysis had been accurate, then why the long French delay in asking for a coastal guarantee? But Grey, for the moment unfamiliar with, indeed unaware of, the details of the past talks, was hard put to refute Cambon's explanations.

The ambassador acted to exploit his advantage. If London insisted on retaining the preamble, then it "would be essential that there should be some understanding between the two Governments that they would at least communicate with each other if there was a menace, and concert

10. "Minute by Sir A. Nicolson," July 24, 1912, *B.D.*, X, pt. 2, no. 401.
11. Asquith, however, thought that "this kind of difficulty is inherent in all such contingent arrangements"; minutes by Asquith, Grey, and Churchill on Nicolson's minute, *ibid.*
12. Grey to Carnegie, July 26, 1912, *ibid.*, no. 402.

beforehand." Perhaps an exchange of private notes, such as he and Lord Lansdowne had done in May 1905, could be arranged. This expedient would enable them, he added, "to say truthfully that no binding agreement existed between us, to take action." To this devious proposal Grey gave an emphatic "no," saying he preferred to leave things as they were. The ambassador was undeterred; either the preamble went or the French got assurances "that, in the event of menace, each Government would ask the other what they were going to do." Faced with this choice, the Foreign Secretary finally admitted the need for consultations but balked at exchanging a "note unless it was to be made public." Further discussions on this point would be resumed, they agreed, when Cambon returned from his holiday.[13]

Grey immediately informed Asquith and Churchill and then the Cabinet of Cambon's demand for some written promise for discussions in case of a crisis. The First Lord still disliked Cambon's assessment of the naval situation. Though he acknowledged not having realized "the extent to wh(ich) the Admiralty had been committed under my predecessor," he continued to favor the "non-committal proviso" because "the present dispositions represent the best arrangements that either power can make independently." And it was not true, he added, "that the French are occupying the Med(iterranea)n to oblige us. They cannot be effective in both theatres and they resolve to be supreme in one. The Germans w(oul)d easily defeat them at sea."[14] Britain had no reason to compensate the French for doing what they would do in any event, that is, operate chiefly in the Mediterranean. In the absence of any Cabinet action on the French demand, Churchill's unyielding attitude toward the French con game held sway within the government.

Sir Francis Bertie made the British position crystal clear to Raymond Poincaré on July 30. Not only did Bertie defend Churchill's preamble against the Premier's objections, he also reminded Poincaré that the French fleet "transfer was a spontaneous decision of the French Government and not in consequence of the conversations between the British and French experts in the same way as the decision of His Majesty's Government to withdraw for the present some of the British ships hitherto stationed there." The Premier conceded that the French move was "spontaneous," but he insisted that the changes would never have occurred had there not been the assurance of British help. Otherwise naval conversations were useless and France would have to provide for its northern coasts. Furthermore: "To begin a Military or Naval convention by saying that it means nothing so far as the Governments are concerned is superfluous and quite out of place in such a Convention." What he really preferred, Poincaré told the ambassador, was a declaration that would ensure immediate discussions in a crisis about "whether

13. *Ibid.*
14. Memo by Churchill, July 29, 1912, *ibid.*, no. 403.

the arrangements made between the experts should be put into force." [15] Noting the attitude of the British Cabinet, Bertie warned his host that such a declaration was unlikely, nor in any case could a decision be reached before September. [16]

During August British policy-makers sporadically reconsidered the wisdom of a non-obligatory proviso as part of any naval arrangement with France. Bertie resumed his earlier pressure for an exchange of notes, calling for two distinct accords, one technical, one political, instead of incorporating both aspects into one settlement. A political statement could, he argued, contain a promise to consult in emergencies. [17] Bertie's solution did not convince Winston Churchill. For months the First Lord had recognized that his new naval dispositions in the Mediterranean required, as he put it, a "definite arrangement" with France without delay. Yet he had consistently made clear that he wanted no alliance, only contingency agreements that would come into effect after a war was declared; thus he disliked Bertie's notion of a separate political declaration. In his famous appraisal of the dangers and limitations of the entente relationship, the First Lord stressed to Sir Edward Grey on August 23 his strong desire to keep unhampered Britain's "freedom of choice," and consequently Britain's ability "to influence French policy beforehand."

> That freedom will be sensibly impaired if the French can say that they have denuded their Atlantic seaboard, and concentrated in the Mediterranean on the faith of naval arrangements made with us. This will not be true. If she did not exist, the French could not make better dispositions than at present. They are not strong enough to face Germany alone, still less to maintain themselves in two theatres. They therefore rightly concentrate their Navy in the Mediterranean where it can be safe and superior and can assure their African communications. Neither is it true that we are relying on France to maintain our position in the Mediterranean. . . . If France did not exist, we should make no other disposition of our forces.
>
> Circumstances might arise which in my judgment would make it desirable and right for us to come to the aid of France with all our force by land and sea. But we ask nothing in return. If we were

15. Bertie to Grey, July 30, 1912, ibid., nos. 404, 405.

16. On July 16, 1912, a Franco-Russian naval convention was signed in Paris that contained provisions for staff talks and for joint war planning. The initial discussions in Paris covered Russian retention of naval supremacy in the Black Sea and French assistance against the Austrians, and possibly the Italians and Germans; "Echange de vues stratégiques entre le Chef d'état-major général de la marine russe et le Chef d'état-major général de la marine française," July 1912, Archives Marine, ES 9; see also Vagts, Defense and Diplomacy, 116–117. Neither the new convention nor Le Temps's disclosure (in early August) of its conclusion had any significant impact upon the Anglo-French naval discussions.

17. Bertie to Grey, Aug. 13, 1912, B.D., X, pt. 2, no. 409; also the memo by Bertie of his interview with George V, July 25, 1912, Bertie Papers, F.O. 800/187.

attacked by Germany, we should not make it a charge of bad faith against the French that they left us to fight it out alone; and nothing in naval and military arrangements ought to have the effect of exposing us to such a charge if, when the time comes, we decide to stand out.

This is my view, and I am sure I am in line with you on the principle. I am not at all particular how it is to be given effect to, and I make no point about what document it is set forth in. But [consider] how tremendous would be the weapon which France would possess to compel our intervention if she could say, "On the advice of and by arrangement with your naval authorities we have left our Northern coasts defenceless. We cannot possibly come back in time." Indeed . . . it would probably be decisive whatever is written down now. *Every one must feel who knows the facts that we have the obligations of an alliance without its advantages, and above all without its precise definitions.*[18]

Churchill had made an eloquent appeal for firmness toward France and a cogent plea for retention of complete control over British foreign policy. He had also recognized how the entente might eventually entangle Great Britain, and, he had perceived the full importance of strategic dispositions in modern warfare. Naval concentrations possess a constant deterrent quality; they also mold the shape of the naval warfare that follows if deterrence fails. To prevent the French from exploiting their situation Churchill wanted it recognized that the current dispositions were the product of national, not entente, decisions. He nevertheless realistically conceded that the respective naval arrangements would inevitably expose each entente partner to a certain dependency upon the other; but to recognize this dependency was one thing, to allow one's partner to exploit what was more apparent than real was quite something else. Hence his resistance in August to the Poincaré-Cambon maneuver to exploit the fact of the naval shift for a closer political relationship; his resistance was, ultimately, to no avail.

On the very same day, August 23, Henry Asquith expressed a willingness "to agree with Bertie that Poincaré's criticism is justified." The Prime Minister had come to feel, Louis Mallet reported to Grey, that the question of a preamble was "a matter of form on which we should give way, if Bertie could suggest some manner of recording this agreement of not too formal a character."[19] Asquith may simply have failed to perceive, though it means he ignored the advice of his colleagues, that the French were subtly seeking to pressure London into a more definite commitment to the Continent. Or he may have reasoned that so long

18. Churchill to Grey, Aug. 23, 1912, quoted in Churchill, *The World Crisis*, I, 115–116, italics added.
19. Mallet to Grey, Aug. 23, 1912, Grey Papers, F.O. 800/94. Three weeks earlier Asquith had expressed a strong dislike for separate agreements; why he altered his view is not clear; Asquith minute on Bertie to Tyrrell, July 31, 1912, *ibid.*, F.O. 800/50.

as the "form" was satisfactory, that is, no open alliance, there would be no harm in accepting a new definition of the entente relationship: Britain would, in the final analysis, retain the decision for peace or war. Always inclined to proceed pragmatically from one crisis to another and to keep all his options open for as long as possible, Asquith may have decided to grant what he regarded as a proper concession, confident that he would still retain a free hand at a moment of crisis. In any event, by late August the French were nearing their long-sought goal of a more precise, written definition of the entente.

In Paris, meanwhile, French naval officials were also laboring over the preamble issue. Admiral Aubert opposed any such statement unless it admitted that the fleet dispositions were the result of staff talks. Delcassé, somewhat more flexible, drafted a preamble stating simply that if the two nations were allies, the French would operate in the Mediterranean, the British in the North Sea; fleet dispositions and consultation were not mentioned.[20] Then, suddenly, before any decision had been made, one of those hazards of modern bureaucratic government manifested itself: a press leak. On September 10 the French press learned that the Third Squadron at Brest would move to the Mediterranean in mid-October.[21] This ill-timed revelation weakened France's negotiating position vis-à-vis London. It also brought instant reactions from the British and the French press.

Generally, the Parisian papers welcomed the news. Some, such as the *Journal des débats*, characterized the shift as a natural extension of the earlier concentration in the Mediterranean. Others, like *Le Temps*, which initially broke the story, cited the transfer as further proof of a Triple Entente naval accord. And *La vie maritime* called it "the absolute confirmation of the *entente cordiale.*" Only *L'éclair*, edited by Delcassé's longtime antagonist Ernest Judet, flatly opposed the move—a position supported of course by the Breton press and politicians.[22] In London Lucien Wolf, writing in the *Daily Graphic*, also claimed the new dispositions were part of an entente accord. But the *Times* insisted that sound naval strategy, not an alliance, had dictated the French shift and the *Westminster Gazette* labeled as "pure nonsense" the idea "of a joint movement between Britain and France to hem Germany in."[23] Suspecting the worst, the *Manchester Guardian* asserted that the fleet develop-

20. Draft preamble by Aubert, n.d. [late August], Archives Marine, ES 10; memo by Delcassé, Sept. 1, 1912, enclosed in Delcassé to Poincaré, Sept. 17, 1912, *D.D.F.*, 3rd ser., III, no. 420; Poincaré, *Au service de la France*, I, 215–217.
21. On Sept. 6, 1912, Aubert ordered the Third Squadron to leave Brest on Oct. 15 for the Mediterranean; Archives Marine, BB4 2708.
22. *Journal des débats*, Sept. 11, 1912; *Le Temps*, Sept. 11, 13, 1912; *La vie maritime*, Sept. 25, 1912; *L'éclair*, Sept. 12–13, Oct. 6, 1912; also see *Le yacht*, Sept. 21, Oct. 12, 1912, and *La moniteur*, Sept. 21, Nov. 30, 1912.
23. Wolf quoted in *Le Temps*, Sept. 13, 1912; *Times*, Sept. 14, 1912; *Westminster Gazette*, Sept. 18, 1912.

ment had been achieved with the connivance of the Asquith government. "And this tremendous revolution in our national policy," it complained, "has been made without the knowledge of Parliament by a little knot of men working by methods of evasion and equivocation. Ministers in the past have been impeached for much less." [24]

Paul Cambon was absolutely appalled by the possible damage caused by the press leak, fearing it would diminish "the principal advantage which a naval accord . . . offered to England." Anxious to resume his elaborate stratagem for closer Anglo-French relations, he emphasized to Arthur Nicolson on September 17 that the French naval moves were temporary, dictated simply by the forthcoming naval maneuvers; a final decision on fleet distribution still depended upon the results of the entente discussions. A somewhat perplexed Undersecretary, mindful of de Saint-Seine's earlier comments and that the French naval maneuvers had already taken place, accepted Cambon's explanation without comment.[25]

Two days later the ambassador enlarged upon these points when he saw the Foreign Secretary. Resuming his earlier campaign to extract something on paper, he reiterated to Grey that any definite naval arrangement depended upon a satisfactory political accord. Surely the two nations could reach an acceptable understanding that would entail no "alliance or any obligation to take action" but that would guarantee consultation. To reinforce the point, Cambon presented Grey with a draft formula (the product of the ambassador's own initiative) briefly stating that if either government feared aggression, consultation would take place immediately. The surprised Foreign Secretary responded that the two powers were already discussing common problems. True, Cambon admitted, but "there was no written understanding." Grey, though fully cognizant of the illegitimate nature of Cambon's assertions about the fleet moves, did not reject the notion of a formula out of hand; nor did he repeat his July demand that such an arrangement be made public. Rather, he promised to discuss the idea with the Prime Minister when he returned. At last Cambon had gotten his foot in the door; whether the door opened wider would depend upon Asquith's response.[26]

Elsewhere other developments were taking place which revealed the complexity of the entente's position in the Mediterranean.[27] Afraid

24. Quoted in Hale, *Publicity and Diplomacy*, 430; for a German view of the press comment, see Kühlmann to Bethmann, Sept. 16, 1912, *G.P.*, XXXI, no. 11595.

25. P. Cambon to Poincaré, Sept. 19, 1912, *D.D.F.*, 3rd ser., III, no. 431; Poincaré, *Au service de la France*, I, 217–219.

26. Grey to Bertie, Sept. 19, 1912, *B.D.*, X, pt. 2, no. 410; P. Cambon to Poincaré, Sept. 21, 1912, *D.D.F.*, 3rd ser., III, no. 448.

27. Things were not helped by a series of sharp, caustic attacks in the French press on British policy in the Near East; the attacks were apparently the work of the Russian Embassy. See, e.g., Poincaré to P. Cambon (tel.), Oct. 11, 1912, *D.D.F.*, 3rd ser., IV, no. 114.

the Italians would misinterpret the news of the French fleet shift, Poincaré had quickly acted to assure Rome that the transfer was not directed against Italy. Provisions for moving the XIX Corps from North Africa had alone necessitated the shift; France, above all, desired continued friendly relations with Italy.[28] The British also sought to assuage any Italian apprehensions: the fleet transfer, Grey told the Italian ambassador, was neither a response to Italian gains against Turkey nor the result of an entente arrangement.

This episode did, however, furnish a convenient opportunity for the entente partners to emphasize to Rome their concern about the future of the Mediterranean, in particular their concern about a possible German role there. On September 21 Grey pointedly stressed to the Italian ambassador that there were other ways for Rome to secure its new possessions in North Africa "than by an extension of the Triple Alliance to the Mediterranean." Italy, for example, could join with Britain and France to form a status quo treaty that would guarantee Italy's recent victories. That such a treaty would also exclude Germany and perhaps require the abandonment of Italian gains in the Aegean Sea was left unstated. Poincaré, who also wanted to strengthen the earlier status quo accord with Spain, warmly endorsed and supported Grey's demarche for a guarantee arrangement with Italy.[29] But until the Italo-Turkish peace settlement could be resolved, the entente partners could expect little success in this venture. And their hopes were further complicated by the outbreak of the first Balkan war in the middle of October.

In late September Sir Edward Grey traveled to Balmoral, that idyllic late summer retreat of British royalty on the banks of the Dee. During his stay two incidents occurred underscoring what Paris and St. Petersburg hoped to glean eventually from the entente and the limits of what they might receive. Serge Sazonov, the Russian Foreign Minister, also visiting at Balmoral, pressed Grey on possible British naval assistance if Russia were to become involved in a war because of the French alliance. Russia was especially afraid that the Germans would bombard its coastal towns in the Baltic. Grey, while responding that this was a question for naval experts, expressed doubts about any British fleet entering the Baltic. Also, he reminded Sazonov that "no British Government could go to war unless backed by public opinion." Thus Britain would never support a French war of revanche or an attempt to encircle Germany. On the other hand, if Germany sought to crush France, he thought Britain would not stand aside: "If Germany dominated the policy of the Continent it would be disagreeable to us as well as to others for we should

28. Poincaré to Laroche (tel.), Sept. 15, 1912, *ibid.*, III, no. 403.
29. Grey to Bertie, Sept. 21, 1912, F.O. Confidential Print, pt. 26, Foreign Office Library; Bertie to Grey, Sept. 20, 1912, Grey Papers, F.O. 800/53; see also chap. xcvi, "Negotiations for an Anglo-Italian Pact, 1912–1914," B.D., X, pt. 2.

be isolated." [30] This significant clarification, while not constituting any firm British commitment to go to war, did make explicit what it would take to bring about such a commitment. Yet it was a verbal clarification, nothing more.

At that very moment Paul Cambon was hard at work trying to translate such an assurance into writing. Moving to exploit Grey's apparent receptivity toward some written statement, the French ambassador returned to the Foreign Office on September 25 with a second formula, this one drafted by Poincaré. It talked of action against a third party and of a common means to conduct such action. Nicolson forwarded the formula to Grey at Balmoral, observing that it presupposed "a defensive alliance. I doubt the Cabinet would take it—don't you?" And he added: "We shall have to sign something but I thought Cambon only asked for [an] interchange of views in certain circum[stances] and this was acceptable." [31] Whether in fact it would be acceptable still depended upon Asquith. But Grey, after Sazonov's pressure and Cambon's demarches, could clearly have had few doubts as he left Balmoral that Britain would have to give France something tangible or else risk the disruption of the entente and the possibility of isolation against Germany.

In Paris, the Poincaré government faced a deadline. It could no longer postpone a response to the British naval proposals of the preceding July. There was no problem on the technical details: the French Staff, finding the Admiralty's ideas "vague," virtually drafted a new convention. The difficulty was whether to include Delcassé's alternative preamble. Although Poincaré strongly disliked the preamble, it was retained because it furnished still another foundation from which to negotiate a written accord with London.[32] By October 1, when the naval counterproposals were transmitted to the Admiralty, the French diplomatic strategy was complete.[33] In a "forward" position were the two formulas to which the British had to respond; in a secondary or "fall-back" position was the naval convention with the preamble. If worse came to worse, the preamble could be utilized to obtain what a conventional political accord could not. As before, everything depended upon Asquith's response.

30. Memo by Grey, Sept. 24, 1912, B.D., IX, pt. 1, no. 805; the King, Asquith, Crewe, and Nicolson saw the memo. Also see Nicolson to Grey, Sept. 30, 1912, ibid., no. 806; Nicolson to Stamfordham, Oct. 2, 1912, ibid., no. 807. For Sazonov's account (October 1912), see Marchand, Un livre noir, II, 345–359.
31. French formula, Sept. 25, 1912, Nicolson Papers, vol. II/1913; Nicolson to Grey, Sept. 25, 1912, ibid.
32. On the preamble question, see P. Cambon to Poincaré, Sept. 21, 1912, D.D.F., 3rd ser., III, no. 446; de Saint-Seine to Aubert, Sept. 21, 1912, ibid., no. 449. An extract of the eventual French reply is in Delcassé to Poincaré, Sept. 17, 1912, ibid., no. 420; the complete reply is in Archives Marine, ES 10.
33. De Saint-Seine to Aubert, Oct. 1, 1912, D.D.F., 3rd ser., IV, no. 15. The technical naval arrangements are discussed in Chapter 13.

The crucial victory for the French forward strategy came on October 11 when the Prime Minister told Grey he saw no harm in Cambon's first formula. "Indeed," Asquith commented, "it is almost a platitude." [34] His attitude made the preamble a dead issue; the question now became one of translating this approval into a form the Cabinet would accept. Ever mindful of radical sensitivities, Asquith and Grey ruled out an exchange of notes unless Parliament was informed. Indeed, for bargaining purposes, the Foreign Secretary told Cambon on October 16 that he saw no need to convert the verbal assurances into writing. But the resourceful French ambassador quickly countered, in a complete change of tactics (and one that was not reported to Paris), that the frequent changes in the French government required that some written accord "to bind France . . . be on the record." For this purpose, he continued, an exchange of private letters that need not be published would serve admirably. This suggestion Grey agreed to consider,[35] and a few days later he gave Asquith's consent for an exchange of letters on condition that the Cabinet approve them. The ambassador accepted. Recognizing that the letters were as much as he was likely to get, Cambon appreciated, even if Asquith did not, that the Cabinet's participation would give the letters "un caractère officiel." [36]

The Grey-Cambon discussions finally reached the Cabinet on October 30. Because the Foreign Secretary had earlier circulated the French formula to the Cabinet and because the French press carried rumors of the negotiations, the Cabinet ministers had ample warning that a turning point had been reached in Anglo-French relations. Surprisingly, therefore, the central point of contention during the session was not the exchange of letters but rather how they would be worded. Some ministers found the formula "vague," and Grey drafted instead a brief, three-paragraph letter acknowledging the staff talks, again declaring that they were nonobligatory, and promising automatic consultation in time of crisis. These modifications satisfied the radicals.[37]

They were also acceptable to Raymond Poincaré, who requested only one apparently slight alteration: an assurance that if the two governments resolved to act, the staff talks would be the basis of their cooperation. This proposal provoked a lengthy wrangle in the Cabinet on November 20 that continued to the next day. The most the ministers would

34. Asquith added: "I am not sure that he and Lansdowne were quite ad idem in their correspondence in May 1905"; Asquith to Grey, Oct. 11, 1912, B.D., X, pt. 2, no. 412. On Oct. 8 Churchill had told Grey that Delcassé's preamble went "a long way toward meeting my view," Grey Papers, F.O. 800/87.
35. Grey to Bertie, Oct. 16, 1912, F.O. 371/1368.
36. The only record of this meeting is P. Cambon to Poincaré, Oct. 31, 1912, D.D.F., 3rd ser., IV, no. 301.
37. The formula had gone to the Cabinet on Oct. 11, 1912. On the Cabinet, see Asquith to George V, Nov. 1, 1912 (covering the Cabinets of Oct. 30 and Nov. 1), Asquith Papers, box 6; Grey to Bertie, Oct. 30, 1912, B.D., X, pt. 2, no. 413; P. Cambon to Poincaré, Oct. 31, 1912, D.D.F., 3rd ser., IV, no. 301.

accept was a promise that in an emergency the staff talks "would at once be taken into consideration and the two governments would then decide what effect should be given to them." In this way, Grey explained to Cambon, neither government would be committed by old plans which might require adjustment in case of war. What Grey did not add, though the French undoubtedly appreciated it, was that the Cabinet had skillfully thwarted Poincaré's attempt to commit Britain to a continental strategy should it decide to help France.[38]

Cambon accepted this change and on November 22 and 23 he and Grey exchanged private letters guaranteeing consultation. The British note read:

> From time to time in recent years the French and British naval and military experts have consulted together. It has always been understood that such consultation does not restrict the freedom of either Government to decide at any future time whether or not to assist the other by armed force. We have agreed that consultation between experts is not, and ought not to be regarded as an engagement that commits either Government to action in a contingency that has not arisen and may never arise. The disposition, for instance, of the French and British fleets respectively at the present moment is not based upon an engagement to co-operate in war.
>
> You have, however, pointed out that, if either Government had grave reason to expect an unprovoked attack by a third Power, it might become essential to know whether it could in that event depend upon the armed assistance of the other.
>
> I agree that, if either Government had grave reason to expect an unprovoked attack by a third Power, or something that threatened the general peace, it should immediately discuss with the other, whether both Governments should act together to prevent aggression and to preserve peace, and if so what measures they would be prepared to take in common. If these measures involved action, the plans of the General Staffs would at once be taken into consideration, and the Governments would then decide what effect should be given to them.[39]

This exchange of letters completed the formal political evolution of the entente. No longer, as had been the case since the second Moroccan crisis, would Anglo-French relations depend entirely upon the intangibles of goodwill and popular support. Paul Cambon's persistent campaign to obtain a written definition of the entente, first begun in 1905, was at last successful. Although Paris would naturally have preferred a more extensive expansion of cross-Channel ties, the letters were

38. Asquith to George V, Nov. 21, 1912, Asquith Papers, box 6; P. Cambon to Poincaré, Nov. 23, 1912, D.D.F., 3rd ser., IV, no. 534.
39. Grey to P. Cambon, Nov. 22, 1912, B.D., X, pt. 2, no. 416; cf. P. Cambon to Grey, Nov. 23, 1912, ibid., no. 417. The original British drafts are in the Grey Papers, F.O. 800/53.

nonetheless a step in that direction. Uncommitted to act, the two governments were committed to consult. Moreover, as Poincaré wrote Delcassé, "the importance of these documents will not escape you; the strategic studies, which have proceeded secretly between the General Staffs of both countries, have henceforth the explicit approval of the British Government." [40] Given the radical strength in the Liberal party, the letters were naturally regarded from the French standpoint as a shoring up of the entente relationship.

The Asquith government, however, viewed the letters from an entirely different perspective. For the radicals the letters constituted definite, unmistakable, written recognition that the highly irregular staff talks did not obligate the British government and that the Cabinet retained its freedom of decision unfettered. But, and this point must be emphasized, the notes were not originally a product of radical attempts to bring the conversations under control. Rather they were a response to French pressure for the consolidation of the entente.[41] It was Cambon's diplomacy, not sudden radical scruples, which occasioned this November restatement that the staff conversations committed neither country. Furthermore, in agreeing to consultation, the Cabinet certainly believed that it had promised nothing beyond what any Cabinet would do in a crisis. When compared with the variety and sweep of the various French demands made since May, the letters looked positively innocuous. This is why the letters provoked, contrary to Grey's later assertions, no real crisis within the Cabinet in late 1912. Most in the Cabinet felt, as Churchill later noted, that "this was the best we could do for ourselves and for them." [42]

Since 1914 the Asquith Cabinet and Grey in particular have been assailed for their alleged failure to understand that the letters actually increased, rather than stabilized Britain's commitment to France. Lord Loreburn, who left the Cabinet in June 1912, gave succinct expression to this opinion in 1919 when he charged that the letters had "implicitly recognized that the duty existed, while agreeing that naval and military conversations and dispositions had not created it—in a formal way." [43] Yet such charges should not obscure the fact that the Cabinet sanctioned the letters precisely because they did want to define the absolute limits of the entente. Admittedly, the Cabinet furnished the French with the written accord which had so long eluded them; on the other hand, the letters offered the Cabinet, and especially its radical members, a means to limit the consequences inherent in their earlier failure

40. Poincaré to Delcassé and Millerand, Nov. 25, 1912, D.D.F., 3rd ser., IV, no. 563. Also see Poincaré, Au service de la France, I, 219–223; Gooch, Before the War: Studies in Diplomacy, II, 166–169.
41. Compare Grey, Twenty-five Years, I, 93–94.
42. Churchill, The World Crisis, I, 116. Also see Marder, Road to War, 306–309; Tyler, British Army, 142–148.
43. Lord Loreburn, How the War Came (London, 1919), 101.

—including that of Lord Loreburn—to stop the military and naval conversations. It was the inability of the radicals in late 1911 to halt the staff talks, not their later endorsement of the Grey-Cambon letters, that determined much of the character of Britain's commitment to France and the Continent. Or, put another way, it was the conversations, not the letters, that were the real culprits. Without the prospect of naval conversations Churchill could never have contemplated a withdrawal from the Mediterranean so calmly nor Cambon have had the opportunity to consolidate Anglo-French ties.

Finally, the Cabinet's decision in July to make the naval conversations official reflected anew one of the essential qualities of the entente relationship—that it was shaped, nurtured, and reinforced by strategic requirements. The Entente Cordiale, conceived in part because of Britain's strategic interests in Moroccan ports, had progressively evolved into a friendly partnership with military and naval features directed against Germany. As a result, by early 1913 there existed not only detailed military and naval preparations but also the guarantee of consultation in times of danger. The quasi-alliance was now largely complete. Paul Cambon had not labored in vain.

13 | Prepared for War: The Entente Military and Naval Arrangements

The Grey-Cambon letters of November 1912 encouraged French hopes for British help in case of a war against Germany. But the ultimate effectiveness of this assistance, if it came, depended upon the preparedness of the British services and upon their coordination with those of the French. The military conversations conducted sporadically until 1910 and intensively thereafter finally attained a definitive status in March 1913. The naval talks, in spite of their more recent origin, were also settled at this time. In both areas only minor adjustments and revisions remained.

The preparation of the B.E.F. and the completion of the staff talks continued to absorb the energies of General Henry Wilson. In the final months before the war he worked assiduously to ready the Expeditionary Force, to propagate the doctrine of continental intervention, and to secure a firm commitment from the Liberal government for the immediate dispatch of the *entire* B.E.F. to France. His efforts were facilitated by changes in command at the War Office. In March 1912 Sir John French, one of the heroes of the Boer War and a former commander at Aldershot, replaced Sir William Nicholson as Chief of the Imperial General Staff. Three months later Haldane became Lord Chancellor and John Seely, also a veteran of the South African campaign, became the new Secretary of State for War. The latter, who possessed neither his predecessor's formidable prestige nor his forensic skills, was subjected to endless importunings from Henry Wilson about the war-readiness of the B.E.F. Equally on the receiving end of Wilson's complaints about the Expeditionary Force was "Johnnie" French, with whom the D.M.O. soon established close ties. Wilson liked the future Earl of Ypres because he was a soldier "pure and simple"; but occasionally he did wish French had "more brains & knowledge. He has neither the one nor the other in any real measure." Still, Wilson found the new C.I.G.S. extremely receptive to his strong views on a host of issues, from intervention on the Continent to conscription to the rights of Ulster. Wilson in turn served as a useful and willing conduit for French's relations with the opposition leadership, especially Bonar Law.[1]

Wilson's campaign for continental intervention benefited from increased public discussion about Britain's military role. The rumors of British military activity in the summer of 1911 prompted, really for the first time since 1906, concern about the purpose and size of Haldane's Expeditionary Force. New interest in the Army first became apparent in the parliamentary debates over the 1912 army estimates. With Leopold Amery and Arthur Lee supplying the pungent questions, Conservative spokesmen asserted that the B.E.F. was "entirely unsuited for [any] sort of European emergency." Charging that many understood that it was "part of our obligation to assist a foreign Power with the Expeditionary Force which should be ready for despatch at short notice," critics such as Amery insisted that the size of the Force (170,000 men) bore no relation to Britain's strategical needs. On July 5, 1912, Amery declared that France's maintenance as a great power was of vital interest to Britain and that consequently London should be prepared to send military assistance. And he added: "If we are to send a force at all, and it is agreed that we should send it—(Hon. Members: 'No.') It is by the great majority of this House, and if we send a force at all we should send it to make sure of victory and not to share in defeat." As it stood, Amery continued, the B.E.F. would be inadequate to meet the German force "that was to march through Belgium to crush the French left. It is upon our Expeditionary Force that the brunt of that march would fall." [2]

But Conservative defense spokesmen were not the only ones talking

1. See, e.g., Mar. 19, Nov. 8, Dec. 2, 1912, Apr. 22, 1913, Wilson Diaries.
2. *Parliamentary Debates: Commons*, 5th ser., 35 (Mar. 6, 1912), 396, 417–418; ibid., 40 (July 4, 1912), 1341–1342. Also see Leopold Amery, *My Political Life*, vol. I (London, 1953), 407–412.

about continental intervention. The *Army Review*, founded by the General Staff in 1911 with Colonel Repington as editor, also advertised such ideas. In the April 1912 issue General French called for an Army "firmly united in the bonds of a common doctrine, not imposed upon us from above so much as accepted by reason of its merits." In July Captain R. W. M. Stevens analyzed the problems of British intervention on the Continent and said that "the first step we could take towards the concentration of superior force on any battlefield would be to place the *whole* Expeditionary Force in the field." [3] Other professional journals also discussed the demands of British military operations in France and Belgium. "Viator" in the *United Service Magazine*, offering some "Topographical Notes on Belgium," declared that it was "a generally accepted axiom that, should this country be drawn into a European conflict, the theatre of war, as far as the British Army's concerned, will be Belgium, where our expeditionary force will take its place on the left flank of the French Army, with a view of arresting a German advance from the east." [4] Finally, the views of Henry Wilson achieved public distribution in November 1913 when the *Times* summarized his lecture entitled "Frontiers, with special reference to those in Europe" given at the University of London. His remarks—which earned him a reprimand from John Seely—included a call for military preparedness and lavish praise of the large army possessed by that other island empire, Japan. Asking his audience, which included Lord Roberts, to ponder the Japanese example, Wilson had concluded his lecture by declaring that "with exceptions so few as to be negligible, the knock-out blow in wars had been and always would be, given not on the sea, but on land." [5]

Neither the Conservative assaults nor the public discussion about a British military role on the Continent brought any clarification from the Asquith government about the purpose of the B.E.F. Seely boasted about having 150,000 men ready for instant mobilization, yet he scrupulously avoided any mention of the Continent. In March 1914 Arthur Lee complained that Seely's chief concern appeared "to be to show that the cost of the Army remains the same, and, having said that, he seemed to think he had completely justified his position. But why is there this total divorce between military expenditure and national strategic requirements which specially disturbs our minds?" Seely's response on this occasion was typical: "It would be most unwise and most wrong for me to give any indication of any sort or kind of what is to be done with the six

3. General French, "Memorandum," *Army Review*, 2 (April 1912), viii; Capt. R. W. M. Stevens, "The Concentration of Superior Force at the Decisive Point. Considered in Relation to the Employment and Training of the Expeditionary Force," *ibid.*, 3 (July 1912), 190. Repington's dual responsibilities as the *Times*' military correspondent and as an editor for the War Office drew parliamentary criticism; *Parliamentary Debates: Commons*, 5th ser., 35 (Mar. 6, 1912), 406–407, 415–416.
4. 46 (February 1913), 505.
5. *Times*, Nov. 6, 1913; Callwell, *Wilson*, I, 130.

divisions of the Expeditionary Force in the event of war." "The real question is," he stressed, " 'is the Expeditionary Force ready to go on expedition?' and to that I answer, it is absolutely ready to go on expedition, and I am persuaded that, wherever it goes, it will fight well." [6]

The government's persistent refusal to comment on the use of the Expeditionary Force was understandable. In the first place, to have mentioned continental intervention would have provoked a crisis with Berlin while giving undue and perhaps erroneous encouragement to Paris. More importantly, it would have antagonized the radicals within the Cabinet and within the Liberal party. Such talk would have alarmed the radicals because of their already well-defined distaste for closer ties with France; it would have angered them because demands for intervention were coupled with calls for compulsory service; and it would possibly have reawakened the traditional radical complaints about the cost of a standing army.

Budgetary considerations were important. Defense costs had skyrocketed during the years of Liberal rule. In 1906 defense spending totaled £59,973,508; in 1913 the estimates ran £74,529,300, an increase of nearly twenty-five percent in just over seven years. Mounting costs of the Anglo-German naval race were chiefly responsible for the increases; in 1906 the naval estimates were £31,472,087, in 1914 £51,580,000. Each additional dreadnought represented an expenditure of roughly £2,000,000. Haldane's tenure at the War Office, on the other hand, brought a reduction and stability to army expenditures. Under his administration the budget ran generally at £27,500,000. The combination of financial savings and budgetary stability effectively shielded both the army estimates and the size of the B.E.F. from critics. Indeed, there was only one serious attempt in the Cabinet to reduce the size of the Expeditionary Force before 1914—in 1908, when Lloyd George and Churchill argued that the Force was too large for any conceivable task it might have in the future. Haldane, citing Britain's possible role on the Continent, managed to override the two future Prime Ministers.[7] There were no further attacks of any consequence on the army budget until late 1912, when concern arose over the progressive but small (£600,000) annual increases in the estimates caused by the development of an aviation capability. But on this occasion the B.E.F. again emerged unscathed and the famous Churchill-Lloyd George row over naval estimates in early 1914 brought no demands for reductions in the army budget.[8]

6. *Parliamentary Debates: Commons*, 5th ser., 69 (Mar. 10, 1914), 1107, 1289. Lord Haldane was equally obscure about the purpose of the B.E.F., though he told the House of Lords in April 1913 that the Force owed its origin "to no calculation of what sort of Army we should require on the Continent or any other particular place"; *Parliamentary Debates: Lords*, 5th ser., 14 (Apr. 21, 1913), 186.

7. See Chapter 4, pp. 99–100.

8. Asquith to George V, Dec. 10, 1912, Asquith Papers, box 6. On the 1913–1914 Cabinet fight over naval estimates, see Churchill, *Young Statesman*, 636–670; Marder, *Road to War*, 311–327.

In this connection it should be stressed that the doctrine of continental intervention originated initially from a consideration of Britain's strategic requirements. The deterioration of Anglo-German relations, not a desire to find an excuse for maintaining a standing army of one hundred eighty thousand men, prompted the organization and development of the B.E.F. Naturally the prospect of action on the Continent appealed to the vanity of professional officers; naturally continental intervention offered a new rationale for the B.E.F., especially after the improvement of Anglo-Russian relations had eased the threat to India. Yet, except for Haldane's mention of the Continent in 1908, this justification of the size and purpose of the Expeditionary Force was muted. After all, the sacrosanct Cardwellian principle remained an effective shibboleth for protection of the B.E.F. The cover offered by the concept of linked battalions had its drawbacks, however, for Cardwell's scheme, along with economic limitations, made it difficult to justify any increase in British military forces to match the expansion of German strength after 1912. An effort in this direction would almost certainly have involved the B.E.F. in a bitter controversy with the radicals. In short, political and economic considerations, coupled with prudence, dictated that the Liberal government refrain from discussing the future role of the Expeditionary Force.

The government could not, however, ignore Conservative denunciations of the newly created Territorial Force and a crescendo of demands for some variation of compulsory service. Lord Roberts and the National Service League had tirelessly agitated for conscription since 1905; after 1911 their clamor attained unprecedented vigor. Roberts and his cohorts assailed the "Terriers" as a wholly ineffective and impractical second-line force for home defense. And indeed, Haldane's progeny offered a most attractive target; in mid-1912, five years after its creation, the Territorial Force was short 50,000 men of its authorized strength of 315,000 with the gap increasing. Such a force, Roberts continually asserted, would endanger Britain in case of a German invasion: what Britain needed was compulsory service, which would ensure that adequate numbers of trained troops were available for home defense.[9] Nor did the propagandists fail to point out that increased manpower could furnish an effective counterweight, if necessary, in a continental war. "Hardly any advocate of the principle" of conscription, the *Westminster Gazette* observed, "can make a speech of ten minutes in its support without revealing to us that what he really has in mind is some European conflict in which the compulsory British army will be engaged

9. On this agitation, see Ropp, "Conscription in Great Britain, 1900–1914," 71–76; David James, *Lord Roberts* (London, 1954), 451–463. The *Nineteenth Century* became the virtual house organ of the movement; see, e.g., the series of articles, "National Safety," 73 (March 1913), 473–499.

against compulsory foreign armies."[10] And Admiral Fisher had no doubts whatever on this score: "Lord Roberts's Rabble wouldn't do as an Army in Flanders (which his backers want!—for they know Invasion is twaddle!) He is their facile dupe! A conscript army and an overseas army would be unequally yoked together." Later Fisher conceded that perhaps he had been "too virulent against these silly asses who want to have an Army in Flanders. *That's the real objective!* You can't have the German Army and the British Navy!"[11]

Although Lloyd George and Winston Churchill occasionally (and privately) favored compulsory service, the Liberal government remained adamantly opposed.[12] Tradition, principle, costs (it would have added at least eight million pounds to the budget), and a steady confidence in Haldane's handiwork constituted the government's response to the barrages from Roberts and his supporters. This response was further justified by the lack of unanimity among ranking Army officers about the value of compulsory service for Britain's home defense needs. The Adjutant General, Sir Spencer Ewart, for example, thought there was "no large body of opinion in the Army in favour of compulsory Service if it was to be limited to 'Home' defence." There were, however, "plenty of 'whole Hoggers' who would like to see out and out conscription for general service in war." Finally, the Liberal leadership could and did warn critics of the Territorial Force that its demise would not necessarily be followed by the institution of some type of compulsory service. Haldane put it bluntly in the House of Lords in April 1913: "All I do say is that the only result of the agitation that is going on, even if it destroys the Territorial Force, would not be to put the nation in any peril, but to hamper it in the use of its Expeditionary Force and compel it to keep part at least of that Force at home."[13] The warning to the continentalists could not have been clearer.

Predictably, Haldane's attitude did not impress the Director of Military Operations. It neither curbed his agitation against the "Terriers" nor halted his efforts for conscription. In constant contact with Lord Roberts, Henry Wilson supplied the conscription forces with crucial information, wrote articles on their behalf, and endlessly canvassed his Unionist-Conservative acquaintances about the defects of Britain's military establishment. Moreover, when John Seely informed the Commons

10. Apr. 12, 1913. Seely complained bitterly to Spender about these editorial comments; Seely to Spender, Apr. [?] 1913. Spender Papers. Add. MSS, 46392. Also see *The History of THE TIMES,* vol. IV, pt. 1: *The 150th Anniversary and Beyond, 1912–1918* (London, 1952), 92–98.
11. Fisher to Balfour, Nov. 22, 1912, Apr. 6, 1913, Balfour Papers, Add. MSS, 49712.
12. Mar. 21, Apr. 19, 1913, Riddell, *More Pages From My Diary,* 130–131, 140–141.
13. Diary, Jan. 23, 1913, Ewart Papers; *Parliamentary Debates: Lords,* 5th ser., 14 (Apr. 21, 1913), 191.

that the General Staff opposed compulsory service, Wilson nearly persuaded French to resign in protest.[14] Curiously and unaccountably, the Liberal government made no direct move to curtail Wilson's blatant participation in Roberts' campaign. In November 1912 Colonel Repington, who with cause bore personal animosity toward Wilson, privately complained to Haldane of the General's "constant intrigues." Because Wilson had General French "in his pocket," the only solution, argued the *Times*'s correspondent, was to replace Wilson with William Robertson. At the same time the government should publish an Army Order "warning officers against deprecating our armed forces in the press in very firm Wellington terms." [15] Repington's appeal brought no results; Wilson continued his intrigues for conscription.

Repington did not, however, immediately abandon his efforts to thwart Wilson. His campaign took a variety of forms. In early 1913 he wrote in the *Times* that unlimited continental intervention was out of the question and asserted that the Royal Navy was worth "500,000 bayonets to the French at the decisive point." An angered Wilson commented privately that the Navy was not worth five hundred bayonets and that the French "did not value it at one bayonet! Except from the moral point." [16] More important, the fragmentary evidence suggests that Repington may have inspired the invasion hearings of 1913 in a circuitous attempt to handcuff the full-blown implementation of Wilson's continental strategy. Although the D.M.O., Hankey, and the Admiralty might all have favored new hearings, it was War Minister Seely who wrote Asquith on January 3, 1913, asking for another invasion study. The Admiralty, Seely alleged, no longer believed an invasion of 70,000 possible; rather it felt that raids up to 8,000 men now constituted the real home defense problem. In these circumstances he thought "the composition of the territorial force and the number of the Expeditionary Force which may be presumed to be free to proceed over sea would require consideration." [17] What prompted Seely's initiative? It may have been, as Henry Wilson first suspected, an attempt to justify reductions in the Territorial Force. More likely it was spurred by Repington, who knew Seely well and who saw, as Seely clearly did not, that new discussions about the danger of raids or an invasion might produce a reaffirmation of the 1908 restrictions on use of the B.E.F. Moreover, it was Repington

14. Callwell, *Wilson*, I, 120, 125.

15. Repington to Haldane, Nov. 27, 1912, Haldane Papers, 5909. Although they agreed on a number of issues—including some form of compulsory service, the ineffectiveness of the Territorial Force, and later the need for a French alliance—the two men shared a profound personal antagonism dating from Wilson's part in Repington's forced resignation from the Army in 1902; Luvaas, *The Education of An Army*, 297, and Mary Repington, *Thanks for the Memory* (London, 1938), 153–158, 190–192.

16. Diary, Feb. 14, 1913, in Callwell, *Wilson*, I, 122; *Times*, Feb. 6–7, 1913.

17. Memo by Seely, Jan. 3, 1913, Asquith Papers, box 24; Jan. 7, Feb. 21, 1913, Wilson Diaries.

who spread the notion (which reached Asquith) that Wilson had inspired the hearings in hopes of securing the release of the entire Expeditionary Force for service on the Continent.[18]

The third major examination of the invasion danger began in January
1913 and extended until May 1914. Among the ministers participating
in the study were Asquith, Lloyd George, Haldane, Morley, McKenna,
Grey, Harcourt, Crewe, Churchill, and Seely; the military and naval experts included Battenberg, A. K. Wilson, Vice Admiral Henry Jackson,
Field Marshal Lord Nicholson, Generals French, Grierson, and Hen-
derson; others on the subcommittee were Hankey, Balfour, and Esher.[19]
    The group's task was, in the Prime Minister's opinion, to consider
whether the strength of foreign navies in the North Sea and the Mediterranean, the introduction of submarines and the wireless, and the
changes in naval construction had altered the danger of invasion since
the 1908 hearings. This narrow conception of the subcommittee's function effectively eclipsed the most significant change that had occurred in
the strategic situation since 1908:

> The strengthening of the French *entente* [as Admiral Jackson de-
> scribed it], whereby it is now at least probable that we shall assist
> the French with the greater part of our Expeditionary Force if they
> are attacked by Germany without direct and wilful provocation,
> or if Germany infringes the neutrality of Belgium, *i.e.* we may now
> have to work with an ally and convey a large military force across
> the Channel, and that at very short notice and with the utmost
> promptitude on the outbreak of the war.[20]

This strategic assumption remained implicit in all of the subcommittee
discussion; indeed, the threat of a raid to block the B.E.F.'s departure
made an invasion seem all the more probable. Yet the subcommittee
made no attempt to review the total context of British grand strategy.
Military intervention on the Continent—the apparent victor of the 1911
showdown between the generals and the admirals—was not reconsidered. Instead the ministers and experts concentrated upon raids, the efficacy of the Territorial Force, and the nature of a German surprise attack. Continental intervention had become the accepted dogma.[21]

18. "Notes of a Conversation," Feb. 14, 1913, *Journals and Letters of Esher*, III,
118–119; a copy of this memo is in the Asquith Papers. On Feb. 20, 1913, General
French told Wilson that "A Court was busy crabbing" on the D.M.O. again, Wilson Diaries.
    19. Henry Wilson, though originally scheduled to be on the subcommittee, was
taken off, a move which he regarded as a "real compliment" to him; Mar. 18, 1913,
Wilson Diaries. The complete records of the investigation are in Cab. 16/28; also
see Marder, *Road to War*, 353–358.
    20. Memo by Vice Admiral Sir Henry Jackson, Chief of the War Staff, Apr. 28,
1913, Cab. 16/28B.
    21. In November 1912 Asquith thought the Admiralty "would never agree to dis-
close their plans, & I think they cannot be blamed. They would discuss *various plans*

The Admiralty's position during the new hearings was simple and un-ambiguous: the danger of raids and of a sudden attack was as great, if not greater, than in 1908. Improved torpedoes and submarines, German superiority in airplanes, the increases in the German fleet, and the new difficulties of intelligence collection—all these conditions warranted re-tention of the 1908 decision to keep two Regular Army divisions at home. Elaborate scenarios were developed by the First Lord and his ad-visers that suggested a raid of 20,000 men at a port like Harwich as plausible and possible. These views were reinforced by naval maneuvers in the summer of 1913, when the "Red Force" landed an estimated 48,000 soldiers at Blyth—in fact, the maneuvers upset even the most ar-dent "blue water" advocates, hitherto supremely confident that the Royal Navy could prevent anything larger than a raiding party from reaching British shores.[22] Although Churchill at no point ever sought to reopen the strategic debate about the use of the British Army, Lord Esher thought the Admiralty's concern over raids was partly dictated by a desire to keep some Army divisions available "for naval strategical pur-poses."[23] Whatever the reason, the Admiralty's desire to retain at least one regular division at home had the practical effect of handicapping the Army's schemes for intervention.

The War Office had equally strong opinions about the danger of an invasion. Henry Wilson, who first viewed the hearings as a government trick to justify a reduction in the Territorial Force, wanted to exploit the sessions for a comprehensive study of British policy. Neither Seely nor General French would go that far. But Seely did constantly seek the sub-committee's approval for the immediate departure of the entire B.E.F. in case of war. Rejecting the 1908 limitations on the number of divi-sions available for overseas action, he told the committee on June 26 that the War Office had never accepted the 1908 ruling. Nor could he "conceive that there was sufficient danger to justify the retention of a third of our military forces in these islands." To do so "would greatly encourage our enemies."[24] Yet the total departure of the B.E.F. meant that home defense duties would fall principally upon the Territorial Forces and any remaining regulars, a prospect that no one regarded with equanimity. Furthermore, the testimony of Lord Roberts, Lord Lovat, and Repington about the dangers of invasion on the one hand and the

without prejudice." This circumspect attitude probably accounts for Asquith's re-luctance to rock the boat; Asquith Papers, box 108.

22. Churchill, *The World Crisis*, I, 158–174; Churchill, *Young Statesman*, 595–608; Churchill to Asquith, Aug. 30, 1913, Asquith Papers, box 13. Naval Staff memo, "Landing from Overseas," June 25, 1913, Cab. 16/28. Developments in aviation helped to buttress the Admiralty's fear of a successful raid or invasion; Robin Higham, *The British Rigid Airship, 1908–1931: A Study in Weapons Policy* (London, 1961), 65–73.

23. Esher to Asquith, June 25, 1913, *Journals and Letters of Esher*, III, 125.

24. Minutes of the 10th meeting of the subcommittee, June 26, 1913, Cab. 16/28A. Also see Seely's memo, Apr. 8, 1913, Cab. 16/28.

ineptness of the "Terriers" on the other left the case for the embarkation of the entire B.E.F. weaker, not stronger. By the end of the summer of 1913 Captain Hankey was able, therefore, to get general agreement from all sides, including Lord Roberts, that at least one regular division would have to be kept at home to defend against raids.[25]

Repeatedly during 1913 Lord Esher attempted to force his colleagues to contemplate overall British strategy for a future war: in particular he wanted a re-evaluation of the War Office's scheme for intervention, a scheme he considered "grotesque" and "wild in the extreme." In April 1913 he charged that there were no improvements in the conditions governing home defense which warranted any alterations in the 1908 decisions. Raids were more, not less, likely; the German fleet was stronger; the Territorial Force was now a proven failure. Also, the new strategic conceptions for the utilization of the B.E.F. far exceeded the guidelines envisaged in the 1907 hearings on India, when a hundred thousand men available in six months was considered adequate. Now, Esher declared, the Army's talk of continental operations had introduced a totally new factor.[26] When none of these challenges provoked any substantial committee response, Esher in desperation raised the red flag of the military conversations. On November 6 he warned that if "by naval and military conventions entered into with our friends and allies, not perhaps specifically, but by inference and assumption, we are pledged to definite acts of war upon which the plans of other nations turn, then, if we are honourably to fulfil our engagements, no other course appears open to us but to change the basis upon which our Army rests, and to adopt the only military system adequate to the needs of continental warfare against Nations in Arms." The British Army, he continued, existed for garrison duty, for overseas reinforcement, and for use as an auxiliary of the Royal Navy. Given the conditions of modern warfare, this force had no business on the Continent.[27]

But even this call for realism stimulated only token discussion in the subcommittee about Britain's military role when on November 12 Henry Wilson briefed the group on his evaluation of possible German invasion threats. At that time Esher and Churchill pressed the D.M.O. about the so-called equilibrium of Triple Entente-Triple Alliance forces, an equilibrium which was the crucial element in Wilson's argument that the B.E.F.'s arrival would decisively influence the course of a war. Under attack Wilson was forced to admit that the Triple Alliance had fifty-

25. Hankey to Asquith, July 29, 1913, Cab. 17/100; Hankey to Balfour, Aug. 27, 1913, Balfour Papers, Add. MSS, 49703.
26. "Note by Lord Esher," Apr. 21, 1913, Cab. 16/28A; "Note by Lord Esher, June 6, 1913," ibid.; "Note by Lord Esher, June 17, 1913," ibid.; Esher to Spender, May 7, 1913, Journals and Letters of Esher, III, 123–124; cf. "Note by the Secretary of State for War on Lord Esher's Memorandum, O.A.–28," Apr. 28, 1913, Cab. 16/28A.
27. "Memorandum by Lord Esher," Nov. 7, 1913, Cab. 16/28A.

seven more divisions and that the Germans could easily spare ten thousand men for a diversionary raid on Britain; nonetheless, he defended his strategic assessment as valid, since none of the "second-class" German divisions "would be put into the front rank at the commencement of a war." There was not, he observed, "as a matter of fact, room for the deployment of this second class." In the hearing Wilson received timely support from John Seely, who insisted that an Expeditionary Force on the Continent would "demobilize" a greater number of German troops than if the same divisions were kept in Britain; "on the whole, it is a wiser operation of war, and makes the conquest of this country as difficult, and probably more so." [28]

Except for this desultory discussion there was no further consideration of the continental strategy by the subcommittee. Still, those ministers present, including Morley and Harcourt, could have had few doubts about either Anglo-French military preparations or the orientation of British strategy. They and others had had a new opportunity to challenge the current military orthodoxy; they had had another chance to verify and limit the military conversations; they had also had a forum for probing the obvious discrepancies between the requirements of military intervention and the British forces available for such action. None of these opportunities was utilized. Esher and the Admiralty did, however, gain some satisfaction from the eventual recommendations of the subcommittee. Alarmed by the increased danger of raids and by the admittedly poor condition of the Territorial Force, the final report of the committee (April 15, 1914) basically reaffirmed the 1908 decisions. Raids were recognized as possible, the figure 70,000 retained as a planning guide for possible invasions, and the Army instructed to keep "the equivalent of two divisions of regular troops" in Britain for home defense purposes.[29]

Henry Wilson was not overjoyed with the "most futile" report he had ever read. He feared that if its conclusions were acted upon, "the whole of the Exped. Force [would be] done away with." To prevent this horrendous prospect, he, Robertson, and General Charles Douglas (who had replaced French as Chief of the Imperial General Staff after the Curragh incident of March in which fifty-eight officers had offered to resign rather than act against Ulster) visited Henry Asquith on May 6. The Prime Minister, who since the Curragh incident was also acting as War Minister, listened to the vehement protests of Douglas and Wilson about the committee ruling. Finally Asquith agreed that he would, if necessary, sanction the dispatch of five, not four, infantry divisions to Europe. The War Office's stated rationale for this clear-cut abandon-

28. Minutes of the 16th meeting of the subcommittee, Nov. 12, 1913, *ibid.*; diary, Nov. 12, 1913, in Callwell, *Wilson*, I, 131.
29. The subcommittee's report is in Cab. 38/26/13; Marder summarizes it, *Road to War*, 356–357.

ment of the C.I.D.'s conclusions rested upon Henry Wilson's unequivocal declaration that no invasion attempt was likely in the event of a war between the alliance systems. This argument, which the subcommittee had not accepted, was now agreed to by the Prime Minister.[30] Why Asquith, whom Simon Lovat thought as "incapable of doing anything except drift" because of "drink, bridge, and holding girls' hands," conceded remains puzzling.[31] He probably yielded to Wilson's pleas because he recognized that any decision about the size of the B.E.F., like the act of intervention, ultimately rested with the Cabinet. To amend the report would not close off any options for him; in the meantime it would appease the generals. In August 1914, despite all of Wilson's prior efforts for a firm commitment, the size of the B.E.F. was an open question.

The campaign for conscription, the assaults upon the Territorial Force, and the efforts to secure a binding commitment on use of the B.E.F. did not monopolize all of Henry Wilson's energies. He also worked to prepare the Expeditionary Force for its projected continental task; this meant perfecting the mobilization arrangements of the Force, assuring its transport across the Channel, and determining its movements and location once in France. Helped by the attitude and interest of Sir John French, the D.M.O. systematically studied the deficiencies of Britain's regular forces. His efforts brought a variety of improvements: the number of horses was increased, new ammunition became available for all divisions, and sufficient gasoline supplies were procured. And yet, despite his efforts, the Force on the eve of war still had serious problems: there was a shortage of officers, the Special Reserve troops were understrength, and essential support equipment was lacking.[32]

Other areas also attracted the attention of Wilson and his staff.[33] The utilization of airplanes for reconnaissance purposes was appreciated and acted upon; the "Secret-Report on Belgium, South of the Line of Charleroi-Namur-Liège, and on Brussels from the Point of View of Aviation—1914" suggests that Wilson fully understood the advantages to be gained from the new methods of surveillance. His staff also calculated

30. May 6, 1914, Wilson Diaries; diary, May 6, 1914, in Callwell, *Wilson*, I, 147. See also "Memorandum by the General Staff on the Recommendations of the Sub-Committee . . . with Respect to Attack on the British Isles from Oversea," May 9, 1914, Cab. 3/2; minutes of the 126th meeting of the C.I.D., May 14, 1914, Cab. 28/27/23. The C.I.D. would not in their 1914 discussions sanction, despite some obvious military advantages, the construction of a Channel tunnel.

31. Dec. 9, 1913, Wilson Diaries.

32. Wilson to French, Apr. 3, 1912, W.O. 106/50; memo by Harper, Apr. 1, 1912, *ibid.*; memo by Harper, Apr. 1, 1913, *ibid.*; Majors Desmond Chapman-Huston and Owen Rutter, *General Sir John Cowans, G.C.B., G.C.M.G.: The Quartermaster-General of the Great War*, 2 vols. (London, 1924), I, 250–270.

33. Wilson's chief assistants were Colonel G. M. Harper, known as "Uncle," and Lt. Col. C. J. Sackville-West, known as "Tit Willow." Harper frequently accompanied Wilson on his jaunts to the Continent; Callwell, *Wilson*, I, 149–150.

the grim, expected casualty figures, known coldly as "wastage rates"; on the basis of five major battles in seven weeks they estimated that a force of 100,000 men would have 53,755 casualties, with 16,127 deaths.[34]

Of all the mobilization arrangements none was so carefully studied and computed as the rail movement of the Expeditionary Force from its bases in Britain and Ireland to the ports of embarkation. No detail, no item was left to chance or doubt. For example, from the 2nd Division at Farnborough, 1,011 soldiers would depart at 5:39 A.M. on the fourth day of mobilization aboard trains numbers 412 and 415, scheduled to arrive in Southampton at 7:24 A.M. These rail moves, which were to begin on the second day, were scheduled to be largely completed by the fifteenth day. All the troops in Britain were slated to embark at Southampton. Duties of the personnel at that port were carefully spelled out: an Embarkation Commandant, assisted by a staff of one hundred sixty-two, would coordinate rail moves into the dock area, allot troops to vessels, and supervise the immediate loading process. To avoid confusion every trainload of troops was treated as a self-contained unit, under no circumstances to be divided between two ships even if it meant sending a ship away slightly empty.[35] In sum, thanks to the diligent Wilson and the cooperation of the railway companies, the B.E.F. was assured of rapid transport from its peacetime posts to the ports of embarkation for the continental adventure.

In cooperation with the Royal Navy, movement of the Force across the Channel was also prepared in detail. The Churchill regime at the Admiralty brought a steady improvement in relations between the two services; the argumentative bickering and infighting of the Fisher years abated, though both sides shied away from prolonged discussions of their respective strategies. The institution of the "High-Level Brigade," an informal group composed of Churchill, Seely, French, Battenberg, Hankey, and others, helped the services coordinate their actions on colonial defense issues, on defense against aerial attack, and especially on the improvement of coastal defenses. Moreover, work on the "War Book" by the C.I.D. subcommittee on interdepartmental coordination also forced the services to clarify their plans.[36] Nonetheless, agreement on transporting the B.E.F. to France remained difficult to achieve. In fact, in late 1912 the Navy momentarily balked altogether on the ferry-

34. Wilson to French, Apr. 15, 1913, W.O. 106/51; a copy of the aerial survey is in Archives Guerre, "Plan XVII: Armée W," box 147b; the casualty estimates are in W.O. 106/45.
35. The rail tables are in W.O. 33/665; also see "Notes of a Meeting of Railway Representatives Held at the War Office, Room 217, 11:30 A.M. 30th Jan. 1913," W.O. 106/50.
36. Minutes of the High Level Brigade, Aug. 14, 1913–May 22, 1914, Cab. 18/27; John E. B. Seely (Baron Mottistone), Adventure (London, 1930), 140–141; "Minutes . . . on the Co-Ordination of Department Action on the Outbreak of War," Cab. 15/1; Hankey, Supreme Command, I, 118–123.

ing operation, causing an angered Henry Wilson to tell the Army Council that "either the Admiralty *must* ship us, or we must make the arrangements ourselves, or I would *go* to Paris and say we were not coming." Wilson refused to let his name "be a guarantee unless we can
carry out my promise."[37] After this outburst there were some improvements: a naval officer was assigned to the Directorate of Military Operations and British naval experts surveyed French ports for landing problems. Still, it took a further overture from Wilson to secure the establishment in early 1914 of a joint War Office-Admiralty committee under Vice Admiral Edmond Slade to resolve a number of outstanding issues; even then some transport tables were still being printed on the
night of the declaration of war, August 4, 1914. Here, too, every detail
was enumerated: there were arrangements for chartering merchant ships,
for hiring stevedores, for diverting traffic from Southampton, for securing frozen meat ships, and for paying the crews of the merchant vessels.
There were even provisions for medals for those helping to ferry the Expeditionary Force to war.[38]

The thoroughness of Wilson's staff work was also evident in his ar-
rangements with the French General Staff. Intensive work during the
Agadir crisis had defined and resolved many aspects of Anglo-French
military cooperation, including the zone of concentration in the Hirson-
Le Cateau-Maubeuge triangle. This staff activity, supplemented by
Wilson's frequent conversations with members of the French Staff, continued to August 1914. By March 1913, however, the British and the
French had settled the crucial problems of unloading and moving the
B.E.F. to the war zone. With only slight modifications, the 1913 schedules were in effect when the war began. The arrangements between the
two staffs may be conveniently divided into four categories: (1) the disembarkation of the Expeditionary Force in the French ports; (2) the
rail movement of the B.E.F. to the zone of concentration; (3) general
logistical support; (4) the command and tactical employment of the
B.E.F.[39]

The British divisions would land at Rouen, Le Havre, and Boulogne.
Advance parties would arrive on the second day of mobilization, combatants on the fourth, and all would be in France by the fourteenth day.
At each port bivouac sites had been preselected, provisions made for
fresh water, French labor assigned to the docks, and even five thousand
pounds set aside for last-minute purchases. Upon disembarkation the

37. Diary, Nov. 12, 1912, in Callwell, *Wilson*, I, 119; Nov. 20, 1912, Wilson
Diaries.
38. Jackson to Battenberg (now First Sea Lord), Nov. 27, 1913, Adm. 116/3109;
the files on the interdepartmental committee are in Adm. 116/1324, 1331–1333,
and W.O. 33/685.
39. The most complete files on the arrangements are in Archives Guerre, "Plan
XVII: Armée W," box 147b, and "Plan XVII," box 148; also see the September
1913 summary prepared in London, W.O. 106/49.

units would remain in their camp areas, normally for forty-eight hours, before moving by train to the staging area.[40]

Rail movements from the ports to the zone of concentration (Le Cateau-Maubeuge-Hirson) were of crucial importance to the Anglo-French planners, for these moves reflected both the complexity and the flexibility of modern transport systems. It would be impossible to land an entire British division as a homogeneous unit at a single French port; Wilson and the French therefore had to plan rail moves which would reunite the disparate elements of each division. In practice the *gare régulatrice* at Amiens had functional responsibility for this task, since all trains, including those from Boulogne, traveled first to Amiens for re-grouping and dispatch northward. From Amiens they could take a northern route by Arras and Douai to the Busigny junction or a southern route by Tergnier and St. Quentin to Busigny. Up to sixty trains a day were scheduled for the movement of the B.E.F., the first shipments to start on the seventh day of British mobilization.[41] Elements of the 3rd Division, for instance, would land at Rouen and Le Havre, proceeding first to Amiens and then on to the Busigny station which controlled detraining. From there the troops would be shuttled along the rail line toward Maubeuge, unloading at Le Cateau, Landrecies, and Aulnoye. The division's mechanical transport would come by road from Boulogne. The entire division was expected to be concentrated by 6:00 P.M. on the fourteenth day of mobilization.[42]

The staff talks in addition settled details for the logistical support of the B.E.F.: the French would supply four days of food to the arriving British troops; food depots were organized; the British were given the right to requisition French goods. The transport and storage of munitions, the selection of airfields, and the definition of jurisdictions between British and French police were also arranged. Nor were communications neglected. Interpreters were assigned, a special code "W" prepared for use between the armies, and telephone lines allocated between the British headquarters at Le Cateau and London. In short, the two staffs attempted to anticipate every conceivable problem involved

40. "Tableau D–1914," Archives Guerre, "Plan XVII: Armée W," box 148; "Instructions sur l'installation dans la place du Havre des éléments W y séjournant temporairement," 1913, *ibid.*, box 147b; "Instructions for Entrainment and Embarkation (Short Voyage) of Units of the Expeditionary Force in Great Britain, Part II," November 1912, *ibid.*

41. "Résumé d'un rapport au sujet de l'organisation du transporte W par voie ferrée," May 13, 1912, *ibid.*; see also Committee of Imperial Defence, *History of the Great War, based on Official Documents:* A. M. Henniker, *Transportation on the Western Front, 1914–1918* (London, 1937), 1–25; Col. Le Hénaff and Capt. Henri Bornecque, *Les chemins de fer français et la guerre* (Paris, 1922), 215–222.

42. "Tableau des débarquements et cantonnements de 3e division d'infanterie," 1913, Archives Guerre, "Plan XVII: Armée W," box 147b. The 1st and 2nd infantry divisions were scheduled to arrive at La Capelle at noon on the fourteenth day; the 5th Division at Landrecies on the fifteenth day; and the 4th and 6th Divisions at Wassigny on the sixteenth and fifteenth days respectively. The cavalry division would be at Maubeuge by 6:00 P.M. on the twelfth day.

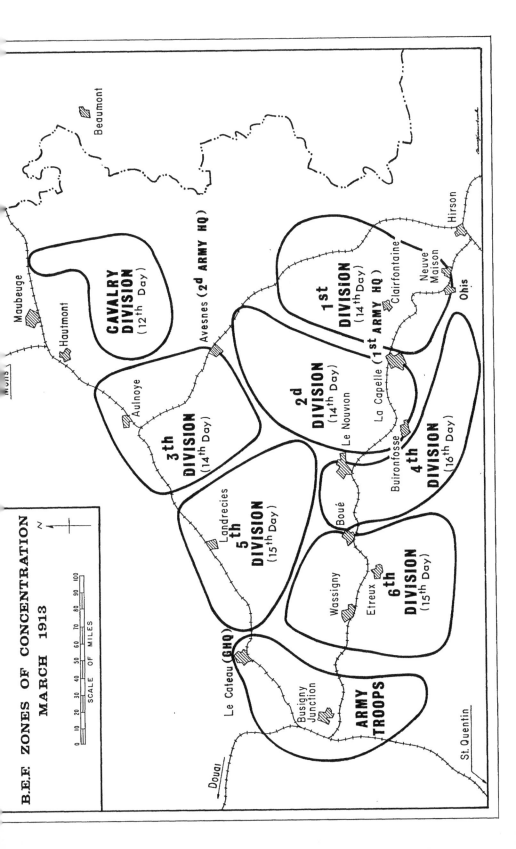

B.E.F. ZONES OF CONCENTRATION
MARCH 1913

SCALE OF MILES

0 10 20 30 40 50 60 70 80 90 100

N

Maubeuge

Beaumont

Mons

Hautmont

CAVALRY DIVISION (12th Day)

Avesnes (2d ARMY HQ)

Hirson

Clairfontaine

Neuve Maison

Ohis

1st DIVISION (14th Day)

La Capelle (1st ARMY HQ)

2d DIVISION (14th Day)

Le Nouvion

Buironfosse

4th DIVISION (16th Day)

Aulnoye

3th DIVISION (14th Day)

Landrecies

5th DIVISION (15th Day)

Boué

Wassigny

Etreux

6th DIVISION (15th Day)

Le Cateau (GHQ)

Busigny Junction

ARMY TROOPS

Douai

St. Quentin

in the establishment of the B.E.F. along the Belgian frontier.[43] The military conversations thoroughly delineated the preliminaries of entente military cooperation; they did not, however, offer much guidance on the problem of wartime cooperation. Although liaison officers were assigned down to brigade level, there was no attempt to define the command relations between the two armies. The British Commander in Chief would act independently and yet at the same time in cooperation with the French Staff; [44] beyond this elementary agreement nothing was settled. Further, the conversations decided little about the tactical employment of the B.E.F. The French, while responsible for selecting the zone of concentration, imposed no other preferences upon Henry Wilson. The General's own views on the tactical employment of the British Army were never spelled out with any clarity. His diary suggests that in August 1913 he expected the British to fight on a twenty-mile front from Andenne to Rochefort in Belgian Luxembourg. To reach this location the B.E.F. would have had to move eastward over fifty miles, crossing the Meuse River in the process. Presumably it would have then linked up with the French forces, especially the Fourth and Fifth Armies, as they moved to the offensive.[45] Whatever Wilson's preferences on the matter, his hopes for offensive action in Belgium were doomed to remain just that, for the German armies did not, as he had expected, obligingly confine their attack below the Meuse.

When war came in 1914 arrangements for the arrival and deployment of the B.E.F. were complete. Henry Wilson, his staff, and the various French bureaus had done their work well. Though their staff work had always remained autonomous, careful liaison and Wilson's personal attention had brought about genuine cooperation and intimacy. And this coordination, coupled with Wilson's own attitude, did much to make the French confident of British help and the D.M.O. equally determined that it should arrive; that he should perhaps have been more skeptical of French strategic intentions and more realistic about the physical and materiel demands of continental warfare would only become apparent later. Nevertheless, Anglo-French coordination far exceeded that established between Paris and St. Petersburg, and also that between Vienna and Berlin. A glance at the latter may be useful.

When first established in 1879, the Dual Alliance did not contain a

43. A convenient summary of these arrangements is in "Appendix K.1," July 1914, *ibid.*, box 148. In May 1914 the French proposed to test the code, using the Dieppe station and a British one located between Brighton and Newhaven, but no such tests actually occurred; "Note pour l'Etat-major de l'armée 3eme bureau," May 13, 1914, *ibid.*, box 147.

44. See "Rapport à M. le Président de la République [Fallières] sur la coopération éventuelle des forces militaires de la Grande Bretagne aux opérations de nos armées du nord-est," March 1912, D.D.F., 3rd ser., II, no. 272.

45. Aug. 21, 1913, Wilson Diaries; Collier, *Brasshat: Biography of Henry Wilson*, 135–136. See also de La Panouse to Millerand, Dec. 11, 1912, Jan. 18, 1913, Archives Guerre, "Plan XVII: Armée W," box 147b.

military convention. In the next three decades the military facet of the Austro-German relationship developed in erratic fashion and there was in fact a total hiatus of exchanges between the two general staffs from 1896 to 1909. Not until the Bosnian crisis of 1908–1909 was there a significant modification in the alliance's laissez-faire approach to military planning. In January 1909, with the approval of the respective civilian ministers, Franz Baron Conrad von Hötzendorf (Chief of the Austro-Hungarian General Staff), initiated correspondence with General von Moltke. During the next three months they exchanged letters reviewing the strategic situation. Moltke spelled out the German plans with clarity and confidence: Germany would deal first with France, and a victory on the banks of the Seine would resolve any problems that might develop on the eastern front; however, just for safety's sake, he wanted Austrian help to check the Russians while victory was being won in the west. Conrad was less sanguine. Anxious to crush the hated Serbians yet fearful of a Russian thrust from Galicia, he wanted some German offensive action in East Prussia to keep the Russians occupied: if he had such assurances from Berlin he would promise in turn to launch an offensive action against Russia that would facilitate Germany's success in the west. Although Moltke disliked Conrad's demands, he finally agreed that the German Eighth Army would launch an attack into Russian Poland. A satisfied Conrad now stood ready to take offensive action against the Russians. This vague agreement of March 1909 was not modified in succeeding years; but in 1914 neither side would, as it turned out, fulfill its share of the concord.[46]

The Berlin-Vienna arrangements, while resembling the Franco-Russian accords, differed substantially from the preparations of the Triple Entente. Both the Franco-Russian and the Austro-German talks were essentially exchanges at the highest staff levels and the resulting accords were sufficiently ambiguous to leave considerable latitude for interpretation. St. Petersburg, on the other hand, had given a precise pledge to attack on a certain day with a specified number of troops; wartime communications between the allies were arranged; rail facilities for the attack were carefully considered. The Anglo-French talks were even more detailed because of the very nature of the operation—the movement of the B.E.F. across the Channel and to the zone of concentration required more staff coordination. Ship and rail movements utilizing foreign facilities simply could not be improvised at the last moment. But

46. Norman Stone, "Moltke-Conrad: Relations between the Austro-Hungarian and German General Staffs, 1909–14," *Historical Journal*, 9 (1966), 201–228; Ritter, *Staatskunst und Kriegshandwerk*, II, 297–307. In 1913 there were discussions among the members of the Triple Alliance that carefully defined their naval cooperation in the Mediterranean and provided for the movement of three Italian army corps to help the Germans; needless to add, this came to little in 1914. On this see Albertini, *The Origins of the War of 1914*, I, 556–565; Vagts, *Defense and Diplomacy*, 102–104; A. F. Pribram, *The Secret Treaties of Austria-Hungary, 1879–1914*, 2 vols. (Cambridge, Mass., 1920), I, 283–305.

the London-Paris talks differed not only in type but also in degree. In the other military talks the Chiefs of Staffs, often themselves ill-informed and vague about the crucial details of logistics and movement, made the arrangements; in the entente talks the responsible and knowledgable planners made the necessary provisions. The complex logistical requirements were recognized; problems of communication between allied armies were anticipated. There was a degree of intimacy and cooperation between the Anglo-French staffs that may be deplored for political reasons, but which represented the best professionalism of the modern military establishment. In comparison even that vaunted stereotype of the military machine and mind, the Prussian staff officer, found his match in the determined efforts of Henry Hughes Wilson to prepare the British Army for war.

The preparations for and coordination of Anglo-French naval arrangements were also under way during 1913 and 1914. These preparations were, of course, just part of the larger naval war plans being elaborated by London and Paris. In Britain the creation of a Naval War Staff and Churchill's own impetuous meddling prompted continuous discussions about the Royal Navy's overall strategy against Germany, especially its plans for action in the North Sea. "War Orders No. 1 (War with Germany)," issued July 1, 1914, was the final embodiment of the Admiralty's deliberations. The destruction of the German fleet, the stoppage of German seaborne commerce, and the protection of the B.E.F. during its Channel crossing were the missions of the Royal Navy in the North Sea. To achieve these goals the Admiralty planned to institute a policy of distant blockade, instead of a close or observational blockade: the Grand Fleet (the name of the Home Fleet on mobilization) would block the area between Scotland and Norway; the Channel Fleet would close the entrance into the Dover-Calais area. From these positions the Navy would conduct periodic sweeps across the North Sea. The blockade and the sweeps with their strangulation of German trade and their constant challenge to German naval pride were confidently expected to entice the German High Seas Fleet to a "showdown" naval battle.[47]

Although Churchill completely approved the strategy of distant blockading, he nevertheless found it too defensive and too passive for his own well-developed bellicose tastes. Repeatedly he urged his naval advisers to consider how the fleet might engage in more vigorous, aggressive action against the German Navy. This desire led him in June 1914 to ask the Naval War Staff to re-examine the much-abused idea of amphibious operations along the German coasts. In particular he contem-

---

47. The war orders and war plans for 1914 are in Adm. 137/1936; also see "War Plans: Home Waters, 1911–1914," Adm. 116/3096; Churchill, *The World Crisis*, I, 152–158; Dewar, *The Navy From Within*, 145–152, 371–381; Marder, *Road to War*, 372–373, 382–383.

plated a close blockade of the Heligoland Bight, which would possibly necessitate the capture of an overseas base such as Borkum. This resurrection of the earlier Fisher-Wilson theme of coastal operations brought no actual change in Admiralty plans before the outbreak of the war; the allure of this kind of operation would, however, stay with Churchill and be evident in his support of the Gallipoli expedition.[48]

In the French Navy, once major strategic guidelines had been decreed in Paris the drafting of war plans remained the responsibility of the fleet commander in chief. In the Mediterranean this task was Vice Admiral Boué de Lapeyrère's. It was not an easy assignment. Preventing the juncture of the Austrian-Italian navies was his principal mission, but he also had another, more complicating one: protection of the XIX Army Corps in its movement from North Africa to metropolitan France. The Admiral persistently protested, much as A. K. Wilson had argued in 1911 in the C.I.D., that protecting troop transports would hinder the execution of his primary mission. The French Navy would be forced into a defensive posture and the enemy would be able to seize the offensive. De Lapeyrère's complaints were unheeded by the Conseil Supérieur de la Défense Nationale. Movement of the XIX Corps became a fixed element in French naval planning, and a special naval division of older vessels was created to cover the ferrying operation. At the same time the French Admiral continued to plan for offensive action against the Italian fleet, operating in the Gulf of Genoa, in the Strait of Messina, and along the Tunisian-Algerian coasts. French ships would, it was hoped, trap the Italians in the Tyrrhenian Sea.[49]

Implicit for the success of the French fleet was the availability of British naval assistance. The continuing expansion of the Austrian and Italian navies, coupled with the formation of a German squadron in the Mediterranean, rendered French naval superiority in that sea virtually nonexistent. British help was imperative. Yet neither admiralty was overjoyed at the prospect of the growing mutual dependence in the Mediterranean. In April 1914 Admiral Pierre Le Bris, Chief of the French Staff, sought to reduce this dependence by advocating the construction of eleven more battleships; these would enable France to strengthen its Mediterranean dispositions and also to re-establish a respectable naval force in the Atlantic. On the latter point the Admiral was supported by de Lanessan and others who constantly trumpeted the danger of France's exposed northern coasts and demanded sharp increases in naval con-

48. Memo by Churchill, June 11, 1914, Adm. 116/3096; Jackson to Oliver, June 29, 1914, *ibid.*; Marder, *Road to War*, 373–377.
49. Delcassé to de Lapeyrère, Nov. 11, 1912, Archives Marine, ED 38; de Lapeyrère to Pierre Baudin (Naval Minister in the Briand-Barthou governments), Sept. 1, 1913, *ibid.*; "Rapport de présentation . . . au sujet du transport du 19e Corps en France à la mobilisation," May 17, 1913, Archives Marine, ES 23; Auguste Thomazi. *La marine française dans la grande guerre, 1914–1918*, 4 vols. (Paris, 1924–1929), II, 17–19.

struction.[50] In London, Winston Churchill found the prospect of dependence useful in defending the five and a half-million-pound increase in his 1914 naval estimates. In January 1914 he reminded his fellow ministers that in 1912 they had disliked "the moral effect of our evacuating the Mediterranean, and the conclusions that would be drawn therefrom, [which] would in fact compromise us too deeply with France"; thus they had adopted the goal of a one-power standard for the Mediterranean. But, he pointed out, to achieve that standard and thereby avoid dependence on France required—now that the Canadian government had reneged on its pledge of assistance—the immediate construction of four and possibly five dreadnoughts during 1914–1915. Such a program would give Britain six dreadnoughts and two "Lord Nelsons" by the end of 1915: the one-power Mediterranean standard would then be a reality.[51] Eventually Churchill got his battleships. However, neither those ships nor the ones urged by Admiral Le Bris would be ready before late 1915; in the meantime the entente partners, despite their own preferences, were dependent upon each other in both the Mediterranean and the Channel.

The entente naval conversations did not become frequent and substantial until late 1912.[52] Before that point, in 1906, 1908, and 1911, the talks had not only been unofficial but brief, cursory, and incomplete. Once the British Cabinet approved the initiation of staff talks and resolved the thorny preamble issue with the Grey-Cambon letters, the way was open for extensive naval exchanges. In late 1912 and early 1913 Captain le Gouz de Saint-Seine, the French naval attaché, shuttled constantly between London and Paris as the staffs worked out the mechanics of naval cooperation. In addition Prince Louis of Battenberg, now the First Sea Lord, traveled to Paris in early March 1913 to thrash out problems with Admiral Le Bris; extensive precautions, including the use of de Saint-Seine's brother's office at 14 Place Vendôme instead of the Naval Ministry, were taken to ensure Battenberg's incognito status.[53] From these discussions there emerged three separate naval con-

50. "Conférence des directeurs militaires," Apr. 30, 1914, Archives Marine, CA 3; Le Masson, "Politique navale et construction de navires de ligne," 997–1008. See also "Le rôle des croiseurs cuirasses allemands," Revue des deux mondes, 6th ser., 20 (Apr. 1, 1914), 560–582; L'excelsoir, Mar. 30, 1914; Le Temps, May 18, 1914. Charles Bos strongly defended the Mediterranean concentration; see, e.g., La vie maritime, 7 (Oct. 10, 1913), 509–511.

51. Memo by Churchill, "Naval Estimates," Jan. 10, 1914, Asquith Papers, box 25.

52. The French files on the naval conversation are complete, Archives Marine, ED 37, ED 38, ES 10; scattered British records are in Adm. 116/3109, 137/818, 1936, 1971; some published documents are in D.D.F., 3rd ser., III–V passim. The unpublished French staff study by Lt. M. B. Touvet, "Guerre de 1914–18: la 2me escadre légère," pp. 30–49, traces the negotiations in detail.

53. De Saint-Seine to Le Bris, Feb. 14, 1913, Archives Marine, ES 10. During 1913 Churchill saw both Poincaré and Baudin, but apparently no records of their conversations survive.

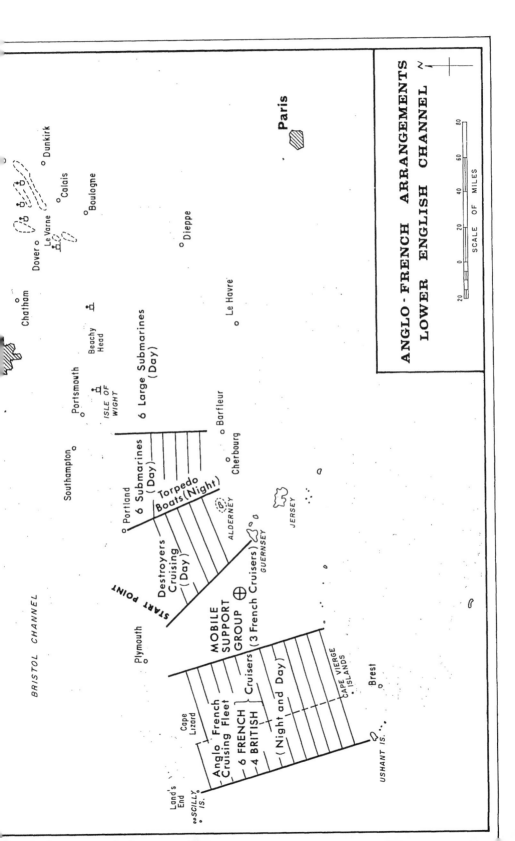

**ANGLO-FRENCH ARRANGEMENTS
LOWER ENGLISH CHANNEL**

ventions (of February 1913), which, along with their subsequent modifications, defined naval cooperation in the upper and lower English Channel and in the Mediterranean.[54]

Arrangements for the upper Channel were drafted by the British Admiralty. "In the event of being allied with the French Government in a war with Germany," the British would assume complete responsibility for the defense of the Strait of Dover. By the second day of mobilization the British would deploy twenty to twenty-four destroyers, two submarine flotillas (twelve to fourteen each), and four small cruisers. As a reinforcement, the French agreed to keep some submarines available and to operate a few torpedo boats between Calais and Boulogne. Orders for both the French and English commanders were completed later in 1913 and commanders were allowed to familiarize themselves with the respective coastal waters.[55] If the entente were to go to war with Germany, Britain had quite clearly become responsible for guarding France's northern coasts.

In the lower Channel arrangements were more complicated. The French had overall command of the Channel area between the Cotentin Peninsula and the English coast, that is, roughly everything west of the Isle of Wight-Barfleur line. Here they expected to deploy six old battle cruisers, two and subsequently three armored cruisers, eighteen destroyers, twelve submarines, six torpedo boats, and some merchant vessels; in addition, four British armored cruisers were scheduled for active duty, serving under the French commander in chief. The coordination of this joint naval force prompted exhaustive staff work, so that by August 1914 the provisions for tactical cooperation in the lower Channel were as precise as their military counterparts. A special "B.G." code was designed; cruising times were established for summer and winter; orders were drafted by the French for the British cruisers, pinpointing their location so that the southernmost British ship would be twenty-five miles off Cape Lizard, with the first French vessel only three miles farther south. The French captains naturally received equally detailed instructions for their role in the Channel defense. Furthermore, one of the earliest "scrambler" systems for identification of ships was devised for the lower Channel. "AKT4V" over the wireless meant that a battleship, accompanied by two light cruisers and a squadron of torpedo boats, was west

---

54. Extracts of the accords, F.O. 6, "Défense de Pas-de-Calais," Jan. 23, 1913; F.O. 7, "Défense de la Manche occidentale," Feb. 10, 1913; and F.O. 10, "Joint Action in the Mediterranean," Feb. 10, 1913, are in de Saint-Seine to Aubert [?], Feb. 14, 1913, D.D.F., 3rd ser., V, no. 397 (D.D.F. errs in naming Aubert—Le Bris had replaced him as Chief of the Naval Staff in January). The complete accords are in M.A.E., "Grande Bretagne," n.s. 22.

55. See, e.g., "War Orders No. 2 for the Admiral of Patrols," May 5, 1913, Archives Marine, ES 10; "Instructions de l'amiral des patrouilles aux flottilles françaises placées sous ses ordres en cas d'alliance," Jan. 27, 1914, ibid. See also "La défense du Pas de Calais," Revue de Paris, 19 (Nov. 15, 1912), 429–448.

of the Cape Lizard-Vierge Islands line and would arrive in "area four" by 9:00 P.M.[56]

The mutual problems of Britain and France in the Mediterranean had originally triggered the need for more satisfactory naval arrangements. Yet, curiously, their plans for cooperation in the Mediterranean were less complete than for the other areas. The Mediterranean convention began with the frank admission that Britain could not promise to maintain a fixed number of ships in that sea, though there were hopes that a British force would always be available to cope with the Austrian Navy. If Britain and France cooperated in a war—a stipulation faithfully inserted in all of the naval conventions, the Mediterranean would be divided into an eastern and a western basin, with each navy patrolling a distinct operational zone. Based at Toulon and Bizerte, the French fleet would protect the XIX Corps in its move to France and operate against the Italian Navy; centered at Malta, the British squadrons would seek to keep the Austrian Navy bottled up in the Adriatic.[57] Unlike the Channel accords, the Mediterranean plans had no provisions for the exchange of war plans between fleet commanders on how this cooperation would be executed, nor any provisions for peacetime cooperation. And the allocation of command responsibility was carefully blurred. Even if the Austrian and Italian fleets managed to join, the entente forces would continue to operate as separate units; they would rely "on their common signal book and pre-arranged means of communication by sight or sound, to ensure [cooperation] being carried out successfully." Only if British naval strength fell below that of the Austrians— a sensitive point to face—would the remaining British ships "join the French Mediterranean Fleet in war, and act under the orders of the French admiral in chief command, always on the understanding that they are subject to recall at any time to England should circumstances require it." As a precaution against this unpleasant contingency, the Admiralty promised to inform Paris periodically of British strength in the Mediterranean.[58]

56. "Instructions pour le Commandant Supérieur du groupe de croiseurs anglais devant concourir à le défense de la Manche occidentale," Nov. 4, 1913, Archives Marine, ES 10; "War Orders No. 2 for the Commander-in-Chief, Home Waters," May 1913, Adm. 137/1971.

57. "Joint Action in the Mediterranean," Feb. 10, 1913, D.D.F., 3rd ser., V, no. 397; also B.D., X, pt. 2, no. 458. In the case of a single-handed fight against the Triple Alliance, British forces would have to withdraw to Malta and Gibraltar and await reinforcements from home; "War Orders No. 1 (revised)," Aug. 20, 1913, Adm. 137/819.

58. In the spring of 1913 Admirals de Lapeyrère and Berkeley Milne were notified of the Mediterranean convention and given new orders that reflected it. But London did not inform Paris until January 1914 of the details of British war plans in the Mediterranean; see de Saint-Seine to Le Bris, Jan. 22, 1914, Archives Marine, ES 10. In mid-1914 the comparative strength of the navies was roughly: Britain, three battle cruisers, four armored cruisers, four light cruisers; France, two dreadnoughts, eleven battleships (six "Dantons" and five "Patries"), six armored cruisers, three light cruisers; Italy, three dreadnoughts, four battleships, six armored cruisers,

The Anglo-French naval arrangements added further reinforcement to the burgeoning entente relationship. In the past naval coordination had been chiefly the product of Fisher's condescension and of hastily contrived, ad hoc accords. After February 1913 responsibilities and duties were carefully defined and incorporated into "conventions"; war orders were prepared by both navies that included provisions for joint Anglo-French action; communications facilities were established and liaison problems investigated. In every instance these arrangements emphasized the mutual dependence of the two navies. The French depended upon British superiority in the North Sea and the Dover straits to protect their coastline; in the lower Channel and in the Mediterranean the stronger French forces shouldered the chief burden of protecting entente interests. The naval agreements, moreover, possessed an entirely different character from the comparable military arrangements. The French Army never based its mobilization plans upon definite British assistance; with the two navies the situation was quite different. Whatever the reasons for the initial dispositions of the two fleets, the naval conventions had the practical effect of enshrining their current strategic locations and of making these concentrations an indispensable part of the respective naval war plans. Both navies had two sets of orders, one for the contingency of going it alone, the other for entente cooperation. Yet the Channel and the Mediterranean arrangements suggest that neither admiralty wanted, expected, or could afford to go it entirely alone against the Triple Alliance. Admiral von Tirpitz' naval program had prompted what no British or French diplomat would have even contemplated ten years before—the forging of a virtual Anglo-French naval alliance.[59]

Nor was the impact of the German naval threat confined to European and Mediterranean waters: there were also Anglo-French naval arrangements in the Far East. The British, despite the progressive concentration of sea power in home waters, still retained in early 1913 four armored cruisers (9,800 to 14,600 tons) and two light cruisers on the China station. The French could supplement this force with three armored cruisers (7,500 tons) and other smaller craft. The Germans, for their part, maintained two first-class cruisers, the *Scharnhorst* and the *Gneisenau*, in the Pacific. Although first mooted in late 1911, entente naval coordination in the Far East was not seriously discussed until July 1912 and arrangements not finally concluded until February 1913. In this case the local naval commanders, Rear Admiral Henri Kerillis for the French and Rear Admiral Sir Alfred Winsloe for the British, and their staffs conducted the negotiations. From their meetings first in Weihai-

five light cruisers; Austria-Hungary, two dreadnoughts, two battleships, three reserve battleships; Germany, one battle cruiser (the *Goeben*), one light cruiser (*Breslau*); see Viscount Hyde and John Leyland, eds., *The Naval Annual, 1914* (London, 1914), 69, 76–81.

59. Churchill, *The World Crisis*, I, 117–119.

wei and then in Saigon, a comprehensive set of naval arrangements resulted which London and Paris subsequently approved. The British
squadron, assisted by the French cruisers *Montcalm* and *Dupleix*, would
conduct offensive operations against the German treaty-port of Tsingtao
and watch the mouth of the Yangtze; French destroyers would protect
the trade routes from Hongkong to Singapore. A special code, reciprocal use of ports, and periodic joint maneuvers were also part of the
accord.[60] Later, fighting instructions were drafted, complete to the point
of declaring: "If the Allied Fleet is superior in numbers, the French
ships should concentrate [their fire] on one ship of the enemy; this ship
will not be fired at by the British." [61] Slightly revised in February 1914,
these arrangements guaranteed effective entente naval coordination in
the Far East.

Anglo-French planning in the Orient merits several observations.
First, the French were the principal beneficiaries of the coordination,
since the British obviously furnished the major naval strength. Second,
the arrangements were the product of on-the-spot discussions between
commanders who in wartime would also have the duty of executing the
provisions; they were not the product of discussions between staff personnel in the naval ministries. Furthermore, the Anglo-French squadrons, because of their distance from Europe, attained a higher degree of
coordination than did forces nearer home. The British Admiralty, which
resisted all French overtures for peacetime signal exercises in the Atlantic or the Mediterranean, permitted them with full abandon in the
distant Pacific.[62] On the other hand, neither the negotiations nor the
arrangements made any mention of Britain's only bona fide ally, Japan:
possible assistance from the British East Indian squadron and from
Australia was noted, but Japanese assistance apparently played no part
in the calculations of the respective entente commanders in the Pacific. Finally, and perhaps most significantly, Anglo-French arrangements in the Orient demonstrated and reflected the worldwide nature
of the entente. What had started as a strategic arrangement over Morocco had not only acquired continental and Mediterranean overtones,
but Asian as well.

In the final months before the war the French sought to expand the
scope of the naval accords, especially naval arrangements in the Mediterranean. For one thing, practical problems arose that indicated the need

60. The records on the Far Eastern talks are in Adm. 137/819 and Archives
Marine, ES 10, ED 38. On the general arrangements, see Kerillis to Delcassé,
July 5, 1912, D.D.F., 3rd ser., III, no. 170; Kerillis to Baudin, Jan. 31, 1913, *ibid.*,
V, no. 303; memo signed by Admirals Albert Huguet and Thomas Jerram, Feb. 6,
1914, Archives Marine, ES 10.
61. "Fighting Instructions," June 14, 1913, Archives Marine, ED 38.
62. Minute by Admiral Jackson, Apr. 16, 1914, Adm. 137/819; "Annexe II à
la lettre au ministre de la Marine," Kerillis to Baudin, Oct. 20, 1913, Archives
Marine, ES 10.

for closer coordination. In the summer of 1913 Pierre Baudin, then the Naval Minister, proposed sending some of the French fleet into the Atlantic to show the flag and to revive sagging Breton enthusiasm for the Navy. Although members of the Conseil Supérieur de la Défense Nationale and the Quai d'Orsay objected, saying that Britain would not like it and that the Anglo-French convention "necessitated" the full French fleet staying in the Mediterranean, Baudin finally won approval for dispatching some ships to the Atlantic. Then, to the consternation of Stephen Pichon, once again Foreign Minister, the British decided to withdraw some units from the Mediterranean for maneuvers. The net effect of these two changes, while the tension continued in the Balkans, was to reduce entente naval strength to below the combined Austro-Italian total. Hastening to assure London that the French regarded the naval accord as remaining in full force, an alarmed Pichon also pushed two of Baudin's ideas for preventing simultaneous withdrawals in the future: a positive commitment from Britain about a strength level in the Mediterranean and improved communications between the fleet commanders in that sea.[63]

Neither of these proposals met with British favor. The Admiralty studiously evaded any promise to keep a definite number of ships in the Mediterranean. To have done so would have, from London's perspective, nullified many of the reasons for entering into a naval convention with France, among them the maintenance of maximum British flexibility in the North Sea. And the Admiralty also rejected a French request to allow the Mediterranean fleet commanders to use the secret "B.G." code during peacetime. The Sea Lords justified this refusal (January 1914) on the grounds that they had not been authorized "to do more than prepare for an alliance between the two countries, and that it is considered the actual use or practice with our joint signal books would go beyond that stage or preparation, and is therefore inadmissible." [64] Further, Battenberg continually emphasized the need for prudence and caution about entente naval preparations. Because the radicals disliked any evidence of closer Anglo-French relations, the entente, he twice warned de Saint-Seine in February 1914, had to be kept out of public view. In keeping with his own advice, Battenberg continued to travel to Paris incognito; his French counterpart, Admiral Le Bris, stayed away from London altogether.[65]

63. Extract from the minutes of the Conseil Supérieur de la Défense Nationale, June 28, 1913, Archives Marine, ES 23; de Saint-Seine to Le Bris, July 9, 1913, ibid., ES 10; Baudin to Pichon, July 29, 1913, D.D.F., 3rd ser., VII, no. 496; Pichon to P. Cambon, July 31, 1913, ibid., no. 505.

64. Le Bris to de Saint-Seine, Jan. 23, 1914, Archives Marine, ES 10; Jackson to de Saint-Seine, Jan. 29, 1914, Adm. 116/3109 (quoted in part in B.D., X, pt. 1, p. 694 n.). Although work on the "B.G." code had begun in 1911, copies were not distributed until August 1913.

65. De Saint-Seine to Le Bris, Feb. 10, 18, 24, 1914, Archives Marine, ES 10; also see de Saint-Seine to Le Bris, May 6, 1914, ibid.

In mid-1914 the French resumed their pressure for closer cooperation in the Mediterranean. On June 11 de Saint-Seine was ordered to request that Britain assume responsibility for watching the *Goeben* and the *Breslau* lest they obstruct French troop moves from North Africa; he was also to reopen the question of peacetime use of the secret codes. For their efforts the French this time got half a loaf. On June 20 Admiral Jackson, Chief of the Naval Staff, promised that Britain's Mediterranean squadron would mask, and bring the German cruisers to combat. This, it should be added, was the sum total of the entente's prewar consideration of the problem created by the introduction of German sea power into the Mediterranean. The renewed French demand for closer communications was again rebuffed, this time with the explanation that such exchanges would be incompatible with Grey's recent parliamentary denials of any Russian naval talks. Such arrangements, Admiral Jackson opined, were in any case unnecessary, for the information about the Triple Alliance navies could easily be exchanged at the ministerial level.[66] The Admiralty was soon to pay, in the escape of the *Goeben* and the *Breslau*, some very embarrassing penalties for its inflexible attitude toward more intimate naval cooperation in the Mediterranean.

66. De Saint-Seine to Le Bris, June 22, 1914, *ibid.*

14 | The Entente on the Eve of War, 1913–1914

Throughout 1912 London and Paris worked to define more precisely the Anglo-French political relationship. The result, after prolonged negotiations and maneuvers, was the exchange of the Grey-Cambon letters pledging each power to consult if danger of war arose. After this exchange of pledges in late November 1912 Anglo-French diplomatic relations entered a more relaxed phase. In succeeding months a series of troublesome but not major crises confronted the two governments, and these occasions furnished the French with continuing opportunities to probe gently probable British intentions in a European conflagration. Paris discovered, though ever so slowly, that the new British commitment to consult heralded no fundamental shift in Liberal foreign policy: British diplomacy appeared as pragmatic and tortuous as ever.

The French could take considerable comfort from the "signals" reaching them from London in early 1913.[1] Paul Cambon, for example,

1. Although Roberta Wohlstetter uses the term "signal" as a label for evidence of

learned that Sir Edward Grey had completely approved George V's warning to Prince Henry of Prussia that Britain might intervene on the Continent "under certain circumstances." Furthermore, conversations with Lloyd George and Churchill at Windsor in January convinced the French ambassador that they too favored strengthening the entente relationship.[2] Two other developments were also welcome news to French policy-makers: Grey's reiteration that no Anglo-German naval talks were contemplated and Churchill's determination, as revealed in the 1913–1914 naval estimates, to keep British naval might unimpaired. And in early April, when there were rumors of another visit by Prince Henry to Britain, Grey took special steps to reassure Paul Cambon, telling him "very privately" of the earlier attempt to elicit "an assurance of neutrality" and pointedly noting that it had been declined. Finally, a British invitation for Raymond Poincaré (now President) to visit London in June and promises that the King would visit Paris in 1914 reinforced the apparent unity and intimacy of the entente partnership.[3]

In the months after November 1912, however, an entirely different matrix of signals was also reaching Paris—information that could give the French leadership much less confidence about London's stance on entente and Triple Entente questions. In December the explosive situation in the Balkans prompted Paul Cambon to sound Grey on what Britain would do if Austria attacked Serbia and Russia then intervened. Refusing to commit himself, the Foreign Secretary would only say that British action would necessarily depend upon British opinion and the attitude of the House of Commons.[4] Grey's patient chairmanship of the ambassadorial conference on Balkan matters further emphasized his reluctance to be "involved in war for a dispute about one or two towns on the Albanian frontier." To the annoyance of Cambon, Grey acted as an

"a particular danger or a particular enemy move or intention," it can be applied with equal validity to information transmitted between alliance partners about their probable intentions; Wohlstetter, *Pearl Harbor: Warning and Decision* (Stanford, 1962), 1–2.

2. P. Cambon to Charles Jonnart, Jan. 23, 1913, *D.D.F.*, 3rd ser., V, no. 248. On the King's conversation, see George V to Grey, Dec. 8, 1912, *B.D.*, X, pt. 2, no. 452; Grey to George V, Dec. 9, 1912, *ibid.*, no. 453; Harold Nicolson, *King George the Fifth: His Life and Reign* (London, 1952), 206–208. On Dec. 5 Prince Louis of Battenberg had written the King suggesting that Prince Henry failed to understand that Britain could not permit Russia or France, "especially France, to be crippled—consequently we *cannot* stand out in certain circumstances"; RA GEO V M520A/1.

3. Grey to Bertie, Apr. 10, 1913, *B.D.*, X, pt. 2, no. 470. In early May London also approved a French request for permission for wartime use of British facilities to communicate between Paris and St. Petersburg; Nicolson to Grey, Apr. 30, 1913, *ibid.*, no. 474.

4. P. Cambon to Poincaré (tel.), Dec. 4, 1912, *D.D.F.*, 3rd ser., IV, no. 622; Grey to Bertie, Dec. 4, 1912, *B.D.*, IX, pt. 2, no. 328; cf. Benckendorff to Sazonov (tel.), Dec. 21/Jan. 3, 1913, Schreiner, *Entente Diplomacy and the World*, no. 768.

"honest broker" in trying to settle the vexing Balkan legacies.[5] Reports of bellicose sentiments in France, including word that French officers were of "the opinion that it would be far better for France if a conflict were not too long postponed," also strengthened Grey's caution about the entente. Britain, he minuted in February, "can be no party to France precipitating a conflict for the revanche" and would have to deprecate "as far as [possible] this aggressive spirit in France." [6]

Other more public and predictable signals also reached Paris during early 1913. On March 10, during the Debate on the Address, Lord Hugh Cecil, a Conservative M.P., asserted that there was a widespread belief that Britain was "under an obligation, not a treaty obligation, but an obligation arising out of an assurance given by the Ministry in the course of diplomatic negotiations, to send a very large armed force out of this country to operate in Europe." Brusquely interrupting Cecil, the Prime Minister immediately declared that he "ought to say that is not true." Asquith's categorical denial alarmed Paul Cambon. He was disappointed, he protested to Grey the next day, that the Prime Minister's statement, though true, "could not have been wrapped in some less abrupt form." The Foreign Secretary, who agreed about the abruptness of the reply, reminded Cambon that the nature of the interruption had prohibited any elaborate explanation of policy. Assured by Grey that the French should attach no importance to the form of the remarks, Cambon let the matter drop.[7] Less easily mollified was Henry Wilson, who had received information "that the Cabinet had decided *not* to help the French on land. . . . What a Cabinet of Cowards, Blackguards, & Fools." [8]

Two weeks later the Prime Minister had another opportunity in the Commons to comment upon the entente relationship. On March 24 Sir William Byles (Liberal) asked whether Britain was under any obligation to France "to send an armed force in certain contingencies to operate in Europe; and, if so, what are the limits of our agreements, whether by assurance or treaty with the French nation." Joseph King (Liberal) wanted to know if "in 1905, 1908, or 1911, this country spontaneously offered to France the assistance of a British Army to be landed on the Continent to support France in the event of European hostilities." Grey, who conceded that the House was entitled to answers on these questions, drafted Asquith's reply:

5. Grey to Buchanan (tel.), Feb. 17, 1913, Grey Papers, F.O. 800/74; see also Grey, *Twenty-five Years*, I, 264.
6. Nicolson to Grey, Feb. 24, 1913, and Grey's minutes quoted in Nicolson, *First Lord Carnock*, 397–398; see also Grey to Bertie, Mar. 4, 1913, F.O. 371/1642.
7. *Parliamentary Debates: Commons*, 5th ser., 50 (Mar. 10, 1913), 42–43; Grey to Bertie, Mar. 11, 1913, B.D., X, pt. 2, no. 466; Cambon to Jonnart, Mar. 11, 1913, M.A.E., "Grande Bretagne," n.s. 10. See also Asquith to Grey, Mar. 14, 1913, Grey Papers, F.O. 800/100; Schoen to Bethmann, Mar. 12, 1913, G.P., XXXIX, no. 15614.
8. Mar. 11, 1913, Wilson Diaries.

As has been repeatedly stated, this country is not under any obligation not public and known to Parliament which compels it to take part in any war. In other words, if war arises between European Powers there are no unpublished agreements which will restrict or hamper the freedom of the Government or of Parliament to decide whether or not Great Britain should participate in a war. The use that would be made of the naval or military forces if the Government and Parliament decided to take part in a war is, for obvious reasons, not a matter about which public statements can be made beforehand.[9]

This response was a noble attempt to please both the French and the radicals, but it cut things very fine. Strictly speaking, the Cabinet was under no obligation to give military assistance to France, nor had it ever given even verbal assurances to this effect; it was only obligated to consult in times of danger. Though acquainted with the staff talks, Asquith, Grey, and most of their colleagues genuinely believed that they retained full freedom in the question of British intervention. But there was another aspect, which Esher expressed well when he wrote on March 12: "Of course there is no treaty or convention, but how we can get out of the commitments of the General Staff with honour, I cannot understand. It seems all so shifty to me." [10] Further, while the staff talks did not commit Britain to intervene, they nonetheless committed the B.E.F. to a form of intervention that a number of M.P.'s could seriously question on military grounds. If the Cabinet decided to intervene, it was in danger of being inflexibly bound to the plans of its military experts. When Asquith spoke of full freedom of action, he deceived not only his parliamentary colleagues but himself as well.

Paul Cambon found Asquith's new commentary on the entente "extremely prudent." But this time he lodged no protest with the Foreign Office, satisfied that the Cecil episode had forced the Prime Minister to be cautious. Moreover, as he reported to Paris, the British press (the *Daily Mail* excepted) treated Asquith's explanation at face value. Sensitive British opinion appeared satisfied.[11]

Britain's refusal to move closer to France, publicly or privately, prompted no direct demarches from Paris. Realistic about the British political environment, the French studiously eschewed blatant demands for the expansion of the entente. Pressure for such a development came

9. *Parliamentary Debates: Commons*, 5th ser., 50 (Mar. 24, 1913), 1316–1317; *B.D.*, X, pt. 2, p. 689 n.
10. Esher to M. V. Brett, Mar. 12, 1913, *Journals and Letters of Esher*, III, 122; Francis R. Flournoy, *Parliament and War* (London, 1927), 206–220.
11. P. Cambon to Pichon, Mar. 25, 1913, M.A.E., "Grande Bretagne," n.s. 22. Lalaing informed Brussels that Britain was not contractually bound to intervene, but that instead London could decide whether to intervene solely on the basis of British interests; Lalaing to Davignon, Mar. 25, 1913, Belg. Arch., "Correspondance politique: Légations," Great Britain, vol. VIII.

instead from Sir Arthur Nicolson, who wanted an open alliance, and more persuasively from Sir Francis Bertie, who stressed that Poincaré wanted something "less vague" than the exchange of private letters. In late June, on the eve of the French President's visit to London, the British ambassador emphasized to Grey that the French feared British military assistance would be dangerously delayed through "protracted discussions." Recognizing that the Cabinet would never accept an alliance, Bertie advocated an exchange of official notes. Such an arrangement, Grey had responded, was most unlikely since it would cause "some resignations" in the Cabinet. Bertie, who thought the Cabinet could "spare" some members, continued to insist that Poincaré would raise the issue of closer relations when he arrived.[12]

Bertie's forecast was inaccurate: Poincaré made no overtures about the entente during his state visit. He was content to interpret his widespread public acclaim as the best indicator of the strength of Anglo-French friendship. The President could be confident that the British, in the words of the Westminster Gazette, regarded the entente as one of "the settled facts of European policy." [13] In the remaining months of 1913 the question of Anglo-French relations disappeared as a topic of intergovernmental discussion. Instead entente diplomacy was monopolized by the continuing Balkan imbroglio and by the ramifications of Italy's territorial acquisitions in the Aegean Sea. On both problems London and Paris pursued similar, and often coordinated, policies: limit amputations of the "Sick Man of Europe" to the Balkan peninsula and force the Italians to disgorge their booty in the Dodecanese. By 1914 the two powers were somewhat successful, or so it appeared, with their Balkan diplomacy.[14] Italy, however, continued to occupy the Aegean islands, and any hope for an Anglo-French-Italian arrangement for the Mediterranean remained just that. Legitimate distrust about Italy's altered relationship to the Triple Alliance did not, it should be added, facilitate an understanding between the three powers.[15]

On a third front, the entente pursued a policy of circumspection and prudence. Developments in Belgium were followed closely. The passage of new military measures and Belgium's apparent determination to defend its neutrality were welcomed by the entente powers, as were indications that the Belgian General Staff was seriously considering all the ramifications of a major war, including the availability and rapidity of

12. Nicolson to Goschen, Mar. 11, 1913, Nicolson Papers, vol. III/1913; memo by Bertie, June 23, 1913, Bertie Papers, F.O. 800/166.
13. June 24, 1913. See also memo by Bertie, July 3, 1913, Bertie Papers, F.O. 800/166; Nicolson to Goschen, June 30, 1913, Nicolson Papers, vol. VI/1913; Poincaré, Au service de la France, III, 238–256.
14. See E. C. Helmreich, The Diplomacy of the Balkan Wars, 1912–1913 (Cambridge, Mass., 1938); A. F. Pribram, Austria-Hungary and Great Britain, 1908–1914, trans. Ian Morrow (London, 1951).
15. See, e.g., Rodd to Grey, Apr. 22, 1914, B.D., X, pt. 2, no. 442; Vagts, Defense and Diplomacy, 103.

British assistance.[16] To ease any Belgian apprehensions London and Paris reiterated their 1912 assurances about respecting the kingdom's neutrality.[17] Nor were the entente capitals unaware of the Kaiser's and Moltke's belligerent statements during King Albert's visit to Berlin in November 1913, statements so formidable that the Belgian monarch had them communicated to the French government.[18] Yet the entente parties never felt confident about how Brussels would react should Germany attack. Major Eugène Génie, the French attaché, could report in January 1914 that the Belgian government "would do nothing to assure loyal and confident cooperation with France in case of a violation of its territory by Germany." [19] And in July 1914 the Belgians were mobilized to thwart an Anglo-French as well as a German attack: three divisions watched the French border and the Belgian coasts, one watched the German frontier. Until the very last moment the Belgian position would tantalize the entente military planners and baffle the entente statesmen.[20] In the end, this unknown quantity, which had first attracted British strategic planners to continental operations, would prove decisive in the realization of their plans.

On the domestic scene, meanwhile, both governments, or rather the Asquith ministry and several French ministries (those of Briand, Barthou, and Doumergue), struggled with problems fraught with international implications. Since 1911 French self-confidence and national pride had grown significantly. Increasingly the French were tiring of German pinpricks, threats, and bullying. This reviving nationalism was further reinforced by the successful efforts to secure parliamentary approval for a three-year service law that would offset the increased manpower of the German Army. Although Caillaux and Jean Jaurès remained politically powerful, their somewhat conciliatory policy toward Germany was thoroughly challenged by the resurging spirit of French nationalism and *revanchisme*. "Defensive patriotism and offensive nationalism had become," Eugen Weber has noted, "difficult to distin-

16. In September 1913, while attending the British maneuvers, Col. G. P. G. Hagemans (on instructions from the Belgian Staff) asked Henry Wilson if Belgium could count on British military assistance. A surprised D.M.O. responded that London could send 160,000 men in fifteen days. This episode created, to say the least, something of a stir in the Belgian Foreign Ministry; see Belg. Arch., "Indépendance neutralité," XIII. Robert Devleeshouwer, *Les Belges et le danger de guerre, 1910–1914* (Louvain, 1958) 177–211.
17. Guillaume to Davignon, Feb. 22, 1913, Belg. Arch., "Indépendance neutralité," XII; Grey to Villiers, Apr. 7, 1913, B.D., VIII, no. 330.
18. J. Cambon to Pichon, Nov. 22, 24, 1913, D.D.F., 3rd ser., VIII, nos. 517, 522; Baron Beyens, *Deux années à Berlin, 1912–1914*, 2 vols. (Paris, 1931), II, 37–47; Albertini, *The Origins of the War of 1914*, III, 440–443.
19. Génie to Noulens, Jan. 6, 1914, quoted in Duchesne, *Les archives de la Guerre et de la Marine à Paris*, 107; Klobukowski to Premier Doumergue, Mar. 3, 1914, M.A.E., "Belgique," n.s. 20.
20. Helmreich, "Belgian Concern over Neutrality," 426–427.

guish." [21] The Zabern incident in late 1913, in which a German officer sanctioned attacks upon Alsatian civilians, served to exacerbate French emotions.

The Asquith Cabinet might occasionally cast a fearful glance at the revival of *revanchisme*, but it was in no position to reproach Paris about the dangers of nationalism. The long-smoldering volcano that was the Irish question threatened to erupt at any time, and there was the very real prospect that an attempt to coerce Ulster would disrupt the British Army. While Lord Morley might regard the Army "as a machine & a tool," there were estimates that perhaps twenty percent of the officers would refuse to execute orders against Ulster.[22] The explosive nature of the situation was painfully revealed on March 20, 1914, when nearly sixty officers tendered their resignations rather than promise to enforce Liberal policy in Ireland. For a moment the Curragh mutiny menaced the effectiveness, indeed the existence, of the military instrument of the British government. Only an ambiguous pledge from the Cabinet about the use of the Army in Ulster saved the situation, though at the expense of Colonel Seely, Field Marshal French, and General Ewart.[23] Asquith, to bridge the gulf within the Cabinet over the episode, took over the War Office. Despite his openly insubordinate behavior, Henry Wilson retained his post as D.M.O.; and in early April he sought to reassure the French Staff of the reliability of the B.E.F.[24]

In early 1914, while the Asquith government struggled with the festering Irish crisis, it also faced new diplomatic demands to clarify its relations with Paris and St. Petersburg. In this instance the significant impetus came from the Russians, who were doubtless disturbed by the unpleasantness of the Liman von Sanders affair and by progress in Anglo-German negotiations over the Baghdad railway.[25] On February 5 Foreign Minister Sazonov mentioned to Sir George Buchanan, the British

21. Weber, *The Nationalist Revival in France*, 128. See also Gilbert Ziebura, *Die deutsche Frage in der öffentlichen Meinung Frankreichs von 1911–1914* (Berlin, 1955); Gordon Wright, *Raymond Poincaré and the French Presidency* (Stanford, 1942); John C. Hunter, "The Strength of France on the Eve of World War I: A Study of French Self-Confidence as Evidenced in the Parliamentary Debates on the Three-Year Service Law of 1913," unpubl. diss. (Harvard University, 1959), and Ralston, *The Army of the Republic*, 343–371.
22. December 29, 1913, Wilson Diaries; Henry Wilson noted that Lord Roberts "was tremendously shocked with Morley's bitterness and likened him to Robespierre." The projected figure of resignations comes from de La Panouse to Noulens, Jan. 8, 1914, Archives Guerre, "Attachés militaires: Angleterre," box 12. Also see the memo by Seely, "Position of the Army With Regard to the Situation in Ulster," Dec. 9, 1913, Cab. 37/117/87.
23. Two recent accounts of the incident are Sir James Fergusson, *The Curragh Incident* (London, 1964), and A. P. Ryan, *Mutiny at Curragh* (London, 1956).
24. On Wilson's role see Callwell, *Wilson*, I, 137–146; the actual diaries add little to Callwell's account.
25. Albertini, *The Origins of the War of 1914*, I, chap. x; B.D., X, pt. 2, chaps. xcii–xcv, xcviii; I. V. Bestuzhev, "Russian foreign policy, February–June 1914," *Journal of Contemporary History*, 1, no. 3 (1966), 93–112.

ambassador, that the Triple Entente needed to be converted into a defensive alliance. Two weeks later Sazonov repeated the idea and argued that a definite British commitment to the Continent would ensure peace since Berlin and Vienna would shrink from such odds. The Tsar, Buchanan was informed, thought a defensive alliance would not entail "any greater risks of war" than Britain already ran. Although Buchanan expressed sympathy for these suggestions, he made clear his doubts about a change in British policy.[26] And the unlikelihood of change was reiterated more forcefully by Sir Edward Grey in the House of Commons on March 18: "The good understandings which have existed and which exist between ourselves and France and Russia have undoubtedly, during the last troublous times, contributed to the peace of Europe." He added: "We remain attached to those good understandings." But Britain would not enter into any "hard and fast alliances," with their "hard and fast obligations." Great Britain would continue to depend upon its own strength for protecting its vital interests.[27]

Grey's comments did not dissuade the Russians from pressing anew for closer ties. In fact, with French assent, St. Petersburg escalated the intensity of the pressure. On April 3 Tsar Nicholas personally sounded Ambassador Buchanan about the possibility of concluding either a defensive alliance or plans for naval cooperation along the lines of the Anglo-French arrangements.[28] At the Foreign Office the permanent officials supported the Russian overtures. For months Arthur Nicolson had insisted that Britain should enter into an alliance relationship with Paris and St. Petersburg. Worried that the French no longer counted upon British military assistance and anxious to appease the Russians, he wanted the elastic entente replaced by more definite agreements. Yet he understood, if he did not like, the political impossibility of such an alliance;[29] thus he and Sir Eyre Crowe urged the acceptance of naval con-

26. Buchanan to Nicolson, Feb. 5, 1914, Nicolson Papers, vol. I/1914; Buchanan to Grey, Feb. 18, 1914, Grey Papers, F.O. 800/74; cf. Benckendorff to Sazonov, Jan. 29/Feb. 11, 1914, Otto Hoetzsch, ed., *Die internationalen Beziehungen im Zeitalter des Imperialismus*, 1st ser., 5 vols. (Berlin, 1931–1934), I, no. 232.
27. *Parliamentary Debates: Commons*, 5th ser., 59 (Mar. 18, 1914), 2186–2190.
28. Buchanan to Grey, Apr. 3, 1914, B.D., X, pt. 2, no. 537; Paléologue to Doumergue (tel.), Apr. 4, 1914, D.D.F., 3rd ser., X, no. 69; Isvolski to Sazonov, Mar. 5/18, 1914, Marchand, *Un livre noir*, II, 249–251. Henry Wilson's diary (June 4, 1913) indicates that Sir John French told the Russian military attaché on June 2 of the details of the projected British help to France. Wilson added: "This fairly took my breath away because Yermiloff has been trying to get this information from us from Huguet & Panouse for 3 years! Not content with this Sir John went this morning to Cambon & proudly told him what he had done!" Neither the available Russian nor the French documents add further illumination to this indiscretion.
29. Nicolson to Hardinge, Jan. 15, 1914, Nicolson Papers, vol. I/1914; Nicolson to Buchanan, Mar. 10, Apr. 7, 1914, *ibid.*, vol. II/1914. Lloyd George's comments in January 1914 about the satisfactory state of Anglo-German relations had given the German press an opportunity to irritate the French; Grey to Lloyd George, Jan. 23, 1914, Lloyd George Papers, C/4/14/12; Lloyd George to Grey, Jan. 26, 1914, *ibid.*, C/4/14/13.

versations as at least a step in the right direction. The Foreign Secretary, as usual, preferred to defer discussions as long as possible, though he indicated a willingness to divulge the contents of the Anglo-French staff talks to the Russians.[30] Grey did not, however, have much opportunity to delay on the Russian maneuver, for it became one of the major topics of discussion during his visit with George V to Paris in late April.

The royal visit, coming on the tenth anniversary of the signing of the entente, provided a splendid public reaffirmation of the cordiality of Anglo-French relations. The importance of the entente to British policy was unmistakably emphasized by the presence of Sir Edward Grey, who in eight years as Foreign Secretary had never left the British Isles in either an unofficial or official capacity. During their hectic four-day stay George V and Grey received rousing, enthusiastic acclaim from the French crowds on the route to Vincennes, at the Opera, and around the Hôtel de Ville. Extravagant toasts and compliments to Anglo-French friendship were in profusion; the King, especially anxious to dispel any doubts about his sincerity to the entente, worked hard on the toasts, which he delivered in acceptable, anglicized French. His counterpart was rather less successful: Ponsonby wrote Arthur Nicolson that some of Poincaré's toasts "read as if they had just been written and had never seen the light before." [31] The impact of the visit was heightened by widespread press coverage. Although British journalists rejected historian Ernest Lavisse' call for still closer Anglo-French relations, suggested in a letter to the *Times* on April 16, the fourth estates in both countries were effusive in their praise of the friendly "understanding." [32]

Grey's presence in Paris afforded a convenient opportunity to examine the health of both the entente and the Triple Entente; the discussions would, as it turned out, be the last review of Anglo-French relations before the war. On April 23 Grey, attended by his private secretary Sir William Tyrrell, met with Gaston Doumergue, the French Premier and Foreign Minister, at the Quai d'Orsay. Paul Cambon and Jacquin de Margerie, a Quai official, were present. Topics as diverse as Albania, Mexico, Italy in the Aegean, and the designs of the Triple Alliance were discussed, but attention centered most upon a French proposal for the initiation of Anglo-Russian naval talks.

Asserting that there was some chance the Russians might desert to the German camp, Doumergue warned that such a development, coupled with Italy's Mediterranean ambitions and the new presence of Germany

30. Crowe, Nicolson, and Grey minutes on Buchanan to Grey, Apr. 3, 1914, B.D., X, pt. 2, no. 537.
31. Ponsonby to Nicolson, Apr. 12, 25, 1914, Nicolson Papers, vol. II/1914; see also Grey, *Twenty-five Years*, I, 268–273.
32. Lavisse and Henry Wickham Steed, with Poincaré's approval, concocted the letter. See *The History of THE TIMES*, IV, pt. 1, 167–171; de Fleuriau to Doumergue, Apr. 20, 28, 1914, D.D.F., 3rd ser., X, nos. 128, 176. If an alliance was out of the question, the *Journal des sciences militaires* wanted at the very least intimate military conversations; 9 (Apr. 25, 1914).

in that sea, would thoroughly endanger the entente. To help avert Russian treachery he implored the Foreign Secretary to draw Britain closer to St. Petersburg. Readily admitting that an alliance was out of the question, Doumergue pressed instead for British defense discussions with the Russians. Although he did not see how they could "amount to much," Grey eventually agreed to seek Asquith's sanction for naval conversations; but he made it clear that the Russians would have to understand that the Anglo-French staff talks left both countries "entirely free to decide whether, in case of war, they would support one another or not."

Doumergue and Grey did not altogether ignore the status of Anglo-French arrangements. The latter displayed no inclination to go further than the private letters of November 1912 in enumerating entente obligations; but he did "reassure" the Premier, who was "touched," that Britain would not refuse its military and naval assistance if France were "unjustly menaced and attacked." British public opinion would force the government to act. And the Foreign Secretary repeated these views when he saw Poincaré later that same day, April 23. While carefully noting that no engagement was possible with the Tsar and that none existed with France, Grey told the French President that "if there were a really aggressive and menacing attack made by Germany upon France, it was possible that public feeling in Great Britain would justify the Government in helping France." [33] This sober assessment of the wellsprings of a democratic foreign policy could have left the French with few illusions about the absolute certainty of British help; on the other hand, Grey's attitude and candor, and his clear definition of what was likely to prompt British action, were of such a character that Poincaré had little reason to complain. Nor could the French forget Grey's pledge that Britain would become more intimate with Russia, a pledge that would have been entirely out of the question even two years before.

Shortly after returning to London Grey asked the Cabinet to consider the advisability of Anglo-Russian naval conversations. On May 12 the Liberal Cabinet, perhaps unduly swayed by Churchill's glowing description of Russia's naval potential in the Baltic, approved the staff talks with only one stipulation: that Grey's letter of November 1912 be sent to St. Petersburg to show precisely the limit of British obligations to France in case of war.[34] As had happened on two previous occasions, November 1911 and November 1912, the apparently inescapable logic of grand strategy compelled a Cabinet filled with radicals to authorize measures which reflected little of their political ideology. In this particular case, however, the ease with which the Russians gained their objective remains astonishing. Eager to maintain its entente relationships and at

33. Grey to Bertie, May 1, 1914, B.D., X, pt. 2, no. 541; "Note du ministre," Apr. 24, 1914, D.D.F., 3rd ser., X, no. 155. See also memo by Bertie, Apr. 24, 1914, Bertie Papers, F.O. 800/166; Poincaré, Au service de la France, IV, 112–113.
34. Asquith to George V, May 14, 1914, RA GEO V R/150.

the same time to take prudent strategic safeguards, the Asquith Cabinet apparently considered the staff talks the perfect, noncommittal way to achieve both goals. In 1911 the Cabinet had regarded the conversations as a grave, indeed dangerous, innovation; by 1914 they were viewed as a convenient political expedient which could be sanctioned in a single session, even when the suppliant was a Romanov.

On May 19 Sir Edward Grey informed Ambassador Benckendorff of the Cabinet's permission for staff talks along the lines established in the Grey-Cambon letters.[35] But before these exchanges could actually begin, Anglo-Russian naval relations became the subject of widespread public speculation. On May 22 the *Berliner Tageblatt* declared that an Anglo-Russian naval understanding had been discussed during the King's visit to Paris.[36] This accurate exposé and the comments it provoked immediately created parliamentary problems for the Asquith government. On June 11 Sir William Byles and Joseph King, the same pair of radicals who had challenged Asquith the year before, asked whether a naval agreement with Russia had been or was being concluded. This time Grey responded for the government, assuring the M.P.'s that the Prime Minister's earlier statement still held true: Britain's freedom of decision remained unimpaired. And he declared that "no negotiations have since been concluded with any Power that would make the statement less true. No such negotiations are in progress, and none are likely to be entered upon so far as I can judge. But if any agreement were to be concluded that made it necessary to withdraw or modify the Prime Minister's statement, which I have quoted, it ought, in my opinion, to be, and I suppose that it would be, laid before Parliament." [37]

Once more the Asquith government had sidestepped the issue of the staff conversations. In his answer the Foreign Secretary drew a careful distinction between a political accord and the allegedly apolitical, contingency-strategical arrangements. In doing so he deliberately misrepresented the Cabinet's recent decision to sanction the Russian naval talks and, of course, grossly falsified the picture of Anglo-French relations;

35. Grey to Bertie, May 21, 1914, B.D., X, pt. 2, nos. 542, 543; P. Cambon to Doumergue (tel.), May 19, 1914, D.D.F., 3rd ser., X, no. 250; Benckendorff to Sazonov, May 6/19, 7/20, 1914, Int. Bez., 1st ser., III, nos. 30, 39.

36. Earlier, on May 9, the *Morning Standard* had inaccurately reported that Isvolski had come to London to continue the talks begun in Paris; see Jagow to Lichnowsky, May 12, 1914, G.P., XXXIX, no. 15873n. Although Bertie thought Poincaré's boasting had caused the *Tageblatt* leak, the culprit was actually Baron de Siebert, a secretary at the Russian Embassy (Bertie to Grey, June 28, 1914, Grey Papers, F.O. 800/55; B.D., X, pt. 2, p. 791n). Also see Hale, *Publicity and Diplomacy*, 441–443.

37. *Parliamentary Debates: Commons*, 5th ser., 63 (June 11, 1914), 457–458. See also Lichnowsky to Bethmann, June 12–13, 1914, G.P., XXXIX, nos. 15881–15882; Benckendorff to Sazonov, May 29/June 11, 1914, Schreiner, *Entente Diplomacy and the World*, no. 852; Grey, *Twenty-five Years*, I, 278–286. In late April Mr. King had asked whether the Cabinet retained freedom of action and Grey referred him to Asquith's 1913 answer.

further, perhaps unwittingly, he conveniently ignored the quite political uses that successive Liberal governments had made of the staff talks. Ever since 1906 the conversations had been a useful and apparently safe way to answer the repeated French and now the Russian overtures for closer political relations. Grey's final comment, that he "supposed" a political accord would be laid before the House of Commons, was little guarantee that Parliament would even necessarily know of a political agreement. The ambiguities of his answer did not pass unnoticed. The *Manchester Guardian*, whose editor, C. P. Scott, knew quite accurately the details of the staff talks,[38] declared on June 12:

> We do not feel satisfied. The natural interpretation of the statement is that there are unpublished agreements, but that they are contingent in their operation either on some future decision of the Executive or of Parliament or on the interpretation of agreements that are published. . . . In other words, unless the agreements amounted to an actual alliance it need not be communicated to Parliament. These answers do not allay uneasiness or diminish the objections we have set forth in discussing the rumors of the naval agreement with Russia. We hope that the questions of yesterday will be followed up by more, in order that we may know exactly where we stand. For, depend upon it, if any agreement has been concluded, there is not a government in Europe which does not know exactly what it is. The secret, in so far as there is one, is a secret from the British Parliament and people, not from any possible enemy.[39]

The parliamentary and press uproar over closer relations with Russia caused Grey and the Admiralty to proceed more cautiously. New troubles with St. Petersburg over Persia likewise dictated a more leisurely approach.[40] Although the Russian naval agent in London, Captain N. Volkov, met with the Admiralty Staff on at least one occasion in early June, he was soon informed that further conversations would be delayed until Battenberg could visit Russia in August. Despite the tempest they caused in mid-1914, the Anglo-Russian naval conversations never in fact had any practical substance.[41]

Russian overtures for closer relations with Britain upset the Germans.

38. Scott had discussed the conversations at length with Lord Esher and Lord Loreburn in early May; memo by Scott, May 4, 1914, Scott Papers, Add. MSS. 50901.
39. Quoted in *G.P.*, XXXIX, pp. 625–626n. On June 13 J. A. Spender reiterated Grey's denial in the *Westminster Gazette*, a journal regarded in Berlin as an organ of the Foreign Office; Lichnowsky to Bethmann, June 13, 1914, *ibid.*, no. 15882.
40. For example, Grey to Buchanan, June 10, 1914, *B.D.*, X, pt. 2, no. 547.
41. Volkov to Chief of the Russian Naval Staff, May 24/June 6, 1914, Schreiner, *Entente Diplomacy and the World*, no. 851; Churchill to Grey, July 7, 1914, *B.D.*, X, pt. 2, no. 559. For the substance of Russian hopes from a naval accord, see "Journal einer Konferenz bei dem Chefs des russischen Admiralstabes," May 13/26, 1914, *Int. Bez.*, 1st ser., III, no. 86.

The possibility of a Triple Entente naval convention was particularly disturbing to a Berlin confident that Anglo-German relations were steadily becoming more intimate. Rumors of naval talks forced the German policy-makers to reconsider two vexing and thoroughly inter-related puzzles: the exact military and naval content of the entente relationship, and the extent of Britain's commitment to France. The solutions accepted by Berlin for these puzzles, as Fritz Fischer has shown, influenced decisively German grand strategy in July 1914.[42]

From 1905 onward, the organs of the German government received frequent reports suggesting possible British military cooperation with the French. During 1905 there were sensational revelations in the French press about a British pledge to send a hundred thousand men to the Schleswig coast. During 1906 and 1907 there were military evaluations concluding that the British had developed plans for intervention on the Continent.[43] Then, in February 1911, the German military attaché in Paris suggested that rumors of Anglo-French staff talks were in fact true. Haldane's frankness about Britain's military preparations during the Agadir tension and his warning in December 1912 provided the Germans with additional evidence of Britain's willingness to defend France against unprovoked attack.[44] These indications were in turn treated with respect in Berlin: Schlieffen amended his final war plans to provide for the contingency of a British arrival, though he did not fear its consequences, and subsequent German plans show that the possibility was heeded. In February 1913 the younger Moltke told the Austrians that he believed Britain was treaty-bound to cooperate with France against Germany, so that he would have to "reckon on her intervention."[45]

On the other hand, German policy-makers had to assimilate a series of consistent denials by Grey, Haldane, and Asquith that military and naval conversations had taken place. The 1906 and 1911–1913 denials were aimed primarily for domestic political consumption; still, Berlin was forced to consider them, and Ambassadors Metternich and Lichnowsky treated them as the truth. There is evidence that some German military planners were sufficiently impressed by the denials to doubt that Britain's intervention would come immediately.[46]

42. Fritz Fischer, *Germany's Aims in the First World War* (New York, 1967), chap. ii.
43. See, e.g., Moltke to Bülow, Nov. 24, 1906, G.P., XXI, pt. 2, no. 7232; Metternich to Bülow, Jan. 31, 1907, *ibid.*, no. 7205.
44. Schoen to Bethmann, Feb. 8, 1911, *ibid.*, XXIX, no. 10520; report of Major Ostertag, Oct. 24, 1911, *ibid.*, no. 10652; Ostertag to Metternich, Dec. 12, 1911, *ibid.*, no. 10670; and *ibid.*, XXXIX, chap. ccxciii.
45. Ritter, *The Schlieffen Plan*, 70–72, 161–164; Ritter, *Staatskunst und Kriegshandwerk*, II, 270–271; Major Baron Bienerth to Conrad, Feb. 19, 1913, quoted in Field Marshal Conrad von Hötzendorf, *Aus meiner Dienstzeit, 1906–1918*, 5 vols. (Vienna, 1921–1925), III, 151–153.
46. Baron Beyens to Davignon, Nov. 25, 1913, Belg. Arch., "Indépendance neutralité," XIII; cf. Beyens, *Deux années à Berlin*, II, 47–53.

The denials had other, more dangerous ramifications as well. Prince Lichnowsky refused to interpret Grey's disavowal of any British convention with France or Russia as meaning that Britain would stand aside if Germany attacked France: for instance, he repeatedly cautioned Berlin in May 1914 that London would not tolerate the destruction of France. But Foreign Minister Gottlieb von Jagow pointedly and caustically asked how the ambassador could reconcile this gloomy assessment with Grey's parliamentary statements that Britain's hands were free.[47] In their own way the staff talks, by forcing Grey to be ambiguous and misleading, had helped to create a kind of creditability gap.

When Grey on June 11 denied to the Commons that negotiations were under way for an Anglo-Russian naval convention, the Wilhelmstrasse faced a peculiar problem. Its own source in the Russian Embassy in London, Baron von Siebert, had flatly indicated that talks were indeed about to begin. Jagow could not directly challenge the Foreign Secretary's veracity, nor could he be very specific for fear of disclosing his source of information. Thus on June 15 he officially accepted Grey's parliamentary explanation and simultaneously warned Ambassador Goschen that, had the rumors been true, "the consequences would have been most serious."[48] But Foreign Minister Jagow was not content to let things rest. Nine days later he had Lichnowsky return to the subject of Anglo-Russian relations during an interview with Sir Edward Grey. The latter reiterated that Britain had no commitment to help France and Russia; but he added that relations within the Triple Entente were intimate and that the three capitals were in touch "in all important matters."[49]

Grey's evasive response occasioned still another German probe. On July 6 Lichnowsky told him that Germany appreciated that there were no secret political agreements with France and Russia. Did this same assurance, the ambassador asked, cover possible "conversational arrangements" with the Russian government? This point-blank inquiry evoked no definite answer; but three days later, after discussing the matter with Nicolson, Grey summoned Lichnowsky to the Foreign Office and leveled with him, spelling out what was meant by intimate relations. He could not deny, he told the diplomat, "that no conversations had taken place between the Military and Naval authorities of France and Russia and ourselves." Such talks had begun in 1906 and had continued from time to time thereafter.

47. Lichnowsky to Bethmann, May 1, 18, 1914, G.P., XXXIX, nos. 15872, 15875; Jagow to Lichnowsky, May 13, 1914, ibid., no. 15874.

48. Goschen to Grey, June 16, 1914, B.D., X, pt. 2, no. 550; Bethmann to Lichnowsky, June 16, 1914, G.P., XXXIX, no. 15883.

49. Grey to Goschen, June 24, 1914, B.D., XI, no. 4; Lichnowsky's report did not contain Grey's additional comment that occasionally the three countries talked "as intimately as Allies"; Lichnowsky to Bethmann, June 24, 1914, G.P., XXXIX, no. 15884.

But everything had been on the footing that the hands of the Governments were quite free. Indeed, if such conversations took place, it was not necessary for me to know what passed. The thing which concerned the Government and myself, and which it was necessary for me to keep in our hands, was whether we should or should not participate if a war arose. If we made any Agreement that entailed obligations upon us, it would not be a secret Agreement. I was pledged to Parliament not to make a secret Agreement of this kind and any such Agreement that was made would be laid before Parliament. . . . It was also true to say that never had there been anything in the nature of preparing an attack upon Germany.[50]

This statement is remarkable for its frankness, balance, and duality. Grey admitted there were military and naval conversations yet skillfully minimized their importance. Moreover, the significance of the talks was partly obscured by his strong insistence that Britain retained full freedom of action and that London planned no attack upon Germany. These comments left Jagow uneasy about the status of Anglo-Russian relations, so uneasy that he secretly sent Albert Ballin to London to investigate and received in turn still another assurance that no convention existed.[51] As a result, Grey's conciliatory tone and his expressions of goodwill toward Germany buttressed the prevailing Bethmann-Jagow belief that Britain would stand aside if Vienna acted over the Serbian affair. As the *Manchester Guardian* had predicted, Grey's disclosures to Lichnowsky, however they might be interpreted, meant that only Parliament and the British people remained ignorant of the military and naval conversations. But their ignorance did not continue much longer. On June 28 Austria's Archduke Franz Ferdinand and his wife Sophie were murdered at Sarajevo, and within five weeks Europe was at war.

50. Lichnowsky to Bethmann, July 6, 9, 1914, G.P., XXXIX, nos. 15886–15887. See also Grey to Sir Horace Rumbold, July 6, 9, 1914, B.D., XI, nos. 32, 41; Nicolson, *First Lord Carnock*, 407–408; E. F. Willis, *Prince Lichnowsky, Ambassador of Peace: A Study of Prewar Diplomacy, 1912–1914* (Berkeley, Calif., 1942), 221–228.
51. Cecil, *Albert Ballin*, 201–209.

15 | The Anglo-French Entente Goes to War: August 1914

In late July 1914 Sir Edward Grey struggled desperately to preserve the peace of Europe. By August 5 his efforts had proven futile: the entente was at war. The long-settled military and naval arrangements quickly went into operation. Both the intricate diplomatic maneuvers to maintain peace and the functioning of the entente's war preparations lie beyond the scope of this study;[1] but there are two questions about August 1914 which must be considered in concluding this work. What effect did the entente and the staff talks have upon Britain's decision to

1. The diplomatic developments can be followed in detail in Albertini, *The Origins of the War of 1914*, II–III; Imanuel Geiss, ed., *Julikrise and Kreigsaus-bruch 1914: Eine Dokumentensammlung*, 2 vols. (Hannover, 1963–1964); and Fischer, *Germany's Aims*, chap. ii. The British and French diplomatic archives do not add any startling new information to that contained in the earlier published volumes on 1914. The execution of the entente's military and naval plans is described in the various official histories and most recently in John Terraine, *Mons: The Retreat to Victory* (New York, 1960); Marder, *The War Years: To the Eve of Jutland, 1914–1916*; and Tuchman, *The Guns of August*.

enter the war? And what role did the conversations play in London's adoption of a continental strategy?

Britain stirred to the dangers of the Austro-Serbian situation very slowly. Although Sir Edward Grey had several discussions with Ambassador Lichnowsky about Vienna's attitude toward Serbia, the bulk of British attentions through most of July were focused on the intractable Irish question. Not until July 20 did the *Times* sound a note of alarm over the deteriorating Danubian situation.[2] The Cabinet did not consider the problem until July 24, when Grey informed his colleagues of the Austro-Hungarian demands upon Belgrade; this ultimatum the Cabinet regarded as "the gravest event for many years past in European politics; as it may be the prelude to a war in which at least 4 of the Great Powers might be involved."[3] Despite this somber evaluation, the Cabinet did not acknowledge or examine the possibility of British involvement in such a war. When Grey saw Paul Cambon on the same day, July 24, there was no mention of British policy should the efforts for peace fail.[4] Yet, by that date, Grey personally doubted that a war between Austria and Serbia could be localized. Implicitly if not explicitly, therefore, he envisaged British intervention as probable if local war could not be prevented.[5]

In St. Petersburg, meanwhile, the Franco-Russian alliance launched its first sortie to secure a British commitment. On July 24 Foreign Minister Sazonov expressed the hope to Sir George Buchanan that the British "would proclaim their solidarity with France and Russia." And French Ambassador Paléologue assured Buchanan "that France would not only give Russia strong diplomatic support, but would, if necessary, fulfil all the obligations imposed on her by the alliance." The British ambassador was cool to this joint overture, observing that Britain "had no direct interests in Servia, and public opinion in England would never

2. *The History of THE TIMES,* IV, pt. I, 177–193; Hale, *Publicity and Diplomacy,* 446–453; J. F. Scott, *Five Weeks: The Surge of Public Opinion on the Eve of the Great War* (New York, 1927), chap. ix.

3. Asquith to George V, July 25, 1914, Asquith Papers, box 7. On July 22 Grey had proposed direct Austro-Russian talks as a way to ease the tension; Grey to Buchanan, July 22, 1914, B.D., XI, no. 79.

4. Grey to Bertie, July 24, 1914, B.D., XI, no. 98; P. Cambon to Bienvenu-Martin (tel.), July 24, 1914, D.D.F., 3rd ser., XI, no. 23; Lichnowsky to Jagow (tel.), July 24, 1914, Max Montgelas and Walther Schüking, eds., *Outbreak of the World War: German Documents Collected by Karl Kautsky* (New York, 1924), no. 157. Also see Ernst Anrich, *Die englische Politik im Juli 1914* (Berlin, 1934), 154–182.

5. Minute by Grey (July 25) on Lichnowsky's memo, July 24, 1914, B.D., XI, no. 100. Grey cabled Buchanan on July 25 that "if war does take place we may be drawn into it by the development of other issues, and I am therefore anxious to prevent war," *ibid.,* no. 112. On Grey's performance in 1914, see Gooch, *Before the War: Studies in Diplomacy,* II, 122–133; Herbert Butterfield, "Sir Edward Grey in July 1914," *Historical Studies,* 5 (1965), 1–25.

sanction a war on her behalf." [6] A declaration of Triple Entente solidarity was therefore out of the question. Upon learning of this exchange,
Grey immediately reaffirmed, in cables to St. Petersburg and Paris, that
Buchanan's views were those of the government; and Bertie was instructed to deliver a memorandum to this effect to the Quai d'Orsay.[7]
In spite of Russian appeals and the advice of Sir Eyre Crowe, who
wanted to promise France and Russia that the British fleet would be
readied the moment another great power mobilized, Grey refused to
link Britain with France and Russia on the Serbian issue. The most he
would do was warn Ambassador Lichnowsky that Britain, though not
committed to any binding agreements, could not remain indifferent to
European complications. But the entente as such remained aloof from
the diplomatic maneuverings.[8]

Grey's caution reinforced the German hope that England would stand
aside; it has also earned him a full measure of historical opprobrium. His
reluctance to intervene more decisively sprang from two sources: first, a
fear that the premature invocation of entente unity would jeopardize
his peace efforts; second, and more importantly, the temper of the
Asquith Cabinet. Thoroughly exhausted by the prolonged crisis over
Ireland, the Cabinet only gradually shifted its concern to foreign affairs.
Indeed, as late as July 27 a session was divided between the Home Rule
tangle and Grey's moves for a four-power conference. Although the ministers on that occasion approved Churchill's order of the day before
keeping the First and Second Fleets together at Portland, there were no
further decisions about Britain's probable position if negotiations failed.
Instead the Cabinet agreed to consider Britain's "precise obligations in
regard to the neutrality of Belgium" at its next meeting—two days
hence.[9] And after the Cabinet Lloyd George told C. P. Scott that "there
could be no question of our taking part in any war in the first instance.
He knew of no Minister who would be in favour of it." [10] While Grey

6. Buchanan to Grey (tel.), July 24, 1914, B.D., XI, no. 101; Paléologue to
Bienvenu-Martin (tel.), July 24, 1914, D.D.F., 3rd ser., XI, no. 19; Sazonov to
Benckendorff (tel.), July 12/25, 1914, Int. Bez., 1st ser., V, no. 48.
7. Grey to Buchanan (tel.), July 25, 1914, B.D., XI, no. 112; "Note de
l'Ambassade de Grande Bretagne," July 25, 1914, D.D.F., 3rd ser., XI, no. 48.
8. Minute by Crowe on Buchanan to Grey (tel.), July 24, 1914, B.D., XI, no.
101; Grey to Rumbold (tel.), July 25, 1914, ibid., no. 116; Lichnowsky to Jagow
(tel.), K.D., no. 180. One who did not, surprisingly, share any enthusiasm for the
Serbian quarrel was Sir Francis Bertie; entry for July 28, 1914, The Diary of Lord
Bertie of Thame, 1914–1918, ed. Lady Algernon Gordon, 2 vols. (New York, n.d.),
I, 3.
9. Asquith to George V, July 28, 1914, quoted in Spender and Asquith, Life of
Asquith, II, 80–81.
10. Memo by Scott, July 27, 1914, quoted in Hammond, C. P. Scott, 177–178;
on the mood of the Cabinet see John, Viscount Morley, Memorandum on Resignation, August 1914 (London, 1928); Churchill, The World Crisis, I, chaps. ix–x;
Grey, Twenty-five Years, I, 298–331, II, 1–18. Also see the questions and answers
about 1914 asked by J. A. Spender in 1929 of various surviving Cabinet ministers;
Spender Papers, Add. MSS, 46386.

did not share the Chancellor of the Exchequer's optimism about non-involvement, he was fully alert to the political potency of the radical bloc in the Cabinet. Ceaselessly vigilant about radical sensitivities ever since the aftermath of Agadir and the crisis over the conversations, he was no less deft in his movements in 1914. Whatever Grey's personal preferences for British policy, and they inclined to a more vigorous role, profound political divisions within the Cabinet shaped and limited his response to French appeals for help, to the aggressive advice of his subordinates, and to the idea of a strong warning to Berlin.[11]

The Foreign Secretary's irenic efforts grew more urgent following Vienna's hasty declaration of war on July 28. As the situation deteriorated, St. Petersburg and Paris intensified their appeals to London for some official sign of support and solidarity. First on July 27 and then again the next day, Russian diplomats urged that Britain end Germany's belief that it would stand aside. Grey's measured response was that the failure of the First Fleet to disperse "ought to dispel this [German] impression," though the Russian Ambassador was also warned not to take this sign as meaning that Britain "promised anything more than diplomatic action." [12] Despite Grey's unwillingness to be more "Servian than the Russians," Ambassador Paul Cambon remained confident that France could depend on British assistance. His confidence, in fact, enabled him to return to Paris on July 25 to help at the Quai d'Orsay until President Poincaré and Premier Viviani, returning by sea from their state visit to Russia, were again in France.[13] Nor was it dampened when he next saw Grey, on July 28, for both agreed that the concentration of the British fleet would emphasize "the anxiety under which the whole of Europe was placed by the Austrian action" and would be interpreted as further proof that Britain would not stand on the sidelines.[14] Cambon was soon to discover that his optimism about the entente was not altogether warranted.

On July 29 the British Cabinet for the first time devoted its entire

11. On July 27 Grey briefly reviewed his peacemaking efforts in the House of Commons and concluded that "no one can say what would be the limit of the issues that might be raised by such a conflict, the consequences of it, direct and indirect, would be incalculable"; quoted in B.D., XI, no. 190. Also see Crowe's strong minute of July 27 on Buchanan to Grey (tel.), July 27, 1914, ibid., no. 170; and Lichnowsky to Jagow (tel.), July 27, 1914, K.D., no. 265.

12. Grey to Buchanan (tel.), July 27, 1914, B.D., XI, no. 177; Bertie to Grey (tels.), July 28, 1914, ibid., nos. 216, 232; Benckendorff to Sazonov (tel.), July 14/27, 1914, Int. Bez., 1st ser., V, no. 122.

13. On July 26 de Fleuriau cabled Paris that Grey, Nicolson, and Benckendorff wanted Cambon back in London; D.D.F., 3rd ser., XI, no. 88. See also Eubank, Paul Cambon, 169–171.

14. Grey to Bertie, July 28, 1914, B.D., XI, no. 238. On the general problem of threats and perceptions in 1914, see Robert C. North, "Perception and Action in the 1914 Crisis," Journal of International Affairs, 21 (1967), 103–122; cf. Robert Jervis, "The Costs of the Scientific Study of Politics: An Examination of the Stanford Content Analysis Studies," International Studies Quarterly, 11 (December 1967), 366–393.

session to the European crisis. A tense, sometimes acrid debate left no doubt that the ministers were unmistakably averse to entanglement in a continental war. And, brushing sentiment aside, the Cabinet had concluded that Britain's obligation to maintain Belgian neutrality was "rather one of policy than of legal obligation." Grey was instructed to notify both the French and German ambassadors that "at this stage we were unable to pledge ourselves in advance, either under all conditions to stand aside, or in any conditions to join in." To put it more specifically, the Asquith Cabinet was under no obligation to France because of the entente relationship. On the other hand, the Cabinet did not confuse its dislike for war with a neglect of purely British interests, for the same sitting authorized Churchill to send the "warning" telegram to the fleet and the C.I.D. to implement the "precautionary stage" of the War Book.[15] Although refusing to commit itself to the Continent, the Cabinet nonetheless took the necessary steps to safeguard Britain's freedom of action. For the moment this did not include intervention in a Balkan quarrel.[16]

After the Cabinet adjourned, Grey crossed Downing Street to the Foreign Office and summoned the German and French ambassadors. Britain, he reiterated to Prince Lichnowsky, intended to stay out of any Austro-Serbian dispute. But in a warning that clearly exceeded the Cabinet's instructions he cautioned that Britain might be forced to intervene if British or French interests became endangered.[17] Although he revealed the gist of this admonition to Berlin to Cambon, he was otherwise brutally blunt with the French ambassador. He began by stressing how different the two Moroccan crises were from the Balkan upheaval. In 1905 and 1911 Germany had seemed determined to crush France on a question which "was the subject of a special agreement between France and us." No such agreement, however, tied Britain to either an Austro-Serbian or Austro-Russian quarrel. "If Germany became involved and France became involved, we had not made up our minds what we should do; it was a case we should have to consider." Moreover, even if France did become involved, the British were "free from engagements, and we should have to decide what British interests required us to do." Nor, added Grey, should France interpret the fleet concentration as implying that Britain planned to participate.[18] Surprisingly, Cambon's reaction to

15. Asquith to George V, July 30, 1914, quoted in Spender and Asquith, *Life of Asquith*, II, 81.
16. The *Westminster Gazette* (July 30, 1914) spoke of Britain's interests in India and the Dominions and warned that Britain did not have "unlimited force" to intervene in Europe.
17. Grey to Goschen, July 29, 1914, B.D., XI, no. 286; Lichnowsky to Jagow (tel.), July 29, 1914, K.D., no. 368. Grey's comments moved the Kaiser to call the British minister a "common cheat," a "common cur!" Also see Albertini, *The Origins of the War of 1914*, II, 508–527.
18. Grey to Bertie, July 29, 1914, B.D., XI, no. 283; P. Cambon to Viviani (tel.), July 29, 1914, D.D.F., 3rd ser., XI, no. 281.

this harsh, discouraging explication of British policy was remarkably restrained. Perhaps he had expected and discounted in advance this stance from the radical Cabinet, confident Grey and Asquith would not desert France or the entente in the last analysis. Or, more probably, he regarded the Foreign Secretary's straight-talk to Lichnowsky as more significant than his distinctions between Morocco and the Balkans. In any event, the French ambassador made no attempt to browbeat Grey about a pledge of support. On that July 29, developments were under way elsewhere that ultimately justified his calm attitude.

In Berlin late that night, Bethmann Hollweg, the German Chancellor, shoved the Belgian question into the teeth of the diplomatic machinery. In an important interview with Sir Edward Goschen, the British ambassador, Bethmann explored the possibility of British neutrality in the event of war. Recognizing that it would "never allow France to be crushed" he offered to give Britain every assurance that French territorial integrity would be maintained "provided that Great Britain remained neutral." In addition he would promise to honor Dutch neutrality. But he would not pledge the same respect for French colonies or, more importantly, for Belgian neutrality.[19]

This maladroit German bid for neutrality profoundly influenced the formation of British policy. In the first place, it disclosed Germany's intention to strike at France and possibly to violate Belgian neutrality in the process. Further, it reinforced the Nicolson-Crowe refrain that Britain had to declare its position in order to preserve peace in Europe. If the policy of deterrence was to work, its premises could not be left in doubt. "It is clear," argued Crowe, "that Germany -is practically determined to go to war, and that the one restraining influence so far has been the fear of England joining in the defence of France and Belgium."[20] Finally, Bethmann's proposal furnished Grey with the perfect issue in his struggle within the Cabinet for intervention. Rather than talk of the Entente Cordiale or the European equilibrium or the dangers of isolation, he could stress the necessity to help tiny Belgium defend its neutrality.

Meanwhile, the return of Poincaré and Viviani on July 29 brought new stability to the French policy process. Almost immediately clarification of the British position was sought, for Grey's insistence that Britain had no engagement to France had reawakened French fears about British dependability. On Thursday July 30 Premier Viviani ordered Paul Cambon to remind Grey of their 1912 letters, especially the provisions for consultation in time of emergency. And the ambassador was to stress

19. Goschen to Grey (tel.), July 29, 1914, B.D., XI, no. 293; Bethmann to Goschen, July 29, 1914, K.D., no. 373; also see Imanuel Geiss, ed., *July 1914: The Outbreak of the First World War: Selected Documents* (New York, 1967), 265–275.

20. Crowe minute on Goschen to Grey (tel.), July 29, 1914, B.D., XI, no. 293; Grey to Goschen (tel.), July 30, 1914, *ibid.*, no. 303.

the contrast between France's peaceful intentions, as evidenced by the withdrawal of French troops from the border (up to ten kilometers away in places), and Germany's widespread military preparations.[21] At the same time President Poincaré appealed to Ambassador Bertie for a British declaration of solidarity with the Franco-Russian alliance, contending that such a statement was the only thing that would persuade Berlin to restrain the Austrians. He warned that "if there were a general war on the continent England would inevitably be involved in course [sic] of it, for protection of her vital interests, and a declaration by her now of her intention to support France, who desires to remain at peace, would almost certainly prevent Germany from embarking on a war."[22]

These varied appeals from Paris, all of which reached Grey on July 30 along with news of the Russian mobilization, occasioned no appreciable change in British policy. That afternoon Grey once again told Cambon that London was indifferent to an Austro-Russian-Serbian struggle and repeated that British public opinion would not support intervention. The ambassador's mention of the 1912 letters and his plea for at least a hypothetical consideration of Britain's position left the Foreign Secretary unmoved. Although he personally was a partisan of intervention, Grey would only promise to bring the entire problem before the Cabinet the next day.[23]

The results of the Cabinet on July 31 could give Paris little cause for hoping that a change in Britain's hands-off policy was imminent. In spite of Bethmann's earlier ambiguity about Belgian neutrality, the Cabinet would go no further than authorizing the Foreign Secretary to sound both France and Germany, à la 1870, about their intentions toward the neutralized state. And even these demarches did not warn that a violation of Belgium might be treated by Britain as a casus belli. Also, the Cabinet flatly refused to meet Cambon's request for some statement of British intentions should war come. Grey conceded, wrote Lord Morley later, "that we were not bound by the same obligation of honour to France as bound France to Russia. He professed to stand by what he had told Cambon in his letter of 1912, that we were left perfectly free to decide whether we would assist France by armed force."[24]

21. Viviani and Abel Ferry (Undersecretary at the Quai d'Orsay) to P. Cambon (tels.), July 30, 1914, D.D.F., 3rd ser., XI, nos. 305, 316; Poincaré, Au service de la France, IV, 373–386, 416–418.
22. Bertie to Grey, July 30, 1914, B.D., XI, nos. 318 (tel.), 320, 373; also see entry for July 30, 1914, Diary of Lord Bertie, I, 4–5.
23. Grey to Bertie, July 30, 1914, B.D., XI, no. 319; P. Cambon to Viviani (tel.), July 30, 1914, D.D.F., 3rd ser., XI, no. 363; Benckendorff to Sazonov (tel.), July 17/30, 1914, Int. Bez., 1st ser., V, no. 288. Asquith on July 30 noted that the City was entirely against intervention.
24. Morley, Memorandum on Resignation, 10; Albertini rightly dates this as applying to the Cabinet of July 31, not Aug. 2 (The Origins of the War of 1914, III, 372). Also see diary, July 31, 1914, Earl of Oxford and Asquith, Memories and Reflections, 1852–1927, 2 vols. (Boston, 1928), II, 10.

Once more Grey had the painful task of informing Paul Cambon of the Cabinet's deliberations. This time, however, he tried to soften the impact with some good news first: that morning he had informed Prince Lichnowsky (with more firmness, in fact, than the divisions within the Cabinet warranted) that if France and Germany became involved in a war, Britain would be "drawn into it." But, he continued, Paris should not interpret this information as signifying a British engagement to France: for instance, the financial situation had grown so acute that Britain might have to remain neutral in order to prevent the collapse of European credit. To this unwelcome news he added the familiar refrain that after all the Cabinet was not obligated to take action, although the preservation of Belgian neutrality might change its position. Angered and embittered, Cambon retorted: "It could not be to England's interest that France should be crushed by Germany." Would it take, he asked testily, a German invasion of French territory to bring about a British decision? For this outburst Grey had no response, except to promise that the Cabinet would discuss any new development.[25]

The interview jolted Paul Cambon. Until this point he had been confident that Grey would be able to persuade the Liberal government to proclaim the unity of the entente. Instead, with Russia mobilizing, with Germany taking precautionary measures, and with Austria at war with Serbia, the British Cabinet refused to act. It was now evident, as in the Moroccan crises, that British interests, with British honor a distant second, were the cohesive elements in Anglo-French relations, and not until these interests appeared directly threatened would the Cabinet realize that noninvolvement was impossible. To convince London that British interests were at stake now became the primary task of French diplomacy. President Poincaré sent George V a personal letter, emphasizing German military preparations and insisting that a display of entente unity was the only way to preserve the peace. The French Embassy in London sent repeated communiqués to the Foreign Office describing German military moves. But neither appeals to royalty nor alarmist intelligence reports were successful in provoking a positive British response.[26]

More successful were Cambon's complaints of Liberal perfidy to the permanent officials at the Foreign Office, to Henry Wilson, and to various Conservative leaders. Of course Nicolson and Crowe agreed completely with the ambassador's laments, and on July 31 both officials stated their position anew to Sir Edward Grey. The preservation of the

25. Grey to Bertie, July 31, 1914, B.D., XI, nos. 352 (tel.), 367; P. Cambon to Viviani (tel.), July 31, 1914, D.D.F., 3rd ser., XI, no. 445; Poincaré, Au service de la France, IV, 433–442; Grey, Twenty-five Years, I, 328–330. For Grey's warning to Lichnowsky, see the ambassador's cable to Jagow, July 31, 1914, K.D., no. 489.

26. Poincaré's letter and the King's reply are in D.D.F., 3rd ser., XI, nos. 457, 550; on the military information see, e.g., Viviani to Cambon (tel.), July 31, 1914, ibid., no. 390.

balance of power, the Assistant Undersecretary asserted, could not be maintained "by a State that is incapable of fighting and consequently carries no weight." Dismissing the current commercial panic as German-inspired and stressing Germany's overture for British neutrality, Crowe insisted that the entente had created "a moral bond" and an "honourable expectation" of British support: it was a question of right or wrong, and on this basis Britain's duty and interests lay in "standing by France in her hour of need." Sir Arthur Nicolson urged that at the least Britain should mobilize its Army so that "if public opinion, at present so bewildered and partially informed, is ready in event of [a] German invasion of France to stand by the latter," the aid would not be too late.[27]

Elsewhere on July 31, General Henry Wilson, behaving more like a party whip than a D.M.O., and George Lloyd worked round the clock to alert Conservatives to the possibility that the Asquith government might leave France in the lurch.[28] Nor were their efforts hindered by Churchill's soundings at the same time for a coalition government that would support Paris.[29]

The strident demands of the *Times* for assistance to France reinforced the French-Conservative-Churchill drive for intervention. On July 30 the Thunderer asserted that England "can no more afford to see France crushed by Germany, or the balance of power upset against France, than Germany can afford to see Austria-Hungary crushed by Russia and that balance upset against Austrian and Hungarian interests." The next day, under the banner "Interests and Duty of Britain," the *Times* insisted that Britain had a moral obligation to France and Russia, that London could not allow the balance of power to be altered or Britain to become isolated against Germany; further, Britain had a distinct naval interest in who controlled the Channel coasts. "France does not threaten our security. A German victory over France could threaten it irremediably." Saturday's paper declared: "We dare not stand aside; our strongest interest is the law of self-preservation."[30]

But by that Saturday night, August 1, the French, the Conservatives, and the "hawks" had little to show for their pressure upon the Asquith Cabinet. That afternoon's *Westminster Gazette* reflected the predominant view of the ministers when it strongly deprecated "the attempt which is being made in some quarters to kindle a war fever . . . and

27. Crowe to Grey, July 31, 1914, B.D., XI, no. 369; Nicolson to Grey, July 31, 1914, *ibid.*, no. 368; also see Nicolson to Grey, Aug. 2, 1914, *ibid.*, no. 446.
28. Callwell, *Wilson*, I, 152–153; George Lloyd to A. Chamberlain, July 31, 1914, Chamberlain Papers, box 14.
29. Churchill, *The World Crisis*, I, 229–230; Lord Beaverbrook, *Politicians and the War, 1914–16* (Garden City, N.Y., 1928), 3–11; Sir Charles Petrie, *The Life and Letters of the Right Hon. Sir Austen Chamberlain*, 2 vols. (London, 1939), I, 369–371; Earl of Birkenhead, *Frederick Edwin, Earl of Birkenhead: The First Phase*, 2 vols. (London, 1933), I, 309–310.
30. Also see *The History of THE TIMES*, IV, pt. 1, 202–211; Hale, *Publicity and Diplomacy*, 461–466.

drive us into the reckless project of embarking our Expeditionary Force on Continental warfare." [31] These sentiments were well represented in Saturday's session of the Cabinet, during which Churchill and Grey both advocated a vigorous, pro-entente policy. The radicals, led by Lord Morley with support from Lloyd George and backed by the major Liberal press organs, remained firmly opposed to intervention in France's quarrel.[32] Even a second equivocal answer from Berlin about its intentions toward Belgium did not shake the radicals' determination to stand aside. Desperate to avoid a Cabinet split and hopeful that the passage of time would bring unity to his government, the Prime Minister on August 1 prudently resisted any attempt to alter Britain's ambivalent stand toward the crisis.[33]

The continuing dalliance of the Liberal government, at a time when France was sliding closer to the abyss, infuriated Paul Cambon. And his heated interview with Grey that Saturday did not help his disposition—the latter repeated again that Britain was under no obligation to France, especially since France was being drawn into war because of its Russian alliance, the terms of which Grey did not even know. Although he assured the ambassador that "this did not mean that under no circumstances would we assist France," Grey emphasized that "it did mean that France must take her own decision at this moment without reckoning on an assistance that we were not now in a position to promise." Stunned, Cambon declared that he could not forward this statement to Paris; he would instead simply notify his government that London had reached no decision. But, interrupted Grey, that would not be true, for the Cabinet had made a decision: it could not ask Parliament to approve the dispatch of the B.E.F. to the Continent. "Such a step had always been regarded here as very dangerous and doubtful. It was one we could not propose, and Parliament would not authorise unless our interests and obligations were deeply and desperately involved."

Grey's pronouncement sorely tried the friendship and the patience of the French diplomat. Britain, he pleaded, *did* have an obligation to help France: for the sake of British opinion France had pulled back its troops from the frontier and thus perhaps ruined its chances for an offensive attack; for the sake of British interests France "had concentrated her fleet in the Mediterranean and had left her northern and western coasts exposed." Grey refused to acknowledge the validity of these contentions,

31. On Spender's role in these crucial days, see his August 1914 memo, Spender Papers, Add. MSS, 46392, and his *Life, Journalism and Politics*, II, 11–19.
32. On radical activity outside the government, see, e.g., the entry, July 31. 1914, Christopher Addison, *Four and a Half Years: A Personal Diary from June 1914 to January 1919*, 2 vols. (London, 1934), I, 31–32; Churchill to Arthur Ponsonby, July 31, 1914, quoted in Churchill, *Young Statesman*, 699–700.
33. Haldane to E. Haldane, Aug. 2, 1914, Haldane Papers, 6012; Asquith, *Memories and Reflections*, II, 10–11; on Lloyd George's position, see Churchill, *Young Statesman*, 700–704; Owen, *Tempestuous Journey*, 264–268.

holding that "it was unreasonable to say that, because France had an obligation under an alliance of which we did not even know the terms, therefore we were bound equally with her, by the obligations in that alliance, to be involved in war." Cambon persevered, countering that surely there was "the obligation of British interests." If Britain failed France, "the *entente* would disappear; and whether victory came to Germany or to France and Russia, [Britain's] situation at the end of the war would be very uncomfortable." [34] The Foreign Secretary, who admitted the pertinence of this harsh prospect, promised that the Cabinet would not ignore such British interests. Further, in a step that may have assuaged Cambon's ruffled feelings somewhat, Grey suggested that a German naval move toward the Channel or a German attack upon Belgium might alter the tone of British opinion.[35] Grey made no definite pledge about the German fleet, but he closed the conversation on a hopeful note: he would remind the Cabinet about France's undefended northern coasts.

Cambon left the Foreign Office extremely discouraged, as well he might. The policy of friendship with Britain—the policy which he had so carefully pursued for sixteen years—was apparently a colossal failure in the moment of truth. Britain had once more become the Perfidious Albion. And indeed, had Cambon known of Grey's momentary proposal that Saturday to pledge British neutrality in return for a German commitment not to attack in the west, he might have completely despaired.[36] Yet, paradoxically, at this nadir in the history of the prewar entente, the prospects for eventual British assistance were growing much greater. The changing probabilities came, it should be emphasized, not from any inherent strength in the entente, but rather from Britain's mounting concern about Belgian neutrality and German sea power. On these issues the Cabinet and therefore Grey were growing less hesitant to act. On August 1, for example, the Foreign Secretary had, despite his talk of a quid pro quo neutrality deal, upbraided Lichnowsky for Jagow's evasive answer on Belgium and warned that "if there were a violation of the neutrality of Belgium by one combatant while the other respected it, it would be extremely difficult to restrain public feeling in this country." [37]

34. Grey to Bertie, Aug. 1, 1914, B.D., XI, nos. 426 (tel.), 447; cf. P. Cambon to Viviani (tel.), Aug. 1, 1914, D.D.F., 3rd ser., XI, no. 532. Nicolson protested the Cabinet's attitude, noting Grey's promises to Cambon that "if Germany was the aggressor you would side with France." The Foreign Secretary responded: "Yes, but he has nothing in writing"; Aug. 2, 1914, Wilson Diaries.

35. Nicolson had pushed the naval issue earlier in the day; Nicolson to Grey, Aug. 1, 1914, B.D., XI, no. 424.

36. Grey to Bertie (tels.), Aug. 1–2, 1914, ibid., nos. 419, 460; Bertie to Grey (tel.), Aug. 1, 1914, ibid., no. 453; Lichnowsky to Jagow (tels.), Aug. 1, 1914, K.D., nos. 562, 570, 596, 603; Bethmann to Lichnowsky (tel.), Aug. 1, 1914, ibid., no. 578; Albertini, The Origins of the War of 1914, III, 380–386.

37. Grey to Goschen, Aug. 1, 1914, B.D., XI, no. 448; Lichnowsky to Jagow (tel.), Aug. 1, 1914, K.D., no. 596.

He refused, moreover, to promise absolute British neutrality even if Germany respected Belgian territory. These intimations, designed to have a sobering effect upon Berlin, also sharpened the focus of British policy. With hopes for peace fading, Belgium emerged as the pivotal issue of Anglo-German relations. But the naval facet of these relations was not ignored either. When Winston Churchill learned late on Saturday night of Germany's declaration of war on Russia, he quickly managed to secure Asquith's assent for total mobilization of the Royal Navy.[38] Britain's unchanging interests—Belgian neutrality and sea power—were not being neglected.

Sunday, August 2, a hot, muggy day in London, was the turning point in Britain's road to war. The morning had hardly begun when Paris, then London, heard of the German occupation of Luxembourg. This action, coupled with Germany's declaration of war against Russia the previous night, gave the meditations of the Cabinet a new sense of urgency. With a European war at hand, the time for British equivocation was ended.[39] Furthermore, the Conservative-Unionist leadership, prodded and inspired by Henry Wilson, had initiated a "Pogrom" to pressure "Squiffy" and his government to act on behalf of France. The result was a letter from Lord Lansdowne and Bonar Law to Asquith on that Sunday morning which contended that "any hesitation in now supporting France and Russia would be fatal to the honour and to the future security of the United Kingdom." The Opposition would support "all measures required by England's intervention in the war." [40] It was in these circumstances then, that the Cabinet held two long, unprecedented Sunday meetings to examine Britain's relationship to Belgium and to the entente.

Sir Edward Grey opened the eleven o'clock session with a strong declaration of support for France. Britain had, he contended, "both moral obligations of honour and substantial obligations of policy in taking sides with France." [41] To support this view he stressed how the French, because of the naval conversations, were safeguarding British interests in the Mediterranean, while entrusting their northern coasts to British care. Churchill, who in 1912 had dismissed this argument as fallacious, now warmly endorsed Grey's insistence that Britain had a moral commitment to assist France in the Channel.[42] Subsequently the Foreign Secretary won, as Lord Morley observed later, general agreement on two

38. Churchill, *The World Crisis*, I, 230–231.
39. For the public mood that day, see G. M. Thomson, *The Twelve Days: 24 July to 4 August 1914* (London, 1964), 162–177, and Geoffrey Marcus, *Before the Lamps Went Out* (Boston, 1965), 264–287.
40. A first draft of the letter mentioned the military and naval conversations; Petrie, *Chamberlain*, I, 370–373. See also Callwell, *Wilson*, I, 153–155.
41. Morley, *Memorandum on Resignation*, 11.
42. Churchill, *The World Crisis*, I, 212–214; Grey, *Twenty-five Years*, II, 1–3; Asquith, *Memories and Reflections*, II, 11–12.

points: "(1) We owed it to France, in view of the Entente, and also of her value to us in the Mediterranean. (2) We could not acquiesce in a Franco-German naval conflict in the narrow seas, on our doorstep so to say." [43] At length, after a "fair discussion," Grey was authorized to promise the French and to warn the Germans that Britain would tolerate no German naval action in the Channel or against the French coasts.

The commitment on the Channel represented a major victory for the entente. After days of evading French requests for assistance, London had finally departed from its hands-off attitude. The alleged content and nature of the naval conversations were instrumental in prompting this commitment; in fact, this was the sole clear-cut instance in which the staff talks exercised a crucial influence upon the Cabinet's deliberations about war or peace. [44] The Cabinet's ability to agree upon the decision was equally a reflection of its own assessment of British naval interests, however. With or without an entente, a belligerent German fleet in the Strait of Dover posed an intolerable threat to British security. Even the presence of a sizable French force in the north would have made little difference to the Admiralty. The naval conversations certainly strengthened the government's determination to guarantee the French coasts; but the dictates of British strategy would have prompted the same decision. And in any case, the British pledge was not the cause of London's entry into the war, for Berlin offered to refrain from operations in the Channel if London would remain neutral. Rather it was the question of Belgium, not naval operations in the Channel or naval conversations, that finally led the Cabinet and Britain to war. [45]

The military talks had even less impact upon the considerations of the Sunday morning Cabinet, a fact Paul Cambon discovered when he saw the Foreign Secretary in the early afternoon. After notifying the ambassador of the Cabinet's decision to defend the coasts, Grey observed that imperial responsibilities and home defense needs would prevent the dispatch of the Expeditionary Force to the Continent. Placing great stress on the morale effect that even two British divisions would have, Cambon asked if the Cabinet's ruling was final. "No," responded Grey, but there was the consideration that "so small a force as two or even four divisions abroad at the beginning of a war would entail the maximum of risk to them and produce the minimum of effect." [46] The B.E.F., regardless of careful preparations, appeared destined to remain a home defense force.

---

43. Morley, *Memorandum on Resignation*, 11–12; also Crewe (Lord Privy Seal) to George V, Aug. 2, 1914, quoted in Spender and Asquith, *Life of Asquith*, II, 82.
44. Albertini, *The Origins of the War of 1914*, III, 524–525 n. 3.
45. "Communication from the German Embassy," Aug. 3, 1914, B.D., XI, no. 531; P. Cambon to Viviani (tel.), Aug. 3, 1914, D.D.F., 3rd ser., XI, no. 670; Lichnowsky to Jagow (tel.), Aug. 3, 1914, K.D., no. 764; Herbert H. Asquith, *The Genesis of the War* (London, 1923), 208.
46. Grey to Bertie (tel.), Aug. 2, 1914, B.D., XI, no. 487; Cambon to Viviani (tel.), Aug. 2, 1914, D.D.F., 3rd ser., XI, no. 612.

Nor was Grey more comforting about London's reaction (which was one of tolerance) toward the German violation of Luxembourg. These timid signs were, however, partly offset by Grey's expressed hope of securing Cabinet permission to make a similar German violation of Belgium a casus belli. Although the veteran ambassador still disliked the hesitancy of the Liberal government, he nonetheless appreciated that the chances for British entry into the war were improving, with or without the B.E.F.[47]

Sir Edward Grey made maximum use of the Belgian issue in the second Cabinet of that seemingly interminable Sunday. Advocating a strong stand on the question of Belgian neutrality, he could bolster his position by citing numerous German violations of French territory, the probability that the German seizure of Luxembourg meant an attack through Belgium, and the actions of Gladstone in the Franco-Prussian War.[48] He could also report that the Belgians were resolved to defend their neutrality; Brussels had just re-emphasized that it would not tolerate even a minor infringement by either side. After another lengthy discussion, the "frocks" took a further step in the direction of war when they agreed that Grey's speech to Parliament the next day should, without using the phrase casus belli, make it evident "that a substantial violation of the neutrality of that country [Belgium] would place us in the situation contemplated as possible by Mr. Gladstone in 1870, when interference with Belgian independence was held to compel us to take action." [49] After the Cabinet adjourned, Grey announced this new decision to a much-relieved Cambon. The entente was intact.

The Cabinet's agreement about Belgium was, at least in retrospect, the watershed for Britain between war and peace. Although the condition—"substantial violation"—still provided a loophole for the radicals to escape through, its vagueness worked even more decidedly in favor of the pro-intervention bloc. For a third time the radicals had, as in the 1911 restrictions on the staff talks and the 1912 Grey-Cambon letters, placed their hopes in words and nuances; they would be no more successful in 1914 than earlier. Furthermore, the willingness to sanction this strong warning on Belgium reflected a slight but distinct shift in the line-up of the Liberal ministers. Burns, Morley, Harcourt, and others, encouraged by C. P. Scott and the Guardian, might still talk of resigning, but the influential Chancellor of the Exchequer had softened his opposition to action.[50] And perhaps most importantly, the limited unity conferred by

47. On Cambon's worried mood that Sunday, see Albertini, The Origins of the War of 1914, III, 406–409.
48. Morley, Memorandum on Resignation, 14–21; Owen, Tempestuous Journey, 265; Lord Riddell, Lord Riddell's War Diary, 1914–1918 (London, 1933), 3–6.
49. Crewe to George V, Aug. 2, 1914, quoted in Spender and Asquith, Life of Asquith, II, 82. See also Villiers to Grey (tel.), Aug. 2, 1914, B.D., XI, no. 476; P. Cambon to Viviani (tel.), Aug. 3, 1914, D.D.F., 3rd ser., XI, no. 638.
50. Memo, Aug. 3, 1914, Scott Papers, Add. MSS, 50901; Hammond, C. P. Scott, 179–181.

the Belgian issue enabled the government to adopt a stance almost certain to involve Britain in war. For this newfound agreement and determination, Britain's traditional, indeed axiomatic concern over the Low Countries—not the entente, nor the staff talks, nor Conservative pressure —was responsible.[51]

In Brussels, meanwhile, the Belgian government had been handed the German ultimatum. The military necessities of the Schlieffen Plan were strengthening the hands of the war party in London.

On Monday morning, August 3, a weary Cabinet reassembled to decide the outlines of Grey's peroration in the Commons that afternoon. The Asquith government, having resolved to resist a major infringement of Belgian neutrality (and in the process help France), now had to secure the support of Parliament. Even as the ministers conferred, reports arrived telling of the German ultimatum to Belgium and of the Belgians' steadfast determination to uphold their independence.[52] This news, though underscoring afresh the dangers of Britain's new policy, immeasurably increased the cohesiveness of the Cabinet. Four ministers—Burns, Morley, Simon, and Beauchamp—had submitted their resignations when the Cabinet met; but their rebellion was more than offset by Lloyd George's decision to remain. The Belgian developments had at last convinced that mercurial Chancellor of the Exchequer that "events" were "too strong for him."[53] The news from Brussels, moreover, heightened the impact of Grey's afternoon explication of past and present British policy.

The House of Commons was jammed. Chairs obstructed the gang ways, and Liberal, Conservative, and Labour members found themselves unaccustomedly sitting next to each other. In the diplomatic gallery Ambassadors Cambon and Benckendorff waited. Finally, at mid-afternoon, Sir Edward Grey arrived. He began with a brief resumé of his efforts to preserve the peace, then turned to the problem of Britain's role in the unfolding war on the Continent. The crisis, he cautioned, had to be approached "from the point of British interests, British honour, and British obligations, free from all passion as to why peace has not been preserved." Likewise, he emphasized that Britain had no secret engage-

51. Spender and Asquith, *Life of Asquith*, II, 89–92; Lloyd George, *War Memoirs*, I, 48, 61, 65–68; Grey, *Twenty-five Years*, II, 7–11; Albertini, *The Origins of the War of 1914*, III, 409–411, 517–524; Ernest R. May, "The Nature of Foreign Policy: The Calculated versus the Axiomatic," *Daedalus* 91 (Fall 1962), 653–667.

52. The news from Brussels arrived at the Foreign Office at 10:55 A.M., Villiers to Grey (tel.), Aug. 3, 1914, *B.D.*, XI, no. 521; Asquith to George V, Aug. 3, 1914, quoted in Spender and Asquith, *Life of Asquith*, II, 82. Before the Cabinet the Conservatives had renewed their pressure for support of France; Petrie, *Chamberlain*, I, 374–377.

53. Memo, Aug. 3, 1914, Scott Papers, Add. MSS, 50901; Morley accused the "splendid *condottiere*" at the Admiralty of having helped to convince Lloyd George in *Memorandum on Resignation*, 24; Beaverbrook, *Politicians and the War*, 14–16.

ments that put "an obligation of honour upon the country." [54] Until the previous day, when the Cabinet had approved the protection of the French coast, London had never promised the Triple Entente more than diplomatic support. This assurance was balanced, some might say tilted, by the Foreign Secretary's subsequent admission that since 1906 he had permitted noncommittal staff talks between Anglo-French military and naval experts—talks, he hastily added, that had been approved by Campbell-Bannerman, Haldane, and Asquith. In addition, letters had been exchanged with the French in 1912 affirming that "these conversations which took place were not binding upon the freedom of either Government." Then Grey read a copy of his letter to Cambon, omitting, probably by accident, the final phrase which said that the plans of the general staffs would be used as a guide to military operations. He insisted that these letters had ensured that "the Government remained perfectly free, and, *a fortiori*, the House of Commons remains perfectly free." In contrast to 1905 and 1911, Britain had no treaty obligations to uphold, no "obligation of honour like the French had to the Russians." Grey, in short, attempted to dispel the fears of the "extreme peace-lovers" that Britain was secretly bound to France.[55] Britain's hands were, supposedly, free.

The Foreign Secretary, continuing in his soft, conversational tone, reviewed recent Anglo-French relations. The entente had created mutual friendship. But did this cordiality imply an obligation? Each listener was to "look into his own heart, and his own feelings and construe the extent of obligation for himself." To encourage this introspection, however, he observed that the French coasts were undefended and that the French fleet was in the Mediterranean "because of the feeling of confidence and friendship which has existed between the two countries." Could Britain, he entreated the Commons and the country, stand idle "if a foreign fleet engaged in a war which France had not sought, and in which she had not been the aggressor, came down the English Channel and bombarded and battered the undefended coasts of France"? Could Britain compel France to withdraw ships from the Mediterranean and thereby expose British interests to possible danger? Because neither British interests nor honor could tolerate such adjustments, the Cabinet, he announced, had promised France naval assistance if the Germans cruised into the Channel.[56]

Having defined Britain's relationship to France, the Foreign Secretary now shifted his attention to Belgium. Patiently he worked to construct a compelling case for British intervention. First he noted the 1839 treaty

54. Grey's speech is in *Parliamentary Debates: Commons*, 5th ser., 65 (Aug. 3, 1914), 1809–1827, and in his *Twenty-five Years*, II, 308–326.

55. Grey, *Twenty-five Years*, II, 309–313. Asquith called the radicals "extreme peace-lovers," Jenkins, *Asquith*, 329.

56. Grey, *Twenty-five Years*, II, 314–316.

on Belgian neutrality and enumerated the duties of the guarantor nations. Then he told his parliamentary colleagues of Germany's refusal to pledge respect for Belgian territory and of the German ultimatum to Brussels. Finally, with all the forensic skill of a trial lawyer, he read King Albert's personal appeal for British diplomatic support in the maintenance of Belgian independence. In these circumstances could Britain, Grey demanded, allow Belgium, probably Holland, and perhaps even France, to lose their independence? Could Britain "run away from those obligations of honour and interest as regards the Belgian treaty"? If Britain stood aside and France and Belgium were beaten, would it still be a great power when the war was over?

The Foreign Secretary at this point paused briefly to outline what intervention would mean for Britain. "For us, with a powerful fleet, which we believe able to protect our commerce, to protect our shores, and to protect our interests, if we are engaged in war, we shall suffer but little more than we shall suffer even if we stand aside." The Cabinet, Grey added, had made no commitment to send the B.E.F. to the Continent. And because the imperial situation was restless, he explained that the government would have to consider carefully "the use which we make of sending an Expeditionary Force out of the country until we know how we stand." [57] In spite of Grey's disclaimer, the B.E.F. was on its way to France within days. In this case, however, his assurances were not an attempt to deceive; rather, they stemmed from the naive ministerial belief in cheap intervention and from the Cabinet's failure to grasp the wider significance of the military conversations. The ministers always believed they would be free to choose the mode of British intervention should war come. They reckoned not upon the energy of Henry Wilson or upon the convincing appeal of a prepared scheme when ranged against improvised alternatives. Grey's minimization of the cost of intervention sprang therefore from a genuine belief that naval action would dominate, and from ignorance.

The pale, drawn Foreign Secretary had been speaking for over an hour now. Rapidly he concluded his remarks: Europe was at war and Britain had to decide whether or not to intervene. It was not a pleasant prospect. "The thought is still with us always of the suffering and misery entailed from which no country in Europe will escape and from which no abdication or neutrality will save us." [58] Yet his comments, coupled with his blunt warnings to Berlin about Belgium and the Channel, clearly indicated that the Asquith government was willing to fight if necessary. And the Cabinet, Grey revealed, was confident that it would be supported by Parliament and the country. As he finished, the resounding applause confirmed his prediction of support: a united Britain would not stand aside.

57. *Ibid.*, 317–323.
58. *Ibid.*, 324.

Grey's remarkable, inconsistently candid review of the entente, the Belgian tangle, and Britain's international position requires no elaborate commentary. After constantly evading the issue since 1910, the Liberal government had at last publicly admitted the existence of staff conversations. Yet even now Grey misrepresented the situation with his contention that the fleet distributions were simply the product of friendship and goodwill. He praised Britain's freedom of decision yet at the same time repeatedly stressed the value of French friendship. His assurances of freedom were, as G. P. Gooch notes, "correct in form but inaccurate in substance; for his whole speech breathed the conviction that [Britain] should be not only endangered but disgraced if [it] left France in the lurch." Furthermore, Grey talked little of how the war began or of the part played by the Franco-Russian alliance in spreading the Serbian quarrel. Instead he emphasized British interests, British obligations to Belgium, and the belief that Britain would suffer little more from intervention than from neutrality. Ever mindful of Berlin's ultimatum to Belgium, of its failure to restrain Vienna, and of Bethmann's crude attempts to purchase British neutrality, Grey and the Cabinet had concluded that Britain could not remain neutral. To win backing for a new course of action the Foreign Secretary had carefully and selectively fashioned a case that not only united the Liberal party, but the country as well. Grey, the seeker of peace, was also the defender of British interests.[59] As it turned out, both he and the nation misunderstood the costs required to preserve those interests.

The sequence of events following Grey's speech can be quickly summarized. Paul Cambon and the French were naturally pleased with both the content and the reception of the address, and their uneasiness about the entente receded. Then, when the German threat to Belgium was officially confirmed, Asquith and Grey (apparently on their own) drafted an ultimatum formally demanding that Germany respect Belgian neutrality;[60] but the ultimatum was not dispatched until two o'clock on Tuesday afternoon, well after the Germans had entered Belgium.[61] Why this delay remains unclear: possibly Grey wanted to avoid any accusation of having acted hastily, perhaps he wanted to make certain the Belgians actually resisted, or he may have preferred a German fait accompli because it would reduce the complications of British intervention.[62] Or, simple military requirements may have influenced the timing of the dispatch, for Churchill asked Battenberg on August 4 at "what time shd the

59. Gooch, *Before the War: Studies in Diplomacy*, II, 132; for a critical view of Parliament's role, see Flournoy, *Parliament and War*, 224–246.
60. There is much confusion over whether the Cabinet actually approved the ultimatum: cf. Spender and Asquith, *Life of Asquith*, II, 92–93; Jenkins, *Asquith*, 329–330; A. J. P. Taylor, *Politics in Wartime and other Essays* (London, 1964), 89–90.
61. Grey to Goschen (tels.), Aug. 4, 1914, B.D., XI, no. 573 (9:30 A.M.), no. 594 (2 P.M.).
62. Albertini, *The Origins of the War of 1914*, III, 489–495, 517–523.

rupture take place. At what hour of daylight or darkness wd it be most convenient to us to begin hostilities. Immediate reply is necessary in order to put the hour into the ultimatum." The admiral's response was: "anytime after midnight tonight." [63] In any case no German assurance was forthcoming by the 11 P.M. (London) deadline on August 4. As Big Ben sounded Churchill wired the fleet: "COMMENCE HOSTILITIES AGAINST GERMANY."

The entente and the staff talks played influential but not decisive roles in the British decision to go to war. Once that step was taken, the impact of the entente and the conversation upon the related question of how the B.E.F. would be employed was crucial and unambiguous: for the staff talks, with an assist from the Admiralty, were responsible for British presence on the western front.[64] But initially during the crisis such a strategic development appeared altogether improbable.

The British services responded to the Serbian imbroglio in piecemeal fashion. This time, unlike 1911, the Admiralty led the way, while the Army, still under Asquith's custody, acted more slowly. Late on Sunday, July 26, Churchill and Battenberg ordered the First and Second Fleets (still in home waters after the Spithead Review) to remain grouped along the south coast. During the next two days the Admiralty took further precautionary steps and on July 29, with the Cabinet's permission, sent warning telegrams to all naval commanders. That night the First (future Grand) Fleet, running with its lights extinguished, sailed past Dover to its war stations in the North Sea, assuming on July 31 its battle stations at Scapa Flow, Cromarty, and Rosyth. There was none of A. K. Wilson's laxity about a possible surprise attack.[65]

Churchill's dispatch of the fleet northward ended, for all practical purposes, any discussion of British naval strategy. The Admiralty's war plans automatically went into operation; there was no opportunity or occasion for the civilian leadership to review naval planning. And there were no challenges to the Admiralty's arrangements with the French over the Channel, the Mediterranean, or the Far East. When the Cabinet agreed on Sunday afternoon (August 2) about a coastal guarantee, Churchill immediately acted to implement the various Anglo-French naval arrangements. Packets containing the "B.G." code were ordered opened in the Channel, though the cipher would be used only if Britain actually entered the war. British naval bases were made available to the French; the Admiralty promised to watch the German fleet should it head for the Mediterranean. Commanders on the China station and in the Mediterranean were instructed to exchange information (using the

63. Minute by Churchill, Aug. 4, 1914, Nicolson Papers, vol. IV/1914.
64. For a general review of this problem, see John Terraine, The Western Front, 1914–1918 (London, 1964), 39–58.
65. Churchill, The World Crisis, I, 205–227; Marder, Road to War, 429–436.

"B.G." codes) about the location of Triple Alliance ships.[66] In brief, the Admiralty's strategy and many of the entente naval preparations were in operation by August 4.

The same could not be said for the Expeditionary Force. At the War Office no significant preparatory measures were taken until July 29 when the Cabinet authorized the "precautionary stage" of the War Book, a step Henry Wilson regarded as "more like business than I expected of this Government." But no army units were recalled from training and the scheduled field exercises for the Territorial Army were not canceled. Even after Germany declared war on Russia, only the Royal Navy received permission for complete mobilization. Finally, on Sunday, August 2, Asquith temporarily entrusted the War Office to its former master once removed, Lord Haldane. Although the D.M.O. regarded this appointment as a "perfect scandal," the Lord Chancellor on Monday morning announced that mobilization would start the next afternoon, August 4. Instead of the desirable simultaneous mobilization of the entente armies, the B.E.F. started with a three-day handicap.[67]

Mobilization orders for the Expeditionary Force made no mention of its possible employment. The strategic use of the Army, despite Wilson's careful planning, remained an open question in the first days of August. The Prime Minister on August 1 pointedly reminded General Sir Charles Douglas, the new Chief of the Imperial General Staff, that he wanted it understood "that the Government had never promised the French an Expeditionary Force." [68] And later that day the Cabinet reaffirmed its opposition to continental involvement: if Britain intervened, naval action would constitute its maximum contribution. Twenty-four hours later the Cabinet reiterated its stand on the Army: the B.E.F. would only be utilized for imperial and home defense tasks. Furthermore, Sir Edward Grey's speech in the Commons the next day gave public currency to the idea of a restricted role for the striking force. And the *Times* on August 4 spoke simply of "Naval Aid for France." Preoccupied with whether or not to intervene in the European struggle, the Cabinet, excepting Churchill and Haldane, had not yet grasped the full strategic ramifications of involvement.[69]

Henry Wilson shared no such illusions. Incessantly active throughout

66. De Saint-Seine to Ministère de la Marine (tel.), Aug. 3, 1914, Archives Marine, Xa 1; Churchill, *The World Crisis*, I, 231–246; "Compte rendu d'un entretien franco-anglais," Aug. 2, 1914, D.D.F., 3rd ser., XI, no. 625; Touvet, "Guerre de 1914–18: la 2me escadre légère," 216–227.

67. De La Panouse to Messimy, July 27, 31, 1914, Archives Guerre, "Attachés militaires: Angleterre," box 12; July 25–Aug. 4, 1914, Wilson Diaries; Callwell, *Wilson*, I, 152–155; Edmonds, *Military Operations*, I, 23–31.

68. Callwell, *Wilson*, I, 154. On Aug. 2 Asquith noted that he personally thought the dispatch of the B.E.F. was "out of the question and would serve no object," Asquith, *Memories and Reflections*, II, 12.

69. Grey to Bertie (tel.), Aug. 2, 1914, B.D., XI, no. 487; even Churchill talked solely of naval operations as late as Aug. 1, Churchill to Lloyd George, Aug. 1, 1914, quoted in Churchill, *Young Statesman*, 703.

the crisis, he centered his efforts at first upon encouraging the French and the Conservatives to pressure the feckless Asquith Cabinet. On July 31, for example, he suggested that the French threaten a break in diplomatic relations unless London backed the entente. In constant contact with the Opposition leadership, he helped instigate the letter of support sent by them to the Cabinet. Not until Monday, August 3, with British participation in the war growing more certain, did the D.M.O. shift his energies from the diplomatic to the strategic problems at hand. Already angered by the Cabinet's delay on mobilization, he regarded Haldane's order on that day as only partially satisfactory for there was no reference in it to embarkation instructions.

Wilson wasted no time in seeking support for dispatch of the Expeditionary Force to France. As before, he relied upon the Conservative hierarchy to badger the government. On Tuesday he complained to a variety of Tory friends, among them Lord Milner, Leopold Amery, John Baird, Leo Maxse of the *National Review*, and Lord Lovat. Repeatedly he emphasized that the delays by Asquith and Grey on the B.E.F. were "sinful,"[70] and his solicitations brought action. Twice on August 4 Arthur Balfour pressured Haldane about the employment of the British Army. Contending that at least four British divisions were required at once to prevent the German Army from crushing France, the former Prime Minister asked: "Is it not a fundamental principle of strategy in a crisis of this particular kind either to keep out of the conflict altogether, or to strike quickly, and strike with your whole strength?" While sympathetic to the appraisal, Haldane insisted that the Expeditionary Force might be better used as the nucleus for a much larger army. This suggestion Balfour flatly rejected, maintaining that a larger army would take six months to develop, which would be too late; and he held that Britain could afford a hundred thousand men without jeopardizing its security. But the acting War Minister remained unconvinced and refused to commit the Cabinet on the matter.[71]

Meanwhile, Henry Wilson sought help for intervention not only from his political friends, but also from the French Embassy and from his like-minded acquaintances at the Foreign Office. On August 4 Cambon lectured Grey on the need for British military help: using a map, he demonstrated how British units would protect the French flank should the Germans come through Belgium. He emphasized that staff preparation hinged upon British embarkation starting on the second day of

70. Callwell, *Wilson*, I, 152–156. General Grierson called the politicians "too sickening for words," MacDiarmid, *Grierson*, 257. Also see Lord Milner's notes, Aug. 4, 1914, Milner Papers, Bodleian Library, Oxford University, box 277.
71. Balfour to Haldane, Aug. 4, 1914, quoted in Maurice, *Haldane*, I, 358–359; notes by Balfour of talk with Haldane, 11 P.M., Aug. 4, 1914, Balfour Papers, Add. MSS, 49724. General Haig had that day written Haldane, urging a delay in committing the B.E.F., quoted in Cooper, *Haig*, I, 128–129. Also see Lansdowne's memo of his Aug. 4 talk with Haldane, quoted in Newton, *Lord Lansdowne*, 440–441.

mobilization (August 6)—a day's delay would thoroughly complicate the arrangements.[72] Arthur Nicolson also pressed the Foreign Secretary for the immediate dispatch of British troops: Britain had to "save France from a rapid advance of the Germans to Paris and from seeing all their eastern defences turned." And the Undersecretary warned Grey on August 5, just prior to the Cabinet, that half-measures would spell disaster, especially if they led to a German victory. Nicolson's concluding sentence graphically spelled out the pressures of the moment: "Pray do not think either Cambon or *any* military man has been speaking to me since I saw you. Forgive me for being so persistent but I feel so deeply that our country's future is at stake." [73]

Recalcitrant Liberal politicians were not the only targets of Henry Wilson's campaign of persuasion; he also had to sell his strategic views to his fellow generals. In particular he argued with Douglas Haig on August 5 about the deployment of the Army. The I Corps commander, who had known of Wilson's plans for intervention since late 1912, now expressed grave doubts about an immediate move. He preferred instead a more gradual build-up of the Empire's resources. Wilson's retort, which reflected perfectly the inadequacies of the prewar planning, was that the war would be far too brief to permit any hesitancy. Not without considerable difficulty, the D.M.O. finally convinced the future Commander in Chief of the desirability of prompt military involvement.[74] And within hours he scored an even more important triumph at the hastily summoned War Council in the Cabinet room.

The importance of the August 5 War Council in the formation of British war strategy cannot be overexaggerated. This "rather motley gathering" [75] had the final opportunity to ratify or to overturn the continental ideas espoused by the General Staff. The type of military strategy, the size of the Expeditionary Force, and the destination of those troops—these questions, regardless of the previous work of the C.I.D., were all within the purview of the War Council. Among those present on this historic occasion were Asquith, Grey, Churchill, and Haldane from the Cabinet (Lord Kitchener attended but did not become War Minister until the next morning); Battenberg from the Navy; Hankey from the C.I.D.; and a variety of past and present military men—Douglas, Roberts, French, Haig, Grierson, Cowans, von Donop, Hamilton, and Wilson.[76]

72. P. Cambon to Doumergue (tel.), Aug. 4, 1914, D.D.F., 3rd ser., XI, no. 754.
73. Nicolson to Grey, Aug. 4, 5, 1914, Grey Papers, F.O. 800/94.
74. Nov. 17, 1912, Wilson Diaries; Callwell, *Wilson*, I, 157–158; cf. Cooper, *Haig*, I, 127–129.
75. Asquith, *Memories and Reflections*, II, 30.
76. There are several accounts of this meeting: Churchill, *The World Crisis*, I, 248–250; Callwell, *Wilson*, I, 158–159; Hankey, *Supreme Command*, I, 169–173; Field Marshal Viscount French, *1914* (New York, 1919), 3–5; Grey, *Twenty-five Years*, II, 66–69; Robert Blake, ed., *The Private Papers of Douglas Haig, 1914–1919* (London, 1952), 68–70.

The meeting began with a consideration of Britain's overall military role in the war. This time the Navy offered no projects for amphibious attacks and there were no demands that the B.E.F. be used primarily for home defense. Instead, the influence of the continental school and the conversations was everywhere pervasive, and convincing. This became apparent when Sir John French, the designated commander of the B.E.F., proposed Antwerp as a possible destination. The D.M.O., who had already argued with the Field Marshal about Antwerp on August 1 and 3, declared flatly that the embarkation schedules could not accommodate a change of this magnitude. He won support against an Antwerp move from Grey and Churchill, the former asserting that Dutch neutrality would render such an operation impractical, the latter that the Navy could not promise protection for transports above the Dover-Calais line. An Antwerp operation was therefore out of the question and so also any lingering thoughts of amphibious assaults along the German coasts.[77]

The assemblage next considered the problems of intervention in France. Assisted by French, Wilson answered and rebuffed questions about the wisdom of immediate intervention, the strength of the Belgian forts, cooperation with the Belgian Army, and the size and quality of French forces. Eventually Wilson and French, backed by Haldane, Grierson, and Roberts, gained general agreement for early aid to France. The decisive factor, Hankey later wrote, "was that the plan for co-operation by our Expeditionary Force on the left of the French Army had been worked out by the two Staffs in great detail, and this could not be said of any other plan." As Churchill noted: "Those who spoke for the War Office knew their own minds and were united." [78]

The War Council, having settled where and when the British would intervene, dealt next with two related issues: the precise destination of the Expeditionary Force and its composition. Since the delay in British mobilization meant that the B.E.F. would be late in reaching Maubeuge, Lord Kitchener pressed for Amiens as the staging area. After some "desultory strategy (some thinking Liége was in Holland) and idiocy," wrote Wilson contemptuously in his diary, the group accepted Lord Roberts' advice to let the French decide on the location of the B.E.F.[79] With Wilson and the French Staff in intimate contact, the odds naturally favored the retention of Maubeuge as the zone of concentration. It should be added, however, that final agreement on this point did not come until August 12 when the D.M.O., French, Lieutenant General Archibald Murray, and Huguet and two other French officers wrangled with Kitchener for three hours over the destination of the B.E.F. In-

77. Esher, who did not participate in these great decisions, still favored amphibious operations; see diary, Aug. 6, 1914, *Journals and Letters of Esher*, III, 175.
78. Hankey, *Supreme Command*, I, 170–171; Churchill, *The World Crisis*, I, 248.
79. Callwell, *Wilson*, I, 158; cf. Lloyd George, *War Memoirs*, I, 74–76.

sisting that the Germans would cross the Meuse and swamp the British while they concentrated, the new War Minister held out stubbornly for Amiens. Full of "colossal ignorance and conceit," Kitchener was, complained Henry Wilson, "incapable of understanding the delays and difficulties of making such a change, nor the cowardice of it, nor the fact that either in French victory or defeat we would be equally useless." [80] Finally and with reluctance Kitchener yielded, accepting Maubeuge as the destination and winning only slight changes in locations of the units. This decision, which made the B.E.F. a virtual adjunct of the French Army, received Asquith's approval that very day. Once again the conversations had forced the hand of the Liberal government.

The August 5 War Council discussed one other aspect of continental intervention, its size. Henry Wilson had already notified the French attaché that Britain would, as Asquith had promised in May, send five divisions if it intervened. But in the Council Churchill completely reversed the Admiralty's position on invasion, offering no objections to the departure of the entire Expeditionary Force for France. The Council consequently recommended that embarkation orders be issued for all six divisions. Wilson had apparently scored still another victory at what he described as "an historic meeting of men, mostly entirely ignorant of their subject."

The next day the Cabinet met to ponder the advice of the War Council. With surprisingly little opposition—aided no doubt by the Burns and Morley resignations—the ministers sanctioned the plan to intervene in France. There were, however, misgivings about sending all six divisions out of Britain. And when a second War Council met that evening (August 6), Kitchener ruled that only four infantry divisions and the cavalry division would depart immediately. A fifth division would go "when circumstances permitted." [81] Ultimately a fifth division did reach France in August, but Wilson's hopes for all six were delayed somewhat longer. Nonetheless, in stark contrast to its mood four days earlier, the Cabinet had authorized continental involvement. As Foch had wisely predicted much earlier, the death of a single British soldier would be sufficient to commit the resources of the British Empire. Four infantry divisions were in fact soon followed by many times that number.

By midnight on Thursday, August 6, the guidelines of Britain's grand strategy were determined. At every point the staff talks, regardless of

80. Aug. 12, 1914, Wilson Diaries; Callwell, *Wilson*, I, 162–163; Huguet, *Britain and the War*, 40–42.
81. Hankey, *Supreme Command*, I, 172–173. Asquith to George V, Aug. 6, 1914, Asquith Papers, box 7; Haldane to Balfour, Aug. 6, 1914, Balfour Papers, Add. MSS, 49724; Asquith, *Memories and Reflections*, II, 31. The Cabinet also discussed operations against German colonial holdings, indeed so thoroughly that Asquith thought they looked "more like a gang of Elizabethan buccaneers than a meek collection of black-coated Liberal Ministers," *ibid*.

the past profusion of noncommittal provisions, had left their impress. On that Thursday the Anglo-French naval authorities had signed a naval alliance which nearly duplicated the terms of the 1913 conventions.[82] On the same day the Cabinet had approved British participation in a continental war on the basis of the staff arrangements, a decision in which the conversations were especially important: the talks had not only enabled Wilson to overcome those who questioned the value of assistance to France, they had also, because of the interlocking transportation schedules, imposed haste and urgency upon London's strategic deliberations. Furthermore, the staff arrangements had effectively preempted Lord Kitchener's freedom to concentrate the B.E.F. where his judgment suggested. Put more strongly, the logistical plans settled by the military conversations had determined the shape of British military strategy. The staff talks, which had bestowed the ability to intervene upon the Asquith Cabinet, also dictated the contours of that intervention. In August 1914 the British government, no less than its French and German counterparts, was committed to a "plan."

The signing of the Anglo-French agreements in 1904 had heralded the start of a diplomatic revolution. Originally those accords had envisaged no more than mutual diplomatic support over Morocco and Egypt. But Berlin's inept diplomacy, the tensions of the naval race, and two Moroccan incidents forged an entente and gave it military and naval overtones. Although the French persistently pressed for a more explicit relationship, the cautious Liberal government refused. All it would concede was to exchange the Grey-Cambon letters promising consultation in times of crisis. Nevertheless, in July–August 1914 Paris and London were linked by mutual interests, the staff talks, and the ambiguous but tenacious Entente Cordiale.

Critics of Britain's entente policy have charged that London had only the obligations of an alliance and none of the compensating advantages. Frequent cooperation between the partners, they insist, created both the expectation of support and a moral commitment to render it. But, without an alliance, London possessed no restraining veto over French diplomacy and strategy. Further, the entente's dependence upon the vagaries of public opinion imposed limitations upon its unity and cohesiveness in the crucial early stages of a diplomatic clash. An alliance, the critics add, would have guaranteed Anglo-French unity in any crisis, given London a more effective way to influence French policy, and permitted no confusion in Berlin about British intentions.[83] Instead of the

---

82. "Protocole des conventions passées entre l'Amirauté britannique et l'Etat-major général de la Marine française," Aug. 6, 1914, Archives Marine, ES 11.
83. Pierre Renouvin, "Britain and the Continent: The Lessons of History," *Foreign Affairs*, 17 (October 1938), 111–127; also Henry A. Kissinger, "Coalition Diplomacy in a Nuclear Age," *Foreign Affairs*, 42 (July 1964), 525–545.

secret, uncertain diplomacy of the entente, an acknowledged alliance with its deterrent effect would have better protected the peace of Europe.

Such criticisms of the entente system usually ignore or minimize the political environment in which Sir Edward Grey operated. To many in Britain "splendid isolation" remained an attractive policy. On the other hand, a vocal group of Britons, including some on the government benches, advocated friendship with Germany. Nor did many politicians or journalists of whatever party relish the thought of being indirectly allied through Paris to St. Petersburg. Moreover, with French nationalism on the upswing, some in both parties feared that a closer cross-Channel relationship might encourage a policy of belligerent *revanchisme*.

Even had an alliance with France been politically possible, there are few grounds for believing that this would necessarily have altered Berlin's course of action in 1914. Lichnowsky had repeatedly warned Berlin that Britain would support France and his admonitions were ignored. And German war plans in any case assumed and discounted the prospect of British intervention.[84]

Finally, critics of the entente system ignore some of the positive benefits it conferred upon the Liberal government. The fundamental premise of Grey's policy was that Britain not allow itself to become isolated against Germany. Thus he steadfastly sought to maintain friendship with France without at the same time losing his ability to influence Paris. The entente was the perfect instrument for his purposes, for by its very uncertainty it exercised a greater restraint upon French policy than an alliance would have. On several occasions, most notably in 1911, misgivings about British dependability helped moderate French action. Even in 1914, with the terms of the Franco-Russian alliance clearly involved, Paris was extremely careful to avoid any appearance of aggressive action lest it forfeit British assistance. The entente, given the composition of the Cabinet and the traditions of British diplomacy, was perhaps the ideal way to protect British interests with a minimum of obligation and risk.[85]

The French leadership naturally preferred an incontrovertible commitment from London. Lacking this guarantee, they could take comfort in the existence of the Grey-Cambon letters and in the fact of the military and naval conversations. The staff talks fostered the hope that the entente could be easily converted into an effective military and naval alliance, thus they were of definite political importance in the main-

84. John Buchan tells an entertaining tale of German attempts in 1914 to discover the contents of the conversations in *The Thirty-Nine Steps* (New York, 1915).
85. Pierre Renouvin, "The Part Played in International Relations by Conversations between the General Staffs on the Eve of the World War," *Studies in Anglo-French History During the Eighteenth, Nineteenth and Twentieth Centuries*, ed. Alfred Colville and Harold Temperly (Cambridge, 1935), 171–172.

tenance of the entente system. The conversations were in fact the British answer to French demands for an alliance; yet, despite their obvious political importance to Anglo-French relations, the staff talks had their most profound impact, rightly enough, upon the development of grand strategy.

The formation of a continental school of British military strategy preceded the staff talks. But the talks when they began encouraged and strengthened the acceptance of this strategy by the General Staff. Thanks to the energies of Generals Grierson, Ewart, and especially Henry Wilson, the liaison with Paris enabled the Directorate of Military Operations to complete the details for intervention on the Continent. This detailed planning, at a time when modern warfare was growing increasingly complex, immensely enhanced the importance and the availability of the B.E.F. More importantly, the conversations provided the Cabinet with the option of intervention and thereby expanded the alternatives open to it in a crisis.

Nevertheless, there were some major disadvantages to a policy of secret, highly restricted staff conversations. Except for those staff officers immediately concerned in the Directorate of Military Operations, few British soldiers were aware of the exact content of the Anglo-French arrangements. Nor were they, or anyone else for that matter, in a position to challenge effectively the fundamental assumptions behind the staff work. This held true even for a man like Haig, who was scheduled to command one of the principal units if war came and who knew the outlines of the planning arrangements. Except for the August 1911 cross-examination in the C.I.D., Henry Wilson never had to defend in detail either his belief in a short war or his exaggerated confidence in the impact of the B.E.F. on a Franco-German conflict. And his claims for the Expeditionary Force facilitated the avoidance of what was the logical corollary of any continental strategy—the capability of developing a large army. The role of the staff expert was buttressed by the secret nature of the conversations, too: as the supplier of information and intelligence he could manipulate the users of his expertise, both military and civilian. The so-called "conservative realism" of the Army staff would go unchallenged even in early August 1914. At least part of the genesis of many British problems on the western front lay in the nature and the illusions of the military conversations.[86]

The influence of the entente upon French military planning was less spectacular. The end of Anglo-French hostility had permitted a reduction of coastal defense forces and the abandonment of plans to invade England. But none of the French war plans before 1914 actually counted upon British assistance; the French Staff regarded the possibility of the

86. The term "conservative realism" is, of course, from Samuel P. Huntington's *The Soldier and the State: The Theory and Politics of Civil-Military Relations* (Cambridge, Mass., 1957); see also Tyler, *British Army*, 174–182.

B.E.F. in the Maubeuge triangle as a welcome bit of flank protection, and no more. Still, the prospect of British divisions—nurtured by the conversations—did exert a negative effect upon French strategic planning. Caillaux and Poincaré prudently discerned that the uncertain variable of British help was a function of another equally uncertain variable, Belgian neutrality. Thus, despite Joffre's repeated attempts to gain approval for a French offensive through Belgium, the French civilian leadership held firm that such a maneuver would ruin any hope of British assistance. This well-founded political consideration left Joffre with no alternative (whatever his last-minute inclinations) but to plan for an *offensive à outrance* in Lorraine, the results of which were unfortunate.

The Anglo-French naval conversations confirmed rather than shaped prewar naval strategy. The Admiralty's 1907 war plans anticipated French domination of the Mediterranean while the British fought in the North Sea. But these schemes, like the 1906 French decision to concentrate chiefly in the Mediterranean, predated the naval conversations. Not until 1912 did the talks become regularized and by then both high commands had settled their basic strategic guidelines. Initially, therefore, the fleet dispositions reflected more the benefits of improved Anglo-French relations than any special coordination between the two admiralties; but by ratifying those dispositions, the conversations did facilitate a further concentration of British naval strength in the north and thereby increase Britain's dependence upon France in the Mediterranean. The result was an apparent moral commitment to France for its services in that sea, a commitment that even the radicals would not overturn in August 1914.

In the case of Britain the military talks also had a significant impact on the institutional problem of interservice cooperation: because they fortified the Army's advocacy of intervention, they indirectly heightened the Admiralty-War Office differences over the use of the British Army in general and the wisdom of amphibious assaults in particular. The Committee of Imperial Defence, which could have provided a perfect forum for the resolution of these differences had Asquith so desired, remained stillborn as an effective coordinator of strategic planning. Although the C.I.D. sponsored valuable hearings and in 1912 influenced the Admiralty's schemes for the Mediterranean, it never adequately considered the ramifications of the strategies of either service. The overall formulation of British strategy continued to be a narrow, departmental affair, free from probing or challenge. The full requirements of continental intervention were, therefore, never appreciated, nor were the limitations of naval blockading as an economic instrument entirely revealed. This lack of firm leadership opened the door to military and naval politicians who lobbied incessantly for their respective strategic plans. The politics of grand strategy was often the politics of personal and service ambition, slightly tempered by concern for national interests.

The Anglo-French entente, lastly, raised for Britain grave questions of constitutional propriety, parliamentary honesty, and the democratic control of foreign policy. The staff talks were deliberately concealed from the Cabinet in 1906 and were only revealed to the entire Cabinet in 1911 when ministerial indiscretions forced a showdown. Equally deliberate were the repeated evasions by Grey and Asquith in the House of Commons about the exact nature of the entente relationship. The Foreign Secretary's contempt for the Cabinet and later for Parliament reflected not only a profound distrust of his colleagues, but an easy willingness to practice secret diplomacy. Yet his radical colleagues, whose pacifist-isolationist attitudes dictated many of his tactics, must share some of the blame for their ignorance of the conversations: Britain's obligation to render diplomatic support to France over Morocco was common knowledge—to make the support meaningful in times of stress would require, as they should have appreciated, British military and naval help that would have to be coordinated in advance. Furthermore, even when the radicals learned of the talks in 1911 their significance was misunderstood and they were allowed to continue under the flimsiest of safeguards. And the radical ministers never challenged the official explications in the Commons about the quantity and quality of the Anglo-French relationship. Britain's secret diplomacy thus carried the seal of radical approval, even if by default.

Lack of candor about the entente had other ramifications as well. First, it convinced many in the 1920's that Britain had become committed to France and against Germany through a policy of stealth and subterfuge. In an age of increasing public interest in foreign affairs and of renewed demands for information about those affairs, the Liberal government continued business as usual, that is, commenting infrequently and elusively about the conduct of foreign policy. From this failure in public relations would stem much of the later disillusionment with the old diplomacy. Second, the secret staff talks left behind a distinct odor, which in turn obscured for many the more important and difficult problem of controlling the various aspects of modern diplomacy. Third, the conversations, it is unnecessary to stress, became a useful weapon in the German arsenal to discredit the verdict of Versailles. And in the 1930's, when Hitler reoccupied the Rhineland, the British proposal for Anglo-French-Belgian staff talks, this time in the open, caused a new wave of recriminations and new caution on behalf of the military planners.[87] Rightly or wrongly, a soi-disant lesson of history had been drawn.

In August 1914 the Entente Cordiale and the conversations provided

87. See the heated correspondence between Lloyd George and Duff Cooper on this point in the *Times*, Mar. 30–Apr. 3, 1936. Also see Doreen Collins, *Aspects of British Politics, 1904–1919* (Oxford, 1965), 117–125.

the overall framework for the conduct of British diplomacy. Although the crucial factor in the Cabinet's reluctant decision to go to war was Britain's traditional interest in Belgium, the shape of that decision owed much to the bureaucratic planning that followed the 1904 entente. Bargaining with one another, sometimes as allies, sometimes as adversaries, diplomats, soldiers, and sailors had determined that, if such a decision were taken, it would be a decision for unreserved alliance with the French, for the dispatch of divisions to fight on the ground in Europe, and for deployment of the Royal Navy primarily against the German High Seas Fleet. Without an appreciation of the process and extent to which their work and that of their counterparts in Paris narrowed the alternatives open to the British and French governments, one has only an imperfect understanding of the onset of World War I and no understanding at all of how that war became the grand carnage it proved to be. In the history of international relations, as in other branches of political history and in economic and social history, faceless groups often play great roles. In 1914 the planning and strategic decisions of some such groups, and individuals within them, would face the final test—the harsh, unyielding reality of war.

Select Bibliography

Manuscripts
Private Papers
Published Documents and Official Histories
General (Books, Articles, Periodicals)

Manuscripts, Private Papers, Published Documents and Official Histories

Application of the fifty-year rule to official archival collections in Belgium, France, and Great Britain * has provided new opportunities for detailed research. In addition, specific sections of the Belgian diplomatic archives up to 1945 are open and those records contain correspondence relevant to the pre-1914 years. Belgian military records before 1914 have, unfortunately, mostly been destroyed. French diplomatic and naval records are open up to and sometimes beyond 1914; the Army records for 1900–1918, though open in 1962, are presently closed and will be reopened in 1969.

The numerous private paper collections now available in Britain, and to a much lesser extent in Belgium and France, are equally revealing. Although some major collections of papers remain closed (most notably the Churchill files), the historian possesses a vast amount of new evidence for reconsideration of the old diplomacy.

Manuscripts

Official Archives

Brussels
> Archives du Ministère des Affaires Etrangères
>> Although they contain little new material on the entente, these papers graphically emphasize the few diplomatic alternatives open to the Belgian government before 1914.

London, Public Record Office
> Admiralty Archives
>> The Admiralty files, especially Adm. 1/, Adm. 116/ and Adm. 137/, are helpful in delineating Britain's naval plans; the files on entente naval cooperation are far less complete.
> Cabinet and Committee of Imperial Defence Archives
>> Includes the complete minutes of the C.I.D. meetings, the records of the prewar subcommittees on invasion and defense of the Empire, and a record of all the memoranda circulated to the Cabinet. Also contains a set (with omissions) of the Prime Ministers' letters to the monarch.
> Foreign Office Archives
>> Because the published *British Documents* concentrate so heavily on Anglo-German relations, the Foreign Office volumes are necessary for a more balanced perspective of entente politics. The Treaty series, covering the actual outbreak of war, adds little on Anglo-French relations.
> War Office Archives
>> Despite their bewildering organization, an invaluable source on British military planning. Directorate of Military Operations files are under W.O. 106. Gaps exist, however, and many files relating to France and Belgium (even those already published in *British Documents*) are difficult to locate.

---

* As of 1967 a thirty-year rule is in effect in Great Britain for official papers.

Paris

Archives du Ministère de la Guerre, Château de Vincennes
  Voluminous records on every phase of France's military preparations before 1914. Numerous boxes for each successive French war plan and a nearly complete file on Anglo-French cooperation (Plan XVII: Armée W, box 147b). Minutes of the Conseil Supérieur de la Guerre are also available.

Archives du Ministère de la Marine
  Hitherto used but slightly. Complete numbered files on Anglo-French relations are in ES 9 and ES 10. Attaché reports are particularly useful, minutes of the Conseil Supérieur de la Marine less so.

Archives du Ministère des Affaires Etrangères, Quai d'Orsay
  Published documents have treated entente relations with reasonable thoroughness; but many unprinted dispatches on the second Moroccan crisis exist. The volumes on Belgium show how closely Paris watched Brussels for some sign of German plans.

Microfilm

German Foreign Ministry Archives (Cambridge University and University of Michigan Projects)
  Add only marginally to Anglo-French relations before 1914; most material was published by German historians and editors in the 1920's.

Private Papers

Belgium: Archives Générales du Royaume, Brussels

Georges Helleputte Papers
J. van den Heuvel Papers
Paul Hymans Papers
François Schollaert Papers
  These collections contain some helpful information on the controversy over Belgium's pre-1914 relations with Britain. Invaluable for a study of the Belgian government in exile during World War I.

France

Paul Cambon Papers, Quai d'Orsay, Paris
  Most published in private correspondence or French documents.
Théophile Delcassé Papers, Quai d'Orsay
  Especially helpful on Delcassé's tenure as Foreign Minister, though somewhat disappointing on Anglo-French relations. Records for his tenure as Naval Minister are sparse.
Stephen Pichon Papers, Bibliothèque de l'Institut de France, Paris
  Not particularly helpful on his first stint at the Quai d'Orsay; do contain much wartime correspondence between Pichon, Camille Barrère, and Raymond Poincaré.

Great Britain

Hugh O. Arnold-Forster Papers, British Museum, London
  A number of memos on army reform and a helpful diary.
Herbert Henry Asquith Papers, Bodleian Library, Oxford University
  A major source, with its complete set of Asquith-monarch letters, Cabinet memoranda, and Asquith's extensive correspondence with troublesome fellow ministers.

Arthur J. Balfour Papers, British Museum
  Abundant documentation of defense matters for the 1900–1905 years and some interesting later personal correspondence (especially with Fisher).
Francis Bertie Papers, Public Record Office
  Useful for Bertie's policy views and for insights into how the Foreign Office worked; the gossip is not without a certain malice.
Henry Campbell-Bannerman Papers, British Museum
  Only a few letters on foreign policy; none on grand strategy.
Austen Chamberlain Papers, University of Birmingham Library, Birmingham
  Some insights on army reform before 1905 and on the war crisis in 1914.
George Clarke (Sydenham) Papers, British Museum
  Somewhat disappointing, these letters deal almost entirely with imperial problems and reveal more about Clarke's correspondents than about Clarke.
Eyre Crowe Papers, Public Record Office
  Of no help before 1914.
Edward VII Papers, Royal Archives, Windsor Castle
  Some interesting papers on army organization and a variety of letters from Esher.
Esher Papers, Watlington Park, Oxfordshire
  Probably the single most important private collection available (excluding the Churchill files) of memos, letters, and journals relating to the problems of British diplomacy and defense between 1904 and 1914.
Spencer Ewart Papers, Williamwood, Kirtlebridge, Dumfriesshire, Scotland
  Though written some time after the relevant event, the diaries are helpful in understanding life in the War Office from 1906 to 1914; few comments on strategy herein.
George V Papers, Royal Archives
  Notes on the trip to Paris in 1914.
Edward Goschen Papers, Public Record Office
  Helpful on Anglo-German relations.
Edward Grey Papers, Public Record Office
  Wide-ranging correspondence with ambassadors, subordinates, and fellow ministers. A number of these letters are not in *British Documents*.
Douglas Haig Papers, National Library of Scotland, Edinburgh
  Of little assistance on the prewar years; the diary entries before 1914 are sporadic and jejune.
Richard B. Haldane Papers, National Library of Scotland
  Nearly devoid of all government memoranda, these contain Haldane's daily letters to his mother and are a useful guide to Liberal politics. Most of the other letters are in Maurice's biography.
Charles Hardinge Papers. Cambridge University Library, Cambridge, and the Public Record Office
  Essential for British imperial policy. Shed only a few new insights on entente politics and not much more on Foreign Office operations.
John Jellicoe Papers. British Museum
  Of no help on Anglo-French relations.
Howard Kelly Papers, National Maritime Museum, Greenwich

Diary, kept while Kelly was an attaché to Brussels and Paris, contains some interesting asides about the life of the various embassies.

Lord Kitchener Papers, Public Record Office
A few scattered references to Anglo-French and continental politics.

Lord Lansdowne Papers, Public Record Office
An extensive assortment of documents, letters, and Foreign Office notes; some private letters to other Cabinet members.

Frank Lascelles Papers, Public Record Office
Clearly reveals the ambassador's problems with the Foreign Office because of his moderate views toward Germany.

David Lloyd George Papers, the Beaverbook Library, London
These were used only from a distance, via correspondence; the indexes suggest that the entente did not much concern Lloyd George except in 1911, and those records are available in the Owen biography.

Reginald McKenna Papers, Churchill College Library, Cambridge

William May Papers, National Maritime Museum
Helpful on prewar naval maneuvers.

Alfred Milner Papers, Bodleian Library
Some items on party politics and the outbreak of war in 1914.

Archibald Murray Papers (private)
Important only after the war is under way.

Arthur Nicolson Papers, Public Record Office (recently moved from the Foreign Office Library)
Major collection, of immense value after 1910. Private correspondence with the ambassadors reveals Nicolson's growing policy differences with Grey. Throughout he is sternly anti-German and pro-Russian.

Gerard Noel Papers, National Maritime Museum
Of only limited help.

Lord Ripon Papers, British Museum
No guidance on the foreign policy of Campbell-Bannerman.

William Robertson Papers, King's College Library, London
A few files on the trials and tribulations of the British Army before 1914 reveal a Robertson with few illusions about the requirements of continental intervention.

Thomas Sanderson Papers, Public Record Office
A few odds and ends.

C. P. Scott Papers, British Museum
Most has appeared in Hammond's biography; a few revealing tid-bits remain.

J. A. Spender Papers, British Museum
Correspondence with Grey and other Liberal leaders makes this an interesting if not always rewarding collection.

Cecil Spring-Rice Papers (private)
A number of the Louis Mallet letters to Spring-Rice reveal the strong anti-German temperament of the Foreign Office in April–May 1905.

Lord Tweedmouth Papers, Naval Library, Ministry of Defence, London
Meager group of letters, mostly dealing with patronage.

William Tyrrell Papers, Public Record Office
Important chiefly after 1914.

Henry Wilson Diaries (private)
For understanding Wilson's strategic thought and schemes the diaries are indispensable; but Callwell has omitted little and remains a reliable guide to Wilson's pre-1914 role.

Published Documents and Official Histories

Austria-Hungary. *The Secret Treaties of Austria-Hungary, 1879–1914*, ed. A. F. Pribram. 2 vols. Cambridge, Mass.: Harvard University Press, 1920–1921.

Belgium. *Amtliche Aktenstücke zur Geschichte der europäischen Politik, 1885–1914 (Die belgischen Dokumente zur Vorgeschichte des Weltkrieges)*, ed. Bernhard Schwertfeger. 9 vols. Berlin: Deutsche Verlagsgesellschaft für Politik, 1925.

France. Assemblée Nationale, Chambre des Députés, session de 1919. *Rapport fait au nom de la Commission d'Enquête sur la rôle et la situation de la metallurgie en France: Question de Briey.* 2 vols. Paris: Imprimerie Nationale, 1919.

France. Assemblée Nationale, Chambre des Députés, session de 1919. *Procès-verbaux de la Commission d'Enquête sur la rôle et la situation de la metallurgie en France: Défense du Bassin de Briey.* 2 vols. Paris: Imprimerie Nationale, 1919.

France. *Journal officiel: debats parlementaires, Chambre des Députés; Sénat.* 1904–1914.

France. Ministère de la Guerre. Etat-major de l'Armée: Service Historique. *Les armées françaises dans la grande guerre.* 68 vols. Paris: Imprimerie Nationale, 1923–1939.

France. Ministère des Affaires Etrangères. *Documents diplomatiques: affaires au Maroc, 1901–1912.* 6 vols. Paris: Imprimerie Nationale, 1905–1912.

France. Ministère des Affaires Etrangères. *Documents diplomatiques français, 1871–1914*, 2nd ser. 14 vols. Paris: Imprimerie Nationale, 1930–1955. 3rd ser. 11 vols. Paris: Imprimerie Nationale, 1929–1936.

Germany. Auswärtiges Amt. *German Diplomatic Documents, 1871–1914*, ed. and trans. E. T. S. Dugdale. 4 vols. New York and London: Harper, 1928–1931.

Germany. Auswärtiges Amt. *Die grosse Politik der europäischen Kabinette, 1871–1914*, ed. Johannes Lepsius, Albrecht Mendelssohn Bartholdy, and Friedrich Thimme. 40 vols. Berlin: Deutsche Verlagsgesellschaft für Politik, 1922–1927.

Germany. Auswärtiges Amt. *Outbreak of the World War: German Documents Collected by Karl Kautsky*, ed. Max Montgelas and Walther Schüking. New York: Oxford University Press, 1924.

Great Britain. Committee of Imperial Defence. *History of the Great War, based on Official Documents: Military Operations*: vol. I, J. E. Edmonds, *France and Belgium, 1914*, 3rd ed. London: Macmillan, 1933.

Great Britain. Committee of Imperial Defence. *History of the Great War, based on Official Documents*: A. H. Henniker, *Transportation on the Western Front, 1914–1918.* London: H. M. Stationery Office, 1937.

Great Britain. Committee of Imperial Defence. *History of the Great War, based on Official Documents: Naval Operations*: vol. I, J. S. Corbett, *To the Battle of the Falklands December 1914.* London: Longmans, Green, 1920.

Great Britain. Foreign Office. *British Documents on the Origins of the War, 1898–1914*, ed. George P. Gooch and Harold W. Temperley. 11 vols. London: H. M. Stationery Office, 1926–1938.

Great Britain. Foreign Office. *Collected Diplomatic Documents Relating to the Outbreak of the European War.* London: H. M. Stationery Office, 1915.

Great Britain. *Parliamentary Debates: Commons.* 4th ser., 1904–1908; 5th ser., 1909–1914.
Russia. *Der diplomatische Schriftwechsel Iswolskis, 1911–1914,* ed. Friedrich Stieve. 4 vols. Berlin: Deutsche Verlagsgesellschaft für Politik, 1924–1926.
Russia. *Entente Diplomacy and the World,* ed. George Abel Schreiner, trans. B. de Siebert. New York: Knickerbocker Press, 1921.
Russia. *Graf Benckendorffs diplomatischer Schriftwechsel,* ed. B. de Siebert. 3 vols. Berlin: Verlag von Walter de Gruyter, 1928.
Russia. *Die internationalen Beziehungen im Zeitalter des Imperialismus,* ed. Otto Hoetzsch. 1st ser., 5 vols. Berlin: Steiner-Verlage, 1931–1934. 3rd ser., 4 vols. to date. Berlin: Steiner-Verlage, 1939——.
Russia. *Un livre noir: diplomatie d'avant-guerre d'après les documents des Archives russes: novembre 1910–juillet 1914,* ed. René Marchand. 2 vols. Paris: Librairie du Travail, 1922–1923.

General: Books, Articles, Periodicals

Among the numerous works on diplomacy and strategy in the final years before World War I, the following were especially helpful: Luigi Albertini, *The Origins of the War of 1914;* Sidney B. Fay, *The Origins of the World War;* Oron J. Hale, *Publicity and Diplomacy with Special Reference to England and Germany, 1890–1914;* William L. Langer, *The Diplomacy of Imperialism;* Arthur J. Marder, *The Anatomy of British Sea Power: A Study of British Naval Policy in the Pre-Dreadnought Era, 1880–1905,* and *From the Dreadnought to Scapa Flow: The Royal Navy in the Fisher Era, 1904–1919* (vol. I: *The Road to War, 1904–1914;* vol. II: *The War Years: To the Eve of Jutland, 1914–1916*); George Monger, *The End of Isolation: British Foreign Policy, 1900–1907;* Gerhard Ritter, *Staatskunst und Kriegshandwerk: Das Problem des "Militarismus" in Deutschland* (vol. II: *Die Hauptmächte Europas und das wilhelminische Reich, 1890–1914*); A. J. P. Taylor, *The Struggle for Mastery in Europe, 1848–1918;* J. E. Tyler, *The British Army and the Continent, 1904–1914.*

Addison, Christopher. *Four and a Half Years: A Personal Diary from June 1914 to January 1919.* 2 vols. London: Hutchinson, 1934.
Albertini, Luigi. *The Origins of the War of 1914,* trans. and ed. Isabella M. Massey. 3 vols. London: Oxford University Press, 1952–1957.
Alexandre, General René. *Avec Joffre d'Agadir à Verdun: souvenirs, 1911–1916.* Paris: Berger-Levrault, 1932.
Amery, Leopold S. *My Political Life,* vol. I. London: Hutchinson, 1953.
Anderson, Eugene N. *The First Moroccan Crisis, 1904–1906.* Chicago: University of Chicago Press, 1930.
André, General Louis. *Cinq ans de ministère.* Paris: Louis Michaud, 1907.
Andrew, Christopher. "France and the Making of the Entente Cordiale," *Historical Journal,* 10 (1967), 89–105.
—— "German World Policy and the Reshaping of the Dual Alliance," *Journal of Contemporary History,* 1, no. 3 (1966), 137–151.
—— *Théophile Delcassé and the Making of the Entente Cordiale.* New York: St. Martin's Press, 1968.

Anrich, Ernst. *Die englische Politik im Juli 1914.* Berlin: Verlag von W. Kohlhammer, 1934.

Army and Navy Gazette.

Army Review.

Arnold-Forster, H. O. *The Army in 1906: A Policy and A Vindication.* New York: E. P. Dutton, 1906.

Arnold-Forster, Mary. *The Right Honourable Hugh Oakeley Arnold-Forster.* London: E. Arnold, 1910.

Asquith, Herbert Henry, Earl of Oxford and Asquith. *The Genesis of the War.* London: Cassell, 1923.

—— *Memories and Reflections, 1852–1927.* 2 vols. Boston: Little, Brown, 1928.

Aston, Major General Sir George. *The Biography of the Late Marshal Foch.* New York: Macmillan, 1929.

—— "The Entente Cordiale and the 'Military Conversations,' " *Quarterly Review,* 258 (April 1932), 363–383.

—— *Memoirs of a Marine: An Amphibiography.* London: John Murray, 1919.

—— *Sea, Land, and Air Strategy.* Boston: Little, Brown, 1914.

Bacon, Admiral Sir R. H. *The Life of Lord Fisher of Kilverstone.* 2 vols. Garden City, N.Y.: Doubleday, 1929.

Balfour, Michael. *The Kaiser and His Times.* Boston: Houghton Mifflin, 1964.

Ballard, Brigadier General C. R. *Smith-Dorrien.* London: Constable, 1931.

Barclay, Sir Thomas. *Thirty Years: Anglo-French Reminiscences, 1876–1906.* Boston: Houghton Mifflin, 1914.

Barlow, Ima Christina. *The Agadir Crisis.* Chapel Hill, N.C.: University of North Carolina Press, 1940.

Barnes, Harry E. *The Genesis of the World War: An Introduction to the Problem of War Guilt.* New York: Alfred A. Knopf, 1926.

Baudry, Lieutenant de Vaisseau Ambroise. *La bataille navale: études sur les facteurs tactiques.* Paris: Berger-Levrault, 1912.

Baumont, Maurice, *et al. Europe de 1900 à 1914.* Paris: Editions Sirey, 1966.

Bayly, Admiral Sir Lewis. *Pull Together!* London: Harrap, 1939.

Beaverbrook, Lord. *Politicians and the War, 1914–1916.* Garden City, N.Y.: Doubleday, 1928.

Belot, Rear Admiral R. de, and André Reussner. *La puissance navale dans l'histoire,* vols. II–III. Paris: Editions Maritimes et d'Outre-Mer, 1960–1963.

Beresford, Admiral Lord Charles. *The Betrayal.* London: P. S. King & Son, 1912.

Berliner Monatshefte (Die Kriegsschuldfrage until 1929).

Bernhardi, General Friedrich von. *Germany and the Next War,* trans. Allen H. Powles. London: E. Arnold, 1913.

Bestuzhev, I. V. "Russian foreign policy, February–June 1914," *Journal of Contemporary History,* 1, no. 3 (1966), 93–112.

Beyens, Napoléon, Baron. *Deux années à Berlin, 1912–1914.* 2 vols. Paris: Plon, 1931.

Binion, Rudolph. *Defeated Leaders: The Political Fate of Caillaux, Jouvenel, and Tardieu.* New York: Columbia University Press, 1960.

Birkenhead, Earl of. *Frederick Edwin, Earl of Birkenhead: The First Phase.* 2 vols. London: Thornton Butterworth, 1933.

Bishop, Donald G. *The Administration of British Foreign Relations.* Syracuse, N.Y.: Syracuse University Press, 1961.

Blake, Robert, ed. *The Private Papers of Douglas Haig, 1914–1919.* London: Eyre & Spottiswoode, 1952.

Bloch, Camille. *The Causes of the World War,* trans. Jane Soames. London: George Allen & Unwin, 1935.

Blunt, Wilfred S. *My Diaries.* New York: Alfred A. Knopf, 1932.

Bond, Brian. "Richard Burdon Haldane at the War Office, 1905–1912," *Army Quarterly and Defence Journal,* 86 (April 1963), 33–43.

Bonham Carter, Victor. *Soldier True: The Life and Times of Field-Marshal Sir William Robertson.* London: Frederick Muller, 1963.

Bonham Carter, Violet. *Winston Churchill: An Intimate Portrait.* New York: Harcourt, Brace & World, 1965.

Bos, Charles. *Refaisons une marine.* Paris: Berger-Levrault, 1910.

Boucher, General Arthur. *La Belgique à jamais indépendante.* Paris: Berger-Levrault, 1913.

––––– *La France victorieuse dans la guerre de demain: étude stratégique.* Paris: Berger-Levrault, 1912.

––––– *L'infantrie sacrifiée.* Paris: Berger-Levrault, 1930.

––––– *Les lois éternelles de la guerre.* 2 vols. Paris: Berger-Levrault, 1923–1925.

Boveri, Margaret. *Sir Edward Grey und das Foreign Office.* Berlin: W. Rothschild, 1933.

Bradford, Admiral Sir Edward. *Life of Admiral of the Fleet Sir Arthur Knyvet Wilson.* London: John Murray, 1923.

Brandenberg, Erich. *Von Bismarck zum Weltkriege,* rev. ed. Leipzig: Im Insel Verlag, 1939.

Bréal, Auguste. *Philippe Berthelot.* 6th ed. Paris: Gallimard, 1937.

Bredt, Johannes V. *Die belgische Neutralität und der Schlieffensche Feldzugsplan.* Berlin: Verlag von George Stilke, 1929.

Brett, Maurice V., and Oliver, Viscount Esher, eds. *Journals and Letters of Reginald, Viscount Esher.* 4 vols. London: Ivor Nicholson and Watson, 1934–1938.

Bridges, Lieutenant General Tom. *Alarms & Excursions.* London: Longmans, Green, 1938.

Brière, Paul. *Un grand français: le vice-amiral François Ernest Fournier.* Mayenne: Floch, 1931.

Bruun, Geoffrey. *Clemenceau.* Cambridge, Mass.: Harvard University Press, 1943.

Buchanan, Sir George. *My Mission to Russia and Other Diplomatic Memories.* 2 vols. Boston: Little, Brown, 1923.

Bülow, Bernhard, Prince von. *Memoirs of Prince von Bülow.* English trans. 4 vols. Boston: Little, Brown, 1931–1932.

Butterfield, Sir Herbert. "Sir Edward Grey in July 1914," *Historical Studies,* 5 (1965), 1–25.

Caillaux, Joseph. *Agadir: ma politique extérieure.* Paris: Albin Michel, 1919.

––––– *Mes mémoires.* 3 vols. Paris: Plon, 1942–1947.

Cairns, John C. "International Politics and the Military Mind: The Case of the French Republic, 1911–1914," *Journal of Modern History,* 25 (September 1953), 273–285.

Callwell, General Sir Charles E. *Field-Marshal Sir Henry Wilson: His Life and Diaries.* 2 vols. London: Cassell, 1927.

––––– *Military Operations and Maritime Preponderance.* Edinburgh and London: William Blackwood & Sons, 1905.

[Cambon, Henri.] *Paul Cambon: Ambassadeur de France, 1843–1924.* Paris: Plon, 1937.

Cambon, Henri, ed. *Paul Cambon: correspondance, 1870–1924.* 3 vols. Paris: Grasset, 1940–1946.

Carew, Tim. *The Vanished Army.* London: William Kimber, 1964.

Carrias, Colonel Eugène. *La pensée militaire allemande.* Paris: Presses Universitaires de France, 1948.

—— *La pensée militaire française.* Paris: Presses Universitaires de France, 1960.

Carroll, E. Malcolm. *French Public Opinion and Foreign Affairs, 1870–1914.* New York: Century Co., 1931.

—— *Germany and the Great Powers, 1866–1914: A Study in Public Opinion and Foreign Policy.* New York: Prentice Hall, 1938.

Cecil, Algernon. *British Foreign Secretaries, 1807–1916: Studies in Personality and Policy.* New York: G. P. Putnam, 1927.

Cecil, Lamar. *Albert Ballin: Business and Politics in Imperial Germany, 1888–1918.* Princeton: Princeton University Press, 1967.

Challener, Richard D. *The French Theory of the Nation in Arms, 1866–1939.* New York: Columbia University Press, 1955.

Chalmers, Rear Admiral W. S. *The Life and Letters of David, Earl Beatty.* London: Hodder & Stoughton, 1951.

Chamberlain, Sir Austen. *Down the Years.* London: Cassell, 1935.

—— *Politics from Inside: An Epistolary Chronicle, 1906–1914.* London: Cassell, 1936.

Chapman-Huston, Major Desmond, and Major Owen Rutter. *General Sir John Cowans, G.C.B., G.C.M.G.: The Quartermaster General of the Great War.* 2 vols. London: Hutchinson, 1924.

Charles-Roux, François. *Trois ambassades françaises à la veille de la guerre.* Paris: Plon, 1928.

Charteris, Brigadier General John. *Field Marshal Earl Haig.* New York: Charles Scribner's Sons, 1929.

Chastenet, Jacques. *Histoire de la troisième république,* vols. III–IV. Paris: Hachette, 1955.

—— *Raymond Poincaré.* Paris: René Julliard, 1948.

Churchill, Randolph S. *Winston S. Churchill,* vol. II: *1901–1914, Young Statesman.* Boston: Houghton Mifflin, 1967.

Churchill, Rogers P. *The Anglo-Russian Convention of 1907.* Cedar Rapids, Iowa: Torch Press, 1939.

Churchill, Winston S. *The World Crisis, 1911–1918.* 4 vols. New York: Charles Scribner's Sons, 1923–1929.

Clarke, I. F. *Voices Prophesying War, 1763–1984.* London: Oxford University Press, 1966.

Colin, Commandant Jean. *Les transformations de la guerre.* Paris: Bibliothèque Philosophie Scientifique, 1911.

Collier, Basil. *Brasshat: A Biography of Field Marshal Sir Henry Wilson.* London: Secker & Warburg, 1961.

Collins, Doreen. *Aspects of British Politics, 1904–1919.* Oxford: Pergamon Press, 1965.

Combarieu, Abel. *Sept ans à l'Elysée avec la Président Emile Loubet.* Paris: Hachette, 1932.

Combes, Emile. *Mon ministère: mémoires, 1902–1905.* Paris: Plon, 1956.

Conrad von Hötzendorf, Field Marshal Franz. *Aus meiner Dienstzeit, 1906–1918.* 5 vols. Vienna: Rikola Verlag, 1921–1925.

Contaime, Henry. *La revanche, 1871–1914.* Paris: Berger-Levrault, 1957.

Contemporary Review.

Conwell-Evans, Thomas P. *Foreign Policy from a Back Bench, 1904–1918: A Study Based on the Papers of Lord Noel-Buxton*. London: Oxford University Press, 1932.

Cooper, Alfred Duff. *Haig*. 2 vols. London: Faber & Faber, 1935–1936.

Cooper, M. B. "British Policy in the Balkans, 1908–9," *Historical Journal*, 7 (1964), 258–279.

Corbett, Sir Julian. *Some Principles of Maritime Strategy*. London: Longmans, Green, 1911.

Craig, Gordon A. *From Bismarck to Adenauer: Aspects of German Statecraft*. Baltimore: Johns Hopkins Press, 1958.

—— *The Politics of the Prussian Army, 1640–1945*, rev. ed. New York: Oxford University Press, 1964.

Cromwell, Valerie. "Communication: Great Britain's European Treaty Obligations in March 1902," *Historical Journal*, 6 (1963), 272–279.

Darrieus, Gabriel. *La guerre sur mer: stratégie et tactique: la doctrine*. Paris: A. Challamel, 1907.

Daveluy, Lieutenant de Vaisseau René. *Etude sur le combat navale*. Paris: Berger-Levrault, 1902.

—— *Etude sur la stratégie navale*. Paris: Berger-Levrault, 1905.

Dehmelt, Bernard Karl. "Bülow's Moroccan Policy, 1902–1905," unpub. diss. University of Pennsylvania, 1963.

Devleeshouwer, Robert. *Les belges et le danger de guerre, 1910–1914*. Louvain: Editions Nauwelaerts, 1958.

Dewar, Vice Admiral K. G. P. *The Navy From Within*. London: Victor Gollancz, 1939.

Dexter, Byron. "Lord Grey and the Problem of Alliance," *Foreign Affairs*, 30 (January 1952), 298–309.

Dickinson, G. Lowes. *The International Anarchy, 1904–1914*. New York: Century Co., 1926.

Digeon, Claude. *La crise allemande de la pensée française, 1870–1914*. Paris: Presses Universitaires de France, 1959.

Domville, Admiral Sir Barry. *By and Large*. London: Hutchinson, 1936.

Duchesne, Albert. *Les archives de la Guerre et de la Marine à Paris et l'histoire de Belgique*. Brussels: Palais des Académies, 1962.

Dugdale, Blanche E. C. *Arthur James Balfour*. 2 vols. New York: G. P. Putnam, 1937.

Dunlop, Colonel John K. *The Development of the British Army, 1899–1914*. London: Methuen, 1938.

Durand-Viel, G. "Delcassé et la marine," *Revue maritime*, n.s. 41 (May 1923), 577–605.

Earle, Edward Mead, ed. *Makers of Modern Strategy: Military Thought from Machiavelli to Hitler*. Princeton: Princeton University Press, 1943.

Edmonds, Sir James E. *A Short History of World War I*. London: Oxford University Press, 1951.

Edwards, E. W. "The Far Eastern Agreements," *Journal of Modern History*, 26 (December 1954), 340–355.

—— "The Franco-German Agreement on Morocco, 1909," *English Historical Review*, 78 (July 1963), 483–513.

—— "The Japanese Alliance and the Anglo-French Agreement of 1904," *History*, 42 (February 1957), 19–27.

Ehrman, John. *Cabinet Government and War, 1890–1940*. Cambridge: Cambridge University Press, 1958.

Engerand, Fernand. *La bataille de la frontière: (août 1914) Briey*. Paris: Editions Bossard, 1920.

Ensor, Sir Robert. *England, 1870–1914.* Oxford: Clarendon Press, 1936.

Esher, Reginald, Viscount. *The Tragedy of Lord Kitchener.* New York: E. P. Dutton, 1921.

Eubank, Keith. *Paul Cambon: Master Diplomatist.* Norman, Okla.: University of Oklahoma Press, 1960.

Falls, Cyril. *The Great War, 1914–1918.* New York: G. P. Putnam, 1959.

Faramond de Lafajolle, Captain. *Souvenirs d'un attaché naval en Allemagne et en Autriche.* Paris: Plon, 1932.

Fay, Sidney B. *The Origins of the World War,* 2nd ed. 2 vols. in 1. New York: Macmillan, 1930.

Fergusson, Sir James. *The Curragh Incident.* London: Faber & Faber, 1964.

Fischer, Fritz. *Germany's Aims in the First World War.* New York: W. W. Norton, 1967.

—— *Griff nach der Weltmacht,* 3rd ed. Düsseldorf: Droste Verlag, 1964.

Fisher of Kilverstone, Admiral of the Fleet Lord. *Memories and Records.* 2 vols. New York: George H. Doran, 1920.

Fitzroy, Sir Almeric. *Memoirs.* 2 vols. London: Hutchinson, n.d.

Flammer, Philip M. "The Schlieffen Plan and Plan XVII: A Short Critique," *Military Affairs,* 30 (1966), 207–212.

Flournoy, Francis R. *Parliament and War.* London: P. S. King & Son, 1927.

Foch, Field Marshal Ferdinand. *De la conduite de la guerre: la manoeuvre pour la bataille.* Paris: Berger-Levrault, 1904.

—— *The Memoirs of Marshal Foch,* trans. T. Bentley Mott. Garden City, N.Y.: Doubleday, Doran, 1931.

—— *Des principes de la guerre: conférences faites en 1900 à l'Ecole Supérieure de Guerre.* Paris: Berger-Levrault, 1903.

Foerster, Wolfgang. "Ist der deutsche Aufmarsch 1904 an die Franzosen verraten worden?" *Berliner Monatshefte,* 10 (2) (November 1932), 1053–1067.

French, Gerald. *The Life of Field Marshal Sir John French.* London: Cassell, 1931.

—— *Some War Diaries, Addresses, and Correspondence of Field-Marshal the Right Honble. The Earl of Ypres.* London: Herbert Jenkins, 1937.

French, Field Marshal Sir John. *1914.* New York: Houghton Mifflin, 1919.

Gall, Wilhelm. *Sir Charles Hardinge und die englische Vorkriegspolitik, 1903–1910.* Berlin: Verlag Dr. Emil Ebering, 1939.

Gardiner, Leslie. *The British Admiralty.* Edinburgh and London: William Blackwood & Sons, 1968.

Gardner, Brian. *Allenby.* London: Cassell, 1965.

Garros, Louis. *L'armée de grand-papa: de Gallifet à Gamelin, 1871–1939.* Paris: Hachette, 1965.

—— "En marge de l'alliance franco-russe, 1902–1914," *Revue historique de l'armée,* 6 (January–March 1950), 29–43.

—— "Préludes aux invasions de la Belgique," *Revue historique de l'armée,* 5 (January–March 1949), 17–37.

Geiss, Imanuel, ed. *Julikrise und Kriegsausbruch 1914: Eine Dokumentensammlung.* 2 vols. Hannover: Verlag für Literatur und Zeitgeschehen, 1963–1964.

—— *July 1914: The Outbreak of the First World War: Selected Documents.* New York: Charles Scribner's Sons, 1967.

—— "The Outbreak of the First World War and German War Aims," *Journal of Contemporary History,* 1, no. 3 (1966), 75–91.

Girardet, Raoul. *La société militaire dans la France contemporaine, 1815–1939.* Paris: Plon, 1953.

Gleichen, Major General Lord Edward. *A Guardsman's Memories: A Book of Recollections*. Edinburgh and London: William Blackwood & Sons, 1932.

Goguel, François. *La politique des partis sous la troisième république*. 2 vols. Paris: Editions de Seuil, 1946.

Gollin, Alfred M. *The Observer and J. L. Garvin, 1908–1914: A Study in Great Editorship*. London: Oxford University Press, 1960.

Gooch, George P. *Before the War: Studies in Diplomacy*. 2 vols. London: Longmans, Green, 1936–1938.

———— *Recent Revelations of European Diplomacy*, 4th rev. ed. London: Longmans, Green, 1940.

Gorce, Paul Marie de la. *The French Army: A Military-Political History*, trans. Kenneth Douglas. New York: George Braziller, 1963.

Gordon, Lady Algernon, ed. *The Diary of Lord Bertie of Thame, 1914–1918*. 2 vols. New York: G. H. Doran, n.d.

Gordon, Donald C. *The Dominion Partnership in Imperial Defense, 1870–1914*. Baltimore: Johns Hopkins Press, 1965.

Gosses, Frans. *The Management of British Foreign Policy Before the First World War, Especially During the Period 1880–1914*, trans. E. C. van der Gaaf. Lieden: A. W. Sijthoff, 1948.

Goudswaard, Johan Marius. *Some Aspects of the End of Britain's "Splendid Isolation," 1898–1914*. Rotterdam: W. L. and J. Brusse, 1952.

Gough, General Sir Hubert. *Soldiering On*. New York: Robert Speller & Sons, 1957.

Grandmaison, Colonel François Loyzeau de. *Deux conférences*. Paris: Berger-Levrault, 1911.

———— *Dressage de l'infantrie en vue du combat offensif*, 3rd ed. Paris: Berger-Levrault, 1908.

Grenville, J. A. S. *Lord Salisbury and Foreign Policy: The Close of the Nineteenth Century*. London: Athlone Press, University of London, 1964.

Grey of Fallodon, Viscount. *Twenty-five Years, 1892–1916*. 2 vols. New York: Frederick A. Stokes, 1925.

Grouard, Lieutenant Colonel A. *France et Allemagne: la guerre éventuelle*, 4th ed. Paris: Librairie Chapelot, 1913.

Grunwald, Constantin de. *Les alliances franco-russes: neuf siècles de malentendues*. Paris: Plon, 1965.

Guihéneuc Collection, Widener Library, Harvard University. (A series of scrapbooks containing press clippings on the French Navy that provide excellent coverage for the years 1900–1914. Oliver F. Guihéneuc was a civil employee in the Naval Ministry.)

Guillen, Pierre. *L'Allemagne et le Maroc de 1870 à 1914*. Paris: Presses Universitaires de France, 1967.

Guinn, Paul. *British Strategy and Politics, 1914 to 1918*. Oxford: Clarendon Press, 1965.

Gwynn, Stephen, ed. *The Letters and Friendships of Sir Cecil Spring-Rice: A Record*. 2 vols. Boston: Houghton Mifflin, 1929.

Haldane of Cloan, Richard, Lord. *An Autobiography*. New York: Doubleday, Doran, 1929.

———— *Before the War*. London: Cassell, 1920.

Hale, Oron J. *Germany and the Diplomatic Revolution: A Study in Diplomacy and the Press, 1904–1906*. Philadelphia: University of Pennsylvania Press, 1931.

———— *Publicity and Diplomacy with Special Reference to England and Germany, 1890–1914*. New York: Appleton-Century, 1940.

Halévy, Elie. A History of the English People in the Nineteenth Century, vol. V: Imperialism and the Rise of Labour, 1895–1905; vol. VI: The Rule of Democracy, 1905–1914. Trans. E. I. Watkin, 2nd ed. London: Ernest Benn, 1951–1952.

Hallgarten, George W. F. Imperialismus vor 1914, 2nd rev. ed. 2 vols. Munich: C. H. Beck'sche, 1963.

Hamilton, General Sir Ian. Compulsory Service. London: John Murray, 1911.

Hamilton, Ian. The Happy Warrior: A Life of General Sir Ian Hamilton G.C.B., G.C.M.G., D.S.O. London: Cassell, 1966.

Hammond, J. L. C. P. Scott of the Manchester Guardian. London: G. Bell, 1934.

Hankey, Lord. The Supreme Command, 1914–1918. 2 vols. London: George Allen & Unwin, 1961.

Hardinge, Charles. Old Diplomacy: The Reminiscences of Lord Hardinge of Penhurst. London: John Murray, 1947.

Hargreaves, J. D. "The Origin of the Anglo-French Military Conversations in 1905," History, 36 (October 1951), 244–248.

Heere, Paul. Die kleinen Staaten Europas und die Entstehung des Weltkrieges. Munich: C. H. Beck'sche, 1937.

Helmreich, Ernst Christian. The Diplomacy of the Balkan Wars. Cambridge, Mass.: Harvard University Press, 1938.

Helmreich, Jonathan. "Belgian Concern over Neutrality and British Intentions, 1906–1914," Journal of Modern History, 36 (December 1964), 416–427.

Heuston, Robert Francis Vere. Lives of Lord Chancellors, 1885–1940. Oxford: Clarendon Press, 1964.

Higgins, Trumbull. Winston Churchill and the Dardanelles: A Dialogue in Ends and Means. New York: Macmillan, 1963.

Higham, Robin. The British Rigid Airship, 1908–1931: A Study in Weapons Policy. London: G. T. Foulis & Co., 1961.

Holsti, Ole R. "The 1914 Case," American Political Science Review, 59 (June 1965), 365–378.

Hosse, Carl. Die englisch-belgischen Aufmarschpläne gegen Deutschland vor dem Weltkriege. Zurich: Amalthea-Verlag, 1930.

Hough, Richard. Dreadnought: A History of the Modern Battleship. New York: Macmillan, 1964.

Howard, Christopher. "The Policy of Isolation," Historical Journal, 10 (1967), 77–88.

—— Splendid Isolation. New York: St. Martin's Press, 1967.

Hubatsch, Walther. Der Admiralstab und die obersten Marinebehörden in Deutschland, 1848–1945. Frankfurt am Main: Verlag für Wehrwesen Bernard & Graefe, 1958.

—— Die Ära Tirpitz: Studien zur deutschen Marinepolitik, 1890–1918. Göttingen: Musterschmidt Verlag, 1955.

Huguet, General Victor Marie. Britain and the War: A French Indictment, trans. H. C. Minchin. London: Menehin, 1928.

Hunter, John C. "The Strength of France on the Eve of World War I: A Study of French Self-Confidence as Evidenced in the Parliamentary Debates on the Three-Year Service Law of 1913," unpub. diss. Harvard University, 1959.

Huntington, Samuel P. The Soldier and the State: The Theory and Politics of Civil-Military Relations. Cambridge, Mass.: Harvard University Press, 1957.

James, David. *Lord Roberts*. London: Hollis & Carter, 1954.

Jameson, Rear Admiral William. *The Fleet that Jack Built: Nine Men Who Made a Modern Navy*. New York: Harcourt, Brace & World, 1962.

Jenkins, Roy. *Asquith*. London: Collins, 1964.

Jervis, Robert. "The Costs of the Scientific Study of Politics: An Examination of the Stanford Content Analysis Studies," *International Studies Quarterly*, 11 (December 1967), 366–393.

Joffre, Field Marshal Joseph J. C. *Mémoires du Maréchal Joffre, 1910–1917*. 2 vols. Paris: Plon, 1932.

―――― *The Memoirs of Marshal Joffre*, trans. T. Bentley Mott. 2 vols. London: Geoffrey Bles, 1932. (This version lacks some of the technical details of the French one.)

―――― *1914–1915: La préparation de la guerre & la conduite des opérations*. Paris: Editions E. Chiron, 1920.

Johnson, Franklyn A. *Defence by Committee: The British Committee of Imperial Defence, 1885–1959*. London: Oxford University Press, 1960.

Jones, Thomas. *Lloyd George*. Cambridge, Mass.: Harvard University Press, 1951.

Jouan, René Marie. *Histoire de la marine française*, 2nd rev. ed. Paris: Payot, 1950.

Joubert, Vice Admiral Henri. *La marine française*. Paris: Editions Alsatia, 1946.

Journal of the Royal United Service Institution.

Journal des sciences militaires: revue militaire française.

Kantorowicz, Hermann. *Der Geist der englischen Politik und das Gespenst der Einkreisung Deutschlands*. Berlin: E. Rowoht, 1929.

Kemp, Lieutenant Commander P. K., ed. *The Papers of Admiral Sir John Fisher*. 2 vols. to date. London: Naval Records Society, 1960–1964.

Kerr, Admiral Mark E. F. *Prince Louis of Battenberg: Admiral of the Fleet*. London: Longmans, Green, 1934.

Keyes, Admiral Sir Roger. *The Naval Memoirs of Admiral of the Fleet Sir Roger Keyes: The Narrow Seas to the Dardanelles, 1910–1915*. 2 vols. New York: E. P. Dutton, 1934–1935.

King, Jere Clemens. *Generals & Politicians: Conflict between France's High Command, Parliament and Government, 1914–1918*. Berkeley: University of California Press, 1951.

Klobukowski, Antony W. *Souvenirs de Belgique: 1911–1918*. Brussels: L'Eventail, 1928.

Kluke, Paul. *Heeresaufbau und Heerespolitik Englands vom Burenkrieg bis zum Weltkrieg*. Munich: R. Oldenbourg, 1932.

Koeltz, General L. *La guerre de 1914–1918: les opérations militaires*. Paris: Editions Sirey, 1966.

Lafore, Laurence. *The Long Fuse: An Interpretation of the Origins of World War I*. Philadelphia: J. P. Lippincott, 1965.

Lanessan, J.-L. de. *Le bilan de notre marine*. Paris: Félix Alcan, 1909.

―――― *Notre défense maritime*. Paris: Félix Alcan, 1914.

―――― *Le programme maritime de 1900–1906*, 2nd ed. Paris: Félix Alcan, 1903.

Langer, William L. *The Diplomacy of Imperialism*, 2nd rev. ed. 2 vols. in 1. New York: Alfred A. Knopf, 1951.

―――― *The Franco-Russian Alliance, 1890–1894*. Cambridge, Mass.: Harvard University Press, 1929.

―――― "Tribulations of Empire: The Mediterranean Problem," *Foreign Affairs*, 15 (July 1937), 646–660.

Lanrezac, General Charles. *Le plan de campagne français et le premier mois de la guerre* (*2 août–3 septembre 1914*). Paris: Payot, 1921.

Lee, Sir Sidney. *King Edward VII.* 2 vols. London: Macmillan, 1925–1927.

Le Hénaff, Colonel, and Captain Henri Bornecque. *Les chemins de fer français et la guerre.* Paris: Librairie Chapelot, 1922.

Le Masson, Henri. "Douze ministres . . . ou dix ans d'hésitations de la marine française," *Revue maritime,* 233 (June 1966), 710–733.

—— "Politique navale et construction de navires de ligne en France en 1914, I," *Revue maritime,* 202 (August–September 1963), 993–1008.

Lichnowsky, Prince. *Heading for the Abyss: Reminiscences.* New York: Payson & Clarke, 1928.

Liddell Hart, Sir Basil H. *The British Way in Warfare.* London: Faber & Faber, 1932.

—— *Foch: The Man of Orleans.* London: Eyre & Spottiswoode, 1931.

—— "French Military Ideas before the First World War," *A Century of Conflict, 1850–1950: Essays for A. J. P. Taylor,* ed. Martin Gilbert. London: Hamish Hamilton, 1966.

—— *Reputations.* London: John Murray, 1928.

Lindberg, Folke. *Scandinavia in Great Power Politics, 1905–1908.* Stockholm: Almquist & Wiksell, 1958.

Lloyd George, David. *War Memoirs.* 6 vols. Boston: Little, Brown, 1933–1937.

Loreburn, Lord. *How the War Came.* London: Methuen, 1919.

Louis, Georges. *Les carnets de Georges Louis.* 2 vols. Paris: F. Rieder, 1926.

Luczynski, Walter. "Belgian Neutrality in *Entente* Diplomacy, 1904–1914," unpub. diss. University of Illinois, 1959.

Lutz, Hermann. *Lord Grey and the World War,* trans. E. W. Dickes. New York: Alfred A. Knopf, 1928.

Luvaas, Jay. *The Education of An Army: British Military Thought, 1815–1940.* Chicago: University of Chicago Press, 1964.

—— "European Military Thought and Doctrine, 1870–1914," *The Theory and Practice of War. Essays Presented to Captain B. H. Liddell Hart,* ed. Michael Howard. London: Cassell, 1965.

MacDiarmid, D. S. *The Life of Lieut. General Sir James Moncrieff Grierson.* London: Constable, 1923.

McGeoch, Lyle A. "The Role of Lord Lansdowne in the Diplomatic Negotiations Connected with the Anglo-French Agreement of April 1904," unpub. diss. University of Pennsylvania, 1964.

McKenna, Stephen. *Reginald McKenna, 1863–1943: A Memoir.* London: Eyre & Spottiswoode, 1948.

Mackintosh, John. *The British Cabinet.* London: Stevens & Sons, 1962.

—— "The Role of the Committee of Imperial Defence before 1914," *English Historical Review,* 77 (July 1962), 490–503.

Macready, General Sir Nevil. *Annals of An Active Life.* 2 vols. London: Hutchinson, 1924.

Magnus, Sir Philip. *King Edward the Seventh.* London: John Murray, 1964.

Manger, J.-B. "Notes sur la crise marocaine de 1905," *Revue d'histoire de la guerre mondiale,* 12 (October 1934), 311–340.

Marchand, A. *Plans de concentration de 1871 à 1914.* Paris: Berger-Levrault, 1926.

Marchat, Henry. "L'affaire marocaine en 1911," *Revue d'histoire diplomatique,* 77 (July–September 1963), 193–235.

Marcus, Geoffrey. *Before the Lamps Went Out.* Boston: Little, Brown, 1965.

Marder, Arthur J. *The Anatomy of British Sea Power: A Study of British Naval Policy in the Pre-Dreadnought Era, 1880–1905.* New York: Alfred A. Knopf, 1940.

—— *From the Dreadnought to Scapa Flow: The Royal Navy in the Fisher Era, 1904–1919,* vol. I: *The Road to War, 1904–1914;* vol. II: *The War Years: To the Eve of Jutland, 1914–1916.* London: Oxford University Press, 1961–1965.

—— *Portrait of An Admiral: The Life and Papers of Sir Herbert Richmond.* Cambridge, Mass.: Harvard University Press, 1952.

Marder, Arthur J., ed. *Fear God and Dread Nought: The Correspondence of Admiral of the Fleet Lord Fisher of Kilverstone.* 3 vols. London: Jonathan Cape, 1952–1959.

Masson, Philippe. "Delcassé, Ministre de la Marine," unpub. diss. University of Paris, 1951.

—— "La politique navale française de 1850 à 1914," *Revue maritime,* 251 (February 1968), 183–203.

Masterman, Lucy. *C. F. G. Masterman: A Biography.* London: Ivor Nicholson and Watson, 1939.

Mathews, J. J. *Egypt and the Formation of the Anglo-French Entente of 1904.* Philadelphia: University of Pennsylvania Press, 1939.

Maurice, Major General Sir Frederick. *Haldane: 1856–1928.* 2 vols. London: Faber & Faber, 1937–1939.

Mendelssohn, Peter de. *The Age of Churchill: Heritage and Adventure, 1874–1911.* London: Thames and Hudson, 1961.

Messimy, Adolphe-Marie. *Mes souvenirs.* Paris: Plon, 1937.

Michon, Georges. *La préparation à la guerre: la loi de trois ans, 1910–1914.* Paris: Librairie des Sciences Politiques et Sociales, 1935.

Midleton, Earl of (St. John Brodrick). *Records & Reactions, 1856–1939.* New York: E. P. Dutton, 1939.

Monger, George. *The End of Isolation: British Foreign Policy, 1900–1907.* London: Thomas Nelson, 1963.

Moniteur de la flotte.

Monteilhet, Joseph. *Les institutions militaires de la France (1814–1932): la paix armée à la paix desarmée,* 2nd rev. ed. Paris: Félix Alcan, 1932.

Morel, E. D. *Morocco in Diplomacy.* London: Smith, Elder & Co., 1912.

Morley of Blackburn, John, Viscount. *Memorandum on Resignation, August 1914.* London: Macmillan, 1928.

Mortimer, Joanne Stafford. "The Moroccan Policy of Bethmann-Hollweg, 1909–1912," unpub. diss. University of Pennsylvania, 1960.

Muret, Pierre. "La politique personnelle de Rouvier et la chute de Delcassé (31 mars–6 juin 1905)," *Revue d'histoire de la guerre mondiale,* 17 (July and October 1939), 209–231, 305–352.

Murray, John A. "Grey and His Critics," *Power, Public Opinion, and Diplomacy: Essays in Honor of Eber Malcolm Carroll,* ed. Lillian Parker Wallace and William C. Askew. Durham, N.C.: Duke University Press, 1959.

The Naval Annual, 1900–1914, ed. T. A. Brassey *et al.* London and Portsmouth: William Clowes & Sons, 1900–1914.

Neilson. Francis. *How Diplomats Make War.* New York: B. W. Huebsch, 1916.

Neton, Albéric. *Delcassé, 1852–1923.* Paris: Académie Diplomatique Internationale, 1952.

Newton, Lord. *Lord Lansdowne: A Biography.* London: Macmillan, 1929.

Nicolson, Sir Harold. *King George the Fifth: His Life and Reign.* London: Constable, 1952.
—— *Sir Arthur Nicolson, Bart., First Lord Carnock: A Study in the Old Diplomacy.* London: Constable, 1930.
Nineteenth Century and After.
Nish, Ian H. *The Anglo-Japanese Alliance: The Diplomacy of Two Island Empires, 1884–1907.* London: Athlone Press, University of London, 1966.
North, Robert C. "Perception and Action in the 1914 Crisis," *Journal of International Affairs,* 21 (1967), 103–122.
Nowell-Smith, Simon, ed. *Edwardian England, 1901–1914.* London: Oxford University Press, 1964.
Owen, Frank. *Tempestuous Journey: Lloyd George, His Life and Times.* New York: McGraw-Hill, 1955.
Padfield, Peter. *Aim Straight: A Biography of Admiral Sir Percy Scott.* London: Hodder & Stoughton, 1966.
Paléologue, Maurice. *An Ambassador's Memoirs,* trans. F. A. Holt. 3 vols. London: Hutchinson, 1923–1925.
—— *Un grand tournant de la politique mondiale, 1904–1906.* Paris: Plon, 1934.
—— *Un prélude à l'invasion de la Belgique: le plan Schlieffen.* Paris: Plon, 1932.
—— *Au Quai d'Orsay à la veille de la tourmente: journal, 1913–1914.* Paris: Plon, 1947.
Patterson, A. Temple, ed. *The Jellicoe Papers: Selections From the Private and Official Correspondence of Admiral of the Fleet Earl Jellicoe of Scapa,* vol. I: 1893–1916. London: Naval Records Society, 1966.
Penson, Lillian M. "The New Course in British Foreign Policy, 1892–1902," *Transactions of the Royal Historical Society,* 4th ser., 25 (1943), 121–138.
—— "Obligations by Treaty: Their Place in British Foreign Policy, 1894–1914," *Studies in Diplomatic History and Historiography in Honour of G. P. Gooch,* ed. A. O. Sarkissian. London: Longmans, Green, 1961.
Petrie, Sir Charles. *The Life and Letters of the Right Hon. Sir Austen Chamberlain.* 2 vols. London: Cassell, 1939.
Playne, Carolyn E. *The Neuroses of the Nations.* London: George Allen & Unwin, 1925.
—— *The Pre-War Mind in Britain.* London: George Allen & Unwin, 1928.
Poincaré, Raymond. *Au service de la France: neuf années de souvenirs.* 10 vols. Paris: Plon, 1925–1933.
Ponsonby, Sir Frederick (Lord Sysonby). *Recollections of Three Reigns.* New York: E. P. Dutton, 1952.
Porter, Charles W. *The Career of Théophile Delcassé.* Philadelphia: University of Pennsylvania Press, 1936.
Pribram, Alfred F. *Austria-Hungary and Great Britain, 1908–1914,* trans. Ian F. D. Morrow. London: Oxford University Press, 1951.
Quarterly Review.
Questions diplomatiques et coloniales.
Reiners, Ludwig. *The Lamps Went Out in Europe,* trans. Richard and Clara Wilson. New York: Pantheon Books, 1955.
Renouvin, Pierre. "Britain and the Continent: The Lessons of History," *Foreign Affairs,* 17 (October 1938), 111–127.

—— *La crise européenne et la première guerre mondiale*, 4th rev. ed. Paris: Presses Universitaires de France, 1962.

—— "Finance et politique: à propos de l'entente cordiale franco-anglaise," *Eventail de l'histoire vivant: hommage à Lucien Febvre*, vol. I. Paris: Armand Colin, 1953, pp. 357–363.

—— "L'orientation de l'alliance franco-russe en 1900–1901," *Revue d'histoire diplomatique*, 80 (July–September 1966), 193–204.

—— "The Part Played in International Relations by Conversations between the General Staffs on the Eve of the World War," *Studies in Anglo-French History During the Eighteenth, Nineteenth and Twentieth Centuries*, ed. Alfred Colville and Harold Temperley. Cambridge: Cambridge University Press, 1935.

Repington, Charles à Court. *The First World War, 1914–1918*. 2 vols. Boston: Houghton Mifflin, 1920.

Repington, Mary. *Thanks for the Memory*. London: Constable, 1938.

Révillon, Tony. *Camille Pelletan*. Paris: Librairie des Sciences Politiques et Sociales, 1930.

Revue belge des livres, documents & archives de la guerre, 1914–1918.

Revue des deux mondes.

Revue d'histoire de la guerre mondiale.

Revue maritime.

Revue militaire des armées étrangères.

Revue militaire générale.

Revue de Paris.

Rich, Norman. *Friedrich von Holstein: Politics and Diplomacy in the Era of Bismarck and Wilhelm II*. 2 vols. Cambridge: Cambridge University Press, 1965.

Riddell, George, Baron. *Lord Riddell's War Diary, 1914–1918*. London: Ivor Nicholson and Watson, 1933.

—— *More Pages From My Diary, 1908–1914*. London: Country Life, 1934.

Ridder, Alfred de. "Encore les conventions anglo-belges," *Revue belge des livres, documents & archives de la guerre, 1914–1918*, 7 (April–June 1931), 218–238.

Ritter, Gerhard. *The Schlieffen Plan: Critique of a Myth*, trans. Andrew and Eva Wilson. London: Oswald Wolff, 1958.

—— *Staatskunst und Kriegshandwerk: Das Problem des "Militarismus" in Deutschland*, vol. II: *Die Hauptmächte Europas und das wilhelminische Reich, 1890–1914*. Munich: R. Oldenbourg, 1960.

Roberts, Field Marshal the Earl. *A Nation in Arms*. London: John Murray, 1907.

Robertson, Field Marshal Sir William. *From Private to Field-Marshal*. Boston: Houghton Mifflin, 1921.

—— *Soldiers and Statesmen, 1914–1918*. 2 vols. New York: Charles Scribner's Sons, 1926.

Ropp, Theodore. "Conscription in Great Britain, 1900–1914: A Failure in Civil-Military Communications?" *Military Affairs*, 20 (1956), 71–76.

—— "The Development of a Modern Navy: French Naval Policy, 1871–1904," unpub. diss. Harvard University, 1937.

—— *War in the Modern World*, 2nd rev. ed. Durham, N.C.: Duke University Press, 1962.

Roskill, Captain S. W. *The Strategy of Sea Power: Its Development and Application*. London: Collins, 1962.

Ryan, A. P. *Mutiny at the Curragh*. London: Macmillan, 1956.

Salaun, Vice Admiral. *La marine française*. Paris: Les Editions de France, 1934.

Sazonov, Serge D. *Fateful Years, 1909–1916*. London: Jonathan Cape, 1928.

Schelling, Thomas C. *Arms and Influence*. New Haven: Yale University Press, 1966.

Schmitt, Bernadotte E. *The Coming of the War, 1914*. 2 vols. New York: Charles Scribner's Sons, 1930.

—— *England and Germany, 1740–1914*. Princeton: Princeton University Press, 1916.

—— "Lord Haldane's Mission to Berlin in 1912," *The Crusades and Other Historical Essays*, ed. L. J. Paetow. New York: F. S. Crofts, 1928.

Schuman, Frederick L. *War and Diplomacy in the French Republic*. New York: McGraw-Hill, 1931.

Schurman, Donald M. *The Education of a Navy: The Development of British Naval Thought, 1867–1914*. London: Cassell, 1965.

Scott, Jonathan F. *Five Weeks: The Surge of Public Opinion on the Eve of the Great War*. New York: John Day, 1927.

Scott, Admiral Sir Percy. *Fifty Years in the Royal Navy*. London: John Murray, 1919.

Seely, John E. B. (Baron Mottistone). *Adventure*. London: Heinemann, 1930.

Selliers de Moranville, General A. *Du haut de la Tour de Babel*. Paris: Berger-Levrault, 1925.

Seton-Watson, Robert W. *Britain in Europe, 1789–1914*. Cambridge: Cambridge University Press, 1937.

Smith-Dorrien, General Sir Horace. *Memories of Forty-Eight Years' Service*. London: John Murray, 1925.

Sommer, Dudley. *Haldane of Cloan: His Life and Times, 1856–1928*. London: George Allen & Unwin, 1960.

Sorb, Captain [Charles Cormier]. *La doctrine de défense nationale*. Paris: Berger-Levrault, 1912. (Excerpts first appeared in *Revue militaire générale*.)

Spectateur militaire.

Spender, John A. *Fifty Years of Europe: A Study in Pre-War Documents*. New York: Frederick A. Stokes, 1933.

—— *Life, Journalism and Politics*. 2 vols. London: Cassell, 1927.

—— *The Life of the Right Hon. Sir Henry Campbell-Bannerman*. 2 vols. London: Hodder & Stoughton, 1923.

Spender, John A., and Cyril Asquith. *Life of Herbert Henry Asquith, Lord Oxford and Asquith*. 2 vols. London: Hutchinson, 1932.

Steinberg, Jonathan. "The Copenhagen Complex," *Journal of Contemporary History*, 1, no. 3 (1966), 23–46.

—— *Yesterday's Deterrent: Tirpitz and the Birth of the German Battle Fleet*. London: Macdonald, 1965.

Steiner, Zara S. "The Formation of British Foreign Policy, 1898–1919, with Special Reference to the Conservative Administration," unpub. diss. Radcliffe College, 1956.

—— "Great Britain and the Creation of the Anglo-Japanese Alliance," *Journal of Modern History*, 31 (March 1959), 27–36.

—— "Grey, Hardinge and the Foreign Office, 1906–1910," *Historical Journal*, 10 (1967), 415–439.

—— "The Last Years of the Old Foreign Office, 1898–1905," *Historical Journal*, 6 (1963), 59–90.

Stieve, Friedrich. *Isvolsky and the World War*, trans. E. W. Dickes. London: George Allen & Unwin, 1926.

Stone, Norman. "Moltke-Conrad: Relations between the Austro-Hungarian and German General Staffs, 1909–14," *Historical Journal*, 9 (1966), 201–228.

Sydenham of Combe, Lord (Sir George Clarke). *My Working Life*. London: John Murray, 1927.

Tabouis, Geneviève. *Jules Cambon par l'un des siens*. Paris: Payot, 1938.

Tardieu, André. *France and the Alliances: The Struggle for the Balance of Power*. New York: Macmillan, 1908.

—— *Le mystère d'Agadir*. Paris: Calmann-Lévy, 1912.

Taylor, A. J. P. *Politics in Wartime and other Essays*. London: Hamish Hamilton, 1964.

—— *The Struggle for Mastery in Europe, 1848–1918*. Oxford: Clarendon Press, 1954.

—— *The Trouble Makers: Dissent over Foreign Policy, 1792–1939*. Bloomington, Ind.: Indiana University Press, 1958.

Temperley, Harold. "British Secret Diplomacy from Canning to Grey," *Cambridge Historical Journal*, 6 (1938), 1–32.

Le Temps.

Terraine, John. *Mons: The Retreat to Victory*. New York: Macmillan, 1960.

—— *Ordeal of Victory*. Philadelphia: J. P. Lippincott, 1963. (A biography of Douglas Haig.)

—— *The Western Front, 1914–1918*. Philadelphia: J. P. Lippincott, 1965.

Thomas, D. H. "The Use of the Scheldt in British Plans for the Defence of Belgian Neutrality, 1831–1914," *Revue belge de philologie et d'histoire*, 41 (1963), 449–470.

Thomas, Mary E. "Anglo-Belgian Military Relations and the Congo Question, 1911–1913," *Journal of Modern History*, 25 (June 1953), 157–165.

Thomazi, Auguste. *La marine française dans la grande guerre (1914–1918)*. 4 vols. Paris: Payot, 1924–1929.

Thomson, George M. *The Twelve Days: 24 July to 4 August 1914*. London: Hutchinson, 1964.

The Times (of London).

The Times. *The History of THE TIMES*. 4 vols. London: Times Publishing Co., 1935–1952.

Tirpitz, Admiral von. *Politische Dokumente*. 2 vols. Hamburg and Berlin: Hanseatische Verlagsanstalt, 1924–1926.

Touvet, Lieutenant de Vaisseau Marie Bernard. "Guerre de 1914–18: la 2me escadre légère," unpub. study at the Archives du Ministère de la Marine, n.d. [1931–1932].

Trevelyan, Sir George M. *Grey of Fallodon*. Boston: Houghton Mifflin, 1937.

Tuchman, Barbara. *The Guns of August*. New York: Macmillan, 1962.

Tucker, Albert V. "The Issue of Army Reform in the Unionist Government, 1903–5," *Historical Journal*, 9 (1966), 90–100.

Tyler, J. E. *The British Army and the Continent, 1904–1914*. London: E. Arnold, 1938.

United Service Magazine.

Vagts, Alfred. *Defense and Diplomacy: The Soldier and the Conduct of Foreign Relations*. New York: King's Crown Press, 1956.

—— *A History of Militarism: Civilian and Military*, rev. ed. New York: Meridian Books, 1959.

—— *Landing Operations: Strategy, Psychology, Tactics, Politics, From Antiquity to 1945.* Harrisburg, Pa.: Military Service Publishing Co., 1946.

—— *The Military Attaché.* Princeton: Princeton University Press, 1967.

Varillon, Pierre. *Joffre.* Paris: A. Fayard, 1956.

Vie maritime, La.

Ward, Sir A. W., and G. P. Gooch, eds. *Cambridge History of British Foreign Policy, 1783–1919,* vol. III: *1866–1919.* Cambridge: Cambridge University Press, 1923.

Weber, Eugen. *The Nationalist Revival in France, 1905–1914.* Berkeley: University of California Press, 1959.

Wegerer, Alfred von. *Der Ausbruch des Weltkrieges.* 2 vols. Hamburg: Hanseatische Verlagsanstalt, 1939.

Westminster Gazette.

White, John A. *The Diplomacy of the Russo-Japanese War.* Princeton: Princeton University Press, 1964.

Williams, Beryl J. "The Strategic Background to the Anglo-Russian Entente of August 1907," *Historical Journal,* 9 (1966), 360–373.

Williamson, Francis T. *Germany and Morocco before 1905.* Baltimore: Johns Hopkins Press, 1937.

Willis, Edward F. *Prince Lichnowsky, Ambassador of Peace: A Study of Prewar Diplomacy, 1912–1914.* Berkeley: University of California Press, 1942.

Willis, Irene Cooper. *England's Holy War: A Study of English Liberal Idealism During the Great War.* New York: Alfred A. Knopf, 1928.

Wilson, Trevor. *The Downfall of the Liberal Party.* London: Collins, 1966.

Wolf, Lucien. *Life of the First Marquess of Ripon.* 2 vols. London: John Murray, 1921.

Wolff, Theodore. *The Eve of 1914,* trans. E. W. Dickes. New York: Alfred A. Knopf, 1936.

Woodward, Ernest L. *Great Britain and the German Navy.* Oxford: Oxford University Press, 1935.

—— *Great Britain and the War of 1914–1918.* London: Methuen, 1967.

Wrench, Sir John E. *Geoffrey Dawson and Our Times.* London: Hutchinson, 1955.

Wright, Gordon. *Raymond Poincaré and the French Presidency.* Stanford: Stanford University Press, 1942.

Wright, Quincy. *A Study of War.* 2 vols. Chicago: University of Chicago Press, 1942.

Wullus-Rudiger, J. *La Belgique et l'équilibre européen,* 2nd ed. Paris: Berger-Levrault, 1935.

Yacht, Le.

Young, Kenneth. *Arthur James Balfour.* London: G. Bell, 1963.

Ziebura, Gilbert. *Die deutsche Frage in der öffentlichen Meinung Frankreichs von 1911–1914.* Berlin: Colloquium Verlag, 1955.

Index

The Politics of Grand Strategy
Britain and France Prepare for War, 1904-1914

The emergence of the Anglo-French entente after 1904 reshaped the international system before the First World War. After Russia's addition in 1907, the Triple Entente confronted the Triple Alliance in crisis after crisis. This study, first published in 1969, chronicles the impact of the entente upon the British decision to pursue a policy of Continental intervention and looks at the ramifications of that decision upon both British and French strategic policies.

Britain's search for support against an assertive Germany represented its first acknowledgement of relative decline in the international system. The British sought to conceal the extent of their policy shift, denying the entente relationship had any military or naval dimension. In fact, from late 1905 to the war, there were secret military and naval conversations between the two governments. Mr. Williamson, focusing upon the content and conduct of the covert planning, examines the assumptions of entente strategy and its operational consequences.

In the years after 1905 the military and naval talks would become a British substitute for a formal alliance commitment to the French; this use of the secret talks, which misled the British cabinet for years and the British parliament down to August 1914, possibly also explains Germany's failure to assess correctly Britain's support for France. Williamson thus helps put Fritz Fischer's arguments about German policy into a comparative framework.

The Politics of Grand Strategy also examines the domestic ramifications of the secret staff planning and the ineptness of radical leadership in the British Cabinet in trying to block the Continental strategy. The author analyzes the problems of civil-military relations, the difficulty of controlling zealous staff officers, and the inherent risks of all forms of strategic planning.

This second edition has a new preface that analyzes the abundant new literature appearing since 1969 on British military and intelligence operations, on the evolution of French strategic planning, and on the clashes of the entente and alliance systems.

Samuel R. Williamson, Jr. received his A.M. in 1960 and his Ph.D. in 1966 from Harvard University and was both a Danforth Fellow and a Fulbright Scholar. Mr. Williamson is currently Vice-Chancello South.

ISBN 1-57392-329-X

90000

ISBN 0-9486

9 781573 923293

The Ashfiel
London and Atlantic H

HUMANITY BOOKS
59 John Glenn Drive • Amherst, N.Y. 14228

CPSIA information can be obtained
at www.ICGtesting.com
Printed in the USA
BVHW01s0941110218

507805BV00006B/98/P

9 781597 404051